FIVE THOUSAND AMERICAN FAMILIES— PATTERNS OF ECONOMIC PROGRESS

VOLUME VI

Accounting for Race and Sex Differences in Earnings and Other Analyses of the First Nine Years of the Panel Study of Income Dynamics

Edited by Greg J. Duncan and James N. Morgan

With Contributions by Richard D. Coe, Mary Corcoran, Greg J. Duncan, Martha Hill, Saul Hoffman, James N. Morgan, and Sandra J. Newman

Conducted Under Contracts with the Office of Economic Opportunity (Responsibility for this project has been transferred to the Office of the Assistant Secretary for Planning and Evaluation, Department of Health, Education, and Welfare)

SURVEY RESEARCH CENTER
INSTITUTE FOR SOCIAL RESEARCH
THE UNIVERSITY OF MICHIGAN

ISR Code No. 3990

Five Thousand American Families—Patterns of Economic Progress, Volume VI
Library of Congress Catalog Card No. 74-62002
ISBN 0-87944-222-0 paperbound
ISBN 0-87944-223-9 clothbound

Published by the Institute for Social Research
The University of Michigan, Ann Arbor, Michigan 48106

Published 1978
Printed in the United States of America

CONTENTS

Preface

A continuing study of this kind provides not only an extended picture of changes experienced by panel members but also a chance to seek answers to the new questions that arise when the data are analyzed.

In the ninth wave of our study, we changed our usual practice of interviewing only the heads of households (defined as the husband in husband-wife families) and interviewed both heads and spouses, where present. The two questionnaires asked identical questions about the skills, work histories, labor force attachment, and earnings of working heads and spouses. In the first part of this volume, we use this information in an attempt to account for earnings differences between the races and sexes. Both the theory and statistical procedure we employ have been developed and used in previous studies of this sort. But the data for these past studies have not been adequate to conduct a fair test of the exploratory power of the hypothesis that earnings differences are caused by skill differences. Our results indicate that even a greatly expanded set of skill measures cannot account for much of the earnings differences between the races and sexes. The analysis of Part I was funded by the U.S. Department of Labor.

Several additional studies are presented in Part II of this Volume. Chapter 6 analyzes responses to questions about education levels required by various jobs and compares those levels to the actual educational attainment of the job holders. It finds that "surplus" education is widespread but also has a wage payoff. The seventh chapter investigates so-called "vintage" effects of the growth rates in earnings of black and white workers using the longitudinal nature of the data. Large effects are found among an older cohort of workers of both races. In the eighth chapter, short- and long-run poverty is investigated with a look at the relative importance of various types of transfer programs in raising individuals above the poverty line. Chapter 8 also examines the composition of the poverty population as the poverty definition is changed. An analysis of the incidence and effects of housing and neighborhood problems constitutes the ninth chapter. A question on actual property taxes paid provides the basis for the analysis presented in the tenth chapter. In Chapter 11, the contribution to or subsidy from families given or received by family members is analyzed and, as in the past, is found to be substantial. The wage analysis of Part I makes use of a fraction of the information obtained in the head-spouse interviews. Descriptive results on many of the remaining questions are presented in Chapter 12. Two of the remaining chapters update data on trends in driving and commuting and in food expenditures. Another chapter summarizes the current work of other researchers who are using the panel data.

This year, to our regret, we have lost Saul Hoffman to the University of Delaware. Otherwise our research staff is unchanged. Richard Coe, Mary Corcoran, and Martha Hill continue to analyze our current data and plan future waves of the study. Dan Hill still spends a quarter of his time with us and directs his own study of electricity pricing during the other three-quarters. Our staff is small, so every member is involved in several aspects of the study. Among many other occupations, Tecla Loup is in charge of pre-editing, Charles Stallman of editing, and Anne Sears of coding. Beverly Harris and Paula Pelletier manage the ever expanding data set; Joan Brinser looks after the respondents and reports to them about the study's findings; Priscilla Hildebrandt shares her computer skills between this and other studies, and Mike Nolte has been taking on some of our computing duties.

Our best wishes go with Wanda Lemon who has moved away and Barbara Browne who left us to care for a new baby. Anita Ernst has taken over their secretarial duties with skill, good humor, and the able help of Virginia Makrucki. Alice Preketes of the SRC Publishing Division was our hard-working editor.

We are grateful to Gordon Goodfellow, our mentor at the U.S. Department of Health, Education, and Welfare, for guiding the study through the complexities of bureaucracy and also for his substantive contributions.

We appreciate the kindness of the following reviewers whose comments improved this volume substantially: Emily Andrews, U.S. Department of Labor; Mary Jo Bane, Harvard University; Francine D. Blau, University of Illinois; Georgianne Baker, Arizona State University; Angus Campbell, Institute for Social Research, University of Michigan; Hugh Conway, Aldona DiPietro, U.S. Department of Labor; Reynolds W. Farley, University of Michigan; Marianne Ferber, Robert Ferber, University of Illinois; Deborah Freedman, University of Michigan; Curt Gilroy, U.S. Department of Labor; Gordon Goodfellow, U.S. Department of Health, Education, and Welfare; David Gordon, New School for Social Research; Edward M. Gramlich, University of Michigan; Patricia Gurin, Institute for Social Research, University of Michigan; Mary Hilton, U.S. Department of Labor; Judith Hybels, Wellesley College; Carol Jusenius, Ohio State University; Tom Juster, Institute for Social Research, University of Michigan; Stanley Lebergott, Wesleyan University; Janice Madden, University of Pennsylvania; Karen Mason, University of Michigan; Stanley Masters, University of Wisconsin; Gilbert Nestel, Ohio State University; Frank Stafford, Institute for Social Research, University of Michigan; Mary H. Stevenson, University of Massachusetts; Ernst Stromsdorfer, U.S. Department of Labor; Phyllis A. Wallace, Massachusetts Institute of Technology; Murray Weitzman, U.S. Bureau of the Census and Arleen Winfield, U.S. Department of Labor.

Greg J. Duncan
James N. Morgan

Ann Arbor

PART I

ACCOUNTING FOR SEX AND RACE DIFFERENCES IN EARNINGS

Chapter 1

A SUMMARY OF PART I FINDINGS

Mary Corcoran and Greg J. Duncan

Introduction

In 1975, white men, on average, earned $6.67 per hour. This was 36 percent higher than the average hourly wage of black men, 60 percent higher than for white women, and fully 78 percent higher than for black women.[1] These wage gaps are not well understood, and indeed, the two leading explanations of them have radically different implications for understanding discrimination and planning public policy. The first, a skill explanation, centers on alleged differences in qualifications: white men earn more than the other three groups because they have more valuable job-related skills. The second, a treatment explanation, claims that a wage gap begins because employers initially treat workers differently according to the employee's sex or race, independent of skills—a bias which usually works to the advantage of white males. This differential treatment might in turn generate the group differences in work skills. If the first theory were true, then pay differentials would fall as skills became more equally distributed through, say, job training programs for the less skilled. If the second theory were true, then job training programs for minorities and women would be less successful in reducing wage differences than programs directed at the institutional causes of discrimination.

Past empirical work has largely focused on the skill explanation and has tried to show how differences in the work skills and hence, the productivity of individual workers lead to the pay differences. (See Mincer and Polachek, 1974; Suter and Miller, 1973.) Thus, since black workers usually have completed less formal education than white workers, they are said to be less qualified than white workers. Supposedly it is rational for employers to pay blacks less because they have fewer skills; the only irrational, or discriminatory pay differential is the wage gap not accounted for by these skills differences.

[1] Throughout this volume, we use the term white to include all racial categories other than black.

If differences in skills account in part for the wage gap, discovering how these differences come about becomes important. For example, the black-white differences in educational quality or attainment, are in part a result of past discrimination in the school system. Or a black may be more likely to drop out of school at age 16 because his family needs his earnings. To the extent that black/white skill differences derive from such causes, it may be misleading to label the resulting wage gap nondiscriminatory—even if this wage gap is not the result of direct employer discrimination.

In the case of sex as opposed to race, it is considerably more difficult to identify a source of differences in skills which could lead to the wage gap. Many economists (e.g., Mincer and Polachek, 1974) say that women's qualifications are lower than men's because women assume the bulk of child care and home care responsibilities. This has several implications regarding job-related skills. First, the majority of women do not work continuously after leaving school but, instead, to fulfill family and child care responsibilities, they intersperse periods of employment with periods of nonmarket work. If women expect to have a less regular lifetime pattern of labor force participation, they may have a shorter work horizon than men and, thus, have clear economic incentives to acquire fewer job skills. In addition, the skills they do acquire may become rusty (and, hence, less valuable) during the time they are out of the labor force to have and raise children. Also, even when women work, they must balance the demands of work and family. Family responsibilities may force women to accept lower paying jobs that are closer to home, to have compatible work schedules, or to have high absenteeism rates in order to care for their children when they are ill.

Some argue that skill differences between men and women which lead to the sex-based wage gap are not really the result of employer discrimination because women choose to place child and home demands above job demands. Many question the assumption that the sex division of labor within the home should be taken as given. They argue that it is important to identify the social institutions and conditions that enforce this sex division of labor. Certainly employer discrimination may also play a role in this if pay differences reinforce the sex division of labor within the home by making it more costly in foregone earnings for men to assume family responsibilities.

On the other hand, proponents of the treatment explanations argue that skill differences, voluntary or not, are not at issue since employers treat equally qualified men and women (or blacks and whites) quite differently. Becker (1957), for instance, has argued that employers may prefer one group of workers to another (men to women or whites to blacks), and that they would be willing to pay a premium to indulge their preferences. Others have argued that employers may treat individual workers on the basis of the characteristics of the group to which they belong (see Aigner and Cain, 1977, for a summary of these arguments). If, for example, the average future labor market attachment of women is less than that of men, then employers with imperfect information about attachment may treat all women as though they had a lower level of attachment.

Bergmann (1971) suggests another possibility. She argues that women workers are "crowded" into a relatively narrow range of occupations, resulting in an oversupply of workers to these "female" jobs and artifically reducing the supply of workers to "male" jobs. According to Bergmann and Adelman (1975) female jobs offer fewer promotions and on-the-job training opportunities than do other jobs, and this produces skill differences between men and women. This argument is a variant of what have been called "segmented labor market" theories. Proponents of these theories (see Cain, 1976) argue that jobs in the labor market fall into one of two sectors, the secondary sector or the primary sector. The secondary sector is composed of relatively small, unprofitable, and unstable firms, and its jobs tend to offer few opportunities for promotion and on-the-job training. Large, stable firms comprise the primary sector and its jobs provide both promotion and training opportunities. Women and blacks tend to be disproportionately restricted to the secondary sector because of hiring discrimination in the primary sector. Discrimination may also exist within the primary sector, as when minorities are relegated to job ladders with lower pay and fewer opportunities for advancement.[2]

Efforts to investigate empirically the sources of the race and sex wage gaps have been hampered by inadequate information on work histories and family responsibilities. Instead, past studies have relied on data sources designed for other purposes. The best of these sources contain measures of years of formal education, verbal ability, and life cycle work patterns. Beyond this, the correspondence between available empirical measures and various theoretical concepts becomes quite remote. The empirical effects of marital status on the relative earnings of men and women, for example, are interpreted as the effect of work commitment. It is impossible to tell, however, if a marital status effect may be a result of discriminatory actions on the part of employers rather than of individual or even average skill differences.

In response to the data deficiencies of past studies, the staff of the Panel Study of Income Dynamics designed a questionnaire which was administered in 1976 to household heads and some 3,500 spouses who were part of a national, representative sample of almost 6,000 families that have been followed since 1968. The analysis reported in the first part of this volume focuses on the 5,212 household heads and spouses who were in the

---

[2]Both the "skills" and the "segmented labor market" explanations take current job structures as given. A third, radical perspective argues that job structures evolved at least in part as a means of worker control and that policies aimed at ending sex and race-wage inequality should focus on changing present job structures (Gordon, 1976).

labor force in 1975. Of this total, 2,250 were white men, 895 were black men, 1,326 were white women and 741 were black women.[3]

The questionnaire was designed to address four hypotheses regarding pay differentials by race and sex. The first is that white men are paid more than black men and white and black women because white men receive more on-the-job training. While this hypothesis is widely believed, evidence to test it has been indirect. The Panel Study data, in contrast, contains responses to a set of direct questions on the training content of jobs.

The last three hypotheses relate to differences in earnings between men and women. They are that women earn less than men because they (1) lose skills when they withdraw from the labor force to have and raise children, (2) have higher absenteeism because of illness of other family members (especially children), and (3) restrict job locations and work hours to those compatible with their household responsibilities. Direct questions on each of these topics were included in the questionnaire. Furthermore, both men and women were asked these questions to see if the men with such limitations suffer the same wage penalties as women with corresponding limitations. Both men and women can restrict job location or work hours either because of family responsibilities or because of personal preferences. Regardless of the reason, similar restrictions should, in the absence of discrimination, bring similar wage penalties to both men and women. Also, some men may drop out of the civilian labor force for a period of years without acquiring additional job skills--perhaps for military service. All respondents who dropped out of the labor force were asked whether, during their period of withdrawal,they had acquired any training or skills that would be useful on a job. If labor markets are efficient, then the wage penalty suffered by men who do not acquire useful job skills while in military service should be similar to that of women who withdraw from the labor force to raise children.

In sum, the Panel Study data contain direct measures of on-the-job training, interrupted work experience, absenteeism, and self-imposed restrictions on job location and work hours. In the analysis presented in the first five chapters, we have described the extent to which these measures differ by race and sex, and estimated the extent to which these differences accounted for differences in pay. We also investigated the extent to which differences in training measures resulted from voluntary choice.

Our data permit us to test the skills explanation to a much greater extent than has been possible with other data sets. We cannot, however, also test the treatment explanation, so we do not include its major explanatory variable—occupation—among our

---

[3]Note that the two goups of women are composed of both wives and unmarried female household heads while both married and unmarried men are included in the two groups of men.

empirical measures. Although differences in occupational distributions explain much of the pay differences between the races and sexes, it is unclear whether the occupational differences result from employer discrimination or voluntary choice. To what extent do women, for example, choose to work in lower paying, female-dominated occupations because they allow flexibility in setting work hours or because they don't penalize those with prolonged work interruptions? An understanding of occupational decisions is obviously crucial for a test of the treatment explanations, and our data tell us very little about this. In this book, we do not control for differences in occupational distributions in attempting to account for pay differences by race and sex. This permits us to estimate the maximum impact of skills on earnings differences.

Analysis

What We Found

Our conclusions can be summarized as follows:

White men differed from black men and from white and black women in ways predicted by the conventional wisdom or stereotypes. White men had completed more formal education than either black men or black women. White men reported training periods on their current jobs which averaged more than twice as long as the training periods of black men or white and black women. White and black women spent less time overall in the labor force than white men, with fewer of their working years being full-time. Also, women were considerably more likely than white men to report being absent from work because of the illness of other family members, to have placed restrictions on hours or job location when looking for work, and to expect to stop work in the near future.

Even after adjusting wages[4] for these large average differences in qualifications, white men still earned substantially more than black men, white women, or black women. Average qualification differences explained less than one-third of the wage gap between white men and black women, less than half of the wage gap between white men and white women, and less than two-thirds of the wage gap between white and black men — substantial but hardly overwhelming amounts given the extensive number of qualification measures included in our data. The earnings advantages enjoyed by white men cannot be entirely or even primarily attributed to the superiority of their skills.

Table 1.1 shows the extent to which different factors accounted for wage differences between white men and the other three groups. Differences in training

---

[4]Wage rates are calculated by dividing total annual labor income by the total annual work hours. Race- and sex-based differences in annual earnings are even larger than differences in hourly earnings because white men work more hours per year than the other groups of workers. Some of these differences in work hours result from larger amounts of involuntary unemployment (and underemployment) incurred by black men and white and black women.

Table 1.1

PERCENTAGE OF THE WAGE GAP BETWEEN WHITE MEN AND OTHER GROUPS OF WORKERS "EXPLAINED" BY VARIOUS FACTORS

(All Working Household Heads and Spouses Aged 18-64)

	Black Men	White Women	Black Women
Formal Education	39	2	11
Work History	3	28	14
Years of Training Completed on Current Job	15	10	8
Indicators of Labor Force Attachment	-2	2	-2
Unexplained	45	58	69
TOTAL	100	100	100

accounted for between 8 and 15 percent of the wage differentials between white men and other workers. Differences in formal education accounted for almost 40 percent of the wage gap between white men and black men and for 11 percent of the wage gap between white men and black women. Differences in work history accounted for 28 percent of the wage gap between white men and white women and about 14 percent of the wage gap between white men and black women.

The most striking finding of the study was that the indicators of labor force attachment explain virtually none of the earnings differences between men and women. Individuals of either sex with lower attachment earned no less than otherwise similar individuals with greater attachment. So while women, on the average, lost more time from work, placed more restrictions on job hours and job location, and more often planned to quit work in the near future, these characteristics were unrelated to wages within each group and hence explained none of the total wage gap between men and women.

Differences in training time on the current job accounted for between 8 and 15 percent of the earnings differences between white men and the other groups. While some of these training differences seemed to be influenced by economic incentives, most were produced by what appeared to be institutional barriers in hiring and promoting blacks and women into the jobs with training.

How We Found It

The remainder of this chapter and the other chapters in the first part of this volume detail our procedures and findings. The next section of this chapter describes each set of qualification measures and the extent to which differences in the measures account for both individual wage differences and average wage differences by race and sex. In the concluding section, we discuss the implications of our results. The two appendices to this chapter describe the statistical procedures used to arrive at estimates of the effects of worker characteristics on individual and on group differences in wages.

The remaining chapters in Part I of this volume treat different sets of qualifications separately and in great detail. Chapter 2 examines the set of work history measures. Since on-the-job training is a central part of most explanations of earnings differences, the entire third chapter is devoted to it. The fourth and fifth chapters focus on self-imposed restrictions and absenteeism, respectively.

Indicators of Attachment to the Labor Force

We used the following five measures of attachment to the labor force in our analyses: absenteeism because of own illness, absenteeism because of illness of others, self-imposed restrictions on work hours and location, self-imposed limits on geographic mobility, and plans to quit work.[5]

The questions used to obtain these measures and the distribution of responses by race and sex are detailed in Figures 1.1 to 1.5. Table 1.2 reports the amount of the wage gap between white men and the other race/sex groups that can be explained by race/sex differences in attachment.

The average time lost from work in 1975 was small for all race/sex groups, but women and black men did lose more time than white men. On the average, white men missed 4 hours from work in 1975 because someone else in the family was sick, compared to 8 hours for black men, 12 hours for white women, and 26 hours for black women. White men lost 36 hours from work because of their own illness compared to 43 for white women, 58 for black women, and 50 for black men. Women were much more likely than men to have imposed limitations on the location of their jobs or hours they would work; only about 14 percent of men reported placing such limitations compared to 34 percent of white women and 22 percent for black women. Surprisingly, the sexes did not differ in the limits they placed on geographic mobility. In each race/sex group, about one-third reported that they could get a better job if they were willing to move. Fewer than one-tenth of all workers planned to quit work in the near future, but most of them were women.

These differences in attachment explained almost none of the sex-based wage gap, largely because attachment, as measured in this study, had a negligible impact on wages.[6] For instance, workers who were frequently absent from work or who had imposed limitations on work hours or job location earned no less or only slightly less than did similarly qualified workers who attended work regularly and imposed no such limitations. Imposing geographic limitations did lower a worker's expected wages, but had almost no effect on race or sex differences in wages since all race/sex groups were equally likely, on

---

[5]We originally used one other measure of labor force attachment, voluntary part-time work, since previous research had suggested lower wages for part-time workers. While women were more likely to be part-time workers, we found that this variable had a large positive effect on the wages of black men that was generated by a very small number of cases, and that it had no significant effect on the wages of white men or white women.

[6]We used the standard statistical procedure of multiple regression to relate wages to our measure of labor force attachment, work history, training, and formal education. In calculating the results for one particular set of predictor variables (such as attachment), the effects of all other sets of predictors have been taken into account. For more details, see the Appendix to this chapter.

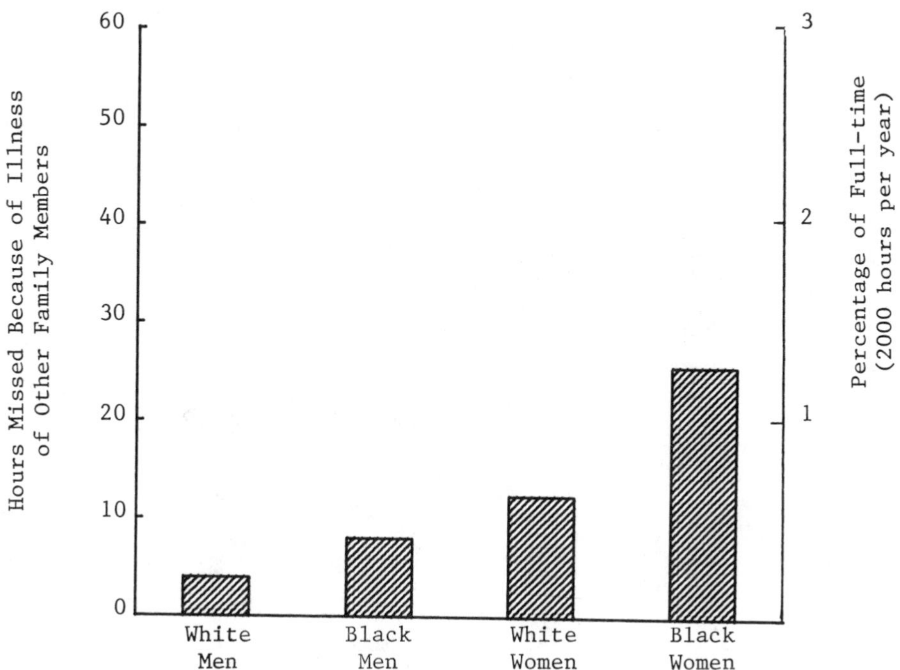

Figure 1.1. ABSENTEEISM BECAUSE OF THE ILLNESS OF OTHERS

When asked "Did you miss any work in 1975 because someone in the family was sick?" women, and especially black women, were much more likely than men to respond affirmatively. When expressed as a fraction of a full time, 2000 hour year, however, the amount of absenteeism for all groups is quite small.

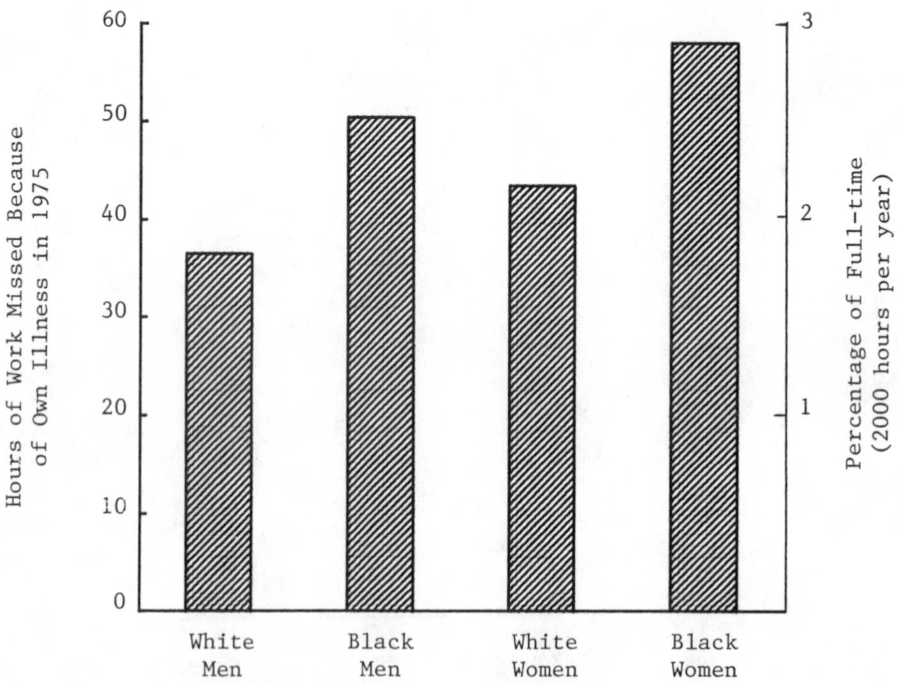

Figure 1.2. ABSENTEEISM BECAUSE OF OWN ILLNESS

Women and black men lost more time from work because they themselves were sick.

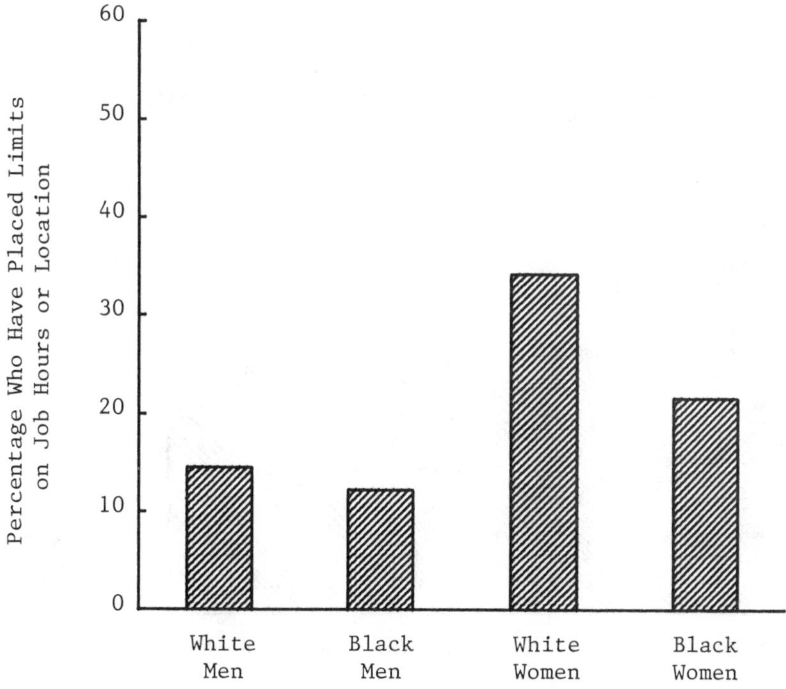

Figure 1.3. SELF-IMPOSED RESTRICTIONS ON LOCATION OR WORK HOURS

Many more women than men gave an affirmative response to the question "Thinking back to when you started your present job, were there some limitations on where you could work or what hours you could work that were factors in taking this job?"

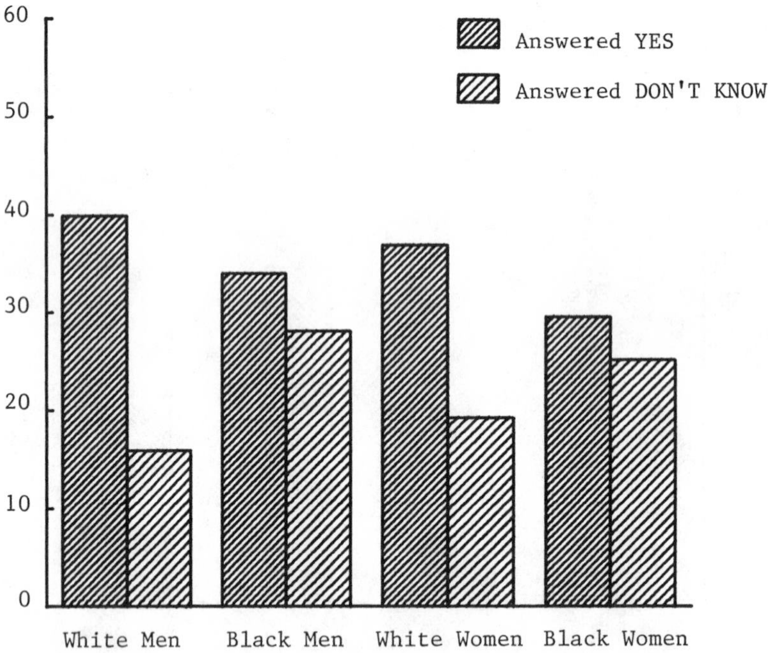

Figure 1.4. SELF-IMPOSED LIMITS ON GEOGRAPHIC MOBILITY

The question "Are there better jobs you could get if you were willing to move and live somewhere else?" showed few differences in affirmative responses across the race/sex subgroups, and blacks were somewhat more likely than whites to say that they didn't know.

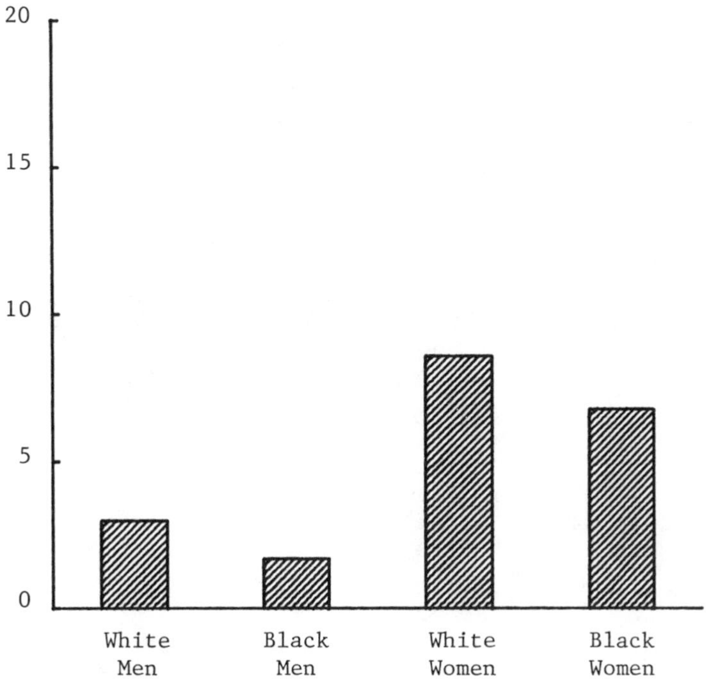

Figure 1.5. PLANS TO QUIT WORK

Although fewer than one-tenth of any of the four groups said they planned to quit work in the next few years for reasons other than to get training, those who do say so are predominately women.

Table 1.2

PROPORTION OF WAGE DIFFERENCES BETWEEN WHITE MEN AND BLACK MEN, WHITE WOMEN AND BLACK WOMEN EXPLAINED BY VARIOUS LABOR FORCE ATTACHMENT MEASURES

(All Working Household Heads and Spouses Aged 18-64)

	Black Men	White Women	Black Women
Hours of Work Missed Because of Illness of Others in 1975	-1	-1	-2
Hours of Work Missed Because of Own Illness in 1975	-1	0	-1
Placed Limits on Job Hours or Location	0	2	1
Knows that There Are Better Jobs Elsewhere	-2	-1	-2
Doesn't Know whether There Are Better Jobs Elsewhere	3	0	1
Plans to Stop Working for Nontraining Reasons	-1	2	1
TOTAL	-2	2	-2

average, to impose such restrictions.[7] Workers who planned to quit work in the near future earned less than did workers with no such plans, but so few workers of either sex planned to quit work that male/female differences in such plans explained, at most, 2 percent of the wage gap between white men and women. Not only did employers fail to reward more reliable workers within the four race/sex subgroups we also found no evidence of reward even to long-term reliable employees for whom information on reliability is readily available and inexpensive.

It may be surprising to learn that differences in attachment explained virtually none of the wage gap between men and women and, indeed, had very little effect on individual worker's wages. Of course, we cannot rule out the possibility that attachment is inadequately measured. But, using a variety of measures, we found that women typically showed less attachment than men with these measures. To the extent that these are valid measures of attachment, these findings suggest that there is little rational economic justification for employers to treat men and women differently on the assumption that it is difficult to sort employees individually and that women as a group are less reliable and less committed than men.

Work History and Training Measures

We split an individual's work history since leaving school into four segments: years out of the labor force since leaving school, years of work experience prior to working for present employer, tenure with present employer prior to present position, and tenure in present position. Tenure in present position was further subdivided into two segments: training completed in present position and post-training tenure. A sixth variable measured the proportion of all years that were full time work.[8] Figures 1.6 to 1.11 show how these measures differed across the four subgroups defined by race and sex. Table 1.3 gives the percentage of the wage gaps between white men and the three other groups that can be accounted for by race/sex differences in work history and training.

As expected, men and women differed considerably both in the amount of time they worked and in the continuity of their work experience. Compared to white men, the

[7]As explained in Chapter 4, responses to the question on self-imposed limits on geographic mobility may be confounded by differences in information about jobs in other locations. Additional analysis in that chapter used the longitudinal aspect of the Panel Study data to test for differences in wage rate changes between husbands and wives who moved as opposed to couples who did not move. In general, these wage differences were minimal although it was found that a greater proportion of wives who moved dropped out of the labor force than did wives who didn't move. Thus, mobility may have an indirect effect on wages by reducing labor force experience.

[8]The definition of "part" and "full" time work was left up to the respondent for this measure, and there is reason to suspect that part-year workers, such as school teachers considered their work as full time.

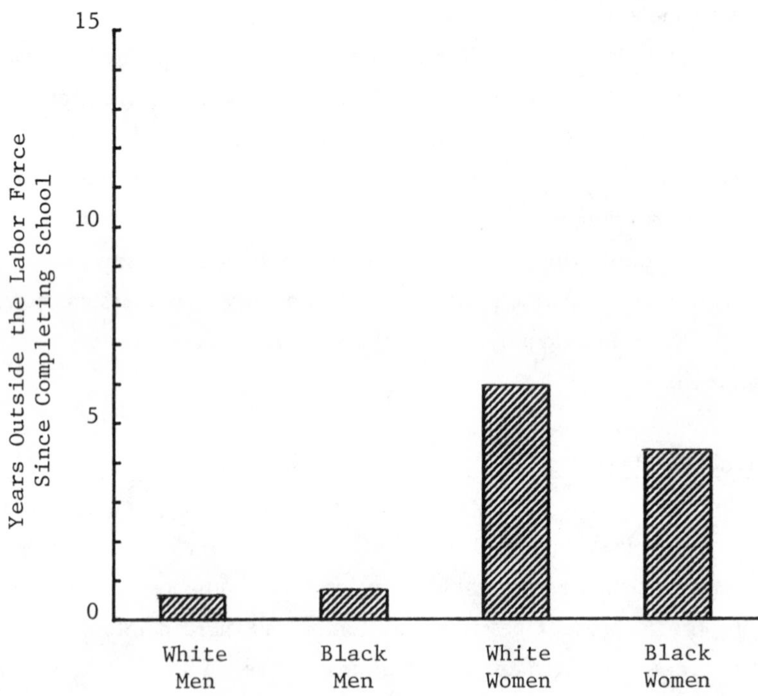

Figure 1.6. YEARS OUTSIDE THE LABOR FORCE SINCE COMPLETING SCHOOL

With respect to work history after finishing their schooling, women spent a much longer time out of the labor force than men.

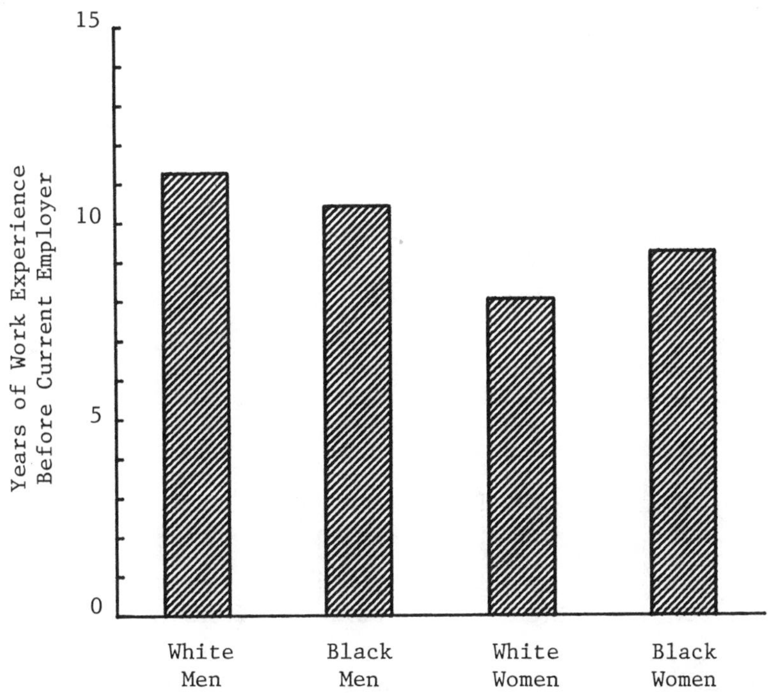

Figure 1.7. YEARS OF WORK EXPERIENCE BEFORE CURRENT EMPLOYER

Women spent somewhat less time in the labor force prior to taking a job with their current employers.

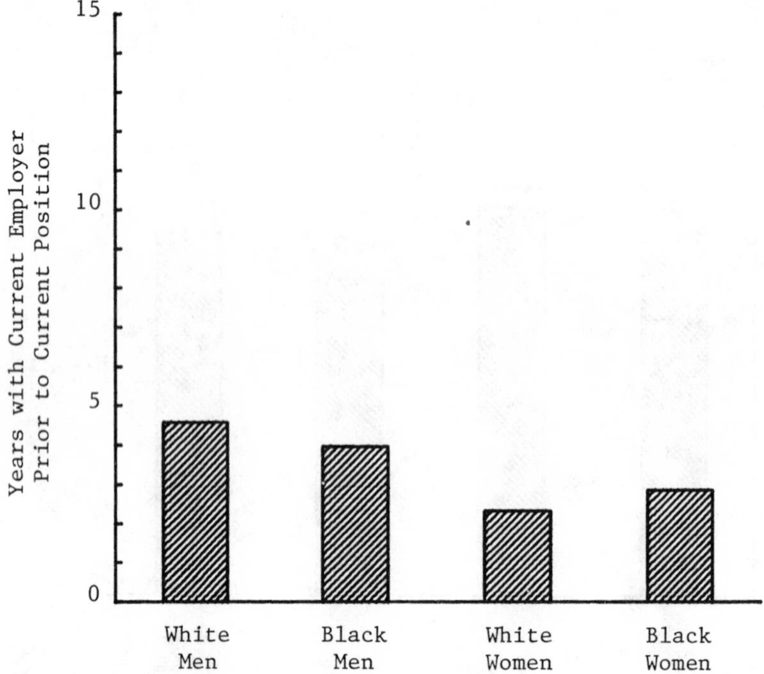

Figure 1.8. YEARS WITH CURRENT EMPLOYER PRIOR TO CURRENT POSITION

Once joining their current employer, women still had fewer years of tenure prior to taking their current position.

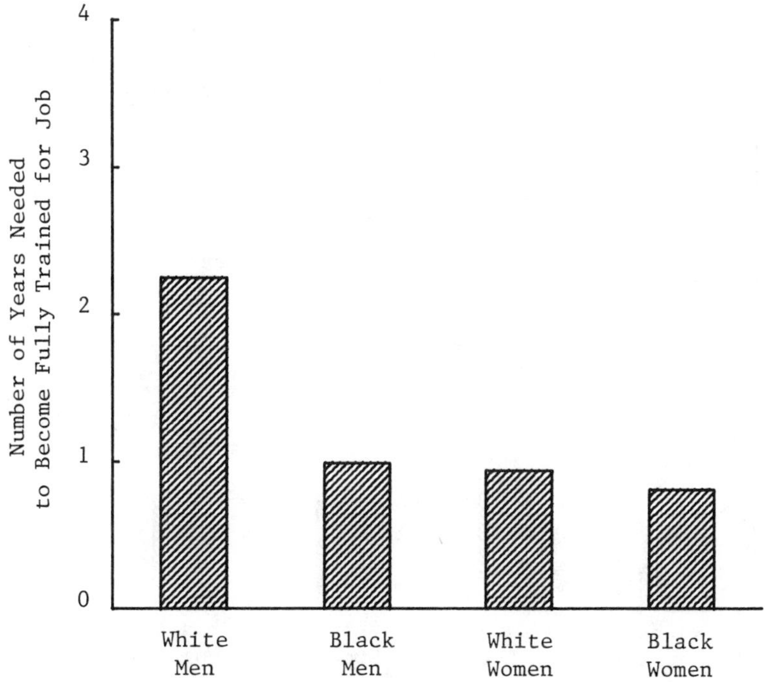

Figure 1.9. ON-THE-JOB TRAINING

In response to the question "How long would it take the average new person to become fully trained and qualified for your job?" white men reported training periods that were more than twice as long as those of the three other groups of workers.

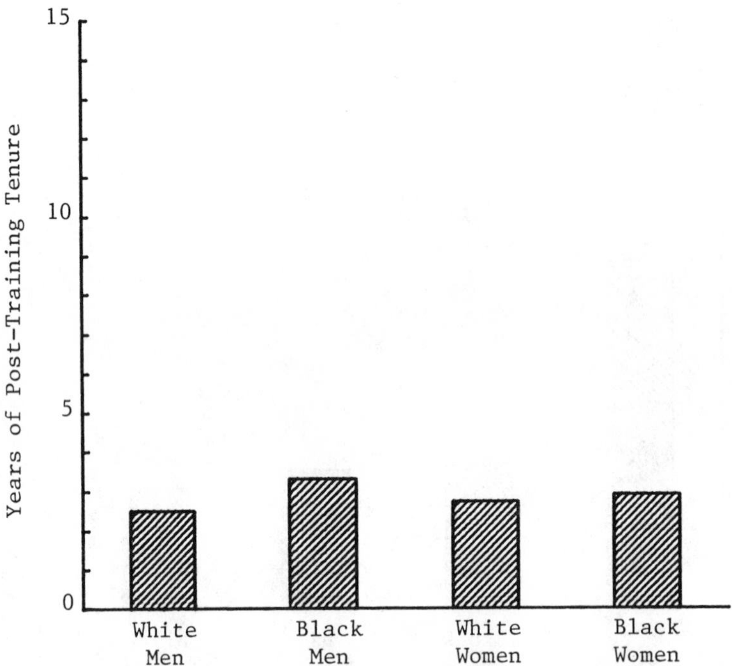

Figure 1.10. YEARS OF POST-TRAINING TENURE ON CURRENT JOB

Women spent about the same amount of time as men in their current position after finishing the training period.

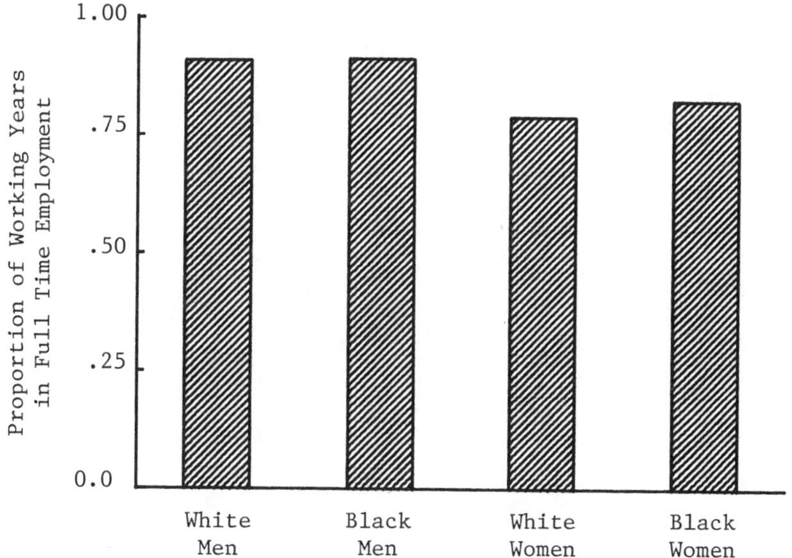

Figure 1.11. PROPORTION OF YEARS WORKED FULL TIME

In addition to working fewer total years, women are also somewhat less likely to work full-time.

Table 1.3

PERCENTAGE OF WAGE DIFFERENCES BETWEEN WHITE MEN AND BLACK MEN, WHITE WOMEN AND BLACK WOMEN EXPLAINED BY VARIOUS WORK HISTORY MEASURES

(All Working Household Heads and Spouses Aged 18-64)

	Black Men	White Women	Black Women
Years Outside the Labor Force Since Completing School	0	6	3
Years of Work Experience Before Present Employer	2	3	1
Years with Current Employer Prior to Current Position	5	12	7
Years of Training Completed on Current Job	15	10	8
Years of Post-Training Tenure on Current Job	-4	-1	-1
Proportion of Total Working Years that Were Fulltime	0	8	4
TOTAL	18	38	22

average white woman had three years less pre-present employer experience, three years less present employer tenure, spent five more years out of the labor force, and was much more likely to work part-time. Differences are similar but smaller when we compare white men to black women. In addition, white men have completed more than twice as much training as black men, white women, or black women.

Past investigations of pay differences by race and sex have indicated that white men's wages rise much more sharply with work experience than do the wages of black men and of women. In contrast with this previous analysis, we broke up work experience into the different segments just described. We found that time spent in a given work segment was equally valuable to all race/sex groups, but that time spent in different segments was not equally valuable. A year of completed training, for instance, raised wages by 5 to 8 percent while a year of pre-employer experience only raised wages 1 to 3 percent. White men had spent relatively more time in the more valuable work segments, especially the training segment, than had the other three groups, and so benefitted more from overall work experience than the rest.

Differences in work history patterns and in training accounted for a considerable portion of the wage gaps between white men and white and black women, largely because women acquired less tenure, completed less training, and were more likely to work part-time. Differences in the proportion of full-time work accounted for 8 percent of the wage gap between white men and white women and 4 percent of the wage gap between white men and black women. Differences in training completed explained 10 percent of the wage gap between white men and white women, 8 percent of the wage gap between white men and black women, and 15 percent of the wage gap between white men and black men. Differences in other tenure components accounted for 11 and 6 percent of the wage gaps between white men and white and black women, respectively.

Surprisingly, the large average differences in years spent out of the labor force since school completion (ranging from 3.5 to 5.2 years) explained very little of the average wage gaps between white men and white and black women. It appears that women are paid less than white men for some reason other than obsolescence of skills because of prolonged periods of labor force withdrawal. Indeed, labor force withdrawals had very small effects on wages even within race/sex groups and even when these withdrawals involved no skill acquisition.[9] Nor did differences in work experience prior to working for one's current employer explain much of the average wage gap between men and women.

[9]Note that labor force withdrawal does reduce wages because work experience is not being accumulated. We find that there is no additional penalty resulting from depreciation or obsolescence of skills. Chapter 2 tests whether withdrawals which involved neither schooling nor training had any effects on worker wages. Such withdrawals had negligible effects on wages for all groups except black men.

Our results (see Chapter 4) show that among white men, married workers earn considerably more than do similarly qualified single workers but that this is not true for women. Some have argued on the basis of similar results that marriage increases men's earnings more than those of women because marriage affects the labor force behavior of men and women quite differently. That is, marital status serves as a proxy for differences in labor market commitment between men and women.[10] In Chapter 4 we find however, that among whites, sex differences in the wage benefits associated with marriage were unchanged even after we adjusted for differences in work commitment, work orientation, and work history.

Black and white men had very similar work history patterns—with one exception. White men had completed twice as much training in their current positions as had black men, and this difference alone accounted for 15 percent of the wage gap between white and black men.

Both the skills and treatment explanations of sex/race wage differentials predict that training accounts for a considerable proportion of the wage gaps between white men and the other three groups. The crucial question is whether race/sex differences in training result from voluntary choice by workers or from the discriminatory hiring and promotion practices of employers. If women and minority workers are crowded into jobs with little opportunity for training it is more appropriate to attribute training-based wage differences to discrimination. In Chapter 3, these issues are explored in some detail. It is concluded that while an individual's chances of engaging in training responded to economic incentives, the most important factors may be involuntary, institutional ones. Women and blacks with similar work horizons and labor force attachment as white men ended up in jobs with less training largely because their prior work experience did not pay off in training opportunities as it did for white men. That is, it appears that employers and firms, when hiring and promoting, may treat women and black men differently than otherwise similarly qualified white men.

Educational Attainment

As Figure 1.12 shows, differences in formal education were greatest between white and black men. White women were most similar to white men, while black women had completed somewhat less education than white women.[11] Because education has a very

---

[10]Another possible explanation for the higher wages of married men reverses the marriage-wage line of causation, i.e., higher wage men are more attractive marriage prospects and are therefore more likely to marry.

[11]Educational distributions do, of course, differ by sex. Women are more likely than men to finish high school, but are less likely to finish college. We investigated possible nonlinear effects of schooling, but found no consistent patterns.

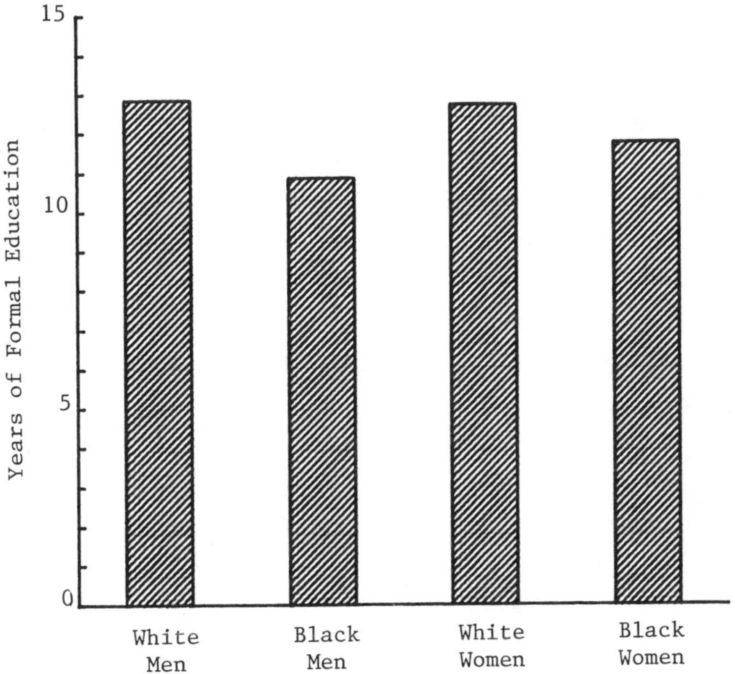

Figure 1.12. FORMAL EDUCATION

Whites have a well-documented advantage in completed education over blacks.

strong effect on wages, differences in educational attainment accounted for a substantial fraction of the pay differences between white men and blacks—especially black men. Differences in formal education accounted for 39 percent of the wage gap between white and black men and 11 percent of the wage gap between white men and black women.

Summary and Implications

We find that the wage advantages enjoyed by white men cannot be explained solely or even primarily by superior qualifications or more attachment to the labor force.[12] Even after adjusting the wage gaps between white men, white and black women, and black men for differences on an extensive list of qualification and attachment measures, white men earned substantially more than did the other groups—particularly women.[13] Given this, we suspect that future investigations of the skills explanation will only confirm these results. That is, those who claim the labor market treats workers fairly in the sense that equally productive workers are paid equally are likely to be wrong. Furthermore, skill augmenting education and training programs alone will probably not eliminate the earnings advantage enjoyed by white men. These results suggest that social scientists should focus more on the treatment explanations of the male/female and black/white wage gaps and less on the skills explanation. Some investigators, for instance might explore the processes by which workers decide to enter certain fields, search for jobs, and acquire jobs. Others might focus on employers' hiring, training, and promotion decisions.

Perhaps our most surprising findings were that virtually none of the indicators of labor force attachment could account for much of the earnings differences between men and women—largely because our indicators of attachment had only trivial effects on wages. Some might argue that we have not included all relevant measures of attachment. This is probably true. But relevant excluded factors are apt to be correlated with our included attachment measures. Since included measures account for none of the gap between white men and the other three groups, it is unlikely that excluded measures will explain very much of the earnings differences. Others may argue that our measures are too imprecise. It is impossible to rule this out entirely. Nevertheless, we used many different

[12]This finding is not unique to us. Most studies which try to adjust the male/female wage gap (Sawhill, 1973; Oaxaca, 1973; Malkiel and Malkiel, 1973; Mincer and Polachek, 1974) or the black/white wage gap (Smith and Welch, 1977) for "skills" differences still leave white men earning considerably more than any other group. Our study generalizes these findings somewhat by including a set of additional skill variables unavailable to past researchers.

[13]It should be noted that the procedure we used to adjust wage gaps tends to overstate the importance of differences in measured qualification.

kinds of measures, and we did find substantial differences in the average values of these measures across the four race/sex groups, with women, as expected, consistently scoring lower than men on attachment. Moreover, we also found that employers do not consistently penalize longer term employees with higher rates of absenteeism, even though the employers have had ample opportunity to gather such information. Thus there appears to be no economic reason for employers to discriminate against women in hiring, promotion, or pay on the basis that women are, on the average, less attached to the labor force than men. If employers justify differential treatment between men and women on the basis of average sex differences in labor force attachment they are clearly behaving unfairly toward many women.[14]

White men's current jobs provided at least twice as much training as did the jobs of women and blacks, and these differences explained a substantial proportion of the wage gaps. By itself, this finding does little to help us understand the extent or operation of discrimination. Do women and black men acquire less skills than white men because they choose to do so or because they are systematically excluded from jobs with good training opportunities? Our evidence (detailed in Chapter 3) indicates that women and black men do not receive the same training opportunities as do similarly qualified white men—a result which suggests that employers treat workers differently on the basis of race and sex. If they do, any wage differences among the four race/sex subgroups which are caused by training differences can also be attributed to discrimination, albeit indirect. This suggests a need for policies (such as affirmative action programs) which ensure equal treatment of these groups in the hiring, promotion, and training decisions, and a need for study of that process.

Women typically have less work experience and are more likely to have worked part-time than white men; these differences in turn affect the wage gap between white men and women. Differences in the average years of experience of men and women are likely

---

[14]In addition to the inequity that results from categorizing whole groups of workers without distinguishing among them, there is an inefficiency in resource allocation that can be costly to society. Arthur Okun commented recently:

> Under conditions of perfect job discrimination, blacks and women (and other victims of prejudice) would get exactly the same jobs they would obtain if not disadvantaged but would merely receive less pay for them. In fact, however, the prevalence of exclusions from good jobs (rather than exploitation involving lower wages) as the technique of discrimination makes substantial inefficiency a by-product of inequality.
>
> Okun, Arthur. "Further Thoughts on Equality and Efficiency." In Income Redistribution, Colin D. Campbell, ed. American Enterprise Institute for Public Policy Research, Washington, D.C. 1977.

In other words, treatment of women as a group without distinction is not only unfair to some of them, but inefficiently assigns them to jobs where they cannot fully use their abilities.

to result in large part from the sex division of labor within the home which may be in turn reinforced by sex discrimination in the labor market. Labor market policies could be designed to enable women and men to combine their family and work roles more efficiently. Such policies might include parental leaves for both sexes, more flexibility in work hours, increasing the availability of part-time work in the more prestigious occupations, or shared jobs.[15] The flexible timing policies would seem especially useful since most of the women (and men) who restrict their job search do so because of concern for the timing of hours, rather than the volume of hours or job location.

It is beyond our expertise to propose a portfolio of specific policies for dealing with unjustified sex and race differences in earnings. But the kinds of policies that might have an effect do become clear from our data. Particularly for blacks, policies which improve the access to and the quality of education could be expected to narrow the wage gaps between the races. Anything that alters the division of labor in the home and the family sex roles toward more equality might well allow women to accumulate more labor force experience, do more full-time work, and hence earn more. But the greatest benefit to those firmly attached to the labor force may derive from policies that equalize access to a job with training and a chance for advancement.

---

[15]Some policies might even provide incentives to break up the sex division of labor in the home. For example, in Sweden parents are guaranteed six paid months of maternity leave for either parent. If parents choose to share maternity leave, they are given seven months, three to one parent and four months to the other.

APPENDIX 1.1

Introduction

In the text of Chapter 1, we summarized the results of our attempts to account for wage differences among white men, black men, white women, and black women. This Appendix details our procedures and findings.

Three steps were involved in the attempt to account for wage differences using the skill and attachment measures available in the Panel Study data. First, we calculated the average values of the measures separately by race and sex. These averages, presented in graphs in the text, are tabulated in Table A1.1a. Next we related all of these measures to wages to determine if individuals with different amounts of these measures are paid accordingly. Third, we combined the information on differences in average skill and commitment measures with information on how these characteristics affect wages in order to calculate the fraction of the wage differences between white men and the other three groups that are "explained" by differences in these characteristics. In addition, we examine the stability of the results by changing the wage rate measure and by using coefficients from a regression in which all four race/sex subgroups are pooled together.

All of the empirical results were obtained from the set of household heads and wives in the Panel who (1) were employed at the time of the spring 1976 interview, (2) had worked at least 500 hours in 1975, and (3) were between the ages of 18 and 64. Note that the women consisted of both wives and female household heads, and also that individuals who were children in families were excluded.[16]

How the Measures Relate to Wages

Although the four groups of workers differed considerably in a number of ways that may affect productivity, it does not necessarily follow that these differences "explain" all of the earnings advantages enjoyed by white men. Differential work experience and attachment will explain the gap only if they have substantial effects on earnings. If, for example, workers who lost time from work to care for other family members are not paid less than workers who miss no work, then the fact that women, on average, tend to miss somewhat more work for this reason will not explain why they earn less than men.

We used multiple regression to estimate the effects of the various measures of education, training, work history, and labor force attachment on wages. Regressions were run separately for the four different groups of workers, and the results are detailed in

[16]The effects of marital status on earnings are examined in some detail in Chapter 4.

Table A1.1a

MEAN VALUES OF INDEPENDENT VARIABLES IN WAGE EQUATION, BY RACE/SEX SUBGROUPS
(All Working Household Heads and Spouses Aged 18-64)

	White Men	Black Men	White Women	Black Women
Formal Education (in years)	12.85	10.96	12.73	11.75
WORK HISTORY				
Years Out of Labor Force since Completing School	0.51	0.63	5.75	4.03
Years of Work Experience before Present Employer	11.27	10.44	8.05	9.27
Pre-employer Work Experience Squared+	225.0	212.9	129.9	161.9
Years with Current Employer Prior to Current Position	4.58	3.96	2.33	2.86
Years of Training Completed on Current Job	1.686	0.791	0.722	0.704
Years of Post-training Tenure on Current Job	2.51	3.31	2.74	2.91
Proportion of Total Working Years that were Full Time	0.909	0.913	0.790	0.826
INDICATORS OF LABOR FORCE ATTACHMENT				
Hours of Work Missed for Others' Illness in 1975	4.01	8.05	12.45	25.68
Hours of Work Missed for Own Illness in 1975	36.5	50.4	43.0	58.0
Limited Job Hours or Location	0.145	0.122	0.342	0.216
Knows there Are Better Jobs Elsewhere	0.399	0.340	0.369	0.295
Doesn't Know Whether there Are Better Jobs Elsewhere	0.159	0.281	0.193	0.252
Plans to Stop Work for Nontraining Reasons	0.030	0.017	0.086	0.068
DEMOGRAPHIC CONTROL VARIABLES				
Size of Largest City in Area (in hundreds of thousands)	3.840	5.484	4.079	5.261
Whether South	0.266	0.542	0.261	0.558
ln 1975 Hourly Wage	1.722	1.461	1.284	1.154
1975 Hourly Wage (Geometric Mean)‡	5.60	4.31	3.61	3.17
Number of Observations	2,250	895	1,326	741

+The square of pre-employer work experience was included in the regressions to allow for a parabolic relationship between experience and wages.

‡These average wage figures differ from those presented in the opening paragraph of the text because these are *geometric* means and the others are *arithmetic* means.

Table A1.1b.[17] We used the natural logarithm form of the hourly wage rate as the dependent variable so that the coefficients can be interpreted as the estimated effects of a one-unit change in an independent variable on the percentage change in wage rate.[18] Thus the ".060" entry in the upper left-hand corner of the table shows that for white men, an additional year of education was associated with a 6.0 percent increase in hourly earnings.

Two striking results emerge from Table A1.1b. First, the relationships between the various independent variables and wages were remarkably uniform across the four subgroups defined by race and sex. Second, differences in attachment did not lead to appreciable differences in pay.

Previous work on pay differences between the sexes and races has found considerable differences in the sizes of the coefficients. For example, the payoff on an additional year of work experience was found to be higher for white men than for any of the other groups. In contrast, our data allowed us to classify work experience into different segments. White men and women spend different amounts of time in the various segments. The coefficients shown in Table A1.1b indicate that the proportional payoff on an additional year spent in any particular segment is quite similar for the four groups. Of the 48 coefficients on the variables for the three minority groups, only 10 are significantly different from the corresponding white male coefficients—two at the 1 percent level of significance and eight at the 5 percent level. Of the 10 differing coefficients, only three were smaller (in absolute value) than the coefficients for white men.[19]

---

[17]Numerous alternatives to the regression model of Table A1.1 were estimated for the four race/sex subgroups and are described in subsequent chapters. The results of Table A1.2 are representative of most of the results from alternative formulations. The data have been weighted for differential sampling and nonresponse rates.

[18]Note that equal percentage changes in wages imply unequal absolute changes in wages. A 10 percent increase from $3.00 per hour is $.30 but is $.60 from $6.00 per hour.

[19]Some readers may be surprised to see that white men and black men have similar coefficients on formal education. This is inconsistent with some past research, but is consistent with a study conducted on several large sets of microdata. Schwartz (1977) found no significant race differences in the effects of education on the national logarithm of annual earnings for men 25 to 64 years with positive earnings in three different national surveys: the 1962 Occupational Changes in a Generation Survey, the 1970 Census, and the 1972 wave of The Panel Study of Income Dynamics.

Table A1.1b

REGRESSION RESULTS FOR SUMMARY WAGE EQUATION, BY RACE/SEX SUBGROUPS
(All Working Household Heads and Spouses Aged 18-64)

	White Men	Black Men	White Women	Black Women
Formal Education (in years)	.060** (.004)	.062** (.006)	.076** (.006)	.079** (.008)
WORK HISTORY				
Years Out of Labor Force since Completing School	-.005 (.007)	-.008 (.010)	-.005** (.002)	.005 (.003)
Years of Work Experience before Present Employer	.013** (.003)	.026** (.005)	.011** (.004)	.011** (.005)
Pre-employer Work Experience Squared	-.0003** (.0001)	-.0006** (.0001)	-.0004** (.0001)	-.0004** (.0002)
Years with Current Employer Prior to Current Position	.024** (.002)	.019** (.003)	.021** (.003)	.017** (.003)
Years of Training Completed on Current Job	.048** (.006)	.065** (.014)	.080** (.013)	.076** (.016)
Years of Post-training Tenure on Current Job	.014** (.004)	.014** (.006)	.022** (.005)	-.012 (.007)
Proportion of Total Working Years that were Full Time	.307** (.060)	.551** (.094)	.262** (.044)	.125* (.057)
INDICATORS OF LABOR FORCE ATTACHMENT				
Hours of Work Missed for Others' Illness in 1975	.0006 (.0005)	-.0003 (.0003)	-.0001 (.0002)	.0003 (.0002)
Hours of Work Missed for Own Illness in 1975	.0002* (.0001)	.0001 (.0001)	-.0002* (.0001)	.0000 (.0001)
Limited Job Hours or Location	-.041 (.030)	.102* (.048)	-.018 (.026)	-.008 (.039)
Knows there Are Better Jobs Elsewhere	-.105** (.024)	-.124** (.037)	-.112** (.028)	-.148** (.039)
Doesn't Know Whether there Are Better Jobs Elsewhere	-.071* (.031)	-.078* (.039)	-.145** (.034)	-.031 (.039)
Plans to Stop Work for Nontraining Reasons	-.169** (.063)	-.222 (.120)	-.056 (.044)	-.285** (.068)
DEMOGRAPHIC CONTROL VARIABLES				
Size of Largest City in the Area (in hundreds of thousands)	.027** (.003)	.018** (.004)	.018** (.003)	.022** (.004)
Whether South	-.060* (.025)	-.095** (.035)	-.034 (.029)	-.089* (.035)
Constant	.334	-.046	-.033	-.009
$\bar{R}^2$	.303	.291	.328	.346
Number of Observations	2,250	895	1,326	741

Note: The numbers on the table are raw score regression coefficients with standard errors in parentheses.

**Significantly different from zero at .01 level.

*Significantly different from zero at .05 level.

While the education and work history measures generally had significant effects on wages, the attachment measures usually did not. Absenteeism because of the illness of others in the family and self-imposed limits on job choice or location had virtually no effect on the wages of any of the four subgroups of workers. Workers who knew of better jobs in other localities but had not moved to take them earned about 10 percent less than those who said no such better jobs existed. Those who did not know whether better jobs were available suffered a somewhat smaller penalty. Those planning to stop work in the next few years also earned less, with the amount varying somewhat across the four subgroups. In general, however, attachment measures did not explain wage differences very well.

Accounting for Wage Differences between White Men and Other Workers

Next we combined the information on differences in the amounts of education, work experience, and work commitment across the race/sex subgroups with the estimated effects of these factors on earnings to see how well they accounted for earnings differences between white men and the other groups of workers. We multiplied the difference between white men and each of the other groups in the average values for each independent variable by its estimated effect (which comes from the wage rate regression equation for white men), and then expressed the product as a fraction of the total difference in wages. As an example, it was shown earlier that white men average nearly 13 years of formal education while the mean for black men is about 11 years. The regression results for white men showed that this two year difference is "worth" 6 percent per year, or about 12 percent altogether. Since the (geometric) mean wages of white men are about 30 percent higher than black men, the differences in educational attainment account for 12/30, or about 40 percent of the total earnings gap between black and white men.[20]

The results of calculating this ratio for each predictor variable are summarized in Table A1.1c. The first entry in the table, 43 percent, comes from the calculation on educational differences between white and black men, as outlined above. The final rows of the table show the fraction of the wage differences that can and cannot be accounted

[20] The statistical basis for this procedure is described in Appendix 1.2.

Table A1.1c

ACCOUNTING FOR WAGE DIFFERENCES BETWEEN WHITE MEN AND OTHER RACE/SEX SUBGROUPS
(All Working Household Heads and Spouses Aged 18-64)

	Percentage of Wage Gap between White Men and Minority Groups Accounted					
	Not Adjusted for South and City Size			Adjusted for South and City Size		
	Black Men	White Women	Black Women	Black Men	White Women	Black Women
Formal Education (in years)	43	2	12	39	2	11
WORK HISTORY						
Years Out of Labor Force since Completing School	0	6	3	0	6	3
Years of Work Experience before Present Employer / Pre-employer Work Experience Squared	3	3	1	2	3	1
Years with Current Employer Prior to Current Position	6	12	7	5	12	7
Years of Training Completed on Current Job	16	11	8	15	10	8
Years of Post-training Tenure on Current Job	-4	-1	-1	-4	-1	-1
Proportion of Total Working Years that were Full Time	0	8	4	0	8	4
INDICATORS OF LABOR FORCE ATTACHMENT						
Hours of Work Missed for Others' Illness in 1975	-1	-1	-2	-1	-1	-2
Hours of Work Missed for Own Illness in 1975	-1	0	-1	-1	0	-1
Limited Job Hours or Location	0	2	1	0	2	1
Knows there Are Better Jobs Elsewhere	-2	-1	-2	-2	-1	-2
Doesn't Know Whether there Are Better Jobs Elsewhere	3	0	1	3	0	1
Plans to Stop Work for Nontraining Reasons	-1	2	1	-1	2	1
DEMOGRAPHIC CONTROL VARIABLES						
Size of Largest City in the Area (in hundreds of thousands)	-17	-1	-7	--	--	--
Whether South	6	0	3	--	--	--
Total Explained	51	42	28	55	42	31
Unexplained	49	58	72	45	58	69
TOTAL	100	100	100	100	100	100

for by our set of 13 explanatory variables.[21] In sum, Table A1.1c shows that differences in educational attainment are most important for black men; differences in work history matter most for women; and training differences are somewhat important for all groups. An equally important finding is that a very large part of wage differences cannot be explained by our long list of productivity-related factors.

Education. We have just seen both that the educational attainment level of white men exceeds that of black men and that education has a strong, positive effect on earnings. So it should not be surprising that the differences in the quantity of education account for a substantial fraction of the wage gap between white and black men. Differences in the quality of education have not been measured in our data and would no doubt increase the explanatory power of education even more. Black women have somewhat more education, on average, than black men, and differences in attainment account for 11 percent of the wage differential between white men and black women.

Work History. A unique aspect of the panel data is that the total work histories of all respondents can be broken down into comparable segments. For black men, the training time on the current job segment is especially important, accounting for 15 percent of the wage gap between white and black men. For both groups of women, the other tenure segments make important contributions as well. Differences between white men and white and black women in the two other segments of employer tenure also explain a substantial part of the wage gaps between white men and white and black women.

Women are also paid less because they spend more time out of the labor force and are less likely to be working full-time when in the labor force. These two factors account for 6 and 8 percent of the wage gap for white women and exactly half that amount for black women.

Labor Force Attachment. Contrary to our initial expectations, the group of attachment variables explain very little of the earnings differences between white men, blacks, and women. None of the measures accounts for as much as 4 percent of the wage

---

[21] Two of the independent variables, Size of Largest City in the Area and Whether South, were included in the regressions to adjust for cost of living and other differences between urban and rural areas and among regions of the country. Because wages are higher in urban areas and because blacks are more likely to be living in urban areas, our treatment of the City Size variable makes a substantial difference in the calculation of how much of the wage differences can be "explained" by the independent variables. In Table A1.1c, these two variables are treated in two different ways. In the first three columns, they are included along with the other independent variables. In the last three columns, the wage differences explained by these two variables have been subtracted from the total wage gap and the explanatory power of the other independent variables is expressed as a fraction of this "adjusted" wage gap. The calculations presented in the text of this chapter are based on the "adjusted" wage gap.

gap, and two of them actually operate in an unexpected direction. White men report less absenteeism because of illness of others in the family, for example, but because absenteeism had a small positive effect on wages it appears that reduced absenteeism among blacks and women would actually increase the wage differences. A more reasonable conclusion would be that this kind of absenteeism produces virtually none of the wage differences. Differences in the extent to which the four groups of respondents have not moved to get better jobs also produces an anomolous result, but this is because white men are more likely to know of better jobs elsewhere. Thus, we may be measuring the amount of job-related information acquired rather than voluntary limits to mobility. Although the remaining measures operate in the expected direction, their contribution to the explanation of wage differences is minimal.

The Effects of Combining the Subsamples and Changing the Wage Rate Measure

Two crucial parts of our analysis are the estimated effects (coefficients) of the independent variables on wages and the portion of the wage gap between white men and the other groups that can be explained by the various independent variables. Our discussion thus far has implicitly assumed a single, correct set of estimates for these two parts, although any data analyst knows that changes in the definition or functional form of variables or additions to the set of independent variables often cause the coefficients to change somewhat. The stability of the coefficients of many of the variables are investigated in later chapters. In this final section of Appendix 1.1, we investigate the sensitivity of the results by first using the average coefficients obtained by pooling the four race/sex subgroups together and second, by using an alternative measure of wage rate.

In our accounting procedure, we had taken differences in average amounts of the various characteristics and valued them with coefficients from the wage equation for white men. Since there were some differences between the coefficients of white men and the other three groups, we also chose to see if differences would arise from valuing characteristics with "average" coefficients obtained by pooling all four groups together rather than the white coefficients. The resulting coefficients, shown in the first column of numbers in Table A1.1d, entitled "Computed Wage Rate" are generally similar to those of white men. The coefficients on the education and training variables are somewhat higher while the coefficients on several of the attachment measures are slightly lower. Using pooled coefficients changes the accounting fractions very little, as shown in the first three columns in Table A1.1e. Educational differences are still very important in explaining wage differences between white and black men, while work history differences

Table A1.1d

REGRESSION RESULTS FOR WAGE EQUATION, WITH ALL RACE/SEX SUBGROUPS COMBINED
(All Working Household Heads and Spouses Aged 18-64)

	Computed Wage Rate	Reported Wage Rate
Formal Education (in years)	.066**	.052**
	(.003)	(.003)
WORK HISTORY		
Years Out of Labor Force since Completing School	-.005**	-.006**
	(.001)	(.002)
Years of Work Experience before Present Employer	.011**	.011**
	(.002)	(.003)
Pre-employer Work Experience Squared	-.0003**	-.0004**
	(.0001)	(.0001)
Years with Current Employer Prior to Current Position	.022**	.025**
	(.001)	(.002)
Years of Training Completed on Current Job	.055**	.031**
	(.005)	(.006)
Years of Post-training Tenure on Current Job	.016**	-.001
	(.003)	(.003)
Proportion of Total Working Years that were Full Time	.291**	.193**
	(.030)	(.040)
INDICATORS OF LABOR FORCE ATTACHMENT		
Hours of Work Missed for Others' Illness in 1975	.0000	-.0002
	(.0002)	(.0002)
Hours of Work Missed for Own Illness in 1975	.0000	-.0001
	(.0001)	(.0001)
Limited Job Hours or Location	-.023	-.046*
	(.017)	(.022)
Knows there Are Better Jobs Elsewhere	-.111**	-.035
	(.015)	(.020)
Doesn't Know Whether there Are Better Jobs Elsewhere	-.094**	-.068**
	(.019)	(.025)
Plans to Stop Work for Nontraining Reasons	-.104**	-.092**
	(.031)	(.041)
DEMOGRAPHIC CONTROL VARIABLES		
Size of Largest City in the Area (in hundreds of thousands)	.023**	.022**
	(.002)	(.002)
Whether South	-.056**	-.063**
	(.016)	(.021)
Black Male	-.101**	-.077
	(.031)	(.041)
White Female	-.255**	-.198**
	(.017)	(.023)
Black Female	-.337**	-.280**
	(.034)	(.054)
Constant	.307	.534
$\bar{R}^2$	.392	.218

Note: The numbers on the table are raw score regression coefficients with standard errors in parentheses. The total number of observations is 5212.

**Significantly different from zero at .01 level.

*Significantly different from zero at .05 level.

Table A1.1e

ACCOUNTING FOR WAGE DIFFERENCES BETWEEN WHITE MEN AND OTHER RACE/SEX SUBGROUPS FOR TWO ALTERNATIVE WAGE RATE MEASURES

(All Working Household Heads and Spouses Aged 18-64)

	Percentage Using Pooled Coefficients and Calculated Wage Rate			Percentage Using Pooled Coefficients and Reported Wage Rate		
	Black Men	White Women	Black Women	Black Men	White Women	Black Women
Formal Education (in years)	44	2	13	42	2	12
WORK HISTORY						
Years Out of Labor Force since Completing School	0	6	3	0	9	5
Years of Work Experience Before Present Employer Pre-employer Work Experience Squared	3	2	1	2	0	0
Years with Current Employer Prior to Current Position	5	11	7	6	16	9
Years of Training Completed on Current Job	17	12	9	12	8	6
Years of Post-training Tenure on Current Job	-5	-1	-1	0	0	0
Proportion of Total Working Years that were Full Time	0	8	4	0	6	3
INDICATORS OF LABOR FORCE ATTACHMENT						
Hours of Work Missed for Others' Illness in 1975	0	0	0	0	1	1
Hours of Work Missed for Own Illness in 1975	0	0	0	0	0	0
Limited Jobs Hours or Location	0	1	0	0	3	1
Knows there Are Better Jobs Elsewhere	-2	-1	-3	-1	0	-1
Doesn't Know Whether there Are Better Jobs Elsewhere	4	1	2	3	1	1
Plans to Stop Work for Nontraining Reasons	0	1	1	0	2	1
Total Explained	66	42	36	64	48	38

play a role in explaining the male/female wage gaps. The conclusion about the unimportance of the attachment measures remains unaltered.

The wage rate measure used in our analysis was calculated by dividing the total 1975 labor income by total 1975 work hours. For wives, the husbands report the income while the wives themselves report their annual work hours. The alternative wage rate measure was a direct report of current rate of salary or hourly wage rate. All employed respondents were asked the question sequences:

D55. Are you salaried, paid by the hour, or what?

1. SALARIED	3. PAID BY HOUR	7. OTHER
D56. How much is your salary? $________ per______ D57. If you were to work more hours than usual during some week, would you get paid for those extra hours of work? 1. YES · 5. NO (GO TO D63) D58. About how much would you make per hour for that overtime? $____________ (PER HOUR) (GO TO D63)	D59. What is your hourly wage rate for your regular work time? $____________ (PER HOUR) D60. What is your hourly wage rate for overtime? $____________ (PER HOUR) (GO TO D63)	D61. How is that? ____________ ____________ ____________ ____________ D62. If you worked an extra hour, how much would you earn for that hour? $____________ (GO TO D63)

The salary reports were converted into hourly earnings by assuming a 40-hour work week. The straight-time hourly rate was used for those paid by the hour. For those who were neither salaried nor hourly, the marginal wage rate reported in question number D62 was used. For 16.7 percent of the respondents, an hourly wage rate was not ascertained.[22] For those cases, we substituted the original hourly earnings measure.

To establish further comparability with the original wage measure, the range of this reported hourly earnings measure was truncated at $.50 and $25.00 and converted to

[22]This includes cases where the reported hourly rate was above $9.98 per hour. Unfortunately, these cases were all coded as $9.98 .

natural logarithms. The simple correlation (r) between these two wage variables is .67. The coefficients from the regression of this alternative wage measure on the same set of independent variables is given in the second column of numbers of Table A1.4. Although the fraction of variance explained in the reported wage equation is only about half as large as in the calculated wage regression, most of the coefficients are similar. Two variables, "Years of Post-training Tenure on Current Job" and "Knows there Are Better Jobs Elsewhere" become insignificant. Changes in the ability of these variables to account for pay differences between the races and sexes, however, are small, as shown in the final three columns of numbers in Table A1.1e. There are some offsetting changes in the explanatory power of some of the work history measures, but our basic conclusions are not affected.

APPENDIX 1.2

The statistical basis of our procedures for accounting for pay differences between the races and sexes has been worked out by Oaxaca (1973) and is summarized in Conte (1976). In this appendix, we describe the procedure, using the group of white men and white women as examples. It applies equally well to accounting for pay differences between white men and the groups of black men and women.

Let (1) $$G = \frac{\overline{W}_{wm} - \overline{W}_{ww}}{\overline{W}_{ww}}$$

where $\overline{W}_{wm}$ is the average hourly wage of white men, and

$\overline{W}_{ww}$ is the average hourly wage of white women.

G, then, is the proportionate average wage advantage of white men relative to white women.

Now (2) $$G + 1 = \frac{\overline{W}_{wm}}{\overline{W}_{ww}}, \text{ so}$$

(3) $$\ln (G + 1) = \ln \overline{W}_{wm} - \ln \overline{W}_{ww}.$$

From the property of least squares estimation,

(4) $$\ln \overline{W}_{wm} = Z_{wm} \hat{\beta}_{wm}$$

and (5) $$\ln \overline{W}_{ww} = Z_{ww} \hat{\beta}_{ww}$$

where Z_{wm} and Z_{ww} are vectors of mean values on the independent variables for white men and women, respectively, and $\hat{\beta}_{wm}$ and $\hat{\beta}_{ww}$ are vectors of estimated coefficients for these two groups.

Substituting (4) and (5) into (3),

(6) $$\ln (G + 1) = Z_{wm} \hat{\beta}_{wm} - Z_{ww} \hat{\beta}_{ww}.$$

Now let

(7) $$\Delta Z = Z_{wm} - Z_{ww} \text{ and}$$

(8) $$\Delta\hat{\beta} = \hat{\beta}_{ww} - \hat{\beta}_{wm};$$

then the wage differential between white men and women can be written either as

(9) $$\ln (G + 1) = \Delta Z \hat{\beta}_{wm} - Z_{ww} \Delta\hat{\beta}$$

or (10) $$\ln (G + 1) = \Delta Z\hat{\beta}_{ww} - Z_{wm} \Delta\hat{\beta} .$$

In words, equation (9) says that the total wage differential can be decomposed into a part resulting from differences in amounts of the independent variables "valued" at the white, male coefficients and a part resulting from differences in coefficients "valued" at the white, female means.[23] Since we find very few differences in coefficients, we ignore the second part of the decomposition. The numbers in Table A1.3 show, for each independent variable i,$(\Delta Z_i \times \hat{\beta}_{iwm}) \div \ln (G + 1)$.

Note that equation (10) represents an alternative method for decomposing the wage differences. In contrast to (9), equation (10) values differences in the mean amounts of the independent variables with the white, female coefficients. Since there were few differences in coefficients across the four race/sex subgroups, this alternative method does not change our conclusions based on use of the white, male coefficients.

---

[23]Note that there is no covariance term in this expression.

References

Aigner, Dennis, and Cain, Glen G. "Statistical Theories of Discrimination in Labor Markets." Industrial and Labor Relations Review 30, No. 2 (January 1977): 175-87.

Arrow, Kenneth J. "Models of Job Discrimination" and "Some Mathematical Models of Race in the Labor Market." Racial Discrimination in Economic Life. Edited by Anthony Pascal. Lexington, Mass.: Lexington Books, 1972.

Becker, Gary. The Economics of Discrimination. Chicago: The University of Chicago Press, 1957.

Bergmann, Barbara. "Occupational Segregation, Wages and Profits When Employers Discriminate by Sex ad Race." College Park, Md.: University of Maryland. Economics of Discrimination Project, Mimeographed. January 1971.

Bergmann, Barbara, and Adelman, Irma. "The 1973 Report of the President's Council of Economic Advisors: The Economic Role of Women." The American Economic Review LXIII (September 1973): 509-15.

Blinder, Alan. "Wage Discrimination: Reduced Form and Structural Estimates." Journal of Human Resources VIII (Fall 1973): 436-55.

Cain, Glen G. "The Challenge of Segmented Labor Market Theories to Orthodox Theory: A Survey." Journal of Economic Literature XIV (December 1976): 1215-57.

Conte, Michael. "Labor Market Discrimination against Women." In Five Thousand American Families—Patterns of Economic Progress, Vol. IV. Edited by G. Duncan and J. Morgan. Ann Arbor, Mich. Institute for Social Research, 1976.

Doeringer, Peter, and Piore, Michael. Internal Labor Markets and Manpower Analysis. Lexington, Mass.: Lexington Books, 1971.

Gordon, David M. "Economic Dimensions of Occupational Segregation: Comment II," In Women and the Workplace. Edited by Martha Blaxall and Barbara Reagan. Chicago: University of Chicago Press, 1976.

Malkiel, Burton, and Malkiel, Judith. "Male/Female Pay Differentials in Professional Employment." The American Economic Review 63 (September 1973).

Mincer, J., and Polachek, S. "Family Investments in Human Capital: Earnings of Wommen." Journal of Political Economy 82, No. 2, Part II (March/April 1974): 576-608.

Oaxaca, Ronald. "Male-Female Wage Differentials in Urban Labor Markets." International Economic Review 14, No. 3 (October 1973).

Polachek, Solomon. "Potential Biases in Measuring Male-Female Discrimination." Journal of Human Resources 70, No. 2 (1975): 205-29.

Sawhill, Isabel. "The Economics of Discrimination against Women: Some New Findings." The Journal of Human Resources VIII, No. 3 (Summer 1973): 386-87.

Schwartz, Joseph, and Williams, Jill. "White-Nonwhite Differences in Income: 1949-1973" In The Effects of Family Background, Test Scores, Personality Traits and Education on Economic Success, Report No. DLMA-NIE-G-74-007-1. Edited by Christopher Jencks and Lee Rainwater. Washington,D.C.: 1977. U.S. Department of Labor.

Smith, James, and Welch, Finis. "Black-White Male Wage Ratios: 1960-1970." American Economic Review 67, No. 3 (June 1977): 323-38.

Stevenson, Mary. "Women's Wages and Job Segregation." Politics and Society, Fall 1973: 83-95.

Suter, Larry E., and Miller, Herman P. "Income Differences between Men and Women." American Journal of Sociology, January 1973.

Chapter 2

WORK EXPERIENCE, WORK INTERRUPTION, AND WAGES

Mary Corcoran

Introduction

Women and black men earn considerably less than white men and, as Figure 2.1 shows, have much flatter wage-experience profiles. White men's earnings rise steadily at a decreasing rate for the first 30 years of experience and then decline somewhat. No other race/sex group shows this steady pattern of earnings increases with work experience over the entire work cycle. Explanations of these two phenomena center on race/sex differences in investments in on-the-job training.

Mincer and Polachek (1974) argue that the differences between white men's and white and black women's earnings and earnings-experience profiles stem from differences in life-cycle patterns of investments in on-the-job training. Women, because they assume the bulk of house and child responsibilities at home, develop quite different patterns of investment in on-the-job training than men. Supposedly men remain in the labor force continuously once they begin full time work, leaving only for military service, additional training, or health reasons. Women not only spend less time overall in the labor market and are more likely to work part-time than men, but they are also less likely to work continuously. Instead, they intersperse periods of paid market work with periods of labor force withdrawal for familial responsibilities, particularly child rearing. This influences wages in three ways. First, women accumulate less total work experience, job tenure, and seniority than men. Second, women's human capital may actually depreciate during periods of labor force withdrawal for child rearing. Third, women who plan to leave the labor force for familial duties such as child rearing, may defer on-the-job training until they reenter the labor market after child rearing, or may have it deferred for them by firms which refuse to hire them for jobs with training.[1] On the other hand, workers who plan to remain continuously in the labor market tend to invest heavily in human capital

[1] Strober and Quester (1974) argue just the reverse; i.e., that women who plan to drop out have great incentive to acquire skills so as to facilitate reentry.

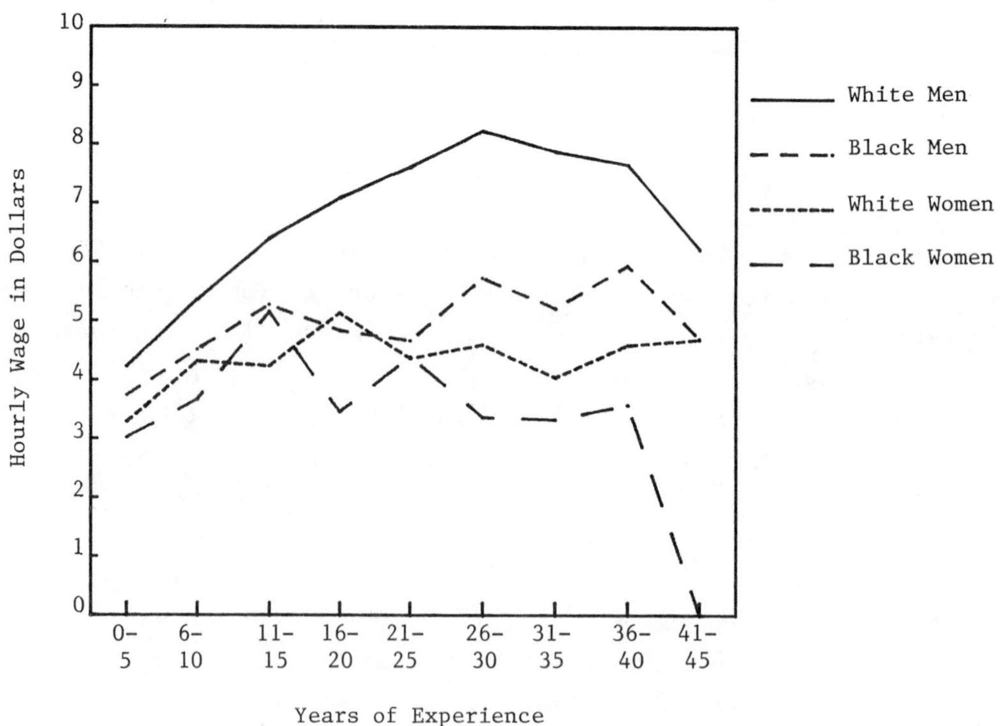

Figure 2.1. HOURLY WAGE BY YEARS OF EXPERIENCE

early in their careers.

Bergmann and Adelman (1973) also use male/female differences in investments in on-the-job training to explain the lower wages and the flatter age-earnings profiles of women workers, but they argue that these low wages and this flatness are the result of "crowding," not of worker choice. Women, they claim, tend to be "crowded" into a narrow range of female-dominated jobs that offer workers little or no opportunity to gain the productivity-enhancing experience (i.e., on-the-job training) that is available in more typically male jobs. This model implicitly assumes that productivity and wages are related. Presumably these "female" jobs offer workers few payoffs for continuous labor market work.

Racial differences in men's age-earnings profiles are not well understood. Welch (1974) has suggested that the apparently flat age-earnings profile of black men is actually a cross-sectional phenomenon.[2] That is, older blacks differ more from younger blacks than older whites do from younger whites. Given the historical growth in opportunities for blacks and differential improvement in the quality of their education, this is not an unreasonable hypothesis. Alternatively some have argued that because blacks traditionally have received lower quality schooling than whites, their investment in human capital may be less efficient. A third explanation is provided by the segmented labor market models (see Cain, 1976, for a discussion of these models). These models divide the labor market into two sectors: a primary sector and a secondary sector. Jobs in the primary sector provide opportunities for both promotion and on-the-job training, but in order to invest in them a worker must first gain access to a job in the primary sector. Segmented labor market theorists further argue that blacks (and women), because of hiring discrimination, tend to be restricted to the secondary sector and hence to jobs which provide few chances to invest in on-the-job training. The "crowding" theory, mentioned above, is clearly a variant of the segmented labor models.

This chapter first describes how patterns of work history differ by race and sex. Here results confirm the popular stereotype that men worked longer and had had more continuous work careers than women. But a surprisingly large minority of men had experienced a period of nonwork since school completion and a surprisingly large minority of women had worked continuously since school completion. It then summarizes the Mincer-Polachek theoretical model relating work history to wages. This is followed by an attempt to specify the relationships between work experience, job tenure, on-the-job training, labor force withdrawals, and wages. This yields two interesting results: work skills do not

---

[2]For a test of this with longitudinal data, see Chapter 7.

appear to become appreciably less valuable during periods of labor force withdrawal—even for white women—and the apparent race/sex differences in the benefits of work experience disappear when experience is separated into segments on the basis of the kinds and amounts of training available in these segments. Finally, the last section investigates the extent to which the race and sex differences in work history and on-the-job training account for race-based and sex-based wage differentials. Average differences between white men and women of both races explained a considerable portion of the wage gap between them, almost entirely because women had less tenure with their present employers, had completed less training, and were less likely to have worked full time than were white men. Differences in work continuity or in the expectation of work continuity had a very modest effect on the wage gap between white men and women. Differences in training completed explained about 15 percent of the wage gap between white and black men—a result which is consistent both with human capital and segmented labor market explanations of the race differences in men's age-earnings profiles.

Analysis

RACE AND SEX DIFFERENCES IN PATTERNS OF LABOR SUPPLY

The Measures of Labor Supply

The ninth wave questionnaires of the Panel Study asked heads and spouses seventeen work history questions (1-17) and two future work plans questions (18-19) listed in Table 2.1. Only workers who interrupted their work careers since 1954 were asked to describe their activities during the interruption on the assumption that memories become quite fallible after 20 years. In addition, all wives under 50 were asked whether they expected to have more children. These work history questions are, of course, retrospective, and ask about interruptions of only a year or more. If women have more intermittent work history patterns than do men, their recollections may well be more subject to error than men's, and this might tend to attenuate relationships between work history measures and wages. To the extent that workers, especially women, are likely to stop work for periods lasting less than 12 months, the continuity of worker careers may be overestimated.

Eleven measures of labor supply were constructed from the questions listed in Table 2.1. Table 2.2 reports the means on these measures by race, sex, and employment status. The first four measure the volume of labor supplied by an individual since age 18; the remaining seven measures can be used to divide an individual's time since leaving school into periods of work and nonwork activities. Most of these measures are self-explanatory,

Table 2.1

WORK HISTORY QUESTIONS

SECTION J: WORK HISTORY

1. How many years have you (HEAD) worked since you were 18?

__________YEARS [00. NONE]

2. How many of these years did you work full time for most of the year?

______________NUMBER OF YEARS [ALL] → (GO TO 4)

3. During the years that you were not working full time, how much of the time did you work? ______________________________

4. Some people have stopped their regular work for a time for such things as military service, family responsibilities, or to go back to school. Have you ever stopped working for a year or more for any of these or other reasons and then gone back to work?

[1. YES] [5. NO] → (SKIP TO NEXT SEQUENCE)

5. Was that only one period, or were there several periods of a year or more when you were not working?

[1. ONE PERIOD] [2. SEVERAL PERIODS]

6. When was the period you were not working? From when to when?

__________ to __________
(MONTH, YEAR) (MONTH, YEAR)

7. What was the most recent period you were not working? From when to when?

__________ to __________
(MONTH, YEAR) (MONTH, YEAR)

IF BEFORE 1955 GO TO QUESTION 18
OTHERWISE GO TO QUESTION 8

8. For what reasons did you stop working the last time? ______________

9. Did you get any training or skills during the time you were not working that you could use in a job?

[1. YES] [5. NO]

10. Why did you go back to work when you did? ______________

11. Did you go back to the same kind of work you had done before?

1. YES → 12. Was it the same job?

- 1. YES → (go to Q15)
- 5. NO → (go to Q13)

5. NO →

13. How did you find the job when you went back to work? Was it through a friend, an employment agency, a want ad, or what?

____

14. How did you get the skills or qualifications for the job? Was it your regular education, previous work experience, some special training, or what?

____

15. About how much did you earn when you went back to work?

$__________ per __________
(HOUR/WEEK/MONTH/YEAR)

16. About how much would you have been earning at that time if you had been working all along?

$__________ per __________
(HOUR/WEEK/MONTH/YEAR)

17. Why is that? _______________

____

18. Do you think you will keep on working for the next few years, or do you plan to quit?

1. KEEP ON WORKING → (go to Q20)

5. PLAN TO QUIT → 19. Why might you stop working?

____

20. Do you expect to have any (more) children? asked only of wives under 50.

1. YES   5. NO   8. DON'T KNOW

but two—Participation Rate and Years between School and Work—merit some explanation. An individual's participation rate is the percentage of time he or she has worked since age 18.[3] For example, an individual who has never worked has a participation rate of 0; an individual who has worked half-time since age 18 has a participation rate of 50; and an individual who has worked full time since age 18 has a participation rate of 100. This participation rate provides a convenient summary of the labor supplied by an individual since age 18. Years between School and Work represents the number of years after a person has left school (and reached 18) before obtaining his (or her) first job. It is defined only for employed persons.[4] This measure is particularly useful when describing employed women's work careers since many women, particularly older women, married either before or soon after school completion, and then delayed labor market entry until their children were raised.

Race/Sex Differences in the Volume and Timing of Work

As Table 2.2 demonstrates, men and women differed dramatically both in the amounts they worked and in their patterns of labor force participation. These differences are somewhat smaller, but are still striking, when we compare currently employed men to currently employed women. For whites, the average employed woman had worked only two-thirds as many years, had worked more part time years, and had a much lower participation rate than did the average employed man. In addition, employed women were three times as likely as men to have delayed labor market entry after school completion. Women who delayed their work careers generally did so for a long time (an average of eight years for white employed women), while men's periods of delay tended to be shorter (3.6 years for the average employed white man).[5]

Overall, white men were just as likely to have interrupted work as were white women. This probably reflects the large number of men who joined the military in World War II and in the Korean War, since when we look only at interruptions after 1954, white

---

[3]Table 2.2, footnote ‡ describes how this variable was constructed.

[4]Table 2.2, footnote ††, describes how this measure was constructed. For nonworking persons, this variable measures the sum of the lengths of any period of nonwork preceding one's first job plus the length of one's current spell of nonemployment. This has no obvious interpretation.

[5]This comparison overstates male/female differences somewhat since white women are more likely than white men to interrupt work two or more times and since the years between school and work measure picks up lengths of all interruptions after the first.

Table 2.2

SUMMARY MEANS ON ELEVEN MEASURES OF WORK EXPERIENCE
(All Male Heads, Female Heads and Spouses Aged 18-64)

	White Men	Black Men	White Women	Black Women
ALL HEADS AND WIVES, 18-64				
Unweighted Number of Observations	2,567	1,147	2,860	1,615
Mean Years Worked Since 18+	20.32	18.54	10.63	12.90
Mean Years Worked Full Time Since 18+	19.14	17.31	8.57	10.23
Mean Years Worked Part-Time Since 18+	1.19	1.22	2.05	2.67
Participation Rate‡	88.60	87.52	48.66	56.22
Percent Who Interrupt after Starting Work⁑	34.0	23.2	29.4	18.6
Percent Who Interrupt Two or more Times after Starting Work⁑	2.9	1.1	9.1	7.5
Mean Years Out During Most Recent Interruption (for those who interrupted)§	2.9	2.8	7.0	3.9
Percent Who Interrupted Since 1955†	13.8	8.2	19.7	12.3
Mean Years Out During Most Recent Interruption Since 1955 (for those who interrupted since 1955)†	2.7	2.8	4.7	2.9
ALL HEADS AND WIVES WHO WORKED MORE THAN 500 HOURS IN 1975				
Unweighted Number of Observations	2,250	895	1,326	741
Mean Years Worked Since 18+	20.01	18.34	13.74	16.04
Mean Years Worked Full Time Since 18+	18.88	17.20	11.24	13.44
Mean Years Worked Part-Time Since 18+	1.11	1.14	2.50	2.73
Participation Rate‡	89.79	90.13	64.55	73.64
Percent with Nonzero Value on Years between School and Work††	15.1	16.6	45.2	50.7
Mean Years between School and Work (for those with nonzero values)††	3.6	2.8	8.0	6.7
Percent Who Interrupt after Starting Work⁑	34.5	23.4	35.5	16.0
Percent Who Interrupt Two or more Times after Starting Work⁑	2.8	1.0	11.6	3.7
Mean Years Out During Most Recent Interruption (for those who interrupted)§	2.8	2.3	7.1	3.4
Percent Who Interrupted Since 1955††	14.4	8.9	24.5	12.2
Mean Years Out During Most Recent Interruption Since 1955 (for those who interrupted since 1955)††	2.7	2.6	4.6	2.6

Table 2.2 (continued)

FOOTNOTES

+These first three measures are calculated directly from questions 1 and 2 in Table 2.1

‡Participation rate

$$= \frac{\text{(years worked full time since 18)} + \text{(years worked part-time since 18)} \times \text{(proportion of time worked)}}{\text{(years worked since 18)}}$$

∻Percentage who interrupt and percentage who interrupt two or more times are estimated directly from the answers to questions 4 and 5 in Table 2.1.

§Years out during most recent interruption is calculated by subtracting the year left from the year returned (answers to questions 6 or 7).

†This is calculated directly from questions 4 through 7.

††Years between school and work is calculated indirectly from years of school, years of work since age 18, and length of most recent interruption. (See footnote §).

Years between school and work = age minus 18 minus years of work since 18 minus length of most recent interruption minus 1 for respondents with less than 12 years of school.

= age minus 6 minus years of school completed minus work experience minus length of last interruption minus 1 for respondents with 12 or more years of school.

This measure is subject to rounding errors in age, years of school, years of work experience, and in the calculation of length of the most recent interruption. For that reason, 1 is subtracted. This variable is also likely to pick up several different kinds of measurement error. For instance, years of school completed does not always exactly equal years spent attending school. The years between school and work variable will pick up such differences in school attendance and school completion. Another problem is sex-related. Women who worked several months or a year after finishing school, then married, dropped out, raised a family, and returned to work, considering it to be unimportant. Finally, for workers who interrupted work twice, years between school and work will be overestimated since they will include time during all interruptions prior to the most recent. Fortunately only a small percentage of people interrupted work more than once.

women were more likely than white men to have interrupted work, and their interruptions occurred more frequently and lasted longer. Less than 3 percent of all employed white men have interrupted work for at least two separate periods of a year or more, compared to one-tenth of employed white women.

Black women worked more years, had a higher average participation rate, and interrupted work less often than white women. Indeed, the average employed black women was less likely to have interrupted work than the average white man, and the length of black women's interruptions were similar to those of white men—at least for interruptions which occurred after 1954. Black women were, however, just as likely as white women to have delayed labor market entry, although for shorter periods of time.

Race differences in men's labor supply were minor with two exceptions: white men were more likely than black men to have interrupted their work careers, and when they delayed starting work they did so for somewhat longer periods.

Sex differences in patterns of labor supply remain, even within similar age groups. (See Appendix 2.1 Table A2.1a.) Differences were larger for white men and women over 35 than for those under 35. This was not true when we compared white men and black women, with the exception that the difference in years worked part time between black women and white men increased across age cohorts.

Table A2.1b in Appendix 2.1 describes the characteristics of workers who report an interruption after 1954. Women and men interrupted work for different reasons, and at different ages. Men generally left work before age 25 for military service while women typically left between the ages of 18 and 34 for childbirth or other family reasons. The stereotype of the continuous male career seems reasonable for men over 25 since less than 20 percent of men who interrupted work did so after age 24. But about 40 percent of all women who interrupted work reported that they left work between the ages of 25 and 34. Finally, more than half of all men who interrupted work reported having acquired job-related training or skills during this nonwork period, compared to only one-fifth of the women. Given this, comparisons of the wage effects of labor force withdrawals across sex groups which do not control for difference in training acquired during withdrawals may be inappropriate. On the multivariate analyses, such controls will be introduced.

Work-History Patterns: A Graphical Presentation

Differences in men's and women's work history patterns are illustrated more clearly in a graphical presentation. The work history patterns of employed workers fall into one of five basic categories described in Figure 2.2. Workers in the first category (Pattern A) worked continuously since school completion. Workers in the next category experienced a

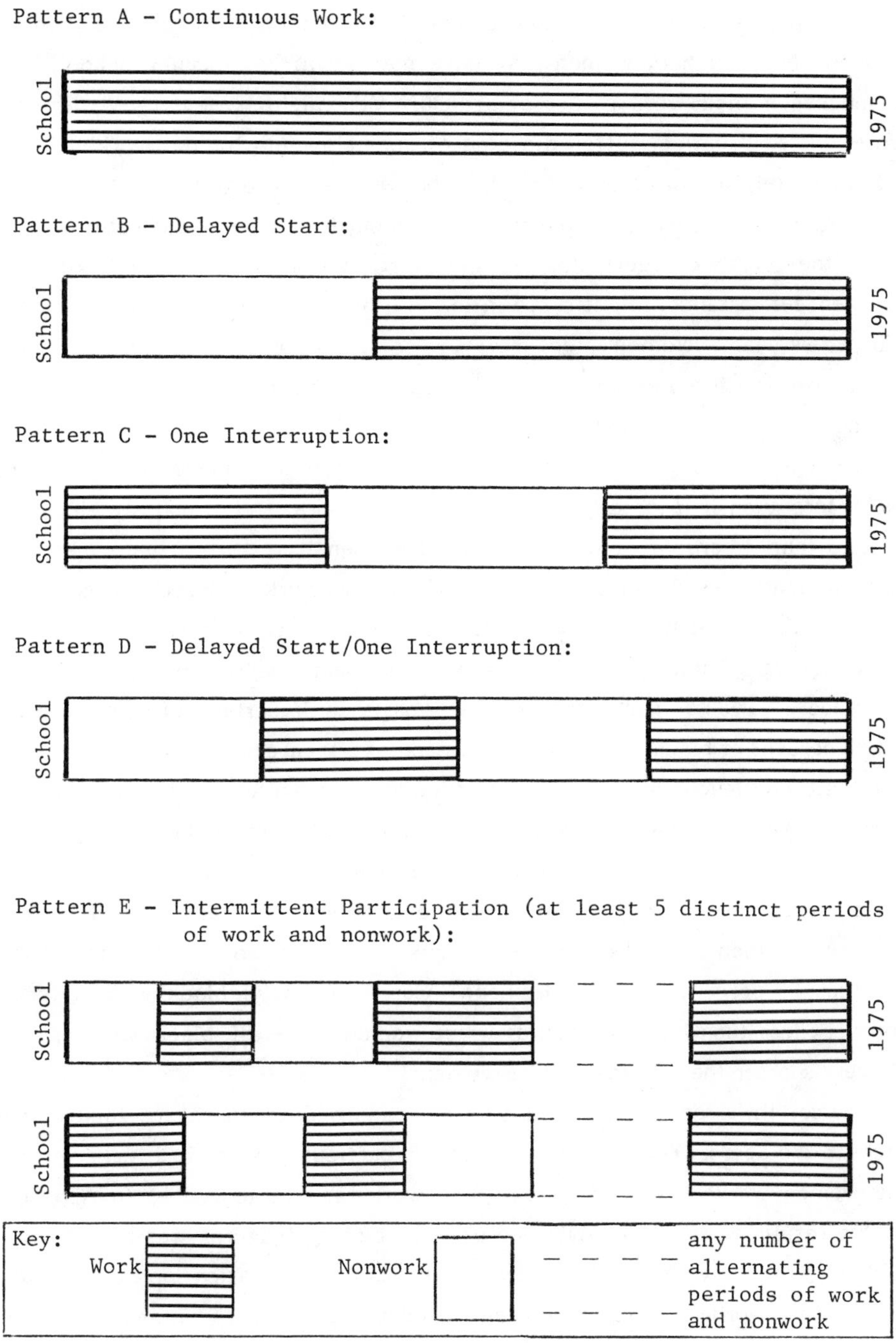

Pattern A - Continuous Work:

School 1975

Pattern B - Delayed Start:

School 1975

Pattern C - One Interruption:

School 1975

Pattern D - Delayed Start/One Interruption:

School 1975

Pattern E - Intermittent Participation (at least 5 distinct periods of work and nonwork):

School 1975

School 1975

Key: Work Nonwork any number of alternating periods of work and nonwork

Figure 2.2. TYPICAL PATTERNS OF LABOR SUPPLY OF EMPLOYED WORKERS

spell of nonemployment between school completion and their first job and then worked continuously. For instance, women may have married after finishing school, raised a family, and begun their work career at age 30. Men might have entered the military, taken an extended vacation, suffered a bout of unemployment, or not worked for health reasons immediately following school completion. Workers who followed Pattern C began work immediately after school completion, dropped out for a period, and returned to work. Workers in the fourth category delayed the start of work and later interrupted their careers. Men, for instance, might serve in the military, work for a few years, then go to school for a few years. Women might marry, raise a child, work for a few years, and then drop out of work to raise another child. Workers in the last category experienced five or more distinct periods of work and nonwork.

Figure 2.3 reports the distribution of each race/sex group across these various patterns. More than half of all employed men had worked continuously since leaving school. Less than 3 percent of white men and less than 1 percent of black men reported having had at least five distinct spells of work and nonwork. Moreover, as Figure 2.3 indicates, men's spells of nonwork were short and were concentrated at the beginning of their work careers. Women's work history patterns, particularly those of white women, were much more variable than those of men. Less than 36 percent of white women, and less than 43 percent of black women had continuous work careers. Moreover, the average length of these continuous work careers, particularly for white women, was shorter than that of men, suggesting that younger, perhaps unmarried women dominated this group. Interestingly, black and white women had quite different labor supply patterns. Black women were much more likely to have worked continuously or to have delayed labor market entry and then worked continuously than were white women (84 percent of black women versus 65 percent of white women). Correspondingly, black women tended to interrupt work less than half as often as white women. Overall, black women's spells of nonwork were shorter than those of white women.

Of course, these comparisons may be misleading since there are fairly large sex differences in the age distributions of workers. In particular, there is a higher proportion of young women workers than of young men workers. Table A.2.1c in Appendix 2.1 presents the results when the distribution of work history patterns was recalculated for workers aged 30 to 44 years.[6] Male patterns of work participation look quite similar to those obtained for workers 18 to 64. But employed women 30 to 44 had more intermittent work history patterns than did employed women in the wider age range. Nonetheless, there still remained a great deal of variation in the work history patterns of women.

[6]This age range was chosen to exclude very young workers, and to be compatible with the National Longitudinal Survey of Women 30 to 44.

WHITE MEN:

Pattern A (54.6 percent)

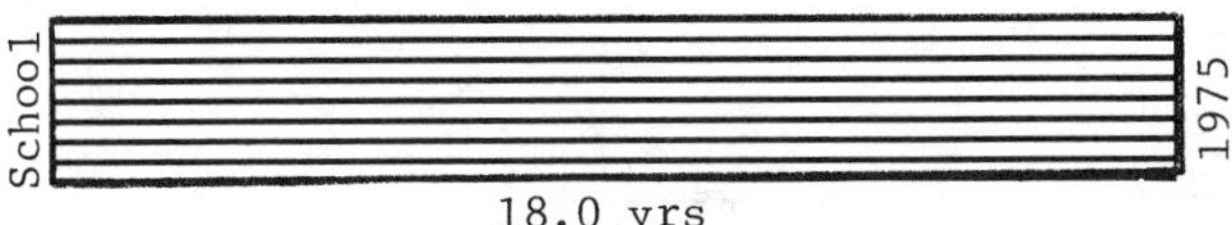

Pattern B (11.1 percent)

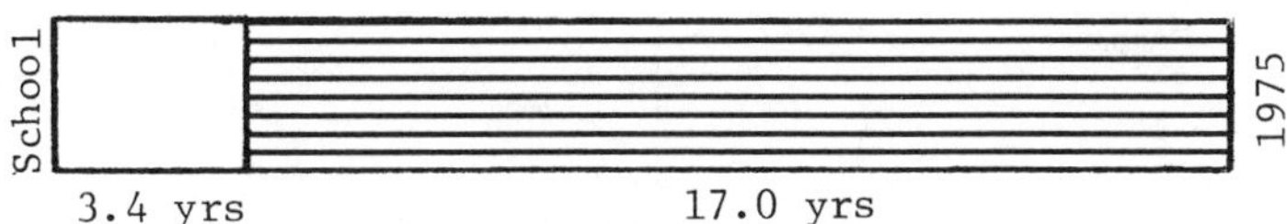

Pattern C (28.5 percent)

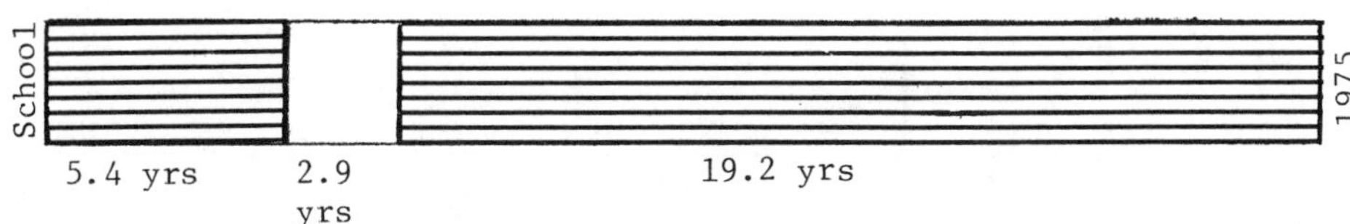

Pattern D (3.2 percent)

Pattern E (2.8 percent)

ALL OTHERS (at least 5 periods of work and nonwork)

$\sum$ work = 21.9 years

$\sum$ nonwork = 4.1 years

Figure 2.3. WORK PATTERNS OF EMPLOYED WORKERS AGED 18-64 BY RACE AND SEX

BLACK MEN:

Pattern A (61.4 percent)

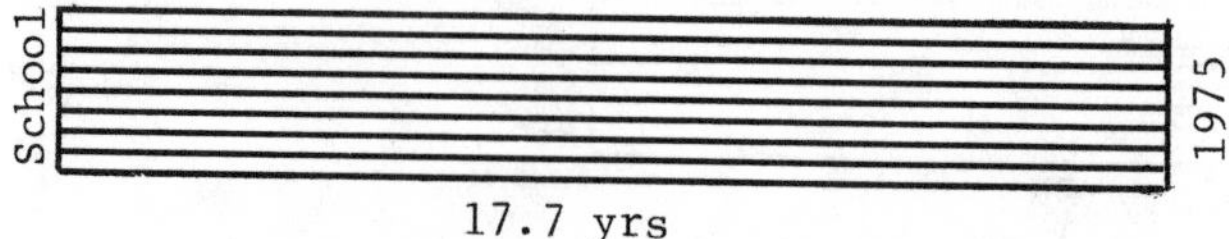

Pattern B (15.1 percent)

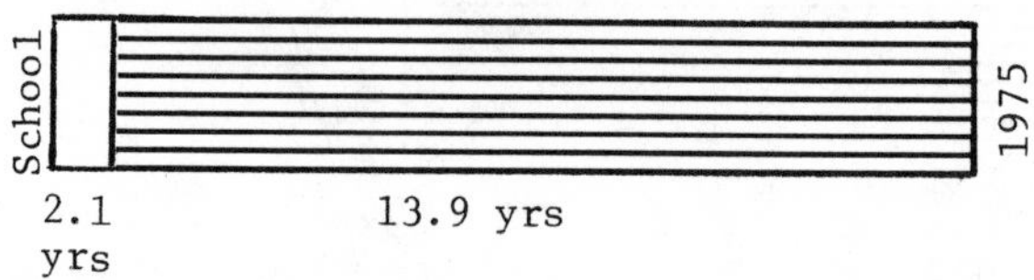

Pattern C (21.8 percent)

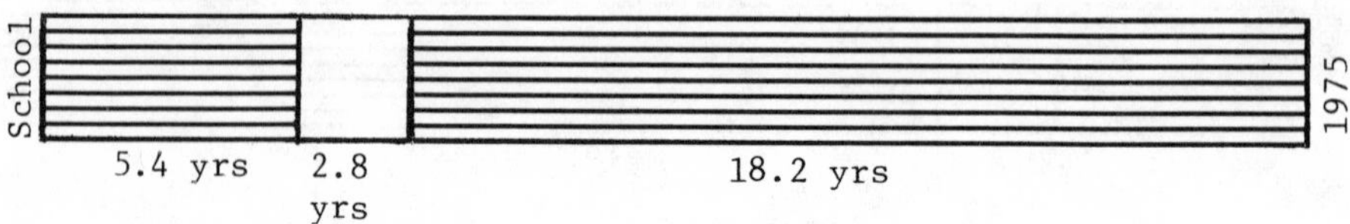

Pattern D (1.0 percent)

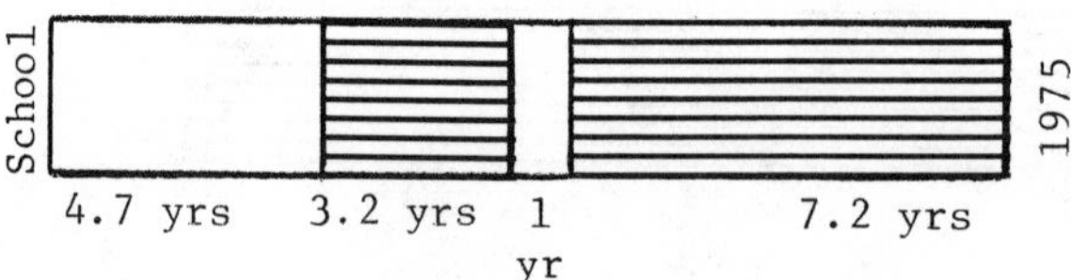

Pattern E (0.7 percent)

ALL OTHERS (at least 5 periods of work and nonwork)

$\sum$ work = 24.7 years

$\sum$ nonwork = 3.7 years

Figure 2.3. (continued)

WHITE WOMEN:

Pattern A (35.6 percent)

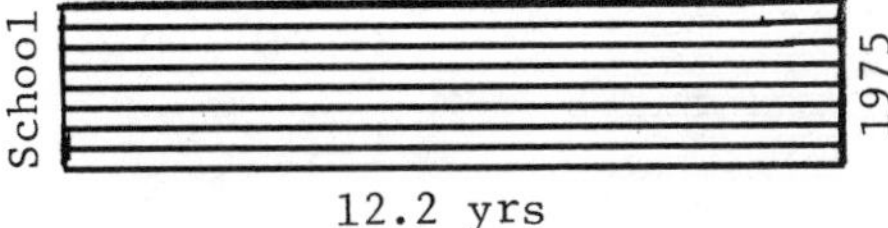

Pattern B (28.9 percent)

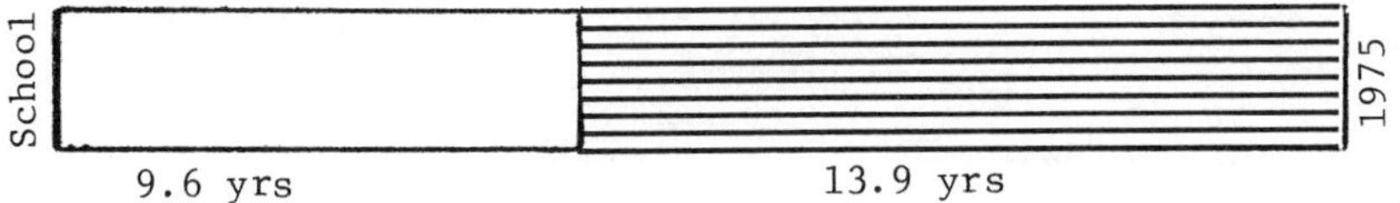

Pattern C (15.3 percent)

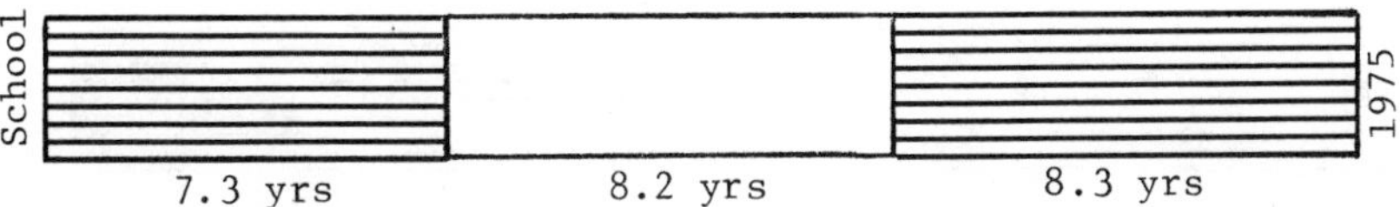

Pattern D (8.4 percent)

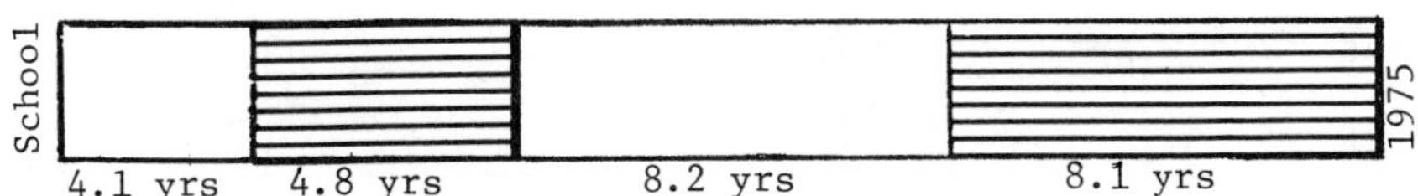

Pattern E (11.8 percent)

ALL OTHERS (at least 5 periods of work and nonwork)

$\sum$ work = 15.6 years

$\sum$ nonwork = 8.9 years

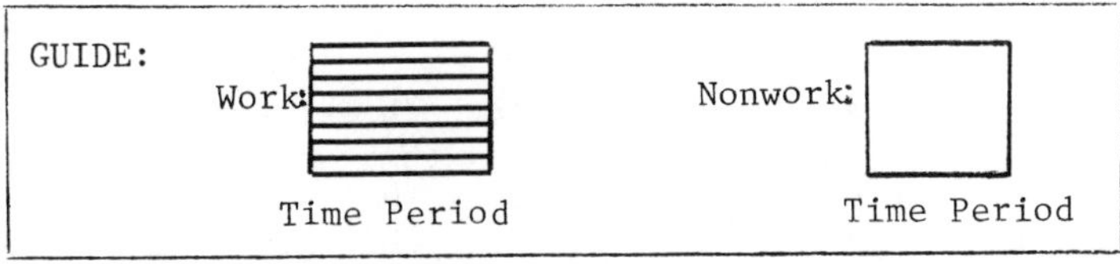

Figure 2.3. (continued)

BLACK WOMEN:

Pattern A (42.4 percent)

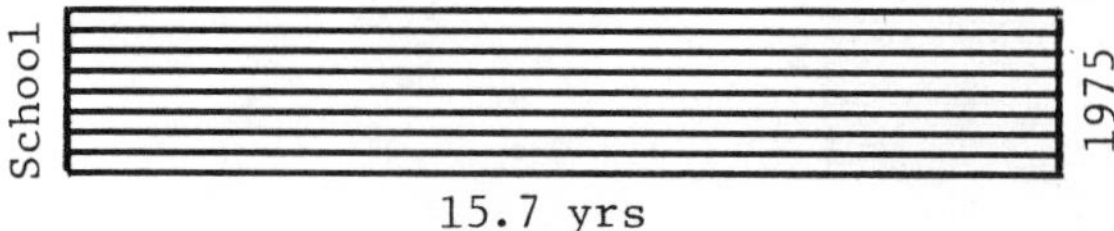

Pattern B (41.8 percent)

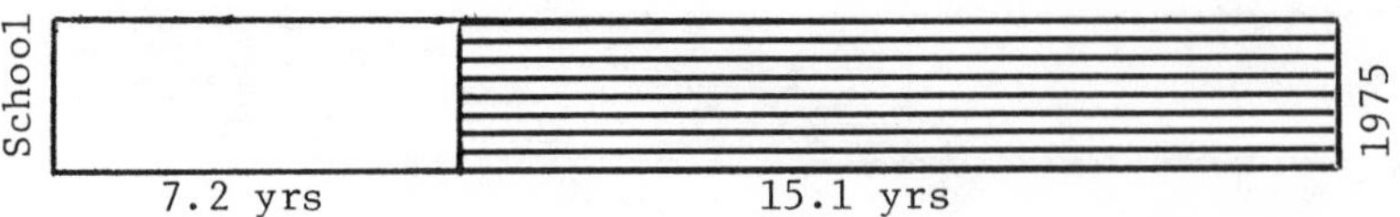

Pattern C (5.4 percent)

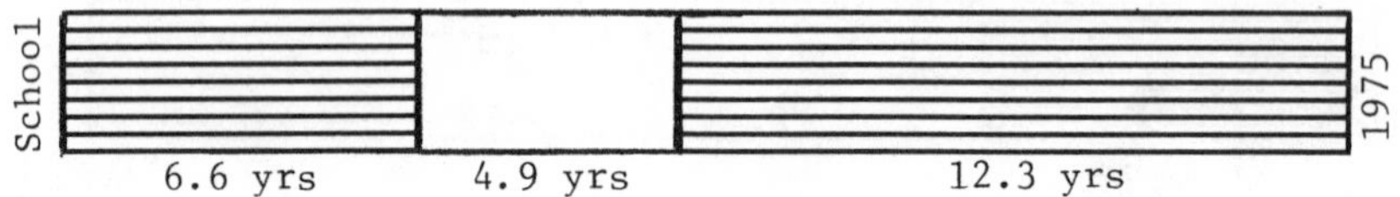

Pattern D (7.0 percent)

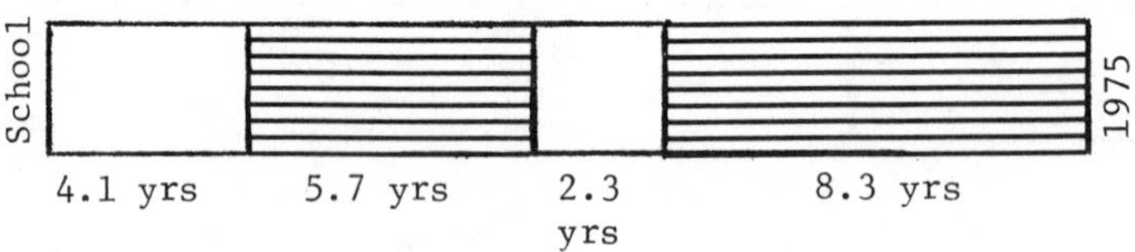

Pattern E (3.7 percent)

ALL OTHERS (at least 5 periods of work and nonwork)

$\sum$ work = 19.3 years

$\sum$ nonwork = 5.5 years

NOTE: In the Panel Study, military service is counted both as part of work experience and as an interruption. In calculating these patterns, I redefined years of work experience since age 18 to exclude time in military service. Pre-work time was then calculated using this new definition.

The numbers under the bar graphs are means.

Figure 2.3. (continued)

About one-quarter of all white women and one-third of all black women had worked continuously since school completion, and black and white women's work history patterns still differed considerably.

WORK HISTORY AND WAGES: THE MINCER-POLACHEK MODEL

In the human capital model, investments in on-the-job training are considered to be critical determinants of wages. (See Mincer and Polachek, 1974.) On-the-job training has a cost since time spent training is assumed to be time diverted from production, and production presumably determines earnings. On-the-job training also has a return in the form of higher later earnings. The following function describes this hypothetical relationship:

$$E_t = E_s + \sum_{i=0}^{t-1} rC_i = Y_t + C_t \qquad (1)$$

Where E_t = earnings capacity in year t;

E_s = earnings which would be received in the absence of any postschool training;

C_i = the dollar cost of investments in human capital in the ith year;

Y_t = earnings in the tth year;

C_t = dollar cost of investments in the tth year, and

r = rate of return to investments in human capital.

If we assume that benefits of an investment increase as the payoff period increases and that the marginal costs of investments are upwardly sloping in a single time period, it can be shown that a declining profile of investment ratios (C_i/E_i) maximizes the present value of expected lifetime earnings. That is, the proportion of one's earning capacity invested in on-the-job training will be high in the early years and then decline rapidly.[7]

Mincer and Polachek (1974) extend this model to account for the possible depreciation of human capital which may result from the discontinuity of women's work experience. They argue that during periods of labor force withdrawal for child rearing and child care, prolonged nonparticipation in the paid labor market may cause the skills acquired at school and work to become less valuable.

The following function adjusts the basic human capital wage model to account for

[7] Duncan and Hoffman provide a more detailed explanation of this model in Chapter 3.

depreciation or obsolescence effects:

$$(2) \quad E_t = E_s + \sum_{i=1}^{t-1} (rC_i - \delta_i E_i)$$

where E_t, E_s, r, C_i are defined as in equation (1);

δ_i = the depreciation rate of human capital in year i, and

E_i = earnings capacity in year i.

The marginal benefits of investments in on-the-job training increase with the length of the payoff period but decline with the length of periods of nonparticipation which follow investments. This suggests that optimal investment patterns will differ depending on the continuity of market activities. Continuously employed workers should concentrate investments early in their careers. Workers who interrupt their work careers for non-market activities will defer investments in on-the-job training until they reenter the labor market after completing these activities so as to minimize the loss from depreciation. Since such workers have a shorter payoff period, their overall volume of investment should be lower than that of workers who remain continuously in the labor force. In their analysis, Mincer and Polachek regard male/female differences in child care responsibilities as exogenously determined.

Equation (3) should capture the investment patterns of continuously employed workers and of workers who withdraw from the labor market for nonmarket activities.

$$(3) \quad Y = a_1 + \sum_{i=1}^{N} (\beta_i e_i + \gamma_i e_i^2) + \sum_{i=1}^{M} \phi_i h_i + \sum_{i=1}^{Q} \lambda_i z_i$$ [8]

where Y = ln (earnings);

z_i = variables other than experience (such as education) which belong in the wage equation;

$e_1,\ldots,e_N$ = distinct periods of work experience for those who interrupt;

$h_1,\ldots,h_M$ = distinct periods of labor force withdrawal (in years), for those who interrupt and 0 for those who do not interrupt;

---

[8] If the rate of investment after labor market reentry is initially high and then declines over time, it is appropriate to include an e_N^2 term. Mincer and Polachek did not incorporate such a term in their analyses of the National Longitudinal Survey, perhaps because this survey looked only at women 30 to 44 years old. Women in this age range are likely to have only recently returned to the labor market; thus values of e_N should be quite small.

$e_1, \ldots, e_{N-1}$ = 0 for those who never interrupt[9];

e_N = total work experience if no interruptions.

β_N is expected to be positive and greater than $\beta_1, \ldots \beta_{N-1}$;

γ_N should be negative;

all values of ϕ_i are expected to be negative.

The experience coefficients in these models (β_i) measure the net rate of return, r, times the ratio of investment (C_i/E_i) in a given time period (see Mincer and Polachek, 1974, pp. 79-80). The coefficients (ϕ_i) in these models measure the net depreciation rate of human capital during the $_i$th period of labor force withdrawal.

This human capital model makes several assumptions which have been questioned by other researchers. First, it assumes the employee decides how much training he or she gets. Advocates of the crowding theory argue that employers play a major role in this decision. Second, work and training are treated as mutually exclusive, that is, time spent in on-the-job training necessarily reduces productivity. Yet there is no direct evidence that this is the case. Third, this model assumes that the intention to drop out is not itself influenced by training and opportunities for investment. But, if crowding theorists are correct, female-dominated jobs provide few incentives for continuous employment.

WORK EXPERIENCE, LABOR FORCE WITHDRAWAL, JOB TENURE, AND EARNINGS—MULTIVARIATE ANALYSES OF INDIVIDUALS

Empirical Measures of Work History

Table 2.3 lists the measures of work experience and of labor force withdrawal used in these analyses and gives their means. Table A2.1d in Appendix 2.1 describes how these measures were constructed. Work experience with one's present employer (employer tenure) will be analyzed separately from other work experience in order to avoid

[9]Theoretical expectations suggest that the pattern of post-interruption investment for those who have dropped out but don't expect to drop out again will resemble the age-specific pattern of investments for workers who do not interrupt work. Given this, it seems appropriate to code total work experience under e_N for those with no interruptions.

Table 2.3

AVERAGE VALUES FOR WORK EXPERIENCE AND INTERRUPTION MEASURES BY RACE/SEX SUBGROUP

(All Working Household Heads and Spouses, Aged 18-64)

	White Men	Black Men	White Women	Black Women
Proportion of Total Working Years that were Full Time	.909	.913	.790	.826
Years between School and Work	.21	.28	3.15	3.07
Years of Pre-interruption Experience	1.66	1.19	2.30	.95
Years Out during Most Recent Interruption	.97	.64	2.52	.54
Years Out during Most Recent Interruption with No Training	.13	.11ǂ	.79	.22
Years of Post-interruption Experience Prior to Working for Present Employer	9.63	9.26	5.77	8.33
Two or More Interruptions	.028	.006+	.118	.037ǂ
Plans to Stop Work for Nontraining Reasons	.030	.017+	.087	.068
Expect More Children	.179	.147	.157	.100
Years Employed by Present Employer Prior to Current Position	4.58	3.96	2.33	2.86
Years Training Completed in Current Job	1.69	.79	.72	.70
Years Post-training Tenure in Current Job	2.51	3.31	2.74	2.91
Years of Work before Present Employer	11.27	10.44	8.05	9.27
Employer Tenure	8.72	8.04	5.74	6.45
Years Out of the Labor Force since Completing School	.51	.63	5.75	4.03

+ Less than 25 cases with non-zero values.

ǂ Less than 50 cases with non-zero values.

confounding effects of general and of firm-specific training.[10] Since women are more likely than men to have worked part-time in the past and part-time work may affect investment behavior, the ratio of full-time employment to all past employment is included.

In Section I, we noted that all employed workers follow one of five possible patterns of labor supply. The first four patterns (which account for more than 95 percent of all workers) can be described exactly using three work experience and two nonwork measures—years between school and work, pre-interruption experience, years out during most recent interruption, post-interruption experience, and employer tenure. <u>Years between school and work</u> is the length of any period of a year or more of nonwork following school completion and preceding one's first job after age 18. <u>Pre-interruption experience</u> is all time spent working with employers other than one's present employer since age 18 and prior to one's most recent interruption. <u>Time out during latest interruption</u> is the length in years of a worker's most recent interruption in his or her work career. <u>Post-interruption experience</u> is all work experience acquired after one's latest interruption with employers other than one's present employer. Workers with no interruptions are coded zero on pre-interruption experience, and their post-interruption experience is defined as all work since age 18 with employers other than one's present employer.[11] The fifth pattern of labor supply described in Section I (pattern E) is a residual pattern which includes all patterns of work participation with at least five distinct periods of work and nonwork—each lasting a year or more. The Panel Study does not provide enough information to allow us to describe this work pattern exactly. For workers who fall into this pattern, years between school and work measures the sum of the length of any period of nonwork following school and preceding one's first job since age 18 and of time spent on all withdrawals from work except the most recent. A dichotomous

---

[10]Including measures of job tenure as independent variables may raise possible problems of simultaneity if, for instance, workers tend to remain in jobs that pay higher than average wages and tend to leave jobs which pay lower than average wages. I have not attempted to deal with this possibility.

[11]Mincer and Polachek argue that workers who interrupt will tend to concentrate investments after labor market reentry. Their patterns of investments during this period should resemble those of workers who have never interrupted. Therefore, it seems reasonable to assign the experience of workers who never interrupt to post-interruption experience. This may, of course, tend to inflate estimated investments after interruptions since workers who never interrupt generally can expect a longer payoff period than workers who do not work continuously.

variable called "two or more interruptions" identifies workers who follow this pattern of intermittent participation.

The above formulation treats identically, all workers who interrupt regardless of their reason for stopping work. But activities during a period of nonwork may well affect the rate at which human capital depreciates. Workers who drop out of the labor force to acquire education or training, for instance, may augment their market skills. Sometimes the military provides opportunities to acquire skills or training that would be valuable in civilian life. Some women who drop out of work to raise children may have taken the opportunity to enroll in training programs either to acquire new skills or to refurbish old ones. Presumably, workers who use periods of labor force withdrawal to acquire work skills may not experience as much depreciation of previously acquired human capital, and the new skills acquired may offset the negative effects of withdrawal. The Panel Study asked all workers who interrupted work since 1955 why they left and whether during the interruption they acquired any skills or training that would be useful on a job. These questions were used to define a second interruption measure—years out during most recent interruption for nontraining reasons. This is probably the best measure of the kinds of interruptions which lead to the depreciation of human capital. Only workers who interrupted work since 1955 for reasons other than schooling <u>and</u> who during their interruption acquired no skills or training which would be useful on a job have nonzero values on this measure.

Two variables—<u>plan to stop work for training reasons</u> and <u>expect more children</u>—were included to test the hypothesis that expectations of employment continuity affect investment decisions. These variables were constructed from questions 18 through 20 in Table 2.1. If workers who expect discontinuous work careers, have invested less intensively than other workers with similar work experience, then these variables should pick up this negative effect.

Few, if any, available surveys measure on-the-job training directly. Instead, patterns in on-the-job training are inferred from experience and/or job tenure coefficients—with experience typically representing general training and with job tenure representing firm-specific training. But these coefficients, in theory, are the product of two unobserved quantities—the average rate of return to a unit investment in human capital and the proportion of earnings capability that is invested in human capital in a given year. That is, black/white or male/female differences in experience coefficients could result either from differential patterns of investment or from differential returns to that investment.

The Panel Study asked all currently employed respondents the following questions about their present employer:

1. How long have you worked for your present employer?

2. On a job like yours, how long would it take the average new person to become fully trained and qualified?

3. How long have you had your present position?

Using these questions, employer tenure was separated into three components: years employed by current employer prior to current position, years of training completed in current job, and years of post-training tenure in current job. Table A2.1d describes how each component was constructed. Together, these components add up to the years of tenure with present employer. Training completed in present position is a direct measure of an individual's on-the-job training, but only of on-the-job training in one's current position.[12]

The other two tenure measures have no clear interpretations. Years employed by present employer prior to current position should include both training and nontraining experience components. But all workers who have never been promoted will have zero values on this measure so that this variable may either pick up unmeasured aspects of worker productivity or unmeasured differences in job characteristics (i.e., workers with zero values may be more likely to be in "dead-end" jobs). Post-training tenure presents similar difficulties. If workers accurately report the training requirements on their job, then any investments in training that occur during post-training tenure would be investments in training for a future job. On the other hand, the more time one spends in post-training tenure, the longer one has gone without a promotion. Nonetheless, these three tenure segments permit a better specification of the quality of work experience with one's employer than would be possible with a single measure of job tenure, since we have a direct measure of on-the-job training in one's current position.

As Table 2.3 demonstrates, men have more experience, more job tenure, and less years of nonwork between school and work than do women. White men also have completed at least twice as much training in their present position as any other race/sex groups. This last difference is consistent either with the hypothesis that white men have a greater economic incentive to invest than women and invest more efficiently than black men or with the crowding and dual labor market hypotheses—i.e., that blacks and women

---

[12]Duncan and Hoffman (Chapter 3) point out two other possible limitations of this variable. The measure of investment volume is imprecise since two jobs with equal reported training periods could vary considerably in training intensity. Also, training requirements are based on self reports. If particular types of workers (e.g., males, whites, college-educated) are more aware of the long-run aspects of jobs than other workers (e.g., women, blacks, high school dropouts), this may result in biased estimates of group differences in returns to completed training.

tend to be confined to jobs which offer few training opportunities.

The ratio of years of full time work to total years of employment is approximately 80 percent for women. This is unexpectedly high given the large proportion of women who work part time or part year in a given year. Perhaps some women in occupations which are full time but not full year, such as teaching, report themselves to be full-time workers.

For blacks, several variables have non-zero values for a very small number of cases. For black men, length of latest interruption with no training, two or more interruptions, and plan to leave for nonschooling reasons each have non-zero values for less than 30 cases. Only 39 black women report two or more interruptions. Coefficients of these variables, even when statistically significant, must be interpreted cautiously, since they are based on so few cases.

Empirical Findings

This section involves five empirical analyses. It begins with the regression of wages on all work experience since age 18 for each race/sex subgroup. Then wages are regressed on a more detailed breakdown of work experience and labor force withdrawal segments. Results provide only limited support for the notion that women's work skills depreciate during periods of labor force withdrawal. This is followed by a replication of Mincer's and Polachek's (1974) analysis of the effects of labor force withdrawals on white, married women aged 30 to 44. Results of this replication suggest that inconsistencies between my results and those of Mincer and Polachek are casued by limiting the sample to women aged 30 to 44. These first three analyses used ordinary least squares to estimate the wage function. But such a procedure can cause problems when these are missing observations on the dependent variable. In this case, we have no observations on nonworking women. In the fourth part of this section, I use a procedure developed by Heckman (1977) to investigate the possibility of selectivity bias in white women's wage equations. Results suggest that the parameter estimates obtained in the first three analyses are not seriously distorted by selectivity bias.

In the last set of analyses, wage equations for white women are run separately by education, by one-digit occupation, and by lifetime work experience to test whether experience and depreciation effects on women's wages vary by these characteristics. There are relatively few differences in effects of either experience or labor force withdrawals by education and occupation.

Before presenting analysis results, I will begin with a caveat. Measures of labor force withdrawal variables for men and women may not be strictly comparable since men and women typically engage in very different activities during periods of labor force withdrawal. To control for this, two measures of labor force interruption were constructed. The first treats all interruptions identically. In the second, only interruptions which involved no training or schooling were defined as labor force withdrawals. Presumably such withdrawals should result in depreciation of work skills for both men and women if Mincer and Polachek's hypothesis holds.

As a first analysis step, the natural logarithm of hourly earnings was regressed on work experience since age 18 separately for race and sex subgroups. This analysis does not treat job tenure separately; nor does it examine effects of periods of labor force withdrawal. The results, shown in Table 2.4 are consistent with past research. White men benefit considerably more from an additional year of work experience than do any other race/sex group. Moreover, this gap in the apparent benefits of experience, as shown in the bottom of Table 2.4, appears to hold for white men and women even after 20 years of work.

Table 2.5 presents the results when the log hourly wage is regressed on an expanded set of work history measures. Results from two equations are presented. The first treats all interruptions identically, regardless of why or when a worker interrupted. The second equation defines interruptions as periods of labor force withdrawal since 1955 which involved neither training nor schooling.[13] These results might be summarized as follows:

1. Staying out of the labor force has surprisingly few significant direct effects on wages, and no effect is significant for more than one race/sex group. Those effects which do exist depend on the timing of workers' labor force withdrawals.

2. Work experience acquired prior to an interruption is worth somewhat less than experience acquired after an interruption for whites—particularly for white men.

3. Returns on work experience differ considerably by kind of work experience. For instance, returns on experience acquired prior to work for one's present employer are almost always lower than returns on experience acquired with one's present employer.[14] In addition, returns on years of training completed always exceed returns on other kinds of

[13]Pre-interruption and post-interruption experience are defined in the same way in equations 1 and 2. Alternatively, people with interruptions for schooling or training could have been treated as if they were employed continuously. This alternate formulation did not affect the general pattern of results for women, but did result in severe multicollinearity problems for men.

[14]The analysis in Table 2.5 does not distinguish whether the work experience prior to one's present employer was in the same or a different field as one's present job. Wage equations were estimated separately for workers who had worked in the same field for most of their life; the coefficients of work history and experience variables were quite similar to those obtained in the full sample of workers.

Table 2.4

REGRESSION RESULTS ON GENERAL WORK EXPERIENCE VARIABLES — *Ln*(WAGE EQUATION), BY RACE/SEX SUBGROUP+

(All Working Household Heads and Spouses Aged 18-64)

	White Men	Black Men	White Women	Black Women
Work Experience Since Age 18	.0476**	.0317**	.0297**	.0211**
	(.0037)	(.0053)	(.0044)	(.0051)
Work Experience Squared	-.0008**	-.0004**	-.0005**	-.0004**
	(.0001)	(.0001)	(.0001)	(.0001)
$\bar{R}^2$	.2531	.2243	.2565	.3023

NOTE: Standard errors are in parentheses.
* Significant at the .05 level.
**Significant at the .01 level.

+Other variables included in the equation are: size of largest city in the area, whether lives in south, years of schooling completed, hours of work missed for illness of self, whether there are better jobs elsewhere if willing to move, doesn't know of better jobs elsewhere, limited work hours or location, and hours of work missed for illness of others.

MTR#4062,4063,4064,4065

RETURNS TO AN ADDITIONAL YEAR OF WORK EXPERIENCE BY RACE/SEX SUBGROUP

After x Years of Work	White Men	Black Men	White Women	Black Women
x = 0 years	.0476	.0317	.0297	.0211
1	.0460	.0309	.0287	.0203
2	.0444	.0301	.0277	.0195
5	.0396	.0277	.0247	.0171
10	.0316	.0237	.0197	.0131
15	.0236	.0197	.0147	.0091
20	.0156	.0157	.0097	.0051

Table 2.5

REGRESSION RESULTS FOR WORK EXPERIENCE VARIABLES
IN *Ln*(HOURLY EARNINGS) EQUATION+
(All Working Household Heads and Spouses Aged 18-64)

Equation 1	White Men	Black Men	White Women	Black Women
Proportion of Working Years that are Full Time	.2715**	.4766**	.2430**	.1205*
	(.0601)	(.0952)	(.0443)	(.0573)
Years between School and Work	-.0091	.0051	-.0088**	.0059
	(.0095)	(.0126)	(.0022)	(.0032)
Years of Pre-interruption Experience Prior to Working for Present Employer‡	.0097	.0533**	.0151*	.0213
	(.0064)	(.0118)	(.0072)	(.0139)
Pre-interruption Experience Squared‡	-.0006*	-.0018**	-.0009**	-.0008
	(.0003)	(.0005)	(.0003)	(.0007)
Years Out during Most Recent Interruption**	-.0075	-.0579**	-.0015	.0035
	(.0095)	(.0172)	(.0025)	(.0081)
Years of Post-interruption Experience Prior to Working for Present Employer	.0226**	.0185**	.0172**	.0218**
	(.0037)	(.0055)	(.0045)	(.0058)
Post-interruption Experience Squared	-.0005**	-.0002	-.0004**	-.0005**
	(.0001)	(.0001)	(.0001)	(.0001)
Two or More Interruptions	-.0032	.0156	.0033	-.1878*
	(.0673)	(.2042)	(.0423)	(.0949)
Plan to Stop Work for Nontraining Reasons	-.1037	-.1530	-.0513	-.2415**
	(.0686)	(.1245)	(.0450)	(.0696)
Expect More Children	-.0168	.1681**	.0290	.1264*
	(.0313)	(.0489)	(.0391)	(.0573)
Years Employed by Present Employer Prior to Present Position	.0408**	.0318**	.0384**	.0353**
	(.0036)	(.0057)	(.0049)	(.0057)
Years Training Completed in Present Position	.0630**	.0736**	.0886**	.0866**
	(.0067)	(.0145)	(.0132)	(.0164)
Years Post-training Tenure in Present Position	.0302**	.0247**	.0347**	.0066
	(.0051)	(.0069)	(.0058)	(.0079)
$\bar{R}^2$	.3095	.2994	.3359	.3709

Equation 2	White Men	Black Men	White Women	Black Women
Proportion of Working Years that are Full Time	.2663**	.3860**	.2418**	.1183*
	(.0600)	(.0956)	(.0442)	(.0569)
Years between School and Work	-.0087	.0059	-.0086**	.0058
	(.0095)	(.0124)	(.0022)	(.0032)
Years of Pre-interruption Experience Prior to Working for Current Employer‡	.0061	.0375**	.0128	.0244
	(.0049)	(.0089)	(.0068)	(.0135)
Pre-interruption Experience Squared‡	-.0006*	-.0012*	-.0008**	-.0008
	(.0003)	(.0005)	(.0003)	(.0006)

Table 2.5 (continued)

	White Men	Black Men	White Women	Black Women
Years Out during Most Recent Interruption With No Training∻	.0073 (.0170)	-.1550** (.0257)	.0037 (.0053)	-.0047 (.0165)
Years of Post-interruption Experience Prior to Working for Present Employer	.0225** (.0037)	.0124* (.0055)	.0178** (.0045)	.0215** (.0057)
Post-interruption Experience Squared	-.0004** (.0001)	-.0001* (.0001)	-.0004** (.0001)	-.0005** (.0001)
Two or More Interruptions	-.0002 (.0073)	-.0585 (.1192)	.0032 (.0450)	-.1863* (.0696)
Plan to Stop Work for Nontraining Reasons	-.1035 (.0673)	-.2886* (.1192)	-.0509 (.0469)	-.2412** (.0676)
Expect More Children	-.0163 (.0313)	.1742** (.0480)	.0360 (.0387)	.1231* (.0570)
Years Employed by Present Employer Prior to Current Position	.0405** (.0036)	.0245** (.0057)	.0388** (.0048)	.0371** (.0057)
Years Training Completed in Current Job	.0635** (.0067)	.0713** (.0143)	.0886** (.0131)	.0871** (.0164)
Years Post-training Tenure in Current Job	.0301** (.0051)	.0226** (.0068)	.0348** (.0055)	.0065 (.0079)
$\bar{R}^2$	.3094	.3188	.3365	.3708

NOTE: Standard errors are in parentheses.
* Significant at the .05 level.
**Significant at the .01 level.

+In all equations, the same variables listed in Table 2.4 footnote +, are included.

‡The pre-interruption experience measure was entered without a squared term in one run. Those equations provided no better fit to the data than those reported in this table.

∻Several different functional forms of the Years Out measures were tried. A quadratic term was added to equations 1 and 2; also several different sets of dummies measuring years out were run. The pattern of results never changed; only black men were penalized for interrupting work.

experience.

4. There are few significant race/sex differences on work history coefficients. This was not true in the simpler model estimated in Table 2.4. Apparently both black and white women and black men had lower returns on general work experience than did white men in that simpler model because they spent less time than white men in the more profitable experience segments.[15]

The spacing of labor force activities after completing school varies appreciably both within and across race/sex groups with 40 percent or more of each race-sex group experiencing some period of labor force withdrawal that lasts at least one year. Yet labor force withdrawals, as measured in Table 2.5, have insignificant or, if significant, small effects on wages and appear to affect only a few individuals. No measure of nonwork time has any significant effect on white men's wages—even when analysis is confined to work interruptions which involved neither training nor schooling. Black men's wages, similar to those of white men, were unaffected by periods of nonwork which followed school completion and preceded one's first job. Black men's wages were negatively and significantly affected by interruptions in their work career which provided neither schooling nor training (about one-quarter of all interruptions for black men). Otherwise, interruptions did not reduce black men's expected wages.[16] But very few black men, only 29 out of 895 black men in our sample, experienced an interruption which involved neither training nor schooling, and the point estimates of penalties for such an interruption seem improbably large—about 15 percent per year out of work.

Periods of labor force withdrawal sometimes lowered women's expected wages. White women who delayed beginning work after school completion earned less than women with otherwise similar education, experience, and tenure. Expected wages dropped about .9 percent for each year of nonwork which followed school completion. But white women's wages were unaffected by interruptions after starting one's work career—even by interruptions which involved no training or schooling. Those white women who had interrupted work frequently (two or more times) earned no less than otherwise similar white women.

---

[15]This could be a statistical artifact. As the number of variables representing work experience increases, so does equation "noise." This, in turn, might obscure race/sex differences in work experience coefficients. However, differentiating between job tenure and all other work experience (i.e., only two independent measures of work experience) also effectively wipes out race/sex differences in work experience coefficients.

[16]When a dummy representing all other interruptions was added to equations in Table 2.5, its coefficient was positive and insignificant.

Black women's expected wages were unaffected by periods of labor force withdrawal except that those who had interrupted work two or more times earned about 19 percent less than other black women. But this applied to only 38 of 741 black women (3.7 percent of the sample).

These data provide only mixed evidence that expectations about work continuity affect the extent to which workers invest in on-the-job training. Whites always had lower coefficients on pre-interruption experience than post-interruption experience, and the effect of an additional year of pre-interruption experience declined faster than that of an additional year of post-interruption experience. We would expect such a result if workers had invested less prior to work interruptions, but the difference between pre-interruption and post-interruption coefficients was significant only for white men. The pre-interruption experience measure also was not significant for either group of whites. For black men, the reverse was true. For black women, pre-interruption and post-interruption experience appeared to be equally valuable.[17] A more consistent finding was that workers who planned to stop work in the near future earned less than otherwise similar workers—perhaps because plans to stop work affected past investment decisions and present productivity. But even here only two of the four coefficients differed significantly from zero, and the causality is unclear. Low wages may discourage workers and encourage plans to leave. Surprisingly, women, black and white, who expected more children earned no less than other women. Indeed, fertility expectations had a significant positive effect on the wages of black men and black women. Blacks who expected more children earned 12 to 17 percent more than other blacks. This result could indicate reverse causation; perhaps higher income blacks are more likely to plan more children than other blacks. Or perhaps this variable differentiates between blacks who are well-organized and plan ahead both for children and careers and blacks who are haphazard in both work and life patterns.

This analysis categorizes an individual's work experience since his or her most recent interruption (all work experience since age 18 for those who never interrupt) into four consecutive segments: post-interruption experience prior to working with one's present employers; experience with one's present employer prior to one's present position; training completed in present position, and years of post-training tenure. Time spent in each of

---

[17] If current job tenure were included in post-interruption experience and in pre-interruption experience (where appropriate), rather than examined separately, both the coefficients of post-interruption experience and of pre-interruption experience increase somewhat, but that of post-interruption experience increases more with the result that for whites and black women, the value of an additional year of post-interruption experience exceeds that of an additional year of pre-interruption experience.

these four segments was not equally valuable. An additional year of training, for instance, raised expected wages 6 to 9 percent while an additional year of post-interruption experience raised wages by only about 2 percent. As might be expected, time spent in training was far more valuable than time spent in other experience segments, and experience with one's present employer prior to one's prsent position (i.e., firm-specific) was generally more valuable than pre-employer experience (general). Surprisingly, work experience acquired after training was completed in one's present position (i.e., a period, presumably during which no investment occurs) significantly increased expected wages for whites and black men. If wages rise with work experience only because work experience is a proxy for on-the-job training, then we would expect these coefficients to be close to zero. Post-training tenure variables may pick up effects of collegiality, seniority, or kinds of firm-specific training (e.g., training for a future job) not captured by the training measure.

Returns to these four distinct work segments were remarkably uniform across race/sex groups[18] in contrast both to previous research and to the results in Table 2.5, both of which indicated that white men's wages rose more sharply with work experience than did women's or black men's. Apparently these race/sex differences in effects of work experience result from the fact that black men and women of both races have spent less time than white men in the more valuable experience segments. White men, for instance, had completed more than twice as much training in their present positions as had any other race/sex group. And men had spent more time than women working for their present employers. This uniformity of race/sex returns to work experience segments is consistent both with the human capital models of wages and with the "crowding" and dual labor market models. Proponents of the human capital model would argue that race/sex differences in time spent in the profitable work segments, particularly the training segment, arise because of rationally motivated race/sex differences in choices about investment. Crowding and dual labor market theorists would argue that access to jobs which offer profitable investment opportunities is restricted by race and sex. If the latter were true, then white men have completed more training solely because they monopolize access to jobs with good training opportunities. In Chapter 3, Duncan and Hoffman ask who gets on-the-job training and why do they get it. Their results provide some support

---

[18]In only three out of 24 possible coefficient comparisons between white men and minority groups across equations (1) and (2) were there any statistically significant race/sex differences in coefficients. The white male coefficients were only absolutely larger than those of other groups in three of these comparisons.

for both the human capital and dual labor market explanations.

Summary Wage Equation

Table 2.6 presents the results of regressing ln (hourly earnings) on a more parsimonious set of experience and labor force withdrawal measures. These new measures were obtained by dropping variables which were insignificant in at least three race/sex subgroups. The pre-interruption and post-interruption experience measures were combined into a single variable measuring years of work experience before present employer. The three labor force withdrawal measures were combined into one variable which measures years out of the labor force since completing school. The expect more children measure was dropped since it has no obvious interpretation—at least in terms of expected work continuity.

Results in Table 2.6 are much the same as those in Table 2.5. Labor force withdrawals have small and usually insignificant effects on expected wages. Returns to completed training are higher than returns to other kinds of experience. Moreover, the coefficients of the various experience and labor force withdrawal measures rarely differ significantly across race/sex groups.

Labor Force Withdrawals and Wages

These results provide little evidence that work skills grow less valuable during periods of labor force withdrawal. Years out of the labor force lowered wages for only a few persons—with the exception of white women. White women's wages were lowered only by labor force withdrawals which followed school completion and preceded one's first job. Interruptions after a work career had started affected expected wages only negligibly.[19] If human capital depreciates during prolonged periods of nonwork, it is unclear why such capital should depreciate at one time and not another. In fact, one would expect that the rate of depreciation of human capital would be greater the greater one's accumulated stock of human capital (see Mincer and Polachek, 1974, p. 94-95). Therefore penalties would be greater for work interruptions than for delays in beginning work since workers who interrupt may have invested in on-the-job training prior to interrupting and hence have more skills to become obsolete. An alternate explanation of these results is that the decision of whether to work after school completion reflects either basic motivational differences between women or affects women's motivations. For

---

[19]Labor force withdrawals do indirectly lower worker wages since periods of nonwork will reduce the amount of work experience and job tenure a worker acquires, and work experience and job tenure each increase wages.

Table 2.6

REGRESSION RESULTS FOR SUMMARY WAGE EQUATION BY RACE/SEX SUBGROUPS+
(All Working Household Heads and Spouses Aged 18-64)

	White Men	Black Men	White Women	Black Women
Years Out of Labor Force since Completing School	-.005 (.007)	-.008 (.010)	-.005** (.002)	.005 (.003)
Proportion of Working Years that were Full Time	.307** (.060)	.551** (.094)	.262** (.044)	.125** (.057)
Years of Work Experience before Present Employer	.013** (.003)	.026** (.005)	.011* (.004)	.011** (.005)
Pre-employer Work Experience Squared	-.0003** (.0001)	-.0006** (.0001)	-.0004** (.000.)	-.0004* (.0002)
Years with Current Employer Prior to Current Position	.024** (.002)	.019** (.003)	.021** (.003)	.017** (.003)
Years of Training Completed on Current Job	.048** (.006)	.065** (.014)	.080** (.013)	.076** (.016)
Years of Post-training Tenure on Current Job	.014** (.004)	.014** (.006)	.022** (.005)	-.012 (.007)
Plans to Stop Work for Non-Training Reasons	-.169** (.063)	-.222 (.120)	-.056 (.044)	-.285** (.068)
$\bar{R}^2$	.303	.291	.328	.346
Number of Observations	2,250	895	1,326	741

* Significant at the .05 level.
**Significant at the .01 level.

+Other variables included are the same as those listed on Table 2.4, footnote +.

instance, women who view themselves primarily as wives and mothers may be most likely to delay starting work, and perhaps these motivational differences persist over time. On the other hand, entering the labor market directly after school completion may itself alter women's perceptions and motivations. That is, women who work for a while after school completion may come to see themselves as potentially attached to the labor force throughout their lives, while women who delay work may not develop such perceptions until they begin work.

A Replication of the Mincer-Polachek Analysis

These empirical results are not necessarily incompatible with Mincer's and Polachek's finding that for a 1967 national sample of white, married women aged 30 to 44 with children, expected wages appeared to depreciate at a net rate of about 1.2 percent per year. These analyses differ from those of Mincer and Polachek in at least four important respects, any one of which might account for this apparent discrepancy. First, the analyses in this chapter include all employed women. As Table 2.7 indicates, unmarried and/or childless women have spent a great deal less time out of the labor force than have other women. Combining unmarried, childless women with ever-married women who have raised children may attenuate the observed effects of labor force withdrawals. A second possibility is that the difference in age ranges across the two analyses affects results. Many of the married women aged 30 to 44 in Mincer's sample may have only recently reentered the labor force after a prolonged absence for child-rearing. If initial wages after a prolonged labor force withdrawal are low relative to a worker's skills because of misinformation about available job opportunities, this might show up as a depreciation effect in a restricted age sample. After workers have been working awhile, they may easily acquire such information and obtain wages more appropriate to their skill levels. Third, the Panel Study (PSID) asked a very different and in some ways less detailed set of work history questions than did the National Longitudinal Survey (NLS). The NLS questions, for instance, focused on work experience at different points in the marriage and child-rearing cycle. The Panel Study ignored interruptions that lasted less than one year. Differences either in data quality or in model specification (because of differences in the wording of questions) may explain some of the differences between the results of this chapter's analysis and those of the Mincer and Polachek analysis. Finally women's work participation patterns are changing over time, and women's labor force withdrawals are likely to be decreasing both in frequency and in duration. This, in itself, may weaken the link between labor force withdrawals and wages for women.

Mincer and Polachek described a married woman's work history using five segments,

Table 2.7

WORK EXPERIENCE AND

YEARS OUT OF THE LABOR FORCE SINCE SCHOOL COMPLETION

(All Female Working Heads and Spouses Aged 18-64 in 1975)

	N	Weighted Percentage of All Employed Female Heads and Wives	Years Out of the Labor Force since School Completion	Years of Work Experience
Ever-Married Women with Children 18-64	878	69.3	8.1	15.3
Unmarried and/or Childless Women 18-64	448	30.7	.6	10.1
All Women 18-64	1326	100.0	5.8	13.7
Married Women 30-44 with Children	270	20.8	6.1	11.7

three periods of work and two periods of nonwork. These segments were based on a woman's activities during different points of the life cycle. These segments included length of work experience prior to one's first child (e_1), time worked after first child and prior to current job (e_2), current job tenure (e_3), time not working after the birth of the first child (h_1), and other nonwork time (h_2). The closest I could come to this specification was to separate women's work histories into years worked prior to current employer, years out of the labor force, and employer tenure. This first variable is in the sum of e_1 and e_2; the second is the sum of h_1 and h_2. Since the coefficients of e_2 and h_2 were insignificant in the Mincer and Polachek analysis, this may attenuate variable coefficients in the PSID replication. Table 2.8 reproduces results from Mincer and Polachek's analysis, and reports the results when ln (hourly earnings) is estimated for married, white women 30 to 44 with children using Panel Study data. The effects of labor force withdrawals are remarkably comparable across these two tables. In Mincer and Polachek's analysis, annual wages drop 1.2 percent for each year not worked, while in the PSID, hourly wages drop 1.4 percent for each year out of the labor force. Neither differences of data quality nor changes in women's labor supply between 1966 and 1975 appear to affect estimated effects of labor force withdrawals across samples. For both ever-married employed women 18 to 64 with children and for all employed women 18 to 64, effects of labor force withdrawals were much smaller, about 0.5 to 0.6 percent per year. Effects were quite comparable across these two groups suggesting that combining unmarried and childless women with ever-married women did not alter effects of labor force withdrawals on wages. Women aged 30 to 44 appear to be much more strongly affected by labor force withdrawals than are otherwise similar women in a wider age range. This is not inconsistent with an argument that women's wages upon return to the labor market are depressed for a short while because of misinformation about job opportunities and/or about their own value as workers.

Sample Selection Bias

At a single point in time, many women will not be employed. If we assume perfect information and rationality, a woman will decide to work only if the benefits she receives from working exceed the benefits of not working. That is, a woman will decide to work if her potential productivity in the market place exceeds her potential productivity outside the market place. Clearly a sample of working women is not a random sample of all women. To the extent that the independent variables in the wage equation influence a woman's market wage relative to her reservation wage, wage functions estimated on all working women may yield biased parameter estimates (Gronau, 1973; Heckman, 1974). Heckman (1977) proposed a relatively simple procedure which provides unbiased parameter

Table 2.8

ESTIMATES OF WAGE EQUATIONS — A COMPARISON WITH THE MINCER-POLACHEK (1974) RESULTS

	NLS White Married Women 30-44 with Children+	PSID White Married Women 30-44 with Children‡	PSID White Ever-Married Women 18-64 Who Ever Raised a Child‡	PSID White Women‡
Years of Work After School and Before First Child (e_1)	.008 (2.8)			
Years of Work Prior to Working for Employer ($e_1 + e_2$)		-.007 (-1.0)	.007 (1.2)	.010 (2.9)
Pre-employer Experience Squared			-.0002 (-1.3)	-.0003 (-2.3)
Years of Nonwork After the Birth of First Child (h_1)	-.012 (-2.5)			
Years Out of the Labor Force since Leaving School ($h_1 + h_2$)		-.014 (-2.9)	-.006 (-2.9)	-.005 (-2.5)
Tenure with Present Employer (e_3)	.012 (2.7)	.016 (2.0)	.021 (8.4)	.024 (11.9)
Years Worked between First Child and Present Job (e_2)	.001 (0.3)			
All Years of Nonwork Except Those in h_1 (h_2)	-.003 (-0.7)			
R^2	.28	.40	.29	.33
N	993	256	858	1326

NOTE: t-statistics are in parentheses.

+This includes only employed women. The following variables were controlled: experience * training, experience * certificate, duration of illness, years residence in county, size of place of residence at age 15, *ln* (hours of work per week on current job), *ln*(weeks of work per year on current job), and number of children.

‡This includes all heads and wives who worked more than 500 hours in 1976. Other control variables include those listed in Table 2.4, footnote + and Proportion of working years that were full time.

estimates. In Appendix 2.2 I discuss this problem and procedure, then detail how I used it with the PSID sample of white women. Table 2.9 presents the results for white women when the natural logarithm of hourly wages is regressed on education, work experience, tenure, and years out of the labor force—using traditional regression and using Heckman's procedure.

The coefficients and R^2's are quite similar across the two equations. All variable coefficients drop somewhat in the corrected regression and returns to years out of the labor force drop by more than half and become insignificant. Selection bias has little effect on parameter estimates with the possible exception of the estimated effect of years of nonwork. It is probably safe to conclude that there is little evidence of selection bias in wage equations estimated on a sample of white working women. Heckman (1977, pp. 3-4) reached a similar conclusion in his empirical analysis of wage functions using the 1967 National Longitudinal Survey for Women Aged 30 to 44.

Estimated Effects of Experience and Labor Force Withdrawals by Education, Occupation and Lifetime Work Experience

Table 2.10 presents estimated wage equations by education, occupation, and lifetime work experience for employed white women. Returns to work experience variables are remarkably similar across education and occupation groups—with one notable exception. Women in professional occupations experienced unusually high returns to pre-employer experience. This suggests that studies should not attempt to generalize about female wages from a sample of professional women.[20] The expected penalties of labor force withdrawals increased slightly with schooling (from .2 percent per year for women with less than 12 years of school to .8 percent per year for college graduates), but effects in all groups were small and usually not significant. The wage penalties associated with labor force withdrawals were no higher for workers who had worked at least half the time since school completion than for similar workers who worked less than half the time since school completion. There is little evidence that work skills depreciated at a higher rate the more human capital a worker had.

ACCOUNTING FOR RACE/SEX DIFFERENCES IN HOURLY EARNINGS

White men and white and black women differed appreciably in the volume and timing of their labor supply as well as the amounts of time spent in different kinds of work ex-

[20]These analyses treat work experience and years out of the labor force as exogenous variables. But few would deny that a woman's earning power is likely to affect her lifetime work commitment. That is, wages, years out of the labor force, and work experience are probably simultaneously determined. In addition, fertility decisions will both affect and be affected by wages, years out of the labor force and work commitment. Specifying and identifying a set of functions which capture these interlocking decisions is beyond the scope of this paper.

Table 2.9

THE REGRESSION OF ℓn (HOURLY WAGES) ON WORK AND NONWORK VARIABLES WITH AND WITHOUT USING HECKMAN'S (1977) CORRECTION FOR SAMPLE SELECTIVITY BIAS.

(All White Working Women Aged 18-64)

	Traditional Regression Corrected for Selection Bias	Traditional Regression
Years of Work Experience before Working for Present Employer	.0088* (.0044)	.0094* (.0045)
Pre-employer Experience Squared	-.0003 (.0001)	-.0003 (.0002)
Proportion of Work that is Full Time	.1913** (.0456)	.2400** (.0456)
Years Tenure with Present Employer	.0202** (.0027)	.0266** (.0022)
Years Out of the Labor Force since Leaving School	-.0015 (.0019)	-.0042* (.0018)
Years of Formal Education	.0860** (.0053)	.0907** (.0052)
λ	-.2687** (.0628)	
Constant	-.0739	-.5390
R^2	.2873	.2774
N	1326	1326

NOTE: Unlike the earlier analyses in this chapter these estimates use unweighted data.

* Significant at the .05 level.

**Significant at the .01 level.

Table 2.10

EARNINGS FUNCTIONS BY SCHOOLING, OCCUPATION, AND LIFETIME WORK EXPERIENCE

(White, Female Household Heads and Spouses Aged 18-64)

	Education			Occupation			Work Experience since School Completion	
	0-11 Years	12 Years	16 or More Years	Profes-sional Technical	Clerical, Sales	Service, Laborers	Worked Less than ½ of Years	Worked More than ½ of Years
Work Experience Prior to Current Employer	.0210* (.0095)	.0087 (.0052)	.0083 (.0127)	.0355** (.0103)	.0102 (.0055)	.0085 (.0107)	.0256 (.0241)	.0070 (.0048)
Pre-Employer Experience Squared	-.0006* (.0003)	-.0003 (.0002)	-.0005 (.0005)	-.0013** (.0004)	-.0003 (.0002)	-.0002 (.0003)	-.0018 (.0020)	-.0002 (.0001)
Years Out of the Labor Force since School Completion	-.0021 (.0035)	-.0059* (.0021)	-.0075 (.0054)	-.0049 (.0049)	-.0057* (.0023)	.0002 (.0036)	-.0025 (.0046)	-.0010 (.0035)
Proportion of Working Years that Are Full Time	.2843** (.1002)	.2741** (.0588)	.3226** (.1091)	.3767** (.0890)	.3483** (.0026)	.3252** (.0984)	.0985 (.0907)	.3445** (.0509)
Employer Tenure	.0229** (.0041)	.0229** (.0026)	.0272** (.0058)	.0270** (.0050)	.0184** (.0029)	.0204** (.0065)	.0221** (.0078)	.0227** (.0022)
Number of Observations	263	810	253	257	533	240	257	1,069

NOTE: Controls are the same as those listed in Table 2.4.

* Significant at the .05 level.

**Significant at the .01 level.

perience, particularly in training. White and black men had quite similar work histories with one exception: white men completed more than twice as much training on their current job as black men.

Table 2.11 reports the percentages of the wage gaps between white men and each of the three other race/sex groups that are accounted for by average race/sex differences on each of the work history components analyzed in Table 2.9.[21] Sex and race differences on the components of labor supply analyzed in Table 2.6 explained a considerable, but by no means an overwhelming percentage of the wage gaps between white men and other race/sex groups. If black men, white women, and black women had the white male means and the white male payoffs to work history and training components, we could explain 20, 41, and 23 percent, respectively, of the wage gaps between them and white men.

For black men, this explanatory power results from differences between white and black men on training completed. For women, most of this explanatory power results from differences between white men and women on training completed, other employer tenure, and proportion of working years that are full time. The substantial male/female differences in work continuity (as measured by years out of the labor force since school completion), plans to stop work, and years worked before working for present employer accounted for only about one-tenth of the average wage gap between white men and white women and about one-twentieth of the wage gap between white men and black women.

Those race/sex differences in work history which explained the largest proportion of the average race/sex wage differences are differences in amount of employer tenure and in training completed. The fact that white men completed more than twice as much training in their present jobs as have any other race/sex subgroup alone accounted for 16 percent of the wage gap between black and white men, 11 percent of the wage gap between white women and white men, and 8 percent of the wage gap between black women and white men. In addition, white men also had more years of employer tenure exclusive of training than did black or white women. These differences explained an additional 11 percent of the wage gap between white men and white women and another 7 percent of the wage gap between white men and black women. It is difficult to interpret these results since it is by no means clear whether blacks and women have completed less training than white men and whether women have lower tenure than white men because of individual investment decisions or because access to jobs with good training opportunities

---

[21]The procedure is to subtract the minority group mean from the white male mean, multiply the difference times the appropriate white male coefficient, and then express the product as a fraction of the difference in ln wages between the minority group and white men. These results are somewhat higher than those reported in Chapter 1 because the simple wage difference was not adjusted for city size and region effects.

Table 2.11

THE PERCENTAGES OF THE WAGE GAPS BETWEEN WHITE MEN AND OTHER RACE/SEX GROUPS ACCOUNTED FOR BY MEAN RACE/SEX DIFFERENCE ON WORK HISTORY SEGMENTS+

	Percentage of Wage Gap Explained		
WORK HISTORY SEGMENT	Black Men	White Women	Black Women
Years Out of the Labor Force Since School Completion	0	6	3
Proportion of Working Years that Were Full Time	0	8	4
Years of Work Experience Before Present Employer; Pre-Employer Work Experience Squared	3	3	1
Years with Current Employer Prior to Current Position	6	12	7
Years of Training Completed on Present Job	16	11	8
Years of Post-Training Tenure on Current Job	-4	-1	-1
Plans to Stop Work for Nontraining Reasons	-1	2	1
TOTAL	20	41	23

+These percentages are estimated by:

$$P = \frac{100B_{wm}(\bar{X}_{wm} - \bar{X}_i)}{\bar{Y}_{wm} - \bar{Y}_i}$$

where:

P = percentage of wage gap explained;

B_{wm} = white male coefficient for the independent variable X in the white male wage equation;

$\bar{X}_{wm}$ = white male mean on X;

$\bar{X}_i$ = minority group mean on X;

$\bar{Y}_{wm}$ = mean of ℓn (hourly earnings) for white men;

$\bar{Y}_i$ = mean of ℓn (hourly earnings) for the minority group.

The choice of the white male coefficient rather than the minority coefficient was arbitrary. However, given the remarkable similarity of coefficients of work history measures across race, and sex groups, this should have little effect on these estimates. Chapter 1 estimates these percentages using coefficients from a wage equation run on the pooled sample. See chapter 1, Appendix 1.2 for a discussion of this point.

and promotion opportunities is restricted by race and sex. Certainly women and blacks have spent proportionally less of their present employer tenure in completing training than have white men. And Duncan and Hoffman (Chapter 3) find that while rational economic incentives do influence the probability that a worker is engaged in training, the most important determinants of required training in one's current job appeared to be institutional factors. Women and blacks with work horizons and work orientation similar to white men were working at jobs with much lower training requirements—primarily because their prior work experience did not pay off in training opportunities as it did for white men. It appears that women and blacks are allocated fewer training opportunities than are otherwise similar white men. To the extent that this is true, race/sex wage differences which arise from race/sex differences in training completed may be attributable to discrimination in job hiring and job assignment. Nor is it clear that male/female differences in employer tenure result solely from the fact that women have worked less overall and so have less job tenure than men. A crowding theorist might argue that women are hired into jobs with lower training and promotion opportunities than are white men, and that this reduces women's incentives to remain with a particular employer, hence reducing women's average tenure.[22]

SUMMARY

Some economists have argued that the extent and continuity of work participation are critical determinants both of wage differences among women and of average wage differences between men and women. Attempts to specify the relationships between work continuity and male/female wage differentials have been hampered by lack of adequate data detailing women's work histories. Before 1977, only one national survey, the National Longitudinal Survey of Mature Women 30 to 44, provided good work history data for women, but this sample has two shortcomings. The range of women's ages is restricted and there is no comparable male sample. Further, two groups of researchers working with the data reached quite contradictory conclusions about how work discontinuity affects wages (Mincer and Polachek, 1974; Sandell and Shapiro, 1977). The ninth wave of the Panel Study of Income Dynamics provides fairly detailed, direct measures of work history and a direct measure of on-the-job training for both men and women in a wide age range.

[22]Some descriptive evidence supports the notion that women are hired into jobs with fewer promotion opportunities. Both black and white women have spent proportionally less of their present employer tenure in the pre-present position tenure segment and proportionally more in the post-training tenure segment than have white men. Workers with zero values on pre-present position tenure have never been promoted; post-training tenure measures time spent with no training or promotions.

This chapter used these data to describe work history patterns by race and sex, to specify how an individual's work history affects his or her wages, and to explore the extent to which average male/female differences on the volume and timing of work experience account for the large average wage gap between men and women.

As expected, men and women differed considerably both in the amount of time they worked and in the continuity of their work experience. Black and white women also differed considerably in patterns of labor supply. For instance, more than half of all employed men have worked continuously since leaving school. Men's spells of nonwork since leaving school are quite short, are concentrated at the start of their work careers—usually beginning before age 25, and very often involve the acquisition of job-related skills. Less than 3 percent of men report at least five distinct spells of employment and nonemployment. Women, particularly white women, report quite different patterns of work participation. More than 60 percent of all employed white women have experienced a spell of nonwork since leaving school, and more than 10 percent report at least five distinct spells of work and nonwork. On the average, periods of labor force withdrawal for women are quite long, rarely involve the acquisition of job-related skills, and are not all concentrated at the start of work careers. Black women's patterns of labor supply fall somewhere in between those of white women and men. As a result of these sex-based differences in the division of time between work and nonwork, women also have less work experience and less tenure with their present employer. In addition, white men have completed twice as much training in their current job as have black men or women.

Probably, the most interesting result of these analyses is that the continuity of work experience does not appear to be a crucial determinant either of individual wages or of average sex-based wage differentials—except to the extent that workers who drop out of the labor force tend to have less tenure on their current jobs. Male/female differences in the frequency and duration of periods of labor force withdrawal for nonmarket activities explained almost none of the wage gap. Further, labor force withdrawals did not always lower women's wages. Very few black women's wages were at all affected by labor force withdrawals. Expected wages dropped about .9 percent for each year not working for white women who were out of the labor force between school completion and the start of their first job. But white women who began and later interrupted their work careers suffered no such penalties. These results are consistent both with the argument that the immediate post-school decision about whether to work either reflects or affects women's career motivations and with the argument that work skills depreciate during periods of nonwork. There is some suggestive evidence that women's wages in the first years following labor market withdrawals may be depressed, perhaps because of a lack of information about the available job opportunities.

At the beginning of this chapter, we saw that white men's earnings increased much more sharply with work experience than did the wages of black men and women. This observation is consistent with past research. When experience was divided into four segments which treated employer tenure and other experience separately and which differentiated between kinds of tenure, experience coefficients became remarkably uniform across race/sex subgroups. That is, white men appeared to benefit more from work experience than did other race/sex groups because white men accumulated more of the valuable kinds of experience, particularly on-the-job training. But it is unclear whether all race/sex groups have equal opportunities to accumulate the more valuable kinds of work experience.

Average differences on time spent in the various segments of work experience do explain a considerable portion of the wage gap between white men and women, almost entirely because women have less tenure with their present employers, have completed less training, and were less likely to have worked full time than white men. This finding is interesting. There appears to be no single aspect of experience or training that provides the explanation for the male/female wage gap. This has potential policy implications since it suggests that women's wage liabilities accumulate over time and cannot be solved by intervening at only one point of the career process.

Finally, these results suggest that studies of sex differences should be extremely cautious about generalizations which are based on analyses of restricted populations. Numerous studies, for instance, use the NLS Panel of Women Aged 30 to 44 years or use samples of professional men and women to study sex differences in wages. But wages of women aged 30 to 44 are apparently affected more strongly by labor force withdrawals than are wages of women in other groups, and work experience prior to one's present job had a much stronger effect on the wages of professional women than on wages of women in other fields.

References

Arrow, Kenneth J. "Models of Job Discrimination" and "Some Mathematical Models of Race in the Labor Market." In Racial Discrimination in Economic Life. Edited by Anthony Pascal. Lexington, Mass.: Lexington Books, 1972.

Ben-Porath, Yoram. "The Production of Human Capital and the Life-Cycle of Earnings." Journal of Political Economy 75 (August 1967): 352-65.

Becker, Gary. The Economics of Discrimination. Chicago: The University of Chicago Press, 1957.

Bergmann, Barbara R. "The Effect on White Incomes of Discrimination in Employment." Journal of Political Economy 79 (March/April 1971): 295-313.

Bergmann, Barbara R. "Occupational Segregation, Wages, and Profits When Employers Discriminate by Sex and Race." College Park, Md.: Economics of Discrimination Project, University of Maryland. Mimeographed. January 1971.

Bergmann, Barbara R. , and Adelman, Irma, "The 1973 Report of the President's Council of Economic Advisors: The Economic Role of Women." The American Economic Review XII (September 1973): 509-13.

Blindner, Alan. "Wage Discrimination: Reduced Form and Structural Estimates." Journal of Human Resources VIII (Fall 1973): 436-55.

Cain, Glen G. "The Challanges of Segmented Labor Market Theories to Orthodox Theory A Survey." Journal of Economic Literature XIV (December 1976): 1215-57.

Doeringer, Peter, and Piore, Michael. Internal Labor Markets and Manpower Analysis. Lexington, Mass.: Lexington Books, 1971.

Heckman, James A. "Sample Selection Bias as a Specification Error." Unpublished paper. The University of Chicago, 1977.

Heckman, James A. "Shadow Prices, Market Wages, and Labor Supply." Econometrica, (July 1974), pp. 679-94.

Mincer, Jacob. Schooling Experience and Earnings. New York: National Bureau of Economic Research, 1974.

Mincer, Jacob, and Polachek, Solomon. "Family Investments in Human Capital: Earnings of Women." Journal of Political Economy 82, No. 2, Part II (March/April 1974): 576-608.

Sandell, Steven, and Shapiro, David. "The Theory of Human Capital and the Earnings of Women: A Re-Examination of the Evidence." Journal of Human Resources, forthcoming.

Stevenson, Mary. "Women's Wages and Job Segregation." Politics and Society, Fall 1973, pp. 83-95.

Strober, Myra, and Quester, Aline, "Comments on Stafford and Johnson." American Economic Review, March 1972.

Welch, Finis. "Black-White Differences in Returns to Schooling." In Patterns of Racial Discrimination, Volume II. Edited by von Furstenberg, George; Horowitz, Anne, and Harrison, Bennett. Lexington, Mass.: Lexington Books, 1974.

Appendix 2.1

Table A2.1a

WORK EXPERIENCE MEASURES BY AGE
(All Heads and Spouses Aged 18-64, Working and Nonworking)

	White Men	Black Men	White Women	Black Women
Number of Observations				
Age 18-24	422	275	607	370
25-34	889	351	860	420
35-44	450	202	505	342
45-54	501	168	496	294
55-64	305	145	392	189
Total	2,567	1,147	2,860	1,615
Weighted Percentage				
Age 18-24	12.2	16.2	15.2	17.5
25-34	30.0	31.7	28.0	25.4
35-44	19.9	21.1	19.3	21.9
45-54	23.3	16.6	20.6	22.4
55-64	14.6	14.4	16.9	12.9
Total	100.0	100.0	100.0	100.0
Mean Total Years Worked				
Age 18-24	3.95	4.03	3.019	2.76
25-34	10.44	8.99	6.786	6.55
35-44	20.42	20.66	10.571	12.30
45-54	29.95	30.10	14.172	20.42
55-64	38.88	39.45	19.543	27.09
Mean Years Worked Full Time				
Age 18-24	2.93	3.17	2.03	1.84
25-34	8.99	7.79	5.31	5.57
35-44	19.15	19.57	8.46	10.13
45-54	28.84	28.35	11.52	16.04
55-64	38.13	38.20	16.41	20.88
Mean Participation Rate				
Age 18-24	79.40	80.40	59.60	55.56
25-34	84.42	80.60	54.91	56.53
35-44	91.50	93.81	43.87	53.03
45-54	93.39	94.32	40.69	58.42
55-64	93.30	93.71	43.70	58.07
Mean Years of Part-Time Work				
Age 18-24	1.02	.86	.99	.93
25-34	1.45	1.20	1.48	.98
35-44	1.27	1.09	2.12	2.17
45-54	1.11	1.75	2.67	4.38
55-64	.75	1.25	3.14	6.21
Mean Length of Latest Interruption (Years) for Those Who Interrupt				
Age 18-24	1.9	2.3+	1.7	--
25-34	2.8	2.6	3.0	2.5
35-44	2.8	2.4	7.0	3.9
45-54	2.7	3.1	9.3	5.3
55-64	3.4	2.9	10.3	5.5

Table A2.1a (continued)

	White Men	Black Men	White Women	Black Women
Percentage Who Interrupted since 1955				
Age 18-24	7.3	4.9+	6.0	5.5
25-34	27.0	18.1	25.6	15.6
35-44	20.4	6.4	35.8	23.4
45-54	3.1	.9	18.1	8.3
55-64	.6	1.9	6.1	4.5
Mean Length of Latest Interruption Since 1955 (Years) for Those Who Interrupted Since 1955				
Age 18-24	1.9	2.3+	1.7	- -
25-34	2.8	2.6	3.0	2.5
35-44	2.6	2.7+	6.2	3.0
45-54	- -	- -	5.5	3.9
55-64	- -	- -	5.5	- -
Proportion Who Interrupted Work at Least Once				
Age 18-24	.074	.070	.069	.062
25-34	.276	.198	.268	.186
35-44	.338	.154	.415	.260
45-54	.507	.420	.405	.170
55-64	.433	.385	.260	.257
Proportion Who Interrupted Work Two or More Times				
Age 18-24	.002	.015	.007	.033
25-34	.020	.011	.060	.051
35-44	.030	.003	.155	.086
45-54	.053	.024	.146	.087
55-64	.028	.003	.076	.140

+Results based on between 15 and 25 observations.

- -Results based on fewer than 15 observations.

Table A2.1b

CHARACTERISTICS OF WORKERS WHO INTERRUPT
(All Heads and Spouses Aged 18-64, Who Interrupted Since 1955)

	White Men	Black Men	White Women	Black Women
Unweighted Number of Observations	398	117	569	201
Weighted Percentage	35.2	2.3	57.6	5.0
Distribution of Years Out				
1	18.6	34.5	27.1	41.8
2	38.6	20.6	18.0	17.4
3-4	36.4	29.9	17.7	19.2
5-6	4.0	7.4	12.2	9.5
7-10	2.5	5.9	11.9	9.7
10 or more	0.0	1.8	13.1	2.4
	100.0	100.0	100.0	100.0
Why Left Work				
Inappropriate	1.7	1.2	.3	2.1
Marriage	0.0	0.0	3.1	2.5
Childbirth	0.0	0.0	44.6	34.6
Other Family Reasons	.8	.5	25.9	32.4
Education of Self	20.9	8.0	8.5	11.4
Military Service	67.0	66.8	.3	.3
Unemployment, Layoff, Fired	1.0	1.4	2.1	5.3
Illness of Self	3.9	7.3	6.6	5.2
Other	2.2	1.8	5.8	1.8
NA, DK	2.4	13.1	2.8	14.4
	100.0	100.0	100.0	100.0
Why Returned to Work				
Inappropriate	1.7	1.2	.3	2.2
Divorce, Widowhood, Separation	0.0	0.0	4.8	5.1
Children Grew Up	0.0	0.0	7.4	9.4
Other Family Pressures	1.0	1.7	5.4	4.0
Finished Education; Discharged from the Military	51.1	33.9	3.5	1.6
Needed Money	25.9	38.6	46.6	50.4
A "Good" Job Came Along	3.3	2.4	5.9	1.9
Health of Self	3.3	2.6	1.7	.2
Other	4.4	2.7	20.4	14.4
NA, DK	9.2	16.9	3.8	10.7
	100.0	100.0	100.0	100.0
How Found Job				
Inappropriate; Same Job	48.2	27.7	20.1	32.9
Friend, Relative	22.3	31.3	31.7	29.8
Employment Agency	8.1	8.7	4.3	6.6
Want Ad, Saw Sign, Sent Letters	19.3	27.1	22.2	16.0
Labor Union Hiring Hall	.6	0.0	.3	1.9
Other	10.4	4.0	17.2	9.4
NA, DK	2.5	1.2	3.9	3.4
	100.0	100.0	100.0	100.0

Table A2.1b (continued)

	White Men	Black Men	White Women	Black Women
Job on Return				
Same Job	24.7	10.0	18.4	24.7
Same Work, Different Job	18.6	14.4	36.1	16.3
Different Work	56.8	75.6	45.5	59.0
	100.0	100.0	100.0	100.0
How Old when Left				
NA, DK	1.9	7.8	2.5	9.5
18-24	81.2	76.1	42.7	30.0
25-34	12.6	10.5	38.7	48.7
35-44	3.0	2.7	13.1	8.4
45-54	.3	.8	2.7	3.2
55-64	.9	2.1	.3	.2
	100.0	100.0	100.0	100.0
Did You Get Training when Out				
Yes	61.2	60.4	19.0	25.3
No	38.8	39.6	81.0	74.7
	100.0	100.0	100.0	100.0

Table A2.1c

RACE/SEX DIFFERENCES IN PATTERNS OF WORK PARTICIPATION

	White Men	Black Men	White Women	Black Women
Percentage Distribution across Patterns:				
Pattern A	55.3	59.8	24.2	34.5
Pattern B	12.7	19.9	28.3	42.2
Pattern C	25.7	18.3	18.3	7.2
Pattern D	3.4	1.7	11.9	11.4
Pattern E	2.9	.3	17.3	4.6
	100.0	100.0	100.0	100.0
Distribution of Years of Work and Nonwork by Patterns:				
A:				
Work	17.7	20.1	17.5	18.5
B:				
Nonwork	3.5	2.3	7.2	6.5
Work	14.0	14.1	10.2	12.0
C:				
Work	5.3	4.1	6.8	6.4
Nonwork	2.9	2.8	7.7	7.6
Work	13.9	11.7	5.7	7.8
D:				
Nonwork	4.2	2.9	5.0	4.3
Work	2.4	5.6	4.2	6.9
Nonwork	2.0	1.2	5.6	2.5
Work	8.9	2.0	4.7	6.9

Table A2.1d

MEASURES OF WORK AND NONWORK

Variable Name		Variable Description
Years of Work Experience Prior to Current Employer (Pre-employer Experience)	=	Years of work since age 18 minus employer tenure.
Proportion of Working Years that Are Full Time	=	$\frac{\text{Years of full time work since age 18}}{\text{Years of work since age 18}}$
Years between School and Work*	=	The length of any period of nonwork (in years) which follows school completion and precedes one's first job after completing school.
	=	Age minus years of school completed minus years out during most recent interruption minus years of work since age 18 minus 1 for workers with 12 or more years of education.
	=	Age minus 18 minus years out during most recent interruption minus years of work since 18 minus 1 for those with 12 or less years of education.
Years Out during Most Recent Interruption+	=	Length of most recent interruption (year returned minus year left) for those who interrupt.
	=	0 for those who never interrupted.
Years of Post-interruption Experience Prior to Working for Present Employer	=	Pre-employer experience if never interrupted.
	=	(1975 minus year returned) minus job tenure, otherwise.
Years of Pre-interruption‡ Experience Prior to Working for Present Employer	=	Pre-employer experience minus post-interruption experience for those who ever interrupt.
	=	0 otherwise.
Two or More Interruptions	=	1 if reported several periods of work interruptions.
	=	0 otherwise.
Years Out during Latest Interruption with no Training After 1955⁘	=	Years out for those who interrupted after 1954 and who did not leave for education and who did not acquire training that would be valuable on a job during their interruption.
	=	0 otherwise.
Plan to Stop Work for Nontraining Reason	=	0 if don't plan to quit work in the near future or if plan to quit work to attend school.
	=	1 otherwise
Expect Children	=	1 if expect to have more children, reported by the wife.
	=	0 otherwise (respondents who are not married or who are over 50 are coded zero).

Table A2.1d (continued)

Work Experience§	= Years of work since age 18.
Years Out of the Labor Force since Leaving School	= Age minus years of school completed minus work experience since 18 for those with 12 or more years of school.
	= Age minus 18 minus work experience since 18, otherwise.
Years with Current Employer Prior to Present Position	= Tenure with present employer minus tenure in in present position (in years).
Years of Training Completed in Current Job	= Years of training required or years in present position, whichever is smaller.
Years of Post-training Tenure in Current Job	= Years in present position minus years of training completed.

---

*This measure is defined as in Table 2.2.

+Military experience is defined as an interruption whenever an individual reports that he interrupted work for the military. This seems reasonable since time in the military often does interrupt regular career experience. On the other hand, time in the military is still allowed to contribute to general work experience as well since military experience constitutes paid employment.

‡If an individual's job tenure is greater than his or her post-interruption experience (that is, if an individual interrupts work and then returns to same employer and still works for that employer), pre-interruption experience is reduced to account for employee tenure that occurred during that period.

∺If workers respond without error, then present position experience should never exceed tenure with present employer and similarly tenure with present employer should never exceed years of work experience. To insure that this was true, all data passed through the following recoding sequence: (1) If present position tenure was greater than employer tenure, the employer tenure was recorded to equal present position tenure; (2) if employer tenure exceeded work experience, then work experience was recoded to equal employer tenure.

§This measure codes as work experience both years worked part-time in college and years in the military after age 18.

APPENDIX 2.2

SAMPLE SELECTION BIAS

Heckman (1974, 1977) describes sample selection bias as a problem which arises because data are missing on the dependent variable in a regression analysis. This problem can be formulated using a simple equation system describing a woman's wage and reservation wage.[1]

Wage: $\ln w_i = \beta_1 x_{1i} + u_{1i}$

reservation wage: $\ln \hat{w}_i = \beta_2 x_{2i} + u_{2i}$

w_i = hourly wage;

$\hat{w}_i$ = reservation wage;

x_{1i} = independent predictors of w_i;

x_{2i} = independent predictors of $\hat{w}_i$.

A woman will work only if her market wage exceeds her reservation wage. That is, if

$$\ln w_i > \ln \hat{w}_i$$

or if

$$(x_{1i}\beta_1 - x_{2i}\beta_{2i}) > (u_{2i} - u_{1i}).$$

Since we will only observe wages when a woman works,

$$E[\ln w/(x_1\beta_1 - x_2\beta_2) > u_2 - u_1]$$

$$= x_1\beta_1 + E[u_1/(x_1\beta_1 - x_2\beta_2) > u_2 - u_1].$$

It can be shown that

$$E[u_1/(x_1\beta_1 - x_2\beta_2) > u_2 - u_1] = \frac{\sigma_{12}}{(\sigma_{22})^{1/2}} \frac{f}{F}$$

where $\sigma_{12} = \mathrm{cov}(u_1,u_2)$,

$\sigma_{22} = \mathrm{var}(u_1 - u_2)$,

---

[1]This description is taken from an unpublished memo on women's shadow and market wage equations by Barbara Devaney, Center for Population Studies, University of Michigan, 1977.

$$f = \frac{1}{\sqrt{2\pi}} \exp\left[- \frac{1}{2} \left(\frac{x_1\beta_1 - x_2\beta_2}{(\sigma_{22})^{1/2}} \right)^2 \right]$$

$$F = \int_{-\infty}^{\frac{x_1\beta_1 - x_2\beta_2}{(\sigma_{22})^{1/2}}} \frac{1}{\sqrt{2\pi}} e^{-1/2\, s^2} \, ds$$

And as a result, consistent estimators can be obtained by estimating

$$ln\ w = \beta_1 x_1 + \hat{\alpha}\frac{f}{F}$$

$$\text{where } \hat{\alpha} = \frac{\hat{\sigma}_{12}}{(\hat{\sigma}_{22})^{1/2}}$$

The wage and reservation wage equations used in this analysis are described below. The wage equation used in this analysis is a simplified version of that shown in Table 2.6. Only work history and school measures are retained.

$\ln w_i = f(e, e^2, p, t, ed, ht)$ <u>wage equation</u>

$\ln \hat{w}_i = f(ed, ht, FI, k_3, k_7, k_{12}, k_{18})$ <u>reservation wage equation</u>

where

w_i and $\hat{w}_i$ are defined as before

e = years of work experience prior to working for present employer

p = proportion of years worked that were full time

t = years of tenure with present employer

ed = years of education

ht = years out of the labor force since leaving school

FI = total family income (in \$100 s) exclusive of own earnings

k_3 = number of children younger than 3 years

k_7 = number of children aged 3 to 6 years

k_{12} = number of children aged 7 to 11 years;

k_{18} = number of children aged 12 to 17 years;

If a woman works, then $\ln w_i$ will be greater than $\ln \hat{w}_i$.

Table A2.2a reports the results of estimating a probit model based on the above two equations.[1] Results appear quite reasonable. The probability that a woman works increases with past experience and with schooling, and is negatively related to other family income, the presence of children, and time spent out of the labor force since school completion.

---

[1]Barbara Devaney of the Population Studies Center, The University of Michigan provided invaluable advice and assistance in setting up and estimating this probit function.

Table A2.2a

PROBIT ESTIMATES OF THE PARAMETERS
DETERMINING THE PROBABILITY THAT A WOMAN WORKS

	$\frac{\beta_2}{(\sigma_{22})^{\frac{1}{2}}}$
Years of Work Experience Before Working for Present Employer	.0124 (.0058)
Pre-employer Experience Squared	-.0010 (.0002)
Proportion of Years Worked Full Time	.5501 (.0870)
Years of Tenure with Present Employer	.2850 (.0024)
Years Out of the Labor Force since Leaving School	-.0557 (.0037)
Years of Education	.0412 (.0068)
Total Family Income Exclusive of Own Earnings (in $100's)	-.0013 (.0003)
Number of Children Younger than 3 Years	-.6548 (.0769)
Number of Children 3 to 6 Years	-.4096 (.0698)
Number of Children 7 to 11 Years	-.0946 (.0358)
Number of Children 12 to 18 Years	.2085 (.0498)
Separated, Widowed, or Divorced	-.0835 (.2234)
Married	-.3552 (.2170)
Constant	.3719
N	2858
Log Likelihood	2036.0

Chapter 3

TRAINING AND EARNINGS

Greg Duncan and Saul Hoffman

Introduction

Most theoretical and empirical work on the determinants of individual earnings have placed special emphasis on an individual's educational attainment and on his or her years of work experience. While the literature about the effects of education on earnings is extensive,[1] the issues involved in the interpretation of the effects of experience on earnings have received considerably less attention. Certainly it is true that earnings tend to rise with years of experience, but the nature of the underlying mechanism which generates that increase is still largely an unresolved theoretical and empirical issue.

An understanding of the way in which experience increases earnings is especially critical for the analysis of wage differentials by race and sex, since previous empirical research has shown that black men and both black and white women have flatter experience-earnings profiles than white males, and that differences in the returns to experience account for a large portion of observed wage differences.[2]

The most widely accepted interpretation of the relationship between experience and earnings is that of the human capital model, which considers years of work experience as a proxy for unobservable investments in on-the-job training. According to the human capital model, wage differentials among individuals are largely the result of differential patterns of investment in on-the-job training and other forms of human capital. An alternative interpretation, frequently associated with the dual labor market model, is that the growth

---

[1]The interpretation of the effects of education on earnings is, of course, still quite controversial. Although most economists agree that education affects earnings by increasing productivity, some argue that the earnings-enhancing effect of education reflects primarily credentialism or the use of education by employers as a screening device. See, for example, Taubman and Wales (1974) or Blaug (1976).

[2]Mincer and Polachek (1974); Blinder (1973).

of earnings with experience reflects seniority and is largely unrelated to increases in individual productivity. Moreover, differences by race or sex in the returns on experience reflect primarily the effects of labor market discrimination. In the absence of any direct measure of on-the-job investments, it has been impossible to distinguish between these—or other—explanations.

This chapter uses three direct measures of training in order to analyze both the determinants of training—who gets training and how much—and its effects on earnings. Our purpose is twofold: first, to test the predictions of life-cycle training models; second, to evaluate the contribution of training differences to observed differences in earnings by race and sex. The analysis of the determinants of training is important precisely because, as we will see, most theoretical explanations of wage differences by race and sex presuppose the validity of the training models.

This chapter first discusses the role of training in the determination of earnings and also reviews the models of optimal investment in training. Special attention is given to those factors which could account for differences in training investments by race and sex. Next it presents basic descriptive information about the training measures, followed by tests of a formal regression model of the determinants of investment in training. Then it considers whether the acquisition of training is costly, as the human capital model asserts. Finally, it looks at the effects of training on the earnings of white men, black men, white women, and black women.

Analysis

EXPERIENCE AND EARNINGS

The Human Capital Model

The basic human capital notion about investment in training is that learning does not cease with the completion of formal schooling. Rather, at some point it simply becomes efficient for an individual to transfer the site of learning to the labor market and to learn in conjuction with work. It is this learning on the job that the human capital model calls investment in on-the-job training, and it is usually asserted that many, if not most, job skills are learned primarily on the job.

What transforms learning on the job into an investment in human capital is that workers are presumed to pay for the on-the-job training they receive.[3] Training and

[3]Becker (1964) first distinguished specific training, which augments productivity only for the current employer, from general training, which augments productivity for other employers as well. Costs of specific training are presumed to be borne by employers, while general training costs are paid by the employees.

production are assumed to be mutually exclusive activities. The acquisition of training, then, involves a necessary sacrifice of output, since both the worker's time, and perhaps resources as well, must be diverted from production to training. Consequently, if a worker is learning while working, he or she is producing correspondingly less and, hence, is paid less. But, according to the model, an individual is willing to accept this wage reduction because the acquisition of on-the-job training will lead to increased earnings in the future.

The key issue for the analysis of earnings differences among individuals in the human capital model is how much on-the-job training an individual acquires. A number of models have attempted to analyze the economic determinants of an individual's decision to invest in on-the-job training; the most well-known of these models are those of Becker (1964), Ben-Porath (1967), and Rosen (1974). In general, these models treat an individual's decision to acquire on-the-job training within the familiar framework of investment theory, modified only to take account of the finiteness of the workspan. It is assumed that individuals are able to choose both the timing and the volume of their investments in on-the-job training, and that they do so in order to maximize the discounted value of their lifetime earnings. Thus, at the simplest level, an individual's decision to invest in training depends on the comparison of the current costs of investment (i.e., depressed earnings) with the present value of the stream of earnings which result from that investment. The investment decision rule involves the conventional comparison of costs and benefits at the margin; that is, an individual should continue to invest in training until the cost of an additional unit just equals its discounted lifetime benefits.

The optimal volume of investment by an individual is a function of several key parameters which influence the costs and benefits of investment and which are thought to vary among individuals at a point in time and for the same individual over the life cycle. The most important of these is the length of the working horizon—the "payoff period"—over which the returns on an investment will be received. Since benefits are greater over a longer working horizon, it is clearly advantageous for an individual to invest in training early in his or her working career when there will be many years over which returns can be earned. Because the marginal costs of investment are assumed to be increasing for any single time period, however, investment costs are reduced if investments are distributed over a number of years. From these conflicting influences, it is possible to demonstrate the existence of an optimal time path of human capital accumulation which, in turn, implies, via the human capital earnings function, a characteristic experience-earnings profile. During the first few working years, investment will be relatively high and, consequently, earnings will be depressed. Thereafter, labor earnings rise, sharply at first and then more gradually, as the optimal rate of investment declines and the returns on previous investments are received.

It is important to emphasize two things about investment in training and its relationship to earnings. First, the human capital model's explanation of individual earnings is derived from and dependent on its theory of the determinants of investments in training. Second, each individual is assumed to be completely free to follow the optimal time path of investment in human capital. Thus, investment in human capital and the resulting life-cycle pattern of earnings are taken to be endogenous in that they are determined by an individual via maximization.

As pointed out in Chapter 2, these models of optimal investment in human capital have been widely used to explain the observed lower wages of women. In this interpretation, a woman's decision to work less regularly and to invest less in herself is considered to be voluntary rather than the result of market forces.

The lower wages of black males are more difficult to explain within a human capital investment framework. There are few significant, voluntary differences in the labor force participation rates of black and white males, so differences in the payoff period are not factors in determining rates of investment in human capital.[4] Explanations of possible differences in investment incentives have focused on labor market discrimination and on differences between whites and blacks in the quantity and quality of schooling. Discrimination operates to reduce the benefits of any human capital investment, while educational differences may influence costs. These effects vary from one formulation of the human capital model to another.[5] In general, the human capital model presents a less satisfactory theoretical explanation for observed differences in wages between white and black males than between men and women.

The Dual Labor Market Model

An alternative explanation of the relationship between labor market experience and earnings and of differences in the returns on experience by race and sex draws on the dual labor market model. The dual labor market model differs from the human capital model primarily in its focus on the characteristics of jobs and job markets, rather than the

---

[4] Recent evidence given in Butler and Heckman (1977) indicates a small decline in labor force participation rates of black males.

[5] For example, discrimination has no effect on investment in the Ben-Porath model, but a negative effect in Rosen's model. The possible effects of educational differences are important in the Ben-Porath model. See Section III for a more complete discussion of this.

characteristics of individuals. Earnings are thought to be largely determined by the labor market in which an individual works rather than the skills (or human capital) he or she possesses. The labor market is assumed to be dichotomized into two sectors, a primary sector and a secondary sector. For all the much-criticized vagueness of the model concerning the distinguishing features of jobs in the two sectors, it is probably reasonable to think of primary sector jobs as "jobs with a future" and secondary sector jobs as "dead-end jobs." Training itself is viewed as being largely technologically determined by the design of jobs, so that a specified amount of training is intrinsic in any given job. An individual acquires training by first gaining access to a job which provides training; that is, jobs and job markets intercede between an individual and investment in on-the-job training.

Another important difference between the primary and secondary labor markets is the existence of highly structured internal labor markets in the primary sector. The concept of an internal labor market was first popularized by Clark Kerr in the early 1950s and then reintroduced by Doeringer and Piore in their subsequent formulation of the dual labor market in the mid-1960s.[6] Kerr had argued that competitive labor markets were increasingly being replaced by what he called "institutional markets," in which customary work rules and practices, frequently formalized by collective bargaining agreements, tended to establish separate markets for those already hired and those seeking employment—an internal labor market for the former group and an external market for the latter. Doeringer and Piore described the internal labor market as an administrative unit "within which the pricing and allocation of labor is governed by a set of administrative rules and procedures."[7] They further argued that most promotion takes place within internal markets according to well-structured job ladders, and that only workers who have gained access to the internal labor market via a limited number of "ports of entry" at the bottom of promotion ladders are considered for higher slots on the job ladder.

Discrimination is an integral part of the dual labor market model, operating both between the primary and secondary sector and within internal labor markets. First, entry-level discrimination is cited as a major institutional barrier between the primary and secondary sector.[8] One result of discrimination, it is argued, is to confine blacks and

---

[6]Kerr (1954) and Doeringer and Piore (1971).

[7]Doeringer and Piore, pp. 1-2.

[8]Doeringer and Piore, p. 133.

women to secondary labor market jobs in disproportionate number, relative to their skills, and once there, they have a very difficult time escaping to the primary sector. The dual labor market theorists argue that hiring decisions typically involve a considerable amount of subjective input, and, consequently, there is ample opportunity to practice discrimination.

Second, internal labor markets, Doeringer and Piore write, "are designed intentionally to 'discriminate'. They do so by conferring special privileges upon the internal labor force not available to those in the external labor force." Although nothing about this requires that the discrimination involved need be in terms of race or sex, in practice, the emphasis has been on this kind of discrimination. Two kinds of discrimination within internal labor markets are usually emphasized. Either all workers may share similar job ladders, but discrimination in promotion may increase as minority group workers seek higher positions in the job hierarchy,[9] or minority group workers may be assigned to different (less favorable) job ladders when they first take primary sector jobs.[10]

If blacks and women are denied access to good jobs in the primary sector, they will tend to acquire less training and, therefore, receive lower wages than white men. The result of this interpretation reflects not optimal individual investments in training, but, rather, the operation of labor market discrimination.

The dual labor market model represents a polar case of a segmented market. Its milder versions can be thought of as predicated on the existence of occupational segregation (either historically or institutionally determined), labor market immobility, and labor market discrimination which becomes more intense at higher levels within job hierarchies. The result is that earnings differentials by race and sex would be expected to increase

---

[9]For a formal neoclassical model of discrimination of this kind, see Kenneth Arrow (1972).

[10]A Federal District Court recently ruled that black pullman porters were subject to this kind of job discrimination. The job classification "pullman porter" had been reserved for blacks. This was true even when porters served as <u>de facto</u> conductors on cars with no (white) conductor: in that event, the porter was assigned to the job classification "porter-in-charge" and paid more than a porter but up to 50 percent less than a regular conductor. Even if a porter served as a porter-in-charge for many years, he would not be promoted to the job of conductor. Similar allegations are regularly made about job discrimination in the construction industry where blacks have been traditionally confined to the less-skilled, lower-wage laborer's union and the travel trades, and prevented from gaining entry into the more highly paid craft unions.

over the life-cycle.

WHO GETS TRAINING?

We will analyze three training measures which were collected as part of the ninth wave of interviewing of the Panel Study of Income Dynamics. These measures are constructed from the fourth and fifth questions from the following sequence:

1. How much formal education is required to get a job like yours?

   ____

2. Do you (also) have to have some work experience or special training to get a job like yours?

   (1) YES (5) NO (GO TO 4)

   3. What kind of experience or special training is that?

   ____

4. On a job like yours, how long would it take the average new person to become fully trained and qualified?

   ________(YEARS) OR ________(MONTHS)

5. Do you feel you are learning things on your job that could lead to a better job or to a promotion?

   (1) YES (5) NO

The entire sequence was designed to obtain information on the formal and informal training components of the respondents' jobs. Questions 1 through 3 deal with pre-job training while the fourth question was intended to measure the volume of the training investment attached to the current job.[11] To help avoid reports of training differences because of skills or experiences unique to the respondent, the phrase "the average new person" rather than "you" was incorporated into the question. The response to Question 4 constitutes our first measure of on-the-job training, "number of years needed to become fully trained and qualified." A second training measure, "whether training for current job," was constructed by comparing the length of the training period to job tenure and by assuming that all training takes place at the beginning of the employment period. If tenure was less than the training period, then the respondent was assumed to be training for his current job. The third training measure, "whether training for a future job," was constructed directly from the fifth question in the sequence.

Admittedly, none of these variables are the precise empirical counterparts of the

---

[11]Note that the second and third questions ask about training prior to current job, so that the response to question 4 should not include such prior training.

theoretical concept of investment in training. In the human capital literature, investments in training are usually measured by the fraction of total potential work time devoted to training rather than working. Our two current training variables are dichotomous rather than continuous. In addition, our measure of the volume of investment attached to the current job is also imprecise, because training in two jobs with equal training periods could have very different intensities and, as a result, unequal amounts of investment. Needless to say, measures of time spent training—crude or otherwise—have not been available to any previous researchers and, for the most part, they have had to content themselves with inferring the time pattern of investment from the life-cycle pattern of change in earnings. While our training measures are imperfect, we would argue that they allow for a far more direct test of the training model than other studies which have tested the training model indirectly via earnings.[12]

Our sample consists of all household heads and spouses in the Panel who were employed at least 500 hours in 1975 and who were between ages 18 and 64.[13]

Before turning to a formal regression model of the determinants of training, it is useful to begin with some descriptive tables. The tables serve two purposes: first, to establish the credibility of the training measures and second, to take a first look at how training differs by race, sex, and several other independent variables.

Table 3.1 presents the mean value for each of the training variables for each of the four race/sex subgroups and also for a series of other independent variables. A fourth training measure, "whether training for either current or future job," is constructed from the two dichotomous training variables and is included as a measure of dead-end jobs with neither current nor future training components. Overall, about one-fifth of the sample were still training for their current job, two-thirds thought they were learning things that could lead to a better job or promotion, and it took, on average, 1.66 years for individuals to be fully trained and qualified on their current jobs. Strikingly large differences exist among the race/sex subgroups. White men held jobs which, on average, required two-and-

---

[12]Keep in mind that our measures of training are based on respondents' reports. There may be some tendency for bias with educated people more conscious of longer run aspects of their jobs, blacks more hopeful about what a job could lead to, and so on. Since the "whether training for a future job" is likely to be affected more by the psychological state of the respondent, we will put more emphasis on findings for the other, more objective training variables. At any rate, our results should be corroborated by studies which have an independent measure of the extent of job training, and perhaps more detail on the process by which these opportunities are distributed to workers.

[13]Female household heads and unmarried male heads are included, so that the group of white and black women includes female heads as well as wives while the groups of white and black men are composed of husbands and unmarried male heads.

Table 3.1

AVERAGE AMOUNTS OF TRAINING BY SEVERAL DEMOGRAPHIC CHARACTERISTICS FOR SEVERAL TRAINING MEASURES
(All Working Household Heads and Spouses Aged 18-64)

			Training Measure			
	Unweighted Number of Observations	Weighted Percentage of Observations	Number of Years Needed to Become Fully Trained and Qualified	Whether Training for Current Job	Whether Training for Future Job	Whether Training for Either Current or Future Job
All	5,225	100.0	1.66	.201	.676	.716
Race/Sex Group						
White Men	2,250	55.7	2.25	.258	.683	.730
Black Men	895	5.3	.99	.091	.785	.801
White Women	1,338	34.6	.94	.141	.642	.678
Black Women	742	4.4	.81	.088	.725	.735
Eta Squared (adj)			.112**	.027**	.005**	.005**
Age						
< 25 Years	1,008	13.5	.91	.255	.785	.807
25-34	1,756	30.5	1.50	.266	.764	.796
35-44	988	20.9	1.86	.180	.687	.731
45-54	950	22.5	2.00	.150	.586	.632
55-64	523	12.6	1.96	.109	.488	.549
Eta Squared (adj)			.033**	.021**	.047**	.040**
Education						
0 Years	67	0.8	1.30	.105	.515	.583
1-5	99	0.9	1.12	.102	.415	.473
6-8	490	7.4	1.27	.077	.488	.520
9-11	914	14.0	1.11	.142	.615	.646
12, High School Diploma	1,192	22.4	1.27	.145	.661	.693
High School Plus Non-academic Training	867	17.3	1.63	.200	.717	.746
Some College	796	16.6	1.75	.255	.715	.765
B.A.	555	13.9	2.34	.311	.754	.806
Advanced Degree	245	6.7	3.16	.313	.749	.820
Eta Squared (adj)			.081**	.034**	.026**	.033**

Table 3.1 (continued)

			Training Measure			
Hours Worked per Week	Unweighted Number of Observations	Weighted Percentage of Observations	Number of Years Needed to Become Fully Trained and Qualified	Whether Training for Current Job	Whether Training for Future Job	Whether Training for Either Current or Future Job
<20 Hours	96	1.9	.85	.103	.508	.545
20-29	223	4.8	.87	.157	.568	.635
30-39	708	14.1	1.38	.158	.641	.677
40-49	3,329	59.5	1.54	.197	.698	.735
50 +	839	19.3	2.54	.264	.678	.726
Not ascertained	30	0.4	1.38	.141	.554	.562
Eta Squared (adj)			.055**	.008**	.007**	.007**
Hourly Earnings (in 1975)						
<$2.00 per hour	520	8.2	.95	.143	.523	.569
$2.00-$2.99	1,018	14.0	.89	.141	.620	.650
$3.00-$3.99	915	15.6	1.00	.179	.683	.709
$4.00-$5.99	1,371	27.1	1.47	.200	.734	.764
$6.00-$7.99	798	18.1	2.06	.233	.708	.754
≥$8.00	603	17.1	3.14	.264	.662	.731
Eta Squared (adj)			.159**	.011**	.015**	.016**

**Significant at .01 level.

a-quarter years of training, while for no other group did the necessary on-the-job training average more than one year. Similarly, over a quarter of the white men were still receiving training for their current job, compared to about 14 percent for white women and only about 9 percent for black men and women. Surprisingly, a higher proportion of blacks than whites reported that they were learning for a future job, 10 percent more for black men and 8 percent more for black women. This latter result could come from the subjective nature of the question upon which it is based.[14]

An individual's age has a strong bivariate relationship with all of the training measures. Younger workers are much more likely to be receiving training on their current job and also to be learning for a future job than are older workers. It appears, however, that the training component of a job increases with age. Workers who are younger than 25 years old have jobs which require less than a year of on-the-job training, while workers who are at least 45 years of age have jobs which entail an average of two years of training. These two facts are not necessarily inconsistent, however, because current training is a function of both the training component and job tenure. The overall situation seems to be one in which workers move through a series of jobs over the life cycle, spending short periods of time in a set of jobs which require relatively little training but provide an opportunity to learn work skills for possible future jobs which provide much more training.

Finally, training increases almost monotonically with education, hours worked per week, and hourly earnings. For all three measures, training is especially low for part-time workers, workers earning less than $3 per hour, and for workers with less than nine years of education.

The distribution of the training variables across occupations, shown in Table 3.2, appeared to be consistent with conventional notions. Among the white-collar workers, professional and technical workers and managers require the longest training period—nearly three years, on average—while secretaries and other clericals require less than a year to be fully trained and sales workers less than a year-and-a-half. In the remaining occupations, there is a clear division between foremen, craftsmen, policemen, and firemen, on the one hand, and operatives, laborers, and service workers, on the other. The training requirements for the skilled blue-collar workers are comparable to those for

---

[14]There is considerable evidence in the psychology literature that blacks are apt to view their own chances for advancement quite optimistically, while continuing to be pessimistic about the chances of blacks in general. See, for example, Campbell and Schuman (1968). More recent support was given by Patricia Gurin in an unpublished memorandum.

Table 3.2

AVERAGE AMOUNTS OF TRAINING BY OCCUPATION FOR SEVERAL TRAINING MEASURES
(All Working Household Heads and Spouses Aged 18-64)

Occupation	Unweighted Number of Observations	Weighted Percentage of Observations	Training Measure: Number of Years Needed to Become Fully Trained and Qualified	Whether Training for Current Job	Whether Training for Future Job	Whether Training for Either Current or Future Job
Physicians, Dentists	13	0.4	5.21	.571	.539	.715
Other Medical	63	1.5	1.95	.201	.810	.810
Accountants	56	1.3	2.40	.448	.807	.891
Teachers, Primary & Secondary	199	4.6	2.57	.236	.687	.746
Teachers, College	50	1.3	3.29	.304	.806	.887
Engineers, Architects, Chemists	92	2.8	2.89	.301	.809	.822
Technicians	113	2.7	1.96	.283	.762	.799
Public Advisors	79	1.7	2.09	.308	.802	.858
Judges, Lawyers	22	0.5	2.51	.389	.597	.727
Other Professional	35	0.8	2.32	.130	.911	.911
Managers, Not Self-Employed	422	11.3	2.76	.335	.785	.840
Managers, Self-Employed	126	3.0	2.14	.125	.438	.476
Secretaries	198	4.3	.80	.135	.747	.773
Other Clerical	644	12.2	.81	.114	.730	.750
Sales Workers	238	5.6	1.40	.229	.732	.774
Foremen	95	2.4	3.13	.285	.743	.772
Other Craftsmen	580	11.3	2.54	.307	.717	.784
Police, Firemen	54	1.1	2.25	.287	.886	.928
Armed Forces	78	1.2	1.52	.381	.860	.895
Transport Equipment Operatives	222	3.2	.52	.075	.464	.478
Other Operatives	762	12.0	.71	.087	.548	.580
Unskilled Laborers--Nonfarm	204	2.1	.63	.084	.603	.624
Farm Laborers	56	0.6	.75	.217	.466	.491
Private Household Workers	73	0.6	.52	.059	.363	.371
Other Service Workers	662	9.9	.60	.097	.560	.596
Farmers	78	1.9	2.86	.098	.395	.446
Eta Squared (adj)			.239**	.070**	.065**	.076**

**Significant at .01 level.

the skilled white-collar workers, while the other blue-collar jobs require the least training of any occupational group, from half a year to about three quarters.

The proportion of workers in each occupation still receiving training for their current job follows a similar pattern. About 10 percent of the operatives, laborers, and service workers and about 12 percent of the clerical workers were still receiving training for their current job, while nearly 30 percent of the professional/technical workers, managers (not self-employed), foremen, and craftsmen were. A relatively low proportion of the operatives, laborers, and service workers—from 35 to 60 percent—report that they are learning skills that might lead to a future job or promotion compared to over 70 percent for most other occupational groups. Thus it appears that the worst jobs do not provide the greatest opportunity for advancement. Respondents in self-employed occupations report long training periods but, not surprisingly, low amounts of training for better jobs.

Since the level of training provided by jobs was shown to be considerably higher for white men than for the other race/sex subgroups, it is helpful to see the extent to which the training differences result simply from differences in the distribution of the subgroups across jobs. This information is given in Table 3.3, which shows training time by occupation for each of the subgroups. Almost without exception, white men report longer training periods within each occupation. While these differences may be caused by different perceptions of identical jobs, a more plausible explanation is that the occupational classification is not detailed enough to distinguish jobs which are truly homogenous with respect to training.

An additional set of descriptive results, given in Appendix Tables A3.1a-A3.1c shows the demographic distribution of the training variables separately by race and sex. In general, the pattern of effects is similar across the four race/sex subgroups. The amount of training increases with age, education, and earnings for virtually all subgroups, while the chances of training for a current or future job diminish with age but increase with education and earnings. Patterns of intercorrelation between current and future training are given in Appendix Table A3.1e.

REGRESSION ANALYSIS OF THE TRAINING DECISION

According to the human capital model, as outlined in the first section of this chapter, individuals choose to acquire training in order to maximize the present value of their lifetime earnings. At every point in time, the decision to invest in training depends on the costs and benefits of acquiring the training, where the benefits are largely a function of the length of the payoff period over which the returns on the investment can be accrued. Therefore, in order to account for differences among individuals in their probability of

Table 3.3

NUMBER OF YEARS NEEDED TO BECOME FULLY TRAINED AND QUALIFIED, BY OCCUPATION, FOR FOUR RACE/SEX SUBGROUPS
(All Working Household Heads and Spouses Aged 18-64)

Occupation	White Men	Black Men	White Women	Black Women
Physicians, Dentists	5.21+	--	--	--
Other Medical	3.82+	--	1.60	--
Accountants	2.94	--	1.32+	--
Teachers, Primary and Secondary	2.88	--	2.38	3.23
Teachers, College	3.59	--	2.80+	--
Engineers, Architects, Chemists	2.95	--	--	--
Technicians	2.48	--	1.18	--
Public Advisors	2.55	--	1.15+	2.22+
Judges, Lawyers	2.51	--	--	--
Other Professional	2.36	--	--	--
Managers, Not Self-employed	3.11	2.98	1.28	2.13+
Managers, Self-employed	2.32	1.41+	1.04+	--
Secretaries	--	--	0.79	0.32
Other Clerical	1.19	0.89	0.72	0.43
Sales Workers	1.93	0.50+	0.58	0.14+
Foremen	3.41	2.06+	--	--
Other Craftsmen	2.62	1.97	0.98+	--
Policemen, Firemen	2.46	0.39+	--	--
Armed Forces	1.56	1.38+	--	--
Transport Equipment Operatives	0.54	0.42	--	--
Other Operatives	0.96	0.62	0.48	0.20
Unskilled Laborers, Nonfarm	0.75	0.36	--	--
Farm Laborers	0.97+	0.37	--	--
Private Household Workers	--	--	0.38+	0.62
Other Service Workers	0.92	0.36	0.53	0.60
Farmers	2.84	--	--	--
Eta Squared (adj)	.190	.284	.183	.392

+Result based on fewer than 25 observations.
--Fewer than 10 observations.

receiving training, it is necessary to include measures of those factors which may influence the costs and benefits of training. For women, it is especially important to consider variables which may influence the length of the payoff period, since their pattern of labor force participation tends to be less regular than that of men.

We use two sets of variables in order to account for the potential benefits of training. The first of these is an individual's work horizon, calculated as the difference between an individual's current age and age 65. This measures the maximum length of the payoff period and, according to the human capital model, the length of the work horizon should be positively related to current investment in training. However, this measure of the work horizon may well overstate the likely payoff period for some individuals, since it assumes that each individual actually chooses to—or is able to—work in every year until age 65. We do not, of course, have any direct information on the actual length of the payoff period, but it is possible to make some inferences about future work commitment on the basis of current and past information. We employ a set of four such measures, two drawn from an individual's past work history, one from his or her current work situation, and the fourth from a question about the future. The two work history variables measure whether the individual ever dropped out of the labor force for a year or more (not counting withdrawals in order to return to school or otherwise learn job skills) or whether the individual ever worked half-time or less since age 18.[15] The current work situation variable measures whether the individual is working part-time (30 hours per week or less) on a voluntary basis. These three variables reflect past and current work commitment and can be treated (and perhaps are treated by employers) as proxies for possible future work commitment. Thus we would expect men and women with these characteristics to be less likely to invest in training than otherwise similar individuals.

The fourth variable is a somewhat more direct indication of future work plans. It is simply a dichotomous measure of whether the wife expects to have more children.[16] Since most women who expect to have more children also expect to drop out of the labor force for at least some period of time, they would be less likely to be acquiring training

---

[15]For some, the part-time work could also be the result of involuntary unemployment. Note that military service that provided some job skills is not counted as an interruption.

[16]Unmarried respondents are scored zero on this variable, so it may seem that the variable, in part, measures the effect of marital status. Inclusion of a direct measure of marital status showed that this was not the case.

currently. For men, the variable should not affect the training decision.

The factors which affect the costs of training are more difficult to handle, both conceptually and empirically. There is, in fact, no clear agreement, even in theory, about the nature and determinants of investment costs; different models characterize training costs in rather different ways. Perhaps the only factor which is hypothesized to affect costs in all formulations is education.[17] It is usually assumed that more education enables an individual to acquire training more easily and efficiently. Because education reduces the training costs, it should be positively related to the probability of training. This is not, however, the only possible explanation of how education might affect training. If employers use education as the basis for screening for jobs which provide training, then more education might increase the probability of training even if it had no effect on its costs.

Finally, our model includes two more variables which reflect an institutionalist perspective on the process by which training is acquired. These two variables are measures of work experience prior to the current job but with the same employer, and all other previous work experience since age 18 but before the current employer.[18] From a human capital perspective, these two variables should have little or no effect, after adjusting for the effects of other variables, including education, work horizon, and future work commitment proxies.[19] In contrast, the prediction from the institutional theories is that prior work experience, especially with the current employer, should affect training opportunities. We included these variables in the model in order to test whether seniority had an independent effect on the probability of receiving training and whether this effect was stronger for some groups of workers than others.

The estimated coefficients and standard errors obtained from regressing each of the two training variables (whether training for current job and whether training for a future job) on identical sets of independent variables for each of the four subgroups are given in

---

[17]An individual's wage rate affects costs, but nevertheless is usually not assumed to affect training decisions. This is especially clear in Ben-Porath's model, where the costs of training are primarily the opportunity costs of time spent training. These opportunity costs are measured by an individual's wage rate, so that although a lower wage rate reduces the benefits of training, it also reduces the costs identically and leaves training decisions unchanged.

[18]There is no problem with multicollinearity between these two variables and work horizon even for men since a variable measuring current job tenure is omitted.

[19]It is possible that experience affects the costs of acquiring training just as education does. If so, then these effects, when adjusted for other variables in the regression analysis, should be similar across the four race/sex subgroups.

Tables 3.4 and 3.5. Since each dependent variable is dichotomous, coefficients can be interpreted as the change in the probability of receiving training that is associated with a unit change in an explanatory variable.

Despite the fact that the two training variables were measured quite differently (the training for current job measure was constructed by comparing the length of the training period to job tenure; the training for future job measure was measured directly from a more subjective question), the direction, significance and, at times, even magnitude of the coefficients are remarkably similar in the two sets of regressions. Education, past work experience, and future work horizon are important predictors for both dependent variables, the latter two being especially important for men. The measures of past and current labor force commitment usually have the expected sign and are statistically significant for at least one of the subgroups. The only group to escape the apparent training penalties for lack of commitment are white men.

Training for Current Job

Since the measure of training for current job is probably more reliable, results for it will be discussed first. A first noteworthy point from Table 3.4 is the importance of education in leading to training opportunities. After the effects of past and prospective work experience have been taken into account, an additional year of education increases the chance of securing on-the-job training by 3 percent for white males, about 2 percent for women, and 1.5 percent for black men. All of these estimated effects are highly significant and are consistent with either a human capital or an institutional explanation. The lower education coefficient for black males could result from school quality differences, although such differences might also be expected to lead to differences between coefficients of white and black women.

In addition to lower education coefficients, black men have lower amounts of education, and these different amounts account for a substantial part of the difference in the fractions of black and white men who receive training. If black men had as much average education as white men and could translate education into training as readily as white men, then the fraction of black men training would increase from 9.1 percent to 14.8 percent.[20]

One of the most important differences among the four sets of coefficients is the effect of past work experience on current training. Past years of work experience have a

---

[20]The average amounts of education for the four race/sex subgroups is given in Appendix Table A3.1f.

Table 3.4

REGRESSION RESULTS FOR WHETHER TRAINING FOR CURRENT JOB, BY RACE/SEX SUBGROUPS
(All Household Heads and Spouses Aged 18-64)

	White Men	Black Men	White Women	Black Women
Education	.030** (.003)	.014** (.003)	.022** (.004)	.021** (.005)
Years of Work Experience Before Present Employer	.052** (.003)	.030** (.003)	.009** (.002)	.008** (.002)
Years with Current Employer Prior to Current Position	.053** (.003)	.034** (.004)	.004 (.002)	.011** (.003)
Interrupted for Nontraining Reasons	.036 (.037)	-.037 (.046)	.017 (.025)	-.074* (.036)
Ever Worked Part-Time?	.004 (.021)	.022 (.022)	-.039** (.020)	.033 (.022)
Expect More Children?	.022 (.025)	-.014 (.028)	-.060* (.030)	-.060 (.037)
If Voluntary Part-Time	.012 (.083)	-.054 (.119)	.044 (.027)	.070 (.038)
Current Work Horizon	.056** (.004)	.033** (.005)	.003 (.004)	.022** (.004)
Work Horizon Squared	-.0001* (.0001)	-.0001 (.0001)	.0001 (.0001)	-.0003** (.0001)
Constant	-2.301	-1.298	-.356	-.583
$\bar{R}^2$	.204	.115	.057	.081
$\bar{Y}$	.258	.091	.141	.088
N	2,250	895	1,338	742

* Significant at .05 level.
**Significant at .01 level.

high payoff in training for men, especially white men, but have very little effect on the chances that women will receive training. Coefficients for white men are nearly twice as large as those for black men and nearly five times as large as the coefficients of the two groups of women. These differences are large enough to account for most of the training advantage that white men have over the other subgroups.[21] This finding is quite important because it suggests something about the process by which individuals receive training opportunities. For white men, the link between time in the labor force and chances of training is strong and direct. For members of minority groups with the same apparent commitment to the labor force (especially women) the association is quite weak. These results are generally consistent with an institutional view of different promotion practices of firms on the basis of race and sex.[22] It is somewhat surprising, however, that the coefficients on the current employer tenure variables are not larger than those on pre-employer tenure. This result suggests that access to training opportunities within the race/sex subgroups is equally increased by both kinds of work experience.

Lack of commitment to the labor force in the past, present, or in the future, may be expected to reduce training incentives or opportunities. Results from the current training regressions show some support for this notion, especially for women. Past labor force interruptions lead to significantly lower chances of training for black women; part-time work in the past lowers the chances that white women are training in their current jobs. A final, quite sensible, piece of evidence is that the expectation of having children reduces the chances of training for women (6 percent and statistically significant for white women; 6 percent but insignificant for black women) but does not have an effect for men.

Since the payoff period is shorter for workers who are nearer to retirement age, a measure of work horizon (65 - age) was included and expected to have a positive effect on

---

[21]As shown in Appendix Table A3.1f, white men average more of both pre-employer and pre-present position work experience than do the other race/sex subgroups. If the minority groups could receive the same training payoff for their years of work experience as white men, their chances of receiving training would increase considerably. Specifically, the increase is 30.7 percent for black men, 46.1 percent for white women and 54.3 percent for black women.

[22]The lower coefficients for blacks and women may also be caused, in part, by a larger amount of error in the measurement of the experience variables. Any such error will tend to bias the coefficients toward zero. It is unlikely that much of the coefficient differences are caused by measurement error, however. If so, one would expect similar differences when these independent variables were used with other dependent variables, which was not the case when these variables were included in wage rate regressions.

training. This is the case for all groups except white women—the group with the least overall attachment to the labor force. Both work horizon and its square were included in the regression to allow for a parabolic work horizon-training profile. The relationship for men is more nearly linear than for black women. For 25-year-old white and black men, an additional horizon year is associated with 5 and 2.5 percent increases, respectively, in the chance of training. For black women, the effect of additional years of work horizon is actually negative until age 30 and becomes increasingly positive thereafter. This pattern is remarkably similar to that predicted by a human capital model applied to the typical life-cycle work pattern of women, but the size of the standard errors of these coefficients caution against overinterpretation.

Training for a Future Job

When the dependent variable is changed from training for current to future job, the pattern of coefficients (shown in Table 3.5) has many striking similarities and some differences. Education, for example, increases the chances of training for a future job in almost exactly the same way as it did for current job training. Black men, as before, benefit the least from additional schooling, while the education coefficients are somewhat higher for women than white men. Given the statistical significance and uniformity of the education coefficients across the eight regressions, we can be quite confident in the result that the chances of training increase with the level of formal education.

As with current training, prior work experience increases the chances of training for a future job much more for white men than for women. The coefficients for black women are actually negative, although none of the coefficients for women are statistically significant at the 5 percent level. For black men, there is an interesting difference in the effects of experience with the current employer and experience prior to the current employer, the former being much more important than the latter. These results are similar to those for current training in suggesting that training opportunities increase with experience much more directly for white men than for women.

Also consistent with findings on current training is the result that the measures of low work commitment have some negative and significant effects on the probability of receiving training for a future job. Black men and women who had worked only part-time (and do not want more work) are also significantly less likely to be training, with the training penalty being twice as large for black women as white women. As with current training, none of these work commitment variables is significant for white men. The only anomalous result from these tables is that black women who expect to have more children are more likely to be training for a future job.

Table 3.5

REGRESSION RESULTS FOR WHETHER TRAINING FOR FUTURE JOB
BY RACE/SEX SUBGROUPS
(All Household Heads and Spouses Aged 18-64)

	White Men	Black Men	White Women	Black Women
Education	.021**	.016**	.025**	.031**
	(.004)	(.005)	(.006)	(.007)
Years of Work Experience Before Present Employer	.011**	.008	.003	-.001
	(.003)	(.004)	(.002)	(.003)
Years with Current Employer Prior to Current Position	.014**	.015**	.004	-.002
	(.003)	(.005)	(.003)	(.004)
Interrupted for Nontraining Reasons	.012	.108	-.053	-.061
	(.042)	(.066)	(.034)	(.057)
Ever Worked Part-Time?	.013	-.109**	-.023	-.088**
	(.024)	(.031)	(.027)	(.034)
Expect More Children?	.022	-.018	-.025	.133*
	(.029)	(.040)	(.042)	(.058)
If Voluntary Part-Time	-.057	.045	-.095*	-.184**
	(.095)	(.173)	(.037)	(.060)
Current Work Horizon	.023**	.032**	.011*	.037**
	(.005)	(.008)	(.005)	(.007)
Work Horizon Squared	-.0001	-.0003**	-.0001	-.0008**
	(.0001)	(.0001)	(.0001)	(.0001)
Constant	-.300	-.095	.110	.069
$\bar{R}^2$	.087	.095	.047	.081
$\bar{Y}$	.683	.785	.642	.725
N	2,250	895	1,338	742

* Significant at .05 level.
**Significant at .01 level.

Additional years of work horizon significantly increase the chances of training for a future job for all four of the race/sex subgroups. Among workers near retirement age, the effect is especially strong for blacks. At age 25, however, additional years of work horizon increase the chances of training by about 1 percent for men, by less than .5 percent for white women, and actually decrease training changes for black women. The pattern of first decreasing and then increasing effects of work horizon for black women is similar to that found for the current training measure, although for future training, the turning point is at age 40, rather than 30.

Amount of Training Required by Job

Our third training variable, a measure of the number of years needed to become fully trained and qualified for the job, can also be related to a set of independent variables, although considerably less information about the training process is obtained. The reason for this is that the previous two training measures were measured currently as were a number of independent variables such as future plans for children. Independent variables in a regression explaining the extent of training needed for the current job are most appropriately dated according to when the respondent first took the job. Some independent variables such as work horizon can be back-dated by subtracting years of current job tenure. Most other independent variables in the prior regressions cannot be back-dated precisely and therefore must be omitted. The only other valid explanatory variables are years of formal education and a measure of whether the respondent placed limitations on location or work hours in his job search.[23] Coefficients and standard errors from the resulting regressions are given in Table 3.6.[24]

As with the other training measures, formal education is a highly significant predictor of the training content of the job, with additional years of education leading to between one-sixth and one-quarter of an extra year of training. The estimated effect of

---

[23]This latter measure is constructed from the question: "Thinking back to when you started your present job, were there some limitations on where you could work or what hours you could work that were factors in taking this job?" The time reference in this question makes it appropriate for explaining total training time but not the current training variables. The educational attainment measure will not be accurate for those who have completed additional schooling since taking their jobs.

[24]We also included a measure of past labor force interruption but it was quite insignificant for all groups and its omission did not change the coefficients of the remaining variables. It was not possible to include a measure of pre-job work experience since it would have been highly colinear with the work horizon variables for men.

Table 3.6

REGRESSION RESULTS FOR NUMBER OF YEARS NEEDED TO BECOME FULLY TRAINED AND QUALIFIED, BY RACE/SEX SUBGROUPS (All Household Heads and Spouses Aged 18-64)

	White Men	Black Men	White Women	Black Women
Education	.167** (.015)	.175** (.017)	.208** (.015)	.280** (.020)
Work Horizon when Took Job	.066** (.023)	.014 (.024)	-.017 (.018)	.003 (.030)
Work Horizon Squared	-.0019** (.0004)	-.0011** (.0004)	.0000 (.0003)	-.0007 (.0004)
Limited Job Hours or Location	-.391** (.121)	-.319* (.151)	-.149* (.076)	.213 (.110)
Constant	.174	-.042	-1.123	-1.921
$\bar{R}^2$	.098	.152	.126	.233
$\bar{Y}$	2.25	.99	.94	.81
Number of Observations	2,225	895	1,338	742

* Significant at .05 level.
**Significant at .01 level.

education is least for white men and greatest for black women.

There is a parabolic relationship between work horizon and volume of training for men, but not for women. White male workers hold jobs with the most training at about age 35 (work horizon = 30 years) while the amount of training continues to increase in the jobs of black men until close to retirement age. As noted before, these life-cycle training results are not necessarily inconsistent with the continuously declining profiles observed for men using the two current training measures. Although the amount of training required by jobs taken by young workers is small, so too, apparently, is their tenure in such jobs. Rapid turnover in jobs with a relatively small amount of training leads to a high probability of still being in the job's training period. Jobs with the largest training content apparently come after years of work experience—and more so for blacks than whites.

The final independent variables, a measure of the limits imposed on job location or hours, has a large and negative effect for men, a more modest negative effect for white women, and, contrary to expectation, an almost significant positive effect for black women. Workers who impose such limits apparently suffer not only wage penalties,[25] but receive less training as well.

The Training Decision—A Summary

If, as most economists believe, differences in on-the-job training play an important role in explaining differences in earnings, then it becomes very important to understand why different individuals receive different amounts of on-the-job training. In the human capital model, training is an investment decision made by an individual worker in response to a comparison of the costs and benefits of the investment. Differential access to jobs with training—a key idea in the dual labor market theory—is not an important factor of the human capital explanation. We have attempted to test these competing explanations by estimating the extent to which training seems to respond to rational investment incentives rather than a set of more institutional factors.

In general, we find some support for both the human capital and institutional models. For men, the chances of training are quite responsive to the length of time over which a training investment could yield returns. This relationship is also strong for black women, but only after the age at which most have stopped having children and the youngest children are old enough to be in school. An investment explanation also would predict that women who expect to interrupt future work to have children would have less of an investment incentive. This indeed seems to be the case for white women. But once measures of

---

[25] This finding is detailed in Chapter 4.

the voluntary aspects of the investment decision have been taken into account, certain institutional factors emerge as being crucial to understanding differences in amounts of training. In particular, prior work experience—both with the same employer and before—has a strong, positive effect on the training chances for white men, but not for blacks or women with similar post- and prospective work experiences. The link between work experience and current training for white men is twice as strong as for black men and more than five times as strong as it is for women. This evidence is quite consistent with internal labor market theories in which minority workers are placed on different promotion ladders from white men, or are relegated to secondary sector jobs with a high degree of turnover.

IS TRAINING COSTLY?

A key difference between the approach to training of the human capital and dual labor market models and, via training, to the determination of individual labor market earnings is the question of whether the acquisition of training is costly. In the human capital model, the costliness of training transforms "learning on the job" into an "investment in on-the-job training." Unless training is costly, the process of acquiring it cannot be characterized and analyzed as a kind of investment activity and, indeed, there would be no optimal life-cycle pattern of investment in training. Moreover, it is the costliness of training, in conjunction with its subsequent benefits in the form of higher earnings, which is assumed to generate the familiar concave experience-earnings profile. In the dual labor market model, the primary sector jobs provide both higher pay and training opportunities.

There are, in general, two possible explanations of why the acquisition of training should entail costs to the individual. The first explanation considers the costs of training as analogous to the costs of education. Economists generally argue that the primary costs of, for example, a college education are not the direct costs of tuition and supplies, but rather the indirect opportunity costs of the potential earnings that are sacrificed because the individual is in school rather than working. Similarly, many economists argue that on-the-job training is also time consuming, even though it usually occurs at the workplace. Ben-Porath, for example, assumes that working and learning are mutually exclusive activities.[26] As a result, an individual who is learning more is working less and hence would earn less in a competitive labor market. The cost of training, then, is the potential earnings which are sacrificed because some portion of the working day is devoted to training rather than working.

Alternatively, even in a pure learning-by-doing context in which training is assumed

[26]Ben-Porath (1967).

to be an automatic consequence of working and is not assumed to be time consuming, training will nevertheless be costly in a competitive labor market. Here, the reasoning follows from Adam Smith's theory of compensating wage differentials. If workers desire training—and, presumably they do since it increases their skills and, hence, their expected future earnings—then, given the requisite amount of information and mobility, the relative supply of labor to jobs offering different amounts of training will assure that, holding skill requirements constant, jobs offering more training will also carry lower current wages. If that were not true, then it would pay workers in jobs with lower training opportunities to offer themselves at lower wages for jobs which have greater training opportunities in the expectation of recouping the lower current wage by higher future wages.

The prediction that training is costly is not a part of the dual labor market model. In it, "good" jobs are those in the internal labor markets of the primary sectors with well-defined promotion ladders, abundant job security, and high wages, and "bad" jobs are those in the competitive, secondary segment of the econony characterized by low pay, high turnover, and little advancement. If the good jobs are allocated through luck, discrimination, or "connections," then individuals who happen to acquire the good jobs will report both more training and higher wages than otherwise comparable individuals in the bad jobs.

We examine the issue of whether training is costly by introducing our two measures of current training into a wage equation. Previous researchers have been unable to address this question because direct measures of training were unavailable. The only empirical evidence for the costliness of training is the concavity of experience-earnings profiles, but an explanation of that kind is completely circular since it is the costliness of training which is assumed to generate the earnings profile in the first place.

Assessing the costliness of training poses a number of empirical problems. A natural empirical procedure for such a valuation would be to use multiple regression to hold constant as many productivity-related variables as possible and then estimate the difference between the wages paid to individuals who are currently training and otherwise similar individuals who are not training.[27] The validity of the resulting estimates depends critically upon the extent to which the most important productivity-related characteristics have been included in the regression equation. If important variables are

---

[27]This procedure is used successfully by Antos and Rosen (1975) to estimate the value of school quality, school neighborhood characteristics, and student racial composition of schools for school teachers' salaries. Thurow and Lucas (1972) attempt to price job characteristics with wage rates and obtain many anomalous results.

omitted, and if these omitted variables have a positive correlation with both training and earnings, then the estimated "cost" of training will be biased and may even appear to increase rather than decrease earnings.[28] This is a potentially serious problem in this case because the individuals who are receiving training tend to be those who also have measured characteristics, such as higher education, which typically lead to higher wages. Since there are possible problems with the model specification, our analysis results concerning the costliness of training are necessarily tentative and somewhat speculative.

As a first attempt to estimate the cost of training, we included the two measures of current training—whether training for current job and whether training for future job—in the wage regressions along with our standard set of productivity-related characteristics.[29] The results, shown in the upper panel of Table 3.7 show that those engaged in either type of training appear to be earning more than those not receiving training. The estimated wage advantage for those training for a current job is significant only for white men; the coefficients on training for a future job are significant for all but the black men.

Since these estimated positive training effects may be the spurious result of unmeasured productivity-related factors, we included an additional variable—training time not yet completed—in the regression, the results for which are given in the second panel of the table. The justification for this variable is that if employers offer jobs with the longest training periods to the most productive workers, then the inclusion of this variable will provide additional control for otherwise unobservable worker characteristics.[30] The use of proxies for unobservable variables is always a precarious empirical procedure, since proxies may measure many things in addition to the desired characteristics. In this case there is the danger that this variable measures unintended features of the job or the worker and itself has a spurious effect on the current training coefficients. As shown in

---

[28]For obvious reasons, there are few published examples in which the wage valuation of job characteristics has unexpected signs. Longitudinal data on workers who change jobs and alter their bundles of job characteristics provide an opportunity for more precise control of productivity-related characteristics. Duncan (1974) uses this strategy and finds several tradeoffs between wages and desirable job characteristics.

[29]In the wage regression reported in this section and in the next, we switch from using a measure of the total amount of training provided by the job to a measure of training time actually completed. The two variables are identical for those who have completed their training period but will differ for respondents who report job tenure that is less than the training period. Wages should respond to completed training and may or may not respond to training time not yet completed. This issue is investigated below.

[30]Frank Stafford suggested this possibility. This line of reasoning also implies that some of the apparent return to completed training may be merely a return to other productivity-related characteristics.

The addition of this variable also introduces some multicolinearity. The simple correlation (r) between training time not yet completed and whether training for current job ranges from .69 to .74.

Table 3.7

IS TRAINING COSTLY?

REGRESSION RESULTS FOR VARIOUS FUNCTIONAL FORMULATIONS
BY RACE/SEX GROUP
(All Working Household Heads and Spouses Aged 18-64)

Independent Variable	White Men	Black Men	White Women	Black Women
REGRESSION #1:				
Training Completed	.057**	.060**	.084**	.062**
	(.006)	(.014)	(.013)	(.015)
Whether Training for Current Job	.080**	.061	.061	.076
	(.030)	(.059)	(.040)	(.061)
Whether Training for Future Job	.047*	.003	.073**	.200**
	(.024)	(.039)	(.027)	(.036)
$\bar{R}^2$	.287	.256	.296	.359
REGRESSION #2:				
Training Completed	.060**	.058**	.084**	.070**
	(.006)	(.014)	(.013)	(.016)
Whether Training for Current Job	-.047	-.073	-.010	.251**
	(.039)	(.078)	(.052)	(.082)
Whether Training for Future Job	.049*	.018	.074**	.202**
	(.024)	(.040)	(.027)	(.036)
Training Time Not Yet Completed	.060**	.064**	.047*	-.160**
	(.012)	(.025)	(.022)	(.051)
$\bar{R}^2$	.294	.260	.298	.367
REGRESSION #3:				
Training Completed	.052**	.046**	.081**	.128**
	(.007)	(.014)	(.015)	(.019)
Whether Training for Current Job	.031	-.217**	.045	.375**
	(.039)	(.082)	(.050)	(.077)
Whether Training for Future Job	.050*	-.004	.074**	.203**
	(.024)	(.039)	(.027)	(.035)
Training Completed times Whether Training for Current Job	.030	.235**	.015	-.197**
	(.016)	(.049)	(.029)	(.033)
$\bar{R}^2$	.288	.274	.296	.389

Table 3.7 (continued)

Independent Variable	White Men	Black Men	White Women	Black Women
REGRESSION #4:				
Training Completed	.053**	.046**	.082**	.126**
	(.007)	(.014)	(.015)	(.019)
Whether Training for Current Job	-.124*	-.274**	-.016	.419**
	(.049)	(.090)	(.058)	(.087)
Whether Training for Future Job	.052*	.005	.074**	.204**
	(.024)	(.040)	(.027)	(.035)
Training Completed Times Whether Training for Current Job	.042**	.216**	.007	-.183**
	(.016)	(.050)	(.029)	(.035)
Training Time Not Yet Completed	.065**	.038	.046*	-.059
	(.012)	(.025)	(.022)	(.054)
$\bar{R}^2$	.296	.275	.297	.389
Number of Observations	2250	895	1338	742

* Significant at .05 level.

**Significant at .01 level.

NOTE: Other variables included in the regressions: whether south, city size, education, pre-employer experience, pre-employer experience squared, pre-present position experience, tenure minus training.

the second panel of Table 3.7, the inclusion of this variable makes a dramatic change in the estimated wage effect of training for a current job. For all but the black women, the apparent wage benefits of training for current job become costs, although these costs are not statistically significant at conventional levels. The coefficients for whether training for a future job, on the other hand, change very little.[31]

An additional refinement is to allow the cost of training to depend on the amount of training completed. It is reasonable to expect training to be more intensive at the beginning of the training period than in its latter stages, and if so, early training costs will also be greater.[32] To account for this possibility, the interaction between training completed and whether training for current job, was added to regression equations 1 and 2. The results, reported in the third and fourth panels of Table 3.7, respectively, support the notion that training costs decrease with the length of the training period, at least for men. There seems to be no such relationship for white women, and costs <u>increase</u> with the training period for black women.

A clearer way to present the results of these final regressions is to evaluate the estimated costs of training for the current job at various points in the training period. This is done for the four race/sex groups in Table 3.8. The group of black men conforms most closely to the expected declining cost profile. Regardless of the inclusion of the training time not yet completed control variable, wages of black men at the beginning of their training period are significantly lower than the wages of otherwise similar individuals who aren't training. For white men, training is estimated to be costly only after the additional control variable is added. There is virtually no wage benefit or penalty for training in a current job for white women, while for black women, training appears to produce a large positive wage effect that declines throughout the training period. These positive and declining wage effects run contrary to expectations and do not conform to any conventional interpretation, dual labor market, human capital, or otherwise.[33]

---

[31]The coefficients on the training time not yet completed variable are also of some interest. For men, additional years of this affect wages to the same extent (6 percent) as do years of completed training. The coefficient for white women is smaller, although still positive and significant, while the coefficient for black women is actually negative and significant.

[32]This follows from the opportunity cost view of training but not necessarily from the compensating wage differential cost formulation.

[33]There are two possible explanations for the anomalous finding for black women. First, the positive wage effect of current training may result from the fact that the earnings equation is most poorly specified for black women. Second, the apparent higher wages for black women who are currently training could reflect short-run disequilibrium rents caused by a sudden increase in the demand for highly-educated black women for jobs which provided training.

Table 3.8

PERCENTAGE OF WAGE DIFFERENCES FOR THOSE CURRENTLY TRAINING AT VARIOUS TIMES IN TRAINING PERIOD

	White Men	Black Men	White Women	Black Women
REGRESSION #3: Not Including "Training Time Not Yet Completed"				
At Beginning of Training Period	3.1	-21.7	4.5	37.5
After One Year	6.1	1.8	6.0	17.8
After Two Years	9.1	25.3	7.5	-1.9
REGRESSION #4: Including "Training Time Not Yet Completed"				
At Beginning of Training Period	-12.4	-27.4	-1.6	41.9
After One Year	-8.2	-5.7	-0.9	23.6
After Two Years	-4.0	16.0	-0.2	5.3

NOTE: Computed from Regressions #3 and #4, Table 3.7.

Our results regarding the costliness of current training were, then, highly sensitive to the various model specification which we considered. The only exception to this was among black males, for whom training appeared to be costly in three of the four specifications. In general, we found strong empirical support for the human capital model's assumption that training was costly only under the strong assumption that a measure of training-time-not-yet-completed legitimately controlled for unobservable productivity-related individual characteristics. Unless one is willing to make that assumption, our results suggest that, with the exception of black males, individuals who are currently training do not earn less than otherwise similar individuals who are not training.

With a single exception, the estimated wage effects of training for a future job are positive in all four of the different formulations reported in Table 3.7. Black women who report training for a future job have the highest wage benefits—20 percent—but the higher wages for white men and women are also statistically significant. Because this reported training variable is more subjective, it may be a less accurate measure of whether training is actually taking place and may merely reflect positive feelings about a job that pays well. Taken at face value, however, these results support the institutional notion of "good" jobs with promotion ladders actually paying more than "bad" jobs held by comparable individuals.

TRAINING AND EARNINGS

Few labor market analysts would dispute the notion that on-the-job training effects earnings; a more relevant issue is the nature and extent of the relationship. The most important empirical dimensions of this association are explored in this section. Specifically, we will investigate the effects of training on earnings, the extent to which training accounts for observed variations in wages by race and sex, and the sensitivity of this estimated effect to changes in functional form and the addition of control variables.

The amount of training completed on the present job can be thought of as one piece of the total work history of an individual.[34] As shown earlier in this chapter, this training segment is more than twice as long for white men as for blacks or women. As important as the length of the training period is the payoff to a given amount of training. Minority workers might earn less because they work in jobs offering less training or because they

---

[34] As mentioned before, a measure of training time actually completed is used in this section in the wage regression and it will differ from total training time for those respondents with job tenure which is less than the total training time required by the job.

have jobs in which the wage benefit of a given amount of training is less or both. Differential benefits will show up as differences in the coefficients on the training variable in the wage equation.

When completed training is included in linear form with other work segments (years of work experience before current employer, years with current employer prior to current position, and years of post-training tenure on current job) and the additional variables of education, whether South, and city size, the estimated benefits of training, shown in the "a" column of Table 3.9, are quite uniform across the four subgroups. An additional year of training raises the wages of white men by 5.4 percent, black men by 5.9 percent, and white and black women by 8.5 percent and 6.6 percent, respectively. Only the coefficient of white women differs significantly from that of white men (t=2.2), and it is larger, not smaller. Thus the payoff on training is highly significant, and roughly uniform across the four race/sex subgroups. It is also approximately equal in magnitude to the estimated wage payoff on additional years of education (not shown in the table).

The training measure makes a modest contribution toward explaining interpersonal variation in wage rates. For white men, the fraction of variance in log wage rates explained (R^2) increases by 2.4 percent when the training variable is added. For the other subgroups, the increase in R^2 is somewhat less: 1.5 percent for black men, 2.3 percent for white women, and 1.7 percent for black women.

To investigate possible nonlinearities in the relationship between training and earnings, the training variable was separated into a set of five dummy variables representing no training, training periods of one to five months, six to 11 months, 12 to 23 months, and two or more years. The estimated coefficients on the training dummies are shown in the bottom half of Table 3.9. With the one to five month dummy omitted to avoid perfect multicollinearity, the coefficients can be interpreted as the proportionate wage difference between workers who have completed a given amount of training and similar workers who have completed between one and five months of training. A summary measure of the usefulness of changing the training variable from linear to categorical form is given by the change in the explained variance of the equation ($\bar{R}^2$).[35] As shown in Table 3.9, the $\bar{R}^2$ actually declines for white men and increases by less than .5 percent for white women. For both black men and women, the increase is greater, 2 percent for each group, although

---

[35]For those concerned with the loss of explanatory power in using a five-category classification rather than some quadratic or cubic form for the training variable, it should be pointed out that even if the relationship between training and earnings were linear, the fraction of explanatory power still available using k classes (in this case k = 5) instead of an infinite set of numbers is $(1-\frac{1}{k^2})$ (in this case, 96 percent). See Aigner, Goldberger, and Kalton (1975).

Table 3.9

REGRESSION RESULTS FOR VARIOUS FUNCTIONAL FORMS FOR THE TRAINING VARIABLE IN THE WAGE EQUATION BY RACE/SEX GROUPS
(All Working Household Heads and Spouses Aged 18-64)

Independent Variable	White Men a	White Men b	Black Men a	Black Men b	White Women a	White Women b	Black Women a	Black Women b
REGRESSION #1:								
Training Completed (linear, in years)	.054** (.006)	.048** (.006)	.059** (.014)	.065** (.014)	.085** (.013)	.080** (.013)	.066** (.015)	.075** (.015)
$\bar{R}^2$	.284	.303	.255	.291	.292	.328	.332	.346
REGRESSION #2:								
No Training	.071 (.111)	.088 (.110)	-.146 (.087)	-.151 (.085)	.123 (.094)	.126 (.092)	-.140 (.133)	-.127 (.133)
1-5 Months	+	+	+	+	+	+	+	+
6-11 Months	.069* (.035)	.057 (.035)	-.086 (.046)	-.046 (.044)	.125** (.036)	.108** (.035)	.149** (.046)	.135** (.046)
12-24 Months	.093** (.031)	.081** (.031)	.216** (.047)	.239** (.046)	.165** (.035)	.143** (.035)	-.011 (.051)	-.003 (.052)
2 or More Years	.229** (.208)	.204** (.028)	.185** (.051)	.194** (.051)	.290** (.045)	.278** (.044)	.384* (.060)	.417** (.061)
$\bar{R}^2$	.282	.300	.274	.308	.296	.331	.355	.383

[a]Other variables included in the equation: whether south, city size, education, years of work experience before present employer, pre-employer experience squared, years with current employer prior to current position, years of post-training tenure on current job.

[b]Also includes: limited job hours or location, hours of work missed for illness of others in 1976, hours of work missed for own illness in 1975, years out of labor force since completing school, proportion of total working years that were full time, knows there are better jobs elsewhere, doesn't know whether there are better jobs elsewhere, plans to stop work for nontraining reasons.

+This category has been omitted to avoid perfect multicolinearity.

*Significant at the .05 level.

**Significant at the .01 level.

the nonlinear functional form does not lend itself to a simple description. In all cases, the wage differences between those who have completed two or more years of training and those who have completed between one and five months is large, positive, and highly significant.

While it is clearly impossible to show that the estimated effects of training do not change with the addition of all possible explanatory factors, we can experiment with the coefficient stability by adding a number of potentially important predictors. Included in the panel data are a set of productivity-related measures that could affect both training and earnings. These consist of voluntary limits on work location or mobility, time lost because of illness of others in the family, past work interruptions, and past incidence of part-time work. When these variables are added, the training coefficients (shown in the "b" columns of Table 3.9) change very little and not consistently in either direction. In no case does the coefficient change by more than a standard error. Further evidence on the stability of the coefficients comes from comparing the coefficients in the linear form of the completed training variable in Table 3.9 with the coefficients obtained when the variables measuring current training and training time not yet completed were added and presented in the top two panels of Table 3.7. Again, the changes are quite minor.

The effects of training on earnings are highly significant and roughly similar for the four groups of workers investigated here. Because the amount of training received by workers of the different races and sexes differs substantially, it is possible that training differences play a major role in explaining wage differences among the four subgroups. The average amount of completed training for white men is 1.69 years, for black men it is .79 years for white and black women, it is .72 and .70 years, respectively.[36] To estimate the extent to which differences in training account for wage differences, we calculate how much the total wage differential between white men and the other groups would fall if the minority workers had jobs with as much training as white men, and if training paid off for blacks and women at the white male rate—4.8 percent. For black men, 16.6 percent of the differential is "explained" by differential amounts of training; for white and black females the fractions are 10.6 percent and 8.4 percent, respectively. Although not overwhelming, the role of training is thus quite important in accounting for wage differentials across the race/sex subgroups.

---

[36]These averages are smaller than those presented in the first section because these are for training completed while those were for the total amount of training time on the job, regardless of whether it was completed or not.

Summary

On-the-job training has been given a central role in the income distribution process, not because of direct evidence on the effects of training on earnings, but rather through a priori theorizing and empirical evidence that was indirect at best. In this chapter, we have used direct training measures to explore the training-earnings relationship, as well as examined questions of who gets training and at what cost.

We have found considerable evidence that time spent in on-the-job training increases earnings, and that the returns to an additional year of training are similar to the returns to additional years of formal schooling. This payoff was quite uniform for men and women and for blacks and whites. We found no evidence that minority workers had a smaller percentage return on training than white men.[37] This does not imply, however, that training is unimportant in explaining wage differentials among groups of workers. While the returns on training are similar, the average amount of training received by white men is much higher than the mean training time of black men and of white and black women. These differential amounts of training "Explain" about 15 percent of the wage gap between white and black men and about 10 percent of the gap between white men and the two groups of women.

Given the importance of training in explaining earnings, and the apparently similar returns on training for all four race/sex subgroups, it is crucial to understand why different individuals are employed in jobs that provide differential amounts of training. A first and perhaps obvious clue is that there are large differences in training times associated with different occupations. Jobs held primarily by white men—the professional, managerial, and craft occupations—have the largest training periods, while the clerical, operative, and unskilled categories into which most minority workers fall provide the least training. Even within a given occupational classification, white men reported longer training times, although this may indicate lack of sufficient detail in occupational codes.

Differences in the occupational distributions of various demographic groups are well-known, and our finding that different occupations provide different amounts of training is not surprising. Of much greater importance in understanding wage differentials is evidence on the extent to which occupational and training differences are the result of voluntary choice rather than institutional forces and labor market discrimination. In this regard, we did find some evidence that training decisions are made in an investment

---

[37] Note that equal percentage increases imply smaller absolute increases for groups with lower wages.

context as the human capital model assumes. The potential length of time over which a training investment might yield returns is an important factor for most groups in explaining whether an individual participated in training and also the expection of more children was a deterrent to training for white women. On the other hand, our analysis found support for the view that training is determined by institutional forces rather than voluntary investment criteria. In particular, time spent with the current employer and in the labor force generally led much more directly to training for white men than for minority workers. This effect was especially important for women, who not only had less labor force experience than men, but were also much less successful in translating that experience into training opportunities. Since our analysis controlled for many of the factors which are usually thought to influence the training decisions of women, this finding suggests that institutional forces and/or discrimination may be a more reasonable explanation of the lower earnings of women than the human capital investment model.

A more definitive, but more difficult, empirical test of the human capital model versus the institutional explanation of training centers around the question of whether training is costly in terms of lower current wages, since this assumption underlies the human capital explanation of training differences. Our evidence on this was mixed. Least ambiguous was the finding that current training is indeed costly for black men. Training appeared to be costly for white men only after a rather strong empirical assumption was made. Current training had no measurable effect for white women and a positive effect for black women. Respondents giving an affirmative response to a more subjective question about training for a future job received higher wages—a result which provides some support for the institutional or dual labor market view.

In sum, our evidence on training provides some new insights into how labor markets operate to produce earnings differences among groups of workers. The labor market appears to be "fair" in the sense that training actually received is rewarded equally, irrespective of race or sex. But there are large differences in the amounts of training received by white men and minority workers. If these differences are the result of voluntary choice, then we would be tempted to downplay the importance of discrimination, and we would anticipate a decline in race/sex wage differences as blacks and women acquired the labor market skills that white men now possess. However, our analysis of the determinants of training suggested that there are important institutional determinants of who gets training. If, as it appears, general labor market work experience does not lead to training opportunities for blacks and women as regularly as it does for white men of similar qualifications and work commitment, then a clear role for public policy is to ensure fair treatment of these groups in the hiring and promotional practices of firms.

References

Aigner, D. J., Goldberger, A. S., and Kalton, G. "On The Explanatory Power of Dummy Variable Regression." International Economic Review 16 (June 1975): 503-10.

Antos, Joseph R., and Rosen, Sherwin. "Discrimination in the Market for Public School Teachers." Journal of Econometrics 3 (February, 1975): 123-50.

Arrow, Kenneth J. "Models of Job Discrimination" and "Some Mathematical Models of Race in the Labor Market." Edited by Anthony Pascal. In Racial Discrimination in Economic Life. Lexington, Mass.: Lexington Book, 1972.

Becker, Gary. Human Capital: A Theoretical and Empirical Analysis with Special Reference to Education. New York: National Bureau of Economic Research, 1964.

Becker, Gary. Human Capital and the Personal Distribution of Income: An Analytic Approach. Ann Arbor, Mich.: Department of Economics, University of Michigan, 1967.

Ben-Porath, Yoram. "The Production of Human Capital and the Life-Cycle of Earnings." Journal of Political Economy 75 (August 1967): 352-65.

Blaug, Mark. "Human Capital Theory: A Slightly Jaundiced Survey." Journal of Economic Literature XIV (September 1976): 827-55.

Blinder, Alan. "Wage Discrimination: Reduced Form and Structural Estimates." Journal of Human Resources VIII (Fall 1973): 436-55.

Butler, Richard, and Heckman, James. "The Government's Impact on the Labor Market Status of Black Americans: A Critical Review." Univeristy of Chicago, 1977. Mimeographed.

Campbell, A., and Schuman, H. Racial Attitudes in Fifteen American Cities. Ann Arbor, Mich.: Institute for Social Research, 1968.

Doeringer, Peter, and Piore, Michael. Internal Labor Markets and Manpower Analysis. Lexington, Mass.: Lexington Books, 1971.

Duncan, Greg J. "Nonpecuniary Work Rewards." In Five Thousand American Families: Patterns of Economic Progress, Vol. II. Edited by James N. Morgan. Ann Arbor, Mich.: Institute for Social Research, 1974.

Johnson, George E., and Stafford, Frank P. "The Earnings and Promotion of Women Faculty." American Economic Review 64 (December 1974): 888-903.

Kerr, Clark. "The Balkanization of Labor Markets." In Labor Mobility and Economic Opportunity. Edited by E. Wight Bakhe. Cambridge, Mass.: MIT Press, 1954.

Mincer, Jacob. Schooling Experience and Earnings. New York: National Bureau of Economic Research, 1974.

Mincer, Jacob, and Polachek, Solomon. "Family Investments in Human Capital: Earnings of Women." Journal of Political Economy 82 (March/April 1974): S76-S108.

Rosen, Sherwin. "Learning and Experience in the Labor Market." Journal of Human Resources VII (Summer, 1972): 326-42.

Taubman, Paul, and Wales, Terence. Higher Education and Earnings. New York: McGraw-Hill, 1974.

Thurow, Lester C., and Lucas, Robert E. B. "The American Distribution of Income: A Structural Problem." Washington, D.C.: U.S. Government Printing Office, 1972.

Table A3.1a

NUMBER OF YEARS TO BECOME FULLY TRAINED AND QUALIFIED
BY SELECTED INDEPENDENT VARIABLES FOR FOUR RACE/SEX SUBGROUPS
(All Working Household Heads and Spouses Aged 18-64)

	White Men	Black Men	White Women	Black Women
All	2.25	.99	.94	.81
Age				
< 25 Years	1.28	.50	.59	.45
25-34	1.95	.70	.96	.62
35-44	2.52	1.09	1.06	.82
45-54	2.65	1.64	.96	1.05
55-64	2.69	1.13	1.08	1.30
Eta Squared (adj)	.048**	.057**	.013**	.033**
Education				
0-5 Years	1.65	.61	.73+	.15+
6-8	1.77	.78	.41	.32
9-11	1.82	.43	.34	.38
12; High School Diploma	1.81	1.31	.70	.90
High School Plus Non-Academic Training	2.28	1.01	.94	.52
Some College	2.33	.93	.95	.78
B.A.	2.79	1.29+	1.50	2.58
Advanced Degree	3.20	--	2.86	3.86+
Eta Squared (adj)	.046**	.199**	.160**	.292**
Hourly Earnings				
< $2.00	1.69	.46	.61	.40
$2.00-$2.99	1.55	.68	.55	.61
$3.00-$3.99	1.53	.40	.68	.46
$4.00-$5.99	1.83	.89	1.07	.99
$6.00-$7.99	2.30	1.33	1.41	2.07
≥ $8.00	3.27	2.51	2.45	2.31+
Eta Squared (adj)	.096**	.121**	.116**	.149**
Marital Status				
Married	2.31	1.13	.94	.96
Single	1.40	.64	1.16	.62
Divorced/Separated/Widowed	2.31	.57	.80	.63
Eta Squared (adj)	.012**	.022**	.005**	.014**

+Results based on less than 25 observations.

--Fewer than 10 observations.

**Significant at .01 level.

Table A3.1b

PERCENTAGE OF WORKERS TRAINING FOR CURRENT JOB
BY SELECTED INDEPENDENT VARIABLES FOR FOUR RACE/SEX SUBGROUPS
(All Working Household Heads and Spouses Aged 18-64)

	White Men	Black Men	White Women	Black Women
All	.258	.091	.141	.088
Age				
< 25 Years	.353	.074	.189	.094
25-34	.349	.103	.167	.101
35-44	.230	.073	.135	.063
45-54	.176	.113	.109	.131
55-64	.135	.079	.084	.011
Eta Squared (adj)	.038**	.003	.010**	.014**
Education				
0-5 Years	.145	.059	.064+	0 +
6-8	.079	.024	.103	.012
9-11	.232	.079	.051	.006
High School Graduate	.191	.086	.099	.165
High School Plus Non-Academic Training	.254	.102	.152	.058
Some College	.312	.141	.177	.163
B.A.	.363	.082+	.222	.253
Advanced Degree	.335	--	.276	.025+
Eta Squared (adj)	.034**	.035**	.031**	.077**
Hourly Earnings				
< $2.00	.220	.107	.115	.021
$2.00-$2.99	.226	.055	.115	.058
$3.00-$3.99	.287	.049	.114	.090
$4.00-5.99	.240	.072	.170	.105
$6.00-$7.99	.266	.110	.159	.180
≥ $8.00	.272	.239	.207	.276+
Eta Squared (adj)	.002**	.029**	.008	.041**
Marital Status				
Married	.247	.094	.123	.073
Single	.345	.105	.263	.087
Divorced/Separated/Widowed	.311	.056	.134	.113
Eta Squared (adj)	.012**	.002	.016**	.003

+Results based on less than 25 observations.

--Fewer than 10 observations.

**Significant at .01 level.

Table A3.1c

WHETHER TRAINING FOR FUTURE JOB OR PROMOTION
BY SELECTED INDEPENDENT VARIABLES FOR FOUR RACE/SEX SUBGROUPS
(All Working Household Heads and Spouses Aged 18-64)

	White Men	Black Men	White Women	Black Women
All	.68	.79	.64	.73
Age				
< 25 Years	.83	.85	.74	.65
25-34	.79	.87	.70	.75
35-44	.68	.78	.65	.86
45-54	.58	.73	.56	.66
55-64	.46	.55	.52	.56
Eta Squared (adj)	.068**	.058**	.027**	.046**
Education				
0-5 Years	.40	.58	.35+	.80+
6-8	.52	.54	.39	.58
9-12	.64	.81	.53	.64
High School Graduate	.62	.87	.66	.81
High School Plus Non-Academic Training	.71	.94	.69	.80
Some College	.73	.81	.68	.69
B.A.	.79	.62+	.69	.82
Advanced Degree	.75	--	.75	.74+
Eta Squared (adj)	.033**	.097**	.034**	.035**
Hourly Earnings				
< $2.00	.53	.68	.51	.48
$2.00-$2.99	.64	.80	.57	.68
$3.00-$3.99	.69	.80	.65	.79
$4.00-$5.99	.73	.79	.73	.85
$6.00-$7.99	.70	.81	.71	.76
≥ $8.00	.66	.73	.62	.94+
Eta Squared (adj)	.009**	.006	.025**	.079**
Marital Status				
Married	.68	.78	.63	.75
Single	.72	.82	.75	.59
Divorced/Separated/Widowed	.76	.79	.63	.75
Eta Squared (adj)	.002	.001	.006	.014**

+Results based on less than 25 observations.

--Fewer than 10 observations.

**Significant at .01 level.

Table A3.1d

MEAN AMOUNTS OF TRAINING BY SEVERAL
JOB CHARACTERISTICS FOR SEVERAL TRAINING MEASURES
(All Working Household Heads and Spouses Aged 18-64)

Education Required to Get Jobs	Unweighted Number of Observations	Weighted Percentage of Observations	Training Measure: Number of Years Needed to Become Fully Trained and Qualified	Whether Training for Current Job	Whether Training for Future Job	Whether Training for Either Current or Future Job
0-5 Grades	1,264	22.0	1.12	.125	.506	.546
6-8	257	4.5	1.23	.122	.535	.573
9-11	165	2.2	.56	.054	.636	.637
12, High School Diploma	2,018	43.0	1.49	.174	.726	.760
Some College	279	7.5	1.91	.255	.805	.843
College Degree	557	15.9	2.69	.328	.766	.806
Advanced Degree	164	4.9	3.20	.363	.752	.838
Eta Squared (adj)			.104**	.040**	.051**	.057**
Other Training Needed to Get Job						
None	2,175	37.6	1.08	.122	.588	.618
Apprenticeship	97	2.7	3.42	.307	.611	.724
Courses; Training Program	485	10.0	1.95	.243	.748	.800
On-the-Job Training	409	8.0	1.60	.236	.729	.769
	96	2.3	2.66	.340	.756	.796
Training; Not Ascertained	287	5.2	2.03	.259	.726	.776
Explicit Skill	434	8.2	1.23	.177	.688	.729
Experience; Background	1,177	26.0	2.17	.260	.743	.782
Eta Squared (adj)			.087**	.028**	.024**	.030**
Job Covered by Union Contract?						
No	3,911	75.4	1.73	.216	.693	.731
Yes	1,314	24.6	1.46	.155	.625	.671
Eta Squared (adj)			.003**	.004**	.004**	.003**

Table 3.1d (continued)

			Training Measure			
Position in Work Hierarchy	Unweighted Number of Observations	Weighted Percentage of Observations	Number of Years Needed to Become Fully Trained and Qualified	Whether Training for Current Job	Whether Training for Future Job	Whether Training for Either Current or Future Job
Self-Employed	413	10.2	2.50	.195	.477	.554
Works for Others; Doesn't Supervise	3,213	54.3	1.13	.153	.639	.674
Works for Others; Supervises without Say over Pay or Promotion	900	18.0	1.70	.203	.769	.802
Works for Others; Supervises *with* Say over Pay or Promotion	699	17.5	2.78	.351	.809	.851
Eta Squared (adj)			.116**	.032**	.043**	.040**

**Significant at .01 level.

Table A3.1e

PERCENTAGE TRAINING FOR CURRENT AND FUTURE JOBS BY RACE AND SEX
(All Working Household Heads and Spouses Aged 18-64)

ALL

		Training for Future Job: No	Training for Future Job: Yes	
Training for Current Job	No	28.4	51.5	79.9
	Yes	4.0	16.1	20.1
		32.4	67.6	100.0

WHITE MEN

		Training for Future Job: No	Training for Future Job: Yes	
Training for Current Job	No	27.0	47.2	74.2
	Yes	4.7	21.0	25.7
		31.7	68.2	99.9

BLACK MEN

		Training for Future Job: No	Training for Future Job: Yes	
Training for Current Job	No	19.9	71.0	90.9
	Yes	1.7	7.4	9.2
		21.6	78.4	100.0

WHITE WOMEN

		Training for Future Job: No	Training for Future Job: Yes	
Training for Current Job	No	32.2	53.8	86.0
	Yes	3.6	10.5	14.1
		35.8	64.3	100.1

BLACK WOMEN

		Training for Future Job: No	Training for Future Job: Yes	
Training for Current Job	No	26.5	64.7	91.2
	Yes	1.1	7.8	8.9
		27.6	72.5	100.1

Table A3.1f

MEAN VALUES OF INDEPENDENT VARIABLES IN WAGE EQUATION BY RACE/SEX SUBGROUPS
(All Working Household Heads and Spouses Aged 18-64)

	White Men	Black Men	White Women	Black Women
Formal Education (in years)	12.85	10.96	12.73	11.75
WORK HISTORY				
Years Out of Labor Force since Completing School	0.51	0.63	5.75	4.03
Years of Work Experience Before Present Employer	11.27	10.44	8.05	9.27
Pre-employer Work Experience Squared	225.0	212.9	129.9	161.9
Years with Current Employer Prior to Current Position	4.58	3.96	2.33	2.86
Years of Training Completed on Current Job	1.606	0.791	0.722	0.704
Years of Post-training Tenure on Current Job	2.51	3.31	2.74	2.91
Proportion of Total Years that were Full Time	0.909	0.913	0.790	0.826
INDICATORS OF WORK ORIENTATION				
Hours of Work Missed for Illness of Others in 1975	4.01	8.05	12.45	25.68
Hours of Work Missed for Own Illness in 1975	36.5	50.4	43.0	58.0
Limited Job Hours or Location	0.145	0.122	0.342	0.216
Knows there Are Better Jobs Elsewhere	0.399	0.340	0.369	0.295
Doesn't Know Whether there Are Better Jobs Elsewhere	0.159	0.281	0.193	0.252
Plans to Stop Work for Nontraining Reasons	0.030	0.017	0.086	0.068
DEMOGRAPHIC CONTROL VARIABLES				
Size of Largest City in the Area (in hundreds of thousands)	3.840	5.484	4.079	5.261
Whether South	0.266	0.542	0.261	0.558
No Training	.01	.03	.02	.01
Less than Six Months Training	.27	.55	.54	.61
6 - 12 Months Training	.14	.14	.17	.15
1 - 2 Years Training	.22	.14	.17	.11
More than Two Years Training	.36	.13	.11	.11
$\ln$ 1975 Hourly Wage	1.722	1.461	1.284	1.154

Chapter 4

SELF-IMPOSED LIMITATIONS ON WORK SCHEDULE AND JOB LOCATION

Martha S. Hill

Introduction

Literature on wage differentials suggests that the male/female wage gap is in part caused by women restricting their work schedules and job location more than men. Women are pictured as receiving lower wages than men as a result of adjusting their labor force activity to accommodate such family responsibilities as child-rearing, housework, and their spouse's career. Such adjustments could include restricting job choice to those jobs that offer compatible work schedules and are closer to home.

If self-imposed limitations on when and where to work reduce productivity, they should, in the context of economic theory, lower wages. Limitations on work schedule or job location could reduce productivity in several ways. Imposing these limitations certainly reduces the range of jobs acceptable to the individual, possibly eliminating some jobs that would make better use of his or her skills. Also, restricting hours worked could lower productivity either by increasing the proportion of work time spent simply preparing to work or by impeding the work done in conjunction with co-workers who have different work schedules.

However, studies espousing the argument that self-imposed limitations on labor force activity account for part of the productivity-related component of the wage gap between men and women have not measured these limitations directly. Instead, they have relied on indirect evidence concerning wage effects. For example, Fuchs (1971), Oaxaca (1973), Malkiel and Malkiel (1973), and Polachek (1975) find evidence of differential effects of marriage and children on the wages of men and women. They ascribe these findings to sex differences in the allocation of human resources between the labor market and the home, with women tending to restrict their labor force activity more than men in response to family responsibilities. But marriage and children may be poor proxies for restriction of labor force activity. At the same time that labor force participation of married women has increased substantially, housework hours of men have increased while housework hours of women have decreased.[1] This suggests that sex differentials in time devoted to the labor market and the home are not as strong as in the past. Also, men as well as women may choose to limit their labor force activity both for family and other reasons. Without direct measurement, the wage effects of these limitations are uncertain.

A new data source, the ninth wave of the Panel Study of Income Dynamics, now provides direct measures of these limitations. This chapter uses these data to explore self-imposed limitations on work schedule and job location, focusing first on the frequency of these limitations by sex and race and then on their wage impact. The first section of this chapter explains the derivation of the measures of limitations on work schedule and job location used in the analysis. The second section investigates the incidence of these limitations. Effects of factors, such as sex, race, marital status, children, age and education, that are thought to alter the incidence of the limitations are explored, first using simple frequency distributions and then with multiple regression analysis. The third section investigates directly the wage effects of imposing limitations on work schedule and job location. The final section tests the validity of attributing wage effects of marriage and children to sex differences in labor force behavior, with limitations on work schedule and job location being included as measures of restricted labor force activity along with controls for on-the-job training, labor force interruption, and absenteeism.

The sample used for most of the ensuing analyses consists of Panel Study household heads and spouses aged 18 to 64, working or only temporarily laid off in the spring/summer of 1976 who also worked at least 500 hours in 1975. These workers are the primary unit of analysis since their wages are observable. For purposes of comparison, however, some data are also presented for nonworking Panel Study household heads and wives.

Analysis

DERIVATION OF MEASURES OF LIMITATIONS ON WORK SCHEDULE AND JOB LOCATION

Three types of measures of self-imposed limitations on work schedule or job location are available from the ninth wave of the Panel Study. These consist of limitations on job location or work hours, restriction of geographic mobility, and voluntary part-time work.

---

[1]"The Use of Time and Technology by Households in the United States" by Frank Stafford and Greg Duncan, a working paper, Department of Economics, University of Michigan, July 1977, shows time diary figures indicating that between 1965 and 1976 housework hours of men increased while housework hours of women decreased, regardless of marital status.

To ascertain self-imposed limitations on job location or work hours, working household heads and wives were asked:[2]

1. Thinking back to when you started your present job, were there some limitations on where you could work or what hours you could work that were factors in taking this job?

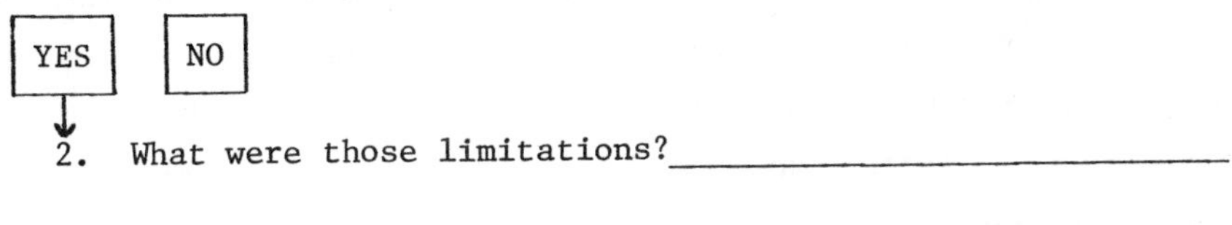

The code for the second question in this set distinguishes limitations on job location, on the amount of work hours, on the timing of work hours, and combinations of these types of limitations. As coded, however, a given type of limitation could encompass diverse forms of restrictions. For example, job location could be restricted to locations close to a suburban home or locations in big cities. Both would be coded as a limitation on job location and could not be distinguished in the analysis, even though the former restriction may lower wages while the later may raise them.

To ascertain restriction of geographic mobility, working household heads and wives were asked:[3]

Are there better jobs you could get if you were willing to move and live somewhere else?

This question was supposed to help test the hypothesis that part of the male/female wage differential is the result of wives being more restricted than husbands in their geographic movement to better jobs. Wording of the question developed from the notion that if this hypothesis were true, then wives who had recently moved would be more likely than their husbands to know of better jobs elsewhere—the jobs they left when they moved. The

---

[2]For nonworking household heads and wives the first question in this set was: "Are there any limitations on when you could work or what hours you could work that would be factors in your taking a job?"

[3]Nonworking household heads and wives were asked the following question if they were either looking for work, unemployed, or thinking of getting a job: "Are there jobs you could get if you were willing to move and live somewhere else?"

question's wording creates interpretation problems, however. It combines willingness to move for a better job with knowledge of the job market, and such knowledge could depend on job satisfaction or the extent of job search.

For analysis purposes, a "yes" response to the question will be treated as indication of explicit restriction of movement to better jobs known to exist elsewhere, a "don't know" response will be treated as indication of restriction because of the lack of knowledge of job prospects in other localities, and a "no" response will be treated as indication of no restriction on geographic mobility.

Since the responses to this question may yield unreliable measures of restricted movement to better jobs, analysis of wage effects of variables based on these responses are supplemented (in the third section of this chapter) with a longitudinal analysis of the effects of actual geographic movement over the panel period on the wages and labor force participation of husbands and wives.

Questions concerning work loads formed the basis of the voluntary part-time work measure. Working household heads and spouses were classified as voluntarily working part-time if they worked 30 or fewer hours per week in 1975, on both the main job and extra jobs combined, and responded that either more work was available on their jobs or they would not have liked to work more had more work been available. The question sequence for determining whether the volume of work hours was voluntarily restricted follows:

1. Was there more work available (on your job/on any of your jobs) so that you could have worked more if you had wanted to?

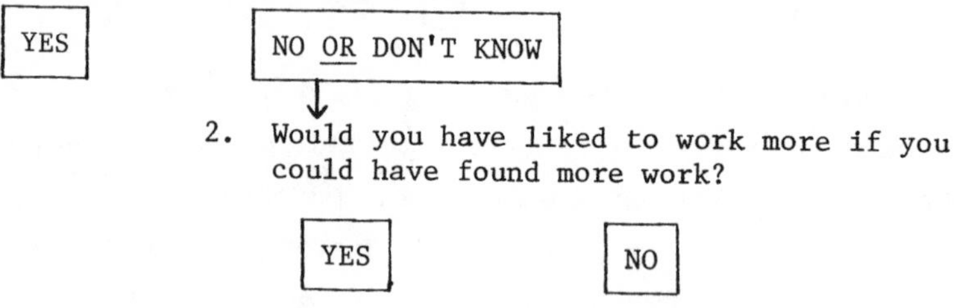

Economists have argued (see Rosen, 1976) that analysis of wage determinants should include hours worked as a predictor of wage level because there may be different markets for jobs with different work hours, e.g., different markets for part-time and full time jobs, and these markets could clear at different wage levels. For this analysis of wage determinants, the voluntary part-time measure of work hours was chosen since the effects of self-restricted work hours were of primary interest.

These questions, admittedly, allow limited measurement of self-imposed work limitations. In addition to the problems already mentioned, they ascertain only the incidence, not the severity, of the restrictions. Only dichotomous variables for whether or not a limitation was imposed can be constructed from them. Thus they allow direct, but not precise, analysis of self-imposed work limitations and their effects on wages.

INCIDENCE OF SELF-IMPOSED LIMITATIONS ON WORK SCHEDULE AND JOB LOCATION

Limitations on Job Locations or Work Hours That Were Factors in Taking the Present Job

The data on job location or work hours limitations indicate, not surprisingly, that women often bear the burden of family responsibilities by adjusting their work schedule and job location to accommodate marriage and child-rearing while men do not. These findings are supported with both bivariate and multivariate analysis. The frequency distribution of limitations on job location or work hours across several individual characteristics of working household heads and wives are highlighted in Table 4.1 (Appendix Table A4.1b contains more comprehensive distributions);[4] the regression results are presented in Table 4.2.

Comprehensive analysis of factors associated with these job limitations is hindered by the lack of detailed information about conditions at the time the limitations were imposed.[5] Thus this analysis concentrates on factors which would not have changed much since that time (race, sex, education, city size, and region), factors which could be back-dated fairly accurately (own age and ages of children), and one other factor (marital status) which could not be back-dated but was crucial to the analysis.[6]

Tables 4.1 and 4.2 show that the frequency of limitations on job location or work hours was about twice as high among women as among men, with whites being somewhat

[4]Many of the tables of frequency distributions of the limitations presented in the text are abridged versions of more comprehensive tables contained in the appendix. The appendix also contains a table of sample distributions for all individual and job characteristics investigated as well as tables of frequency distributions of the limitations for nonworking household heads and wives.

[5]The limitations apply to the time when the job was obtained.

[6]Ages were backdated by subtracting years on the job from the age given in 1976. The Panel Study contains two measures of years on the job: years with present employer and years in present position. The former measure was used for this back-dating since its code was more comprehensive. (Time with present employer was coded from 0 to 998 months, whereas time in present position was coded from 0 to 98 months.)

Table 4.1

MEAN VALUES ON WHETHER LIMITATIONS ON JOB LOCATION OR WORK HOURS WERE FACTORS IN TAKING PRESENT JOB, BY SELECTED INDIVIDUAL CHARACTERISTICS
(Working Household Heads and Spouses Aged 18-64)

	Entire Sample	White Men	Black Men	White Women	Black Women
All	.215	.145	.122	.342	.216
Marital Status (in 1976)					
Married, Spouse Working	.254	.154	.096	.385	.280
Married, Spouse Not Working	.128	.116	.079	.255	.150
Single	.252	.253	.245	.283	.055
Widowed	.226	---	---	.235	.294
Divorced	.245	.182	.047	.295	.161
Separated	.234	.220+	.144	.327	.164
Eta squared (adj)	.019**	.011**	.053**	.013	.041**
Age of Children when Started Working for Present Employer‡					
No Children Less than 18 Years Old	.197	.164	.140	.268	.134
Preschool Children Only	.198	.150	.165	.340	.258
School-age Children Only	.259	.111	.011	.400	.271
Preschool and School-age Children	.227	.119	.104	.487	.288
Eta squared (adj)	.004**	.004	.020**	.027**	.028**
Age when Started Working for Present Employer⁑					
Less than 25 Years	.197	.149	.133	.292	.235
25-34 Years	.221	.156	.163	.377	.163
35-44 Years	.256	.127	.066	.410	.310
45-54 Years	.187	.110	.042	.290	.072
55-64 Years	.177	.179	.017+	.221	---
Eta squared (adj)	.003**	.002	.017**	.013**	.032**
Education (in 1976)					
Less than 8 Years	.108	.099	.108	.117	.178
9-11 Years	.166	.145	.049	.235	.119
12 Years	.226	.119	.106	.375	.268
13-15 Years	.271	.200	.246	.392	.263
16 Years	.235	.161	.257+	.392	.203
17 Years or More	.218	.167	---	.330	.281+
Eta squared (adj)	.011**	.008**	.041**	.024**	.025**

---Fewer than 10 observations.

+10-24 Observations.

‡Variable is based on wife's report of children's years of birth and individual's report of length of time worked for present employer.

⁑Variable is based on individual's report of age in 1976 and length of time worked for present employer.

**Significant at .01 level.

Table 4.2

REGRESSIONS ON WHETHER LIMITATIONS ON JOB LOCATION OR WORK HOURS WERE FACTORS IN TAKING PRESENT JOB

(Working Household Heads and Spouses Aged 18-64)

Independent Variable	White Men	Black Men	White Women	Black Women
Education (in years)	.0056* (.0025)	.0025 (.0037)	.0203** (.0050)	.0231** (.0065)
Age (in years)†	.0003 (.0009)	-.0010 (.0012)	.0006 (.0013)	-.0036* (.0018)
If Both Preschool and School-Aged Children†	-.0291 (.0221)	.0175 (.0314)	.2468** (.0426)	.1216** (.0429)
If Preschool Children Only†	.0010 (.0199)	.0715* (.0308)	.0874* (.0434)	.0865 (.0506)
If School-Aged Children Only†	-.0365 (.0247)	-.0765* (.0308)	.1373** (.0325)	.1518** (.0373)
Whether Single	.1013** (.0308)	.1238** (.0342)	-.0273 (.0447)	-.2124** (.0471)
Whether South	.0358* (.0173)	.0574* (.0244)	-.0572 (.0303)	-.0501 (.0333)
City Size (in hundred thousands)	.0030 (.0018)	.0093** (.0028)	.0088** (.0031)	.0001 (.0038)
Constant	.0463	.0150	-.0337	.0393
Number of Observations	2,250	895	1,326	741
$\overline{Y}$	.145	.122	.342	.216
$\overline{R}^2$	.0104	.0507	.0473	.0644

* Significant at .01 level.

**Significant at .05 level.

† Variable has been back dated to conditions at time individual began working for present employer.

more likely than blacks to impose such limitations. Fully one-third of the white women and one-fifth of the black women reported such restrictions compared to less than 15 percent of the white men and about 10 percent of the black men. Interestingly, this large male/female differential was also present in the responses of nonworking household heads and spouses to the question of whether these limitations would be factors in taking a job.[7] (See Appendix Table A4.1e.)

Marital status and children had very different effects on women's and men's decisions about restrictions. Apparently greater family responsibilities caused women to restrict their work hours or job location, whereas fewer family obligations allowed men to limit when or where they would work.

Effects of children on the likelihood of women imposing job restrictions were clearly positive. Both with and without controls for other factors, women with children were more likely to impose job restrictions than were women without children. School-age children had a larger positive impact on the incidence of these restrictions than did preschool children. Since working women with children must make child care arrangements if their children are not in school while they are working, it may be that working women with school-age children try to constrain their work schedules to take advantage of the effectively free child care services provided by the public school system, whereas working women with preschool children are more likely to make child care arrangements to suit their work schedules.

Effects of children on the likelihood of men imposing job restrictions were generally quite small and opposite to those of women. For white men, children had no significant effect, although the incidence of restrictions was somewhat higher among the childless than among those with children. For black men, children had both negative and positive effects depending on the children's ages. Both with and without controls for other factors, black men with school-age children, only, were least likely to restrict job location or hours, whereas black men with preschool children, only, were most likely to impose job restrictions.

As with presence of children, marital status generally had opposite effects for men and women. Among men, those who were single were most likely to impose job limitations both in a bivariate and multivariate context. Among black women, however, those who were single had the lowest incidence of such restrictions. Among white women, the effect of being single was also negative, but small and insignificant. These differences could reflect selectivity factors associated with marriage. It may be that men (women) with

---

[7] Racial variation in the frequency of job location/work hours limitation was, however, virtually nonexistent among nonworking household heads and wives. (See Appendix Table A.4.1e.)

stronger labor force attachment are more (less) likely to marry. Or it could reflect sex differences in family responsibilities. It could be that pressures of supporting a family tend to compel men to work even if the hours or the job location are undesirable, whereas home duties tend to force women to restrict work hours or job location.

Education also affected the incidence of self-imposed job limitations. The effects were similar for men and women, however. Bivariate frequencies show that men with at least some college education and women with at least high school education were most likely to restrict job location or work hours. In a multivariate context, education had positive effects on the likelihood of imposing job limitations, particularly for women. Possibly workers, especially women workers, with higher education can be more selective about work schedule and job location because they have a wider range of jobs to choose from, or they may choose to be more restrictive in order to devote more time to child-rearing.[8]

The frequency of self-imposed limitations on job location or hours also varied with age. Black men under age 35 and all women aged 35 to 44 had particularly high frequencies of job limitations. However, when marital status and children were controlled, age showed no strong effect on the likelihood of imposing these limitations. No doubt, the bivariate age effects were mostly reflecting effects of marital status and children.

For every coded type of limitation on job location or work hours, women registered higher frequencies of limitations than did men. (See Table 4.3). This sex difference was especially pronounced with respect to limitations on timing of work hours—the most common type of job limitation. About 14 percent of the white women and 8 percent of the black women, as compared to about 4 percent of the men, restricted when they would work. Interestingly, for nonworking female household heads and spouses this timing restriction was also the most common type of job restriction that would be a factor in their taking a job. (See Appendix Table A4.1f.) These results indicate that an increased supply of jobs with flexible work schedules would be very helpful to women.

Since timing of work hours was the most common restriction, its determinants were investigated using multiple regression.[9] The results were so similar to those of Table 4.2,

---

[8]Panel Study data presented in Chapter 12, Table 12.3 show an increase in mean hours of child care with wive's education for working wives with children under age 12. This trend held as well when number in the family unit, age, and race were controlled.

[9]A variable measuring whether or not limitations only on timing of work hours were factors in taking the present job was regressed on variables measuring education, age, presence of children, marital status, region, and city size.

Table 4.3

PERCENTAGE DISTRIBUTION OF RESPONSES ABOUT WHAT TYPES OF LIMITATIONS ON JOB LOCATION OR WORK HOURS WERE FACTORS IN TAKING PRESENT JOB, BY RACE AND SEX

(Working Household Heads and Spouses Aged 18-64)

Type of Limitation	White Men	Black Men	White Women	Black Women
Job Location Only	4.1	2.7	6.9	4.5
Amount of Hours Only	1.6	0.6	4.3	1.7
Timing of Hours Only	4.2	4.1	13.7	8.4
Job Location and Amount of Hours Only	0.6	0.1	2.4	0.4
Other	1.9	1.6	4.7	4.5
Not Ascertained or Don't Know Type of Limitation	2.1	3.1	2.2	2.1
None; Not Ascertained or Don't Know Whether any Limitation	85.5	87.8	65.8	78.4
Total	100.0	100.0	100.0	100.0
Number of Observations	2,250	895	1,338	742

however, that they are not discussed in detail here. (See Appendix Table A4.1g for the results.)

Restriction of Geographic Mobility

Women are usually assumed to be more restricted in job choice than men because of geographic immobility. Since wives's careers tend to be secondary to those of their husbands, women are thought to be more restricted in their ability to move for better jobs. However, analysis of the measures of restriction of geographic mobility as defined in the first section of this chapter suggests that women are no more likely than men to restrict geographic moves to better jobs, and that marriage does not increase the likelihood of such restrictions among women. Unfortunately, measurement problems make these results somewhat tenuous.

Across the four race/sex subgroups, responses to whether better jobs were available if the respondent were willing to move were similar. (See Table 4.4.) Approximately one-third responded "yes" to this question, indicating explicit restriction of movement to better jobs known to exist elsewhere. About one-fifth responded "don't know". The remaining 40 to 45 percent indicated that they felt they were in their best job locality by answering "no". Race differences in responses were more pronounced than sex differences. Blacks were somewhat less likely to answer "yes" and more likely not to know.

The frequency distributions presented in Table 4.5 suggest that factors associated with explicitly restricting geographic mobility were similar across race and sex, and that family responsibilities were not strong impediments to geographic mobility.[10] First, number of children had virtually no effect on the frequency of reporting that there were better jobs available elsewhere, especially among whites, both women and men. Within each race/sex subgroup, the frequency of such reports among those with no children is almost equivalent to the subgroup average with no clear pattern of effect of number of children. Also, effects attributable to the presence of a working spouse were similarly nonexistent, and, in fact, within each race/sex subgroup single respondents were more likely to say there were better jobs elsewhere than were married respondents. Age and education also had similar effects within each subgroup. Working household heads and wives under age 35 and those with higher levels of education more frequently reported that there were better jobs they could get elsewhere. These trends in effects of family responsibilities and age were present among nonworking household heads and wives as well. (See Appendix Table A4.1h for details.)

---

[10] All working household heads and wives who reported that there were better jobs they could get if they were willing to move were assigned a value of 1 on the dependent variable, and all others were assigned a value of 0.

Table 4.4

PERCENTAGE DISTRIBUTION OF RESPONSES ABOUT WHETHER BETTER JOBS AVAILABLE IF WILLING TO MOVE, BY RACE AND SEX

(Working Household Heads and Spouses Aged 18-64)

Whether Better Jobs Available if Willing to Move	White Men	Black Men	White Women	Black Women
Yes	39.9	34.0	36.9	29.5
Don't Know	15.9	28.1	19.3	25.2
No; Not Ascertained	44.2	37.9	43.8	45.3
Total	100.0	100.0	100.0	100.0
Number of Observations	2,250	895	1,326	741

Table 4.5

MEAN VALUES FOR WHETHER BETTER JOB AVAILABLE IF WILLING TO MOVE, BY SELECTED INDIVIDUAL CHARACTERISTICS

(Working Household Heads and Spouses Aged 18-64)

	Entire Sample	White Men	Black Men	White Women	Black Women
All	.381	.399	.340	.369	.295
Marital Status (in 1976)					
Married, Spouse Working	.383	.408	.315	.373	.259
Married, Spouse Not Working	.356	.367	.331	.296	.177
Single	.477	.491	.385	.485	.456
Widowed	.275	---	---	.203	.541
Divorced	.374	.474	.532	.346	.154
Separated	.417	.474+	.394	.473	.256
Eta Squared (adj)	.006**	.006	.012	.016**	.064**
Number of Children (in 1976)					
None	.383	.404	.366	.370	.275
One	.393	.406	.280	.410	.249
Two	.383	.408	.345	.348	.297
Three	.356	.367	.439	.293	.480
Four	.399	.424	.394	.348	.274
Five	.305	.295	.159	---	.215
Six or More	.207	.115+	.140	---	.586+
Eta Squared (adj)	.002	.004	.018**	.004	.024**
Age (in 1976)					
Less Than 25 Years	.449	.451	.446	.448	.455
25-34 Years	.452	.485	.397	.416	.331
35-44 Years	.344	.362	.358	.324	.270
45-54 Years	.351	.357	.157	.381	.251
55-64 Years	.250	.270	.305	.227	.110
Eta Squared (adj)	.020**	.022**	.040**	.021**	.039**
Education (in 1976)					
Less Than 8 Years	.251	.265	.165	.263	.238
9-11 Years	.313	.353	.365	.258	.250
12 Years	.363	.382	.348	.350	.290
13-15 Years	.421	.413	.344	.444	.439
16 Years	.478	.483	.817+	.450	.416
17 Years of More	.479	.487	---	.475	.130+
Eta Squared (adj)	.019**	.017**	.079**	.022**	.024**

---Fewer than 10 observations.

+10-24 observations.

**Significant at .01 level.

Since bivariate findings can be misleading, restrictions on geographic mobility were also analyzed in a multivariate context by regressing the restriction measures against the following variables:

Measures of the Desirability of the Present Job

Earnings (annual labor earnings measured in thousands of dollars)

If Extra Pension (if the individual was covered by more than one pension plan, including social security)

Years with Present Employer

If Plan to Quit Work

Measures of Knowledge of Better Jobs

Pre-Employer Experience (years worked since age 18—years with present employer)

Education (in years)

If Born in State of Residence

Number of Miles to City Center

Measures of Attachment to Local Area

If Own Home

Measures of Economic Need for a Better-Paying Job

Other Family Income/Family Needs (This variable was constructed by subtracting the individual's earnings in 1976 from total family income, then dividing the residual by the Panel Study's measure of family money income needs.)

Measures of Family Responsibilities

Number of Preschool Children (number of children in the family unit under age 6)

Number of School-Aged Children (number of children in the family unit aged 6-17)

If Married, Spouse Working

If Married, Spouse Not Working

If Separated, Divorced, Widowed (the excluded category of marital status is that of single)

Two measures were used to try to distinguish between restrictions resulting from lack of knowledge of job prospects in other localities and those explicitly resulting from lack of movement given knowledge of job prospects. The first measure was used to form the dependent variable used in the regressions presented in Table 4.6.[11] The second measure formed the dependent variable used in the regressions presented in Table 4.7.[12]

The regression results, like the bivariate frequency distributions, suggest that marriage does not impede geographic mobility to better jobs, particularly for women. Marriage had no significant positive effect on either measure of restriction of mobility. Thus, the stereotype of a wife's job choice being constrained by her husband's job location could be true, but these results suggest that marriage is not a powerful force in restricting the movement of women to better jobs.

Unlike the bivariate results, the regression results suggest that children tend to restrict the geographic mobility of women but not men. For white women the likelihood of not knowing whether there were better jobs elsewhere significantly increased with number of school-age children (see Table 4.6); for black women the likelihood of knowing that there were better jobs elsewhere significantly increased with number of school-age children (see Table 4.7). For men there were no significant effects of the number of children on either restriction measure.

It is possible that genuine effects of the factors restricting movement to better jobs are masked by measurement problems. For example, responses to whether respondents knew of better jobs elsewhere could depend on the extent of the job search, and the extent of the job search could vary systematically with factors such as sex, marital status, and presence of children.[13] Some findings, however, do lend some credibility to these measures of restricted geographic mobility, including the results concerning the effects of

---

[11]All working household heads and wives who didn't know whether or not there were better jobs available if they were willing to move were assigned a value of 1 on this dependent variable, and all others were assigned a value of 0.

[12]This dependent variable was defined only for working household heads and wives who knew whether or not there were better jobs available if they were willing to move. Workers who said there were better jobs available were assigned a value of 1 on this dependent variable, and those who said there were not better jobs available were assigned a value of 0. Cases where the respondent didn't know whether or not there were better jobs available (and, hence, had a value of 1 on the dependent variable of Table 4.6) were eliminated from the regressions of Table 4.7.

[13]It is possible that family considerations cause married workers, particularly working wives, and workers with children to search the job market more narrowly than other workers. If so, these factors could increase restriction of movement to better jobs without increasing the likelihood of workers knowing that there were better jobs elsewhere.

Table 4.6

REGRESSIONS ON DOESN'T KNOW WHETHER THERE ARE BETTER JOBS ELSEWHERE
(Working Household Heads and Spouses Aged 18-64)

Independent Variable	White Men	Black Men	White Women	Black Women
Earnings (in thousands of dollars)	-.0009 (.0009)	.0031 (.0039)	-.0062* (.0031)	.0123* (.0057)
If Extra Pension	-.0143 (.0171)	.0007 (.0325)	-.0171 (.0235)	-.0340 (.0347)
Years with Current Employer	.0011 (.0012)	-.0033 (.0025)	.0058** (.0020)	-.0074** (.0026)
Years of Work Experience Before Present Employer	.0012 (.0010)	-.0018 (.0018)	.0020 (.0015)	-.0004 (.0020)
Education	-.0058** (.0029)	-.0200** (.0061)	-.0126** (.0047)	-.0273** (.0083)
If Born in State of Residence	.0151 (.0171)	.1104** (.0336)	-.0048 (.0237)	.0083 (.0362)
Number of Miles to City Center	-.0005 (.0004)	-.0010 (.0009)	-.0003 (.0005)	-.0012 (.0010)
If Plan to Quit Work	-.0327 (.0428)	-.2031* (.0914)	.0167 (.0376)	.2043** (.0621)
If Own Home	.0218 (.0200)	.0547 (.0367)	-.0082 (.0273)	-.0438 (.0376)
Other Family Income/Family Needs	-.0009 (.0085)	-.0098 (.0285)	.0136* (.0068)	.0232 (.0231)
Number of Preschool Children	-.0008 (.0142)	-.0129 (.0248)	.0053 (.0068)	-.0373 (.0231)
Number of School-age Children	.0024 (.0069)	-.0035 (.0118)	.0311** (.0111)	.0076 (.0126)
If Married, Spouse Working	-.0396 (.0364)	-.0969 (.0603)	-.0912* (.0436)	.0467 (.0670)
If Married, Spouse Not Working	-.0132 (.0366)	-.1745** (.0607)	-.0057 (.0531)	-.0348 (.0886)
If Separated, Divorced, Widowed	-.0557 (.0442)	-.0409 (.0591)	-.0357 (.0428)	-.1390* (.0575)
Constant	.2457	.5540	.3816	.5864
Number of Observations	2,250	895	1,326	741
$\bar{Y}$	.159	.281	.193	.252
$\bar{R}^2$	.0032	.0362	.0220	.0598

* Significant at .01 level.
**Significant at .05 level.

Table 4.7

REGRESSIONS ON KNOWS THERE ARE BETTER JOBS ELSEWHERE
(Working Household Heads and Spouses Aged 18-64, Responding Either Yes or No to Question on which Dependent Variable is Based)

Independent Variable	White Men	Black Men	White Women	Black Women
Earnings (in thousands of dollars)	-.0051** (.0013)	-.0160** (.0050)	-.0140** (.0045)	-.0283** (.0075)
If Extra Pension	-.0363 (.0248)	-.1018* (.0429)	-.1023** (.0324)	-.0776 (.0460)
Years with Current Employer	-.0047** (.0017)	-.0002 (.0032)	-.0022 (.0029)	-.0035 (.0032)
Years of Work Experience Before Present Employer	-.0041** (.0014)	-.0034 (.0024)	-.0012 (.0021)	-.0013 (.0026)
Education	.0236** (.0042)	.0415** (.0079)	.0279** (.0064)	.0379** (.0112)
If Born in State of Residence	-.0640* (.0248)	-.0132 (.0428)	-.0719* (.0325)	.0164 (.0473)
Number of Miles to City Center	.0026** (.0005)	-.0001 (.0011)	.0035** (.0007)	.0027* (.0013)
If Plan to Quit Work	-.0211 (.0621)	-.0461 (.1015)	-.1209* (.0513)	-.0096 (.0934)
If Own Home	-.0292 (.0289)	-.1831** (.0447)	-.0291 (.0368)	-.1369** (.0503)
Other Family Income/Family Needs	-.0169 (.0124)	.0093 (.0399)	-.0007 (.0102)	.0172 (.0312)
Number of Preschool Children	-.0390 (.0206)	-.0360 (.0311)	-.0090 (.0335)	.0194 (.0339)
Number of School-age Children	-.0026 (.0101)	-.0117 (.0155)	-.0023 (.0156)	.0465** (.0164)
If Married, Spouse Working	.0472 (.0529)	.1354 (.0797)	-.1162 (.0600)	-.1473 (.0892)
If Married, Spouse Not Working	.0275 (.0533)	.1318 (.0786)	-.1434 (.0739)	-.3007* (.1192)
If Separated, Divorced, Widowed	.0120 (.0635)	.1877* (.0799)	-.1089 (.0590)	-.1225 (.0753)
Constant	.3484	.2757	.3674	.2604
Number of Observations	1,884	621	1,077	499
$\bar{Y}$	.476	.483	.459	.396
$\bar{R}^2$	.0571	.1243	.0702	.1258

* Significant at .01 level.
**Significant at .05 level.

control variables in the regressions.[14] Within subgroups, workers with more desirable jobs—those with higher annual labor earnings and those with extra pension plans—were less likely to report that better jobs were available in other localities. Also within subgroups, workers presumably with greater knowledge of better jobs in other localities—those with higher education, those not residing in their state of birth, and those living further away from cities—were more likely to report that they knew of better jobs that they could get if they were willing to move.

Voluntarily Working Part Time

Voluntary restriction of work hours to part-time was much more common among women than among men. About 15 percent of the white women and 10 percent of the black women, compared to less than 1 percent of the men, were voluntarily working part-time. (See Table 4.8.)

As indicated by Table 4.8 (and substantiated by regression results presented in Table A4.1i) family responsibilities apparently had differential effects by sex and race on the incidence of voluntary part-time work. Fewer family responsibilities tended to encourage voluntary part-time work among men and black women, perhaps because having no family to support freed them to work less. Greater family responsibilities tended to encourage voluntary part-time work among white women, no doubt because of greater conflict between home duties and labor market work.

Among men, those who were single, those with no children, and those under age 25 registered the highest incidence of voluntary part-time work. Among black women, those who were single, those with no children, and those aged 55 to 64 registered higher than average incidence of voluntary part-time work. On the other hand, among white women, those who were married and those with children had the highest incidence of voluntary part-time work.

WAGE EFFECTS

As results of the previous section indicate, some men as well as women impose restrictions on work schedule or job location. If these restrictions affect wages as eco-

---

[14] Frequency distributions across occupation also suggest that reports of whether better jobs were available elsewhere were not entirely unrealistic. (See Appendix A4.1c.) Among all four race/sex subgroups, professional or technical workers were most likely to report that there were better jobs that they could get if they were willing to move; these are workers who could probably qualify for a wide variety of jobs. Among white men, farmers and self-employed businessmen were least likely to report better jobs available elsewhere; these are workers whose skills may be specifically tailored to their given locality.

Table 4.8

MEAN VALUES FOR WHETHER VOLUNTARILY WORKING PART-TIME BY SELECTED INDIVIDUAL CHARACTERISTICS

(Working Household Heads and Spouses Aged 18-64)

	Entire Sample	White Men	Black Men	White Women	Black Women
All	.061	.010	.006	.148	.090
Marital Status (in 1976)					
Married, Spouse Working	.092	.010	.001	.198	.092
Married, Spouse Not Working	.018	.005	.001	.130	.072
Single	.046	.049	.032	.038	.101
Widowed	.048	---	---	.054	.080
Divorced	.056	.000	.000	.077	.132
Separated	.033	.000+	.003	.074	.024
Eta squared (adj)	.019**	.012**	.020**	.033**	.008**
Number of Children (in 1976)					
None	.058	.017	.012	.106	.136
One	.059	.002	.002	.159	.073
Two	.071	.009	.001	.229	.020
Three	.064	.008	.003	.212	.048
Four	.053	.000	.000	.263	.073
Five	.050	.000	.000	---	.228
Six or More	.039	.000+	.000	---	.023+
Eta squared (adj)	.001	.004	.004	.020**	.030**
Age (in 1976)					
Less than 25 Years	.045	.029	.032	.061	.090
25-34 Years	.053	.006	.001	.147	.018
35-44 Years	.065	.010	.001	.165	.087
45-54 Years	.070	.003	.002	.194	.133
55-64 Years	.074	.015	.000	.160	.185
Eta squared (adj)	.002	.006	.020**	.014**	.032**

---Fewer than 10 observations.

+10-24 observations.

**Significant at .01 level.

nomic theory suggests, then they should lower wages. And in the absence of discrimination, they should affect wages in a similar fashion for male and female workers with similar qualifications. That is, after controlling for other possible productivity-related factors, wage effects of a given type of job restriction should be the same across all workers, male or female, black or white.

Wage effects of the limitations were investigated by regressing the natural logarithm of the hourly wage rate on the measures of job limitations and other possible productivity-related factors. The results of such regressions are presented in Table 4.9. At first glance these results may appear replete with race/sex differences. Comprehensive investigation, however, reveals that wage effects of self-imposed limitations on work schedule and job location were often similar across race and sex.

Limitations that Were Factors in Taking the Present Job

Results provide only weak evidence that limiting job location of work hours lowers workers' wages. The first set of regressions in Table 4.9 indicates no significant associated wage penalties. For each subgroup except black males, the coefficients on the variable measuring this limitation are negative but insignificant. But for black males, the coefficient is actually positive and significant at the .05 level.

Wage effects of limitations on job location or work hours could, of course, vary by type of limitation. To test this, the job location or work hours limitation was broken down by type in Regression #2 (Table 4.9). With no limitation on job location or work hours as the excluded category, Regression #2 contained variables representing limitation of job location, limitation of either amount or timing of work hours, and combinations of limitations of job location, amount of hours, and timing of hours.[15]

As indicated by the coefficients on these variables in Regression #2, present wage effects of most types of job location or work hours limitations were insignificant across all the race/sex subgroups. Only one type of limitation registered a significant negative effect and for only one subgroup. White women imposing combinations of limitations had significantly lower wages than white women imposing no limitations. Limitations only on job location also registered significant effects, but they were positive rather than negative. Blacks, both men and women, who limited job location had significantly higher wages than blacks imposing no limitations on either job location or work hours. This may indicate that blacks who limit job location merely eliminate less desirable jobs or it may indicate that the effects of restricting job location are simply ill-based.[16]

[15]This latter category includes nonascertained limitations on job location/work hours.

[16]Of the 24 black women restricting only job location, most had wages below the average for black women but three of them with exceptionally high weights had wages well above the average for black women. These three women were either professional, technical, or managerial workers. Only 19 black men restricted job location. Three of these had exceptionally high weights and above average wages.

Table 4.9

EFFECTS OF WORK SCHEDULE AND JOB LOCATION LIMITATIONS ON WAGE RATES
(Working Household Heads and Spouses Aged 18-64)

Independent Variable	White Men	Black Men	White Women	Black Women
REGRESSION #1				
Limited Job Hours or Location	-.0415 (.0301)	.1025* (.0481)	-.0220 (.0264)	-.0071 (.0386)
Knows there Are Better Jobs Elsewhere	-.1052** (.0235)	-.1216** (.0370)	-.1109** (.0279)	-.1490** (.0385)
Doesn't Know whether there Are Better Jobs Elsewhere	-.0699** (.0307)	-.0821* (.0386)	-.1460** (.0334)	-.0251 (.0394)
Voluntarily Working Part-Time	.0800 (.1066)	.5855** (.1983)	.0456 (.0364)	-.1252* (.0596)
$\bar{R}^2$	.3024	.2973	.3285	.3638
REGRESSION #2:				
Limited Either Amount or Timing of Job Hours	-.0596 (.0458)	.0557 (.0740)	.0013 (.0329)	-.0343 (.0520)
Limited Only Job Location	.0551 (.0531)	.2570** (.0952)	.0548 (.0495)	.1912* (.0799)
Placed Combined Limits on Amount of Job Hours, Timing of Job Hours, or Job Location	-.0890 (.0504)	.0496 (.0736)	-.1316** (.0435)	-.0817 (.0624)
Knows there Are Better Jobs Elsewhere	-.1050** (.0235)	-.1202** (.0372)	-.1125** (.0279)	-.1615** (.0387)
Doesn't Know whether there Are Better Jobs Elsewhere	-.0701* (.0307)	-.0922* (.0389)	-.1455** (.0333)	-.0249 (.0393)
Voluntarily Working Part-Time	.0732 (.1066)	.5903** (.1982)	.0537 (.0364)	-.1285* (.0594)
$\bar{R}^2$	.3030	.2984	.3329	.3694
REGRESSION #3				
Limited Job Hours or Location	-.0965* (.0420)	-.0547 (.0646)	-.0274 (.0351)	.0164 (.0507)
Limited Job Hours or Location × Years with Present Employer	.0066 (.0035)	.0197** (.0054)	.0010 (.0044)	-.0036 (.0051)
Knows there Are Better Jobs Elsewhere	-.1064** (.0235)	-.1164** (.0368)	-.1111** (.0279)	-.1506** (.0385)
Doesn't Know whether there Are Better Jobs Elsewhere	-.0696* (.0307)	-.0884* (.0383)	-.1460** (.0334)	-.0246 (.0394)
Voluntarily Working Part-Time	.0859 (.1066)	.5844** (.1969)	.0459 (.0364)	-.1244* (.0597)
$\bar{R}^2$	.3032	.3068	.3280	.3634

* Significant at .05 level.
**Significant at .01 level.

NOTE: Other variables in these regressions: whether south, city size, formal education, years out of labor force since completing school, years of work experience before present employer, pre-employer work experience squared, years with current employer prior to current position, years of training completed on current job, years of post-training tenure on current job, proportion of total working years that were full time, hours of work missed for illness of others in 1975, hours of work missed for own illness in 1975, and plans to stop work for nontraining reasons.

The apparent absence of wage penalties associated with these limitations could be caused by measurement problems. Both wages and the incidence of limitations on job location or work hours are measured as of the present time, although the limitations would have been imposed in the past, at the time of taking the present job. Wage-reducing effects of these limitations could diminish with time on the job. Possibly with more time on the job, the worker's ability to compensate for productivity-reducing aspects of these limitations would increase.

To test this hypothesis, an interactive term which was the product of limited job hours or location and years with present employer was added to the wage regressions (See Regression #3 in Table 4.9). This addition allows separation of the wage effects of limitations on job location or work hours into two components—initial wage effects (wage effects at 0 years with present employer) and tenure or time specific wage effects. As indicated by the results of Regression #3, only white men were penalized initially for limiting job location or work hours, and only the wages of black men were affected significantly by the interaction term. Thus, both initial and present wage effects of imposing limitations on job location or work hours appear to be generally inconsequential, particularly for women.

Other measurement problems could also contribute to these results. As mentioned earlier, the same coded limitation could encompass quite diverse restrictions. This diversity could mask effects of limitations on wages if restrictions with opposite wage effects were coded identically.

Restriction of Geographic Mobility

Two different measures of restricted geographic mobility are included in the wage analysis—a measure of the lack of movement to better jobs known to exist elsewhere and a measure of the lack of knowledge of job prospects elsewhere. Individuals with either restriction earned less than those who said there weren't better jobs available elsewhere.[17] This is apparent in all three sets of regressions in Table 4.9.

---

[17]The effects of these variables could be somewhat circular in that respondents earning low wages could be more likely to feel that there must be better jobs elsewhere than those earning high wages. However, the occupational distribution on restriction of geographic mobility (see footnote 14 and Appendix Table A4.1c.) argues against this factor dominating the results.

The wage penalties for knowing there were better jobs elsewhere (but not having moved to get them) were remarkably similar across the four subgroups, averaging about 10 percent. Thus, both the frequency and the wage effect of such immobility varied little with sex or race.

The wage penalties for lack of knowledge of job prospects elsewhere were more race/sex-specific. Even though such ignorance was about equally common for men and women and somewhat more common for blacks than whites, it reduced wages of white women by a large percentage, reduced wages of men by a lesser percentage, and had no significant effect on the wages of black women.

Voluntarily Working Part Time

Voluntary restriction of work hours to part-time, per se, did not tend to result in lower wages for working household heads and wives. For whites, both men and women, such restriction had no significant effect on wages. For black men, the apparent effect of this constraint was to increase wages substantially rather than to decrease them; however, this anomalous result was precipitated by a very small number of outliers.[18] Only for black women is there any evidence of this self-imposed work constraint lowering wages.

Longitudinal Evidence Concerning The Effects of Geographic Mobility on the Wages and Labor Force Participation of Husbands and Wives

The measures of restricted geographic mobility included in this chapter were intended to be used to test the hypothesis that part of the male/female wage differential is the result of wives being more restricted than husbands in their geographic movement to better jobs. Because of several problems with these measures, however, one could argue that tests of this hypothesis using these measures are not reliable. Thus, in order to more adequately investigate one basis for this hypothesis, that wives are more likely than husbands to lose rather than gain a better job when the family moves, Panel Study data were examined for effects of actual geographic mobility on the wages and labor force participation of husbands and wives.

Table 4.10 summarizes the findings. The figures presented in this table were derived from a Multiple Classification Analysis, a form of dummy variable regression, of Panel

---

[18] Two truck drivers and one service worker precipitate this finding. Out of the seven black men voluntarily working part-time, these three workers earned very high wages, whereas the remaining four earned wages close to the average for black men.

Table 4.10

MEAN CHANGES IN WAGES AND LABOR FORCE PARTICIPATION OF HUSBANDS AND WIVES BY GEOGRAPHIC MOVEMENT

Geographic Movement between 1970 and 1975	Change in Relative Wages of Husband and Wife			Percentage Change in Husband's Wage			Percentage Change in Wife's Wage			Percentage of Husbands Who Left the Labor Force			Percentage of Wives Who Left the Labor Force		
	N	Unadjusted mean	Adjusted mean+	N	Unadjusted mean	Adjusted mean‡	N	Unadjusted mean	Adjusted mean∺	N	Unadjusted mean	Adjusted mean‡	N	Unadjusted mean	Adjusted mean∺
Moved to Different County	51	-.089	-.049	192	.743	.697	59	.719	.672	223	.087	.126	223	.216	.211
Moved within Same County	199	.040	.073	545	.626	.558	220	.682	.599	623	.086	.118	632	.126	.116
Did Not Move	345	.068	.048	966	.513	.552	394	.717	.758	1206	.108	.087	1206	.095	.099
Eta Squared		.0037			.0125**			.0003			.0012			.0138**	
Beta Squared		.0019			.0042*			.0061			.0029*			.0116**	
$\bar{Y}$		.047			.570			.708			.100			.116	
Standard Deviation		.700			.710			.899			.300			.320	
Total Number of Observations		595			1703			673			2061			2061	

*Significant at .05 level.

**Significant at .01 level.

+Adjusted for the effects of number of children, race, and age and education of both the husband and wife.

‡Adjusted for the effects of number of children, race, and age and education of the husband.

∺Adjusted for the effects of number of children, race, and age and education of the wife.

Study families with the same head and spouse from 1970 through 1976. Table 4.10 contains both unadjusted means distributed according to the geographic movement of the family and comparable means adjusted for the effects of age, education, number of children, and race measured as of 1976. Means for five dependent variables are presented:[19]

Change in relative wages of husband and wife, measured as the ratio of the wife's wage to her husband's wage in 1975 minus the corresponding ratio in 1970. This measure was obtained for families in which the husband and wife were working in both 1970 and 1975.

Percentage Change in husband's wage, measured as the ratio of (husband's wage in 1975 minus husband's wage in 1970) to husband's wage in 1970. This measure was obtained for families in which the husband was working in both 1970 and 1975.

Percentage Change in wife's wage, measured as the ratio of (wife's wage in 1975 minus wife's wage in 1970) to wife's wage in 1970. This measure was obtained for families in which the wife was working in both 1970 and 1975.

Percentage of husbands who left the labor force.

Percentage of wives who left the labor force.

The figures in this table indicate that, on average, although the wife's wage does not increase as much as her husband's wage when the family moves, the geographic movement has no strong detrimental effect on her wage if she is able to continue working. In terms of percentage change in own wage, husbands' wages increased significantly more with geographic movement whereas wives' wages did not. In terms of change in the relative wages of the husband and wife, couples who moved to a different county averaged the lowest increases in the wages of the wife relative to the husband. However, wives' wages did not significantly decline with geographic movement, and the effects of geographic movement on the relative wages of the spouses were insignificant. In general, the control variables, particularly age, education, and number of children, were better predictors of wage changes than was geographic mobility.

Although geographic movement had little effect on the wages of wives who continued to work, it apparently did reduce the wives' ability or desire to continue working.[20]

[19]Change in relative earnings, change in own work hours and own commuting hours of husbands and wives, and percentage of husbands and wives entering the labor force were also investigated. Of these variables, only change in commuting hours of husbands varied significantly (at the .01 level) with geographic movement once demographic factors were controlled for; husband's commuting hours tended to increase with greater geographic movement.

[20]These results are consistent with Sandell's (1977) findings.

Even with demographic controls, wives tended to be more likely than husbands to leave the labor force as a result of moving, particularly if the move was to a different county. There is, then, the possibility of an indirect effect of mobility on the wives' wages by reducing the amount of labor market experience.

EFFECTS OF MARRIAGE AND CHILDREN ON WAGES

As mentioned in the introduction to this chapter, various studies have found evidence of differential effects of marriage and children on the wages of men and women and have attributed these findings to differential restriction of labor force activity. However, the analysis in this chapter has indicated that not all forms of self-imposed limitations on work schedule and job location were most common among married women with children, and that the wage effects of some limitations were similar across both sex and race. Of course, restriction of labor force activity can take other forms, such as less on-the-job training, interrupted labor force participation, and absenteeism.

Since the Panel Study data allow direct measurement of all of these forms of restricted labor force activity, plus wages, marital status, and number of children present in the household, it is now possible to test whether marital status and number of children serve as proxies for degree of restriction of labor force activity. This can be done by comparing wage effects of marital status and children first without and then with controls for restriction of labor force activity, as in Regressions #4 and #5 of Table 4.11. Apparently the number of children variable serves as a proxy for degree of restriction of labor force activity but marriage variables do not.

Results show that the detrimental effect of children on women's wages is mostly caused by restriction of labor force activity. The negative effect of number of children on the wages of white women becomes insignificant once intervening variables measuring labor force activity are controlled for, and the positive effect for black women becomes large enough to be significant.

Results also show, however, that the wage effects of marital status represent something other than differential restriction of labor force activity. Particularly among whites, the wage effects of marital status persist even with extensive controls for differences in labor market behavior. Marriage, both past and present, clearly entails much larger wage advantages, independent of worker qualifications, for white men than for any other race/sex subgroup. This is certainly inconsistent with the conclusions of Fuchs (1971), Oaxaca (1973), Malkiel and Malkiel (1973), and Polachek (1975). And it may at first seem inconsistent with their empirical findings; but it is not. These studies can be

Table 4.11

EFFECTS OF MARITAL STATUS AND CHILDREN ON WAGE RATES
(Working Household Heads and Spouses Aged 18-64)

Dependent Variable = ℓn Wage Rate

Independent Variable	White Men	Black Men	White Women	Black Women
REGRESSION #4:				
If Married	.3105**	.1808**	.0087	.0165
	(.0521)	(.0614)	(.0526)	(.0618)
If Widowed, Divorced, Separated	.2399**	-.0202	.0570	.1174
	(.0632)	(.0639)	(.0552)	(.0634)
Number of Children under Age 18	-.0009	-.0005	-.0643**	.0117
	(.0099)	(.0115)	(.0140)	(.0125)
Expect More Children?	-.0762*	.0999	.0625	.1201
	(.0375)	(.0557)	(.0496)	(.0676)
$\bar{R}^2$	.2566	.2324	.2294	.2951
REGRESSION #5:				
If Married	.3148**	.0940	.0582	-.0162
	(.0501)	(.0584)	(.0485)	(.0575)
If Widowed, Divorced, Separated	.2467**	-.0453	.0738	.1185*
	(.0608)	(.0608)	(.0514)	(.0582)
Number of Children under Age 18	.0130	-.0044	-.0152	.0302**
	(.0091)	(.0111)	(.0125)	(.0117)
Expect More Children?	-.1085**	.1422**	-.0076	.1567*
	(.0352)	(.0532)	(.0453)	(.0634)
Number of Observations	2,250	895	1,326	741
$\bar{R}^2$	.3189	.3075	.3277	.3789

* Significant at .05 level.

**Significant at .01 level.

NOTE: Other variables in regression #4: whether south, city size, education, age-education-6, and age-education-6 squared.

Other variables in regression #5: whether south, city size, formal education, years out of labor force since completing school, years of work experience before present employer, pre-employer work experience squared, years with current employer prior to current position, years of training completed on current job, years of post-training tenure on current job, proportion of total working years that were full time, hours of work missed for illness of others in 1975, hours of work missed for own illness in 1975, and plans to stop work for nontraining reasons, limited job hours or location, knows there are better jobs elsewhere, and doesn't know whether there are better jobs elsewhere.

misleading since their conclusions imply something not indicated in their findings. Attributing differential wage effects of marriage to differential restriction of labor force activity implies positive wage effects of marriage for men and negative wage effects of marriage for women. The evidence presented in those studies, however, shows no such negative effect for women. What it does show is simply a larger positive wage effect of marriage for white men than for white women.

What actually causes the advantageous effect of marriage on the wages of white men? One possibility is that characteristics which make men more desirable marriage partners also make them more productive workers. For example, married men could be more productive than single men because, on average, they are in better health. Or they may have stronger work motivation, although the controls for labor market experience should have captured a large part of that effect. Another possibility is the presence of paternalistic attitudes among employers which lead them to feel that men with greater family responsibilities deserve higher wages. In any case, the positive effect of marriage on the wages of white men, unmatched among other subgroups of workers, is apparently not caused primarily by more stable patterns of labor force activity.

Summary

In this chapter we have examined the incidence and wage effects of self-imposed limitations on work schedule and job location. Three forms of these limitations were investigated in this analysis: limitations on job location or work hours when looking for work, restriction of geographic mobility, and voluntary part-time work.

With respect to incidence, we found that women, particularly white women, were more likely than men to restrict their work hours or job location when looking for work. This trend held for all forms of this limitation, particularly the most common form—restriction of timing of work hours. Women also were more likely than men to voluntarily work part-time. However, men appeared to be just as likely as women to restrict geographic mobility.

Conflicts between family responsibilities and labor market work contributed to the large sex differentials in the incidence of limitations on job location or work hours and voluntary part-time work. Family responsibilities seemed to have little detrimental effect on geographic mobility, however.

Wage effects of self-imposed limitations on work schedule and job location were often similar across the four race/sex subgroups. Some, but not all, forms of these restrictions resulted in wage penalties.

Limitations on job location or work hours generally had little effect on wages, particularly for women. Also, voluntarily choosing to work part-time tended to have no significant effect on wages, particularly among white workers.

Restriction of geographic mobility, as measured by whether better jobs were known to be available elsewhere, did result in lower wages for all race/sex subgroups. Workers who knew of better jobs elsewhere but had not moved to take them paid a price for this immobility, and the price, as a percentage of wages, was similar across race and sex. Workers who did not know about their job prospects in other localities paid a price for this ignorance. This price, as a percentage of wages, was highest for white women and lowest for black women.

Since measurement of restrictions on geographic mobility was recognized as problematic, actual effects of geographic movement on the wages and labor force participation of husbands and wives were also investigated. Findings indicated that wives left the labor force in greater numbers if the family moved, but those wives who found jobs did not tend to suffer significant wage penalties as a result of moving.

We also investigated the validity of attributing sex differential wage effects of number of children and marital status to differences in labor force activity. Number of children did serve as a proxy for differences in labor force activity, but marital status did not. Independent of worker qualifications, marriage offers white men a large wage advantage not available to women or black men.

References

Fuchs, Victor R. "Differences in Hourly Earnings Between Men and Women." Monthly Labor Review 94 (May 1971).

Malkiel, Burton G., and Malkiel, Judith A. "Male-Female Pay Differences in Professional Employment." The American Economic Review, (September 1973).

Oxaca, Ronald. "Male-Female Wage Differentials in Urban Labor Markets." International Economic Review 14, No. 3 (October 1973).

Polachek, Simon. "Potential Biases in Measuring Male-Female Discrimination." Journal of Human Resources X, No. 2 (Spring 1975).

Rosen, Harvey. "Taxes in a Labor Supply Model with Joint Wage Hours Determination." Econometrica, May 1976.

Sandall, Steven H. "Women and the Economics of Family Migration." The Review of Economics and Statistics, November 1977.

APPENDIX 4.1

Table A4.1a

DISTRIBUTIONS ON SEVERAL INDIVIDUAL CHARACTERISTICS BY RACE AND SEX

(Working Household Heads and Spouses Aged 18-64)

	Entire Sample		White Men		Black Men		White Women		Black Women	
	Number of Observations	Weighted Per-centage	Number of Observations	Weighted Per-centage	Number of Observations	Weighted Per-centage	Number of Observations	Weighted Per-centage	Number of Observations	Weighted Per-centage
All	5212	100.0	2250	100.0	895	100.0	1326	100.0	741	100.0
Marital Status (in 1976)										
Married, Spouse Working	2622	48.9	1018	43.2	374	40.6	874	59.6	356	48.1
Married, Spouse Not Working	1510	29.4	1014	44.1	333	31.2	113	8.5	50	5.0
Single	442	9.2	119	6.8	95	15.2	121	11.4	107	13.9
Widowed	124	2.7	12	0.8	12	1.0	58	5.2	42	9.6
Divorced	324	7.4	67	4.1	29	2.5	131	12.7	97	13.2
Separated	190	2.4	20	1.0	52	9.4	29	2.7	89	10.1
Number of Children (in 1976)										
None	2081	45.2	878	40.9	291	41.0	686	53.4	226	40.8
1	1197	20.8	521	20.8	208	20.2	285	20.7	183	22.6
2	997	19.1	485	21.3	157	18.5	215	15.6	140	18.9
3	536	9.6	235	10.9	105	10.7	96	7.5	100	9.2
4	223	3.4	83	4.3	63	3.4	27	1.9	50	4.4
5	111	1.2	29	1.1	44	4.3	12	0.7	26	2.5
6+	67	0.7	19	0.8	27	1.8	5	0.3	16	1.5
Age of Youngest Child (in 1976)										
No Children	2081	45.2	878	40.9	291	41.0	686	53.4	226	40.8
Less than 2 Years	554	7.1	279	8.8	126	7.3	79	4.1	70	7.1
2-5 Years	1016	14.8	436	17.3	227	19.2	166	10.2	187	14.3
6-13 Years	1181	24.1	489	24.2	207	23.7	289	23.5	196	27.1
14-17 Years	380	8.9	168	8.8	44	8.8	106	8.9	62	10.6
Age of Children when Started Working for Present Employer										
No Children under 18 Years Old	2320	46.6	1059	46.5	379	49.8	639	47.0	243	41.1
Preschool Children Only	1065	17.6	522	21.5	213	19.4	174	11.8	156	12.2
School-age Children Only	986	20.6	318	15.4	118	13.0	350	29.2	200	29.1
Both Preschool & School-age Children	841	15.1	351	16.6	185	17.7	163	12.0	142	17.7

Table A4.1a (continued)

	Entire Sample		White Men		Black Men		White Women		Black Women	
	Number of Observations	Weighted Per-centage	Number of Observations	Weighted Per-centage	Number of Observations	Weighted Per-centage	Number of Observations	Weighted Per-centage	Number of Observations	Weighted Per-centage
Years Worked for Present Employer										
Less than 1 Year	852	14.7	339	12.7	131	11.1	276	18.9	106	11.9
1 Year	520	9.2	195	7.8	82	9.3	170	11.6	73	6.8
2-4 Years	1425	23.8	556	21.4	246	26.1	376	26.3	247	31.5
5-9 Years	1333	26.0	594	26.8	222	24.9	295	24.0	222	31.7
10 Years or More	1082	26.4	566	31.2	214	28.7	209	19.2	93	18.1
Age when Started Working for Present Employer										
Less than 25 Years	2191	36.1	955	37.5	418	43.9	533	33.0	285	33.5
25-34 Years	1573	31.3	757	34.5	273	30.9	335	26.3	208	30.2
35-44 Years	893	20.0	329	17.0	115	14.8	286	24.8	163	26.1
45-54 Years	466	10.3	171	8.7	73	6.9	146	13.6	76	9.0
55-64 Years	89	2.2	38	2.2	16	3.4	26	2.2	9	1.2
Hours Worked per Week on Main Job (in 1975)										
Less than 20 Hours	94	1.9	6	0.2	5	0.5	56	4.6	27	2.9
20-29 Hours	220	4.7	28	1.2	14	1.2	129	10.7	49	7.2
30-39 Hours	707	14.2	174	8.1	74	10.1	295	22.6	164	29.7
40-49 Hours	3326	59.6	1400	61.0	681	72.8	763	55.6	482	57.1
50 or More Hours	838	19.4	633	29.2	112	15.0	80	6.3	13	2.5
NA	27	0.2	9	0.3	9	0.4	3	0.2	6	0.5
Age (in 1976)										
Less than 25 Years	1008	13.6	364	11.6	205	15.3	291	16.3	148	15.5
25-34 Years	1751	30.5	811	31.6	289	31.4	422	29.2	229	25.8
35-44 Years	985	20.9	416	20.8	171	23.3	237	19.9	161	26.0
45-54 Years	946	22.4	440	23.7	136	18.6	230	20.8	140	23.1
55-64 Years	522	12.6	219	12.2	94	11.4	146	13.8	63	9.5
Average Hourly Earnings (in 1975)										
$0.50-$1.99	501	7.7	119	5.0	87	7.1	171	11.5	124	14.1
$2.00-$2.99	1032	14.2	244	8.1	205	18.1	304	21.0	279	33.8
$3.00-$3.99	916	15.7	297	11.3	169	14.1	298	22.2	152	21.7
$4.00-$5.99	1372	27.1	627	26.3	249	29.7	361	29.2	135	18.7
$6.00 or More	1391	35.2	963	49.2	185	31.0	192	16.1	51	11.7

Table A4.1a (continued)

	Entire Sample		White Men		Black Men		White Women		Black Women	
	Number of Observations	Weighted Per-centage	Number of Observations	Weighted Per-centage	Number of Observations	Weighted Per-centage	Number of Observations	Weighted Per-centage	Number of Observations	Weighted Per-centage
Annual Earnings (in 1975)										
Less than $5,000	1295	20.1	220	8.4	197	16.2	508	36.3	370	46.3
$5,000-$7,499	1045	16.0	275	9.8	225	19.3	343	24.3	202	26.3
$7,500-$9,999	861	15.7	351	13.6	172	19.0	238	18.8	100	14.4
$10,000-$14,999	1143	23.8	678	29.3	213	29.8	189	15.7	63	10.7
$15,000-$19,999	527	13.7	413	20.9	68	10.6	40	4.2	6	2.3
$20,000 or More	341	10.6	313	18.0	20	5.1	8	0.8	0	0.0
Occupation (in 1976)										
Professional, Technical	722	17.6	368	17.6	35	5.2	257	20.3	62	11.6
Manager, Official, Proprietor, Not Self-employed	421	11.3	305	15.8	28	5.0	74	6.0	14	3.7
Self-employed Businessman	123	2.9	95	4.5	10	0.5	17	0.9	1	0.0
Clerical and Sales	1074	22.0	250	11.0	90	17.0	533	40.1	201	25.9
Craftsman, Foreman	807	16.0	598	25.9	178	18.0	19	1.5	12	1.3
Operative	983	15.2	383	15.2	278	25.9	182	13.4	140	16.8
Laborer, Service Worker	993	13.1	174	6.8	270	28.0	240	17.7	309	40.6
Farmer, Farm Manager	78	1.9	74	3.3	3	0.3	1	0.0	0	0.0
NA; DK	11	0.1	3	0.1	3	0.2	3	0.1	2	0.1
Education (in 1976)										
Less than 8 Years	624	8.6	226	9.5	222	19.9	73	5.6	103	8.3
9-11 Years	926	14.2	304	12.9	237	19.9	190	13.8	195	27.4
12 Years	2048	39.5	833	35.7	309	39.2	591	45.2	315	43.1
13-15 Years	766	15.9	365	16.3	96	14.8	219	15.9	86	12.6
16 Years	480	11.9	286	13.9	23	4.7	145	10.6	26	5.4
17 or More Years	368	9.9	236	11.8	8	1.6	108	9.0	16	3.3
Family Income (in 1975)										
Less than $2,499	66	1.3	16	0.8	15	1.0	23	2.0	12	1.7
$2,500-$4,999	281	3.6	57	2.3	90	7.9	54	4.5	80	7.5
$5,000-$7,499	545	7.5	163	5.9	135	12.3	103	7.9	144	19.2
$7,500-$9,999	641	8.5	205	6.9	158	13.8	133	9.2	145	16.4
$10,000-$12,499	669	11.1	272	10.7	139	15.1	156	11.0	102	12.4
$12,500-$14,999	633	11.6	295	12.2	106	12.0	154	10.8	78	8.4
$15,000-$19,999	1007	21.0	488	22.3	149	21.8	259	18.9	111	20.1
$20,000-$24,999	647	15.2	343	16.5	59	7.3	209	15.7	36	5.1
$25,000 or More	723	20.2	411	22.3	44	8.9	235	20.0	33	9.1

Table A4.1b

MEAN VALUES FOR WHETHER LIMITATIONS ON JOB LOCATION OR WORK HOURS WERE FACTORS IN TAKING PRESENT JOB, BY SEVERAL INDIVIDUAL CHARACTERISTICS (Working Household Heads and Spouses Aged 18-64)

	Entire Sample	White Men	Black Men	White Women	Black Women
All	.215	.145	.122	.342	.216
Marital Status (in 1976)					
Married, Spouse Working	.254	.154	.096	.385	.280
Married, Spouse Not Working	.128	.116	.079	.255	.150
Single	.252	.253	.245	.283	.055
Widowed	.226	---	---	.235	.294
Divorced	.245	.182	.047	.295	.161
Separated	.234	.220+	.144	.327	.164
Eta Squared (adj)	.019**	.011**	.053**	.013	.041**
Age of Children when Started Working for Present Employer‡					
No Children Less than 18 Years Old	.197	.164	.140	.268	.134
Preschool Children Only	.198	.150	.165	.340	.258
School-age Children Only	.259	.111	.011	.400	.271
Preschool & School-age Children	.227	.119	.104	.487	.288
Eta Squared (adj)	.004**	.004	.020**	.027**	.028**
Years Worked for Present Employer					
Less than 1 Year	.271	.185	.138	.381	.222
1 Year	.272	.167	.128	.397	.363
2-4 Years	.241	.168	.182	.355	.191
5-9 Years	.183	.108	.074	.326	.249
10 or More Years	.171	.140	.101	.271	.142
Eta Squared (adj)	.010**	.006	.015**	.008	.017**
Age when Started Working for Present Employer⁑					
Less than 25 Years	.197	.149	.133	.292	.235
25-34 Years	.221	.156	.163	.377	.163
35-44 Years	.256	.127	.066	.410	.310
45-54 Years	.187	.110	.042	.290	.072
55-64 Years	.177	.179	.017+	.221	---
Eta Squared (adj)	.003**	.002	.017**	.013**	.032**
Hours Worked per Week on Main Job (in 1975)					
Less than 20 Hours	.559	---	---	.615	.254
20-29 Hours	.444	.230	.024+	.510	.172
30-39 Hours	.281	.155	.310	.350	.308
40-49 Hours	.195	.156	.113	.286	.161
50 or More Hours	.138*	.116	.050	.323	.430+
NA	.009	---	---	---	---
Eta Squared (adj)		.006	.042**	.037**	.033**
Average Hourly Earnings (in 1975)					
$0.50-$1.99	.215	.126	.153	.285	.210
$2.00-$2.99	.247	.154	.082	.343	.173
$3.00-$3.99	.277	.186	.041	.379	.256
$4.00-$5.99	.224	.141	.215	.345	.230
$6.00 or More	.166	.138	.086	.322	.250
Eta Squared (adj)	.010**	.002	.039**	.003	.006

Table A4.1b (continued)

	Entire Sample	White Men	Black Men	White Women	Black Women
Annual Earnings (in 1975)					
Less than $5,000	.308	.183	.122	.385	.199
$5,000-$7,499	.260	.158	.059	.354	.240
$7,500-$9,999	.214	.139	.151	.308	.257
$10,000-$14,999	.189	.155	.163	.306	.122
$15,000-$19,999	.164	.160	.117	.194	---
$20,000 or More	.094	.092	.025+	---	---
Eta Squared (adj)	.024**	.006	.017**	.009	.016**
Occupation (in 1976)					
Professional, Technical	.249	.168	.072	.367	.313
Manager, Official, Proprietor, Not Self-employed	.194	.151	.061	.389	.307
Self-employed Businessman	.176	.155	.056+	.295+	
Clerical and Sales	.310	.200	.305*	.366	.228
Craftsman, Foreman	.116	.123	.026	.066+	.440+
Operative	.163	.130	.142	.232	.156
Laborer, Service Worker	.239	.145	.075	.356	.179
Farmer, Farm Manager	.032	.032	---	---	---
NA; DK	.385+				
Eta Squared (adj)	.029**	.011**	.078**	.015	.021**
Education (in 1976)					
Less than 8 Years	.108	.099	.108	.117	.178
9-11 Years	.166	.145	.049	.235	.119
12 Years	.226	.119	.106	.375	.268
13-15 Years	.271	.200	.246	.392	.263
16 Years	.235	.161	.257+	.392	.203
17 or More Years	.218	.167	---	.330	.281+
Eta Squared (adj)	.011**	.008**	.041**	.024**	.025**
Family Income (in 1975)					
Less than $2,499	.124	.158+	.015+	.114+	.088+
$2,500-$4,999	.263	.204	.163	.368	.137
$5,000-$7,499	.199	.153	.068	.287	.195
$7,500-$9,999	.190	.145	.178	.275	.075
$10,000-$12,499	.191	.156	.104	.268	.163
$12,500-$14,999	.232	.166	.237	.335	.394
$15,000-$19,999	.211	.147	.081	.341	.309
$20,000-$24,999	.233	.134	.033	.420	.177
$25,000 or More	.221	.126	.133	.394	.328
Eta Squared (adj)	.002	.002	.033**	.017	.058**

---Fewer than 10 observations.

+10-24 observations.

‡Variable is based on wife's report of children's years of birth and individual's report of length of time worked for present employer.

⁑Variable is based on individual's report of age in 1976 and length of time worked for present employer.

**Significant at .01 level.

Table A4.1c

MEAN VALUES FOR WHETHER BETTER JOBS AVAILABLE IF WILLING TO MOVE, BY SEVERAL INDIVIDUAL CHARACTERISTICS
(Working Household Heads and Spouses Aged 18-64)

	Entire Sample	White Men	Black Men	White Women	Black Women
All	.381	.399	.340	.369	.295
Marital Status (in 1976)					
Married, Spouse Working	.383	.408	.315	.373	.259
Married, Spouse Not Working	.356	.367	.331	.296	.177
Single	.477	.491	.385	.485	.456
Widowed	.275	---	---	.203	.541
Divorced	.374	.474	.532	.346	.154
Separated	.417	.474+	.394	.473	.256
Eta Squared (adj)	.006**	.006	.012	.016**	.064**
Number of Children (in 1976)					
None	.383	.404	.366	.370	.275
1	.393	.406	.280	.410	.249
2	.383	.408	.345	.348	.297
3	.356	.367	.439	.293	.480
4	.399	.424	.394	.348	.274
5	.305	.295	.159	---	.215
6+	.207	.115+	.140	---	.586+
Eta Squared (adj)	.002	.004	.018**	.004	.024**
Age of Youngest Child (in 1976)					
No Children	.383	.404	.366	.370	.275
Less than 2 Years	.396	.388	.468	.426	.305
2-5 Years	.422	.445	.354	.386	.389
6-13 Years	.368	.372	.308	.378	.312
14-17 Years	.326	.368	.172	.301	.196
Eta Squared (adj)	.002	.003	.018**	.002	.012
Age (in 1976)					
Less than 25 Years	.449	.451	.446	.448	.455
25-34 Years	.452	.485	.397	.416	.331
35-44 Years	.344	.362	.358	.324	.270
45-54 Years	.351	.357	.157	.381	.251
55-64 Years	.250	.270	.305	.227	.110
Eta Squared (adj)	.020**	.022**	.040**	.021**	.039**
Average Hourly Earnings (in 1975)					
$0.50-$1.99	.377	.441	.421	.336	.320
$2.00-$2.99	.425	.452	.335	.437	.338
$3.00-$3.99	.406	.460	.282	.391	.270
$4.00-$5.99	.397	.435	.394	.345	.366
$6.00 or More	.340	.352	.300	.318	.076
Eta Squared (adj)	.004**	.009**	.010	.008	.035**
Annual Earnings (in 1975)					
Less than $5,000	.416	.461	.308	.412	.381
$5,000-$7,499	.383	.437	.355	.373	.225
$7,500-$9,999	.369	.416	.338	.321	.340
10,000-$14,999	.398	.425	.388	.346	.096
$15,000-$19,999	.339	.352	.281	.284	---
$20,000 or More	.344	.346	.241+	---	---
Eta Squared (adj)	.003**	.007	.007	.006	.053**

Table A4.1c (continued)

	Entire Sample	White Men	Black Men	White Women	Black Women
Occupation (in 1976)					
Professional, Technical	.465	.489	.565	.434	.392
Manager, Official, Proprietor, Not Self-employed	.452	.466	.390	.422	.186
Self-employed Businessman	.223	.233	.167+	.160+	
Clerical and Sales	.359	.369	.412	.359	.264
Craftsman, Foreman	.377	.384	.297	.301+	.560+
Operative	.313	.355	.288	.252	.255
Laborer, Service Worker	.391	.429	.318	.409	.308
Farmer, Farm Manager	.180	.166	---	---	---
NA; DK	.300+	---	---	---	---
Eta Squared (adj)	.017**	.023**	.026**	.016	.015
Education (in 1976)					
Less than 8 Years	.251	.265	.165	.263	.238
9-11 Years	.313	.353	.365	.258	.250
12 Years	.363	.382	.348	.350	.290
13-15 Years	.421	.413	.344	.444	.439
16 Years	.478	.483	.817+	.450	.416
17 Years or More	.479	.487	---	.475	.130+
Eta Squared (adj)	.019**	.017**	.079**	.022**	.023**
Family Income (in 1975)					
Less than $2,499	.478	.527+	.403+	.459+	.412+
$2,500-$4,999	.434	.468	.358	.435	.395
$5,000-$7,499	.407	.399	.381	.442	.344
$7,500-$9,999	.438	.533	.270	.383	.341
$10,000-$12,499	.390	.426	.344	.357	.303
$12,500-$14,999	.416	.438	.418	.393	.236
$15,000-$19,999	.376	.394	.347	.361	.267
$20,000-$24,999	.354	.355	.284	.360	.270
$25,000 or More	.333	.348	.290	.321	.125
Eta Squared (adj)	.005**	.011**	.008	.006	.022**

---Fewer than 10 observations.

+10-24 observations.

**Significant at .01 level.

Table A4.1d

MEAN VALUES FOR WHETHER VOLUNTARILY WORKING PART TIME, BY SEVERAL INDIVIDUAL CHARACTERISTICS
(Working Household Heads and Spouses Aged 18-64)

	Entire Sample	White Men	Black Men	White Women	Black Women
All	.061	.010	.006	.148	.090
Marital Status (in 1976)					
Married, Spouse Working	.092	.010	.001	.198	.092
Married, Spouse Not Working	.018	.005	.001	.130	.072
Single	.046	.049	.032	.038	.101
Widowed	.048	---	---	.054	.080
Divorced	.056	.000	.000	.077	.132
Separated	.033	.000+	.003	.074	.024
Eta Squared (adj)	.019**	.012**	.020**	.033**	.008
Number of Children (in 1976)					
None	.058	.017	.012	.106	.136
1	.059	.002	.002	.159	.073
2	.071	.009	.001	.229	.020
3	.064	.008	.003	.212	.048
4	.053	.000	.000	.263	.073
5	.050	.000	.000	---	.228
6+	.039	.000+	.000*	---	.023+
Eta Squared (adj)	.001	.004	.004	.020**	.030**
Age of Youngest Child (in 1976)					
No Children	.058	.017	.012	.106	.136
Less than 2 Years	.036	.000	.000	.177	.010
2-5 Years	.045	.009	.000	.157	.050
6-13 Years	.073	.004	.004	.198	.076
14-17 Years	.090	.006	.000	.243	.055
Eta Squared (adj)	.003**	.004	.005	.019**	.020**
Age (in 1976)					
Less than 25 Years	.045	.029	.032	.061	.090
25-34 Years	.053	.006	.001	.147	.018
35-44 Years	.065	.010	.001	.165	.087
45-54 Years	.070	.003	.002	.194	.133
55-64 Years	.074	.015	.000	.160	.185
Eta Squared (adj)	.002	.006	.020**	.014**	.032**
Average Hourly Earnings (in 1975)					
$0.50-$1.99	.092	.015	.000	.144	.162
$2.00-$2.99	.103	.000	.006	.190	.060
$3.00-$3.99	.087	.037	.000	.139	.071
$4.00-$5.99	.042	.003	.002	.107	.034
More than $6.00	.039	.008	.013	.183	.212
Eta Squared (adj)	.012**	.011**	.004	.009	.041**
Annual Earnings (in 1975)					
Less than $5,000	.208	.053	.033	.292	.123
$5,000-$7,499	.061	.016	.000	.102	.027
$7,500-$9,999	.025	.009	.000	.043	.064
$10,000-$14,999	.014	.002	.001	.043	.155
$15,000-$19,999	.008	.003	.003	.050	---
More than $20,000	.007	.008	.000+	---	---
Eta Squared (adj)	.100**	.019**	.023**	.099**	.027**

Table A4.1d (continued)

	Entire Sample	White Men	Black Men	White Women	Black Women
Occupation (in 1976)					
Professional, Technical	.078	.007	.000	.174	.159
Manager, Official, Proprietor, Not Self-employed	.038	.004	.000	.154	.447
Self-employed Businessman	.054	.048	.000+	.107+	---
Clerical and Sales	.097	.022	.000	.143	.022
Craftsman, Foreman	.003	.003	.000	.000+	.000+
Operative	.024	.009	.008	.059	.009
Laborer, Service Worker	.117	.009	.014	.210	.118
Farmer, Farm Manager	.017	.017	---	---	---
NA; DK	.000+	---	---	---	---
Eta Squared (adj)	.028**	.010	.005	.018	.096**
Education (in 1976)					
Less than 8 Years	.029	.012	.001	.084	.078
9-11 Years	.063	.008	.006	.141	.127
12 Years	.066	.002	.009	.157	.046
13-15 Years	.061	.016	.005	.142	.073
16	.059	.023	.000+	.130	.206
17 Years or More	.066	.009	---	.182	.250+
Eta Squared (adj)	.002	.005	.001	.003	.034**
Family Income (in 1975)					
Less than $2,499	.025	.000+	.000+	.043+	.020+
$2,500-$4,999	.120	.093	.060	.153	.144
$5,000-$7,499	.045	.021	.000	.075	.079
$7,500-$9,999	.054	.014	.001	.114	.063
$10,000-$12,499	.051	.003	.005	.126	.109
$12,500-$14,999	.047	.013	.000	.121	.020
$15,000-$19,999	.060	.003	.001	.172	.116
$20,000-$24,999	.063	.011	.000	.160	.013
$25,000	.073	.005	.000	.197	.152
Eta Squared (adj)	.004	.019**	.042**	.012	.019

---Fewer than 10 observations.

+10-24 observations.

**Significant at .01 level.

Table A4.1e

MEAN VALUES ON WHETHER LIMITATIONS ON JOB LOCATION OR WORK HOURS WOULD BE FACTORS IN TAKING A JOB, BY SEVERAL INDIVIDUAL CHARACTERISTICS
(Nonworking Household Heads and Spouses)

	Unweighted Number of Observations	Weighted Percentage of Observations	Whether Limitations on Job Location/ Work Hours Would Be Factors in Taking a Job
All	3,546	100.0	.260
Race/Sex Subgroup			
White Men	550	23.0	.144
Black Men	277	2.7	.157
White Women	1,784	66.5	.298
Black Women	935	7.8	.316
Eta Squared (adj)			.024**
Age			
Under 25	654	10.5	.469
25-34	640	15.4	.516
35-44	436	10.3	.441
45-54	477	13.2	.319
55-64	503	15.1	.150
65 or Older	836	35.5	.061
Eta Squared (adj)			.178**
Marital Status			
Married, Spouse Working	1,592	42.9	.411
Married, Spouse Not Working	855	28.5	.111
Single	246	4.7	.464
Widowed	480	17.0	.288
Divorced	184	4.2	.466
Separated	189	2.6	.473
Eta Squared (adj)			.061**
Number of Children in Family Unit			
0	1,720	60.8	.142
1-2	1,179	27.1	.439
3-4	496	10.1	.462
5 or More	151	2.0	.399
Eta Squared (adj)			.112**
Age of Youngest Child			
No Children	1,720	60.8	.142
1 Year	431	7.3	.485
2-5 Years	626	13.4	.476
6-12 Years	502	11.0	.447
13-17	269	7.5	.337
Eta Squared (adj)			.118**
Employment Status			
Unemployed	421	7.2	.461
Retired	677	28.3	.091
Housewife	1,931	53.7	.327
Student	135	3.3	.491
Other	382	7.5	.128
Eta Squared (adj)			.085**

**Significant at .01 level.

Table A4.1f

PERCENTAGE DISTRIBUTION OF RESPONSES ABOUT WHAT TYPES OF LIMITATIONS ON JOB LOCATION OR WORK HOURS WOULD BE FACTORS IN TAKING A JOB

(Nonworking Household Heads and Spouses)

Type of Limitation	Entire Sample	White Men	Black Men	White Women	Black Women
Job Location Only	3.9	5.5	1.0	3.5	3.1
Amount of Hours Only	2.4	0.8	3.2	2.6	4.7
Timing of Hours Only	11.6	3.4	1.6	14.7	12.4
Job Location and Amount of Hours Only	1.4	1.0	0.0	1.6	1.4
Other	6.0	3.4	9.5	6.6	7.9
NA; DK on Type of Limitation	0.7	0.3	0.4	0.8	3.1
None; NA or DK Whether any Limitation	74.0	85.6	84.3	70.2	68.4
Total	100.0	100.0	100.0	100.0	100.0
Number of Observations	3,546	550	277	1,784	935
Weighted Percentage of Total Observations	100.0	23.0	2.7	66.5	7.8

Table A4.1g

REGRESSIONS ON WHETHER LIMITATIONS ON TIMING OF WORK HOURS WERE FACTORS IN TAKING PRESENT JOB
(Working Household Heads and Spouses Aged 18-64)

Independent Variable	White Men	Black Men	White Women	Black Women
Education (in years)	-.0005 (.0014)	.0076** (.0022)	.0051 (.0037)	.0094* (.0045)
Age (in years)†	-.0008 (.0005)	-.0001 (.0007)	-.0005 (.0010)	-.0012 (.0012)
If Both Preschool and School-age Children†	-.0094 (.0125)	.0334 (.0189)	.1509** (.0314)	.0443 (.0295)
If Preschool Children Only†	-.0134 (.0113)	.0070 (.0185)	.0487 (.0321)	.0241 (.0348)
If School-age Children Only†	-.0191 (.0140)	-.0211 (.0217)	.0965** (.0240)	-.0323 (.0256)
Whether Single	.0638** (.0175)	.0899** (.0206)	-.0199 (.0330)	-.0965** (.0324)
Whether South	.0043 (.0098)	.0401** (.0146)	-.0102 (.0224)	-.0530* (.0229)
City Size (in hundred thousands)	.0020* (.0010)	.0050** (.0017)	-.0016 (.0023)	-.0035 (.0026)
Constant	.0677	-.1074	.0485	.0732
Number of Observations	2,250	895	1,326	741
$\overline{Y}$	.042	.041	.138	.084
$\overline{R}^2$	.0115	.0620	.0213	.0285

* Significant at .01 level.

**Significant at .05 level.

†Variable has been back dated to conditions at time individual began working for present employer.

Table A4.1h

MEAN VALUE OF WHETHER JOBS AVAILABLE IF WILLING TO MOVE,
BY SEVERAL INDIVIDUAL CHARACTERISTICS
(Household Heads and Spouses, Unemployed or Thinking of Getting a Job)

	Unweighted Number of Observations	Weighted Percentage of Observations	Whether Limitations on Moving for Known Job Opportunities
All	1,315	100.0	.358
Race-Sex Group			
White Men	165	19.7	.388
Black Men	140	3.0	.234
White Women	553	66.5	.381
Black Women	457	10.9	.202
Eta Squared (adj)			.016**
Employment Status			
Unemployed	421	25.7	.494
Retired	41	5.1	.388
Permanently Disabled	41	2.6	.363
Housewife	678	55.1	.472
Student	125	10.9	.502
Other	9	0.6	.202
Eta Squared (adj)			.028**
Age			
Under 25	477	26.3	.405
25-34	400	31.9	.404
35-44	203	17.7	.293
45-54	153	15.3	.333
55-64	61	5.9	.270
65 or Older	21	2.9	.150
Eta Squared (adj)			.017**
Marital Status			
Married, Spouse Working	698	59.7	.375
Married, Spouse Not Working	202	15.2	.331
Single	174	10.2	.407
Widowed	49	3.5	.135
Divorced	85	6.6	.431
Separated	107	4.9	.198
Eta Squared (adj)			.017**
Number of Children in Family Unit			
0	414	36.8	.384
1	306	19.9	.359
2	284	23.7	.367
3	155	11.3	.353
4	82	5.0	.222
5	35	2.1	.160
6 or More	39	1.2	.360
Eta Squared (adj)			.009**
Age of Youngest Child in Family Unit			
No Children	414	36.8	.384
Under 2	264	15.2	.410
2-5 Years	365	26.6	.338
6-13 Years	214	15.5	.319
14-17 Years	58	5.9	.262
Eta Squared (adj)			.007**

**Significant at .01 level.

Table A4.1i

REGRESSION ON WHETHER VOLUNTARILY WORKING PART-TIME
(Working Household Heads and Spouses Aged 18-64)

Independent Variable	White Men	Black Men	White Women	Black Women
Education (in years)	.0006 (.0007)	-.0007 (.0009)	.032 (.0039)	.0012 (.0047)
Years of Work Experience Before Present Employer	-.0000 (.0003)	-.0003 (.0003)	-.0004 (.0013)	.0002 (.0013)
Years with Current Employer Prior to Current Position	-.0005 (.0003)	-.0004 (.0005)	-.0039 (.0021)	.0176** (.0019)
Years in Current Position	-.0000 (.0007)	-.0006 (.0010)	.0035 (.0035)	.0008 (.0040)
Number of Preschool Children	-.0015 (.0038)	-.0036 (.0042)	.0155 (.0218)	-.0137 (.0165)
Number of School-aged Children	-.0001 (.0018)	.0008 (.0021)	.0370** (.0096)	.0044 (.0079)
If Married, Spouse Working	-.0387** (.0097)	-.0265** (.0101)	.0783** (.0373)	-.0975 (.0408)
If Married, Spouse Not Working	-.0412** (.0097)	-.0285** (.0101)	.0648 (.0463)	-.0727 (.0544)
If Separated, Divorced, Widowed	-.0466** (.0119)	-.0280** (.0101)	.0118 (.0377)	-.0728** (.0354)
If Someone Other than Head Requires Extra Care	.0127 (.0112)	-.0009 (.0099)	-.0311 (.0661)	-.0085 (.0415)
Other Family Income/Family Needs	.0040 (.0023)	-.0021 (.0049)	.0239** (.0059)	.0356* (.0141)
If Plan to Quit Work	.0334** (.0116)	.0044 (.0157)	-.0253 (.0332)	-.1214** (.0392)
Whether South	.0016 (.0049)	-.0110 (.0058)	-.0540* (.0226)	-.0011 (.0231)
City Size (in hundred thousand)	.0002 (.0005)	-.0013 (.0007)	.0013 (.0024)	.0055* (.0025)
Constant	.0369	.0590	-.0116	.0352
Number of Observations	2,250	895	1,326	741
$\bar{Y}$	.010	.006	.148	.090
$\bar{R}^2$	.0134	.0142	.0566	.1501

* Significant at .05 level.

**Significant at .01 level.

Chapter 5

ABSENTEEISM FROM WORK

Richard D. Coe

Introduction

The belief that employers reward dependable, reliable employees is virtually axiomatic in our society. Individuals who are frequently absent from work are considered to be more susceptible to being fired, more likely to be passed over for promotions, and less likely to receive merit wage increases. In the context of economic theory, dependability is one indicator of productivity, and less dependable workers suffer a penalty in the form of lower wages for their relative unproductiveness.

The importance of absenteeism emerges most clearly when one considers the question of wage differentials between men and women and, to a lesser degree, between blacks and whites. It is well documented that in the United States men earn considerably higher wages than women, on the average, and that whites receive higher wages than blacks, again on the average. Some observers consider these differences as evidence of sexual and racial discrimination operating in our society, or, more radically, as inherent in our capitalistic economy. Other commentators tend to view these wage differentials as reflections of differing productivity among individual workers which, although lamentable, are justifiable, at least from the perspective of the employer. Part of this differing productivity can be traced to differences in absenteeism. Women, it is alleged, are more prone to miss work because of family responsibilities, most notably in order to care for their children. Black workers, because of their generally more deprived upbringing, may suffer from poorer health and consequently miss more days of work because of their own illness.

In this chapter we investigate absenteeism from work among the different racial and sexual subgroups of the population. We examine three distinct types of absenteeism—hours of work missed because of illness of someone else in the family, hours of work missed because of a person's own illness, and excess vacation hours taken (or not taken, as the case may be). The first section of this chapter discusses the interview questions which were used to measure these components of absenteeism. It is followed by descriptive tables of average hours of work missed for these three reasons by various family characteristics of the race/sex subgroups. Next, absenteeism because of family responsibilities is treated as a dependent variable, and regression analysis is used to isolate the factors which are associated most strongly with this occurrence. Finally, the separate components of absenteeism are treated as explanatory variables in a wage equation, to see if absenteeism is indeed penalized by lower wages. The results are then summarized.

THE SOURCE OF DATA ON ABSENTEEISM

The following sequence of questions was asked of all heads and wives who reported themselves working at the time of the interview (Spring 1976).

D38. Did you miss any work in 1975 because someone else in the family was sick?

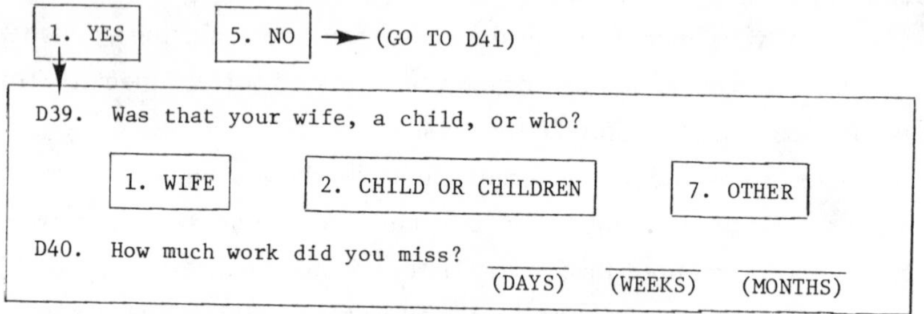

1. YES

5. NO → (GO TO D41)

D39. Was that your wife, a child, or who?

1. WIFE   2. CHILD OR CHILDREN   7. OTHER

D40. How much work did you miss? ______ (DAYS) ______ (WEEKS) ______ (MONTHS)

D41. Did you miss any work in 1975 because you were sick?

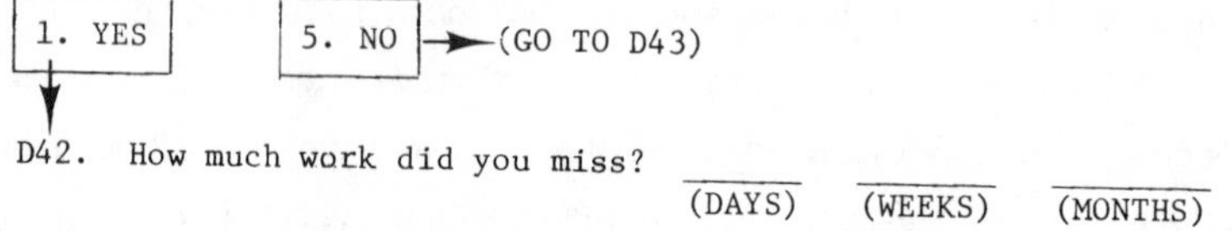

1. YES

5. NO → (GO TO D43)

D42. How much work did you miss? ______ (DAYS) ______ (WEEKS) ______ (MONTHS)

D43. How many weeks of paid vacation do you get each year? ______________ (WEEKS)

D44. Did you take any vacation or time off during 1975?

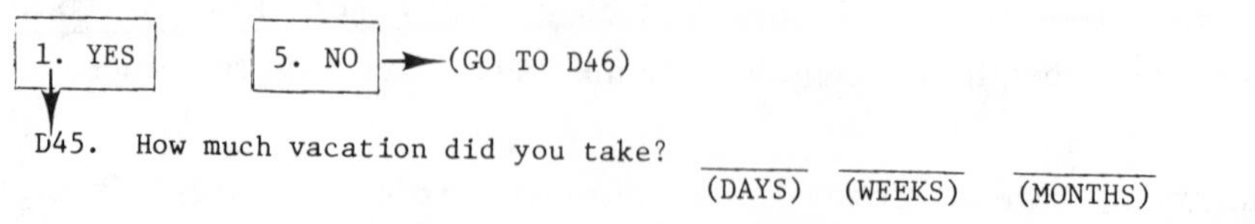

1. YES

5. NO → (GO TO D46)

D45. How much vacation did you take? ______ (DAYS) ______ (WEEKS) ______ (MONTHS)

To determine the number of hours missed because of illness of other family members, the number of days reported in D40 was multiplied by 8. (If the answer was in weeks, 40 hours was multiplied by the number of weeks missed. If the answer was in months, 152 hours, representing 40 hours multiplied by the 4-1/3 weeks assumed to be in a month, was multiplied by the number of months missed.) A similar procedure was used with D42 to determine hours missed because of own illness.

Excess vacation hours were defined as the difference between the number of hours of paid vacation and the number of hours of vacation taken. The variable could have both positive and negative values, a negative value indicating that the individual did not take all the vacation time to which he was entitled. A week was assumed to contain 40 hours of work.

DESCRIPTIVE TABLES OF ABSENTEEISM

This section presents the highlights of the average hours of work missed for the different components of absenteeism, by selected family or individual characteristics.

Absenteeism Because of Family Responsibilities

Table 5.1[1] shows the proportion of the different race/sex subgroups who reported missing any work because of the illness of other family members and the family member whose illness caused it. Table 5.2 categorizes the proportion of workers with specific characteristics who missed work because of family responsibilities and the average hours of work missed in 1975. Several points emerge from these tables. First, absenteeism because of illness of other family members is not a pervasive phenomenon; only about 10 percent of the men and 23 percent of the women reported missing any work for this reason. The average hours of work missed for the entire sample was correspondingly low—8 hours a year. Those who did miss work because of family responsibilities, however, missed a substantial amount of work—an average of 54 hours a year for the entire sample.

Absenteeism for family responsibilities varied greatly across the race/sex subgroups. Women were much more prone than men to miss some work, and while there was no racial difference in the propensity to take off some time because of illness of others, blacks, on average, missed about twice as many hours as whites (controlling for sex). Across the entire sample of workers, women averaged three times as many hours missed as men, but this differential was lowered considerably when one looked only at those who missed some work.

There was a marked sexual difference with respect to whose illness caused the absenteeism, as seen in Table 5.1. Of the men who missed work, most did so to care for

[1]More complete tables are presented in the Appendix, together with a table showing the distribution of the sample by the characteristics of interest.

Table 5.1

PROPORTION OF SAMPLE WHO MISSED ANY WORK BECAUSE OF ILLNESS OF OTHER FAMILY MEMBERS AND FAMILY MEMBER WHO CAUSED SUCH ABSENTEEISM BY RACE/SEX SUBGROUPS

(All Working Household Heads and Spouses Aged 18-64)

	Entire Sample	White Men	Black Men	White Women	Black Women
Missed Work for Illness of Others					
Yes	14.8	10.2	9.1	21.8	24.9
No	85.2	89.8	90.9	78.2	75.1
Family Member Ill					
Spouse	4.4	5.3	5.5	2.9	2.4
Child	6.9	2.1	1.6	14.2	16.4
Other	3.3	2.4	2.0	4.6	6.0
Inap; Missed No Work	85.2	89.9	90.0	78.2	75.1
Not Ascertained; Don't Know	0.3+	0.4+	-- +	0.2+	-- +
Number of Observations	5,225	2,250	845	1,338	742

+Less than 25 observations

JOB 683221,648628

Table 5.2

MEAN HOURS MISSED AND WHETHER MISSED ANY WORK BECAUSE OF ILLNESS OF OTHERS, BY RACE/SEX SUBGROUPS, FOR SELECTED FAMILY CHARACTERISTICS, 1975

(Working Household Heads and Spouses Aged 18-64)

Family Characteristic	Entire Sample (N = 5225)		White Men (N = 2252)		Black Men (N = 895)		White Women (N = 1338)		Black Women (N = 742)	
	Whether Missed	Mean Hours Missed	Whether Missed	Mean Hours Missed	Whether Missed	Mean Hours Missed	Whether Missed	Mean Hours Missed	Whether Missed	Mean Hours Missed
All	.148	8.1	.102	4.0	.091	8.0	.218	12.3	.249	25.7
Whether Missed for Illness of Others										
Yes	1.00	54.0	1.00	39.2	1.00	88.0	1.00	56.6	1.00	103.2
No	0.0	0.0	0.0	0.0	0.0	0.0	0.0	0.0	0.00	0.0
Family Member										
Spouse	1.00	53.3	1.00	36.7	1.00	104.2	1.00	75.7	1.00	161.2
Child	1.00	52.7	1.00	31.7	1.00	45.6	1.00	52.7	1.00	87.4
Other	1.00	63.1	1.00	55.8	1.00	77.1	1.00	58.1	1.00	123.1
Inap; Missed no Work	0.00	0.0	0.00	0.0	0.00	0.0	0.00	0.0	0.00	0.0
Not Ascertained, Don't Know	1.00+	17.8+	1.00+	18.2+	--	--	1.00+	16.0+	1.00+	24.0+
Whether Someone Else Requires Extra Care										
Yes	.298	24.8	.254	12.7	.248	53.6	.363	26.4	.295	65.4
No	.141	7.5	.096	3.7	.077	3.9	.211	12.0	.245	23.1
Number of Children Aged 13 or Younger										
None	.089	5.3	.071	4.2	.032	2.3	.113	6.3	.140	12.4
One	.227	11.6	.140	4.5	.110	5.9	.372	21.4	.315	29.6
Two	.229	12.1	.150	3.9	.219	29.3	.389	23.1	.415	50.4
Three	.174	9.2	.062	2.2	.185	13.8	.451	20.7	.418	47.6
Four or More	.171	10.5	.135	3.3	.082	5.2	.616	50.4	.344	37.7
Marital Status										
Married	.155	8.2	.108	3.8	.116	10.6	.241	14.2	.320	35.0
Single	.048	1.5	.022	1.3	.035	1.8	.059	1.0	.155	5.0
Widowed	.175	19.5	.195	54.4	.029	5.7	.174	12.5	.178	15.8
Divorced	.190	10.1	.096	4.6	.000	0.0	.253	11.7	.139	22.0
Separated	.160	10.2	.120	3.0	.027	1.0	.232	15.3	.214	19.2

+Less than 25 Observations.

Job #683221, 648628

their wives, while women who missed work overwhelmingly did so to care for their children. For example, 54 percent of the white men who missed work did so to care for their wives, while only 21 percent stayed home to care for their children. Of the white women who were absent, however, 65 percent missed work to care for their children, and only 13 percent to care for their husbands. But those women who were absent to care for their husbands missed a lot of work—an average of 76 hours for white women and 161 hours for black women (Table 5.2).

As might be expected, single workers were generally less likely to miss work because of someone else's illness and averaged fewer hours missed. When compared to the widowed, divorced, or separated, marriage had a notably positive influence on absenteeism of black workers, but did not appear to be correlated with more absenteeism for white workers.

Finally, a word should be said concerning the effect of having someone else in the family who requires a lot of extra care for health reasons. This was not a widespread occurrence, as only about 4 percent of the white workers and 8 percent of the black workers were in this position. (See Appendix Table A5.1a.) Predictably, the presence of such a person in the household leads to a greater likelihood of missing work, and of missing more hours of work. The result was especially noticeable for men, and black men in particular. Black men who did not live with someone who required extra care averaged only about 4 hours of work missed annually because of someone else's illness. Black men who did have such a person in the household, however, averaged over 50 hours of work missed annually.

As shown in Appendix Table A5.1b, the likelihood of missing work and the average number of hours missed did not vary systematically according to family size, the age of the worker, family income, the worker's wage rate, or whether he/she was salaried.

Absenteeism Because of One's Own Illness

Missing work because of one's own illness was much more common than missing work because of someone else's illness. Forty-nine percent of the workers missed at least some work because they were ill, and the average amount missed for the entire sample in 1975 was 40 hours, or one week. Those workers who were absent because they were sick averaged 83 hours of work missed in 1975.

The variation across race/sex subgroups in the propensity to miss work and the number of hours missed because of one's own illness was not as pronounced as was absenteeism because of family responsibilities, as shown by Table 5.3. Female workers were slightly more likely to miss work than male workers—53 percent compared to 46 percent.

Table 5.3

MEAN HOURS MISSED AND WHETHER MISSED ANY WORK BECAUSE OF OWN ILLNESS, BY RACE/SEX SUBGROUPS, FOR SELECTED FAMILY CHARACTERISTICS, 1975

(All Working Household Heads and Spouses Aged 18-64)

Family Characteristic	White Men		Black Men		White Women		Black Women	
	Whether Missed	Mean Hours Missed	Whether Missed	Mean Hours Missed	Whether Missed	Mean Hours Missed	Whether Missed	Mean Hours Missed
All	.462	36.5	.468	50.4	.530	43.0	.517	58.0
Whether Missed for Own Illness								
Yes	1.00	79.0	1.00	107.5	1.00	81.1	1.00	112.2
No	0.0	0.0	0.00	0.0	0.00	0.0	0.00	0.0
Whether Missed for Illness of Others								
Yes	.644	39.5	.646	37.9	.684	42.6	.611	54.4
No	.441	36.1	.451	51.6	.487	43.1	.487	59.2
Whether Someone Else Requires Extra Care								
Yes	.514	45.2	.705	104.0	.531	93.3	.610	109.4
No	.460	36.2	.447	45.5	.529	40.4	.509	53.3
Number of Children Aged 13 or Younger								
None	.432	39.0	.441	47.7	.529	40.0	.503	59.2
One	.491	34.3	.543	57.5	.561	54.8	.565	33.2
Two	.515	32.5	.353	31.3	.503	34.0	.571	72.9
Three	.433	28.8	.540	42.4	.465	34.0	.395	100.4
Four or More	.504	58.0	.626	115.0	.416	160.3	.371	35.6
Marital Status								
Married	.451	35.9	.487	53.4	.508	41.0	.495	60.8
Single	.541	31.8	.577	48.1	.678	44.5	.502	39.1
Widowed	.604	69.7	.171	50.3	.365	43.4	.448	31.4
Divorced	.505	30.5	.246	31.3	.573	50.3	.556	83.1
Separated	.531	115.7	.240	35.5	.577	51.6	.671	62.0
Age								
18-24	.539	37.1	.443	44.0	.595	36.9	.566	59.8
25-34	.504	27.4	.464	34.7	.620	42.9	.563	53.8
35-44	.501	46.7	.490	58.8	.491	50.1	.593	44.4
45-54	.374	35.3	.502	50.3	.480	51.4	.386	85.5
55-64	.385	44.6	.417	84.8	.392	27.2	.427	37.3

JOB 681733,681743

There was no racial difference in the propensity to miss some work because of one's own illness; however, black workers missed more hours of work on the average. This is especially true when one looks only at those workers who missed some work: whites who missed some work missed an average of 80 hours while blacks missed 110 hours in 1975.

There is some indication that the propensity to miss work because of one's own illness is positively related to the needs of other members of the family. Both those workers who missed some work to care for other family members and those workers who were in a household where someone else required a lot of extra care were more likely to miss some work because of their own illness. Furthermore, the presence of someone else in the family who required extra care had a substantial positive effect on the average number of hours missed for one's illness—at least twice as many hours missed for all race/sex subgroups except white men. (This hours effect did not hold for those workers who missed work because of the illness of some other family member.)

None of the other characteristics studied appeared to have any noticeable effect on absenteeism because of own illness. A possible exception was the presence of a large number (four or more) of younger children in the household, which resulted in a substantially higher average number of hours missed for all the race/sex subgroups except black women. The fact that the age of the worker had no effect on absenteeism because of one's own illness is somewhat surprising since it might be expected that older workers would be more prone to illness. Such does not appear to be the case.[2]

Excess Vacation Hours

Excess vacation hours were defined as the difference between paid vacation hours and the number of vacation hours taken. From this definition it is apparent that this variable measures two distinct aspects of the individual worker: his taste for vacation (perhaps indicating his degree of work commitment), and the amount of paid vacation his job grants. Thus, this variable measures a combination of a worker's individual attributes and characteristics of his job.[3]

Table 5.4 presents the average amount of paid vacation hours, of vacation hours actually taken, and excess vacation hours for the entire sample of the race/sex subgroups, as well as the average amounts of these variables by occupation. As the first row shows, women take more excess vacation time, on the average, than men. White women workers

[2] This fact may be a result of frequently ill older workers dropping out of the labor force.

[3] It should be noted that this variable makes no allowance for accumulated vacation time. Thus, excess vacation hours may be overstated for some individuals.

average 55 hours per year; black women workers average 34 hours per year. White men, on the other hand, average only 13 hours per year, while black men had the lowest average of all, 1.2 hours annually. These figures also indicate a racial difference in excess vacation hours: blacks, on the average, take fewer excess vacation hours than whites. Despite these sex and race differences, the distribution of mean excess vacation hours does not appear to vary systematically with any of the individual and family characteristic variables which were examined in the context of absenteeism because of family responsibilities and absenteeism because of one's own illness. (See Appendix Table A5.1d for the distributions.)

As can be seen from Table 5.4, the occupational distribution of the race/sex subgroups accounts for part of the differences in excess vacation time taken. To begin with, women are more likely to be school teachers than men, an occupation which has considerable unpaid vacation time in the form of summer vacations.[4] (Incidentally, school teachers also have considerably more paid vacation time than other occupations.) Women are also more heavily concentrated in clerical, sales, laborer, or service jobs which have lower amounts of paid vacation time, especially laborer and service jobs. (Black men are also concentrated more heavily in laborer and service jobs than their white counterparts.) These two occupations account for a substantial part of the excess vacation time of women workers, particularly white women.

But even when the disproportionate effect of school teachers is controlled, the conclusion remains that women take more excess vacation time than men. And blacks take less excess vacation time than whites. Women received fewer paid vacation hours than men, on the average, but they take more actual vacation time. These two factors combine to give women substantially higher excess vacation time than men. Black men have considerably less paid vacation time than white men, while black and white women have virtually the same average amount of paid vacation time. But black men and women both take less vacation time than white men and women (about 16 hours less per year, when school teachers are not counted), and thus have lower excess vacation time.

---

[4]Teachers often have the option of spreading their pay for the school year (usually nine months) over the full year. There is no *a priori* way of knowing how these individuals would respond to the question of how much paid vacation they get. Judging from the results presented in Table 5.4, it would seem that many teachers consider summer vacation as unpaid vacation time. This is not conclusive, however, since it is not known how many teachers who reported substantial excess vacation hours were actually paid over a full year. This same ambiguity may also partly explain why teachers have large amounts of paid vacation time.

Table

VACATION HOURS BY OCCUPATION
(All Working Household Heads

Occupation	White Men (N = 2250)				Black Men (N = 895)			
	Weighted Percentage of Observations	Paid Vacation Hours	Vacation Hours Taken	Excess Vacation Hours	Weighted Percentage of Observations	Paid Vacation Hours	Vacation Hours Taken	Excess Vacation Hours
All	100.0	90.1	102.8	12.7	100.0	78.4	79.6	1.2
(All Nonteachers)	(97.5)	(88.5)	(94.0)	(5.5)	(99.0)	(78.1)	(78.1)	(0.0)
Professional, Technical	17.6	114.1	176.3	62.2	5.2	104.8	166.4	61.6
(Teachers, Primary & Secondary)	(2.5)	(152.7)	(450.2)	(297.5)	(1.0)+	(105.3)	(229.4)	(124.1)
Managers, Officials, and Proprietors, Not Self-Employed	15.8	110.3	103.7	-6.6	5.0	88.9	80.9	-8.0
Self-Employed	4.5	30.9	87.6	56.7	0.5+	11.1	37.8	26.7
Clerical, Sales	11.0	88.2	85.9	-2.3	17.0	93.8	103.4	9.7
Craftsmen, Foremen	25.9	88.4	91.6	3.2	18.0	75.0	67.2	-7.8
Operatives	15.2	90.8	79.3	-11.5	25.9	81.0	75.1	-5.9
Laborers, Service Workers	6.8	69.0	71.5	2.4	28.0	63.6	62.4	-1.2
Farmers, Managers	3.3	6.6	41.0	34.4	0.3+	40.0	29.5	-10.5
Not Ascertained, Don't Know	0.1+	53.6	218.7	165.1	0.2+	80.0	40.0	-40.0

+Less than 25 Observations.

5.4

FOR THE RACE/SEX SUBGROUPS, 1975

and Spouses Aged 18-64)

White Women (N = 1338)				Black Women (N = 742)			
Weighted Percentage of Obser-vations	Paid Vacation Hours	Vacation Hours Taken	Excess Vacation Hours	Weighted Percentage of Obser-vations	Paid Vacation Hours	Vacation Hours Taken	Excess Vacation Hours
100.0	82.1	137.5	55.4	100.0	77.0	110.8	33.7
(91.6)	(70.1)	(107.6)	(37.5)	(93.6)	(71.6)	(91.5)	(20.0)
20.1	149.9	284.4	134.5	11.6	127.2	308.8	181.5
(8.4)	(212.2)	(461.5)	(249.3)	(6.4)	(150.5)	(385.6)	(235.2)
6.0	88.7	94.8	6.1	3.7	96.0	108.7	12.7
1.2+	3.4	59.4	56.0	0.0+	0.0	0.0	0.0
40.2	71.0	101.2	30.2	25.9	88.2	105.8	17.5
1.5+	105.5	103.5	-1.9	1.3	45.3	52.3	6.9
13.2	67.1	84.1	17.1	16.9	58.9	50.4	-8.6
17.7	42.2	115.8	73.6	40.6	62.3	84.8	22.5
0.0+	0.0	40.0	40.0	--	--	--	--
0.1+	156.9	132.3	-24.6	0.1+	13.3	46.7	33.3

ABSENTEEISM BECAUSE OF OTHER FAMILY MEMBERS

The results presented in the previous section showed that absenteeism because of family responsibilities varied greatly across the race/sex subgroups of workers. In this section we use regression analysis to determine what factors account for these differentials. The analysis used two alternative dependent variables: whether the individual missed any work because of the illness of other family members, and the hours of work missed for this reason. The following independent variables were used:

1. Number of children in household aged 1 to 2.

2. Number of children in household aged 3 to 5.

3. Number of children in household aged 6 to 13.

4. Number of children in household aged 14 to 17.

5. Number of other nonworking adults. If the taxable income of other family members besides the head and wife was at least $2,000, then the number of other labor income receivers was subtracted from the number of adults in the household (excluding head and wife) to arrive at this variable. If the taxable income of other family members was less than $2,000, then this variable equalled the number of adults in the household, excluding head and wife. These individuals may be available as substitute caretakers, or they may result in an additional person to care for if ill.

6. Number of other working adults. If the taxable income of other family members was $2,000 or more, this variable equalled the number of other labor income receivers; otherwise, this variable equalled zero.

7. If someone else in the household besides the spouse required a lot of extra care. This dichotomous variable was coded 1 if the head reported that someone else in the household (not including a spouse) required a lot of extra care.

8. A working spouse present, earning at least $1 an hour more than the individual. This variable measures, in combination with the other dummy variables listed below, whether the worker was married, whether his/her spouse was working, and the wage differential between the spouses if both worked. The variable was coded 1 if the worker was married to a spouse who worked at least 500 hours in 1975 and whose wage rate was at least $1 an hour greater than the individual's wage rate. The wage differential provides a measure of the opportunity cost of one spouse staying home as compared to the other. The omitted group from this series of dummy variables are those workers without a spouse.

9. A working spouse present, earning within $1 an hour of the individual. This variable was coded 1 if the worker was married to a spouse who worked at least 500 hours in 1975. In addition, the difference in the wage rate between the spouses had to be less than $1 an hour.

10. A working spouse present, earning at most $1 an hour <u>less</u> than the individual.

This variable was coded 1 if the worker was married to a spouse who worked at least 500 hours in 1975 and the spouse's wage rate was at most $1 an hour less than the individual's wage rate.

11. Nonworking spouse present, who was not disabled. This variable was coded 1 if the worker was married to a spouse who worked less than 500 hours in 1975. In addition, the spouse did not require a lot of extra care or did not report a disability which severely limited his/her ability to work.

12. Nonworking spouse present, who was disabled. This variable was coded 1 if the worker was married to a spouse who worked less than 500 hours in 1975 and who either required a lot of extra care or reported a disability which severely limited his/her ability to work.

13. If could have worked less if wanted to. This dichotomous variable was coded 1 if answered "yes" to question "Could you have worked less if you had wanted to?" A measure of job flexibility.

14. Family money income.

The results of the regression analysis are presented in Table 5.5 and provide some insight into the source of the racial and sexual variations in absenteeism because of family responsibilities. The major source of the differential absenteeism between white men and white women shows up quite clearly as resulting from the presence of children under the age of 14 in the household. White men are virtually unaffected by the presence of children in the household; white women, on the other hand, show a marked increase in absenteeism resulting from the presence of young children. The effect of very young children (under the age of three) is especially pronounced on the number of hours missed by white women. The presence of a disabled spouse also has a more adverse effect on white women than white men, although both are significantly affected. The presence of such a person results in an average increase of 25 hours of missed work a year for white women, but only nine hours a year for white men (compared to no spouse being present in the household).

The source of the sexual differences in absenteeism because of family responsibilities between black men and women is more difficult to pinpoint. Surprisingly, the number of children younger than age three has a strong positive effect on the absenteeism of black men, but no significant effect on the hours of work missed by black women. The opposite result holds with respect to the number of children between the ages of six and 13. The presence of a disabled spouse in the household (as compared to not having a spouse) has a roughly similar effect on the absenteeism of black men and black women. (In the hours missed equation, the coefficient on this variable for black women is 16 hours higher than for black men—a difference exactly equal to the difference between white

Table 5.5

REGRESSION RESULTS FOR WHETHER MISSED WORK AND HOURS OF WORK MISSED FOR ILLNESS OF OTHER FAMILY MEMBERS, BY RACE/SEX SUBGROUPS

(All Working Household Heads and Spouses Aged 18-64)

	White Men (N=2250)		Black Men (N =895)		White Women (N =1338)		Black Women (N=742)	
Independent Variable	Whether Missed	Hours Missed	Whether Missed	Hours Missed	Whether Missed	Hours Missed	Whether Missed	Hours Missed
Constant	.061	5.5	.015	-1.1	.126	9.6	.145	18.3
Number of Children Aged 1-2	.098** (.016)	1.6 (1.1)	.099** (.024)	20.4** (3.6)	.223** (.038)	30.9** (5.6)	.112** (0.42)	3.6 (7.2)
Number of Children Aged 3-5	.013 (.015)	-0.7 (1.0)	.044* (0.20)	-7.0* (3.1)	.234** (.034)	8.5+ (5.0)	.088* (.035)	-7.2 (6.0)
Number of Children Aged 6-13	-.001 (.007)	-0.3 (0.5)	.008 (.010)	0.6 (1.6)	.109** (.015)	4.0+ (2.1)	.102** (.018)	13.3** (3.1)
Number of Children Aged 14-17	-.001 (.011)	-0.4 (0.7)	-.018 (.015)	2.1 (2.3)	-.029 (.018)	-2.3 (2.7)	-.071** (.023)	0.2 (3.9)
Number of Other Non-working Adults	-.019 (.018)	-0.8 (1.2)	.034+ (.018)	13.6** (2.8)	-.016 (.033)	-3.7 (4.8)	-.006 (.027)	-6.7 (4.6)
Number of Other Working Adults	-.004 (.010)	-0.7 (0.7)	-.024+ (.014)	-1.6 (2.1)	.013 (.017)	1.0 (2.5)	-.020 (.033)	1.6 (5.6)
If Someone Else Required Extra Care, Excluding Spouse	.112** (.041)	5.9* (2.8)	-.010 (.039)	30.1** (5.9)	.203** (.076)	16.6 (11.2)	-.045 (.066)	31.5** (11.4)
Working Spouse, Earning At Least $1/Hour More	-.019 (.035)	-3.4 (2.3)	.283** (.052)	81.1** (8.0)	.009 (.030)	8.2+ (4.4)	.102* (.049)	8.6 (8.4)

Table 5.5 (continued)

Independent Variable	White Men (N=2250) Whether Missed	White Men (N=2250) Hours Missed	Black Men (N=895) Whether Missed	Black Men (N=895) Hours Missed	White Women (N=1338) Whether Missed	White Women (N=1338) Hours Missed	Black Women (N=742) Whether Missed	Black Women (N=742) Hours Missed
Working Spouse, Earning Within $1/Hour	.032 (.027)	-1.2 (1.8)	-.024 (.033)	-2.0 (5.1)	.017 (.034)	2.6 (5.0)	.133** (.049)	23.1** (8.3)
Working Spouse, Earning At Most $1/Hour Less	.025 (.023)	-2.4 (1.6)	.007 (.030)	-7.7+ (4.6)	.084* (.043)	0.1 (6.3)	.256** (.077)	117.1** (13.3)
Nonworking Spouse, Not Disabled	.018 (.022)	-1.8 (1.5)	.033 (.029)	-5.8 (4.4)	-.095 (.067)	-4.8 (9.8)	.151 (.097)	18.9 (16.7)
Nonworking Spouse, Disabled	.163** (.047)	9.2** (3.1)	.431** (.064)	31.6** (9.8)	.167* (.080)	25.5* (11.8)	.315* (.161)	47.9+ (27.6)
Could Have Worked Less If Wanted To	.008 (.014)	0.4 (0.9)	.049* (.023)	13.7** (3.5)	-.064* (.025)	-7.2+ (3.7)	-.154** (.042)	-15.4* (7.1)
Family Money Income (Hundreds of Dollars)	.0000 (.0001)	.001 (.004)	.0001 (.0001)	-.0023 (.022)	.0001 (.0001)	-.02 (.02)	.0001 (.0003)	-.082+ (.050)
$\bar{R}^2$ (Adjusted)	.023	.006	.137	.264	.116	.034	.104	.147

**Significant at .01 level.
* Significant at .05 level.
+ Significant at .10 level.

men and white women. However, this higher coefficient is not quite significant at the .05 level for black women, while the lower coefficient for black men is significant at the .01 level.) Thus, the two major sources of the inequality in absenteeism between white men and women do not hold for black men and women. It would seem that the equation is not capturing a major source (or sources) of the sexual differences between blacks, as evidenced by the large difference in the constant terms, particularly in the hours missed equation. (Black women have a constant term of 18.3 hours; for black men the corresponding figure is -1.1 hours.) It also appears that the hours missed by black women are adversely affected by the presence of a working husband.[5] It might be expected that the presence of a working husband means that the working wife is more likely to stay home to care for other family members, especially children. But the results for the number-of-children variables cast some doubt on this explanation. However, when one recalls from Table 5.1 that black women who missed work to care for their husbands missed an exceptionally large amount of work on the average, it would seem that the most likely source of increased absenteeism among black women married to a working husband is the responsibility of caring for a frequently-ill-but-not-disabled husband.[6] The working white wife does not seem to face a similar burden.

These results also point to the source of the racial differences in absenteeism because of family responsibilities. A comparison of the results for white and black men indicates that white men simply do not have much responsibility to care for other family members, clearly not as much as black men. The absenteeism of black men, as compared to white men, is much more adversely affected by the presence of very young children, other nonworking adults, and someone who requires a lot of extra care, whether or not it be a spouse. The major source of the different amounts of absenteeism between black and white women workers appears to stem from the fact mentioned above, that black female

---

[5]Somewhat surprisingly, the effect of a working husband is most pronounced if the husband earns less than the wife. In addition, if the wife earns at least $1 an hour more than the husband, the effect is to sharply increase the hours missed of the husband.

[6]Further investigation into this issue yielded the following information. Thirty-three black working women missed 100 hours or more of work in 1975 to care for another member of the household. All were married. In 26 of these cases, the husband worked more than 500 hours in 1975. In these 26 cases six wives missed work to care for the husband, 15 for a child, and five for some other family member. Although the majority of these cases involved caring for a child, the percentage (unweighted) who missed to care for a husband was greater than the percentage (weighted) in the sample as a whole (see Table 5.1). In the multivariate analysis, the effect of children was controlled, and thus the implication remains that the presence of a frequently ill working husband has a significantly positive effect on the absenteeism of black women resulting from illness of other family members.

workers who are married to a working husband miss a substantial amount of work, probably to care for him. The absenteeism of white female workers is unaffected by marriage unless the husband is disabled.

ABSENTEEISM AND WAGE DIFFERENTIALS

Calculated Wage Rate

There are some marked differences across the race/sex subgroups of the sample in the amount of absenteeism from work, particularly in the absenteeism due to illness of other family members. The evidence presented so far supports the view that women are indeed more likely to be absent from work because of family responsibilities. The crucial question now is whether such absenteeism is translated into a wage penalty, and whether this may account for some of the observed differentials in wage rates across the race/sex subgroups.

In order to answer this question, the three components of absenteeism—hours of work missed because of illness of other family members, hours missed because of one's own illness, and excess vacation hours taken—were entered into the basic wage equation presented in Chapter 1. Assuming that increased absenteeism implies less productivity, it was expected that all of these variables would have a negative effect on wage rates. These expectations were not totally confirmed, as shown by Table 5.6. (The complete regression results are presented in Appendix Table A5.1e.)

In general, adding the absenteeism measures to the basic wage equation explained little of the individual wage differentials, as virtually all of the variables were statistically insignificant. For white men and black women, all of the components of absenteeism had a non-negative effect on wage rates, but all were insignificant except for hours missed by white men for their own illness, which was significantly positive at the .05 level. The wage rates of white women were negatively affected by all of the measures of absenteeism, but only hours missed because of their own illness had a statistically significant effect. None of the absenteeism measures had a statistically significant effect on the wage rates of black men.

The only firm conclusion that can be drawn from these results is that missing work because of family responsibilities does <u>not</u> result in lower wage rates. Although women were more likely to be absent from work because of family responsibilities, those women who missed work for this reason did not receive lower wages as a result. Thus no support is found for the belief that part of the wage differential between men and women can be explained or justified on the basis of differing individual productivity resulting from differences in family responsibilities. This does not eliminate the possibility that employ-

Table 5.6

ABSENTEEISM AND CALCULATED WAGE RATES

(All Working Household Heads and Spouses Aged 18-64)

	Dependent Variable: ℓn Calculated Wage Rate			
Independent Variable	White Men (N=2250)	Black Men (N=895)	White Women (N=1338)	Black Women (N=741)
Hours Missed for Illness of Other Family Members	.0006 (.0005)	-.0003 (.0003)	-.0001 (.0002)	.0003 (.0002)
Hours Missed for Own Illness	.0002* (.0001)	.0001 (.0001)	-.0002* (.0001)	.0000 (.0001)
Excess Vacation Hours	.0000 (.0001)	-.0003 (.0002)	-.0001 (.0001)	.0001 (.0001)
$\bar{R}^2$	.302	.293	.329	.360

* Significant at .05 Level.
**Significant at .01 Level.

Note: Other variables in the regression equations included: formal education, years out of labor force since completing school, years of work experience before present employer, pre-employer work experience squared, years with current employer prior to current position, years of training completed on current job, years of post-training tenure on current job, proportion of total working years that were full time, whether placed limits on job hours or locations, knows there are better jobs elsewhere, doesn't know whether there are better jobs elsewhere, plans to stop work for nontraining reasons, size of largest city in the area, whether south.

For the complete regression results, see Appendix Table A5.1e.

ers discriminate across the board on this basis, applying a stereo-type of frequently absent women to their hiring or promotional decisions, thus relegating women as a group to lower paying jobs. Such a policy should be recognized for what it is: discrimination *per se* on the basis of sex, with no productivity-grounded justification on the individual level.

The results do show that white women are penalized for being absent because of their own illness. The fact that white women miss more work than white men for this reason, however, accounts for only a very small fraction of the wage differential between these groups. White women stay home on average 6.5 hours a year more than white men because they are sick. At a wage penalty of .02 of 1 percent per hour missed, this amounts to a total wage penalty of .13 percent, or .3 percent of the average differential in wage rates between white men and white women. Moreover, white men are *not* penalized for such absenteeism,[7] and thus the wage penalty imposed on white women, while arguably related to productivity differences, still results in women being inordinately penalized for missing work.

Reported Wage Rate

The wage rate measure used in the previous section was calculated by dividing the individual's income from labor earnings by the actual number of hours worked during the year. In determining these hours of work, hours spent on vacation, hours missed because of one's own illness, hours missed because of illness of others, and hours missed because of strikes or temporary layoffs were all subtracted to arrive at the actual number of hours worked. There is, thus, some possibility that entering the three absenteeism measures into the regression of this calculated wage rate may result in a positive bias in the coefficient, even if the true effect is neutral.[8] Similarly, a small negative effect of absenteeism might be neutralized by the definitional interrelatedness of the variables, and could partially account for the results reported in the previous section.

In an attempt to control somewhat for this potential problem, the identical regression used in the previous section was run using the reported wage of the individual as the dependent variable. Respondents were asked their salary or their hourly wage for their regular work time. If they were neither salaried nor paid by the hour, they were asked how much they would have earned had they worked an extra hour. The answers to these

[7]The significantly *positive* coefficient on this variable for white men is probably caused in part by the method by which the wage rate variable was constructed. More will be said on this point in the section below on reported wage rates.

[8]Indeed, in results not reported here, total vacation hours taken (rather than excess vacation hours) had a consistently positive and significant effect on wage rates.

questions formed the reported wage rate variable. Two points should be noted concerning this measure. First, it is not dated exactly with the response for the absenteeism variables. The expected wage was asked of the respondents' current job, at the time of interview (Spring 1976). The absenteeism variables were asked concerning the year 1975. Some job change may have occurred in the interim. Second, the reported wage was only coded up to $9.98 per hour. For the results presented below, individuals who were coded $9.98 for reported wage were assigned their calculated wage rate—the wage rate used in the previous section.[9] Thus, any differences in results between the two dependent variables can be attributed to those individuals whose reported wage was less than $9.98 per hour.

Table 5.7 presents the results. (For the complete results, see Appendix Table A5.1f.) As was expected, use of the reported wage rate rather than the calculated wage rate resulted in more negative coefficients for virtually all the absenteeism variables, across all race/sex subgroups. Two differences from the results for the calculated wage rate are worthy of note. The negative effect of excess vacation hours is particularly pronounced with all groups but black women suffering a statistically significant wage penalty. Furthermore, black and white men have identical coefficients, which are greater (absolutely) than those of women. The explanation for this change is not clear. Perhaps at lower paying jobs the commitment of the worker toward his job is crucial, regardless of race. Or perhaps lower paying jobs are less likely to have paid vacations, thus <u>any</u> vacation taken would be excess vacation as defined here.

The other major change concerns the wage rates of black men. When reported wage rates are used as the dependent variable, black men show a penalty for absenteeism because of family responsibilities. They are the only group which shows a significant effect for this variable. These results provide some support for the hypothesis that black men who have family responsibilities which frequently cause them to miss work are relegated to lower paying jobs. When these missed hours are accounted for in calculating effective wage rates, this penalty disappears. But this still may have a negative effect on the labor <u>income</u> of black men.

Interactions between Absenteeism and Tenure

It is tempting to explain the general lack of wage penalties for absenteeism by arguing that employers do not know what the absenteeism record of a prospective

[9]The percentages of the different race/sex subgroups who had reported wages in excess of $9.97 per hour, and thus were assigned their calculated wage rate for this analysis, were as follows: white men, 23.7 percent; black men, 5.5 percent; white women, 6.0 percent; black women, 6.2 percent.

Table 5.7

ABSENTEEISM AND REPORTED WAGE RATES

(All Working Household Heads and Spouses Aged 18-64)

	Dependent Variable: ℓn Reported Wage Rate			
Independent Variable	White Men (N=2250)	Black Men (N=895)	White Women (N=1338)	Black Women (N=741)
Hours Missed for Illness of Other Family Members	.0001 (.0008)	-.0029** (.0004)	-.0001 (.0002)	.0001 (.0002)
Hours Missed for Own Illness	-.0001 (.0001)	.0001 (.0001)	-.0003** (.0001)	-.0000 (.0001)
Excess Vacation Hours	-.0006** (.0001)	-.0006** (.0002)	-.0002* (.0001)	-.0002 (.0001)
$\bar{R}^2$	.164	.234	.234	.354

* Significant at .05 Level.
**Significant at .01 Level.

Note: Other variables in the regression equations included: formal education, years out of labor force since completing school, years of work experience before present employer, pre-employer work experience squared, years with current employer prior to current position, years of training completed on current job, years of post-training tenure on current job, proportion of total working years that were full time, whether placed limits on job hours or locations, knows there are better jobs elsewhere, doesn't know whether there are better jobs elsewhere, plans to stop work for nontraining reasons, size of largest city in the area, whether south.

For the complete regression results, see Appendix Table A5.1f.

employee is likely to be. In the absence of individual information, the employer resorts to the average behavior of groups and thus prefers to hire men, especially white men, because, as a group, their rates of absenteeism are less. If this were true, then there would be no individual wage penalties for absenteeism, but the wages of women as a group would be lower because of their higher absenteeism. While this argument might be plausible for employees who have just been hired, it does not hold for longer-term employees. Absenteeism is simple and inexpensive to monitor; if it has a substantial effect on productivity, then cost-conscious employers should use it as a criterion for decisions about pay and promotions. This suggests that wage penalties for absenteeism should depend on employee tenure. In the context of the regression analysis of the wage-absenteeism relationship, it means that an absenteeism-tenure interaction variable should have a negative (and significant) coefficient.[10]

To test for such interactions, we added two new variables to the regression equations reported in Tables 5.6 and 5.7: "Hours missed because of illness of other family members times years with present employer" and "Hours missed because of own illness times years with present employer." The coefficients on these two new variables as well as the coefficients on the two absenteeism variables are shown in Table 5.8.[11] Of the 16 coefficients on the interaction variables, five are statistically significant at the 5 percent level, but two of these five are positive rather than negative. Of the remaining three coefficients, only one—for black women—is significant at the 1 percent level. There is no evidence of a negative absenteeism-tenure interaction for either white women or black men. In sum, with the possible exception of black women, it does not appear that employers consistently penalize tenured employees who missed substantial amounts of work time because of either their own illness or the illness of other family members.

Summary

The purpose of this chapter was to investigate the question of whether frequent absenteeism from work resulted in wage penalties for individual workers. Particular attention was devoted to absenteeism because of family responsibilities, which is widely thought to be a source of lower wages for working women. Although absenteeism because of family responsibilities was not a widespread phenomenon, it was found that women were indeed more prone to be absent for this reason, averaging three times as many hours

---

[10]This assumes that those with higher rates of absenteeism in 1975 were also likely to have higher rates of absenteeism in previous years as well.

[11]The excess vacation hours variable was dropped from these runs.

Table 5.8

THE EFFECTS OF AN ABSENTEEISM-TENURE INTERACTION ON WAGE RATES
(All Working Household Heads and Spouses Aged 18-64)

Independent Variable	White Men	Black Men	White Women	Black Women
	Dependent Variable: ℓn Calculated Wage Rate			
Hours Missed for Illness of Other Family Members Times Employer Tenure	-.00010* (.00049)	.00001 (.00010)	.00000 (.00004)	-.00007** (.00002)
Hours Missed for Own Illness Times Employer Tenure	.00001 (.00001)	-.00002 (.00002)	-.00000 (.00002)	-.00000 (.00002)
Hours Missed for Illness of Other Family Members	.00215* (.00090)	-.00037 (.00037)	-.00017 (.00048)	.00092** (.00030)
Hours Missed for Own Illness	.00008 (.00013)	.00025 (.00017)	-.00021 (.00014)	.00009 (.00016)
	Dependent Variable: ℓn Reported Wage Rate			
Hours Missed for Illness of Other Family Members Times Employer Tenure	-.00004 (.00007)	.00059** (.00011)	-.00001 (.00004)	-.00005* (.00002)
Hours Missed for Own Illness Times Employer Tenure	.00002 (.00002)	.00003 (.00002)	.00004* (.00002)	-.00003 (.00002)
Hours Missed for Illness of Other Family Members	.00074 (.00132)	-.00410** (.00042)	.00009 (.00051)	.00053* (.00026)
Hours Missed for Own Illness	.00025 (.00020)	.00036 (.00020)	-.00050** (.00015)	.00018 (.00014)

* Significant at .05 Level.
**Significant at .01 Level.

Note: Other variables in the regression equations included: formal education, years out of labor force since completing school, years of work experience before present employer, pre-employer work experience squared, years with current employer prior to current position, years of training completed on current job, years of post-training tenure on current job, proportion of total working years that were full time, whether placed limits on job hours or locations, knows there are better jobs elsewhere, doesn't know whether there are better jobs elsewhere, plans to stop work for nontraining reasons, size of largest city in the area, whether south.

missed a year as men. The primary source of this absenteeism for white women is the responsibility of caring for younger children. For black women, on the other hand, caring for a frequently ill working husband appears to be the major source of increased absenteeism because of family responsibilities, a situation which white women do not seem to face to such a degree. But while women were more likely to miss work because of family responsibilities, this absenteeism did not translate into wages lower than the wages of women who were not absent and no evidence was discovered to support the view that a portion of the observed wage differentials between men and women can be accounted for by the fact that women are more often absent from work than men.

There were also some racial differences in the amount of absenteeism to care for other family members. Blacks averaged approximately twice as many hours missed as whites. Compared to their white counterparts, black men were much more responsible for the care of other members in the household; significant effects were found for the presence in the household of very young children, other nonworking adults, and someone who required a lot of extra care. In addition, black men were the only group for whom some evidence was found to indicate that they suffered a wage penalty for absenteeism—a significant negative effect on reported wage rates was discovered. This result, however, did not hold when our standard calculated wage rate was used. The differences in absenteeism because of family responsibilities between white and black women were more difficult to pinpoint, but apparently resulted from the responsibility of black working wives to care for their husbands.

The distribution of hours missed because of personal illness showed little variation across the race/sex subgroups. However, there was evidence indicating that white women are penalized in the form of lower wages for this type of absenteeism. A significant negative coefficient was found for this variable in the wage equation for white women. For the other race/sex subgroups, absenteeism because of the workers own illness had either an insignificant or positive effect on wages.

The distribution of the difference in vacation hours taken and paid vacation hours varied substantially across the race/sex subgroups, with whites and women taking more excess vacation time than blacks and men, on the average. The sex differences appeared to be based partly on the differences in the occupational distributions of the sexes, with women being more heavily concentrated in jobs with little or no paid vacation. The source of the racial inequality in excess vacation hours was not apparent and may be based on differences in taste for vacation, or work commitment. There was some evidence that this variable had a significantly negative effect on wage rates, but this negative effect was statistically significant only when we looked at reported wage rates rather than calculated wage rates.

Table A5.1a

NUMBER OF OBSERVATIONS AND WEIGHTED PERCENTAGE OF OBSERVATIONS, BY RACE/SEX SUBGROUPS, FOR SELECTED FAMILY CHARACTERISTICS, 1975

(Working Household Heads and Spouses Aged 18-64)

Family Characteristics	White Men		Black Men		White Women		Black Women	
	Number of Observations	Weighted Percentage of Observations	Number of Observations	Weighted Percentage of Observations	Number of Observations	Weighted Percentage of Observations	Number of Observations	Weighted Percentage of Observations
All	2,250	100.0%	895	100.0	1,338	100.0	742	100.0
Whether Missed for Own Illness								
Yes	1,069	46.2	388	46.8	720	53.0	358	51.7
No	1,181	53.8	507	53.2	618	47.0	384	48.3
Whether Missed for Illness of Others								
Yes	262	10.2	107	9.1	296	21.8	171	24.9
No	1,988	89.8	788	90.9	1,042	78.2	571	75.1
Whose Illness								
Spouse	146	5.3	55	5.5	40	2.9	26	2.4
Child	52	2.1	25	1.6	198	14.2	113	16.4
Other	54	2.4	27	2.0	56	4.6	31	6.0
Inap; Missed No Work	1,990	89.9	788	90.9	1,042	78.2	571	75.1
Not Ascertained, Don't Know	8	0.4	0	0.0	2	0.2	1	0.0
Whether Someone Else Requires Extra Care								
Yes	83	3.7	57	8.3	63	4.9	51	8.4
No	2,167	96.3	838	91.7	1,275	95.1	691	91.6
Number of Children Aged 13 or Younger								
None	1,049	49.8	339	50.2	798	62.1	289	51.9
One	537	21.1	237	21.9	299	21.3	192	21.7
Two	439	19.0	164	14.1	167	11.8	154	17.2
Three	168	7.6	86	8.8	61	4.2	71	6.6
Four or More	57	2.6	69	4.9	13	0.6	36	2.6
Marital Status								
Married	2,032	87.3	707	71.9	999	68.4	407	53.1
Single	119	6.8	95	15.2	121	11.3	107	13.9
Widowed	12	0.8	12	1.0	58	5.1	42	9.6
Divorced	67	4.1	29	2.5	131	12.5	97	13.2
Separated	20	1.0	52	9.4	29	2.6	89	10.1

Table A5.1a (continued)

Family Characteristics	White Men		Black Men		White Women		Black Women	
	Number of Observations	Weighted Percentage of Observations	Number of Observations	Weighted Percentage of Observations	Number of Observations	Weighted Percentage of Observations	Number of Observations	Weighted Percentage of Observations
Age								
18-24	364	11.6	205	15.3	291	16.1	148	15.5
25-34	811	31.6	289	31.4	426	29.2	230	25.9
35-44	416	20.8	171	23.3	240	19.9	161	26.0
45-54	440	23.7	136	18.6	234	20.9	140	23.1
55-64	219	12.2	94	11.4	147	13.8	63	9.5
Family Size								
One	187	10.9	156	25.0	194	18.4	93	18.1
Two	592	24.5	112	13.4	482	33.8	163	23.5
Three	509	20.5	188	17.4	267	19.3	159	22.5
Four	495	22.3	141	17.3	211	15.2	120	15.7
Five	268	12.3	107	12.3	103	7.9	89	9.4
Six	115	5.9	71	4.5	46	3.4	52	4.0
Seven or More	84	3.6	120	10.1	35	2.1	66	6.8
Family Income (1975)								
$ 4,999 or Less	73	3.1	105	8.9	77	6.5	92	9.2
$ 5,000 - 7,499	163	5.9	135	12.3	104	7.9	144	19.2
$ 7,500 - 9,999	205	6.9	158	13.8	134	9.2	146	16.4
$10,000 - 12,499	272	10.7	139	15.1	156	10.9	102	12.4
$12,500 - 14,999	295	12.2	106	12.0	156	10.8	78	8.4
$15,000 - 19,999	488	22.3	149	21.8	263	19.1	111	20.1
$20,000 or More	411	22.3	44	8.9	238	20.0	33	9.1
Hourly Wage								
Less than $1.50	56	2.6	43	3.9	93	6.4	47	5.8
$1.50 - 1.99	63	2.5	44	3.2	92	6.2	82	8.6
$2.00 - 2.49	107	3.2	76	6.1	131	8.9	147	15.3
$2.50 - 2.99	137	5.0	129	12.0	166	11.4	125	17.4
$3.00 - 3.99	297	11.3	169	14.1	297	21.9	152	20.9
$4.00 - 5.99	627	26.3	249	29.7	360	28.8	135	19.9
$6.00 or More	963	49.2	185	31.0	199	16.3	54	12.0
Whether Salaried								
Yes	974	46.2	223	30.8	599	46.1	253	38.2
No	1,276	53.8	672	69.2	739	53.9	489	61.8

Table A5.1b

MEAN HOURS MISSED AND WHETHER MISSED ANY WORK BECAUSE OF ILLNESS OF OTHERS, BY RACE/SEX SUBGROUPS, FOR SELECTED FAMILY CHARACTERISTICS, 1975

(Working Household Heads and Spouses Aged 18-64)

Family Characteristics	White Men		Black Men		White Women		Black Women	
	Whether Missed	Mean Hours Missed	Whether Missed	Mean Hours Missed	Whether Missed	Mean Hours Missed	Whether Missed	Mean Hours Missed
All	.102	4.0	.091	8.0	.218	12.3	.249	25.7
Whether Missed for Illness of Others								
Yes	1.00	39.2	1.00	88.0	1.00	56.6	1.00	103.2
No	0.0	0.0	0.0	0.0	0.0	0.0	0.0	0.0
η^2		.344		.281		.162		.344
Whose Illness								
Spouse	1.00	36.7	1.00	104.2	1.00	75.7	1.00	161.2
Child	1.00	31.7	1.00	45.6	1.00	52.7	1.00	87.4
Other	1.00	55.8	1.00	77.1	1.00	58.1	1.00	123.1
Inap; Missed No Work	0.00	0.0	0.00	0.0	0.00	0.0	0.00	0.0
Not Ascertained, Don't Know	1.00	18.2	--	--	1.00	16.0	1.00	24.0
η^2	.991	.371	1.00	.301	1.00	.166	1.00	.369
Whether Someone Else Required Extra Care								
Yes	.254	12.7	.248	53.6	.363	26.4	.295	65.4
No	.096	3.7	.077	3.9	.211	12.0	.245	23.1
η^2	.010	.007	.026	.082	.006	.001	.001	.012
Number of Children Aged 13 or Younger								
None	.071	4.2	.032	2.3	.113	6.3	.140	12.4
One	.140	4.5	.110	5.9	.372	21.4	.315	29.6
Two	.150	3.9	.219	29.3	.389	23.1	.415	50.4
Three	.062	2.2	.185	13.8	.451	20.7	.418	47.6
Four or More	.135	3.3	.082	5.2	.616	50.4	.344	37.7
η^2	.016	.001	.059	.037	.109	.019	.074	.040
Marital Status								
Married	.108	3.8	.116	10.6	.241	14.2	.320	35.0
Single	.022	1.3	.035	1.8	.059	1.0	.155	5.0
Widowed	.195	54.4	.029	5.7	.174	12.5	.178	15.8
Divorced	.096	4.6	.000	0.0	.253	11.7	.139	22.0
Separated	.120	3.0	.027	1.0	.232	15.3	.214	19.2
η^2	.006	.048	.018	.007	.020	.005	.032	.020

Table A5.1b (continued)

Family Characteristics	White Men		Black Men		White Women		Black Men	
	Whether Missed	Mean Hours Missed	Whether Missed	Mean Hours Missed	Whether Missed	Mean Hours Missed	Whether Missed	Mean Hours Missed
Age								
18–24	.109	3.5	.111	8.4	.190	8.1	.242	15.7
25–34	.124	3.9	.079	3.7	.314	20.1	.376	33.7
35–44	.105	3.4	.103	17.3	.252	11.8	.214	26.4
45–54	.077	4.8	.110	5.4	.145	6.4	.183	26.0
55–64	.083	4.1	.045	5.0	.109	10.8	.169	17.2
η^2	.004	.001	.005	.012	.034	.008	.032	.006
Family Size								
One	.056	5.8	.027	0.8	.068	2.0	.082	6.4
Two	.085	4.4	.056	6.2	.176	10.7	.190	17.7
Three	.124	4.1	.115	6.6	.313	19.0	.359	29.1
Four	.128	3.9	.114	3.5	.294	19.7	.238	24.2
Five	.099	2.6	.127	7.5	.294	12.3	.444	58.8
Six	.095	2.8	.063	4.2	.339	12.0	.422	71.0
Seven or More	.099	2.4	.188	41.1	.312	16.9	.183	24.5
η^2	.006	.002	.029	.056	.050	.011	.072	.046
Family Income (1975)								
$ 4,999 or Less	.098	5.6	.081	5.2	.112	8.8	.134	9.7
$ 5,000 - 7,499	.116	4.4	.037	3.4	.186	14.0	.177	17.6
$ 7,500 - 9,999	.122	4.0	.124	8.9	.185	11.6	.297	39.9
$10,000 - 12,499	.134	5.2	.066	4.4	.213	10.4	.288	29.0
$12,500 - 14,999	.112	4.7	.101	4.4	.225	12.8	.126	5.5
$15,000 - 19,999	.087	4.1	.153	19.0	.254	18.6	.403	48.2
$20,000 - 24,999	.081	2.4	.027	0.4	.234	12.1	.263	10.8
$25,000 or More	.104	3.8	.059	5.7	.233	8.2	.144	6.3
η^2	.004	.002	.021	.015	.007	.005	.053	.043
Hourly Wage								
Less than $1.50	.049	2.0	.191	25.0	.182	6.7	.093	3.7
$1.50 - 1.99	.082	7.2	.018	0.5	.186	21.2	.291	53.2
$2.00 - 2.49	.137	4.7	.068	7.2	.160	12.8	.205	15.4
$2.50 - 2.99	.098	4.1	.055	2.1	.271	15.2	.224	20.4
$3.00 - 3.99	.132	4.3	.056	2.1	.201	10.0	.291	20.9
$4.00 - 5.99	.081	2.7	.110	16.1	.244	15.4	.305	33.7
$6.00 or More	.109	4.5	.096	4.1	.217	6.7	.220	32.5
η^2	.004	.002	.039	.022	.006	.005	.015	.023
Whether Salaried								
Yes	.109	4.2	.077	6.1	.212	8.1	.275	29.1
No	.097	3.9	.098	8.9	.223	16.0	.233	23.5
η^2	.000	.000	.001	.001	.000	.005	.002	.001

Table A5.1c

MEAN HOURS MISSED AND WHETHER MISSED ANY WORK BECAUSE OF OWN ILLNESS, BY RACE/SEX SUBGROUPS, FOR SELECTED FAMILY CHARACTERISTICS, 1975

(All Working Household Heads and Spouses Aged 18-64)

Family Characteristics	White Men		Black Men		White Women		Black Women	
	Whether Missed	Mean Hours Missed	Whether Missed	Mean Hours Missed	Whether Missed	Mean Hours Missed	Whether Missed	Mean Hours Missed
All	.462	36.5	.468	50.4	.530	43.0	.517	58.0
Whether Missed for Own Illness								
Yes	1.00	79.0	1.00	107.5	1.00	81.1	1.00	112.2
No	0.0	0.0	0.00	0.0	0.00	0.0	0.00	0.0
η^2		.120		.179		.106		.141
Whether Missed for Illness of Others								
Yes	.644	39.5	.646	37.9	.689	42.6	.611	54.4
No	.441	36.1	.451	51.6	.487	43.1	.487	59.2
η^2	.015	.000	.013	.001	.027	.000	.011	.000
Whether Someone Else Requires Extra Care								
Yes	.514	45.2	.705	104.0	.531	93.3	.610	109.4
No	.460	36.2	.447	45.5	.529	40.4	.509	53.3
η^2	.000	.000	.020	.016	.000	.008	.003	.011
Number of Children Aged 13 or Younger								
None	.432	39.0	.441	47.7	.529	40.0	.503	59.2
One	.491	34.3	.543	57.5	.561	54.8	.565	33.2
Two	.515	32.5	.353	31.3	.503	34.0	.571	72.9
Three	.433	28.8	.540	42.4	.465	34.0	.395	100.4
Four or More	.504	58.0	.626	115.0	.416	160.3	.371	35.6
η^2	.005	.002	.020	.017	.002	.008	.010	.013
Marital Status								
Married	.451	35.9	.487	53.4	.508	41.0	.495	60.8
Single	.541	31.8	.577	48.1	.678	44.5	.502	39.1
Widowed	.604	69.7	.171	50.3	.365	43.4	.448	31.4
Divorced	.505	30.5	.246	31.3	.573	50.3	.556	83.1
Separated	.531	115.7	.240	35.5	.577	51.6	.671	62.0
η^2	.003	.006	.036	.001	.018	.001	.013	.009

Table A5.1c (continued)

Family Characteristics	White Men		Black Men		White Women		Black Women	
	Whether Missed	Mean Hours Missed	Whether Missed	Mean Hours Missed	Whether Missed	Mean Hours Missed	Whether Missed	Mean Hours Missed
Age								
18-24	.539	37.1	.443	44.0	.595	36.9	.566	59.8
25-34	.504	27.4	.464	34.7	.620	42.9	.563	53.8
35-44	.501	46.7	.490	58.8	.491	50.1	.593	44.4
45-54	.374	35.3	.502	50.3	.480	51.4	.385	85.5
55-64	.385	44.6	.417	84.8	.392	27.2	.427	37.3
η^2	.017	.004	.002	.014	.026	.004	.028	.011
Family Size								
One	.542	44.4	.453	45.3	.626	40.0	.454	32.7
Two	.433	34.5	.459	65.8	.503	40.0	.520	70.9
Three	.445	31.0	.472	39.3	.564	42.0	.577	51.8
Four	.463	31.7	.435	35.9	.468	47.8	.569	70.6
Five	.482	49.0	.512	48.2	.470	63.8	.497	60.3
Six	.444	31.2	.365	58.3	.539	12.9	.272	41.3
Seven or More	.463	52.6	.563	85.4	.451	68.4	.534	78.9
η^2	.004	.004	.007	.013	.013	.006	.017	.009
Family Income (1975)								
$ 4,999 or Less	.372	63.6	.430	67.6	.431	42.1	.350	39.2
$ 5,000 - 7,499	.471	59.3	.556	48.9	.553	63.1	.528	38.3
$ 7,500 - 9,999	.513	43.4	.428	51.6	.496	56.2	.600	93.4
$10,000 - 12,499	.531	40.6	.554	68.3	.576	57.9	.404	41.9
$12,500 - 14,999	.475	32.6	.478	23.6	.535	39.5	.506	81.9
$15,000 - 19,999	.479	37.1	.387	49.2	.518	42.2	.687	81.7
$20,000 - 24,999	.458	34.9	.276	20.9	.622	44.1	.120	9.1
$25,000 or More	.402	25.2	.646	65.8	.480	22.8	.534	30.5
η^2	.007	.009	.038	.014	.011	.010	.076	.030
Hourly Wage								
Less than $1.50	.231	12.6	.510	99.5	.303	55.5	.346	24.0
$1.50 - 1.99	.393	32.5	.388	30.9	.362	67.4	.413	30.5
$2.00 - 2.49	.282	12.9	.425	40.7	.401	32.1	.414	47.6
$2.50 - 2.99	.383	35.9	.501	33.9	.532	42.7	.474	97.1
$3.00 - 3.99	.469	48.4	.269	26.7	.524	47.0	.696	68.2
$4.00 - 5.99	.496	41.2	.545	60.6	.599	40.3	.480	44.2
$6.00 or More	.477	34.3	.484	55.4	.636	34.0	.624	56.2
η^2	.013	.004	.035	.015	.040	.006	.051	.020
Whether Salaried								
Yes	.461	23.7	.579	46.5	.589	30.7	.518	44.8
No	.462	47.5	.419	52.1	.479	53.5	.517	66.2
η^2	.000	.011	.022	.000	.012	.008	.000	.005

Table A5.1d

MEAN EXCESS VACATION HOURS, BY RACE/SEX SUBGROUPS, FOR SELECTED FAMILY CHARACTERISTICS, 1975

(Working Household Heads and Spouses Aged 18-64)

Family Characteristics	White Men (N=2250)	Black Men (N=895)	White Women (N=1338)	Black Women (N=742)
All	12.7	1.2	55.4	33.7
Whether Missed for Own Illness				
Yes	10.0	4.7	56.3	12.7
No	15.0	-1.9	54.3	56.5
η^2	.000	.001	.000	.018
Whether Missed for Illness of Others				
Yes	-4.1	2.1	48.7	17.9
No	14.6	1.1	57.2	38.9
η^2	.002	.000	.000	.003
Whether Someone Else Requires Extra Care				
Yes	15.4	14.9	43.6	35.9
No	12.6	-0.0	56.0	33.5
η^2	.000	.002	.000	.000
Number of Children Aged 13 or Younger				
None	16.0	1.8	54.8	47.5
One	9.6	1.1	52.9	5.8
Two	6.5	3.1	66.3	45.6
Three	10.6	3.3	46.8	-1.0
Four or More	25.2	-13.9	46.5	-1.3
η^2	.001	.001	.001	.015
Marital Status				
Married	11.2	4.7	58.8	28.6
Single	39.2	-6.5	80.1	32.7
Widowed	-19.6	3.4	33.2	94.8
Divorced	8.6	8.4	32.9	32.9
Separated	5.5	-14.9	9.4	4.4
η^2	.004	.005	.007	.017

Table A5.1d (continued)

Family Characteristics	White Men (N=2250)	Black Men (N=895)	White Women (N=1338)	Black Women (N=742)
Family Size				
One	28.7	-4.8	60.0	18.3
Two	15.1	-8.9	45.0	66.3
Three	4.3	37.2	55.0	20.8
Four	8.3	16.3	72.5	51.3
Five	15.2	-8.7	52.5	12.8
Six	8.9	-12.1	55.0	7.2
Seven or More	19.4	15.7	74.4	8.1
η^2	.004	.046	.003	.018
Age				
18-24	11.6	-11.7	24.8	-39.9
25-34	18.9	0.0	64.8	37.4
35-44	10.0	-20.5	75.9	37.9
45-54	5.2	29.5	53.3	42.3
55-64	16.9	20.2	44.6	110.9
η^2	.002	.004	.009	.054
Family Income (1975)				
$ 4,999 or Less	14.1	-4.1	77.1	41.3
$ 5,000 - 7,499	6.7	-1.7	41.7	18.1
$ 7,500 - 9,999	8.8	18.8	27.1	2.8
$10,000 - 12,499	0.7	4.3	52.8	65.7
$12,500 - 14,999	13.3	-10.8	42.1	17.0
$15,000 - 19,999	6.6	-12.2	59.9	41.5
$20,000 - 24,999	8.4	-5.0	42.1	37.5
$25,000 or More	29.9	32.1	81.2	67.0
η^2	.007	.026	.010	.018
Hourly Wage				
Less than $1.50	12.7	26.6	102.5	25.1
$1.50 - 1.99	30.2	-15.4	34.9	12.1
$2.00 - 2.49	9.1	6.4	55.5	7.8
$2.50 - 2.99	20.2	28.8	58.7	63.4
$3.00 - 3.99	1.1	-10.4	29.3	3.2
$4.00 - 5.99	1.0	-8.1	44.9	32.4
$6.00 or More	20.2	2.2	95.8	98.5
η^2	.007	.029	.020	.038
Whether Salaried				
Yes	13.2	11.0	60.8	59.6
No	12.2	-3.2	50.7	17.6
η^2	.000	.006	.001	.016

Table A5.1e

COMPLETE REGRESSION RESULTS FOR ABSENTEEISM AND CALCULATED WAGE RATES
(All Working Household Heads and Spouses Aged 18-64)

Independent Variable	Dependent Variable: ℓn Calculated Wage Rate			
	White Men (N=2250)	Black Men (N=895)	White Women (N=1338)	Black Women (N=741)
Constant	.336	-.035	-.041	-.007
Formal Education (in years)	.060** (.004)	.063** (.006)	.077** (.006)	.078** (.008)
Work History				
Years Out of Labor Force Since Completing School	-.006 (.007)	-.009 (.010)	-.005** (.002)	.005 (.003)
Years of Work Experience Before Present Employer	.013** (.003)	.027** (.005)	.010* (.004)	.011* (.005)
Pre-Employer Work Experience Squared	-.0003** (.0001)	-.0006** (.0001)	-.0004** (.0001)	-.0004* (.0002)
Years With Current Employer Prior to Current Position	.024** (.002)	.019** (.003)	.021** (.003)	.016** (.003)
Years of Training Completed On Current Job	.048** (.006)	.068** (.014)	.081** (.013)	.073** (.016)
Years of Post-Training Tenure on Current Job	.014** (.004)	.015** (.006)	.023** (.005)	-.012 (.007)
Proportion of Total Working Years that Were Full Time	.310** (.060)	.522** (.095)	.257** (.044)	.126* (.058)
Indicators of Work Orientation				
Limited Job Hours Or Location	-.041 (.030)	.102* (.048)	-.015 (.026)	-.007 (.039)
Knows there are Better Jobs Elsewhere	-.105** (.024)	-.119** (.037)	-.111** (.028)	-.149** (.039)
Doesn't Know whether there Are Better Jobs Elsewhere	-.071* (.031)	-.072 (.039)	-.144** (.033)	-.032 (.039)
Plans to Stop Work for Nontraining Reasons	-.170** (.063)	-.233* (.120)	-.054 (.044)	-.279** (.069)

Table A5.1e (continued)

Independent Variable	White Men (N=2250)	Black Men (N=895)	White Women (N=1338)	Black Women (N=741)
Demographic Control Variables				
Size of Largest City in the Area (hundreds of thousands)	.027** (.003)	.018** (.004)	.018** (.003)	.022** (.004)
Whether South	-.060* (.025)	-.093** (.035)	-.034 (.029)	-.090** (.035)
Measures of Absenteeism				
Hours of Work Missed for Illness of Others in 1975	.0006 (.0005)	-.0003 (.0003)	-.0001 (.0002)	.0003 (.0002)
Hours of Work Missed for Own Illness in 1975	.0002* (.0001)	.0001 (.0001)	-.0002* (.0001)	.0000 (.0001)
Excess Vacation Hours Taken in 1975	.0000 (.0001)	-.0003 (.0002)	-.0001 (.0001)	.0001 (.0001)
$\bar{R}^2$	.302	.292	.329	.360

* Significant at .05 level.
**Significant at .01 level.

Table A5.1f

COMPLETE REGRESSION RESULTS FOR ABSENTEEISM AND REPORTED WAGE RATES
(All Working Household Heads and Spouses Aged 18-64)

Independent Variable	Dependent Variables: ℓn Reported Wage Rate			
	White Men (N=2250)	Black Men (N=895)	White Women (N=1338)	Black Women (N=741)
Constant	.475	1.008	.268	.128
Formal Education (in years)	.052** (.006)	.025** (.007)	.065** (.006)	.072** (.008)
Work History				
Years Out of Labor Force Since Completing School	-.012 (.011)	-.009 (.011)	-.005** (.002)	-.001 (.003)
Years of Work Experience Before Present Employer	.009 (.005)	.035** (.006)	.013** (.005)	.005 (.005)
Pre-Employer Work Experience Squared	-.0003* (.0001)	-.0013** (.0002)	-.0004** (.0001)	-.0003 (.0002)
Years With Current Employer Prior to Current Position	.026** (.002)	.008* (.003)	.021** (.003)	.024** (.003)
Years of Training Completed On Current Job	.032** (.009)	.073** (.016)	.046** (.014)	.007 (.015)
Years of Post-Training Tenure on Current Job	-.002 (.006)	.009 (.007)	.007 (.005)	-.020** (.006)
Proportion of Total Working Years that Were Full Time	.227* (.088)	.120 (.110)	.132** (.047)	.141** (.052)
Indicators of Work Orientation				
Limited Job Hours Or Location	-.043 (.044)	.085 (.056)	-.047 (.028)	-.066 (.035)
Knows there Are Better Jobs Elsewhere	.058 (.034)	-.186** (.043)	-.157** (.030)	-.120** (.035)
Doesn't Know whether there Are Better Jobs Elsewhere	-.051 (.045)	-.003 (.045)	-.133** (.035)	-.009 (.036)
Plans to Stop Work for Nontraining Reasons	-.111 (.092)	-.134 (.139)	-.053 (.046)	-.222** (.062)

Table A5.1f (continued)

Independent Variable	White Men (N=2250)	Black Men (N=895)	White Women (N=1338)	Black Women (N=741)
Demographic Control Variables				
Size of Largest City in the Area (hundreds of thousands)	.027** (.004)	-.004 (.005)	.017** (.003)	.024** (.004)
Whether South	-.098** (.036)	-.189** (.041)	-.025 (.031)	.0002 (.032)
Measures of Absenteeism				
Hours of Work Missed for Illness of Others in 1975	.0000 (.0008)	-.0029** (.0004)	-.0000 (.0002)	.0001 (.0002)
Hours of Work Missed for Own Illness in 1975	-.0001 (.0001)	.0001 (.0001)	-.0003** (.0001)	-.0000 (.0001)
Excess Vacation Hours Taken in 1975	-.0006** (.0001)	-.0006** (.0002)	-.0002* (.0001)	-.0002 (.0001)
$\bar{R}^2$	.164	.234	.234	.354

* Significant at .01 level.
**Significant at .05 level.

PART II

OTHER ANALYSES

Chapter 6

THE ECONOMIC VALUE OF SURPLUS EDUCATION

Greg J. Duncan and Saul Hoffman

Introduction

Nearly half of the U.S. work force in 1976 reported that their formal education exceeded the education level required by their jobs.[1] To some, this overeducation constitutes a "great training robbery." The implicit assumption of this view is that the surplus education provides little or no economic benefit and, therefore, reflects a major misallocation of educational resources. To a proponent of the human capital model, on the other hand, educational requirements are irrelevant. The skills confered by any amount of education, whether surplus or required, should pay a return similar to that from any other investment. This chapter will use data gathered from a recent national sample of workers on educational requirements, attainments, and other demographic characteristics to examine the extent, determinants, and benefits of surplus education.

BACKGROUND

Although concern with the mismatch between the educational requirements of jobs and the actual educational attainments of the work force was voiced much earlier,[2] Ivar Berg popularized the subject in his book, Education and Jobs: The Great Training Robbery (1970). In the course of his general attack on the benefits of education, Berg cites evidence from several studies which show a low or even negative correlation between educational attainment and performance. For example, to the assertion "Better-educated people are more promotable," he finds "the argument was unsupported by any evidence that better-educated people compare favorably with their less educated peers who started

---

[1]This is based on an estimate made from the Panel Study data which are described herein.

[2]In 1949, for example, Seymour Harris wrote: ". . . in the light of our college graduates' vocational expectations the numbers are, and will be increasingly excessive. . . a large proportion of the potential college students within the next twenty years are doomed to disappointment after graduation. . ." (1949, p. 64, emphasis in original).

at some given point on the organizational ladder" (p. 79).

These facts contradict the predictions of the human capital model. As Blaug states in his recent review of the human capital literature; "Nothing is more alien to the human-capital research program than the . . . notion of technologically-determined educational requirements for jobs" (1976, p. 846). Obviously, if there are no educational requirements, there can be no such thing as surplus education. This is clearest in the human capital life-cycle investment and earnings models (Ben-Porath, (1967), Ryder, Stephen, and Stafford (1976), and Heckman (1976)) in which individuals simply rent to employers that portion of their stock of human capital which they do not use for investment (or leisure) purposes. What is striking about these models in this context is that there is virtually no reference to jobs at all. Individuals are assumed to rent their human capital independently of the job they hold. In effect, this omission confirms Blaug's statement: jobs are ignored in these models, because skill requirements are implicitly assumed to be infinitely flexible. Consequently, the concept of surplus education is irrelevant.

Some human capital theorists would probably concede the existence of some educational requirements, but would nevertheless predict a minimal amount of surplus education. They would argue, instead, that the operation of a competitive labor market would assure that, in equilibrium, the relative supply of and demand for labor of a given quality should be equal. In the short run, however, mismatches could occur, and the existence of workers with surplus education is certainly possible as a temporary phenomenon.[3] Presumably, for those workers, the economic return to surplus education would be lower than that to required education.

A third approach is more institutional and contains elements of the "screening hypothesis," "credentialism," and the internal labor market theories.[4] It assumes that employers treat educational qualifications as an inexpensive guide to "trainability," where trainability is a function of ability, motivation, background, and perhaps race and sex as well. How the employer treats applicants with educational qualifications which exceed the standard relative to those who just meet it is not discussed explicitly by proponents of this approach. The rigid nature of jobs presupposed by many screening theorists, however, would seem to limit severely the possible economic benefits to those who are overqualified. In addition, discriminating employers may be more likely to recognize and reward surplus education among white men than among minority workers whose race and sex are most important to the screening procedure. It also is possible that direct labor

---

[3]See Freeman (1975).

[4]Blaug (1976) reviews this literature also.

market discrimination may be an increasing function of a worker's skill. If that were the case, and if discrimination operated via the allocation of individuals to jobs rather than wage differentials among individuals in the same job, then we would expect blacks and women to have more surplus education than white males.

In sum, the alternative views of how education interacts with jobs provide some contradictory hypotheses. To strict believers of rigid, educational requirements for jobs, such as Berg, surplus education should have no payoff, and those who have deficit education for the jobs into which they were hired should not be penalized. Proponents of the human capital view would not expect pervasive mismatches between required and completed education level and, barring short run imbalances, would predict that the benefits to surplus education and the penalty for deficit education should be similar to the payoff to the educational level required by the jobs. The institutional theories could possibly accomodate both of these positions, but its single prediction would probably be closer to Berg's view, especially for minority workers.

Analysis

DATA

We used data from the ninth wave of the Panel Study of Income Dynamics.[5] Parallel interviews were conducted both with household heads, arbitrarily taken to be the husband in a married couple, and also with their wives. The interviews provide information, when weighted, on a representative national sample of about 3,000 men and 2,000 women who worked during 1975.[6] Educational requirements were ascertained from the following question: "How much formal education is required to get a job like yours?" and was coded in the following categories: 1. 0-5 grades, 2. 6-8 grades, 3. 9-11 grades, 4. 12 grades, 5. Some college; associate degree, 6. College degree; B.A. or B.S., 7. Advanced or professional degree, and 8. Don't know, not ascertained. The vast majority (90.3 percent) of respondents were able to state these educational requirements; the remainder have been excluded from subsequent analysis.[7]

---

[5]See A Panel Study of Income Dynamics, 1977, for details.

[6]Note that the sample is representative of men and women who were heads or spouses, and excludes adults who were children or siblings of the household head.

[7]The fraction of respondents reporting educational requirements varied little by race and sex, ranging from 88.8 percent for black women to 93.3 percent for black men. Some respondents mentioned different requirements now versus when they first took the job. For them, current educational requirements were coded.

DESCRIPTIVE ANALYSIS

Before turning to an estimation of the possible economic benefits of surplus education, we first describe the extent and simple demographic correlates of actual versus required educational attainment. Table 6.1 presents the distribution of the educational requirements of jobs along with the corresponding distribution of actual educational attainment by race and sex. For jobs in all four race/sex groups actual attainment levels exceed the level of education required. About a fifth of all jobs require no more than a grade school education, and almost 7 percent more require less than a high school education. In contrast, less than 2 percent of the working population have only a grade school education and only about 21 percent have less than a high school education. The educational requirements of the jobs held by white men are fairly similar to those of white women, somewhat higher than those of black women, and much higher than for black men. More than a third of the jobs held by black men require a grade school education or less, and for over half of their jobs, completion of high school is not required. For all four race/sex subgroups, average completed education was about a year-and-a-half greater than that required by the jobs these individuals held.

In Table 6.2, each individual is classified according to whether he or she reported having more education than is required for the job ("surplus education"), less than is required ("deficit education"), or the same as the required amount. The estimates of the number of individuals having surplus or deficit education are conservative since both actual and required education were coded into educational brackets, and any differences between actual and required education within brackets were ignored.[8] Overall, only about 46 percent of the sample just met the educational requirements of their jobs while 42 percent reported having more education than their jobs required. The remaining 12 percent actually had less education than required by their jobs, but for most of these individuals either the job requirements have inflated since they began working or else they have some high school but without a diploma working in jobs which require a high school diploma. Only black men appear to differ from the overall pattern; they are the only group in which the number of individuals having surplus education (48.5 percent) is greater than the number who have exactly the required amount (39.4 percent), and they also have the largest average amount of surplus education.[9]

---

[8]The brackets were those noted above for educational requirements. Measurement error in reports of actual or required education will impart a downward bias to estimates of the number of workers with actual education equalling required education.

[9]This result for black men could be caused, in part, by the lower quality of education that blacks receive. If educational requirements are measured in white school quality "units," then an identical quality-adjusted amount of surplus education would show up in our measures of surplus education as being larger for blacks than whites.

Table 6.1

COMPLETED EDUCATION AND FORMAL EDUCATION REQUIRED FOR JOBS, BY RACE/SEX SUBGROUPS

(All Working Household Heads and Spouses Aged 18-64)

	All		White Men		Black Men		White Women		Black Women	
Education Level	Percentage Completed	Percentage Required	Percentage Completed	Percentage Required	Percentage Completed	Percentage Required	Percentage Completed	Percentage Required	Percentage Completed	Percentage Required
None, 0-5 Grades	1.5	21.9	1.5	20.9	8.4	36.8	0.7	20.4	1.3	28.4
6-8 Grades	6.8	4.5	7.6	4.8	11.2	8.7	4.6	3.5	7.9	4.1
9-11 Grades	13.3	2.2	11.9	1.4	18.9	6.5	13.1	2.4	26.7	4.2
12 Grades, High School Diploma+	39.7	43.0	35.4	41.1	40.2	37.2	46.1	46.2	42.0	49.8
Some College	16.6	7.5	17.6	7.4	16.1	5.7	15.5	8.3	12.2	4.8
B.A. Degree	14.7	16.0	16.8	18.1	3.8	3.1	14.3	15.6	5.1	7.6
Advanced Degree	7.4	4.9	9.2	6.4	1.6	1.9	5.7	3.5	3.9	1.1
Total	100.0	100.0	100.0	100.0	100.0	100.0	100.0	100.0	100.0	100.0
Average Years of Education‡	12.7	11.3	13.0	11.6	11.0	9.4	12.8	11.4	11.8	10.3

+This category includes individuals who had nonacademic training in addition to high school.

‡The required education average is calculated by assigning the following numbers to the Required Education Level categories:

0-5 grades = 5
6-8 grades = 8
9-11 grades = 11
12 grades = 12

Some College = 14
B.A. Degree = 16
Advanced Degree = 18

The actual education variable was coded in years with a maximum of 18.

Table 6.2

COMPARISON BETWEEN ACTUAL EDUCATION LEVEL AND EDUCATION REQUIRED FOR JOBS, BY RACE/SEX SUBGROUPS
(All Working Household Heads and Spouses Aged 18-64)

	All	White Men	Black Men	White Women	Black Women
Percentage whose Actual Education Level Equals Education Required	46.1	44.7	39.4	49.5	46.4
Percentage whose Actual Education Level Exceeds Education Required (Surplus Education)	42.0	41.7	48.5	41.3	42.7
Percentage whose Required Education Exceeds Actual Education (Deficit Education)	11.9	13.6	12.1	9.2	10.9
Total	100.0	100.0	100.0	100.0	100.0
Average Difference between Actual and Required Education (in years)	1.49	1.45	1.82	1.49	1.61
Average Surplus Education+	1.80	1.83	2.21	1.68	1.82
Number of Observations	4,689	2,034	798	1,195	662

+Surplus education equals 0 if actual education is less than or equal to required education.

The fractions of respondents in various occupations who report surplus and deficit education is given in Table 6.3. In general, surplus education is most prevalent among lower status occupations and among the self-employed. Less than one-third of professionals, clerical workers, and managers who do not work for themselves have amounts of education that exceed the requirements for their jobs while, except for craftsmen, over half of the workers in all other occupations report surplus education.

Occupational classification accounts for much less of the variance in the incidence of deficit education than it does for surplus education. Non-self-employed managers, craftsmen, and operators are somewhat more likely than average to report deficit education, while service workers, laborers, and professionals are the least likely to do so.

Additional descriptive information on the demographic correlates of surplus and deficit education was obtained from two dummy variable regressions which included as predictors completed education, pre-employer work experience, current employer tenure, race, and sex. The dependent variables are dichotomous, equalling one if the respondent reported any surplus (regardless of how much) or any deficit. All independent variables are categorical to allow for nonlinear relationships. Results from these regressions are presented in Table 6.4. They show both the unadjusted and regression-adjusted mean values of the dependent variables by category of each independent variable. Also shown are the bivariate measure of association between each independent and dependent variable, eta squared, and its multivariate analogue, beta squared.[10]

In general, the completed education and current employer tenure variables are important predictors of the incidence of surplus and deficit education. High school and—contrary to popular notions—college graduates are <u>least</u> likely to have surplus education,[11] while more than half of those having either advanced degrees or between six and 11 grades of education have more education than their jobs required. High school and college graduates are also least likely to report deficit education. Adjustments for differences in labor force experience, job tenure, race, and sex have very little effect on these patterns.

Nearly two-fifths of the work force have completed high school only. The incidence of surplus education in this group is low, but because there are so many of them, over one-

---

[10]The eta squared, or squared correlation ratio, is simply the fraction of variance of the dependent variables that is explained by the independent variable, before adjustments are made for the effects of the other predictors. The beta squared can be thought of as a regression-adjusted fraction of variance explained. The difference between the size of the eta squared and beta squared shows the extent of adjustment when the effects of other predictor variables are taken into account. See Andrews et. al. (1973) for further details.

[11]Those with zero to five years of education have no surplus education by definition.

Table 6.3

UNADJUSTED MEAN PROPORTIONS WITH SURPLUS AND DEFICIT EDUCATION, BY OCCUPATION

(All Working Household Heads and Spouses Aged 18-64)

Occupation	Unweighted Number of Observations	Weighted Percentage of Observations	Whether Surplus Education	Whether Deficit Education
Professional	686	18.5	.33	.09
Manager, Not Self-employed	387	11.6	.31	.19
Self-employed Manager	110	2.9	.51	.12
Clerical	785	16.8	.31	.10
Sales Worker	214	5.6	.51	.11
Craftsmen and Foremen	710	15.6	.39	.15
Operators	854	14.6	.57	.14
Laborers	235	2.7	.61	.09
Service Workers	631	10.0	.56	.07
Farmers	67	1.7	.54	.13
Not Ascertained	10	0.1	.87	.00
All	4,689	100.0	.42	.12
			η^2=.050	η^2=.013

Table 6.4

UNADJUSTED AND REGRESSION-ADJUSTED MEAN PROPORTIONS WITH SURPLUS AND DEFICIT EDUCATION, BY VARIOUS DEMOGRAPHIC CHARACTERISTICS
(All Working Household Heads and Spouses Aged 18-64)

Independent Variable	Unweighted Number of Observations	Weighted Percentage	Whether Surplus Education: Unadjusted	Whether Surplus Education: Adjusted	Whether Deficit Education: Unadjusted	Whether Deficit Education: Adjusted
Completed Education			η^2=.127	β^2=.129	η^2=.141	β^2=.134
0-5 grades	130	1.3	.00	.01	.15	.13
6-8 grades	414	6.8	.54	.57	.27	.24
9-11 grades	796	13.5	.54	.54	.38	.38
12 grades	1,831	39.2	.24	.24	.06	.06
13-15	699	15.9	.67	.66	.12	.13
College degree	456	12.5	.36	.35	.03	.04
Advanced degree	363	10.8	.60	.60	.00	.00
Pre-employer Work Experience			η^2=.001	β^2=.002	η^2=.007	β^2=.003
1-5 years	1,970	37.0	.42	.43	.10	.11
5-10 years	1,103	24.7	.43	.42	.10	.12
10-15 years	600	13.7	.45	.45	.13	.11
15-20 years	357	8.5	.39	.39	.13	.12
20 or more	659	16.1	.40	.30	.18	.15
Current Employer Tenure			η^2=.015	β^2=.017	η^2=.031	β^2=.022
0-1 years	754	14.5	.51	.49	.07	.06
1-2 years	468	9.2	.45	.46	.07	.09
2-5 years	1,274	23.5	.45	.46	.08	.10
5-10 years	1,205	26.0	.41	.42	.12	.11
10-20 years	611	15.6	.37	.37	.16	.15
20 or more	377	11.1	.29	.27	.26	.23
Race/Sex			η^2=.001	β^2=.002	η^2=.004	β^2=.003
White Men	2,034	56.0	.42	.42	.14	.13
Black Men	798	5.4	.48	.52	.12	.08
White Women	1,195	34.2	.41	.41	.09	.11
Black Women	662	4.4	.43	.43	.11	.07
$\bar{R}^2$			.143		.165	

fifth of those with surplus education are in this category. Fully one-quarter of those with surplus education are college dropouts, most of whom have jobs which require only a high school education. College graduates, on the other hand, constitute only one-tenth of the overeducated, while those with advanced degrees and high school dropouts each accounts for about 15 percent of this group.

The relationship between job tenure and both of the dependent variables is monotonic. Those individuals with the greatest tenure are least likely to report surplus education and most likely to report deficit education. These findings are consistent with the view that educational credentials for some jobs have risen over time, and that individuals with these jobs are allowed to remain even though they might be unable to obtain similar jobs with other employers. For these individuals, it would appear that firm-specific training does substitute for formal educational requirements. However, the lack of any significant relationship between pre-employer work experience and either surplus or deficit education suggests that general labor market experience is not treated similarly by employers. This latter result is somewhat surprising, since both education and labor market experience are usually assumed to provide general training, and would, therefore, be expected to substitute for each other. Indeed, this apparent non-substitutability supports either a fairly strong credentialist interpretation of educational requirements or a belief that training is very job-specific.

THE ECONOMIC VALUE OF SURPLUS EDUCATION

Completed education is the sum of the education level required by the job and the difference between completed and required education. As a first estimate of the value of the difference, we include in a wage equation the years of required, surplus, and deficit education along with the following set of control variables: years of labor force experience, experience-squared, whether south, and city size.[12] Since the dependent variable is the natural logarithm of the wage rate, coefficients measure the estimated percentage increase in wages associated with an additional year of the given type of education after controlling for the effects of the other independent variables. Results obtained when completed education was included with the control variables are given in the top panel of Table 6.5. The estimated coefficients for the three additive components of completed education (i.e., required, surplus, and deficit) are presented in the lower panel of Table 6.5.

---

[12] The experience variable is constructed from the question: "How many years have you worked since you were 18?"

Table 6.5

EFFECTS OF EDUCATION ON *ln* HOURLY WAGE RATE, BY RACE/SEX SUBGROUP

(All Working Household Heads and Spouses Aged 18-64)

	White Men	Black Men	White Women	Black Women
REGRESSION #1				
Completed Education (in years)	.058** (.004)	.059** (.006)	.089** (.005)	.103** (.007)
$\bar{R}^2$	.251	.214	.263	.309
REGRESSION #2				
Required Education (in years)	.063** (.004)	.076** (.007)	.091** (.005)	.105** (.007)
Surplus Education (in years)	.029** (.006)	.040** (.008)	.052** (.008)	.047** (.010)
Deficit Education (in years, scored negatively)	.042** (.011)	.048** (.013)	.014 (.020)	.038 (.024)
$\bar{R}^2$	.279	.261	.314	.413
Number of Observations	2,034	798	1,187	662

NOTE: Other variables included in the regressions were years of labor force experience, experience squared, southern location, city size.

**Significant at .01 level.

The most striking result from Table 6.5 is that surplus education indeed pays off for all four of the race/sex subgroups, with the return to additional years of surplus education being almost exactly half the return to an additional year of required education. In every case, the benefit to surplus education is positive and highly significant and, contrary to the prediction of the internal market theory, it is somewhat less for white men than for others. The proportionate increase in wages associated with an additional year of surplus education is estimated to be 2.9 percent for white men, 4.0 percent for black men, 5.2 percent for white women, and 4.7 percent for black women.[13]

Also striking is the fact that men who hold jobs for which they are underqualified are penalized for their deficit education. Each additional year of deficit education reduces earnings of white men by 4.2 percent and black men by 4.8 percent.[14] The estimated effects of deficit education for the two groups of women are in the same direction as men (i.e., deficit education reduces wages) but the coefficients are not statistically significant at conventional levels.

To investigate the robustness of these results, the following alternative specifications were estimated:

1. A multiplicative interaction term between required education and the sum of the surplus and deficit education was added to test whether the return to surplus or deficit education depended on the level of required education. The coefficient for the interaction variable was not significant at the 5 percent level for any of the four subgroups.

2. The entire set of regressions was reestimated only for those between 21 and 35 years of age. If surplus education results from short run mismatches between individuals and jobs, then those with least time in the labor market might benefit the least from overqualification. In fact, the coefficients for surplus education did fall somewhat for white men and white women but remained statistically significant at the 1 percent level for all but the white men. For this latter group, the coefficient was significant at the 10 percent level.

   In contrast, the coefficients on the deficit education variables increased considerably when the sample was restricted to young people, indicating a larger wage penalty for years of deficit education. For the younger group, this may result because older workers find that the educational requirements of their jobs have inflated well after they took the jobs and this has not affected their wages.

3. A variable measuring the square of required education was added into the equation. If the returns to additional years of education decline with the level

---

[13]Only the surplus education coefficient for white women is significantly different from the white, male coefficient.

[14]Since deficit education is scored negatively, a positive coefficient indicates a negative relation between years of deficit education and wages.

of required education, then the smaller coefficient for surplus education may be more similar to the payoff on additional years of required education than is indicated in Table 5. The coefficient for the squared term was significant but positive for both groups of women, indicating increasing returns on additional years of required education. Coefficients on the quadratic term for both groups of men were quite insignificant.

4. The self-employed were omitted from the sample. Both the definition of educational requirements and the measurement of hourly earnings for the self-employed are problematic and so the regressions of Table 5 were reestimated after the self-employed had been omitted. Since fewer than 5 percent of the blacks and women are self-employed, it is not surprising that the coefficients for these groups changed very little. The coefficient for the surplus education variable differed the most, increasing to .042 for black men, to .058 for white women and to .053 for black women. For white men, the surplus education coefficient rose from .029 to .038, and the deficit education coefficient fell from .042 to .025. It would appear, then, that the self-employed have considerably smaller payoffs on surplus education than those working for others, but the coefficient for surplus education in this latter group is still less than two-thirds the size of the coefficient for required education.

In sum, the results do not provide clear support for any of the three models. The notion that surplus education is without economic value is most clearly refuted by these data; payoffs on additional years of surplus education were positive and highly significant for all four groups studied. The fact that the estimated value of surplus education is about half that of required education was contrary to predictions from the most rigorous versions of the human capital model. That the differences may result from short run disequilibrium is a possibility, although the fact that the benefits of surplus education did not decline uniformly for all groups of young workers contradicts the disequilibrium explanation. Even the vague predictions of the credentialists are not supported by the finding that surplus education benefits white men <u>less</u> than minority workers.

Summary and Conclusions

Almost half of the workers in the United States have more education than is required by their jobs. Surplus education occurs more frequently among blacks and workers in low status occupations and less frequently among those with high school and college degrees. We should be neither alarmed nor complacent about the pervasiveness today of workers who have more education than their jobs require. If wages reflect productivity, then our results suggest that much of the surplus education is indeed productive, since the payoff on surplus education was found to be positive and highly significant for all major demographic groups. But the fact that the payoff on surplus education was only half that of required education suggests some potential misallocation of educational resources. While the smaller payoffs may result, in part, from temporary mismatches between people and jobs, the evidence suggest that much of it may be permanent. If so, and if the surplus education is not obtained only for consumption purposes, then it becomes important to continue to monitor the distribution of required and actual educational attainment in the work force.

References

Andrews, Frank M., Morgan, James N., Sonquist, John A., and Klem, Laura. Multiple Classification Analysis (2nd edition). Ann Arbor: Institute for Social Research, 1973.

Ben-Porath, Yoram. "The Production of Human Capital and the Life Cycle of Earnings." Journal of Political Economy, 75 (August 1967): 352-65.

Berg, Ivar. Education and Jobs: The Great Training Robbery. (New York: Praeger, 1970.)

Blaug, Mark. "The Empirical Status of Human Capital Theory: A Slightly Jaundiced Survey." Journal of Economic Literature, 14 (September 1976): 827-55.

Freeman, Richard B. "Overinvestment in College Training?" Journal of Human Resources, X (Summer 1975): 287-311.

Harris, Seymour. The Market for College Graduates. Cambridge: Harvard University Press, 1949.

Heckman, James J. "A Life Cycle Model of Earnings, Learning and Consumption." Journal of Political Economy, 84 (August 1976): S11-S44.

A Panel Study of Income Dynamics: Procedures and Tape Codes 1976 Interviewing Year. Ann Arbor: Institute for Social Research, 1976.

Ryder, Karl E., Stafford, Frank P., and Stephen, Paula E. "Labor, Leisure, and Training Over the Life Cycle." International Economic Review, 17 (October 1976): 65174.

Chapter 7

BLACK-WHITE EARNINGS DIFFERENCES OVER THE LIFE CYCLE

Saul Hoffman

Introduction

Ever since the publication in 1957 of Gary Becker's The Economics of Discrimination, economists have attempted to analyze the nature and source of black-white income differences. The research presented here considers black-white earnings differentials within a life-cycle context. It attempts to integrate economic theories of life-cycle earnings patterns with the empirical analysis of black-white earnings differences in order to investigate the effects of labor market experience on the earnings of black and white males. The specific issue addressed here is whether labor market discrimination against blacks tends to increase over the life cycle of an individual. Previous research on labor market discrimination has rarely emphasized this potential source of earnings differences both because the theoretical basis was developed only recently and because the appropriate data were unavailable.

The theoretical interest of economists in the life-cycle pattern of individual labor market earnings has increased tremendously in recent years. This upsurge of interest corresponds roughly to the development and wide-spread acceptance of the human capital model in the period since the early 1960's. The life-cycle perspective marked the point of departure for the human capital model, and the analysis of life-cycle earnings remains one of its most central features. The explanation of life-cycle earnings patterns also figures prominently in the major alternative model of the labor market, the dual labor market model. Empirical analysis of the poverty population also focused attention on life-cycle earnings. If, as appears to be the case, a relatively large fraction of the poverty population at any moment is only temporarily poor, then an understanding of the nature and determinants of change in individual earnings is crucial for informed public policy.[1]

[1]Morgan, et al. (1974).

Analysis of differences in black-white earnings in terms of age or years of work experience is still very much an unresolved empirical issue. Previous empirical work on this topic has shown, virtually without exception, that black-white earnings differences do, in fact, appear to increase over the life cycle. The implication of this finding—that the labor market itself is a vehicle for promoting and intensifying these differences—is serious, both for the nature and focus of government policies aimed at minority workers as well as for economic theory. Indeed, Glen Cain included the finding in his list of "neoclassical puzzles"—empirical results which orthodox economic theory has been unable to account for satisfactorily and which have become the focus of the alternative segmented labor market theories.[2]

A possible problem with all of these empirical studies, however, is their reliance on cross-sectional rather than longitudinal data. As a result, the apparent life-cycle findings were actually drawn from the earnings of a number of individuals of different ages rather than from the life-cycle pattern of earnings of a single individual. It was possible, then, that the cross-sectional result might misrepresent the life-cycle earnings profiles of black and white workers and that the finding of increasing "life-cycle" discrimination might be simply a statistical artifact of the cross-section. Finis Welch has made this argument in a series of recent papers, citing what he calls "vintage effects"—the relative differences between older black and white workers and between younger ones—as a plausible explanation of the cross-sectional finding.[3]

This chapter reexamines the issue of black-white life-cycle earnings, paying careful attention both to alternative theories of life-cycle earnings and to the implications of the vintage hypothesis for empirical work. In order to test the vintage hypothesis and to estimate black-white life-cycle earnings patterns, a cross-sectional earnings function and a pooled cross-section and time-series earnings function are estimated using longitudinal data on individual earnings from the Panel Study of Income Dynamics. The pooled results provide an improved estimate of life-cycle earnings differences, and the comparison of the cross-sectional and pooled results provides a test of the vintage hypothesis.

Analysis

MODELS OF BLACK-WHITE LIFE-CYCLE EARNINGS DIFFERENCES

This issue of black-white life-cycle earnings differences is closely tied to economic models of labor market earnings, since most of these models place primary emphasis on

---

[2]Cain (1976).

[3]Welch (1973, 1974).

the explanation of the life-cycle pattern of individual earnings. There are at least two possible explanations of increasing black-white earnings differences over the life-cycle, each corresponding to a different model of the labor market. Discrimination itself may be constant over the life cycle, but the relative productivity of black and white workers—and hence, their earnings—may diverge over the life cycle or relative individual productivity may be constant. Likewise discrimination may increase over the life-cycle. The constancy of discrimination is explained by the human capital model, while the increasing discrimination is best explained by dual or segmented labor market models.

The Human Capital Model[4]

According to the human capital model, the life-cycle pattern of individual labor market earnings simply reflects an individual's life-cycle pattern of productivity which, in turn, depends on self-investment over time in human capital. Thus, if for any reason whatsoever, blacks invest in less human capital than do otherwise similar whites, then their productivity, and hence their earnings, will diverge from that of white workers over the life cycle.

The crucial question with respect to black-white life-cycle earnings differences is whether there are reasons to expect that blacks will tend to invest in less human capital than otherwise similar whites. There are at least two factors which might give blacks incentive to acquire less human capital. One is labor market discrimination which may lower the value of any investment and thereby reduce the optimal amount of investment in any period.[5] Thus, the presence of—and future expectation of—discrimination may operate indirectly to exacerbate current income differences by reducing the incentives to acquire job skills. Second, the costs of investment may differ systematically between blacks and whites. In most human capital models, the costs of investment are assumed to be a function of the individual's ability to learn.[6] Since blacks tend to have less education than whites and, perhaps, poorer quality education as well, their investment costs might be greater and, hence, they would have an incentive to acquire less human capital.

---

[4]A full presentation of the human capital model and its implications for life-cycle earnings is presented in Chapter 3. The discussion here assumes familiarity with the basic outline of the human capital model; it draws heavily on the life-cycle accumulation models of Ben-Porath (1967) and Rosen (1972).

[5]This effect is stronger in the life cycle model of Rosen (1972) than in the model of Ben-Porath (1967), as a result of differences in the way the costs of investment are characterized. See Hoffman (1977) for a further discussion of this.

[6]This point is emphasized in Ben-Porath's model.

Thus, it is conceivable that black-white skill differences might increase over the life cycle as a result of differential rates of investment in on-the-job training.

The Dual Labor Market Model

The dual labor market model differs from the human capital model primarily in its focus on the characteristics of jobs, and job markets, rather than the characteristics of individuals. Earnings are thought to be largely determined by the labor market in which an individual works rather than the skills (or human capital) he or she possesses. The labor market is assumed to be dichotomized into a primary sector and a secondary sector. For all the much criticized vagueness of the model concerning the distinguishing features of jobs in the two sectors, it is probably reasonable to think of primary sector jobs as "jobs with a future" and secondary sector jobs as "dead-end jobs." Training itself is viewed as being largely technologically determined by the design of jobs, so that a specified amount of training is intrinsic in any given job. An individual acquires training by first gaining access to a job which provides training; that is, jobs and job markets intervene between an individual and investment in on-the-job training.

Discrimination is an integral part of the dual labor market model. Entry-level discrimination is cited as a major institutional barrier between the primary and secondary sector. One result of discrimination, it is argued, is to confine blacks and women to secondary labor market jobs in disproportionate numbers, relative to their skills, and, once there, they have a very difficult time escaping to the primary sector. The dual labor market theorists argue that hiring decisions typically involve a considerable amount of subjective input, consequently, there is ample opportunity to practice discrimination. Moreover, those blacks who are able to find primary sector employment are assumed to face increasing discrimination in promotions.

The dual labor market model represents a polar case of a segmented market. In its milder versions, it can be thought of as a model which is predicated on the existence of occupational segregation (either historically or institutionally determined), labor market immobility, and labor market discrimination which becomes more intense at higher levels within job hierarchies. If blacks are denied access to good jobs in the primary sector, they will tend to acquire less training and, therefore, receive lower wages than white men. In this interpretation, this result reflects not optimal individual investments in training, but rather, the operation of labor market discrimination in which earnings differentials by race would be expected to increase over the life cycle.

CROSS-SECTIONAL STUDIES AND THE VINTAGE HYPOTHESIS

It is certainly true that in simple bivariate cross-sectional analyses, blacks tend to

Table 7.1

AVERAGE NONWHITE INCOME AS A PERCENTAGE OF AVERAGE WHITE INCOME BY AGE, 1949, 1959, 1969, MALES ONLY

Age	1949 (median)	1959 (median)	1959 (mean)	1969 (mean)
18-24	70	70	67	85
25-34	59	61	61	70
35-44	55	59	57	64
45-54	54	55	52	58
55-64	49	52	51	54

SOURCE: Freeman (1973), p. 85.

have flatter age-earnings profiles than do whites. Table 7.1 summarizes the results from the 1950, 1960, and 1970 Censuses. The table clearly shows that significant earnings differentials existed at the time of entry into the labor force, and that the differentials increased with age. Although the earnings gap has narrowed since 1950 for all age groups, the magnitude of the cross-sectional decline with respect to age has been relatively constant.

Since the mid-1960s, most analyses of black-white earnings differences have been based on cross-sectional survey data which provided information on individual earnings (rather than just cell means) as well as basic demographic data and, depending on the data set, other individual characteristics as well. In general, these studies (see, for example, Hanoch (1965), Hall (1973), and Blinder (1973)) estimated separate earnings functions for blacks and whites and then examined differences in the estimated coefficients. Virtually all of these studies found clear evidence of increasing black-white earnings differences with respect to age or years of labor market experience in the form of lower regression coefficients for blacks than for whites. This was true regardless of the data source used or the set of independent variables included in the analysis. Indeed, the evidence was so strong that Robert Hall concluded from his analysis of the Survey of Economic Opportunity data that "the whole notion of a career with steady advancement is relevant only for white males."[7]

One problem common to all of these studies is that they attempted to infer the life-cycle effects of discrimination on the labor market earnings of a single individual from the cross-sectional effects of discrimination on different persons of different ages. A procedure of this kind is appropriate only if the factors which affect the relative earnings of blacks have been constant over the time period covered by the cross section. Otherwise, there is no reason to expect that the life-cycle earnings pattern of a young black will resemble that inferred from the cross section.

An argument of this kind is implicit in the vintage hypothesis which has been advanced recently by Welch. He argues that the cross-sectional results of previous studies reflect not the life-cycle effects of discrimination, but rather "vintage effects" in the form of an improvement over time in the relative quality of schooling available to blacks and/or a secular decline in discrimination. That is, the lower relative earnings of older black workers might result either from large differences between older blacks and older whites in the quality of education or from the lingering effects of the more severe labor market discrimination which older blacks faced when they first entered the labor market.

---

[7]Hall (1973), pp. 393-94.

In his own work, Welch has emphasized improvements over time in the quality of education available to black school children, particularly in the South. He cites, for example, a number of nominal input measures of educational quality, such as per capita expenditures, pupil-teacher ratios, and length of school year, all of which have increased relatively more rapidly for blacks than whites during the twentieth century. Thus, he argues that younger black workers—who are more recent vintages and who, therefore, received a better quality education—produce work of higher quality relative to whites than do older blacks, and, consequently, they receive relatively higher wages.

Formally, Welch's vintage hypothesis implies that conventional cross-sectional earnings equations are misspecified since the two vintage-related factors—quality of education and the severity of labor market discrimination—are invariably omitted from the equation. Since these two omitted variables are assumed to influence earnings, and since they are correlated with years of work experience, it can be shown that the estimated cross-sectional coefficient on years of work experience will understate the true life-cycle parameter.[8] Moreover, it is likely that this underestimate will be greater for blacks than for whites, since the vintage effects of school quality and discrimination are, presumably, greater for blacks than for whites. The prediction of the vintage hypothesis, then, is that the estimated cross-sectional difference in the returns on experience for blacks and whites is likely to be larger than the corresponding life-cycle difference. Note, however, that there is nothing in the vintage hypothesis that suggests that the true life-cycle coefficients for blacks and whites are necessarily equal.

ESTIMATING A LIFE-CYCLE EARNINGS MODEL

In principle, a life-cycle model could be estimated with cross-sectional data, if the model is properly specified by incorporating direct measures of vintage effects. The problem is that available vintage measures are crude at best: there are no appropriate summary measures of discrimination, and although some information on school quality is available, it is usually limited to per capita expenditures in highly aggregative form and measured across geographical units in varying ways. It is highly doubtful, therefore, that the model specification can be improved very much in this way. Virtually all of the bias would likely remain.

Ideally, in order to examine black-white life-cycle earnings differences, one should use longitudinal data on the earnings of a set of individuals, all of whom are of the same

---

[8]The appendix to this chapter provides a formal treatment of the specification error problem and its implications for the cross-sectional estimation of life-cycle effects in the presence of vintage effects.

vintage. Because we are primarily interested in differences in the life-cycle pattern of earnings between blacks and whites rather than in the life-cycle earnings of any single individual, we could combine all blacks and all whites in pooled cross-section and time-series regressions. The estimated equation, then, would be of the form:

$$(1)\ Y_{it} = \beta_0 + \beta_1 X_{it,1} + \dots \beta_{EXP} EXP_{it} + \dots \beta_k X_{it,k} + \varepsilon it,$$

where Y_{it} is the earnings of the ith individual in year t,

$X_{it,\,k}$ is the kth independent variable, measured for the ith individual in year t; and EXP is a measure of years of work experience.

The problem here is that the actual data available to economists falls far short of a complete life-cycle series on individual earnings for a representative sample of workers of the same vintage. The most extensive longitudinal data set currently available is the Panel Study of Income Dynamics. At the time of this analysis, the Panel Study provided information on eight consecutive years of earnings data for a representative national cross section of households. These individuals, of course, belong to many vintages rather than one, and for any single vintage, there are simply not a sufficient number of observations to perform a separate analysis.

A natural procedure to increase the sample size is to pool observations across a number of vintages. The effect of this procedure, however, is to introduce some cross-sectional bias into the equation. The potential estimation problem is shown in Figure 7.1. Assume that earnings information is available for N consecutive years and that we want to estimate the returns on experience for the group of workers who had from x to (x+z) years of work experience in the first year for which information is available. In year one, the cross-sectional, experience-earnings profile might look like A_1B_1; in year two assume that the experience-earnings profile, now covering the range from (x+1) to (x+z+1) years of experience, shifts up to A_2B_2, and so on through year N. In this example, the true life-cycle earnings profile is A_1A_N, which, obviously, is rather different than that estimated using cross-sectional data. The experience-earnings profile, estimated from a pooled model, would be similar to A_1B_N; its exact slope would depend on the scatter of points in each of the cross sections. Thus, the pooled model provides a much better estimate of the life-cycle profile than does the cross-sectional estimation, but it is not an unbiased estimate. It is, however, possible to use the comparison of the cross-sectional results with the pooled results in order to extrapolate to the true life-cycle effect. The appendix to this chapter provides details on the extrapolation procedure.

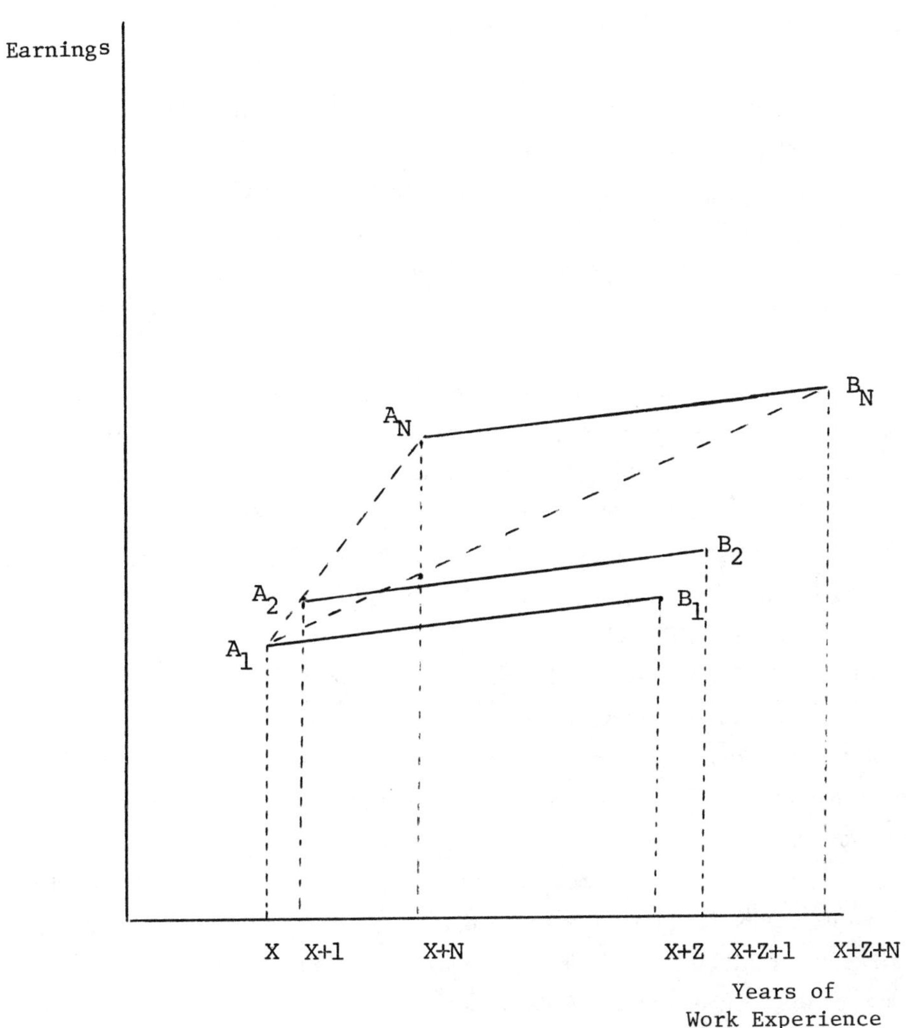

Figure 7.1. GRAPHICAL REPRESENTATION OF EFFECTS OF POOLING ON ESTIMATION OF LIFE-CYCLE RETURNS TO EXPERIENCE

CROSS-SECTIONAL AND POOLED ESTIMATES OF BLACK-WHITE LIFE-CYCLE EARNINGS

The general empirical procedure involved estimating identical earnings equations using cross-sectional and pooled data. The cross-sectional model was estimated using data for 1967, while the pooled analysis used annual data from 1967 through 1974. The pooled analyses focused on two cohorts of black and white males, those individuals between ages 20 and 29 in 1967 and those between 30 and 39 in 1967.[9] The corresponding 1967 cross-sectional cohorts covered seven more years than the pooled cohorts—ages 20 to 36 and 30 to 46 in 1967—so that identical portions of the experience-earnings profile would be compared in the cross-sectional and pooled equations. Only individuals who were in the labor force in each year—either "working now or laid off temporarily" or "looking for work, unemployed"—were included in the analysis.[10] This requirement eliminated individuals who were retired, disabled, or in school at any time during the eight years. It did not, however, necessarily exclude individuals who worked few or even zero hours in any single year; to do so might bias black-white comparisons of whether the incidence of long-term unemployment differed by race. Finally, individuals who were farmers or self-employed workers in any year were also eliminated from the sample, since earnings for these two groups are notoriously difficult to measure and interpret.

All of the earnings equations were estimated in two versions, first with experience in linear form only and then, again, adding experience-squared. Since the experience parameter was already allowed to vary by age by virtue of the separate estimation for the two age groups, the test for nonlinearity within each cohort was treated as simply an empirical issue. Only for the younger cohort of white males was the quadratic term statistically significant, and, consequently, it was eliminated from the model for the older cohorts and for the younger cohort of blacks.

---

[9]These two cohorts correspond roughly to those individuals who would have completed high school in the postdesegregation period (1955-1966) and in the postwar, predesegregation period, respectively.

[10]These are not the Bureau of Labor Statistics definitions of labor force status, but are answers to the question, "Now we would like to know about your present job—are you working now, looking for work, retired, a housewife, or what?" There is no response category for dropping out of the labor force other than returning to school, retiring, or becoming disabled.

The dependent variable used in this analysis is the natural log of real hourly earnings.[11] The set of independent variables used in this analysis are drawn from both the theoretical literature concerning the human capital model and the dual labor market model as well as from previous empirical work. In addition to the experience variable, the other independent variables were years of education, a test score measure,[12] union status, city size, region, the unemployment rate in the individual's county of residence, and a series of dummy variables for industry of employment. The equations were estimated by OLS regression.[13]

The cross-sectional and pooled results for the younger cohort of workers are presented in Table 7.2. Even within this relatively narrow age range, the cross-sectional results show a different pattern of returns on experience for blacks and whites. First, as noted above, the white experience-earnings profile is parabolic while that for blacks is linear throughout.[14] Over almost all of the relevant range of experience, the annual rate of increase in earnings for whites is greater than that for blacks. For example, the return on an additional year of work experience for a white worker with eight years of work experience is about 4.5 percent annually. At 12 years of experience, the return on an additional year of experience is still almost one-and-a-half percentage points higher (3.16 percent versus 1.75 percent) for whites than for blacks.

The pooled results, however, suggest that the cross-sectional model does not accurately reflect the longitudinal pattern of earnings. This is especially true for black work-

---

[11]For individuals with suspiciously large year-to-year fluctuations in wage rates, the original interviews were checked for possible interviewer or coding errors. Out of approximately 11,000 cases (1,400 cases x 8 years), only about 25 had obvious errors which needed to be corrected. The most common error involved interviewer or respondent confusion between work hours per day and work hours per week, causing an obvious but easily remedied five-fold variation in wage rates.

[12]This variable measures the respondent's score on a 13-item sentence completion test, drawn from the verbal portion of the Lorge-Thorndike Intelligence Test. For further information on the test, see A Panel Study of Income Dynamics, Vol. II, pp. 367-71.

[13]Maeshiro (1976) has shown that in an autoregressive model which includes a trended independent variable such as experience, the familiar Cochrane-Orcutt transformation is likely to result in less efficient estimates than the OLS estimator. For this reason, and also because the pooled equation provides a biased estimate of p, since it is still misspecified, OLS was used.

[14]The F-statistic for the inclusion of experience-squared in addition to years of experience in linear form was 10.7 for whites and 1.4 for blacks. The critical value of F for one additional variable and approximately 200 degrees of freedom is 3.84. When the white equation was estimated without experience-squared, the estimated coefficient on experience was .0375. In this form, the difference between the black and white coefficients on experience is statistically significant at the 1 percent level.

Table 7.2

1967 CROSS SECTION AND 1967-1974 POOLED EARNINGS FUNCTIONS FOR COHORT OF YOUNG BLACK AND WHITE MALES

Variable	Cross Section (Age 20-36 in 1967)		Pooled (Age 20-29 in 1967)	
	White	Black	White	Black
Experience	.0772** (.0126)	.0175** (.0060)	.0905** (.0088)	.0242** (.0038)
Experience Squared	-.0019** (.0006)	---	-.0027** (.0004)	---
South	-.0339 (.0373)	-.0384 (.0740)	-.0087 (.0189)	-.0625* (.0367)
City Size	.0002** (.0001)	.0005** (.0001)	.0002** (.0001)	.0004** (.0001)
Union	.1581** (.0394)	.1951** (.0630)	.1104** (.0200)	.1197** (.0287)
County Unemployment Rate	.0162* (.0095)	.0110 (.0271)	.0116** (.0035)	-.0077 (.0060)
Education	.1000** (.0080)	.0430** (.0132)	.1020** (.0045)	.0480** (.0068)
Test Score	.0095 (.0096)	.0086 (.0128)	.0044 (.0054)	.0189** (.0069)
Agriculture & Mining	-.1035 (.1109)	-.0947 (.1351)	-.1514** (.0771)	-.2596** (.0743)
Manufacturing Durables	.1616** (.0652)	.1774** (.0950)	.0827** (.0340)	-.0090 (.0464)
Construction & Transportation	.1236** (.0651)	.1308 (.0910)	.0084 (.0342)	.1173** (.0465)
Trade	.0031 (.0684)	-.0321 (.1094)	-.0591 (.0354)	-.0938* (.0514)
General Services	.0535 (.0771)	.1814 (.1250)	-.0324 (.0413)	-.1100* (.0594)
Professional Services	-.0592 (.0737)	.2425* (.1246)	-.1737** (.0396)	.1571** (.0639)
Government	.0862 (.0799)	-.0476 (.1274)	.0149 (.0417)	.0097 (.0611)
Constant	-1.0272	-.4576	-.8331	-.2093
N	534	230	2008	896
$\bar{R}^2$	.363	.348	.288	.309

* Significant at .05 level.

**Significant at .01 level.

ers, for whom vintage effects are clearly evident. The returns on an additional year of experience increased substantially for black workers, from 1.75 percent in the cross-section to 2.42 percent in the pooled model.[15] Compounded over eight years, this yields an average growth in earnings of 18 percent compared to 13 percent in the cross-sectional earnings profile. For whites, the returns on experience change only slightly from the cross section to the pooled model. The pooled experience-earnings profile is somewhat more concave than the cross-sectional one; the predicted rates of growth of earnings with experience are equal for workers with eight years of experience.[16] This means that for white workers with more than five years of work experience in 1967, the predicted earnings growth in the cross section actually exceeded that of the pooled model.

The pooled model still shows some evidence of increasing life-cycle earnings differences, although considerably less than indicated by the cross-sectional regressions. For the older group of black workers within the younger cohort—those with 10 or more years of work experience in 1967—the predicted eight-year rate of growth of earnings exceeded that for similar whites. For the younger workers, however, earnings for whites still appeared to increase more rapidly with experience. Indeed, the pooled regression results suggest that the black-white earnings gap was almost zero at the time of entry into the labor market and grew rapidly through the first decade of experience. This finding should be interpreted with caution, however, since the sample unfortunately contained relatively few blacks with less than four years of work experience in 1967.[17] More weight can be given to the results for workers with slightly more experience; for example, for workers with six years of experience in 1967, the earnings of whites increased about 33 percent compared to about 18 percent for otherwise similar black workers. As a result, the aver-

---

[15]In a one-tailed test of the hypothesis that the pooled coefficient is greater than the cross-sectional coefficient, the null hypothesis could be rejected at about the 80 percent level of confidence.

[16]When the pooled model was estimated without experience-squared, the coefficient on experience fell to .0341, compared to .0375 in the cross-sectional equation. In this form, the equation suggests that vintage effects were negative for all of the whites in this age cohort.

[17]There were only 12 blacks with four years of experience or less in 1967. This was, in part, a function of the way experience was defined and the age filter that was used. Experience in 1967 was defined as age minus years of education minus six (constrained to be no more than age minus 16) and the minimum age in the sample was 20. Thus, no high school graduate could have less than two years of work experience in 1967. The most likely candidates for very low experience in 1967 were young (20-22) high school graduates or slightly older (23-24) high school graduates or slightly older (23-24) college graduates. It turned out that there were very few blacks in either category.

age earnings of the black workers fell from about three-quarters that of whites at six years of experience to about two-thirds after 13 years.[18]

The predicted cross-sectional and pooled experience-earnings profiles are plotted in Figure 7.2. The equations are evaluated for an individual who belongs to a labor union, does not live in the South, is employed in durable goods manufacturing, and who has mean values for all other independent variables.[19] The two predicted profiles are virtually identical for whites, differing only slightly in level and slope. For blacks, however, the pooled equation is well above the cross-sectional one. Moreover, the rate of change of earnings, shown by the slope of the experience-earnings profile, is greater for blacks at all levels of experience in the pooled equation. Still, in both models, the white experience-earnings profile lies well above that for blacks.

The cross-sectional and pooled results for the 30 to 39 years old cohort are shown in Table 7.3. For this cohort of workers, there is clear evidence of vintage effects. Once again, the cross-sectional results show clear differences not only in the level of earnings, but also in the rate of change of earnings with experience. The real earnings of white workers increased by about 0.85 percent with each additional year of experience, while earnings for blacks actually fell by 0.40 percent per year. Although the black coefficient is not significantly different from zero at conventional levels, the difference between the black and white coefficients is statistically significant at the 10 percent level. If the individual life-cycle pattern of earnings followed that inferred from the cross section, then black-white earnings differences would increase by 1.25 percent per year and by over 9 percent over the eight-year period.

In the pooled model, however, these apparent life-cycle differences in the returns on experience disappear. For both blacks and whites, earnings growth outpaced that of the vintage of workers who precede them. For whites, the vintage effect is moderate again; the pooled returns on an additional year of work experience are a quarter of a percentage point higher than in the cross-sectional model.[20] For blacks, the vintage effects are

---

[18]That the more rapid growth in the earnings of whites may be a result of greater investments in on-the-job training is suggested by the data presented in Chapter 3, Appendix Table A3.1b. Overall, white men are two-and-one-half times more likely to be training for their current jobs than black men. Among those in the youngest age group, this difference is considerably higher.

[19]Because the dependent variable was in logarithmic form, the average hourly earnings shown in the figure are the geometric means for workers with the specified set of characteristics.

[20]The difference between the two coefficients is not statistically significant at conventional levels.

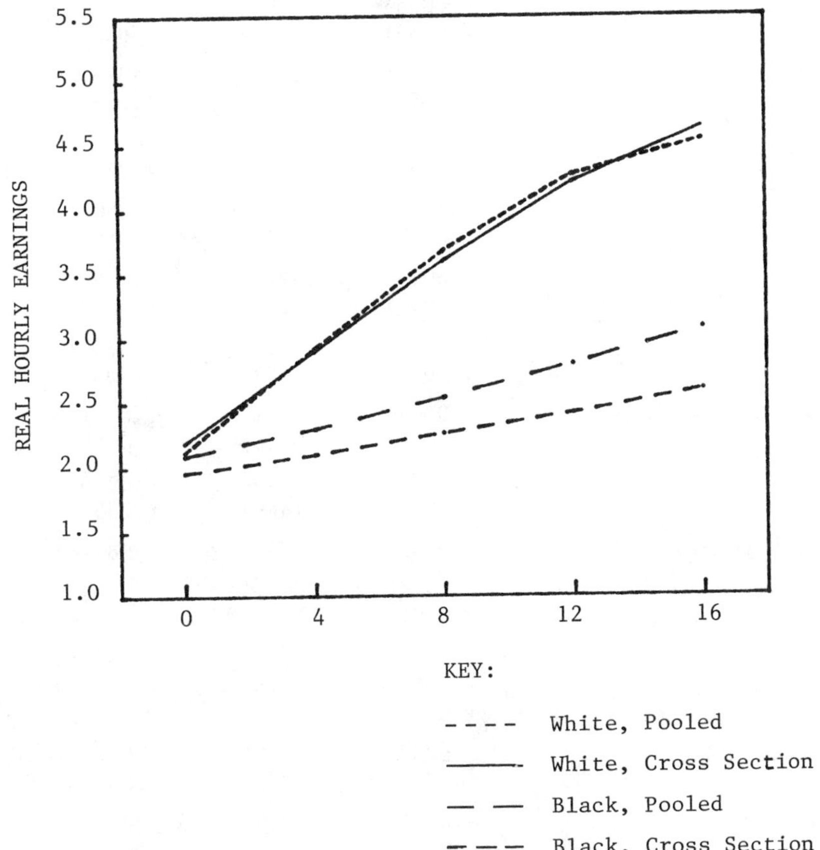

Figure 7.2. 1967 CROSS SECTION AND 1967-1974 POOLED EXPERIENCE-EARNINGS PROFILES FOR BLACK AND WHITE MALES.

(Cross Section, Ages 20-36 in 1967, and Pooled, Ages 20-29 in 1967)

Earnings profiles are evaluated for workers who belong to a labor union, work in durable-goods manufacturing, do not live in the South, and have mean values for all other independent variables.

Table 7.3

1967 CROSS SECTION AND 1967-1974 POOLED EARNINGS FUNCTIONS FOR COHORT OF MIDDLE-AGED BLACK AND WHITE MALES

Variable	Cross Section (Age 30-46 in 1967)		Pooled (Age 30-39 in 1967)	
	White	Black	White	Black
Experience	.0085** (.0032)	-.0040 (.0061)	.0113** (.0020)	.0126** (.0036)
South	-.0936** (.0353)	-.0277 (.0807)	-.0737** (.0178)	.0138 (.0343)
City Size	.0004** (.0001)	.0005** (.0001)	.0004** (.0001)	.0006** (.0001)
Union	.1068** (.0357)	.2528** (.0760)	.0801** (.0168)	.1820** (.0294)
County Unemployment Rate	.0035 (.0090)	.0225 (.0242)	.0057* (.0030)	.0159** (.0053)
Education	.0722** (.0068)	.0363** (.0137)	.0732** (.0036)	.0356** (.0055)
Test Score	.0304** (.0084)	.0091 (.0125)	.0231** (.0045)	.0186** (.0052)
Agriculture & Mining	-.0874 (.0994)	-.4869** (.1449)	-.0916* (.0558)	-.5127** (.0651)
Manufacturing Durables	.0465 (.0535)	.1572 (.1075)	.0871** (.0279)	.1149** (.0473)
Construction & Transportation	.0497 (.0550)	.1684** (.0953)	.0989** (.0295)	.1297** (.0438)
Trade	-.0860 (.0611)	.0675 (.1194)	-.1017** (.0342)	-.0083 (.0555)
General Services	-.0837 (.0685)	.2400* (.1372)	-.0044 (.0361)	-.0265 (.0560)
Professional Services	-.0776 (.0608)	.1849 (.1284)	.0134 (.0314)	.0530 (.0528)
Government	-.0534 (.0665)	.2748** (.1325)	-.0565* (.0334)	.1261 (.0542)
Constant	-.1818	-.1096	-.1507	-.3349
N	628	252	2528	1040
$\bar{R}^2$	.378	.448	.369	.469

* Significant at .01 level.

**Significant at .05 level.

extremely strong, with each additional year of experience yielding a 1.26 percent increase in real earnings rather than the slight decline predicted by the cross section. The difference between the cross-sectional and pooled estimate for black workers is statistically significant at the 5 percent level, and there is now no statistically significant difference between the estimated black and white returns on experience.

The corresponding experience-earnings profiles, again evaluated for union members in durable goods manufacturing who do not live in the South, are shown in Figure 7.3. The difference in the level of earnings of black and white workers is large in both models, but in the pooled model, the differences decline slightly over the life-cycle.

As noted above, the estimated coefficients on experience are biased even in the pooled models, but it is possible to use the comparison of the cross-sectional and pooled results to extrapolate to the true life-cycle parameter. These extrapolated coefficients are presented in Table 7.4, along with the corresponding cross-sectional and pooled estimates. Because the extrapolation procedure is based on some strong assumptions—namely, that the cross-sectional model is correctly specified except for the omitted vintage effects and that the earnings model is itself stable over time except for changes in the returns to experience—it is probably prudent to think of the true life-cycle parameter as being bracketed by the pooled and extrapolated estimates.[21]

In general, since vintage effects were stronger for blacks than for whites, the effect of extrapolation is to narrow still further the black-white differences in returns on experience. For the younger workers in the 20 to 29 age cohort, the remaining differences are still sizeable, but they narrow rapidly with experience. For workers with eight years of experience in 1967, the apparent cross-sectional difference of almost 3 percent per year fell to about 2.5 percent in the pooled model and finally to about 1.25 percent when the coefficients were extrapolated. For the older workers in this cohort—for example, those with 12 years of experience in 1967—the extrapolated black returns are greater than the returns on experience for white workers. This is also true for the entire 30 to 39-year-old cohort, where the extrapolated black coefficient is over two percentage points greater than that for whites. Assuming that the pooled and extrapolated estimates bracket the true parameter value, the results suggest that differences in earnings growth did exist in the first eight to 10 years of work, but that thereafter, earnings differences were maintained or even reduced. For both cohorts, the pooled and extrapolated results indicate a far more optimistic life-cycle situation than would be inferred from cross-sectional results.

[21]In Table 7.4, the returns on experience in the younger cohort are evaluated at various levels of experience to allow for the nonlinear returns to experience for whites. For the blacks in this cohort, the returns are constant at all levels of experience, since the experience term was, as noted above, entered in linear rather than quadratic form.

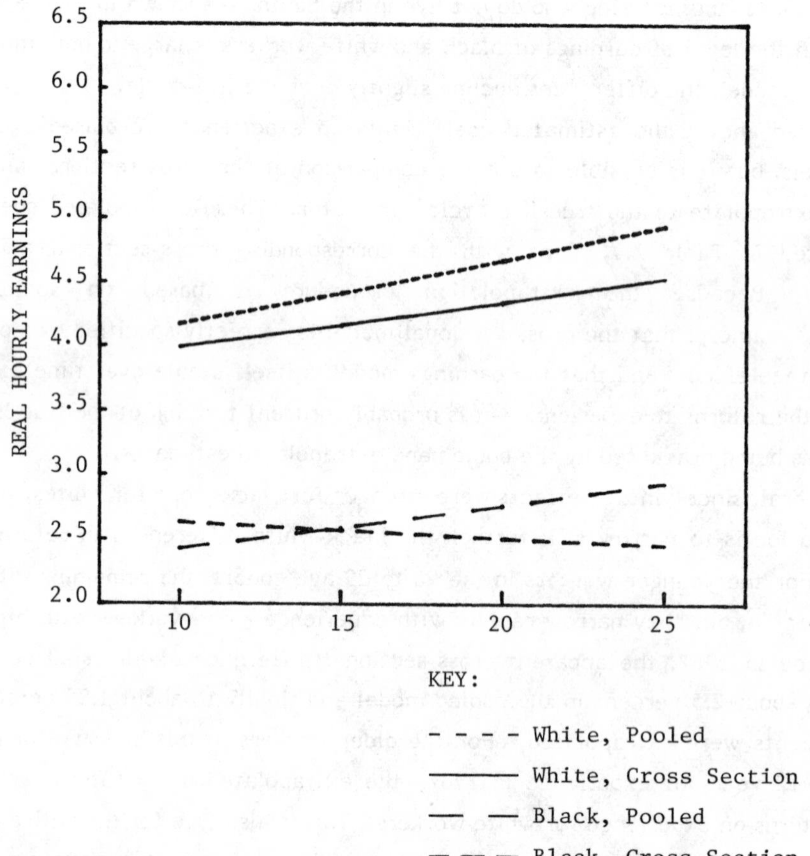

Figure 7.3. 1967 CROSS SECTION AND 1967-1974 POOLED EXPERIENCE-EARNINGS PROFILES FOR BLACK AND WHITE MALES

(Cross Section, Ages 30-46 in 1967, and Pooled, Ages 30-39 in 1967).

Earnings profiles are evaluated for workers who belong to a labor union, work in durable-goods manufacturing, do not live in the South, and have mean values for all other independent variables.

Table 7.4

CROSS-SECTIONAL, POOLED, AND EXTRAPOLATED COEFFICIENTS ON YEARS OF WORK EXPERIENCE FOR BLACK AND WHITE WORKING MALES

	Age 20-29 with:			Age 30-39
	4 Years Work Experience (1967)	8 Years Work Experience (1967)	12 Years Work Experience (1967)	
White				
Cross Section	.0620	.0468	.0316	.0085
Pooled	.0689	.0473	.0257	.0113
Extrapolated	.0757	.0479	.0164	.0158
Black				
Cross Section	.0175	.0175	.0175	-.0040*
Pooled	.0242	.0242	.0242	.0126
Extrapolated	.0353	.0353	.0353	.0396

NOTE: The full regression included years of education, union status, a test score measure, city size, region, county unemployment rate, and industry of employment.

*Not significantly different from zero at .05 level.

Summary

Three results stand out in the comparison of the cross-sectional, pooled, and extrapolated results. One is the very striking evidence of vintage effects for the older cohort of black workers and the very high extrapolated estimate of their returns on additional years of work experience. Since it is difficult to imagine that the normal operation of the labor market actually favors blacks over whites, it is possible that this finding reflects the effects of minority hiring and affirmative action programs. Related to this is the finding of negative vintage effects for the white workers in the older part of the 20 to 29 cohort. For this group of workers, the pooled and extrapolated returns are lower than in the cross-section; in effect, they were unable to match the earnings growth of either the cohort of whites which preceded them or of their companion cohort of black workers. It is at least plausible that the steeper experience-earnings profile of the older black workers came, at least in part, at the expense of a decline in the experience-earnings profile of whites in the same cohort. This would be the case if, for example, minority hiring and affirmation action programs enabled black workers to acquire jobs and, especially, promotions, which might previously (i.e., in the decade or so before 1967) have been given disproportionately to whites.

Finally, although the older black workers in these two cohorts appeared to fare well compared to the older whites, this was not the case for the younger blacks. Even using the extrapolated coefficients, the difference in earnings between the younger black and white workers clearly increased over the first ten years of experience.

References

Becker, Gary. The Economics of Discrimination. Chicago: The University of Chicago Press, 1957.

Ben-Porath, Yoram. "The Production of Human Capital and the Life-Cycle of Earnings." Journal of Political Economy 75 (August 1967).

Blinder, Alan. "Wage Discrimination: Reduced Form and Structural Estimates." Journal of Human Resources 7 (Fall 1973).

Cain, Glen G. "The Challence of Segmented Labor Market Theories to Orthodox Theory: A Survey." Journal of Economic Literature XIV (December 1976).

Doeringer, Peter B., and Piore, Michael J. Internal Labor Markets and Manpower Analysis. Lexington, Mass.: Heath-Lexington Books, 1971.

Freeman, Richard B. "Comment." In Discrimination in Labor Markets. Edited by Orley Ashenfelter and Albert Rees. Princeton, N.J.: Princeton University Press, 1973.

Hall, Robert E. "Wages, Income, and Hours of Work in the U.S. Labor Force." In Income Maintenance and Labor Supply. Edited by Glen C. Cain and Harold Watts. Chicago: Rand-McNally, 1973.

Hanoch, Giora. "An Economic Analysis of Earnings and Schooling." Journal of Human Resources 1 (Summer 1967).

Hoffman, Saul. "Black-White Life-Cycle Earnings Differences and the Vintage Hypothesis: A Longitudinal Analysis." Unpublished Ph.D. dissertation, The University of Michigan, 1977.

Kmenta, Jan. Elements of Econometrics. New York: MacMillan, 1971.

Maeshiro, Asatoshi. "Autoregressive Transformation, Trended Independent Variables, and Autocorrelated Disturbance Terms." The Review of Economics and Statistics 58 (November 1976).

Morgan, James N. "Changes in Global Measures." In Five Thousand American Families-Patterns of Economic Progress, Volume I. Edited by James N. Morgan. Ann Arbor, Mich.: Institute for Social Research, 1974.

Rosen, Sherwin. "Learning and Experience in the Labor Market." Journal of Human Resources 7 (Summer 1972).

Survey Research Center. A Panel Study of Income Dynamics: Study Design, Procedures, Data Available. Ann Arbor, Mich.: Institute for Social Research, 1972.

Welch, Finis. "Education and Racial Discrimination." In Discrimination in Labor Markets. Edited by Orley Ashenfelter and Albert Rees. Princeton, N.J.: Princeton University Press, 1973.

Welch, Finis. "Black-White Differences in Returns to Schooling." In Patterns of Racial Discrimination, Volume II. Edited by George von Furstenberg, Anne Horowitz, and Bennet Harrison. Lexington, Mass.: Lexington Books, 1974.

APPENDIX 7.1

IMPLICATIONS OF THE VINTAGE HYPOTHESIS FOR THE CROSS-SECTIONAL ESTIMATION OF BLACK/WHITE LIFE-CYCLE EARNINGS DIFFERENCES

According to the vintage hypothesis, earnings are a function not only of the conventional cross-sectional explanatory variables, but of two other variables as well: the quality of an individual's education and the extent and strength of discrimination at the time an individual entered the labor market. We can express this model as:

$$(1)\quad Y = X\beta + \varepsilon$$

where $X = [X^* \mid Q \mid D]$ and $\beta = \begin{bmatrix} \beta^* \\ \hline \beta_Q \\ \hline \beta_D \end{bmatrix}$

Here, X^* is a (N x K-2) matrix of conventional explanatory variables and Q and D are (N x 1) vectors representing the quality of an individual's education and a composite summary measure of labor market discrimination, respectively; β^*, β_Q, and β_D are the corresponding regression parameters. Both Q and D are, in turn, hypothesized to be functions of vintage:

$$(2)\quad Q = \alpha_1 V + \eta$$

$$(3)\quad D = \alpha_2 V + \mu$$

In most cross-sectional analyses, however, Q and D are omitted, and the estimated equation is

$$(4)\quad Y = X^*\beta^* + \varepsilon^*.$$

The cross-sectional equation is, therefore, misspecified.

Solving for $\hat{\beta}^*$, as estimated from equation (4), we have:

$$(5)\quad \hat{\beta}^* = (X^{*\prime}X^*)^{-1}X^{*\prime}Y$$

$$= (X^{*\prime}X^*)^{-1}X^{*\prime}(X\beta + \varepsilon)$$

$$= (X^{*\prime}X^*)^{-1}X^{*\prime}\left\{[X^* \mid \ell \mid D]\begin{bmatrix}\beta^* \\ \hline \beta_{\ell} \\ \hline \beta_D\end{bmatrix} + \varepsilon\right\}$$

$$= (X^{*\prime}X^*)^{-1}X^{*\prime}X^*\beta^* + (X^{*\prime}X^*)^{-1}X^{*\prime}\ell\beta_{\ell}$$

$$+ (X^{*\prime}X^*)^{-1}X^{*\prime}D\beta_D + (X^{*\prime}X^*)^{-1}X^{*\prime}\varepsilon.$$

Taking expectations,

$$(6)\quad E(\hat{\beta}^*) = \beta^* + \beta_{\ell}E[X^{*\prime}X^*)^{-1}X^{*\prime}\ell] + \beta_D E[X^{*\prime}X^*)^{-1}X^{*\prime}D].$$

Finally, substituting for ℓ and D from equations (4) and (5),

$$(7)\quad E(\hat{\beta}^*) = \beta^* + \beta_{\ell}E[X^{*\prime}X^*)^{-1}X^{*\prime}(\alpha_1 V + \eta)]$$

$$+ \beta_D E[(X^{*\prime}X^*)^{-1}X^{*\prime}(\alpha_2 V + \mu)$$

$$(8)\quad E(\hat{\beta}^*) = \beta^* + \beta_{\ell}\alpha_1 E[(X^{*\prime}X^*)^{-1}X^{*\prime}V] + \beta_D\alpha_2 E[X^{*\prime}X^*)^{-1}X^{*\prime}V].$$

The two bracketed expressions in (8) can be thought of as the (K-2 x 1) vector of "coefficients" from the auxiliary regression[1] of V on X*. For the coefficient of interest here, the cross-sectional coefficient on years of work experience, the corresponding expression is simply:

$$(9)\quad E(\hat{\beta}^*_{exp}) = \beta_{exp} + Z_{exp}(\alpha_1\beta_{\ell} + \alpha_2\beta_D),$$

where Z_{exp} is the coefficient on experience from the auxiliary regression.

As equation (9) clearly shows, the coefficient on years of work experience, estimated from cross-sectional data, will be biased unless the second term on the right-hand side of (9) equals zero. It is useful to think of the

[1]Since both V and X* are non-stochastic, the auxilliary regression can be viewed as a purely descriptive regression only. See Kmenta (1971), pp. 391-94.

bias as being composed of two multiplicative terms, one Z_{exp}, reflecting the multiple regression relationship between vintage and years of work experience, and the other, $\alpha_1\beta_Q + \alpha_2\beta_D$, reflecting the effects of vintage, operating through quality of education and discrimination, on earnings. Unless at least one of these two components is equal to zero, the estimated cross-sectional coefficient will be biased.

According to the vintage hypothesis, the second of the two multiplicative terms in (9) will be negative: $\alpha_1 < 0$ (school quality is negatively related to vintage), while $\beta_2 > 0$ (earnings are a positive function of school quality); similarly, $\alpha_2 > 0$ (discrimination is positively related to vintage) and $\beta_D < 0$ (discrimination reduces earnings). As for the first component of the bias, Z_{exp}, in any cross-section, vintage, measured by an individual's age, is related to years of work experience by the identity, $V = Exp + M$, where M equals an individual's age at the completion of school and entry into the labor market.[2] When differences among individuals in educational attainment are controlled for in the auxiliary regression, the auxiliary coefficient on years of work experience is approximately equal to one in a cross section.

The net result, then, is that the bias is negative; that is, the cross-sectional estimate of the effects of work experience on earnings is less than the true life-cycle parameter when vintage effects are present.

The further contention of the vintage hypothesis is that if equations (1), (2), and (3) are estimated separately by race, then α_1 is more negative for blacks (the quality of education is more strongly related to vintage for blacks than for whites) and that α_2 is more positive for blacks

---

[2]This identity assumes regular labor force participation and no unemployment after an individual enters the labor market.

(a stronger relationship between vintage and discrimination). Consequently, it is easy to see from (9) that the bias in the estimated coefficient on experience will be greater (more negative) for blacks than for whites.

The procedure for extrapolating to the true life-cycle parameter draws on equation (9) in which the bias is represented as the product of the effects of vintage on earnings ($\alpha_1\beta a + \alpha_2\beta_D$) and the relationship between vintage and experience (Z_{exp}). The derivative of (9) with respect to Z_{exp} is $\partial E(\hat{\beta}*_{exp})/\partial Z_{exp} = \alpha_1\beta_Q + \alpha_2\beta_D$. Since α_1, α_2, β_Q, and β_D are parameters, the derivative is a constant, and its value can be estimated by performing two auxiliary regressions--for example, one cross-sectional, and the other pooled over several vintages--and then using the two pairs of estimated values of $E(\hat{\beta}*_{exp})$ and Z_{exp} to compute the finite approximation of the derivative. It is possible, then, to extrapolate to the true value of β_{exp} by using (9) since all the terms are known. The true life-cycle value of β_{exp} can be computed as:

$$\beta_{EXP} = \hat{\beta}^*_{EXP:P} - (Z_{EXP:P}) \left(\frac{\hat{\beta}^*_{EXP:P} - \hat{\beta}^*_{EXP:CS}}{Z_{EXP:P} - Z_{EXP:CS}}\right)$$

Chapter 8

DEPENDENCY AND POVERTY IN THE SHORT AND LONG RUN

Richard Coe

Introduction

Since the War on Poverty was announced, there have been reports about how many people are poor, whether poverty is being eliminated, and how successful government anti-poverty programs are in pushing people above the poverty line. Repeated counting of the poor requires agreement on how we measure poverty, but periodically we should look behind these accepted numbers in order to assure ourselves that we aren't being misled concerning the nature and extent of poverty in the United States.

We intend to examine two aspects of the nature of poverty. The first involves determining what sources of income are responsible for lifting people above the poverty line. The official poverty definition used by the Census Bureau counts money received from all sources equally as income. However, it is of interest to know how many people are dependent, but not poor, because some form of welfare kept them out of poverty. Our society has numerous mechanisms by which we attempt to provide individuals with the resources necessary for their existence. Foremost among these are the labor and capital markets in which people exchange the use of their labor services or the use of money or physical assets for a monetary return in the form of wages, salaries, rent, interest, or dividends. An increasingly important mechanism of support, however, is the transfer system in which people receive money without a direct exchange of services or use of capital.[1] There are numerous types of transfer payments. There are <u>contributory</u> transfers, both private and public, where people contribute money at one stage in their life or when they are employed and are thus entitled to payments at some other time in their life or when they are unemployed. Private contributory transfer programs include private pension plans and injury-related income replacement plans. Public contributory

[1] The rising importance of transfer payments in our economy has recently received increased attention from economists, most notably from members of the Association for the Study of the Grants Economy.

transfer programs include the Social Security program, workmen's compensation, and unemployment benefits.[2] There are also noncontributory transfers, both private and public, where individuals are not necessarily required to make any monetary contribution in order to receive payments. No doubt the largest of the private noncontributory transfers are those occuring within the household, particularly between parents and children. (This type of transfer is the subject of Chapter 11, and will not be discussed in this chapter.) Other private noncontributory transfers occur between households, as when elderly parents are supported by an adult offspring or a wife by a former spouse.[3] Finally, there are public noncontributory transfers, which include Aid to Families with Dependent Children, General Asistance, and Supplemental Security Income, as well as a host of in-kind programs, such as public housing and food stamp subsidies.

In evaluating the nature and extent of poverty it might be argued that we should be concerned not only with whether a family is above the poverty line, but with the mechanism of support on which it relies. Our concern may not be restricted to eliminating poverty per se, but may also encompass eliminating dependency on noncontributory transfers. If so, then the source of income becomes as crucial as the amount, and it is this issue which we wish to address first.

Our second concern is with the time period over which poverty is measured. The official poverty counts are based on annual incomes of families, a time span which fails to distinguish between those families which have an occasional bad year and those which are persistently in straitened circumstances. This distinction would seem crucial for our understanding of the nature of poverty, and how we devise programs to combat it. For example, a short-run emergency insurance program (such as unemployment insurance)

---

[2]Although workers do not make direct cash payments to the workmen's compensation or unemployment benefits funds, as they do to the Social Security Trust Fund, economic theory leads us to believe that workers contribute to these funds via reduced wages. The same line of reasoning applies to the employer's share of the Social Security tax.

[3]These classifications are, of course, arbitrary to a degree, and the example of alimony perhaps best illustrates this. We classify alimony as a noncontributory transfer, but one could certainly argue that such transfers are not "noncontributory" in a moral or even economic sense. The rationale behind alimony payments is that the time and energy devoted by one spouse to efforts around the home were essential to the success of the other spouse and to the family, and that the spouse who expended such efforts is entitled to some return. Our distinction, however, is between situations where prior monetary contributions result in legal entitlements to subsequent benefits versus other situations.

would seem most appropriate for families suffering an atypical hard year, while longer run educational opportunity or job training programs may be most appropriate to eliminate persistent dependency.

Data available from the Panel Study of Income Dynamics enable us to examine the effect of different sources of transfer income and different time horizons on the measurement of poverty. The second part of this chapter defines the various measures used in the analysis. Then it analyzes the sources of transfer income and the incidence of poverty in a one-year time perspective. It is followed by an examination of different time horizons and the measurement of poverty, and a look at the sources of income over a nine-year time horizon.

Analysis

DEFINITIONS OF DIFFERENT MEASURES OF INCOME

The analysis which follows will employ five measures of income, defined as follows:

Taxable Income of the Family (Income I). Taxable Income of the Family consists of all wages, salaries, bonuses, overtime, commissions, income from professional practice or trade, net income from farming or from owning a business, income from market gardening, roomers and boarders, and dividends, interest, rent, trust funds, or royalties received by all members of the household. It is meant to measure the income received by the family from exchanging the use of their labor and/or money and physical assets in the labor and capital markets. This measure corresponds closely, but not exactly, to the definition of adjusted gross income used by the Internal Revenue Service.[4]

Taxable Income Plus Private Contributory Transfers (Income II). This measure consists of Income I plus other retirement pay, pensions, and annuities. It does not include Social Security payments.

Taxable Income Plus Private and Public Contributory Transfers (Income III). This measure consists of Income II plus Social Security payments, unemployment benefits, and workmen's compensation payments.

Taxable Income, Private and Public Contributory Transfers, Plus Private Noncontributory Transfers (Income IV). This measure equals Income III plus alimony, child support,

---

[4]Perhaps the most notable difference from the Internal Revenue Service definition of adjusted gross income is the omission of capital gains income. Also omitted are alimony payments received and the taxable portion of private retirement payments.

and money received from friends and relatives who were not members of the household.

Taxable Income, Private and Public Contributory Transfers, Plus Private and Public Noncontributory Transfers (Income V). This measure consists of Income IV plus AFDC payments, other welfare, and Supplemental Security Income payments.[5] As a measure of total family monetary resources, it is virtually equivalent to the income measure used by the Census Bureau to determine the number of people in poverty. Benefits from in-kind public noncontributory transfer programs (e.g., food stamps, public housing) are not included in this measure.

SOURCES OF INCOME AND THE EXTENT OF POVERTY

Impact on the Poverty Poverty Population of the Different Types of Income

Table 8.1 relates the sources of income to the percentage of various subgroups of the population who were in poverty. The first page is for a one-year period, 1975. The first row shows the percentage of individuals who would be in poverty if income included only what the family received through the labor and capital markets (e.g., wages, salaries, rents, dividends, and interest).[6] As shown in the final column of row one, these sources of income maintain 80 percent of the population above the poverty line. Those individuals left behind are disproportionately in families where the head is either 65 years or older, black, disabled, unmarried with children, or female. (These groups are not mutually exclusive.)

When private contributory transfer income (i.e., pensions, annuities, and other retirement pay, not including Social Security income) is added to taxable income, an additional 2.5 percent of the population is lifted above the poverty line. Individuals living in families headed by an elderly or disabled person were particularly aided by this source

---

[5]This definition of Income V (and, for that matter, of Incomes II, III, and IV) is not entirely correct for all years. Only in years 1974 and 1975 was the transfer income of other household members besides the head and wife divided into its separate components. For the years 1967 through 1973, the total transfer income of others was added to Income IV to form Income V, in addition to the public noncontributory transfer income of the head and wife. This no doubt resulted in an overstatement of the amount of public noncontributory transfers received by the family. Appendix Table A8.1a shows the potential effect of this overstatement on the results reported in this chapter.

[6]It should be emphasized at this point that the individual is the unit of analysis in this chapter, but the economic well-being of the individual is measured by the resources of the family to which he belongs.

Table 8.1

INDIVIDUALS BROUGHT ABOVE THE POVERTY LINE
BY VARIOUS KINDS OF TRANSFER INCOME
(All Sample Individuals in 1976)

	Household Head in 1976 was . . .													
	Age 65 or Older		Black		Disabled		Unmarried with Children		Female		Employed at Least 1500 Hours in 1975		All	
Income Definition	Per-cent-age Poor	Per-centage Brought out of Poverty	Per-cent-age Poor	Per-centage Brought out of Poverty	Per-cent-age Poor	Per-centage Brought out of Poverty	Per-cent - age Poor	Per-centage Brought out of Poverty	Per-cent-age Poor	Per-centage Brought out of Poverty	Per-cent-age Poor	Per-centage Brought out of Poverty	Per-cent-age Poor	Per-centage Brought out of Poverty
1975														
1 Taxable Income	61.0		43.2		66.8		51.0		49.7		4.6		20.4	
		12.4		1.3		10.2		0.2		2.6		0.0		2.5
11 Taxable Income plus Private Contributory Transfers	48.6		41.9		56.6		50.8		47.1		4.6		17.9	
		30.9		5.5		22.9		5.6		12.9		0.6		5.8
111 Taxable Income plus Private and Public Contributory Transfers	17.7		36.4		33.7		45.2		34.2		4.0		12.1	
		0.9		1.1		1.6		7.2		4.6		0.5		1.1
1V Taxable Income, Private and Public Contributory Transfers, plus Private Noncontributory Transfers	16.8		35.3		32.1		38.0		29.6		3.5		11.0	
		3.2		6.8		5.6		9.3		7.0		0.4		2.1
V Taxable Income, Private and Public Contributory Transfers, plus Private and Public Noncontributory Transfers	13.6		28.5		26.5		28.7		22.6		3.1		8.9	

Table 8.1 (continued)

Income Definition	Household Head in 1976 was . . .													
	Age 65 or Older		Black		Disabled		Unmarried with Children		Female		Employed at Least 1500 Hours in 1975		All	
	Percentage Poor	Percentage Brought out of Poverty	Percentage Poor	Percentage Brought out of Poverty	Percentage Poor	Percentage Brought out of Poverty	Percentage Poor	Percentage Brought out of Poverty	Percentage Poor	Percentage Brought out of Poverty	Percentage Poor	Percentage Brought out of Poverty	Percentage Poor	Percentage Brought out of Poverty
All Years 1967-1975														
I Taxable Income	22.4		20.3		30.6		19.7		18.4		0.8		5.9	
		6.3		1.2		6.8		0.9		2.3		0.1		1.1
II Taxable Income plus Private Contributory Transfers	16.1		19.1		23.8		18.8		16.1		0.7		4.8	
		10.7		4.1		9.8		3.2		5.1		0.1		1.8
III Taxable Income plus Private and Public Contributory Transfers	5.4		15.0		14.0		15.6		11.0		0.6		3.0	
		0.5		0.7		0.8		1.1		1.2		0.0		0.3
IV Taxable Income, Private and Public Contributory Transfers, plus Private Noncontributory Transfers	4.9		14.3		13.2		14.5		9.8		0.6		2.7	
		2.8		7.6		7.1		7.9		5.2		0.4		1.6
V Taxable Income, Private and Public Contributory Transfers, Plus Private and Public Noncontributory Transfers	2.1		6.7		6.1		6.6		4.6		0.2		1.1	

Table 8.1 (continued)

	Household Head in 1976 was . . .													
	Age 65 or Older		Black		Disabled		Unmarried with Children		Female		Employed at Least 1500 Hours in 1975		All	
Income Definition	Percentage Poor	Percentage Brought out of Poverty	Percentage Poor	Percentage Brought out of Poverty	Percentage Poor	Percentage Brought out of Poverty	Percentage Poor	Percentage Brought out of Poverty	Percentage Poor	Percentage Brought out of Poverty	Percentage Poor	Percentage Brought out of Poverty	Percentage Poor	Percentage Brought out of Poverty
Any Year 1967 1975														
I Taxable Income	76.5		72.8		81.3		72.0		71.0		23.4		38.3	
		5.8		0.3		3.2		0.3		1.3		0.3		1.5
II Taxable Income plus Private Contributory Transfers	70.7		72.5		78.1		71.7		69.7		23.1		36.8	
		30.6		3.1		18.6		4.1		10.1		1.8		6.2
III Taxable Income plus Private and Public Contributory Transfers	40.1		69.4		59.5		67.6		59.6		21.3		30.6	
		5.9		1.1		4.3		8.3		6.5		2.8		3.5
IV Taxable Income, Private and Public Contributory Transfers, plus Private Noncontributory Transfers	34.2		68.3		55.2		59.3		53.1		18.5		27.1	
		4.2		2.5		4.3		4.8		5.6		1.1		2.0
V Taxable Income, Private and Public Contributory Transfers, plus Private and Public Noncontributory Transfers	30.0		65.8		50.9		54.5		47.5		17.4		25.1	

of support. For example, 12.4 percent of the individuals living in a family with a head aged 65 or more were moved above the poverty line as a result of such income. Individuals who were in families headed by a black person, an unmarried person with children in the household, or by a head who worked at least 1,500 hours were virtually unaffected by this type of income.

Public contributory transfer payments had a substantial impact on the extent of poverty, as shown in the third row of Table 8.1. Approximately 6 percent of the population is moved out of poverty when Social Security payments, workmen's compensation, and unemployment benefits are added to family income. As might be expected, the elderly and the disabled are most aided by these mechanisms of support, as 31 percent of the elderly and 23 percent of the disabled are pulled above the poverty line. Again, the working poor, blacks, and unmarried parents are least affected by these types of transfers.

Private noncontributory transfers lifted 1.1 percent of the population out of poverty. The major beneficiaries of this type of transfer were individuals in families headed by an unmarried parent and/or by a female, whose income undoubtedly increased as a result of the inclusion of alimony and child support payments. Other transfers between families, as when children help support an elderly parent, are also included in this category, although their effects are surprisingly small.

Adding public noncontributory transfer payments (i.e., payments from Aid to Families with Dependent Children, Supplemental Security Income, and general assistance programs) to form total family money income resulted in an additional 2.1 percent of individuals being moved out of poverty. The benefits from such transfers flowed most noticeably to individuals in families where the head was either an unmarried parent, female, or black. (Again, these groups are not mutually exclusive.) The working poor are little affected by these types of transfers.

Even after all sources of monetary income are counted, however, 8.9 percent of all individuals remain in poverty,[7] indicating that the various support mechanisms adopted by

---

[7]The Panel Study has consistently yielded lower counts of the poverty population than the Census Bureau estimates. The year 1975 is no exception. While the Panel Study shows 8.9 percent of all individuals were in poverty in 1975, the Census Bureau estimates that 12.3 percent of all individuals were in families where income was not sufficient to provide for basic needs. The source of discrepancy has not been pinpointed. Minarik concluded that the Panel Study requires better income reporting from its respondents than does the Census Bureau, and this could result in fewer poor persons. McClelland concluded that the Panel Study slightly underrepresents lower socioeconomic status famlies, which would also result in a lower count of poor persons. It should also be noted that children born into the panel since 1972 are not included in this analysis, which may result in a downward estimate of the aggregate poverty population.

See J. Minarik, "New Evidence on the Poverty Count," working paper (Washington, D.C.: The Brookings Institution, 1973), and McClelland, K., "Why Different Surveys Yield Different Results: Education and Earnings in the Census and the Panel Study of Income Dynamics," in <u>Effects of Family Background, Test Scores, Personality Traits and Schooling</u>

our society are not completely fulfilling the purpose of providing individuals with the necessary resources to meet basic needs. Although the exchange sector of our economy provides the basic resources for the vast majority of members of our society, certain subgroups of our population rely heavily on the various transfer systems. While the elderly and the disabled receive substantial support from contributory transfer payments, presumably built up over their working lifetimes, other segments of our society—primarily the blacks and individuals in a family headed by an unmarried parent—are dependent on noncontributory transfers to lift them out of poverty. Despite the aid these groups do receive, they are still disproportionately poor. These figures also illustrate the fact that the working poor are aided very little by the various transfer systems. Although most people who work are not poor, fewer than one-third of those who work but do not earn enough to raise themselves above the poverty line receive sufficient transfer income to enable them to climb out of poverty.

Composition of the Poverty Population

The first page of Table 8.2 presents a similar story by showing the composition of the poverty population when different measures of income are counted. When only the taxable income of the family is counted, individuals in families headed by a person aged 65 or more comprise 35.5 percent of the poverty population. When total family money income is used, however, such individuals comprise only 18.1 percent of the poverty population, indicating that they are benefitted disproportionately (in terms of being lifted out of poverty) compared to those individuals living in families headed by a person under the age of 65.[8] Public contributory transfer payments provided the biggest relative gain for this group. In contrast, individuals in families headed by a black person comprised 27.2 percent of the population when only income from the exchange sector of the economy was counted. This percentage rose to 41.3, however, when money income from all sources was included in the income measure, indicating that blacks benefitted relatively less than nonblacks from the aggregate of transfer systems. A similar situation existed for the working poor, who accounted for only 16 percent of all those individuals whose taxable income failed to meet their minimal needs but accounted for one-quarter of the poverty population after all money income was counted.

---

on Economic Success, edited by Christopher Jencks and Lee Rainwater, Report No. DLMA-NIE-G-74-007-1, (Washington, D.C.: U.S. Department of Labor, 1977).

[8]If both groups had benefitted relatively equally by the various transfers in terms of being lifted above the official poverty line, then individuals in families headed by a person aged 65 or more would have comprised 35.5 percent of the poverty population no matter what income measure was used.

Table 8.2

COMPOSITION OF THE POVERTY POPULATION
BY VARIOUS KINDS OF TRANSFER INCOME AND BY DIFFERENT TIME HORIZONS

(All Sample Individuals in 1976)

Income Definition	Percentage of Poverty Population in a Household Whose Head in 1976 was . . .					
	Age 65 or Older	Black	Disabled	Unmarried with Children	Female	Employed at Least 1500 Hours in 1975
1975						
I Taxable Income	35.5	27.2	21.4	23.7	44.0	16.0
II Taxable Income plus Private Contributory Transfers	32.2	30.1	20.7	26.9	47.5	18.1
III Taxable Income plus Private and Public Contributory Transfers	17.3	38.7	18.2	35.4	51.0	23.4
IV Taxable Income, Private and Public Contributory Transfers, plus Private Noncontributory Transfers	18.1	41.3	19.2	32.7	48.7	22.3
V Taxable Income, Private and Public Contributory Transfers, plus Private and Public Noncontributory Transfers	18.1	41.3	19.6	30.6	46.0	25.0

Table 8.2 (continued)

Income Definition	Percentage of Poverty Population in a Household Whose Head in 1976 was . . .					
	Age 65 or Older	Black	Disabled	Unmarried with Children	Female	Employed at Least 1500 Hours in 1975
All Years, 1967-1975						
I Taxable Income	45.4	44.5	34.2	31.8	56.8	9.2
II Taxable Income plus Private Contributory Transfers	39.9	51.1	32.5	37.1	60.5	10.9
III Taxable Income plus Private and Public Contributory Transfers	21.4	64.5	30.6	49.2	66.3	13.3
IV Taxable Income, Private and Public Contributory Transfers, plus Private Noncontributory Transfers	21.5	67.6	31.8	50.5	65.2	14.5
V Taxable Income, Private and Public Contributory Transfers, plus Private and Public Noncontributory Transfers	22.1	77.0	35.9	56.2	73.9	13.6

Table 8.2 (continued)

Income Definition	Percentage of Poverty Population in a Household Whose Head in 1976 was . . .					
	Age 65 or Older	Black	Disabled	Unmarried with Children	Female	Employed at Least 1500 Hours in 1975
Any Year, 1967-1975						
I Taxable Income	23.7	24.5	13.9	17.8	33.5	43.2
II Taxable Income plus Private Contributory Transfers	22.8	25.4	13.9	18.5	34.2	44.3
III Taxable Income plus Private and Public Contributory Transfers	15.6	29.2	12.8	21.0	35.2	49.3
IV Taxable Income, Private and Public Contributory Transfers, plus Private Noncontributory Transfers	15.0	32.4	13.4	20.7	35.4	48.2
V Taxable Income, Private and Public Contributory Transfers, plus Private and Public Noncontributory Transfers	14.2	33.8	13.3	20.6	34.2	49.0

Average Amounts of Different Types of Income

Examining the percentage of individuals who are brought above the poverty line by various types of transfer payments ignores the fact that many individuals may benefit by the different types of income, but not sufficiently to lift them out of poverty. An alternative way of evaluating the different types of transfer systems is to measure the average amount of various transfers received by the entire recipient population (Table 8.3) and by those groups in poverty under the different definitions of income (Table 8.4). Table 8.3 reemphasizes the fact that the exchange sector of our economy is by far the most important mechanism by which people acquire their command over resources. Almost 94 percent of the population were in families with some connection with the labor or capital markets, and the average amount acquired from these sources by those families was $15,499, clearly the largest source of income. But some segments of the population have much less connection to these exchange markets, most notably the aged and the disabled. Public noncontributory transfers reached the fewest members of the population; only 8.5 percent of the population were in families which received any income of this type in 1975. Again, however, certain segments of the population were much more dependent than others on this source of income—individuals in families headed by a black person, a disabled person, a female, or an unmarried person with children in the household. It should also be noted that private noncontributory transfers reached more individuals than either public noncontributory transfers or private noncontributory transfers, this differential being especially pronounced when one looks at the nine-year figures. The average amount of private noncontributory transfers received by recipient families was relatively low, however.

Table 8.4, instead of looking at the entire population, focuses only on those individuals who were in families which were poor under the different definitions of income. It shows the percentage of individuals who were in poor families (by the different definitions) who received any of the various types of transfers, and the average amount they received. For example, of all those individuals who were in families headed by an individual age 65 or older and whose taxable income was not sufficient to raise the family above the poverty line, 62.8 percent were in families which received some taxable income. Their average taxable income was $1,222.

The figures presented in Table 8.4 enable us to distinguish between two distinct aspects of the effect of the different transfer systems on the poverty population, namely, the amount of income received by those persons who are connected to the various systems, and the percentage of poor individuals who are connected at all with the various systems. For example, of those individuals in families whose income exclusive of any public noncontributory transfers was insufficient to raise them above poverty, only 57

Table 8.3

INDIVIDUALS WHO WERE IN FAMILIES WHICH RECEIVED DIFFERENT TYPES OF INCOME, AND THE AVERAGE AMOUNTS OF THAT INCOME
(All Sample Individuals in 1976, N = 15,702)

	Household Head in 1976 was...													
	Age 65 or Older		Black		Disabled		Unmarried with Children		Female		Employed at Least 1500 Hours in 1976		All	
Type of Income	Percentage Who Were Recip-ients	Aver-age Amount	Percentage Who Were Recip-ients	Aver-age Amount	Percentage Who Were Recip-ients	Aver-age Amount	Percentage Who Were Recip-ients	Aver-age Amount	Percentage Who Were Recip-ients	Aver-age Amount	Percentage Who Were Recip-ients	Aver-age Amount	Percentage Who Were Recip-ients	Aver-age Amount
1975														
Taxable Income	63.3	$8,438	84.2	$10,454	67.3	$6,565	78.4	$8,342	79.8	$7,346	100.0	$19,696	93.9	$16,506
Private Contributory Transfers	43.8	3,055	8.4	2,238	34.4	3,108	7.6	1,737	15.3	2,163	3.6	2,500	10.6	3,179
Public Contributory Transfers	88.2	3,243	31.4	1,904	70.0	3,041	29.2	2,935	40.0	2,633	13.8	1,558	27.8	2,529
Private Noncontributory Transfers	9.4	1,117	17.1	1,088	13.3	850	40.0	1,773	28.9	1,550	11.3	1,522	13.5	1,533
Public Noncontributory Transfers	14.9	1,107	31.4	2,503	31.4	1,876	37.4	2,955	27.3	2,601	2.2	1,182	8.5	2,224
9-Year Average, 1967-1975														
Taxable Income	96.3	8,208	98.3	8,800	96.4	6,714	98.3	8,879	98.3	8,469	100.0	18,379	99.4	15,719
Private Contributory Transfers	59.6	1,780	22.1	742	50.0	1,470	20.4	794	29.5	1,014	12.8	727	21.0	1,229
Public Contributory Transfers	93.0	1,983	55.0	784	84.6	1,508	56.6	1,083	63.3	1,223	36.8	438	48.8	889
Private Noncontributory Transfers	40.7	344	51.1	331	49.4	306	73.5	687	62.7	596	37.9	422	41.7	427
Public Noncontributory Transfers	36.7	777	60.4	1,556	55.9	1,182	62.9	1,655	55.6	1,423	20.2	743	27.5	1,040
Percentage Distribution of Sample Individuals	11.9		12.9		6.6		9.5		18.1		70.7		100.0	

NOTE: All figures are in 1975 dollars.

Table 8.4

FRACTIONS OF SAMPLE INDIVIDUALS WHO WERE POOR IN 1975 BY DIFFERENT DEFINITIONS OF INCOME WHO WERE IN FAMILIES WHICH RECEIVED DIFFERENT TYPES OF INCOME, AND THE AVERAGE AMOUNTS OF THAT INCOME

	Household Head in 1976 was...													
	Age 65 or Older		Black		Disabled		Unmarried with Children		Female		Employed at Least 1500 Hours in 1976		All	
Poverty Definition 1975	Percentage	Average Amount	Percentage	Average Amount	Percentage	Average Amount	Percentage	Average Amount	Percentage	Average Amount	Percentage	Average Amount	Percentage	Average Amount
Percentage Income I Poor Who Received any Taxable Income	62.8	$1,222	63.4	$3,485	51.1	$2,077	57.5	$2,933	59.4	$2,127	100.0	$ 5,322	70.4	$ 2,797
Percentage Income I Poor Who Received any Private Contributory Transfers	45.0	2,905	10.6	2,475	33.9	3,029	6.4	1,611	16.8	2,120	1.0	2,276	24.9	3,241
Percentage Income II Poor Who Received any Public Contributory Transfers	94.8	3,020	44.2	2,079	74.8	2,930	28.9	3,234	48.2	2,659	29.7	1,743	55.6	2,884
Percentage Income III Poor Who Received any Private Noncontributory Transfers	8.8	872	22.7	1,039	12.1	933	42.7	1,716	37.0	1,620	26.5	1,366	25.9	1,593
Percentage Income IV Poor Who Received any Public Noncontributory Transfers	59.8	1,186	70.2	2,702	75.2	2,154	80.8	3,177	70.7	2,919	28.9	2,021	57.0	2,641
Percentage Income V Poor Who Received any Public Noncontributory Transfers	50.3	970	63.2	2,256	69.9	1,780	74.6	2,699	61.6	2,390	21.7	1,808	46.8	2,255

Table 8.4 (continued)

Poverty Definition	Household Head in 1976 was . . . Age 65 or Older		Black		Disabled		Unmarried with Children		Female		Employed at Least 1500 Hours in 1976		All	
All Years, 1967-1975	Per-centage	Aver-age Amount	Per-centage	Aver-age Amount	Per-centage	Aver-age Amount	Per-centage	Aver-age Amount	Per-centage	Aver-age Amount	Per-centage	Aver-age Amount	Per-centage	Aver-age Amount
Percentage Income I Poor Who Received any Taxable Income	83.6	$ 626	91.6	$2,166	88.3	$ 992	91.5	$1,437	90.7	$1,035	100.0	$ 5,882	89.9	$ 1,512
Percentage Income I Poor Who Received any Private Contributory Transfers	69.6	1,519	26.1	1,002	55.9	1,377	22.1	875	34.8	1,028	3.9	1,200	44.3	1,476
Percentage Income II Poor Who Received any Public Contributory Transfers	95.7	1,938	60.9	1,078	81.8	1,860	54.5	1,625	67.6	1,456	66.9	630	73.8	1,665
Percentage Income III Poor Who Received any Private Noncontributory Transfers	67.1	258	57.9	323	60.0	299	70.4	432	66.6	425	23.8	269	55.9	372
Percentage Income IV Poor Who Received any Public Noncontributory Transfers	89.0	1,164	95.2	2,863	93.8	2,137	98.8	3,215	96.3	3,032	78.2	2,155	93.8	2,746
Percentage Income V Poor Who Received any Public Noncontributory Transfers	73.9	377	89.7	1,819	86.6	1,192	97.4	2,283	92.1	1,926	43.4	555	84.8	1,711

Table 8.4 (continued)

Poverty Definition	Household Head in 1976 was . . . Age 65 or Older: Per-centage	Age 65 or Older: Aver-age Amount	Black: Per-centage	Black: Aver-age Amount	Disabled: Per-centage	Disabled: Aver-age Amount	Unmarried with Children: Per-centage	Unmarried with Children: Aver-age Amount	Female: Per-centage	Female: Aver-age Amount	Employed at Least 1500 Hours in 1976: Per-centage	Employed at Least 1500 Hours in 1976: Aver-age Amount	All: Per-centage	All: Aver-age Amount
Any Year, 1967-1975														
Percentage Income I Poor Who Received any Taxable Income	95.2	$4,448	97.7	$5,863	95.6	$4,159	97.7	$5,852	97.6	$5,734	100.0	$ 10,385	98.1	$ 8,053
Percentage Income I Poor Who Received any Private Contributory Transfers	64.1	1,719	24.6	761	51.2	1,446	21.9	803	32.1	1,062	19.0	643	33.1	1,326
Percentage Income II Poor Who Received any Public Contributory Transfers	97.5	2,110	60.5	903	87.7	1,798	59.3	1,254	69.3	1,362	52.2	678	67.3	1,268
Percentage Income III Poor Who Received any Private Noncontributory Transfers	51.5	359	58.6	337	56.3	335	78.9	617	70.7	546	59.4	548	60.5	495
Percentage Income IV Poor Who Received any Public Noncontributory Transfers	69.5	820	78.2	1,697	78.4	1,384	88.1	1,892	78.9	1,676	48.4	1,121	60.7	1,423
Percentage Income V Poor Who Received any Public Noncontributory Transfers	65.2	762	77.4	1,699	76.6	1,367	87.1	1,942	76.4	1,714	45.2	1,142	57.5	1,434

NOTE: All figures are in 1975 dollars.

percent were in families which received any public noncontributory transfers. From Table 8.1, however, we know that public noncontributory transfers lifted only 19.1 percent of the Income IV poor above the poverty line (2.1 percent ÷ 11.0 percent). Therefore, of the 57 percent of the Income IV poor who received public noncontributory transfers, only one-third (19.1 percent ÷ 57.0 percent) received such transfers in an amount sufficient to raise them above the poverty line. The implication for public policy is that higher payment levels for noncontributory transfer programs would significantly reduce the fraction of individuals who were in poverty as officially defined. It seems clear, however, that such an increase in payments would still leave many individuals in poverty, since 43 percent of the Income IV poor are not connected at all to the public noncontributory transfer system. (It deserves reemphasis here that not all such programs are included in this analysis.) For public policy purposes, this would indicate that any program which has as its goal the elimination of poverty would have to reach a substantial number of individuals who are not currently participants in the public noncontributory transfer system. Existing public noncontributory transfer programs, of course, are not intended to cover the entire poverty population, so part of this nonparticipation can be attributed to explicit decisions made by policy makers. Aid to Families of Dependent Children, for example, restricts eligibility primarily to single parent famlies with dependent children in the household and imposes a work requirement if no child in the household is under the age of six.[9] But even though 80 percent of the Income IV poor individuals who are in households headed by a single parent with children under 18 in the family unit receive some public noncontributory transfers, there remains one-fifth of such individuals who may be eligible for such transfers but are not receiving any.[10] Thus it would appear that nonparticipation in the transfer systems by eligible families may be hindering efforts to alleviate poverty.

The results in Table 8.4 confirm the findings presented in Table 8.1 with respect to which subgroups of the population benefit the most from the different transfer systems. The elderly and the disabled are the most likely recipients of contributory transfer payments, both public and private. Individuals in families headed by a black person or by an unmarried person with children in the household are not likely to be recipients of contributory transfer payments, but are aided by public noncontributory transfers. Finally, the working poor are not aided much by any of the various transfer systems.

---

[9] In certain cases, two-parent families are also eligible for AFDC payments. Examples would be where one of the parents is incapacitated or unemployed.

[10] It is possible that some of these families are ineligible for nonincome reasons, such as having excess assets.

DIFFERENT TIME HORIZONS AND THE EXTENT OF POVERTY

The above discussion was based on poverty measured during a single year, in accordance with the official definition of poverty employed by the Census Bureau. This section takes a longer run view of the nature of poverty. We focus both on the persistence of poverty by looking at the fraction of individuals in various subgroups of the population who were in families whose income fell below their minimum needs level in every one of the nine years between 1967 and 1975 (inclusively) and on the transitory nature of poverty by looking at those individuals who were in families which were in poverty in any one of the nine years between 1967 and 1975.

The most startling result from the figures presented in Table 8.1 is that poverty is much less persistent but much more pervasive than might be thought by looking at single year poverty statistics. While 8.9 percent of all individuals were poor in 1975, only 12 percent of these were poor in every one of the nine years (1.1 percent of the entire population).[11] While this is still a significant number of people to face such severe hardship, it does indicate that many of the one-year poor may be only temporarily below the line. But coupled with this heartening finding is the discovery of the pervasiveness of temporary poverty. Although only 8.9 percent of the population was poor in the single year 1975, one-quarter of the population (25.1 percent) was in poverty in at least one out of the nine years between 1967 and 1975. It would seem that despite the fact that many families are able to escape the continual confines of poverty, a substantial portion of our population is faced with the threat of falling from their precarious position above the poverty line.

Changing the time horizon also has a dramatic impact on the composition of the poverty population, as shown by Table 8.2. Those subgroups of the population which are disproportionately in poverty on an annual basis are generally in a much worse situation when poverty is viewed over a nine-year period. For example, blacks accounted for 41.3 percent of the poor individuals in 1975, but an astonishing 77.0 percent of the persistently

---

[11]The arbitrariness of the official poverty line should be noted at this point. A family could be moved above the poverty line in one year by the addition of a small amount of money to family income. Although it would remain poor in the other eight years, it would still be classified as moving out of persistent poverty. It could be argued quite forcibly that a family which was poor in eight out of nine years was persistently poor.

poor individuals. Individuals in families headed by an unmarried person with children in the household and/or by a female also accounted for a much larger percentage of the persistently poor than of the one-year poor. On the other hand, these groups comprise a smaller percentage of the transitory poor than of the one-year poor. For example, blacks comprise 33.8 percent of the individuals who were poor in at least one of the nine years, as compared to 41.3 percent of the 1975 single year poor. These results indicate that the more favored groups of our society—such as whites, and male-headed families— although not free from the threat of poverty, are likely to be poor for only a limited time. The more disadvantaged groups of individuals, however, are much more likely to be in continual poverty, as well as in one-year poverty. The policy implications of these findings are important. If policy makers use one-year poverty statistics to allocate the funds for programs aimed at eliminating persistent poverty, they may under-allocate funds to blacks, to unmarried parents with children, and to female-headed families. On the other hand, funds for programs aimed at providing emergency aid to families who are temporarily in difficult circumstances may be over allocated to such groups, and under allocated to whites and other groups who, although not usually poor on an annual basis, are likely to fall intermittently below the poverty line.

PERMANENT AND TRANSITORY POVERTY AND DIFFERENT SOURCES OF INCOME

We now turn to the effects the different sources of income have on permanent and transitory poverty. Table 8.1 shows again that the exchange sector of the economy is the primary vehicle for keeping the vast majority of individuals out of persistent poverty. Only 5.9 percent of the individuals are in families whose taxable income was lower than their minimum needs level in every one of the nine years from 1967 through 1975. At the same time, the labor and capital markets were not particularly efficient in preventing transitory poverty; almost 40 percent of the sample individuals were in families whose taxable income failed to meet minimum needs in at least one of the nine years. For certain subgroups of the population—the elderly, the blacks, the disabled, the unmarried parents with children in the household, and the female-headed families—this failure was particularly pronounced. Over 70 percent of those in families headed by such individuals were unable in at least one year to meet their minimum needs with income derived from the labor and capital markets.

Of the other types of income, public contributory transfer payments continued to have the largest absolute impact on poverty. Such payments lifted 1.8 percent of the individuals out of persistent poverty, and 6.2 percent out of transitory poverty. The elderly and the disabled were the main beneficiaries of such transfers, as was found for the one-year period 1975. Public noncontributory transfers also had a major impact, lifting 1.6 percent of the population out of persistent poverty. This represents 59.3

percent of those individuals whose income exclusive of public noncontributory transfers was not sufficient to bring them above the poverty line in any of the nine years. In absolute terms, the major beneficiaries of such transfers were individuals in families headed by a black person, a disabled person, or an unmarried person with children in the household. Over 7 percent of the individuals in each of these groups were brought out of persistent poverty by such payments. In relative terms, however, these groups were not aided by such transfers as much as were the individuals who were not in such families. This can be seen from the figures in Table 8.2, which show the composition of the population of persistently poor individuals with and without public noncontributory transfers included in family income. Without the inclusion of such transfers, blacks, for example, comprised 67.6 percent of the persistently poor population; with the inclusion, 77.0 percent. This increase in the percentage of the poverty population accounted for by black individuals indicates that on a relative basis blacks benefitted less than nonblacks from public noncontributory transfer payments. This happens despite the fact that on an absolute basis blacks benefitted more than nonblacks. This occurs because among the blacks and nonblacks who were persistently poor without the inclusion of public noncontributory transfers, a smaller percentage of blacks than nonblacks were lifted out of persistent poverty by the inclusion of such transfers. Specifically, although 7.6 percent of the black individuals were lifted out of poverty by public noncontributory transfers, this accounted for only 53 percent of the 14.3 percent of black individuals who were in persistent poverty without the inclusion of such transfers. As mentioned above, for the entire population, such transfers lifted 59 percent of the persistently poor out of poverty, thus indicating that a higher relative percentage of nonblacks than blacks were lifted out of persistent poverty by public noncontributory transfers.

Although public noncontributory transfers are relatively efficient in eliminating persistent poverty, they are one of the most ineffective in eliminating transitory poverty. Such transfers lifted only 2 percent of the entire population out of transitory poverty, which represents less than 10 percent of the transitory poor when public noncontributory transfers were excluded from income. This result is tempered somewhat by the figures presented in Table 8.4, which indicate that the average annual amount of public noncontributory transfers received by the Income IV poor over the nine-year period compares favorably to the average annual amounts of other types of transfers received by families who were poor under alternative definitions of income. These payments apparently are not sufficient to prevent these families from occasionally falling below the poverty line.

SUMMARY AND CONCLUSIONS

This chapter has attempted to examine how our perception of the nature and extent of poverty is affected if we place poverty in a long-run perspective and if we examine the sources of income which push individuals above the poverty line. Perhaps the most important finding of the study is that poverty, as officially defined with respect to a family's minimum level of needs, is much less persistent but more pervasive than might be thought from a look at the official one-year poverty figures. Of the individuals who were poor in the one-year period 1975, only 12 percent were in poverty in every one of the nine years between 1967 and 1975. On the other hand, while only 8.9 percent of the population was poor in 1975, fully one-quarter of the sample individuals were in poverty in at least one of the nine years between 1967 and 1975. Viewing poverty over a longer time horizon than one year also dramatically alters the composition of the poverty population. Individuals in families headed by a black person, a female, or an unmarried person with children in the household, while disproportionately poor on a one-year basis, comprise an even larger fraction of the persistently poor. For example, blacks comprised 41.3 percent of the poverty population in 1975, but they accounted for a shocking 77.0 percent of the individuals who were in families which were poor in <u>every</u> one of the nine years between 1967 and 1975. The implication for public policy is that decision makers should be cautious in using the official annual poverty figures to allocate the resources earmarked for public anti-poverty programs depending on the precise goal of the individual program. If, for example, the program is aimed at eliminating long-run poverty, the use of one-year poverty figures to allocate the program's funds would result in an under-allocation of such resources to black families.

APPENDIX 8.1

The different types of transfer payments were added to taxable income to evaluate their effect on poverty in an arbitrary order. The rationale for adding contributory transfers before noncontributory transfers was that the receipt of contributory transfers is more a product of an individual's own actions than is the receipt of noncontributory transfers, which depend much more on the action of other individuals. Thus persons who must rely on noncontributory transfers in order to climb above the poverty line are arguably more dependent than individuals who do not need such transfers in order to meet their minimum needs. The rationale for adding public transfers after private transfers was that the receipt of public transfers is conditioned on the actions of the community as a whole, while the receipt of private transfers does not require such concerted agreement. Thus, persons who must rely on public transfers to provide for minimum needs are dependent on the agreement of a larger number of people than are those who rely on private transfers.

Given the political importance of public noncontributory transfer payments, it is interesting to determine whether the conclusions presented in this chapter concerning such transfers are dependent on the choice of ordering. As in Table A8.1a, adding public noncontributory transfers to taxable income before adding in any other transfers does not significantly alter any of the conclusions in this chapter concerning the effect of public noncontributory transfers on the extent of poverty. Changing the order in such a manner somewhat decreases the effect of public noncontributory transfers on one-year poverty, increases its already relatively large effect on persistent poverty, and greatly decreases its minor effect on transitory poverty.

It also should be mentioned in relation to Footnote 5 of the text, that including the entire transfer income of others in years 1967 through 1973 as public noncontributory transfer income does not alter the effect of such transfers on persistent or transitory poverty.

Table A8.1a

INDIVIDUALS BROUGHT ABOVE THE POVERTY LINE
BY ADDING IN PUBLIC NONCONTRIBUTORY TRANSFERS FIRST

	Household Head in 1976 was...													
	Age 65 or Older		Black		Disabled		Unmarried with Children		Female		Employed at Least 1500 Hours in 1975		All	
Income Definition	Percentage Poor	Percentage Brought out of Poverty	Percentage Poor	Percentage Brought out of Poverty	Percentage Poor	Percentage Brought out of Poverty	Percentage Poor	Percentage Brought out of Poverty	Percentage Poor	Percentage Brought out of Poverty	Percentage Poor	Percentage Brought out of Poverty	Percentage Poor	Percentage Brought out of Poverty
1975														
Taxable Income	61.0		43.2		66.8		51.0		49.7		4.6		20.4	
Taxable Income plus Public Noncontributory Transfers	59.7	1.3	38.0	5.2	63.6	3.2	43.0	8.0	44.3	5.4	4.3	0.6	18.9	1.5
All Years, 1967-1975														
Taxable Income	22.4		20.3		30.6		19.7		18.4		0.8		5.9	
Taxable Income plus Public Noncontributory Transfers	19.5	2.9	11.6	8.7	23.6	7.0	12.4	7.3	12.9	5.5	0.3	0.5	4.2	1.7
Taxable Income plus All Transfer Income of Others	18.0	1.5	11.0	0.6	22.0	1.6	11.9	0.5	11.7	1.2	0.3	0.0	3.9	0.3
Any Year, 1967-1975														
Taxable Income	76.5		72.8		81.3		72.0		71.0		23.4		38.3	
Taxable Income plus Public Noncontributory Transfers	76.5	0.0	71.6	1.2	80.9	0.4	70.6	1.4	69.9	1.1	22.8	0.6	37.8	0.5
Taxable Income plus All Transfer Income of Others	75.4	1.1	71.4	0.2	80.5	0.4	70.6	0.0	69.3	0.6	22.7	0.1	37.6	0.2

Chapter 9

RESIDENTIAL PROBLEMS, DISSATISFACTION, AND MOBILITY

Sandra J. Newman and Greg J. Duncan

Introduction

Over the last three decades, the growth in the nation's real income has permitted most Americans to upgrade significantly the quality of their housing. Nevertheless, housing quality has remained a salient policy issue: although this improvement has been dramatic for all income groups, housing problems continue to be concentrated among the poor, and the severity of these problems has tended to reflect the severity of their poverty.[1] In fact, the panoply of housing legislation, spanning from the National Housing Act of 1937 through the most recent amendments to the Housing and Community Development Act of 1974, has always reiterated essentially the same goals: "to provide a decent home and suitable living environment" to all citizens.[2]

These housing goals have remained elusive. As a result, increased effort has been directed at developing a rudimentary understanding of the basic processes which influence housing deterioration, neighborhood stabilization and change, and constraints on housing and mobility decisions.

One subset of this large range of unresolved questions concerns the nature of relationships between housing and neighborhood quality, housing and neighborhood satisfaction, and mobility behavior. Underlying this area of research is the important policy issue of identifying target populations who are living in inadequate residential environments and are either unable to move or are forced to bear the monetary and often emotional costs of changing residences in an attempt to find even minimally adequate housing. If the inadequacies of the dwelling and surrounding neighborhood play a significant role in bringing about discontent or moves which otherwise would not be undertaken, it may be

[1]Housing and Community Development Act of 1974, 88 State. 633.

[2]United States Housing Act of 1949, 63 Stat. 413.

wiser to invest in rehabilitating and upgrading the standing housing stock and existing neighborhoods instead of demolishing old, and reconstructing new, communities—a concept which continues to occupy a prominent position in housing and community development policies.

Analysis

The research we report in this paper covers a number of these behavioral relationships and processes which underlie land development. At a basic level, we sought to identify those subgroups within the population who suffer disproportionately from a range of housing and neighborhood problems. In addition, we hoped to determine whether discontent with the residential environment is affected by specific problems and inadequacies in that environment and also whether these problems have strong and direct influences on household mobility decisions.

Set in the context of the growing body of literature on household mobility behavior, this work represents an evaluation of the "push" factors of origin areas which motivate dissatisfaction, intentions to move, and actual mobility rather than the "pull" characteristics of alternative destinations. Following the "stress response" framework developed by Rossi (1955), Wolpert (1965), Butler, et al. (1969), Brown and Moore (1970), Clark and Cadwallader (1973) and Speare (1974), we view thinking about moving as a response to defects in the residential environment. At the same time, we modify and extend past studies in several ways. First, the data are national rather than local or regional in scope. They were collected as part of the eighth and ninth waves of the Panel Study of Income Dynamics. Second, because we have collected information on the causes of both intended and actual moves, we were able to analyze the actual and planned moves of people who gave locational (rather than job-related or involuntary) reasons for their mobility decisions. If the effects of environmental conditions on decisions to move are of concern, then the failure to distinguish between housing or locational mobility and job-induced mobility in some past analyses may have yielded misleading and imprecise results. Third, as Clark and Cadwallader (1973) have noted, "In the analysis of residential mobility, a model is needed which can take into account the perception of the <u>overall</u> environment around the household, as it is within this context that the household makes its decisions."[3] (Emphasis added.) Therefore, potential sources of stress included in the analysis are not limited to the physical or structural problems with the individual housing units but encompass structural and social neighborhood conditions, as well. Regardless of whether one group of these factors is more important than the other or they are mutually

---

[3] Clark and Cadwallader, p. 30.

reinforcing, both must be included in the analysis.[4] Finally, by including a variety of measures of specific housing and neighborhood problems, we have been able to test the effects of these variables on satisfaction more completely than has been the case to date.

In order to assess both the direct and indirect effects[5] of housing and neighborhood problems, a wide range of factors were included in the model of mobility decision making. These measures can be divided into five categories: 1. background variables (i.e., demographic and socio-economic characteristics); 2. housing and neighborhood variables (i.e., indicators of housing and neighborhood quality and condition); 3. social-psychological variables (i.e., satisfaction or dissatisfaction with the house and with the neighborhood); 4. intentions (i.e., the expectation of a move); and 5. behavior (i.e., actual mobility).

The framework for the analysis is shown in Figure 9.1. The assumed causal ordering of the factors runs from left to right and is indicated by arrows.[6] The ultimate outcome measure, at the far right, is actual mobility, which is assumed to be determined by all other factors in the model.[7] The measure of actual mobility is dichotomous, equalling 100 if the family moved for a consumptive reason[8] within one year after the time they reported about problems and satisfactions, and zero if the family did not move or moved for some other reason. Moving leftward, the penultimate outcome is the expectation of mobility. The expectations are measured concurrently with the problems, satisfactions, and background factors. Expectations, in turn, help to determine actual mobility and thus play the role of an intervening variable between satisfaction, problems, and background factors on the one hand, and actual mobility on the other. Expected mobility took one of four values between zero and 100 depending on the degree of certainty the respondents

---

[4]Lansing and Mueller, June 1964, p. 20.

[5]That is, whether the environmental conditions affect discontent and mobility directly or operate through other intervening factors.

[6]This mobility model is quite similar to one used by Speare (1974), although it was developed independently. The main difference is the inclusion of the housing and neighborhood problem variables in our model, though several background variables differ as well.

[7]The additional arrow leading to actual mobility represents the effects of all determinants of mobility not contained in the model.

[8]Consumptive moves are those residential shifts motivated by housing or neighborhood considerations. The 0-100 scale is used so that changes in the variable can be interpreted as changes in the probability that a family moved, measured in percentage units.

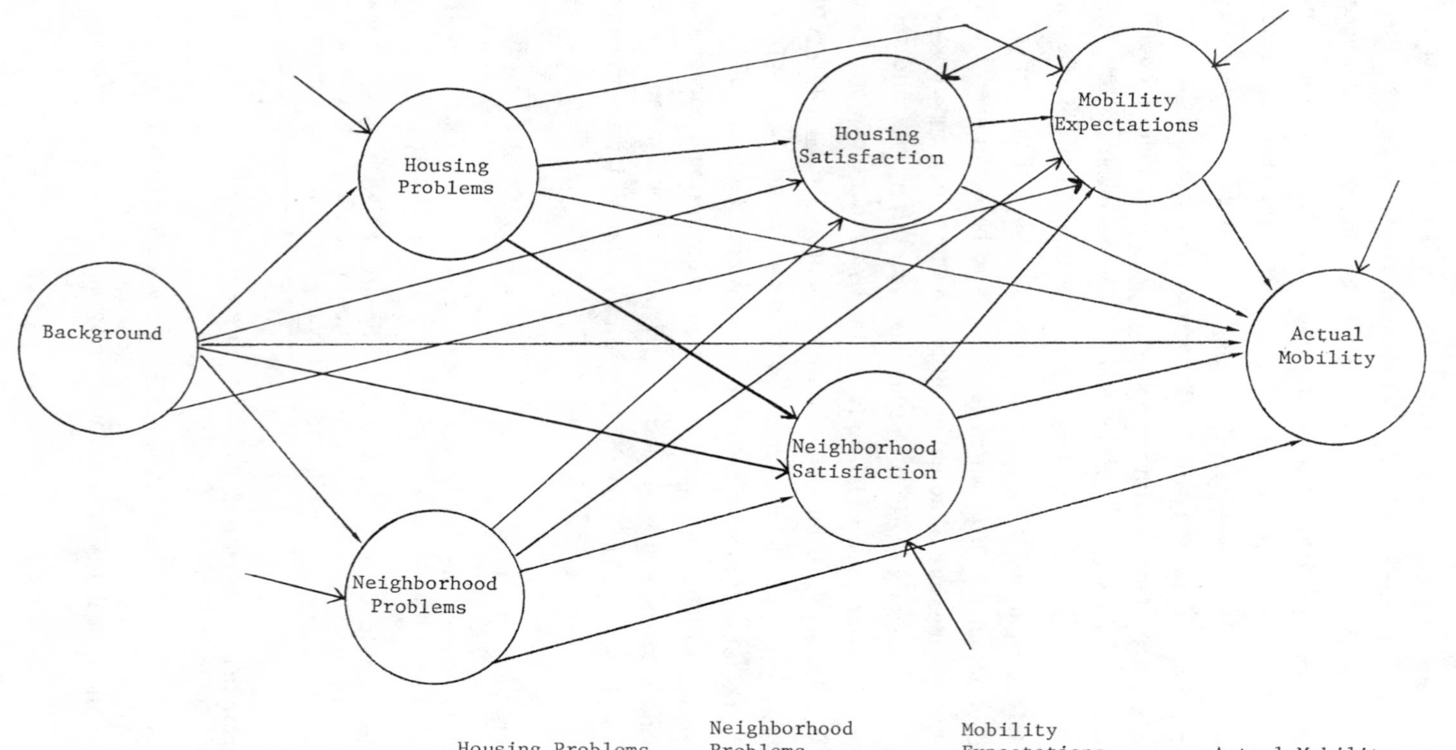

<u>Background (measured in 1975)</u>

1. Whether Single Family House
2. Whether Owns
3. Age of Head
4. Total Family Income
5. Actual-Required Number of Rooms
6. Whether Black
7. Whether Welfare Income
8. City Size
9. Whether School-age Children
10. Family Size

<u>Housing Problems (measured in 1975)</u>

1. Plumbing
2. Structure
3. Security
4. Vermin
5. Heat

<u>Neighborhood Problems (measured in 1975)</u>

1. Neighborhood Unclean
2. Bad for Children
3. Congestion
4. Theft
5. Personal Crime

<u>Mobility Expectations (measured in 1975)</u>

Whether Expect to Move for Consumptive Reasons in 1975

<u>Actual Mobility (measured in 1976)</u>

Whether Actually Moved for Consumptive Reasons between 1975 and 1976

Figure 9.1. FRAMEWORK FOR ANALYSIS OF HOUSING AND NEIGHBORHOOD PROBLEMS

were able to attach to their moving intentions.[9]

Separate questions on housing and neighborhood satisfaction were used to form the two satisfaction variables. Each satisfaction variable was measured by a four-point scale ranging from "extremely satisfied" to "extremely dissatisfied." As shown in Figure 9.1, they also act as intervening variables, being determined by the problem and background variables and helping to determine expected and actual mobility.

The housing and neighborhood problems were assumed to occur at an early phase of the mobility process, being causally prior to the general measures of satisfaction as well as prospective and actual mobility, and determined only by a set of background variables. Respondents were asked two questions about each of five housing problems and five neighborhood problems.[10] The first questions determined whether the particular problem existed, while the respondent's evaluation of whether the problem was a big or small problem (in those cases where the problem was reported to exist) was the purpose of the second questions. The scaling of the housing and neighborhood indicators incorporated both the incidence and evaluation of problems; if the problem did not exist, it was coded 0, small problems were coded .5 and big problems were coded 1.[11] The housing indicators included assessments of plumbing, the structural soundness and condition of the dwelling unit, security from break-ins, adequacy of insulation and heating, and the presence of roaches and rodents. The neighborhood conditions included cleanliness of streets and yards, quality of the neighborhood as a place for children, degree of crowding, noise and traffic, and safety—in terms of burglaries and robberies, muggings, rapes, the presence of drugs, and too few police. Needless to say, these 10 measures do not exhaust the full range of possible sources of environmental inadequacy, stress, and discontent. Nevertheless, they are the indicators which have most often yielded significant results in past research both at the Survey Research Center and elsewhere, and were chosen on that basis.[12]

---

[9]The questions were: "Do you think you might move in the next couple of years?" and "Would you say you definitely will move, probably will move, or are you more uncertain?" Those responding "definitely" in the second question were coded 100, "probably" were coded 67, "more uncertain" were coded 33, and "no" were coded zero.

[10]A list of the questions on housing and neighborhood problems is included in Appendix 1.

[11]We experimented with alternative ways of scaling the problem variables but found that analysis results were unaffected by these changes.

[12]Rodgers (1975); Marans and Rodgers (1975); U.S., Department of Commerce (1975); Newman (1974); Lansing, Marans, and Zehner (1970); Butler (1969); Lansing and Marans (1969); Rossi (1955).

Eleven variables were included which characterized the demographic, socio-economic, and locational situation of the respondents. These variables are crucial for at least two reasons. First, background variables show the incidence of housing and neighborhood problems among different subgroups and signal those groups which are especially burdened. Second, in the event that differences in reported satisfaction and mobility actually stem from differences in demographics rather than housing and neighborhood problems, excluding these demographic measures would yield incorrect or misleading results. The background measures in the model are: race; the life cycle variables of age of household head, family size, and whether the respondent has school-aged children; and six variables describing the location and economic status of the household: whether the family lives in a single family house, whether the family owns (or is buying) its home, the size of the largest city in the SMSA, the crowding measure of actual minus required number of rooms,[13] total family income, and whether the family receives any of its income from welfare sources (e.g., General Assistance, Aid to Families with Dependent Children, and other cash sources of welfare income).

The crowding measure is grouped with the background factors rather than with the housing and neighborhood problems because it results from changes in family size and life cycle rather than from an environmental state external to the household. Regardless of how it is categorized, however, the overriding importance of crowding in the mobility process demonstrated by past research requires that its effects be taken into account.

The causal structure depicted in Figure 9.1 serves not only as a conceptual framework for the analysis but also, with a few key assumptions, as an empirical basis as well. The model can be expressed in equation form as follows:

(1) Housing $\text{problem}_i = f_{1i}$ (background)

(2) Neighborhood $\text{problem}_j = f_{2j}$ (background)

(3) Housing satisfaction $= f_3$ (housing problems, neighborhood problems, background)

(4) Neighborhood satisfaction $= f_4$ (neighborhood problems, housing problems, background)

(5) Mobility expectations $= f_5$ (housing satisfaction, neighborhood satisfaction, housing problems, neighborhood problems, background)

---

[13] In computing required rooms, a base of two rooms (exclusive of bathrooms) was allowed for head and spouse or for a single head. One additional room was allocated for each single person aged 18 or older, one room for a married couple other than head and spouse, and one room for every two children of the same sex under age 18. Children under age 10 were paired regardless of sex if this reduced the room requirement.

(6) Actual mobility = f_6 (mobility expectations, housing satisfaction, neighborhood satisfaction, housing problems, neighborhood problems, background)

There is one equation for each variable that is, itself, determined by other variables in the model. These endogenous (or dependent) variables are dependent upon all variables which have arrows running to them. With the additional assumption that all of the f-functions are linear and additive, each of the equations can be estimated with multiple regression.[14]

The equations in the model form the basis for the rest of this paper. In the next section, each of the problem measures are treated as dependent variables (as in equations (1) and (2)) and their relationship to the 10 background factors is discussed. Then the results for equations (3) and (4) are described; namely, the association between each satisfaction measure and the aggregation of problem measures from each of the two domains. The fourth section presents the examination of the effects of housing and neighborhood problems along with housing and neighborhood satisfaction on prospective and actual mobility (equations (5) and (6)). The results are summarized and discussed further in the last section of the paper.

Incidence of Housing and Neighborhood Problems among Panel Households

As shown in Table 9.1, the incidence of each of the 10 housing and neighborhood problems among all panel households tended to be fairly low, though housing problems were slightly less prevalent than were neighborhood problems. The proportion of respondents who ranked each of these conditions as a "big" problem was also extremely small; the largest fraction was 8.3 percent which was associated with the item assessing the neighborhood as a poor place for children. Of the respondents reporting big problems, however, most concerned neighborhood rather than housing matters.

The pattern of intercorrelation among the various housing and neighborhood problems is best seen in a correlogram, which is shown in Figure 9.2. The strengths of the zero-order correlations are represented by dashed, solid, and double lines. In general, the correlogram shows much stronger associations among the neighborhood problems than among the housing problems with "security" being the only house-related problem having strong links crossing over to several of the neighborhood problems. As might be expected, the three crime-related problems tended to occur together, although none of the zero-order correlations exceeded .50.

---

[14]Additivity means that the effects of a given independent variable on the dependent variable do not vary by the level of some other independent variable. In other words, additivity means that there are no interactions among the independent variables in each equation. It must also be assumed that the error term associated with each equation is independent of the variables in that equation, and that the error terms are independent of one another.

Table 9.1

INCIDENCE OF HOUSING AND NEIGHBORHOOD PROBLEMS AMONG PANEL HOUSEHOLDS

	Percentage of Respondents Reporting:		Total Percentage Reporting Problems+:
	A Small Problem	A Big Problem	
Housing Problems			
1. Heat	9.3	6.4	16.0
2. Plumbing	10.1	4.8	15.0
3. Structure	10.2	4.1	14.5
4. Vermin	9.0	3.3	12.4
5. Security	6.9	5.1	12.2
Neighborhood Problems			
1. Theft	10.0	7.3	17.5
2. Bad for Children	8.7	8.3	17.4
3. Congestion	9.0	7.1	16.3
4. Neighborhood unclean	10.1	5.0	15.6
5. Personal Crime	4.5	4.6	9.4

+Because a very small proportion of respondents could report that a particular problem existed but did not indicate whether the problem was big or small, the "total" fractions are not simple sums of the percentage reporting a small problem plus the fraction reporting a big problem.

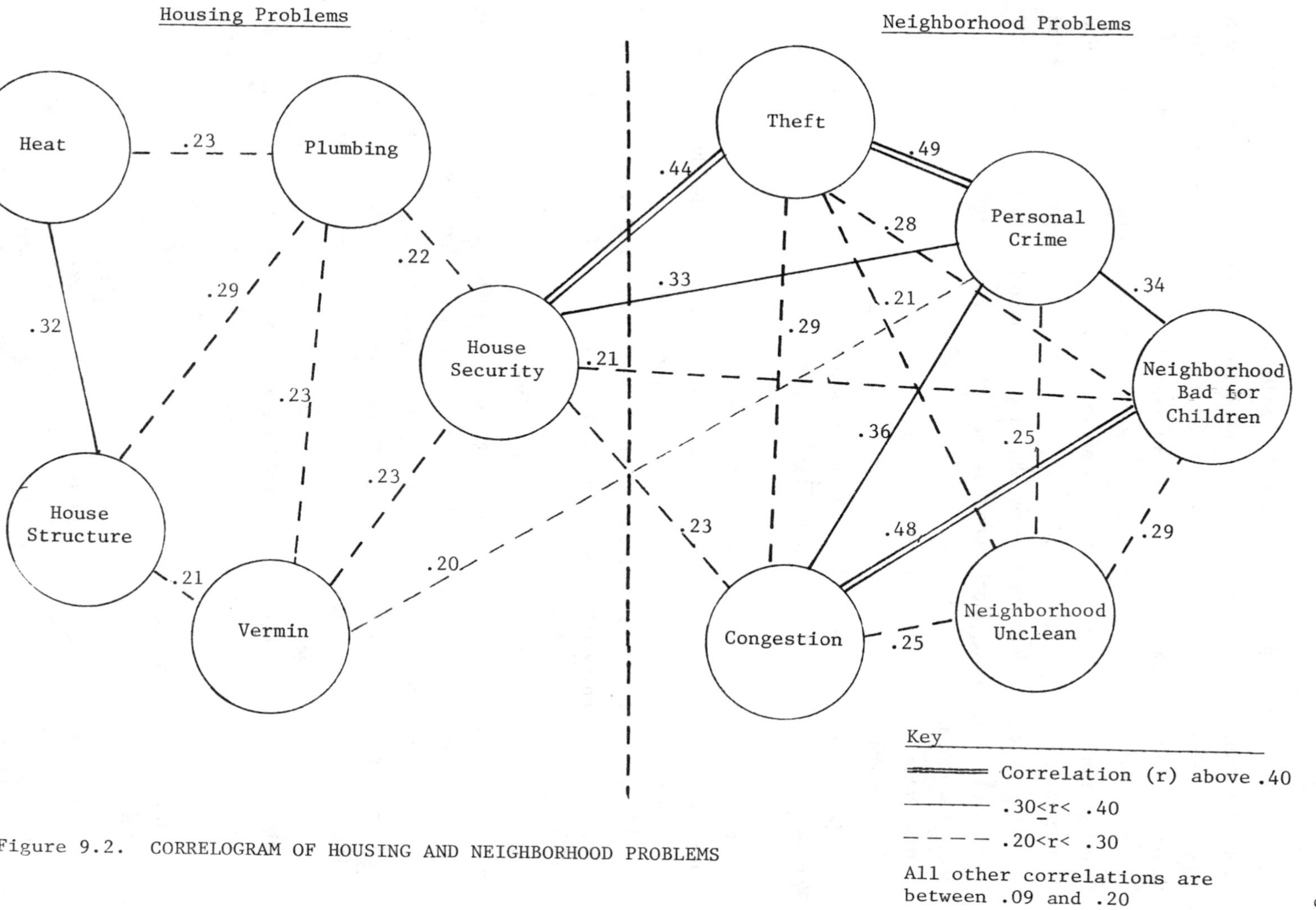

Figure 9.2. CORRELOGRAM OF HOUSING AND NEIGHBORHOOD PROBLEMS

A first way to distinguish subgroups in the population who report a higher incidence of problems in their residential settings is to examine the zero-order correlations between each problem variable and each background variable. The strongest relationships which result from this analysis indicate that blacks are more likely than others to suffer from vermin in their housing units and from crime-ridden, poorly kept up neighborhoods. They are joined by renters and those living in multiple family housing in their tendency to live in neighborhoods which are considered to be poor places for children and in congested areas. All other correlations were below .20, which is somewhat surprising in view of stereotype notions of strong associations between such factors as crowded living quarters or location within large central cities, for example, and the environmental stresses of structural problems, vermin, neighborhood congestion and crime. Similarly, very few of the basic demographic characteristics of individuals, such as age, education, income, or family size are strongly related to any particular self-reported housing or neighborhood problems. As noted, only race helps to distinguish a population subgroup which is beset by a number of these problems.

The stability of these zero-order correlations between pairs of variables can be examined with multiple regression anslysis in which the effects of all the background factors are considered simultaneously. As indicated earlier, the first two equations in the path model actually encompass 10 multiple regressions in which each of the 10 problem measures are dependent variables with the group of background factors as independent variables.

A summary of the results of these 10 regressions is shown in Table 9.2. None of the regression models is very powerful in accounting for the incidence of each of the problem variables. The proportion of variance explained by the models (adjusted for degrees of freedom) ranges from .025 in the prediction of plumbing problems to .103 in the prediction of problems with vermin in the dwelling unit. However, the form of the relationships revealed in the two-way correlation analyses is supported by the regression results.

It is evident that particular population groups endure multiple problems in their residential environments: blacks, for example, are significantly more likely than non-blacks to suffer from every problem asked about with the sole exception of poor insulation and heat in their houses. Thus, although problems do not tend to occur together in the population as a whole, particular demographic groups live in residential settings beset by many inadequacies.[15]

---

[15]These conditions were described as problems by the residents themselves rather than by an interviewer or some other objective observer. Conceptually, it is self reports of housing and neighborhood conditions rather than interviewer ratings which are particularly useful in trying to relate people's perceptions and evaluations to their actions. Procedurally, as well, interviewer ratings have always been problematic; even after extensive training by experts, enumerator evaluations have proved to be unreliable (U.S., Department of Commerce, 1977).

Table 9.2

DIRECTION AND STATISTICAL SIGNIFICANCE OF BACKGROUND VARIABLES IN PREDICTING HOUSING AND NEIGHBORHOOD PROBLEMS

	Housing Problems					Neighborhood Problems				
Independent Variables	Plumbing	Structure	Lack of Security	Vermin	Heat	Neighborhood Unclean	Neighborhood Bad for Children	Congestion	Theft	Personal Crime
Single Family House	++	++	++	++			--	--		-
Whether Owns	--	--		--	--		-	--		
Age of Head					--		-	-		
Income	-	--			--		-			
Actual minus Required Rooms			--	--	+					-
Education			+	--		--	-	-		
Black	++	++	++	++		++	++	+	++	++
Welfare			++	++	++	+	++	++		++
City Size			++				++	++	++	++
School Aged Children							--	--	-	
Family Size		++						++		
$\bar{R}^2$	.025	.045	.044	.103	.037	.041	.096	.080	.040	.066

++Coefficient is positive and significant at .01 level.

--Coefficient is negative and significant at .01 level.

+Coefficient is negative and significant at .05 level.

-Coefficient is positive and significant at .05 level.

Individuals who receive some income from welfare are almost as burdened as blacks, escaping only from problems with plumbing and structural components in their housing and burglaries and robberies in their neighborhoods (in the sense that they are not any more or less likely to have these problems than any other group). Living in an SMSA with a large central city population is associated with lack of security in the housing unit as well as problems of theft, personal crime, congestion, and inadequate neighborhoods for children. Interestingly, city size is not a significant predictor of problems with neighborhood cleanliness. Occupants of single family homes are substantially less troubled by neighborhood congestion or the inadequacies of their neighborhoods as a place to raise children, but it is surprising to see that they are more likely than others to be bothered by all of the housing problems that were asked about except lack of sufficient heat. Owners are also less likely to report problems with congestion or inadequacies in their neighborhoods with respect to children which, given the physical and social nature of most communities of owned homes, is an expected result. Similarly, families with school-aged children are less prone to complain about these neighborhood problems (and also about theft), which suggests that these features of neighborhoods probably play a prominent role in the assessment and selection of alternative communities by families in the child-rearing phase of the life cycle.

It is surprising to find that crowding within the dwelling unit is associated with only two housing problems—vermin and lack of security from break-ins—and with only one neighborhood problem—personal crime. Even more startling is the finding that insufficient heat in winter is most apt to occur in houses with an excess of rooms. It may be that this lack of crowding results not only from an excess of rooms relative to the number of inhabitants, but from a housing unit which is large in absolute square footage terms, as well. To the extent that large houses are frequently difficult to heat evenly, this crowding measure may be acting, in part, as a proxy for dwelling unit size.

Problems and Satisfaction

The mobility model specifies that housing and neighborhood satisfaction are determined by both the problem measures and the background variables. The estimated coefficients obtained from regressing each of the satisfaction measures on the problem and background variables are shown in Table 9.3. For example, the first number in the table, -.20, can be interpreted as the change in the four point housing satisfaction scale associated with having a serious plumbing problem as opposed to no plumbing problems. That estimated coefficient is statistically significant at the 5 percent level. In general, the results presented in Table 9.3 show that housing problems were the most important de-

Table 9.3

EFFECTS OF HOUSING AND NEIGHBORHOOD PROBLEMS ON HOUSING AND NEIGHBORHOOD SATISFACTION

	Dependent Variable			
	Housing Satisfaction		Neighborhood Satisfaction	
Housing Problem				
Plumbing	-.20*	(.08)	-.14	(.08)
Structure	-.76**	(.08)	-.35**	(.08)
Security	-.42**	(.08)	-.04	(.08)
Vermin	-.26**	(.09)	-.09	(.08)
Heat	-.41**	(.07)	.07	(.07)
Neighborhood Problem				
Neighborhood unclean	-.05	(.08)	-.69**	(.07)
Bad for children	-.06	(.07)	-.42**	(.07)
Congestion	-.15*	(.08)	-.65**	(.07)
Theft	.14*	(.07)	-.22**	(.07)
Personal Crime	-.12	(.09)	-.04	(.09)
$\bar{R}^2$	.214		.237	

* Significantly different from zero at .01 level.
**Significantly different from zero at .05 level.

NOTE: The number on the table are raw score regression coefficients with standard errors in parentheses. Other variables in both regressions included: whether single family house, whether owns, age of head, total family income, actual minus required rooms, education of head, whether black, whether welfare, city size, whether school-aged children, and family size.

terminants of housing satisfaction while neighborhood satisfaction was best explained by neighborhood problems. By far, the most important housing problems were those related to the structure of the house; respondents with serious structural problems scored fully three-quarters of a point lower on the housing satisfaction scale. Interestingly, structural problems were also significant predictors of neighborhood satisfaction, perhaps because structural problems in a given house are likely to be found in neighboring ones, as well, and the upkeep and condition of neighborhood dwellings have historically been primary indicators of contentment with the neighborhood.

Problems with security and heat were the next most important determinants of housing satisfaction, and below them came problems with plumbing and vermin. While the coefficients on these variables were statistically significant, their importance was considerably less than that of the structural problems.

For neighborhood satisfaction, congestion and cleanliness were more important than either of the two indicators of crime problems, a finding which is consistent with the results obtained by Marans and Rodgers (1975) in their analysis of neighborhood satisfaction using data from the 1971 study of quality of life in America. The incidence of serious problems with congestion and cleanliness reduced neighborhood satisfaction by two-thirds of a point, while theft problems reduced it by one-fifth of a point, and the effects of personal crime problems were not statistically significant at conventional levels.

It is curious to find that crime does not play a significant role in generating feelings of dissatisfaction with the neighborhood environment, but some recent research suggests that this may not be an idiosyncratic result. It has been shown that there is practically no relationship between the overall crime rate in a geographic area and the levels of dissatisfaction with neighborhood safety as reported by the residents.[16] Additionally, individuals who have been victimized are apparently no more dissatisfied with the safety of their neighborhoods than are those who were not crime victims!

The subset of background variables, which were also significant predictors of housing and neighborhood satisfaction, is consistent with the findings of past research.[17] For example, older respondents, owners, and those living in single family houses were more satisfied with both their house and their neighborhood. In addition, crowding emerged as a crucial determinant of housing satisfaction, being second only to structrual problems in its

---

[16] Quality of Life in the Detroit Metropolitan Area: Public Safety. Working paper, Institute for Social Research, Ann Arbor, Mich.: August, 1975.

[17] Butler, et al., (1969); Marans and Rodgers (1974).

ability to account for interpersonal differences in reports of housing satisfaction. In fact, crowding had a strong and pervasive influence on discontent with the residential environment, in general, being significant in predicting neighborhood satisfaction as well as housing satisfaction. It may also be similar to the structural problems in the sense that crowded dwelling units may tend to cluster within specific geographic areas thereby indicating something about the environment surrounding the dwelling unit as well as inside it. The significance of the neighborhood congestion variable supports this interpretation. Only two other background variables were significant at the 5 percent level—owners were more satisfied with their housing than renters and neighborhood dissatisfaction increased with city size.

Problems and Mobility

As portrayed in Figure 9.1, the link from the housing and neighborhood problems to actual mobility is both direct and indirect, with both satisfaction reports and mobility expectations operating as intervening variables. A desirable feature of the path model is that it is possible to decompose the _total_ effects of problems on mobility into _direct_ effects which operate independently of the intervening variables and _indirect_ effects which operate through them.[18] In this section, we first estimate the total effects of problems on mobility and then decompose those total effects which are statistically significant.[19]

The most startling result of this analysis is the generally minimal total effects of housing and neighborhood problems on actual mobility, with plumbing being the only statistically significant housing problem and congestion the only significant neighborhood

---

[18]This is best seen through a simple example. Suppose that there are three variables: problems (P), satisfaction (S), and actual mobility (A), and that

(1) $A = a_1 + b_1 S + b_2 P$

and (2) $S = a_2 + b_3 P$.

To understand the relationship between problems (P) and actual mobility (A), it is helpful to substitute equation (2) into (1) to get:

(3) $A = (a_1 + b_1 a_2) + (b_1 b_3 + b_2) P$.

Thus the total effect on A of a unit change in P can be decomposed into two parts—1. b_2, which comes from equation (1) and shows the _direct_ effect of P on A after controlling for the effects of S, and 2. $b_1 b_3$, the _indirect_ effect of P on A which operates through S. This indirect effect is the product of b_1, the effect of S on A, controlling for the effects of P, and b_3, which is the effect of P on S.

[19]The _total_ effects are estimated in an equation with actual mobility as the dependent variable and the problem and background measures as independent variables.

problem. Families with serious plumbing or congestion problems had mobility rates that were about 6 percentage points higher than families without such problems. Of all the housing problems included in the analysis, faulty plumbing may be the most serious and least conducive to adaptation by household members. It is difficult to develop a similar argument for the neighborhood congestion variable, however. It seems plausible that there are some other correlates of congestion which affect mobility but have not been included in the analysis. For example, if congestion implies something about conditions of high population density, and density, in turn, is associated with inadequate public services, then some of the congestion effect may be a result of the poor services. Aside from these two variables, however, the measures of satisfaction and expected mobility had little impact; almost all of the effects of the problems on actual mobility operated independently of these variables.

Without further investigation, it was not obvious how to interpret the absence of effects of almost all the housing and neighborhood problems on actual mobility. Because a sizable proportion of those with housing and neighborhood problems also had low mobility rates, they may have overwhelmed the relationship between problems and mobility of the most mobile groups.[20] In order to test this possibility, the model was estimated a second time for a special subsample of individuals generally considered to be among the most mobile: heads of households who rent and are 35 years of age or younger. If anything, the results of this second estimation indicate even more strongly that specific deficiencies which exist in the residential environment have essentially no influence on residential mobility. As before, plumbing problems had a positive and significant total effect on actual mobility. This time, however, none of the neighborhood problems were significant; the only other significant problem was housing structure, and it reduced rather than increased the chance of moving. Our overall conclusion, therefore, is that the housing and neighborhood problems we have measured have very little effect on mobility, either for the population as a whole or for highly mobile subgroups within it. And because the total effects of problems on mobility are generally small and insignificant, it is not worthwhile to examine the possibility that either or both satisfaction measures act to intervene between the problems and actual mobility.

In contrast to the housing and neighborhood problems which seem to have little effect on actual mobility, many of the background factors and one of the satisfaction

---

[20]These low mobility rates could stem from viewing the search for adequate housing which is affordable as a futile gesture, resulting in a truncated process which ends with dissatisfaction or even intentions but no actual movement. Alternatively, if a search is actually undertaken, it may have been unsuccessful. Unfortunately, we have no direct measures of either of these two phenomenon.

measures display sizable impacts on shifts in residence. As shown in the first column of Table 9.4, age of the household head, the presence of school-aged children, owning rather than renting, living in a single family house, and lack of crowding all had highly significant, negative, total effects on mobility. As in past research, we find age effects to be the most powerful, with each additional year reducing the chance of moving by three-tenths of a percentage point. The income measure was also statistically significant but with a positive effect on actual mobility.

Comparing the strength of the two satisfaction measures in predicting mobility shows housing satisfaction to be clearly more important, with a one-unit increase along the four-point scale being associated with a 2.2 percentage point drop in the chance that a move took place. While the housing satisfaction measure was statistically significant at the .01 level, the neighborhood satisfaction variable was not quite significant at the .05 level, and the size of its effect was half the size of the housing satisfaction measure. Virtually all research in this area, dating back to Rossi's 1955 study, have found housing concerns to carry the greatest weight in the residential mobility decision.[21]

The satisfaction and mobility expectation measures play the role of intervening variables between the background variables on the one hand, and actual mobility on the other. Since the total effects of the background variables are large and significant, it is possible to examine the extent to which the housing and neighborhood satisfaction and expectations act as intervening variables and carry the indirect effects of the background variables to mobility. This information is given in the remaining columns of Table 9.4. Housing satisfaction does indeed play a role in explaining the effect of crowding on mobility; the indirect effect accounts for almost one-sixth of the total effect. Statistically significant but quantitively less important indirect effects are also found for the housing satisfaction variable in accounting for the total effects of age and ownership on mobility. In general, neighborhood satisfaction has a considerably smaller effect as an intervening variable.[22] Mobility expectations, however, play a more important role in intervening between these two background variables and mobility.

Summary and Conclusions

In this paper, we have explored three facets of the process of residential change and mobility: the incidence of housing and neighborhood problems, the relationship between

---

[21] Rossi (1955).

[22] An additive index of housing problems and neighborhood problems was constructed and substituted for the individual items at each phase of the path model. The results were essentially unchanged.

Table 9.4

TOTAL, DIRECT AND INDIRECT EFFECTS OF SEVERAL BACKGROUND VARIABLES ON ACTUAL MOBILITY

			Indirect Effect Operating through:			
Background Variable	Total Effect =	Direct Effect +	House Satis-faction	Neighbor-hood Satis-faction	Mobility Expec-tations	Other+
Age of Household Head	-.309** (.037)	-.238** (.037)	-.014	-.005	-.052	.000
Whether School-aged Children	-5.02** (1.62)	-5.01** (1.60)	.005	-.021	-.231	.237
Owns	-6.63** (1.48)	-4.55** (1.48)	-.265	-.048	-1.450	-.317
Whether Single Family House	-4.83** (1.42)	-4.22** (1.42)	-.201	-.182	-.241	.014
Income (in thousands of dollars)	.232** (.060)	.221** (.059)	.000	.001	.017	-.007
Actual minus Required Number of Rooms	-1.215** (.402)	-.932* (.400)	-.198	-.033	-.044	-.008

* Significantly different from zero at .05 level.
**Significantly different from zero at .01 level.

+The "Other" category is composed of indirect effects operating through the problem variables and indirect effects operating through more than one intervening variable.

NOTE: Total and direct effect numbers are raw score regression coefficients with standard errors in parentheses. Background variables with insignificant total effects were included in the regressions, but the results are not shown. Indirect effects where paths running from background variable to intervening variable are significantly different from zero at the .05 level are underlined.

these problems and satisfaction with house and neighborhood, and the impact of these problems on actual mobility behavior.

Although the 10 housing and neighborhood problems measured were not pervasive in the sample as a whole, a number were conspicuous among several population subgroups. Blacks were in the worst position, suffering more than any other demographic group from both housing and neighborhood problems. Those on welfare were almost as burdened. Renters tended to have a host of housing problems but may have found some compensation in their somewhat lower incidence of neighborhood ills. It is families with young children, though, who are least likely to live in neighborhoods which are deficient in terms of the atmosphere for children, congestion, traffic, noise, and crime. In part, this may be the result of self-selection, as it may indicate those concerns which were most prominent during the residential search process undertaken by these families.

As expected, we also found links between problems and reports of housing and neighborhood satisfaction. More than one-fifth of the variance in each of the satisfaction measures (i.e., housing satisfaction and neighborhood satisfaction) was accounted for by the 10 indicators of locational problems as well as the background factors. Although housing problems were stronger predictors of housing satisfaction, and neighborhood satisfaction bore the strongest relationship to neighborhood problems, the two most important variables in each model—structural inadequacies of the individual dwelling unit and unkempt neighborhood structures—suggest that responses to both of these environments are in fact linked to one another. Structural soundness, maintenance, and upkeep emerge as underlying dimensions which unify the responses to these two levels of the residential setting. Similarly, crowding within the housing unit and congestion in the neighborhood may represent a second dimension linking people's reactions to the house and neighborhood.

The third proposition examined, namely, that housing and neighborhood problems play a direct and strong role in affecting actual mobility, was not upheld by the analyses. Very little evidence was found which demonstrated a relationship between these two stages of the mobility process either for the sample as a whole or for a subsample of young renters—acknowledged to be among the most mobile subgroups in the population. The striking weakness of this segment of the model is clearly shown in Table 9.5 which lists the total R^2's and partial R^2's of each predictor group in the path structure. The net gain in explanatory power associated with each set of independent variables above that contributed by the background factors is marginal, at best.

The only environmental stress variables which displayed significant impacts on mobility were plumbing problems and neighborhood congestion. Although the latter was

Table 9.5

TOTAL AND PARTIAL R^2's OF BACKGROUND, HOUSING AND NEIGHBORHOOD PROBLEMS, HOUSING AND NEIGHBORHOOD SATISFACTION, AND MOBILITY INTENTIONS ON ACTUAL MOBILITY

	Total R^2	Partial R^{2+}
Background	.10	.10
Housing and Neighborhood Problems (over and above background)	.11	.01
Housing and Neighborhood Satisfaction (over and above problems and background)	.12	.01
Mobility Intentions (over and above satisfaction, problems and background)	.14	.02

+Calculated as follows: $\frac{R^2_{with} - R^2_{without}}{1-R^2_{without}}$ where R^2_{with} is the fraction of variance in actual mobility explained by the predictor variable group plus all prior prediction groups, and $R^2_{without}$ is the factor of variance in actual mobility explained by all prior predictor variables.

important for both satisfaction and behavior, structural problems in the housing unit had the greatest influence on housing satisfaction, while problems with plumbing were most important in predicting actual mobility both totally and directly. This may indicate that structural problems are depressing yet tolerable, but plumbing problems are more than can be endured.

Like Speare's work on the residential mobility of a Rhode Island sample, we found that the effects of several background variables on actual mobility operate indirectly through housing satisfaction. The largest effects were for crowding, age, and tenure. At the same time, the assumption that satisfaction is a good proxy for specific environmental problems in predicting actual mobility behavior has clearly not been supported by this investigation.

There are at least three aspects of this research which are salient from a policy perspective. First, the national goals of decent housing and suitable environments for all citizens make even the low incidence of the housing and neighborhood problems reported in these national data unacceptable. Of particular concern are a few demographic groups, primarily blacks and those receiving some income from welfare sources, who continue to outdistance the rest of the population in both the incidence and range of environmental deficiencies. It may be the case that the proportion of these particularly vulnerable groups living in substandard housing has fallen since the 1950s, but it also seems clear that the improvement in their environmental conditions has not been great enough to eliminate all of the major problems besetting their residential environments.[23]

Second, the analysis demonstrates relatively strong relationships between the specific measures of environmental stress and the satisfaction of people's needs in their residential settings. By and large, the defects having the greatest effect on satisfaction could be remedied through repair and rehabilitation. Further, as just noted, the demographic correlates of the environmental problems and discontents indicate a further deterioration in the welfare of several vulnerable population groups who already face a host of difficulties in their lives. Given that the major goal of public policy at any level is the achievement of societal needs and, therefore, societal well-being, this research has isolated a number of policy targets—both physical and social—at the residential level.

Third, the failure of our mobility decision model to reveal any strong or direct effects of specific housing and neighborhood problems on mobility behavior clearly does not support our contention that environmental stress results in moves that otherwise might not occur. Two explanations for this failure seem possible. First, because the reports on housing and neighborhood problems were collected in one year while those on

---

[23]Housing in the Seventies, pp. 6-22.

actual mobility were collected in the subsequent year, it may be the case that repairs made in the interim cancelled the necessity for moving, at least for housing-based reasons.[24] A much more negative interpretation of the operation of housing markets, and one that also seems much more likely, is that the desire to move among those with serious housing and neighborhood problems is indeed strong, but impediments to searching for and finding suitable housing intervene between the desire and the behavior.[25] These impediments may range from feelings of frustration and futility which proscribe any search, to failure in finding appropriate housing even if a search is made. Perhaps if the former group thought that better housing were within reach or if the latter group eventually found suitable accommodations, the amount of mobility would be greater.

---

[24] Consistent with this interpretation is the finding that crowding does have an impact on mobility, because while faulty plastering or poor insulation can be repaired, expansion of dwelling unit space is quite a bit more difficult, particularly for renters.

[25] It might be argued that one year is too short a time period to observe actual mobility. Other analyses, however, have shown that while less than half of those expecting to move for housing and neighborhood reasons actually move within a three year period, about two-thirds of those who <u>do</u> move do so within one year. See Duncan and Newman (1976), p. 179.

References

Brown, Lawrence, and Moore, E. "The Intraurban Migration Process: A Perspective." In The Internal Structure of the City. Edited by L. S. Bourne, New York: Oxford University Press, 1971, 200-09.

Butler, Edgar, et al. Moving Behavior and Residential Choice: A National Survey. Washington, D.C.: Highway Research Board, 1969.

Clark, W. A. V., and Cadwallader, M. "Locational Stress and Residential Mobility." Environment and Behavior, March 1973, 29-41.

Duncan, Greg J., and Newman, Sandra J. "Expected and Actual Residential Mobility." Journal of the American Institute of Planners, 42, No. 2 (April 1976): 174-86.

Housing and Community Development Act of 1974, 88 State. 633.

Institute for Social Research. "Working Papers on the Detroit Quality of Life Study." Ann Arbor, Michigan, 1974. Mimeographed.

Lansing, John B., and Marans, Robert W. "Evaluation of Neighborhood Quality." Journal of the American Institute of Planners, 35, No. 3 (May 1969): 195-99.

Lansing, John B.; Marans, Robert W., and Zehner, Robert B. Planned Residential Environments. Ann Arbor, Mich.: Institute for Social Research, 1970.

Lansing, John B., and Mueller, Eva, with Nancy Barth. Residential Location and Urban Mobility. Ann Arbor, Mich.: Institute for Social Research, June 1964.

Marans, Robert, and Rodgers, Willard. "Toward an Understanding of Community Satisfaction." In Metropolitan America in Contemporary Perspective. Edited by Amos Hawley and Vincent Rock. New York: Halsted Press, 1975.

Newman, Sandra. "The Residential Environment and the Desire to Move." Ann Arbor, Mich.: Institute for Social Research, 1974. Mimeographed.

Rodgers, Willard, et al. Quality of Life in the Detroit Metropolitan Area. Ann Arbor, Mich.: Institute for Social Research, 1975. Mimeographed.

Rossi, Peter. Why Families Move: A Study in the Social Psychology of Urban Residential Mobility. New York: The Free Press, 1955.

Speare, Alden. "Residential Satisfaction as an Intervening Variable in Residential Mobility." Demography, 11, No. 2 (May 1974): 173-88.

U. S., Department of Commerce, Bureau of the Census. Annual Housing Surveys, Part B: Indicators of Housing and Neighborhood Quality. Washington, D.C.: Government Printing Office, 1975.

U. S., Department of Commerce, Bureau of the Census. Measuring the Quality of Housing: An Appraisal of Census Statistics and Methods. Washington, D.C.: Government Printing Office, 1967.

U. S., Department of Commerce, Bureau of the Census. Minutes of the Census Advisory Committee on Housing for the 1980 Census. Washington, D.C.: Government Printing Office, 1977.

U. S., Department of Housing and Urban Development. Housing in the Seventies. Washington, D.C.: Government Printing Office, October, 1973.

United States Housing Act of 1954, 68 Stat. 590.

United States Housing Act of 1949, 63 Stat. 413.

United States Housing Act of 1937, 60 Stat. 888.

APPENDIX 9.1

Table A9.1a

Questions Used to Form Housing and Neighborhood Problem Variables

Plumbing: "Do you have any problem with the plumbing where you live--things like not enough hot water, toilets that don't flush well, or old sinks and tubs?" (If yes:) "Is that a big problem or a small one?"

Structure: "How about the structure of your home--any problems with sagging floors or ceilings, walls that crack and crumble, and things like that?" (If yes:) "Is that a big problem or a small one?"

Security from break-ins: "Is there any problem with lack of security from break-ins?" (If yes:) "Is that a big problem or a small one?"

Vermin: "How about rats, cockroaches, and things like that--any problems there?" (If yes:) "Is that a big problem or a small one?"

Heating: "Is poor insulation or getting enough heat a problem?" (If yes:) "Is that a big problem or a small one?"

Neighborhood unclean: "How about the general cleanliness of the streets in your immediate neighborhood? Are there unkempt yards or grounds, houses poorly kept up, or infrequent and sloppy garbage pickup?" (If yes:) "Is that a big problem or a small one?"

Bad for children: "Is this a poor neighborhood for kids, with too few places to play, too many ways for kids to get in trouble, and things like that?" (If yes:) "Is that a big problem or a small one?"

Congestion: "Is this a crowded area with too many people, too much noise, and bad traffic?" (If yes:) "Is that a big problem or a small one?"

Burglaries: "How about burglaries and robberies--is this a problem where you live?" (If yes:) "Is that a big problem or a small one?"

Personal Crime: "How about muggings, rapes, pushers, junkies, or too few police --any problems there?" (If yes:) "Is that a big problem or a small one?"

Table A9.1b

REGRESSION RESULTS FOR MOBILITY MODEL
WHEN ALL INDEPENDENT VARIABLES ARE INCLUDED

Variable	Coefficient	Standard Error
Background		
Single family house	-4.221**	(1.419)
Whether owns	-4.554**	(1.477)
Age of head	- .238**	(.037)
Income (in thousands of $)	.221**	(.059)
Actual-required rooms	- .932*	(.400)
Education	- .089	(.178)
Black	- .951	(1.782)
Welfare	2.037	(2.662)
City size	- .0026*	(.0012)
School-aged children	-5.007**	(1.596)
Family size	- .738	(.485)
Problems		
Plumbing	5.638*	(2.301)
Structure	1.630	(2.390)
Security	-1.533	(2.480)
Vermin	-3.151	(2.579)
Heat	-3.909	(2.050)
Neighborhood clean	- .399	(2.274)
Good for children	-3.726	(2.207)
Congestion	4.151	(2.281)
Theft	1.111	(2.148)
Personal crime	-2.040	(2.613)
Housing satisfaction	- .634	(.635)
Neighborhood satisfaction	- .817	(.636)
Mobility expectations	.173**	(.020)

$\bar{R}^2$ = .136

Number of observations = 2642

**Significantly different from zero at .01 level.

*Significantly different from zero at .05 level.

Chapter 10

AN EMPIRICAL NOTE ON THE RESIDENTIAL PROPERTY TAX

Richard D. Coe and Martha S. Hill

Introduction

Who pays the residential property tax and how much they pay have long been of interest to economists and public policy makers. The theoretical issues involved in determining who bears the ultimate burden of the tax have evoked considerable controversy over the last decade. Measurement questions concerning the amount of tax that different individuals pay have long plagued researchers in this area. Hopefully data from the Panel Study of Income Dynamics can shed some light on this latter issue.[1]

For the first eight years of the Panel Study, the annual property tax paid by homeowners in the sample was estimated by assigning an effective property tax rate to each homeowner and applying that to the reported market value of the house in which the family resided. The assignment was based on the region of the country in which the family lived and the distance from the nearest city of 50,000 or more.[2] In the ninth year of interviewing, homeowners were asked directly the amount of their yearly property taxes in 1975, including city, county, and school taxes. In addition, renters were asked their monthly rent.

Utilizing this information, this chapter sets out to fulfill two very limited purposes. First, we look at the relationship of property taxes paid in 1975 as a percentage of 1975

[1]Two previous studies on the incidence of the residential property tax have utilized data from the Panel Study of Income Dynamics. See Barlow (1974) and Aaron (1974, 1975).

[2]Maynes and Morgan (1957). The Assigned effective tax rates were as follows:

Distance from Nearest City of 50,000 or More	New England States	All Other States
0-5 miles	.025	.020
5-49 miles	.020	.015
50 or more miles	.015	.010
Not ascertained	.020	.015

family money income and as a percentage of average annual income over a nine-year period, 1967-1975. This analysis is based on the simple assumption that consumers of housing services bear the burden of the residential property tax, thus we ignore the complex theoretical questions involved in a general equilibrium analysis of the incidence of the tax.[3] Second, we compare the reported property tax payments of homeowners with two alternative estimating procedures—the procedure employed in the first eight years of the Panel Study and a procedure which incorporates the effective property tax rates for various cities as reported in the Census of Governments (1972). We also look at some alternative ways of estimating the property tax paid by renters. In addition, some general descriptive information on various aspects of the residential property tax is presented in the Appendix tables.

Analysis

BASIC DATA DESCRIPTION

In order to assess the impact of the tax on families at differing levels of economic welfare, it is necessary to determine a measure of economic welfare. Perhaps the most common measure is annual family money income. We use 1975 family money income as one way of ranking families according to relative economic status. This measure, however, has been repeatedly criticized as failing to reflect fully the relative economic position of a family. One common criticism is the failure to account for differences in family size. A single-member family with an annual money income of $8,000 is clearly in a better economic position than a six-member family with the same annual income, *ceteris paribus*. To control for this, we have related 1975 family money income to a needs standard which accounts for family size and economies of scale. This needs standard is virtually equivalent to the needs standard employed by the Bureau of Census in determining the number of families in poverty.

Both of these measures are based on a one-year accounting of a family's resources and needs. But some families may experience abnormally low or high levels of income in any given year, because of factors such as unusual overtime in a particular year or perhaps excessive unemployment or illness. It is certainly arguable that two families with the

[3]We also ignore other theoretical problems, such as the fraction of the tax which is actually levied on the land and not the building, and which is theoretically borne by the owner of the land rather than the consumer of the services of the building.

same income or income/needs ratio in a given year are not in the same economic position if one family is only temporarily at that level of income while the other family is always at that level. In short, an annual measure of economic welfare does not accurately reflect a family's longer run, or normal, level of economic welfare, and a longer run measure is a better measure of a family's true economic position. This point may be especially crucial in examining the impact of the residential property tax, since housing consumption decisions, which under our incidence assumptions are a primary determinant of the burden of the tax, are thought to be based on a family's long-run level of income. In order to control for this, we have ranked families according to average annual income and average income/needs ratio over the nine-year period 1967-1975.

Table 10.1 gives the decile breakpoints for these four measures of relative economic welfare. As expected, the nine-year measure compresses the distribution of economic welfare. Table 10.2 gives the unweighted number of observations of homeowners and renters in each decile. The weighted percentages of these two groups in each decile appear in Tables 10.3 and 10.4. In the aggregate, our analysis includes 2,519 renters and 2,507 homeowners. On a weighted basis, 60.1 percent of our sample consists of homeowners.

Two caveats must be noted concerning our sample selection. First, respondents who replied that they neither owned nor rented their dwelling unit were omitted from the sample. This group comprised 5.4 percent (weighted) of the entire Panel Study sample. Over 60 percent of this group received their housing as a gift. Under these circumstances it is impossible to determine who actually paid the property taxes.

More troublesome were homeowners whose property tax payments were not ascertained from the interview. This group comprised 8.8 percent of all homeowners, and they were omitted from the analysis. The omission of this large a group poses some questions as to the representativeness of the sample upon which the results are based. Fortunately, this omitted group is fairly evenly divided among different income levels (see Appendix Table A10.1a), thus we believe that the results are not seriously biased by their exclusion.

One final point should be mentioned before the results of this study are presented. Except for the exclusions mentioned above, the sample consists of all Panel Study families in the ninth year of interviewing. Many of these families underwent substantial changes in family composition over the nine-year period. Some original families divorced or separated, and thus became two families. Other families in 1976 were headed by individuals who were originally children of sample families but who formed their own households. These changes are significant in the calculation of nine-year average annual income and income/needs, since this calculation will include income and needs level for

Table 10.1

DECILE BREAKPOINTS FOR DIFFERENT MEASURES OF RELATIVE ECONOMIC WELL-BEING

Decile	Range for 1975 Income	Range for 1975 Income/Needs+	Range for Nine-Year Average Income‡	Range for Nine-Year Average Income/Needs+
1	$ 0- 3,499	0.00-1.08	$ 0- 5,395	0.00-1.19
2	3,500- 5,604	1.09-1.56	5,396- 7,983	1.20-1.83
3	5,605- 7,682	1.57-2.08	7,984-10,165	1.84-2.26
4	7,683-10,019	2.09-2.51	10,166-12,175	2.27-2.69
5	10,020-12,199	2.52-3.00	12,176-14,251	2.70-3.11
6	12,200-14,729	3.01-3.55	14,252-16,390	3.12-3.61
7	14,730-17,663	3.56-4.18	16,391-18.744	3.62-4.11
8	17,664-21,366	4.19-5.03	18,745-21,705	4.12-4.85
9	21,367-27,314	5.04-6.38	21,706-26,676	4.86-6.04
10	27,315 or more	6.39 or more	26,677 or more	6.05 or more

+Income and needs expressed in 1975 dollars.

‡Income expressed in 1975 dollars.

Table 10.2

NUMBER OF OBSERVATIONS FOR DIFFERENT MEASURES OF ECONOMIC WELL-BEING, BY DECILES

	By 1975 Income Decile		By 1975 Income/Needs Decile		By Nine-Year Average Income Decile		By Nine-Year Average Income/ Needs Decile	
Decile	Home-owners	Renters	Home-owners	Renters	Home-owners	Renters	Home-owners	Renters
1	162	430	198	559	199	480	198	638
2	162	428	227	408	238	529	315	609
3	213	396	241	356	245	407	254	312
4	206	394	255	275	261	281	259	219
5	250	254	240	222	258	241	243	193
6	276	205	279	168	265	161	272	170
7	288	164	260	170	271	128	224	130
8	300	133	264	142	246	121	263	99
9	322	75	260	120	270	94	247	84
10	328	40	283	59	254	77	232	65
TOTAL	2507	2519	2507	2519	2507	2519	2507	2519

the family in which the sample individual as a member in each individual year. For example, a split-off child will have averaged in the income and income/needs ratio of his parents' household for the years he was in that household. This presents some difficult interpretation problems which are common in most analyses of longitudinal data for which the family is the appropriate unit of analysis but undergoes pervasive family composition changes.[4] The optimal solution to this problem is not clear; we have opted to include all families in the analysis (with the noted exceptions) and caution the reader of the problem.[5]

THE RESIDENTIAL PROPERTY TAX AS A PERCENTAGE OF INCOME

One-Year Analysis

Previous research, operating on the assumption that the consumers of housing services bear the burden of the residential property tax, has found that the tax accounts for a larger percentage of the annual money income of families with lower annual incomes than of families with higher annual money incomes.[6] In other words, the residential property tax is regressive in incidence. Our results confirm these findings, as shown in Table 10.3. For this table, families were ranked according to their 1975 money income. For homeowners, the reported property tax payments were taken as a percentage of income, the results being reported in column 2. For renters, 15 percent of annual rent was used as an estimate of the property tax levied on their dwelling unit, and this estimate was taken as a percentage of annual income. The results for renters are reported in column 5. For both groups, annual income was assumed to be at least $1,000, in order to avoid extreme (and unrealistic)[7] results. In column 7, the results for the two groups are combined to present an aggregate picture of the burden of the tax.

---

[4]In 1968 there were 4,802 sample families. In 1976 this number had increased to 5,862, exclusive of sample families which were lost over the sample period. Thus family composition change is clearly a widespread occurence.

[5]Barlow (1974) limited his analysis to families with the same head and spouse over the relevant time period. Aaron (1974, 1975) made no reference to the problem, a particularly acute omission with respect to his analysis because he limited his sample to recent movers, which would presumably include many split-offs.

[6]See, for example, Netzer (1966).

[7]It is possible for a family to have zero or even negative income in a given year, if, for example, the family business or farm suffered a large loss. Calculating percentages with very low or negative bases is unenlightening for purposes of the present study. Calculating percentages with a zero base is, of course, difficult.

Table 10.3

PROPERTY TAXES AS A PERCENTAGE OF 1975 INCOME, BY 1975 INCOME DECILE

	(1)	(2)	(3)	(4)	(5)	(6)	(7)	(8)
	Homeowners			Renters		All		
1975 Income Decile	Weighted Percentage of Observations	Reported Taxes as Percentage of 1975 Income	Effective Taxes as Percentage of 1975 Income	Weighted Percentage of Observations	15 Percent of Annual Rent as Percentage of 1975 Income	Weighted Percentage of Observations	Reported Taxes or 15 Percent of Annual Rent as Percentage of 1975 Income	Effective Taxes or 15 Percent of Annual Rent as Percentage of 1975 Income
1	6.2	9.0+	9.0+	13.4	7.5+	9.1	8.1+	8.1+
2	5.9	5.3	5.2	14.4	4.3	9.3	4.7	4.7
3	7.5	4.1	3.8	12.8	3.2	9.6	3.7	3.5
4	6.9	4.3	3.9	14.3	2.7	9.8	3.3	3.2
5	8.8	3.0	2.5	11.7	2.4	10.0	2.7	2.5
6	10.0	3.1	2.5	10.0	2.0	10.0	2.7	2.3
7	11.6	3.2	2.6	8.1	1.9	10.2	2.8	2.3
8	12.5	2.5	1.9	7.4	1.5	10.5	2.2	1.8
9	14.3	3.0	2.2	5.0	1.7	10.6	2.8	2.1
10	16.3	2.4	1.6	2.8	1.3	10.9	2.3	1.5
TOTAL	100.0	3.6+	3.0+	100.0	3.3+	100.0	3.4+	3.1+

+Figure based on assigning $1,000 income to families with income less than $1,000.

As the results presented in these columns clearly demonstrate, the residential property tax is regressive for both homeowners and renters, and for the population as a whole. Among homeowners in the lowest income decile, property taxes paid in 1975 equalled 9.0 percent of family money income for that year, on the average; for homeowners in the highest income decile the average was only 2.4 percent. The equivalent figures for renters were 7.5 percent and 1.3 percent. For the population as a whole, families in the lowest income decile paid an average 8.1 percent of their income to the property tax, while families in the highest income decile paid only 2.3 percent. It should be noted, however, that the regressive pattern of the residential property tax is most pronounced in the lowest two income deciles, and is more moderate as one moves up the income ladder past that point.

These results ignored the fact that homeowners who itemize their income tax deductions can deduct property tax payments made on their homes.[8] The effect of this deduction is to shift part of the property tax burden of homeowners to the federal treasury. The portion of the tax which is shifted will equal the homeowner's marginal income tax rate times his property tax payment, the remainder[9] being borne by the homeowner. Columns 3 and 8 show the effect of the federal income tax deduction on the incidence of the property tax on homeowners and the population as a whole, under the assumption that all homeowners itemize deductions on their federal income tax return.[10] As expected, the regressivity of the tax is more pronounced. The burden of the tax on lower income households is virtually unaffected. The burden on higher income households is reduced on the order of 20 to 33 percent.

Recalculating these same estimates, but ranking families according to their income/needs ratio rather than their money income, results in little change in the incidence pattern of the residential property tax, as shown in Table 10.4. The burden on families in the lowest decile is lessened, but the tax remains regressive.

Nine-Year Analysis

The preceding analysis utilized single-year measures of econoic well-being and the percentage of single-year income which was devoted to the payment of the residential

[8] Section 164, Internal Revenue Code, 1954, as amended as of July 22, 1977.

[9] This remainder will equal one minus the marginal tax rate times the property tax payment.

[10] It is also assumed, in estimating the marginal tax rate, that all married homeowners file joint returns.

Table 10.4

PROPERTY TAXES AS A PERCENTAGE OF 1975 INCOME, BY 1975 INCOME/NEEDS DECILE

	(2)	(3)		(4)	(5)	(6)	(7)	(8)
	Homeowners			Renters		All		
1975 Income/ Needs Decile	Weighted Percentage of Obser- vations	Reported Taxes as Percentage of 1975 Income	Effective Taxes as Percentage of 1975 Income	Weighted Percentage of Obser- vations	15 Percent of Annual Rent as Percentage of 1975 Income	Weighted Percentage of Obser- vations	Reported Taxes or 15 Percent of Annual Rent as Percentage of 1975 Income	Effective Taxes or 15 Percent of Annual Rent as Percentage of 1975 Income
1	5.2	8.1+	8.1+	14.6	6.9+	9.0	7.3+	7.3+
2	7.0	5.1	5.0	13.0	3.9	9.4	4.5	4.4
3	7.6	4.2	3.9	12.3	3.3	9.5	3.7	3.6
4	9.2	3.9	3.4	11.0	2.8	9.9	3.4	3.1
5	9.4	3.7	3.2	10.9	2.6	10.0	3.2	2.9
6	11.1	3.1	2.5	8.3	2.4	10.0	2.9	2.5
7	11.6	3.0	2.3	9.2	2.0	10.6	2.6	2.2
8	11.9	3.1	2.4	8.2	2.0	10.4	2.8	2.3
9	12.5	2.7	2.0	7.8	1.7	10.6	2.4	1.9
10	14.4	2.5	1.6	4.7	1.5	10.5	2.8	1.6
TOTAL	100.0	3.6+	3.0+	100.0	3.3+	100.0	3.4+	3.1+

+Figure based on assigning $1,000 income to families with income less than $1,000.

property tax in order to ascertain the incidence of the tax. As mentioned earlier, it is often argued that such single-year measures do not reflect a family's true level of relative economic well-being or its true resource base from which to pay the tax. In Tables 10.5 and 10.6 we incorporate two modifications into the preceding analysis in order to analyze the effects of using longer run measures of economic resources. First, families are ranked according to their annual income and income/needs ratios, averaged over the nine-year period from 1967 to 1975, inclusive. Second, the amount of 1975 residential property taxes paid are calculated as a percentage of annual income averaged over the same nine-year period[11].

These two changes resulted in a pronounced decrease in the regressivity of the residential property tax, particularly at the lower end of the income scale. When families are ranked according to average annual money income (Table 10.5), the percentage of average annual income which is accounted for by the tax (excluding the federal income tax offset) is 4.3 percent for families in the lowest income decile and 2.5 percent for families in the highest income decile. When families are ranked according to average income/needs ratio (Table 10.6), the regressivity of the tax is reduced even more, with families in the lowest decile bearing a burden equal to 3.4 percent of their nine-year average income while families in the highest decile pay 2.6 percent of their income to the tax. By either ranking, the tax is essentially proportional past the third income decile. Only when the federal income tax deduction for property taxes is factored into the estimates does the tax exhibit a noticeably regressive pattern. Families in the higher income brackets benefit substantially from this deduction, while families in the lower income deciles are virtually unaffected. The incidence pattern is still substantially less regressive than was found when single-year measures were employed, however.

A COMPARISON OF DIFFERENT METHODS OF ESTIMATING PROPERTY TAX BURDENS

Homeowners

Previous years of the Panel Study have estimated the property tax paid by homeowners by applying to reported house value an estimated effective tax rate developed by Maynes and Morgan.[12] The actual rates used are reported in Footnote 2, on page 1. The

[11]The reader is reminded that to some extent the preceding analysis controlled for possible abnormally low incomes by assuming a $1,000 minimum level of family money income.

[12]Maynes and Morgan (1957).

Table 10.5

PROPERTY TAXES AS A PERCENTAGE OF 9-YEAR AVERAGE INCOME, BY 9-YEAR AVERAGE INCOME DECILE

	Homeowners			Renters		All		
9-Year Average Income Decile	Weighted Percentage of Obser-vations	Reported Taxes as Percentage of 9-Year Average Income	Effective Taxes as Percentage of 9-Year Average Income	Weighted Percentage of Obser-vations	Reported Taxes as Percentage of 9-Year Average Income	Weighted Percentage of Obser-vations	Reported Taxes or 15 Percent of Annual Rent as Percentage of 9-Year Average Income	Effective Taxes or 15 Percent of Annual Rent as Percentage of 9-Year Average Income
1	7.1	4.3	4.2	12.1	4.2	9.1	4.3	4.2
2	7.2	3.6	3.4	14.1	3.1	10.0	3.3	3.2
3	7.5	3.5	3.1	12.4	2.3	9.4	2.9	2.7
4	8.3	3.1	2.7	11.1	2.2	9.4	2.6	2.4
5	9.2	2.6	2.2	11.1	1.8	10.0	2.3	2.0
6	11.0	2.7	2.2	8.7	1.8	10.1	2.4	2.0
7	11.4	3.0	2.4	8.3	1.6	10.2	2.5	2.1
8	11.6	2.9	2.2	8.7	1.5	10.5	2.4	2.0
9	12.8	3.1	2.3	7.3	1.3	10.6	2.6	2.0
10	13.8	2.9	1.9	6.3	1.2	10.8	2.5	1.7
TOTAL	100.0	3.1	2.5	100.0	2.3	100.0	2.8	2.4

Table 10.6

PROPERTY TAXES AS A PERCENTAGE OF 9-YEAR AVERAGE INCOME, BY 9-YEAR AVERAGE INCOME/NEEDS DECILE

	Homeowners			Renters		All		
9-Year Average Income/ Needs Decile	Weighted Percentage of Obser- vations	Reported Taxes as Percentage of 9-Year Average Income	Effective Taxes as Percentage of 9-Year Average Income	Weighted Percentage of Obser- vations	Reported Taxes as Percentage of 9-Year Average Income	Weighted Percentage of Obser- vations	Reported Taxes or 15 Percent of Annual Rent as Percentage of 9-Year Average Income	Effective Taxes or 15 Percent of Annual Rent as Percentage of 9-Year Average Income
1	4.2	3.3	3.2	11.4	3.5	7.1	3.4	3.4
2	8.3	3.3	3.1	15.4	2.9	11.2	3.1	3.0
3	7.8	3.4	3.1	12.1	2.5	9.5	3.0	2.8
4	9.2	3.1	2.6	10.6	2.3	9.8	2.7	2.5
5	10.0	2.9	2.3	11.0	1.9	10.4	2.5	2.2
6	12.2	3.4	2.8	10.2	1.7	11.4	2.8	2.4
7	10.4	3.3	2.6	9.0	1.6	9.8	2.7	2.2
8	12.7	2.7	2.1	7.7	1.7	10.7	2.5	2.0
9	12.6	3.0	2.2	7.1	1.6	10.4	2.6	2.1
10	12.7	2.9	2.0	5.5	1.3	9.8	2.6	1.8
TOTAL	100.0	3.1	2.5	100.0	2.3	100.0	2.8	2.4

burden of the tax for 1975 based on these rates is reported in column 3 of Table 10.7, using 1975 family money income as the measure of ability. The burden based on the reported property tax payment is presented in column 2. A third method of estimating the property tax paid by homeowners is to apply to reported house value the effective tax rates by county[13] as reported in the 1972 Census of Local and State Governments. These estimates are reported in column 4 of Table 10.7.

The estimates based on the Maynes-Morgan procedure parallel extremely closely the reported property tax payments of homeowners. Burden estimates based on the effective property tax rates reported in the Census of Governments are consistently higher than the tax burdens reported by the panel and those based on the Maynes-Morgan tax rates. This is probably a result of the fact that the Census rates are reported for the largest counties in the country, and these rates are no doubt higher than those found in more rural areas. A comparison by city size of the property tax rates based on the reported taxes and on the Census data (Appendix Tables A10.1b and A10.1c) support this explanation. The property tax rates for the larger cities are comparable, for the smaller cities the Census rates are consistently higher than the reported rates. Despite these differences, the overall pattern of regressivity is unchanged under the different estimating procedures.

Renters

For the results concerning the burden of the residential property tax, we used 15 percent of annual rent as an estimate of the property taxes borne by renters.[14] We also estimated the amount of tax paid by renters by applying the Maynes-Morgan and the Census tax rates to an estimate of the market value of the rental unit. To derive an estimate of the market value of a rental unit, we multiplied monthly rent by 100, a procedure adopted by Aaron.[15] A comparison of the burden on renters as calculated under these alternative procedures is presented in Table 10.8.

The estimates based on 15 percent of annual rent and those based on the Maynes-Morgan tax rates are very similar. As with homeowners, the estimates based on the Census tax rates are consistently higher than the estimates derived by the alternative procedures. Again, this can be attributed to the fact that the Census tax rates do not

[13]The details of translating the estimates of effective tax rates for the 126 selected counties reported in the Census of Governments to an effective rate for every county represented in the Panel Study sample are described in the Appendix.

[14]The Michigan state income tax uses 17 percent of annual rent as an estimate of the property tax paid by renters.

[15]See Aaron (1974) p. 215.

Table 10.7

SELECTED ESTIMATES OF PROPERTY TAX INCIDENCE FOR HOMEOWNERS BY 1975 INCOME DECILE

	(1)	(2)	(3)	(4)
		As a Percentage of 1975 Income		
1975 Income Decile	Weighted Percentage of Observation	Reported Taxes	Dwelling Unit Value Times Estimated Tax Rate‡	Dwelling Unit Value Times Census Tax Rate‡
1	6.2	9.0+	9.0+	12.5+
2	5.9	5.3	6.8	8.9
3	7.5	4.1	4.6	6.0
4	6.9	4.3	4.0	5.5
5	8.8	3.0	3.3	4.4
6	10.0	3.1	3.2	4.5
7	11.6	3.2	3.0	4.3
8	12.5	2.5	2.7	3.6
9	14.3	3.0	2.8	4.0
10	16.3	2.4	2.2	3.1
TOTAL	100.0	3.6+	3.6+	5.0+

+Figure based on assigning $1,000 income to families with income less than $1,000.

‡Dwelling Unit Value = Reported 1976 House Value.

Table 10.8

SELECTED ESTIMATES OF PROPERTY TAX INCIDENCE FOR RENTERS, BY 1975 INCOME DECILE

	(1)	(2)	(3)	(4)
		As a Percentage of 1975 Income		
1975 Income Decile	Weighted Percentage of Observations	15 Percent of Annual Rent	Dwelling Unit Value Times Estimated Tax Rate‡	Dwelling Unit Value Times Census Tax Rate‡
1	13.4	7.5+	6.5+	9.0+
2	14.4	4.3	3.8	5.0
3	12.8	3.2	3.0	3.7
4	14.3	2.7	2.5	3.2
5	11.7	2.4	2.2	3.0
6	10.0	2.0	1.8	2.5
7	8.1	1.9	1.7	2.2
8	7.4	1.5	1.4	1.8
9	5.0	1.7	1.6	2.1
10	2.8	1.3	1.1	1.6
TOTAL	100.0	3.3+	3.0+	3.9+

+Figure based on assigning income of $1,000 families with income less than $1,000.

‡Dwelling unit value = 100 x 1975 average monthly rent.

reflect the generally lower property tax rates which exist in rural areas. The overall pattern of regressivity does not vary in any significant way under any of these procedures.

Homeowners and Renters Combined

The separate alternative estimates of the burden of the tax on homeowners and renters can be combined in a number of different ways[16] to yield an estimate of the burden of the tax on the population as a whole. Four different combinations are presented for comparison in Table 10.9. Column (1) combines the reported taxes for homeowners and 15 percent of annual rent for renters to produce an estimate of the aggregate incidence of the tax. (Column (2) of Table 10.7 and column (2) of Table 10.8.) The reader will recognize this combination as that upon which the aggregate incidence results reported earlier were based. Column (3) combines the results which applied the Maynes-Morgan estimated property tax rates to the value of the dwelling unit—either the reported house value of homeowners or 100 times monthly rent for renters. (This represents a combination of column (3) of Table 10.7 and column (3) of Table 10.8.) Column (4) combines the results which applied the Census estimate of effective property tax rate to the value of the dwelling unit. (A combination of column (4) of Table 10.7 and column (4) of Table 10.8.) Column (5) combines the reported taxes for homeowners and the dwelling unit value times the Census tax rate for renters. (Column (2) of Table 10.7 and column (4) of Table 10.8.)

All of these combinations yield similar patterns of the incidence of the residential property tax. The tax is clearly regressive under any of these combinations when single year money income is used as the measure of ability-to-pay and of relative economic well-being.

Summary and Conclusion

This chapter attempts to fulfill two limited purposes. First, we examine, under highly simplified incidence assumptions, how our concept of the burden of the property tax changes if we extend the time horizon over which we measure the ability-to-pay and the relative economic well-being of different households. Second, we examine how sensitive our estimates of the property tax burden are to selected alternative measures of the property tax payments which each household faces.

With respect to the first issue, we find that when single-year family money income is used as a measure of ability-to-pay and as a measure of relative economic well-being,

[16]Nine, to be exact.

Table 10.9

SELECTED ESTIMATES OF PROPERTY TAX INCIDENCE FOR HOMEOWNERS AND RENTERS COMBINED, BY 1975 INCOME DECILE

		As a Percentage of 1975 Income			
	(1)	(2)	(3)	(4)	(5)
1975 Income Decile	Weighted Percentage of Observations	Reported Taxes or 15 Percent of Annual Rent⁑	Dwelling Unit Value Times Estimated Tax Rate‡	Dwelling Unit Value Times Census Tax Rate‡	Reported Taxes or Dwelling Unit Value Times Census Tax Rate‡,⁑
1	9.1	8.1+	7.5+	10.4+	9.0+
2	9.3	4.7	5.0	6.4	5.1
3	9.6	3.7	3.8	4.8	3.9
4	9.8	3.3	3.1	4.2	3.7
5	10.0	2.7	2.8	3.7	3.0
6	10.0	2.7	2.6	3.7	2.9
7	10.2	2.8	2.6	3.7	2.9
8	10.5	2.2	2.3	3.1	2.3
9	10.6	2.8	2.6	3.6	2.8
10	10.9	2.3	2.1	2.9	2.4
TOTAL	100.0	3.4+	3.4+	4.6+	3.7+

+Figure based on assigning $1,000 income to families with income less than $1,000.

‡Dwelling unit value refers to reported 1976 house value for homeowners and 100 times 1975 average monthly rent for renters.

⁑Reported taxes are used for homeowners and the other method of estimating taxes is used for renters.

the residential property tax is quite clearly regressive. This regressivity is accentuated by the federal income tax deductibility of property tax payments available to homeowners. This conclusion is unchanged when families are ranked according to a single-year income/needs measure in order to account for family size. When a nine-year measure of relative economic well-being and of ability-to-pay is used, however, the regressivity of the tax is sharply reduced, and the tax becomes essentially proportional throughout most of the income range. But the availability of the federal income tax offset reintroduces a distinct element of regressivity to the overall burden of the tax, although still to a less pronounced degree than was found for the one-year estimates.

A comparison of alternative procedures for estimating the property tax payments of different households resulted in no significance changes in the pattern of the incidence of the residential property tax.

Several assumptions were employed to derive these results, some of questionable validity. In particular, the assumption that consumers of housing services bear the ultimate burden of the tax is one of controversial theoretical validity. In addition, the interpretative problems of using nine-year measures of income and income/needs for all households, including those which have undergone substantial changes in family composition, should also be remembered in analyzing these results.

References

Aaron, Henry. Who Pays the Property Tax?. Washington, D.C.: The Brookings Institution 1975.

Aaron, Henry. "A New View of Property Tax Incidence." Papers and Proceedings of the American Economic Association, May 1974.

Barlow, Robin. "The Incidence of Selected Taxes by Income and Class." Five Thousand American Families—Patterns of Economic Progress, Vol. II. Edited by James N. Morgan. Ann Arbor, Mich.: Institute for Social Research, University of Michigan, 1974.

Maynes, E. S., and Morgan, J. H. "The Effective Rate of Real Estate Taxation." Review of Economics and Statistics, Vol. 39 (February 1957).

Netzer, Dick. Economics of the Property Tax. Washington, D.C.: The Brookings Institution, 1966.

Other Empirical Studies on the Incidence of the Property Tax

Bishop, George. Tax Burdens and Benefits of Government Expenditures by Income Class, 1961 and 1965. New York: Tax Foundation, Inc., 1967.

Brownlee, O. H. Estimated Distribution of Minnesota Taxes and Public Expenditure Benefits. Minneapolis, Minn.: University of Minnesota Press, 1960.

Gillespie, W. Irwin. "The Effect of Public Expenditures on the Distribution of Income." In Essays in Fiscal Federalism. Edited by Richard Musgrave. Washington, D.C.: The Brookings Institution, 1965.

Morgan, J. N.; David, M.; Cohen, W., and Brazer, H. Income and Welfare in the United States. New York: McGraw-Hill, 1962.

Musgrave, Richard, and Daicoff, Darwin. "Who Pays the Michigan Taxes?" In Michigan Tax Study Staff Papers. Edited by Harvey Brazer. Lansing, Mich.: Michigan Tax Study, 1958.

Pechman, Joseph, and Okner, Benjamin. Who Bears the Tax Burden? Washington, D.C.: The Brookings Institution, 1974.

Pealy, Robert, et al. "The General Property Tax." In Michigan Tax Study Staff Papers. Edited by Harvey Brazer. Lansing, Mich.: Michigan Tax Study 1958.

University of Wisconsin Tax Study Committee. Wisconsin's State and Local Tax Burden. Madison, Wis.: University of Wisconsin, 1959.

APPENDIX 10.1

Derivation of the Census of Governments Tax Rate

As used in this chapter, The Census of Governments Tax Rate for a given household is equivalent to a value derived for its 1976 county of residence from data presented in the 1972 Census of Governments, Vol. 2, Part 2. Table 12 in that publication presents effective tax rates as of 1971 on residential (nonfarm) real property classified by major cities and balance of the county for selected counties.[17] These rates form the basis for what this chapter terms the Census of Governments Rax Rate.

A county included in Table 12 for which effective residential tax rates were available by major cities was assigned a value on the Census Tax Rate equivalent to the effective residential tax rate averaged over all major cities listed for the county. A county included in Table 12 for which rates were available only for balance of the county was assigned the balance of the county rate.

Any county not listed in the 1972 Census of Governments Table 12 was assigned a value on the Census Tax Rate equivalent to a computed average rate for its respective state. This average rate equalled the averaged balance of the county effective residential tax rate when such rates were available for at least one county in the state. When effective residential tax rates were only available by major cities, this average rate for the state was computed as the average of the Census Tax Rates derived for all counties within the state that were listed in Table 12. For states not listed in Table 12, this average rate for the state was set equal to the average of such rates for surrounding states (i.e., Vermont's average rate is equivalent to the average of the average rates for New Hampshire and Maine, and Wyoming's average rate is equivalent to the average of the average rates for Montana and Idaho.)

[17] Table 12 "Property Tax Rates and Assessment-Sales Price Ratios for Real Property Involved in Measurable Sales, for Selected Local Areas: 1971", pp. 110-43.

Table A10.1a

DISTRIBUTION OF REPORTED PROPERTY TAX PAYMENTS BY FAMILY MONEY INCOME, 1975

(All Homeowners, N = 2976)

Family Money Income						Percentage Paying Property Taxes of:					
	None	$1-99	$100-199	$200-299	$300-399	$400-499	$500-749	$750-999	$1000-1499	$1500 or more	Don't Know	TOTALS
$0-4999	0.7	3.8	1.8	1.1	0.9	0.3	0.7	0.2	-	0.1	1.5	11.2
$5000-7499	0.6	2.1	1.9	0.9	0.6	0.6	0.8	0.5	0.1	-	1.2	9.4
$7500-9999	0.3	1.2	1.4	0.9	0.9	0.7	0.7	0.4	0.2	0.2	1.2	7.9
$10,000-12,499	0.4	1.4	1.8	1.5	1.1	1.0	1.3	0.3	0.2	0.1	1.2	10.2
$12,500-14,999	0.4	0.9	1.7	1.3	1.4	1.2	1.1	0.7	0.4	0.2	1.1	10.4
$15,000-19,999	0.5	1.0	2.5	2.1	2.8	2.0	3.3	1.6	1.1	0.4	1.4	18.6
$20,000-24,999	0.2	0.7	1.3	1.3	1.4	0.8	3.3	1.8	1.0	1.0	0.6	13.6
$25,000 or more	0.0	0.2	0.6	1.1	1.4	1.9	3.8	2.8	3.1	3.1	0.7	18.7
TOTALS	3.0	11.3	13.1	10.0	10.7	8.6	15.1	8.2	6.0	5.2	8.8	100.0

- No Observations for this cell.

Figures are percentages of the total sample.

Table A10.1b

PROPERTY TAXES AS A PERCENTAGE OF HOUSE VALUE, BY HOUSE VALUE AND CITY SITE

Reported Property Taxes Divided By House Value

	City Size						
1975 Reported House Value	500,000 or more	100,000-499,999	50,000-99,999	25,000-49,999	10,000-24,999	Less Than 10,000	All
$1-9,999	.091	.032	.019	.015	.016	.012	.026
$10,000-19,999	.023	.015	.014	.017	.014	.009	.015
$20,000-29,999	.019	.015	.014	.013	.011	.009	.014
$30,000-39,999	.022	.014	.014	.014	.011	.009	.015
$40,000-49,999	.021	.014	.013	.013	.011	.009	.015
$50,000-74,999	.024	.012	.014	.013+	.011+	.010+	.018
$75,000 or more	.020	.014+	.014+	.013+	.006+	.004+	.015
TOTAL	.024	.015	.014	.014	.012	.010	.016

+Fewer than 20 observations.

Table A10.1c

CENSUS OF GOVERNMENTS TAX RATE, BY HOUSE VALUE AND CITY SIZE

Census Tax Rate

	City Size						
1975 Reported House Value	500,000 or more	100,000-499,999	50,000-99,999	25,000-49,999	10,000-24,999	Less Than 10,000	All
$1-9,999	.022	.019	.017	.017	.016	.013	.016
$10,000-19,999	.023	.017	.018	.022	.017	.016	.018
$20,000-29,999	.023	.021	.020	.020	.017	.017	.020
$30,000-39,999	.026	.019	.021	.021	.019	.016	.021
$40,000-49,999	.026	.019	.022	.022	.017	.016	.022
$50,000-74,999	.026	.019	.022	.018+	.015+	.017+	.023
$75,000 or more	.026	.021+	.016+	.019+	.015+	.013+	.022
TOTAL	.025	.019	.020	.020	.017	.016	.020

+Fewer than 20 observations.

Chapter 11

INTRA-FAMILY TRANSFERS REVISITED: THE SUPPORT OF DEPENDENTS INSIDE THE FAMILY

James N. Morgan

Introduction

Despite a growing aggregate of institutional and government income maintenance programs to support otherwise dependent people, the vast bulk of the support for those who are not currently earning or receiving enough to be independent comes from within the family. Most family help (the technical name is transfers) occurs within individual households rather than between households, i.e., money or time given to helping relatives who live elsewhere. In a national survey reported in 1962, we distinguished between private and government, contributory and noncontributory transfers to families, and in 1973 we published some estimates, based on the current panel study, of the amount of intra-family transfers.[1] This chapter reexamines intra-family transfers using our latest data which have more detail about incomes and hours of housework and child care. We find such transfers are still huge, however we estimate them.

Analysis

Assumptions and Definitions of Terms

We do not know exactly who consumes how much of the family income, but we can make some reasonable assumptions. We assumed that individuals consume in the sense that they benefit from all the family income, even if some of it is saved or is used to pay taxes. We started with the food needs that are the basis of the poverty standard. Taking as base the 1967 figure of $7 a week for food for an adult male, we assumed the consumption of those aged six to 13 would be 6/7th of that, those three to five years old

[1] See Morgan et al. (1962), especially Chapters 13 and 14, and Baerwaldt and Morgan (1973).

would be 4/7th, and those under three would be 2/7th's. Thus a family with one four-year old child has a total needs index of 18. Each adult is assumed to consume 7/18th of the family income, and the child 4/18th's. We felt that the sex differences in food needs, and the age differences after age 14, were not usable, since other differences may well offset them. Older people may eat less but they require more medical care. Women may eat less than men, but may have higher expenditures elsewhere, e.g., medical care. We need not worry about economies of scale, or the cost of one more family member, since we are concerned only with allocating the income of a given family among its members—no one is marginal. Our earlier estimates (Baerwaldt and Morgan 1973) tried three different ways of estimating who consumes which part of the family income according to food needs.[2]

The earlier study also tried varying definitions of income. Here we restricted ourselves to the most inclusive definition which included nonmoney components for which we have information. We added to family money income the subsidy value of any food stamps, the imputed return on net equity in an owned home (imputed rent), and the value of time spent on housework and child care. We used 5 percent of home equity as an estimate on the nonmoney income it produces. We used two different methods for valuing housework and child care, eschewing any attempt to value it as the cost of hiring a housekeeper. One estimate used simply $5 an hour across the board—a little high for the value of housework, a little low for the real, if not the market, value of child care. As an alternative, we used each individual's average hourly earnings in market work, or an estimate of what those earnings would be for those not currently working for money.[3] This estimate was not based simply on the wages of similar individuals, because of the possible self-selection bias—those who can earn more are more likely to work. Instead we estimated a "shadow wage" using an equation developed by Barbara Devaney for white wives, allowing for the fact that market work cannot be less than zero hours, so people not working for money can have expected wages well below their reservation wage.[4] The use of such an alternative "opportunity cost" value of time assumes that rational marginal

[2]For estimates of intra-family transfers, see Baerwaldt and Morgan (1973), especially Chapter 13. For background materials on estimating needs see Orshansky (1977).

[3]Some are critical of the opportunity cost approach, arguing that houseworkers do not get paid more for more education or more experience. They would prefer an estimate of the cost of hired help, plus a differential. See Ferber and Brinbaum (1977), pp. 19-28.

[4]Even for a working woman, the value of her home production may well be below what she earns on the market, which is why she decided to work for money, and the reverse may be true for women who do not work for money. Self-selection bias can be great when interpersonal differences in aptitudes and propensities are great. But women's market wages, as a result of discrimination, may also generally understate their

choices are possible between more housework-and-child-care and more market work.[5] The shadow wage so estimated is related positively to years of education and work experience (or lack of it) as well as to the numbers of younger children because the value of time devoted to them is higher; it is negatively related to the number of older children who presumably free mother to go to work, lowering her reservation wage. The actual estimating equation was:

natural log of shadow wage = -.05792 + .081 (years of education)
+ .00344 (age minus years of work since 18 = "home time")

+ .00132 (home time)^2 + .0058 (husband's wage rate)

+ .000004 (income net of husband's and wife's earnings)

+ .153 (number of children under three)
+ .08 (number of children three to five)

+ .016 (number of children six to 13)
- .022 (number of children 14-17).

We cavalierly applied this equation also to the few nonworking male heads and to blacks, heads or spouses. We omitted the housework of others (not head or spouse) both from those "others' " family income and from their contribution to it since we lacked individual information about these "others" necessary to estimate their potential hourly earnings. (They were included in the $5 an hour calculations.)

---

productivity and the value of their time. Finally, market alternatives may differ from one area to another, so nonworking mothers may be concentrated in market areas where their earning opportunities are less than their skills would justify. It is market wage after taxes that really counts, but the tax on wages differs depending on family income. And separate valuation of child care, if we could estimate the hours separately, would recognize its higher skill requirements.

Whatever the valuation, however, there are such large differences in the hours reported spent on housework and child care by people of different ages and sexes, that some account needs to be taken of it in assessing intra-family transfers.

[5]Devaney (1977). Instead of iterative procedures to solve the maximum likelihood equations of the Tobin method, which are often expensive and unreliable, she uses a method that treats the problems as one of regression with censored dependent variables. Conditional estimates of wages for those not working are produced using a regression only for those who are, and these are used to recalculate the regression for the full sample. This provides a new set of estimated wages for those not working which can be resubstituted and the regression calculated again, and again, until the sequence of parameter estimates converges. The result is equivalent to Tobin's but the calculations easier and the convergence assured. (See also Hartley (1976).)

Multiplying each individual's reported hours of housework and child care by an estimated value per hour, and adding the individual's own earnings and other income, gave an estimate of that individual's total contribution to the family income. Subtracting that individual's share in the consumption of that income yielded a positive net contribution to the family or a negative net subsidy from the family. For individuals other than head or spouse, we ignored housework and child care in the opportunity cost version. We did not know their hourly earnings nor did we have the background facts to estimate a shadow wage. Hence the estimate of total family income includes the value of housework and child care only when done by the husband, wife, or single head.

Income from capital was recorded separately if it went to individuals other than the head or wife, but we evenly divided the rest of capital income (rent, interest, dividends, and business and farm profits) between husband and wife. The same was true for transfer incomes, which were identified if they went to an individual other than head or wife, but otherwise were lumped together. We divided head-and-spouse transfer income evenly between them, even though some of it may well have been for the benefit of children. Indeed some of the transfer income of single female heads is for child support, yet is credited to the head.

This estimation of the net contribution to the family or net subsidy from the family of each individual thus included a kind of shaky redistribution inside the family of transfer incomes from outside the family. Since the original designation of who "contributed" is uncertain, and since we might object to counting this redistribution anyway, we also provided an estimate of net contribution-subsidy that excluded transfer income from both income and consumption, and hence from net contribution or subsidy. We provided then the following estimates for each individual:

Total contribution to the family—earnings, capital and transfer income, and value of housework and child care hours.

Net contribution—total contribution minus estimated consumption of the family income. If negative, this is a subsidy from the family.

Adjusted net contribution, excluding transfer income from outside the family from both individual income and contribution, and from individual consumption.

Hours of housework, or value of housework, when valued at hourly earnings or shadow wage estimate of what they might be.

Empirical Results

The appendix tables give these averages for individuals grouped by age and sex or by education and sex—the latter segregating those other than head and spouse since their education was not known or in the case of children, unfinished. Clearly, heads, spouses, and other people aged 25 to 64 are on the average net contributors to others in the family, while those younger and older are the beneficiaries of subsidy from intra-family transfers.

Figures 11.1 through 11.3, depict the age patterns for men and women, first valuing housework at $5 an hour and even including work of others in the family, then valuing it at actual or estimated hourly earnings, and finally looking at blacks only, using the $5 an hour for housework and child care. The obvious pattern of early dependency, middle-aged productivity, and aged dependency appear as expected. Comparison of Figures 11.1 and 11.2 shows the effects of different valuations of housework and child care: using market alternative opportunity cost increases the estimated contribution of men relative to women. Given the discrimination against women in the labor market, however, their market alternatives may under-value their child care and house work. Likewise, it is difficult to believe that just because a man earns $20 an hour on his job, he is worth that much taking out the garbage or minding the children.

The reader can produce other estimates using different valuations of housework and child care, by using the average hours given in the Appendix tables. For example, deducting $2 times the average number of hours would give an estimate of average net contribution at $3 an hour for housework and child care. Or one could remove considerations of housework and child care altogether by deducting $5 times the hours, or deducting the average assigned value given in Tables A11.1c and A11.1d.

All in all, women appear to receive an economic subsidy during the years when many of them are raising children and their husbands are getting their peak earnings, but this depends on the valuation of housework and child care time, since the total hours of money and nonmoney work are clearly greater for women during those years than for men (see Chapter 12).

Since actual earnings account for most of the contributions people make, the second of each pair of tables in the Appendix shows the relation of education to average net contribution, separately for men and women, segregating those other than head or spouse into the "education not ascertained" category. As expected, the more the education, the greater the net contribution people make to their families. For blacks, the pattern is less clear and less dramatic.

Since education affects men's market wages more than women's, and drives them well above the $5 an hour we assigned to housework and child care time, it is the highly educated men who are credited with the largest average net contributions. Again, one can argue with the valuations of time, saying that women should be able to earn as much as men, hence all their time should be worth as much.

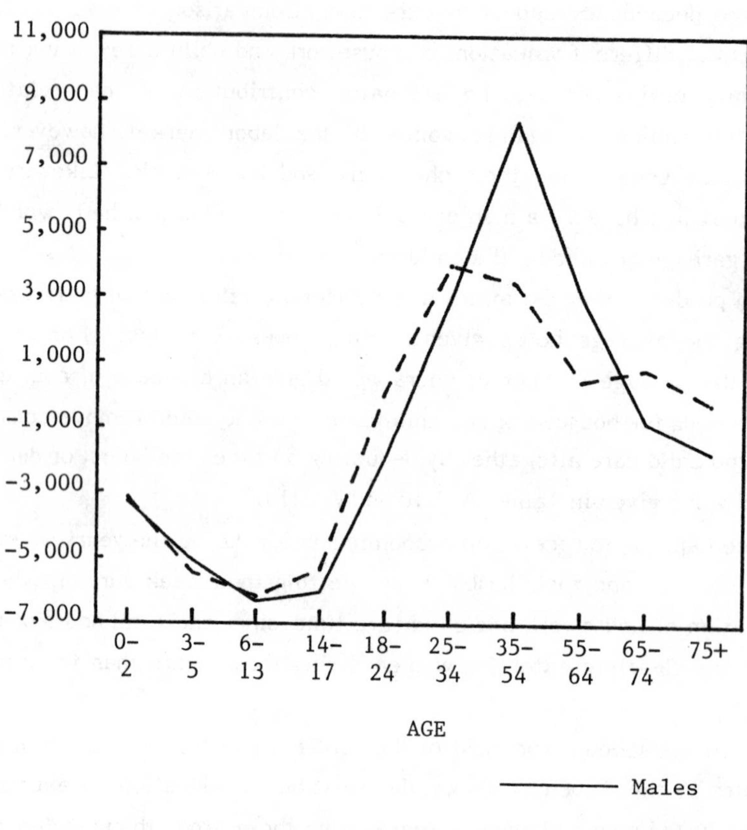

Figure 11.1. AVERAGE NET INDIVIDUAL CONTRIBUTION TO FAMILY (OR SUBSIDY FROM FAMILY) BY AGE AND SEX, 1976

Valuing Housework and Child Care at \$5/hour Exluding Redistribution of Transfer Income)

Source: Appendix Table A11.1a

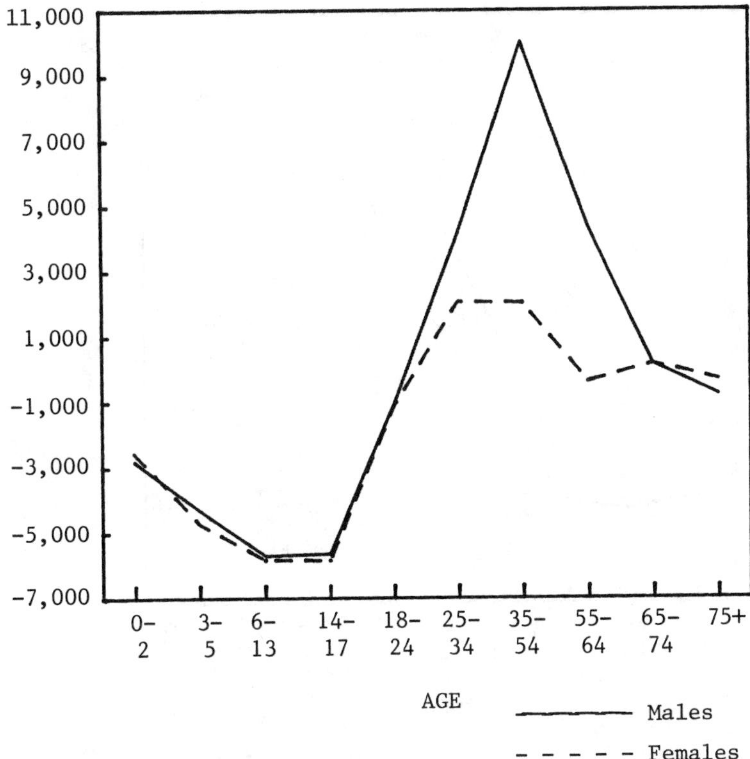

Figure 11.2. AVERAGE NET INDIVIDUAL CONTRIBUTION TO FAMILY (OR SUBSIDY FROM IT) BY AGE AND SEX

Valuing Housework and Child Care at Foregone Market Wage Rates Excluding Redistribution of Transfer Income

Source: Appendix Table A11.1c

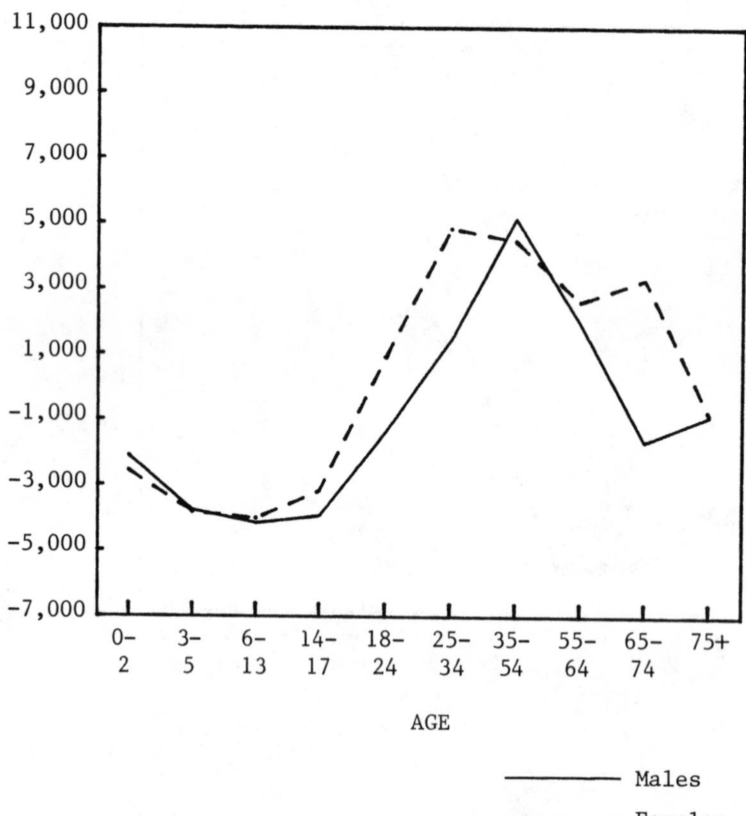

Figure 11.3 AVERAGE ADJUSTED NET INDIVIDUAL CONTRIBUTION TO FAMILY (OR SUBSIDY FROM FAMILY) BY AGE AND SEX FOR BLACK FAMILIES

Valuing Housework and Child Care at $5/hour Excluding Redistribution of Transfer Income

Source: Appendix Table A11.1e

Estimating Aggregates

In the national income accounts, the flows of money that go to people who did not currently earn it are also called transfer incomes. Likewise, national income accounting for family transfers should count only the aggregate of the net subsidies received, or the aggregate of the net contributions made, but not both since that would count a dollar transfer twice—once when contributed, once when received. On the other hand, averaging to obtain the net contributions of a group can eliminate offsetting amounts completely. Indeed, except for errors and rounding, the overall average net contribution for the whole population should be zero. If we ignore the sign, add up the contributions and subsidies, and divide by two, we have the amount of transfer flow for either a group or for the whole sample. The Appendix tables give such average estimates for the subgroups by age and sex or education and sex, but a more important estimate is the aggregate amount of intra-family transfer in comparison with the transfers in the national accounts.

Estimating aggregates from a sample is best done by estimating an average per person and then multiplying by an outside, more precise, estimate of the aggregate number of persons. Estimating averages in our sample necessitated using weights to take account of different sampling and response rates, and all the data we have given are so weighted. Some of the individuals were not sample members, yet we had to include them to balance out the families we studied for this purpose. They were given the same weights as the other family members. Actually, weights used in estimating a weighted average of 17,937 cases will make very little difference. Other sources of variation plus conceptual and measurement problems are probably more serious.

At any rate, assuming 215 million individuals in the United States population, we have four estimates of the aggregate volume of intra-family transfers. Two estimates use the $5 an hour valuation of housework, and the other two use foregone market wages, actual or estimated. Two include the redistribution within the family of transfer incomes from outside, two exclude it. The estimated aggregates are in billions of dollars:

Redistribution inside the family of transfers from outside:	Housework and Child Care Valued at:	
	$5 per Hour	Market Wage of Individual
Included	$552	$528
Excluded	$534	$511

Our estimates for 1970 (Baerwaldt and Morgan, 1973) were $313 billion using a much lower wage for housekeepers or child tenders to value housework and child care, $398 billion valuing housework at estimated opportunity wage cost.

As fractions of the Gross National Product, these estimates are comparable, since GNP was $982 billion in 1970 and $1,516 billion in 1976. The intra-family transfers amount to about a third of the gross national product. The implication is that the family is still the main source of support for dependent persons in our society. Government income maintenance programs, including Social Security and welfare, and private transfers such as pensions, account for only a small fraction of the total. This proportion, however, may increase in the future because of the elimination of many state relative-responsibility requirements, and the tendency of older people to live alone. Expanded social responsibility for children, mentally retarded, and disabled people could also increase the relative and absolute amount of public transfers.

Summary

We have estimated the extent to which some contribute more than they consume of the family's income (including nonmoney components) while others receive a subsidy. The results depend heavily on how one values unpaid work, but the beneficiaries are mostly children and the aged, just as they are the main beneficiaries of nonfamily transfer systems—Social Security, welfare, private pensions, child support payments. But the aggregate amounts are huge by any definition. They remind us of the great importance of the family in society, and the need to be aware of the impact of social policies and historic trends on how the family functions.

References

Baerwaldt, Nancy, and Morgan, James. "Trends in Intra-Family Transfers." In Surveys of Consumers 1971-1972. Edited by Lewis Mandell et al. Ann Arbor: Institute for Social Research, 1973.

Devaney, Barbara. The Labor Supply of Married Women: An Analysis of the Allocation of Time to Market and Nonmarket Activities. Unpublished Ph.D. Dissertation, The University of Michigan, 1977.

Ferber, Marianne A., and Brinbaum, Bonnie G. "The 'New Home Economics,' Retrospects and Prospects." Journal of Consumer Research, 4 (June 1977).

Hartley, Michael. The Tobit and Probit Models: Maximum Likelihood Estimation by Ordinary Least Squares. Discussion Paper 374. Buffalo: State University of

New York at Buffalo, 1976.

Morgan, James N., David, Martin, Cohen, Wilbur, and Brazer, Harvey. Income and Welfare in the United States. New York: McGraw-Hill, 1962.

Orshansky, Mollie. The Measure of Poverty, Technical Paper 1, Documentation of Background Information and Rationale for Current Poverty Matrix. Washington, D.C.: U.S. Department of Health, Education and Welfare, 1977. (A compilation of articles, mostly from the Social Security Bulletin.)

APPENDIX 11.1

Table A11.1a

INTRAFAMILY TRANSFERS BY AGE AND SEX OF INDIVIDUALS
(Valuing Housework/Child Care at $5 per Hour)

Age and Sex	Mean Total Dollar Contribution	Mean Net Dollar Contribution	Mean Net Dollar Contribution Excl. Transf. from Outside the Family	Mean Dollar Flow Ignoring Sign (Excl. Transf.)	Mean Hours of Housework and Child Care	Number of Cases
Males						
Younger than 3	8	-3,299	-3,198	3,198	0	548
3 - 5	60	-5,087	-4,867	4,868	12	540
6 - 13	478	-6,340	-6,101	6,104	93	1,532
14 - 17	1,334	-6,038	-5,673	6,051	176	875
18 - 24	7,277	-1,897	-1,795	3,514	328	1,371
25 - 34	14,535	2,939	2,921	4,504	520	1,362
35 - 54	19,029	8,396	8,292	8,935	416	1,385
55 - 64	14,933	3,019	2,936	4,885	295	480
65 - 74	9,762	-814	-934	3,117	435	284
75 or Older	7,310	-1,743	-1,920	2,547	415	134
Females:						
Younger than 3	5	-3,171	-3,058	3,061	0	514
3 - 5	68	-5,466	-5,286	5,286	14	552
6 - 13	801	-6,167	-5,896	5,919	159	1,435
14 - 17	2,211	-5,328	-5,008	5,248	408	854
18 - 24	9,577	164	179	3,697	1,290	1,622
25 - 34	14,727	3,990	3,799	5,340	1,909	1,412
35 - 54	13,438	3,434	3,165	5,152	1,555	1,762
55 - 64	12,299	451	377	3,217	1,225	635
65 - 74	11,277	825	726	2,426	1,114	413
75 or Older	8,223	-242	-414	1,899	820	227
All	8,972	-92	-78	4,972	700	17,937

N = 17,937

NOTE: Even young children can have interest or dividend income of their own.

MTR 1181

Table A11.1b

INTRAFAMILY TRANSFERS BY EDUCATION AND SEX OF INDIVIDUALS
(Valuing Housework/Child Care at $5 per Hour)

Education and Sex	Mean Total Dollar Contribution	Mean Net Dollar Contribution	Mean Net Dollar Contribution Excl. Transf. from Outside the Family	Mean Dollar Flow Ignoring Sign (Excl. Transf.)	Mean Hours of Housework and Child Care	Number of Cases
Males: (Husbands or male heads)						
Cannot Read and Write	8,308	846	595	3,021	383	113
0-5 Grades	8,044	537	313	3,019	431	164
6-8 Grades	10,125	1,307	1,199	3,844	407	537
9-11 Grades	12,231	3,072	2,961	4,608	499	753
12 Grades	14,025	3,378	3,324	4,729	452	773
High School & Training	15,376	4,146	4,058	5,211	495	610
Some College, no Degree	15,705	4,331	4,269	5,567	459	600
Bachelor's Degree	20,787	6,949	6,966	7,897	448	401
Graduate Work	25,442	10,329	10,307	10,904	420	195
Other Males or Education not Ascertained+	1,235	-5,333	-5,103	5,332	94	4,365
Females: (Wives or female heads)						
Cannot Read and Write	9,591	2,362	1,765	2,107	1,168	65
0-5 Grades	8,602	1,540	1,345	2,419	1,188	154
6-8 Grades	11,122	2,558	2,304	3,159	1,412	669
9-11 Grades	12,537	3,963	3,603	4,414	1,722	1,142
12 Grades	13,671	3,011	2,863	4,692	1,805	1,359
High School & Training	13,556	2,648	2,524	4,017	1,536	736
Some College, no Degree	13,699	2,228	2,075	4,212	1,488	590
Bachelor's Degree	14,254	1,100	1,068	4,404	1,306	351
Graduate Work	16,775	1,143	1,125	3,751	1,107	111
Other Females or Education not Ascertained+	1,801	-4,941	-4,715	5,068	240	4,249
All	8,973	-90	-76	4,970	700	17,937

N = 17,937

+Includes all individuals other than heads and wives.

MTR 1181

Table A11.1c

INTRAFAMILY TRANSFERS BY AGE AND SEX OF INDIVIDUALS
(Valuing Housework/Child Care at Shadow Wage)

Age and Sex	Mean Total Dollar Contribution	Mean Net Dollar Contribution	Mean Net Dollar Contribution Excl. Transf. from Outside the Family	Mean Dollar Flow Ignoring Sign (Excl. Transf.)	Mean Dollar Value of Housework and Child Care	Number of Cases
Males:						
Younger than 3	0	-2,821	-2,720	2,720	0	548
3 - 5	0	-4,306	-4,086	4,086	0	540
6 - 13	12	-5,699	-5,461	5,461	0	1,532
14 - 17	452	-5,643	-5,278	5,651	0	875
18 - 24	6,798	-1,063	-960	3,476	1,160	1,371
25 - 34	14,764	4,156	4,138	5,428	2,829	1,362
35 - 54	19,766	10,026	9,921	10,372	2,819	1,385
55 - 64	15,145	4,397	4,313	5,573	1,687	480
65 - 74	8,809	160	40	2,262	1,221	284
75 or Older	6,301	-767	-944	1,511	1,068	134
Females:						
Younger than 3	0	-2,555	-2,442	2,442	0	514
3 - 5	0	-4,716	-4,537	4,537	0	552
6 - 13	6	-5,827	-5,556	5,556	0	1,435
14 - 17	270	-5,837	-5,516	5,553	100	854
18 - 24	6,693	-1,147	-1,132	3,178	3,565	1,622
25 - 34	11,894	2,063	1,872	4,267	6,714	1,412
35 - 54	10,956	2,032	1,763	4,436	5,294	1,762
55 - 64	10,155	-373	-447	3,200	3,981	635
65 - 74	8,803	168	68	1,907	3,174	413
75 or Older	6,598	-308	-481	1,634	2,474	227
All	7,861	-38	-23	4,798	2,387	17,937

N = 17,937

MTR 1181

Table A11.1d

INTRAFAMILY TRANSFERS BY EDUCATION AND SEX OF INDIVIDUALS
(Valuing Housework/Child Care at Shadow Wage)

Education and Sex	Mean Total Dollar Contribution	Mean Net Dollar Contribution	Mean Net Dollar Contribution Excl. Transf. from Outside the Family	Mean Dollar Value of Housework and Child Care	Number of Cases
Males:					
Cannot Read and Write	7,256	2,246	1,995	864	113
0-5 Grades	6,863	1,874	1,650	974	164
6-8 Grades	9,585	2,747	2,639	1,497	537
9-11 Grades	11,875	4,545	4,434	2,138	753
12 Grades	14,082	4,800	4,746	2,316	773
High School & Training	15,508	5,563	5,476	2,607	610
Some College, No Degree	16,036	5,480	5,419	2,626	600
Bachelor's Degree	21,900	5,116	8,133	3,355	401
Graduate Work	27,004	11,406	11,384	3,665	195
Other Males or Education not Ascertained+	780	-4,734	-4,503	17	4,365
Females:					
Cannot Read and Write	6,265	1,129	531	2,513	65
0-5 Grades	4,888	409	214	2,226	154
6-8 Grades	7,636	1,086	831	3,572	669
9-11 Grades	8,702	2,004	1,644	4,773	1,142
12 Grades	10,511	1,091	944	5,863	1,359
High School & Training	11,254	1,481	1,358	5,379	736
Some College, no Degree	11,861	1,136	984	5,605	590
Bachelor's Degree	14,216	987	956	6,493	351
Graduate Work	18,786	2,084	2,066	7,544	111
Other Females or Education not Ascertained+	645	-4,871	-4,644	41	4,249
All	7,861	-36	-21	2,387	17,937

N = 17,937

+Includes all individuals other than heads and wives.

MTR 1181

Table All.1e

INTRAFAMILY TRANSFERS FOR BLACKS ONLY
BY AGE AND SEX OF INDIVIDUALS
(Valuing Housework/Child Care at $5 per Hour)

Age and Sex	Mean Total Dollar Contribution	Mean Net Dollar Contribution	Mean Net Dollar Contribution Excl. Transf. from Outside the Family	Mean Dollar Flow Ignoring Sign (Excluding Transfers)	Number of Cases
Males:					
Younger than 3	0	-2,116	-1,927	1,927	241
3 - 5	81	-3,772	-3,442	3,446	252
6 - 13	500	-4,160	-3,698	3,712	741
14 - 17	1,246	-3,940	-3,366	3,427	436
18 - 24	5,801	-1,368	-1,136	2,839	622
25 - 34	11,116	1,448	1,396	3,069	421
35 - 54	13,049	5,171	4,971	5,645	404
55 - 64	10,041	1,963	1,708	3,686	162
65 - 74	6,331	-1,659	-1,931	3,026	60
75 or Older	4,662	-880	-910	2,169	22
Females:					
Younger than 3	12	-2,576	-2,423	2,427	236
3 - 5	43	-3,822	-3,493	3,494	258
6 - 13	812	-4,016	-3,592	3,669	697
14 - 17	2,250	-3,162	-2,647	2,923	448
18 - 24	8,143	924	941	3,247	764
25 - 34	12,173	4,857	4,329	5,000	502
35 - 54	11,705	4,485	3,756	4,442	709
55 - 64	10,482	2,623	2,252	3,385	221
65 - 74	8,873	3,314	3,004	3,807	93
75 or Older	5,770	-822	-1,417	2,754	39
All	6,243	-57	-48	3,640	7,328

N = 7,328

Table A11.1f

INTRAFAMILY TRANSFERS FOR BLACKS ONLY
BY EDUCATION AND SEX OF INDIVIDUALS
(Valuing Housework/Child Care at $5 per Hour)

Education and Sex	Mean Total Dollar Contribution	Mean Net Dollar Contribution	Mean Net Dollar Contribution Excl. Transf. from Outside the Family	Mean Dollar Flow Ignoring Sign (Excluding Transfers)	Number of Cases
Males:					
Cannot Read and Write	7,332	913	450	2,926	76
0-5 Grades	6,739	225	70	2,450	110
6-8 Grades	10,192	2,844	2,643	4,266	184
9-11 Grades	9,566	1,872	1,696	3,357	340
12 Grades	12,668	3,584	3,530	4,367	241
High School & Training	14,126	3,762	3,635	4,614	137
Some College, no Degree	14,011	2,467	2,397	3,642	119
Bachelor's Degree	16,003	2,146	2,077	3,730	25
Graduate Work	20,076	5,139	5,235	9,074	9
Other Males or Education not Ascertained+	1,019	-3,524	-3,116	3,296	2,120
Females:					
Cannot Read and Write	8,455	3,309	2,329	2,629	39
0-5 Grades	8,566	2,433	2,057	2,423	78
6-8 Grades	9,709	3,860	3,138	3,764	306
9-11 Grades	11,644	4,501	3,746	4,299	562
12 Grades	12,418	4,289	3,860	4,757	414
High School & Training	11,800	3,483	3,245	3,788	213
Some College, no Degree	13,949	5,015	4,199	4,913	141
Bachelor's Degree	14,636	3,213	2,864	3,340	38
Graduate Work	19,003	2,713	2,813	5,975	13
Other Females or Education not Ascertained+	2,018	-2,789	-2,441	3,291	2,163
All	6,243	-56	-47	3,640	7,328

N = 7,328

+Includes all individuals other than heads and wives.

MTR 1181

Table A11.1g

INTRAFAMILY TRANSFERS FOR BLACKS ONLY
BY AGE AND SEX OF INDIVIDUALS
(Valuing Housework/Child Care at Shadow Wage)

Age and Sex	Mean Total Dollar Contribution	Mean Net Dollar Contribution	Mean Net Dollar Contribution Excl. Transf. from Outside the Family	Mean Dollar Value of Housework and Child Care	Number of Cases
Males:					
Younger than 3	0	-1,498	-1,309	0	241
3 - 5	0	-2,911	-2,581	0	252
6 - 13	0	-3,390	-2,927	0	741
14 - 17	80	-3,348	-2,774	1	436
18 - 24	4,800	-591	-360	1,084	622
25 - 34	10,520	2,386	2,334	2,560	421
35 - 54	13,155	6,641	6,441	2,564	404
55 - 64	9,749	3,382	3,127	1,790	162
65 - 74	5,581	-610	-882	1,459	60
75 or Older	3,365	-297	-328	419	22
Females:					
Younger than 3	0	-1,798	-1,645	0	236
3 - 5	0	-2,730	-2,400	0	258
6 - 13	4	-3,430	-3,005	0	697
14 - 17	141	-3,608	-3,093	46	448
18 - 24	4,657	-526	-509	2,362	764
25 - 34	9,670	3,689	3,161	4,865	502
35 - 54	8,806	3,280	2,540	3,796	709
55 - 64	7,126	1,132	761	2,858	221
65 - 74	5,643	1,941	1,630	1,769	93
75 or Older	4,329	-458	-1,052	1,026	39
All	4,779	13	22	1,616	7,328

N = 7,328

Table A11.1h

INTRAFAMILY TRANSFERS FOR BLACKS ONLY
BY EDUCATION AND SEX OF INDIVIDUALS
(Valuing Housework/Child Care at Shadow Wage)

Education and Sex	Mean Total Dollar Contribution	Mean Net Dollar Contribution	Mean Net Dollar Contribution Excl. Transf. from Outside the Family	Mean Dollar Value of Housework and Child Care	Number of Cases
Males:					
Cannot Read and Write	6,151	1,880	1,418	1,110	76
0-5 Grades	5,427	1,296	1,140	833	110
6-8 Grades	9,951	4,440	4,239	2,163	184
9-11 Grades	8,435	2,484	2,308	1,927	340
12 Grades	12,197	4,655	4,601	2,975	241
High School & Training	14,433	6,139	6,012	3,257	137
Some College, no Degree	14,284	3,237	3,167	3,180	119
Bachelor's Degree	16,714	2,806	2,736	3,616	25
Graduate Work	22,924	6,981	7,078	5,491	9
Other Males or Education not Ascertained+	425	2,769	-2,361	5	2,120
Females:					
Cannot Read and Write	4,772	1,606	626	2,108	39
0-5 Grades	4,656	991	614	2,131	78
6-8 Grades	6,171	2,373	1,650	2,918	306
9-11 Grades	7,892	2,735	1,980	3,907	562
12 Grades	9,971	3,349	2,920	4,881	414
High School & Training	9,573	2,769	2,531	4,307	213
Some College, no Degree	11,124	3,768	2,952	5,317	141
Bachelor's Degree	13,611	2,619	2,270	6,852	38
Graduate Work	20,197	2,033	2,128	6,332	13
Other Females or Education not Ascertained+	579	-2,743	-2,396	18	2,163
All	4,779	14	23	1,616	7,328

N = 7,328

+Includes all individuals other than heads and wives.

MTR 1181

Chapter 12

A POTPOURRI OF NEW DATA GATHERED FROM INTERVIEWS WITH HUSBANDS AND WIVES

James N. Morgan

Introduction

This chapter contains relatively simple data based on paired interviews taken in 1976 with husbands and wives in our sample. Some of the questions asked were new, others had been included in previous interviews with husbands. The interviews also contained a series of parallel questions asked of both husbands and wives. The result is a rich set of data. The bits of it we look at here include:

1. The cost in hours and dollars of housework and child care, for families of different sizes.

   Detailed information about child care provisions and costs for working mothers and on how nonworking mothers saw the possibilities for child care if they went to work for money.

   The expectations of wives about additional children and working for pay, and how they thought their husbands felt about these things.

2. Parallel questions about their jobs when both husband and wife were working.

3. Education, work experience, and earnings. (Since previous analysis of the relation of wives' earnings to their education and work experience were based on husbands' reports on all three, it seemed useful to see whether a different relationship appeared when we used the wife's report on her own education, work experience, and earnings.)

Analysis

Family Size Related to Housework and Child Care

Single family heads and husbands were asked about hours spent on housework by themselves and by others in the family (excluding the wife), while wives were asked the following more extensive sequence, starting with the same question about housework that had been asked of husbands and single heads:

> About how much time do you spend on housework in an average week—I mean time spent cooking, cleaning, and doing other work around the house?
>
> Do you pay for any help with the housework from someone outside your household? How much does this cost you per week?

In addition, those with children under 12 in the home were asked:

> You said you spend _____ hours a week on housework. Are there times in addition to that when you are looking after the children or taking them places? About how many hours a week would that amount to on the average?
>
> Are there times when your husband looks after the children or takes them places? About how many hours a week would that amount to on the average?

The subset of those wives with children under 12 who also worked for money were asked:

> How are the children taken care of while you work?
>
> > What about the time they aren't in school?
> >
> > How many hours per week are they taken care of?
>
> Do you pay for this with money, doing something in return, or what?
>
> > How much does that cost you per week?
> >
> > How much time does that take per week?

(We omit the skip sequences, and adjustments for only one child, etc.)

> In the past year how many times did someone have to stay home from work to take care of the children because these arrangements broke down? Who was that, was it you, your husband, or someone else?

Such questions do not, of course, elicit the kind of precision that time diaries do, but they avoid the interpersonal variability from asking only about yesterday or last week. Husbands might also include in their housework hours the same time their wives reported they were taking care of the children. When we present averages of the dollar costs they include a substantial proportion of zeroes, since only a minority pay for child care or housework. We present the averages, however, so they can be added up to form a picture of the total costs of housework and child care for families of different sizes.

Ignoring some minor discrepancies arising from the fact that not all wives were interviewed, and not all had husbands present, we have the average hours of housework for 5,863 Families, where:

> 650 Single male heads reported 468 hours of housework a year
>
> 1,670 Single female heads reported 886 hours
>
> 3,542 Husbands reported 301 hours of housework
>
> 3,472 Wives reported 1473 hours of housework.

The wives can be divided into four groups: those with and without children under 12 in the house, and those working and not working for money:

> There were 820 wives with no children under 12 and no paid employment—who did 1,513 hours of housework per year.
>
> 995 nonworking wives with children under 12 who averaged 1,932 hours of housework.
>
> 865 working wives with no children under 12 averaged 1,084 hours of housework.
>
> And there were 787 working wives with children under 12, who averaged 1387 hours of housework in 1975 and 1,244 hours of work for money on their job. These same working wives with children also reported that their husbands put in 468 hours of child care, that they paid $385 for child care, and that they put in 19 hours repaying others for child care.

A series of multivariate analyses revealed little or no relationship between any of these investments of hours or dollars on the one hand, and race, age, or education on the other, for any of the various subgroups according to sex and marital status, presence of children, and whether the wife worked. The only exception: the very highly educated reported larger expenditures for child care and extra housework as did the younger working mothers of children under 12. The multivariate adjustments of family size effects for their relation to age, education, or race are so small that we can use the unadjusted subgroup means to show the differences in hours and dollar cost according to family size.

Table 12.1 shows hours of housework according to family size, for different heads (single male, single female, and married) and for wives, whether working for money or not and with or without children under 12. The patterns are all meaningful—including the decrease in hours for large families but no children under 12, where the older children presumably take some of the load off the parents. The table also gives average annual expenditures for having housework done, which are small even allowing for the fact that these averages include zeroes for the majority who do not pay for housework.

Husbands do not appear to do more housework in larger families, even according to their own reports, whereas women do, particularly when the large family also contains children under 12.

Table 12.2 focuses on employed (for money) mothers with children under 12 (the first column repeats the data on house-work hours from Table 12.1). They average well over half time in paid work (last column) regardless of family size, do not receive more help from the husband, or spend appreciably more for paid help as family size increases. What does happen is that "others," mostly the older children, help more with the house-

Table 12.1

ANNUAL HOURS OF HOUSEWORK, BY NUMBER IN FAMILY, FOR GROUPS ACCORDING TO SEX-MARITAL STATUS AND WORK STATUS OF MOTHERS

							Nonworking Wives		Working Wives		Dollars Paid Annually for Help with Housework	
Number in Family	Single Women	Single Men	Hus-bands	All Heads	All Wives	Others‡	No Children under 12	Children under 12	No Children under 12	Children under 12	All Heads	All Wives
1	729	436	-	613	-	-	-	-	-	-	-	-
2	960	661	325	455	1,184	235	1,375	-	951	-	$ 53	$ 70
3	1,164	+	294	461	1,424	447	1,700	1,602	1,242	1,145	34	43
4	1,309	+	293	400	1,627	414	1,828	1,855	1,204	1,455	44	51
5	1,413	-	257	360	1,789	641	1,827	2,142	1,430	1,440	59	66
6	1,335	-	329	403	1,871	747	+	2,101	1,581	1,665	53	60
7	1,400	-	268	430	1,766	877	+	2,229	+	1,326	13	15
8 or More	1,310	-	249	382	2,190	875	+	2,462	+	1,719	28	32
All Sizes	885	468	301	479	1,473	455	1,513	1,932	1,084	1,387	$ 34	$ 57
Number of Cases	1,670	650	3,542	5,862	3,472	5,862	820	995	865	787	5,862	3,459
Eta Squared	.12	.05	.00	.02	.11	.28	.06	.08	.08	.06	.01	.00

-No Cases.
+Fewer than 25 cases. They show the same pattern in a forthcoming article using detailed time-diary data that separates child care time.
‡This is an average per family, not per other person.

MTR 1185

Table 12.2

HOURS AND DOLLAR COSTS OF HOUSEWORK AND CHILD CARE FOR WORKING MOTHERS, BY FAMILY SIZE

(Reported by Wives Who Work for Money and Have Children under 12)

Number in Family	Housework Hours			Dollars Paid for Housework	Child Care Hours			Dollars Paid for Child Care	Wife's Work Hours for Money (paid work hours)
	Wife	Husband	Others		Wife	Husband	Wife in Exchange		
3	1,145	349	33	16	937	497	16	559	1,391
4	1,455	346	158	44	894	494	14	388	1,151
5	1,440	295	576	39	634	424	31	289	1,187
6	1,665	442	759	32	534	412	38	182	1,228
7	1,326	333	988	0	819	460	0	81	1,407
8 or More	1,719	310	1,319	83	731	418	0	354	1,126
All	1,387	344	320	34	812	468	19	385	1,244
Eta Squared	.06	.01	.36	.01	.02	.01	.01	.05	.02

work. But mother is left with a combination of time demands that require a great deal of "overtime" work. These mothers work, paid and unpaid, a total of around 3,500 hours a year regardless of the family size.

One might infer something about the marginal time-costs of adding one more family member, by adding everyone's housework and child care times, including paid time (assuming perhaps $3 an hour). The totals increase by only a few hundred hours per added person, implying substantial economies of scale in living together.

Table 12.3 shows the pattern of expenditures of money and time for housework and child care according to the wife's education. Clearly the higher hourly earnings that go along with higher education are not being extensively used to reduce the time burden on married working mothers. Indeed, better-educated mothers even when they are in paid employment report spending more time on child care. This has been noted by Russell Hill and Frank Stafford in their analyses of investments in children.[1]

Child Care Provisions of Working Mothers

Working mothers were asked how their children were cared for while they worked, with a probe about the time when they were not in school. The proportion mentioning various methods (some mentioned two) as a percentage of all families, was:

	PERCENT
Day-care center, nursery school	1.1
Baby sitter, friend, neighbor	3.1
Husband or wife or both, split shifts, etc.	4.0
Relative, or siblings over 12	1.4
Relatives not in dwelling	2.1
Self-care	0.8
Public school (mostly as a second mention)	4.2

Table 12.4 shows the patterns of replies about details according to the wife's age, education, race, and the number in the family.

The younger, better educated mothers with fewer children were most likely to pay money for part or all of the child care; the older, less educated mothers with more children more often got it without paying in either money or reciprocal time. Blacks also were more likely to pay and less likely to get free care.

[1]Hill and Stafford (1974) had to infer child care time components of a total of housework and child care, whereas we have asked about child care separately in the 1976 questions. They show the same pattern in a forthcoming article using detailed time-diary data that separate child care time.

Table 12.3

EXPENDITURES OF TIME AND MONEY FOR HOUSEWORK AND CHILD CARE, BY EDUCATION OF WIFE

	Dollar Expenditures				Hour Expenditures			
Education of Wife	All Wives	Working Wives with No Children under 12	Working Wives with Children under 12	Paid for Child Care	In Return for Child Care	Wives' Child Care	Husbands' Child Care	Wives' House-work
6 - 8 Grades	33	17	34	215	14	657	441	1,377
9 - 11 Grades	14	13	34	262	14	797	625	1,397
12 - High School	18	17	5	418	15	620	438	1,472
12 plus Non-academic	77	44	35	365	12	787	453	1,325
Some College	97	146	14	434	15	1,038	410	1,359
College Graduate	172	134	31	463	24	1,203	410	1,255
Advanced or Professional Degree	225	173	257	487	0	758	500	1,357
Eta Squared	.03	.04	.08	.03	.02	.05	.02	.01

Table 12.4

REPORTS ON CHILD CARE PROVISION WHILE WORKING, BY WIVES WITH CHILDREN UNDER 12 IN FAMILY NOW AND WORKING FOR MONEY AS WELL

	Percentage Who Pay Money for Child Care	Percentage Getting Free Child Care	Percentage Reporting Care Problems Once a Month or More	Percentage Reporting No Child Care Problems	Percentage of Wives Who Stayed Home to Care for Child	Number of Observations‡
Age of Wife						
18-24	68	20	3	61	22	163
25-34	53	35	4	57	21	391
35-44	13	69	1	57	24	170
45-54	17	54	9	68	7	53
55 or Older+						
Education						
Less than 6 Grades+						
6-8 Grades	21	48	11	61	10	46
9-11 Grades	32	55	5	59	21	162
High School	42	42	3	59	27	261
High School plus nonacademic	42	47	0	63	14	131
Some College	41	46	5	48	20	97
College Degree	50	27	2	61	15	58
Advanced Degree+						
Number of Persons in Family						
Fewer than 3+						
3	59	29	2	50	27	255
4	43	41	4	63	18	244
5	26	55	4	65	17	133
6	20	63	6	46	25	67
7	9	80	6	63	16	45
8 or more	36	62	12	61	22	43
Race						
Nonblack	40	45	4	58	21	501
Black	45	41	6	58	25	287
All	40	45	4	58	21	788

+ Categories with fewer than 50 cases are omitted.

‡Not the same as proportion of wives (complex sample).

MTR #1186

We also inquired about problems with child care:

> "In the past year how many times did someone have to stay home from work to take care of the children because these arrangements broke down?"
>
> "Who was that? Was it you, your husband, or someone else?"

Only a small minority, one in 20, reported breakdowns as often as once a month, and the majority said it never happened. When it did, usually the wife stayed home. There were no significant differences according to age, education, family size, or race, with the possible exception of a tendency for older, less educated mothers to be less likely to stay home with the children in emergencies.

Child Care Possibilities Perceived by Nonworking Mothers

A sequence of questions was also asked of mothers with children under 12 at home who were not working for money. They were asked about possible child care if they went to work, and about other possible problems. Table 12.5 gives an overview of their replies according to their ages, education, number in the family, and race. A substantial minority said they could not arrange for child care at all, 24 percent, and another 8 percent thought it would cost $2 an hour or more. Overall, the expected cost per hour was:

	PERCENT
Nothing	19.6
Less than $1	34.7
1.00-1.99	18.2
2.00 or more	8.3
Don't Know	19.2

The better educated wives thought in terms of organized day-care or paid baby sitters and higher per-hour cost, while the less educated thought in terms of relatives, friends, or self-care by the children.

Those with larger families were more likely to report that child care could not be arranged at all or that it would be done by relatives, friends, or self-care. Blacks more often reported that care simply could not be arranged.

Mothers were also asked:

> "Do you think that your going to work would cause any problems for your family?"
>
> "What kinds of problems? Why is that?"

Women with large families, blacks, and older mothers were less likely to expect problems than better educated mothers if they took a job for money. The kinds of problems varied from technical details to objections from white husbands (black husbands were not seen as objecting) or concern for the needs of the children. The only major

Table 12.5

REPORTS ON POSSIBLE CHILD CARE IF THEY WORKED FOR MONEY, BY WIVES WITH CHILDREN UNDER 12 NOT CURRENTLY WORKING FOR MONEY

	Percentage who Could Not Arrange Child Care	Percentage Who Would Expect to Use			Percentage Who Would Expect Cost to be $2/Hour or More	Percentage Who Would Expect That Going to Work Would Cause Problems	Percentage Whose Problems Focus On			Number of Observations§
		Organized Care+	Individual Care‡	Relative or Self-Care			Children	Husband	No Care Available	
Age										
18-24	21	20	24	34	3	40	13	7	7	314
25-34	21	25	33	18	7	53	15	13	6	406
35-44	26	14	25	30	10	43	12	10	6	191
45-54	38	4	17	35	0	33	15	4	7	68
Education										
Less than 6 Grades⁑										
6-8 Grades	29	6	3	59	0	27	4	9	6	81
9-11 Grades	23	15	24	34	3	40	10	15	5	268
12-High School	26	18	24	30	7	47	15	10	8	343
High School plus Nonacademic	24	26	37	13	3	52	16	13	9	116
Some College	29	21	36	10	13	37	10	2	8	94
College Degree	9	32	45	10	12	68	24	11	0	52
Advanced Degree⁑										
Number of Persons in Family										
Fewer than 3⁑										
3	12	26	31	29	5	49	13	11	5	290
4	25	25	29	19	6	49	15	10	6	295
5	24	12	33	29	7	45	11	12	6	190
6	35	12	27	21	9	43	20	12	7	97
7	38	0	9	53	5	35	12	5	14	50
8 or More	40	21	10	28	5	34	11	3	4	75
Race										
Nonblack	23	20	29	25	6	49	15	11	6	683
Black	36	17	17	27	6	17	6	2	6	314
All	24	20	28	25	6	46	14	11	6	997

+Such as day-care centers or nursery schools.

‡Baby sitter or friend.

⁑Categories with fewer than 50 cases are omitted.

§Not the same as proportion of wives--complex sample.

MTR #1186

pattern seemed to be more mention of no care available for those with very large families.

More Children Vs. Working Wives: Husbands' Attitudes and Wives' Plans

We find no evidence that expected future children compete with present jobs. In fact, 53.6 percent of wives under 50 who expect more children are working, compared to 52 percent of wives under 50 who do not expect more children.

On the other hand, wives' reports of their husbands' attitudes appear to support the notion that some women do not work because their husbands oppose it.

Husbands' Feelings about Wife Working as reported by Wives	Percentage of Husbands of Wives under 50	Percentage of Their Wives Who Are Working
Very much in favor	32	74.3
Somewhat in favor	25	60.8
Neither for nor against	17	44.3
Somewhat against	13	31.9
Very much against	13	14.7
	100	

MTR #1179

Perceptions of others' feelings can, of course, be distorted to fit the facts, but it seems likely that some reality is reflected here.

Even greater agreement on current goals appears with husbands' desires about more children:

Wife Says Husband Wants More Children	Percentage of Wives Reporting	Percentage of Wives Who Expect More Children
Very much	30	82.1
Somewhat	12	60.1
Neither for nor against	11	13.6
Somewhat against	13	10.8
Very much against	34	1.6
	100	

MTR #1179

Did the husbands who wanted more children oppose their wives working? No. Only a tenth of the husbands fit that stereotype.

If we ignore the strength of approval or disapproval, we find a fourth of the husbands approving both more children and their wives having a job, while some 13 percent disapproved of both. Ten percent wanted more children and did not want their wives to work, while a whopping 26 percent did not want more children and wanted their wives to work. A fourth of the husbands were ambivalent on one or both issues; only 3 percent were noncommittal on both.

In the previous waves of the panel study we asked the husband the questions about the number of children had and desired, whereas most fertility studies have interviewed the wives. Since marriages break up, and there is always some ambiguity about the treatment of children of prior marriages (or liaisons), it is interesting to compare the number of children the husband reported with the number the wife reported in the ninth wave. Heads were asked (and the sequence repeated for new heads each year):

> Do you have any children who do not live with you? How many? When were they born? Did you have any children who are not now living? When were they born?

To this we add the number of children currently living with the family. In the ninth wave, spouses were asked:

> Have you ever raised any children, or are you raising any now? How many (was/is) that in all? When were they born? (Were/are) any of them children who were not born to you?

If we eliminate the few cases (8.8 percent) where wives report children not born to themselves, we can see whether husband and wife report the same number of children—remembering the various valid reasons for different numbers. In 51.1 percent of the cases they report the same number; 16.3 percent of these reported zero for both. The major discrepancies come from women who report having raised children (born to them) but whose husbands reported no children, or where the wife reports more children than the husband (again even after eliminating cases where some of them were not born to her). Presumably many of these were children from prior marriages of the wife.

For 3,542 married couples in the sample in the ninth wave, we can compare the husband's report on his wife's years of school with the wife's report. The rank correlation (Tau-B was .82, far higher than the .54 for number of children (with its definitional difficulties). The two agreed to the year in 72.6 percent of the cases. In 8 percent of the cases the husband reported that his wife had more education than she said she did, and the wife reported more for herself in 11.2 percent of the cases, including a few zeroes which may reflect difficulties with definitions or concepts or editing. Clearly, using the husband's report on the wife's education is unlikely to do much damage. In fact, in 40 percent of the cases, they both reported 12 grades (high school for the wife) although the husband reported 12 grades 47 percent of the time, and the wife 44 percent. The differences were rather well balanced in both directions, apparently one or the other spouse being more precise in reporting 11 or 13 grades rather than just saying high school.

In order to compare the expectations and desires of husbands and wives, we have to go back to the fourth and fifth waves of the survey, during which heads were asked what they thought was the ideal family size (1971) and what they expected their completed family size to be (1972). These comparisons require restricting the analysis to families with the same head and wife since the 1971 interview. There are 2,245 such families.

If we start with the husband's expected completed family size in 1972, and subtract the number he already had in 1971 and the number younger than six in 1976, we should have an indication of whether the husband was still expecting more children in 1976, assuming that he had not changed his mind. We can compare this with the wife's answer to the 1976 question:

Do you expect to have any more children?

Number of Added Children Head Presumably Still Expects	Number of Cases	Percentage of Wives Expecting More	Percentage of Wives Saying Husband Wanted More Children
None	1,360(est)	5	16
One	123	43	56
Two	66	77	78
Three or More	33	60	76

Number of Added Children Head Presumably Still Expects to Reach Ideal	Percentage of Wives Expecting More	Percentage of Wives Saying Husband Wanted More Children
None	5	12
One	15	27
Two	28	34
Three or More	16	33

MTR #1179

There is a problem, however, with the question asked of wives. We asked those wives who said that they wanted more children:

How many children do you expect to have altogether?

Some people thought that we were asking how many more children they expected. Consequently some gave a number smaller than the number of children they already had.

How Husbands and Wives See Their Jobs When Both Work

In the 1976 wave of interviewing the 2,934 couples who were both in the labor force (or only temporarily out of work) were asked parallel questions about their jobs. By examining the joint distributions of their replies, we can go beyond comparing two distributions and ask whether the jobs and attachments to the labor market of husbands and wives are more or less alike than pure chance would allow. For example 24 percent of the husbands reported that they wanted more work than they had last year, and 15.5 percent of the wives said they wanted more work. If there were no tendency for their replies to be related, then one would expect .24X.155, or .037 (3.7 percent) of the couples to have both spouses wanting more work. In fact both say they wanted more work in 5.7 percent of the cases, so there is some positive association—a tendency for both to say the same things. When the replies are more detailed, we use a statistical measure of association, usually a rank correlation coefficient, Kendall's Tau-b. In the case of wanting more work, Tau-b is .07, positive but small.

Job Attachment

We shall look first at attachment to the job, and perceived job opportunities.[2] Both were asked:

> If you were to get enough money to live as comfortably as you would like for the rest of your life, would you continue to work?

Seventy-one percent of the husbands said yes, they would continue work; 57 percent of the wives said yes; and for 43 percent of the couples both said yes, which is about what one would expect if the two responses were independent (.71 x .57 = .404). Of course there were twice as many cases in which the husband said he would continue and the wife said she would quit, as there were the reverse (26 versus 13). Figure 12.1 shows parallel age patterns—declining but with a reversal for those still working after age 65.

Working couples are presumably subject to double constraints against moving, and some feel that these impinge more seriously on wives. We asked:

> Are there better jobs you could get if you were willing to move and live somewhere else?

Forty-one percent of the husbands and 43 percent of the wives said yes, a startlingly small difference. In 19 percent of the couples, both said yes. Both responses are about what two independent (unrelated) responses would produce.

Even without moving, wives might restrict where or what hours they worked more than their husbands. We asked:

---

[2]This question was asked only if the respondents reported that there was not more work available on his/her job. Actually husbands were more likely to report refusing available work because the work was too hard; wives were somewhat more likely to give family-related reasons.

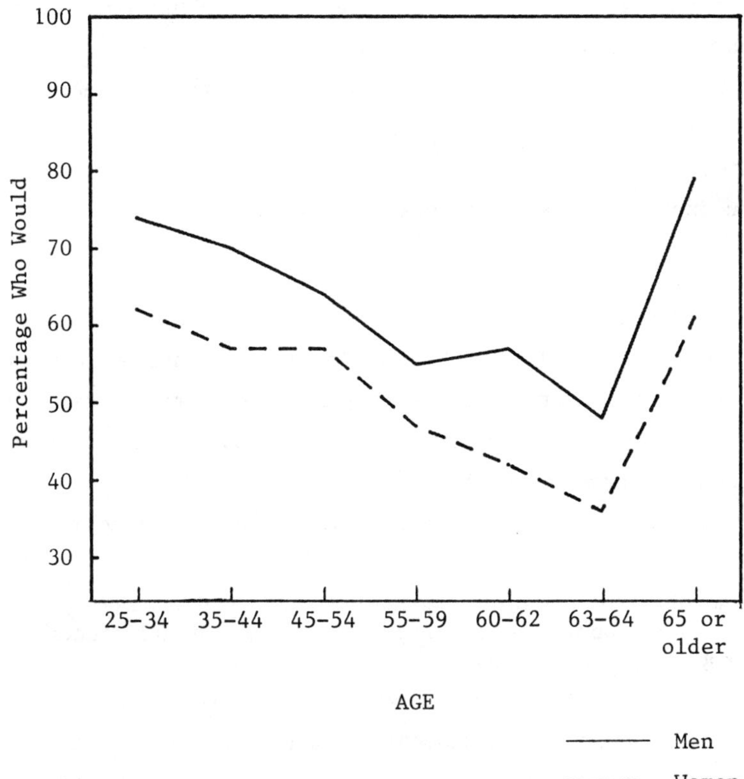

Figure 12.1. PERCENTAGE WHO WOULD CONTINUE TO WORK IF THEY GOT ENOUGH MONEY TO LIVE AS COMFORTABLY AS THEY WOULD LIKE FOR REST OF LIFE

(For Married Couples, but Working)

> Are there better jobs around here that you might get if you were willing to go farther to work or work different hours?

Twenty-two percent of the husbands said there were, but 38 percent of the wives said so! There is truth to some stereotypes. These differences in both "better job" situations may even be greater than reported if women are more likely not even to get or remember information about alternative opportunities, feeling unable to move anyway. Figure 12.2 shows that the awareness of alternative opportunities declines with age; perhaps reflecting reality.

To the questions:

> Do you think you will keep on working for the next few years, or do you plan to quit?

and

> Why might you stop working?

only 3 percent of working husbands and 13 percent of the wives answered that they might stop. More than half of the husbands in this group planned to retire, and more than half of the wives expected to stop working for family reasons. Apparently wives are only a little less attached to the labor force than husbands.

Almost identical answers were given by husbands and wives to the job security question:

> If you should lose your present job, what would you say were your chances of finding another job just as good as your present job in all respects? Would they be very good, good, not so good, or not good at all?

Sixty percent of the husbands and 63 percent of the wives said "Good" or "Very good." If the two replies had been independent (uncorrelated), 38 percent of the couples would have had both spouses confident about their employability. (.60 x .63 = .38) In fact it was 41 percent, indicating a small positive correlation—the Tau-b rank correlation coefficient was .13. This confidence also declined with age, although with reversals for women at ages 63-65 and still working, and for men 65-71 and still working (Figure 12.3).

When we come to more numerical measures such as annual hours of unemployment or illness, the whole distribution is important. Overall we can say that a tenth of the husbands and a tenth of the wives reported more than five weeks of unemployment (more than 220 hours). There was a mild positive correlation in the tendency for unemployment to hit two in the same family (Tau-b = .12).

Similarly with hours missed from work because of illness of the person or some other family member, 12 percent of the husbands and 14 percent of the wives reported losing more than 5 weeks. Again the correlation, Tau-b, was .12. The resulting final work hours differed, however, because more wives work part time:

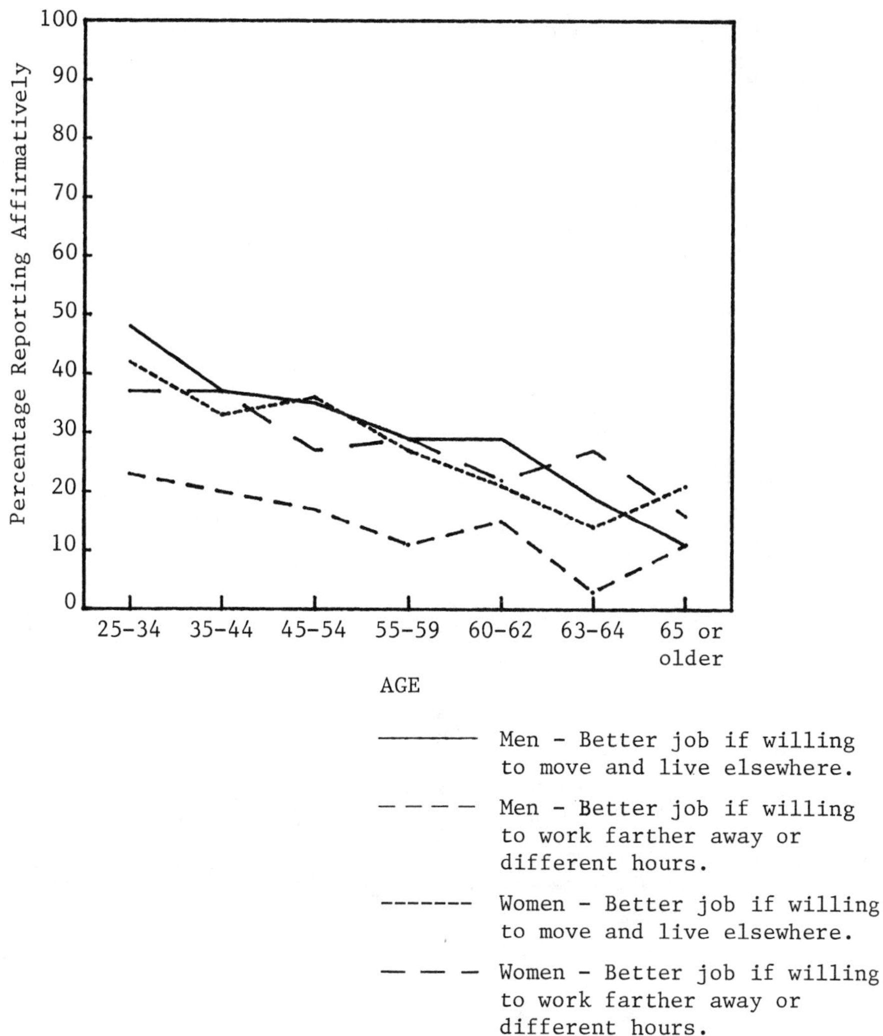

Figure 12.2. DISTRIBUTION OF RESPONDENTS WHO BELIEVED THERE WERE BETTER JOBS AVAILABLE IF HE/SHE WERE WILLING TO MOVE AND LIVE ELSEWHERE, OR BETTER JOBS "AROUND HERE" IF WILLING TO GO FARTHER TO WORK OR WORK DIFFERENT HOURS.

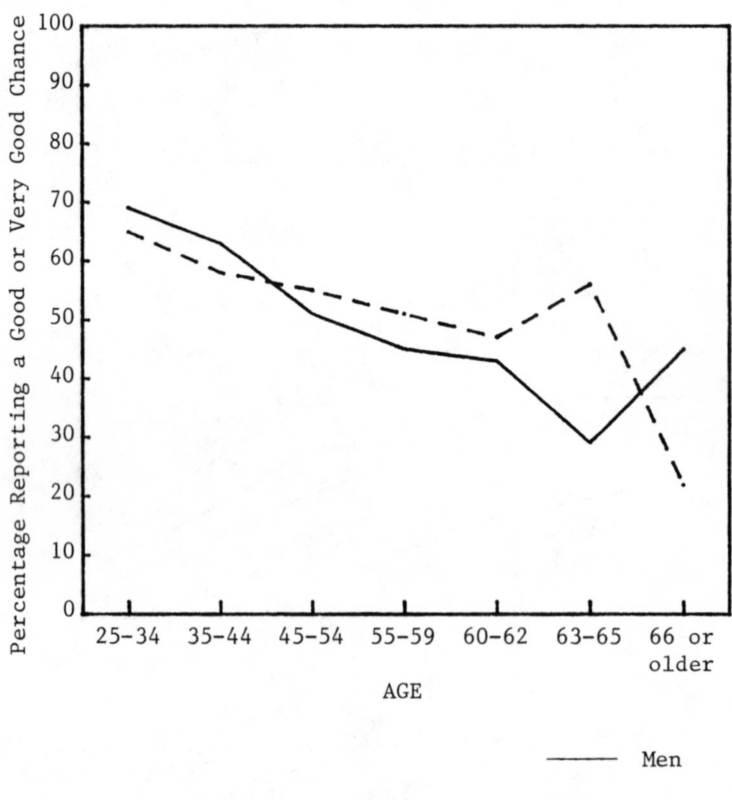

Figure 12.3. DISTRIBUTION OF THOSE BELIEVING THERE IS A VERY GOOD OR GOOD CHANCE OF FINDING ANOTHER JOB AS GOOD AS PRESENT ONE.

Annual Hours of Work for Money in 1975	Percentage of Husbands	Wives
1-219	1	8
220-379	0	4
380-979	3	17
980-1579	9	24
1580 or More	87	48
	100	101

MTR #1183

If we regard 1,580 or more hours a year as practically full time, then in 44 percent of the working couples both spouses were working full time. (Tau-b = .11)

Commuting

Husbands tended to spend more time commuting than did their working wives, 64 percent reporting 100 hours a year or more, as against 45 percent of the wives. But there was a visible tendency for both or neither to have long commuting—both spent 100 hours a year or more in 33 percent of the cases (Tau-b = .14).

Annual Hours Commuting	Percentage of Husbands	Wives
None (work at home)	8	9
1-19	2	8
20-59	13	20
60-99	13	18
100-139	17	16
140-219	23	15
220-379	19	11
380 or more	5	3
	100	100

MTR #1183

A curious difference appears in the reports of husbands and wives on how they get to work:

Mode of Commuting	Percentage of Husbands	Percentage of Wives
Public Transportation	5	6
Car Pool	6	7
Drives by Self	72	64
Walks	2	4
Drives with Spouse	5	11
Other	2	1
Not Reported or Inappropriate (not currently employed)	8	7
	100	100

MTR #1183

In a majority of the cases where the wife said she drove with her husband, the husband said he drove himself to work, despite the question wording:

> Do you use public transportation to get to work, have a car pool, drive by yourself, walk, drive with your wife, or what?

It is likely that as soon as the phrase "drive by yourself" appeared, the male respondent stopped listening, if he did the driving, whereas the wife kept listening until she heard the phrase, "ride with your husband." In addition, some wives may only go to work a few days a week. However, the amount of husband-wife pooling is clearly closer to 11 percent than to 5 percent.

The rank correlation between husband and wife's miles to work was .18.

Miles to Work	Percentage of Husbands	Percentage of Wives
Less than 1	8	6
1	11	15
2	5	6
3-4	12	15
5-9	21	24
10-14	16	15
15-19	11	7
20-29	9	5
30	5	3
Not Obtained	1	3
	99	99

MTR #1183

The low correlation between husband and wife's commuting miles and the relatively little driving together implies that, for the most part, they work in widely different places.

Rewards from Work and Types of Work

How good are the jobs? Starting with the most obvious and working down to details, we look first at hourly earnings:

Hourly Earnings	Percentage of Husbands	Percentage of Wives
Less than $2	5	17
$2-$2.49	3	9
$2.50-$2.99	6	13
$3-$3.99	14	21
$4-$5.99	28	24
$6 or More	44	15
	100	100

Tau-b = .21

MTR #1183

Of course part of the difference is not a result of discrimination but of differences in work experience as seen below in answers to the work history questions:

Years of Work for Money Since 18	Percentage of Husbands	Percentage of Wives
Less than 5	7	24
5-9	20	30
10-14	15	19
15-19	11	11
20-24	11	7
25-29	12	4
30 or More	23	5
	99	100

Tau-b = .54

MTR #1183

Nineteen percent of the husbands and 23 percent of the wives reported working for federal, state, or local governments—a substantial number. In 7 percent of the couples both husband and wife worked for government, a small positive correlation (Tau B = .15).

Twelve percent of the husbands and 6 percent of the wives were self-employed. In 2 percent of the families both spouses were self-employed.

Twenty percent of the husbands but only 9 percent of wives and 2 percent of couples (hardly greater than chance Tau B = .07) had some say over the pay or promotion of others working under them. This particular characteristic of a job is associated with higher pay, other things being equal.

Looking the other way in the work hierarchy, we asked whether the respondent's boss had a boss over him, indicating that the respondent was at least two levels down from supreme authority. Seven-and-a-half percent of the husbands and 70.2 percent of the wives said their boss had a boss, and both said so 53 percent of the time, practically uncorrelated incidence.

Husbands and wives did not differ much on "How much formal education is required to get a job like yours?" but their answers were positively correlated (.21) presumably because their actual education tended to be correlated, and to affect their jobs.

Education Required by Job	Percentage of Husbands	Percentage of Wives
0-5	17	20
6-8	5	3
9-11	2	2
12-High School	40	41
College	7	7
Degree	15	15
Advanced Degree	5	3
NA	9	12
	100	100

Both also were asked:

Do you also have to get some work experience or special training to get a job like yours?

What kind of experience or special training is that?

Experience or Training	Percentage of Husbands	Percentage of Wives
Apprenticeship	4	0
Courses, Training Program	9	13
On the Job Training, Training on Previous Job (not a program)	8	6
Training plus Experience (no mention of any of the above)	3	2
Training, Not Clear How Acquired	7	3
Explicit Skill, No Mention How Acquired	7	11
Experience or Background, No Mention of Specific Skills	27	22
None or NA	35	42
	100	99

This question was followed by:

On a job like yours, how long would it take the average new person to become fully trained and qualified?

Months	Years	Percentage of Husbands	Percentage of Wives
Less than 1	0	1	2
1-5	1	25	52
6-17	1	25	27
18-29	2	12	6
30-41	3	7	3
42-53	4	8	3
54-65	5	9	2
66 and Over	6 or More	5	1
Always Learning More		4	1
NA		4	4
		100	100

Tau-b = .14

Husbands mentioned a wider variety of types of training for their job, but fewer formal courses or training programs. The huge difference was in the amount of on-the-job learning on the present job that was seen as required. More than half the wives said it took less than half a year to get up to standard, but half the husbands said it took them more than a year and a half. Not only were the present jobs better in the sense of taking longer to learn, but for husbands they were also more likely to be seen as leading to a still better job as shown in the answers to:

> Do you feel you are learning things in your job that could lead to a better job or to a promotion?

Seventy-one percent of husbands said yes compared to 65 percent of wives (Tau-b = .12).

Sixty-six percent of husbands and 50 percent of wives answered yes to:

> Do you have some skills or job experience that you cannot use in your present job?

In addition, 26 percent and 27 percent, respectively, thought that they might want to get a job some day which used those skills or experience (Tau-b = .03).

Comparisons of the reports on how long it takes to learn the job, and whether it teaches skills that could lead to a better job, are interesting since they show different age patterns. Men have two diametrically opposite age patterns: the young report more often that they are learning things that could lead to a better job, while the older men report more often than the younger that their present job required five or more years to become qualified. The same age patterns appeared for women, but at a far lower level. Figure 12.4 shows the vast difference, and the rarity of women reporting jobs that require much training, or that provide access to better jobs.

Finally, as an examination of multiple coverage, and difference in fringe benefits, we asked:

> How many employee retirement or pension plans are you covered by, including Social Security?

Number of Retirement Plans	Percentage of Husbands	Percentage of Wives
One	37	51
Two	53	36
Three	6	2
Four	1	0
None	3	2
NA	1	9
	101	100

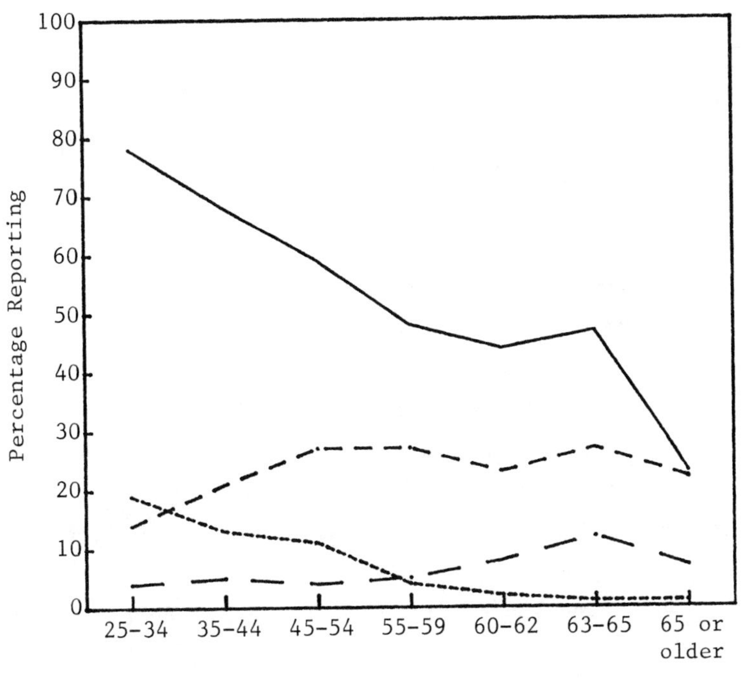

——— Men - Learning things in job that could lead to better job or to a promotion.

— — — — Men - Job requires five or more years of learning.

------- Women - Learning things in job that could lead to better job or to a promotion.

— — — Women - Job requires five or more years of learning.

Figure 12.4. PROPORTIONS REPORTING THAT IT TOOK FIVE OR MORE YEARS TO BECOME FULLY TRAINED AND QUALIFIED ON THE JOB, AND REPORTING THEY WERE LEARNING THINGS ON THE JOB THAT COULD LEAD TO A BETTER JOB OR PROMOTION.

More important than the fact that husbands are more likely to have a second pension, is the fact that families with two earners are likely to have three or more pensions. In fact, for these working couples, the number of pension plans involved is:

Number of Pension Plans	Percentage of Families
One	4
Two[3]	27
Three	35
Four or More	31

As background for interpreting all these similarities and differences, it is useful to know that husbands and wives tend to have similar amounts of education, rank correlation = .52, and similar ages, rank correlation = .85. Since we often use the husband's report on the wife's education, it is important to note that the rank correlation between these two reports on the same fact is very high: .87.

Since husbands and wives tend to be of similar age, education, and race, it is not surprising that their jobs are similar. Indeed, there is a surprising lack of correlation in what they report about their jobs. It is not common for both to work for the government, belong to a union, face unemployment, or want more work at the same time. Most of the differences are as expected: less work experience and lower wages for wives, somewhat less attachment to work, and some restrictions on location and hours of work, indicated by knowledge of better jobs available.

Husband's versus Wife's Report on Wife's Earnings

Since in the study the respondents for married couples have generally been the husbands, analyses of the wives' earnings have been based on the husbands' reports of wives' earned income and work hours, as well as education and years of work experience since 18. Even in 1976 when the wives also were interviewed, the husbands were asked about wives' earnings and hours, but the wives were also asked about their education, work experience, wage rate (not total earnings), and hours of work. The wage rate questions were:

[3]Remember if a husband wife are both covered by Social Security, the wife cannot collect benefits both on her own and as a dependent. She is encouraged to take whichever is larger.

Are you salaried, paid by the hour, or what?

Salaried: How much is your salary? \$______ per ______

Paid by Hour: What is your hourly rate for your regular work time?

\$______

Other: If you worked an extra hour, about how much would you earn that hour? \$______

(The first two groups were also asked about overtime pay rates, but we ignore that here.)

If we take units with the same head and spouse for the 1975 and 1976 interviews, we can compare the results of using the husbands' 1975 reports on their wives' education and experience, and their 1976 reports on wives' earnings, with the 1976 reports by the wives on all three.

The rank correlations on the background facts were .85 for the two reports on education and .75 for the two reports on years of experience.[4]

For the wives' hourly earning figure we have an average earning of \$4.39 by husbands' report, with a standard deviation of \$3.02, and an average earning of \$4.07 by wives' report, with a standard deviation of \$1.75. The distributions are quite similar despite the different standard deviation which probably reflects the truncation of wife-reported earnings at \$10.00.

Hourly Earnings	Percentage of Husbands Reporting	Percentage of Wives Reporting
Less than \$1.00	3	0
\$1.00-1.49	3	1
\$1.50-1.99	7	2
\$2.00-2.49	10	13
\$2.50-2.99	12	14
\$3.00-3.99	21	27
\$4.00-5.99	26	29
\$6.00 or More	17	15
	99	101

[4]These differ from the correlations reported earlier because here we consider only working wives with the same husband since 1975.

The discrepancies were balanced:

Wife versus Husband	Percentage
Wife Two or More Brackets Higher	9
Wife One Bracket Higher	17
Same Bracket	51
Wife One Bracket Lower	17
Wife Two or More Brackets Lower	7
	101

Since so much analysis hinges on the relationship of education and work experience with earnings, comparable regressions seemed in order. To make the comparison fair we truncated both hourly earnings figures at $10 per hour since the wives' reports were already so truncated. Although this affects few cases, they can have a substantial effect on regression results. We used MCA (dummy variable or categorical regression) since that also provides information on the pattern of effects, without any appreciable loss in the power of the predictors. The gross and net power of education and work experience using the two different sets of estimates, were as follows:

	Husbands' Reports		Wives' Reports	
All Wives	Gross Effect (Eta^2)	Net Effect ($Beta^2$)	Gross Effect (Eta^2)	Net Effect ($Beta^2$)
Education	.191	.186	.182	.191
Work Experience	.040	.030	.061	.062
R^2 (adjusted)		.212		.257
Black Wives Only				
Education	.243	.258	.313	.312
Work Experience	.016	.026	.098	.080
R^2 (adjusted)		.239		.373

Using the wives' reports produces higher correlations of earnings with education and experience, primarily because of the larger estimated effect of work experience. Repeating the analysis for black wives reveals an even greater improvement in the correlation, including a higher association of earnings with education. Our ability to explain male/female differences in earnings on the basis of difference in education and experience would apparently be greater if we used the wife's reports on the facts.

Do the two reports produce different patterns of the effects of education or experience on earnings? Figures 12.5 and 12.6 show the shapes. The regression used log earnings, for statistical reasons, so the numbers are really geometric mean earnings

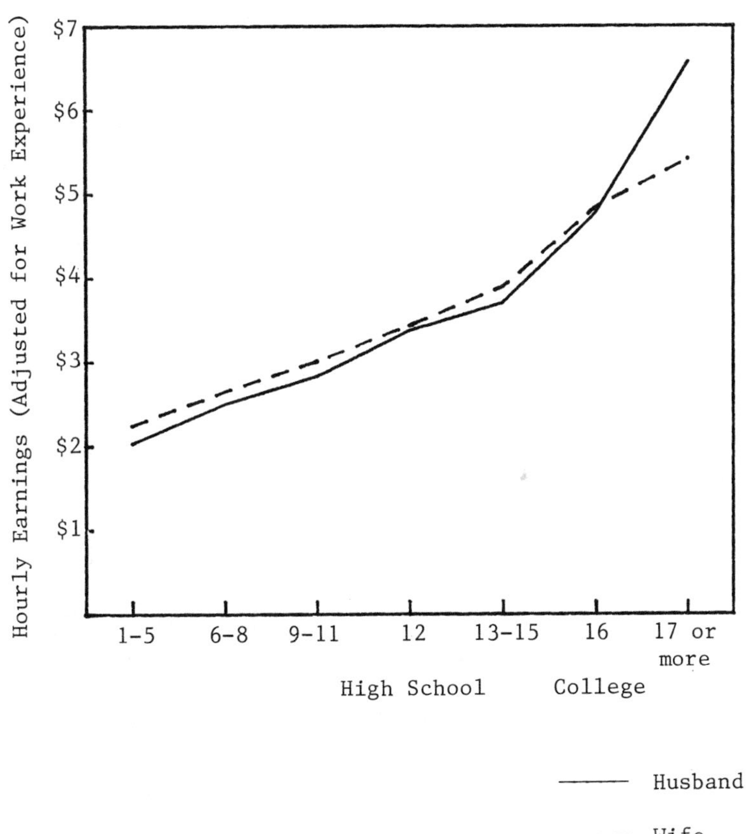

Figure 12.5. WIFE'S HOURLY EARNINGS BY EDUCATION ADJUSTED FOR YEARS OF WORK EXPERIENCE COMPARING HUSBAND'S AND WIFE'S REPORTS

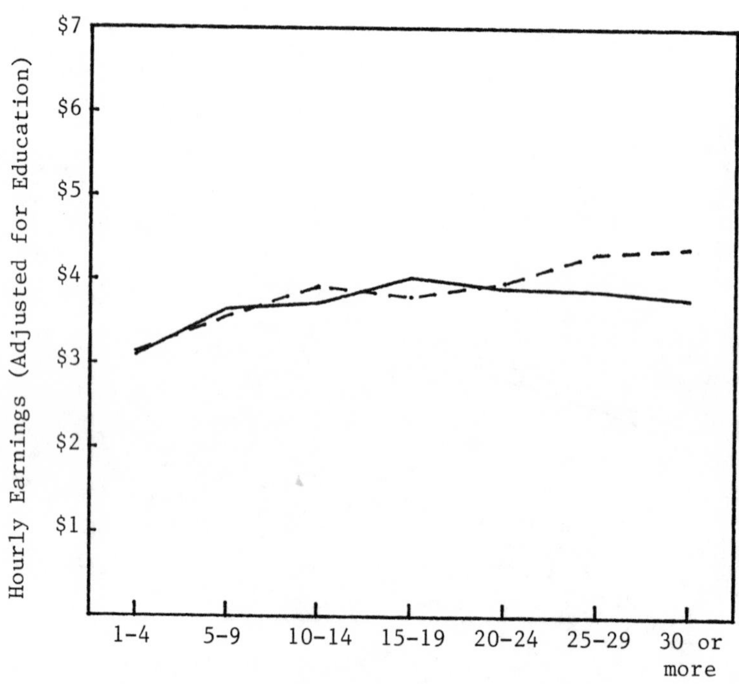

Figure 12.6. WIVES' HOURLY EARNINGS BY YEARS OF WORK EXPERIENCE, ADJUSTED FOR EDUCATION COMPARING HUSBAND'S OR WIFE'S REPORTS.

adjusted for the other predictor. The pattern of effects is quite similar for education, except for the small group of wives with advanced education beyond college. The pattern for years of experience is different indicating that in the numerical regressions the experience-squared term would have been insignificant and the experience term would have had a larger coefficient if we had used the wives' reports.

The truth, as is frequently the case, is that there are differences, but they probably would not affect the main conclusions of the analyses that have been conducted. The direction of the effect is, however, that using the husband's report leaves more of the wife's earnings unexplained by her experience and education and more of the difference in earnings between the sexes seemingly unexplained by education and experience. Thus, some of this unexplained wage gap can be attributed to husbands' inaccurate reporting.

Do Husbands and Wives Have the Same Sense of Personal Efficacy?

Four self-rating questions in the area of personal control or personal efficacy were asked of all heads in 1975 and of wives in 1976. Using only stable pairs in which the wife was interviewed in 1976, we can compare each husband's attitude in 1975 with that of his wife in 1976. As in the other comparisons, the correlation is low. The rank correlations between spouses' responses using the full five categories of response ranged from .22 down to .10 (Table 12.6).

A simpler way to determine the relative independence of the replies is to focus on the most self-confident answer to each question. If 50 percent of the husbands and 50 percent of the wives gave such a response, then .50 x .50 or 25 percent of the time they both would give that response even if their replies were in fact totally uncorrelated. Columns 3 and 4 in Table 12.6 present the actual percentage of couples in which husband and wife both gave the "best" answer, and the percentage expected if there were no relationship between their replies.

The replies were sufficiently uncorrelated so that we cannot use one spouse's replies to such questions to represent those of the other spouse. This does not mean that one spouse's attitudes would not affect the other spouse's behavior, of course.

It is interesting to compare self-esteem not only of husbands and wives, but also of unmarried male and female heads of households. We simplify the picture by combining the four answers into a single index by adding the scores, the sum ranging from 4 to 20, and subtracting from 20 so a high score is high self-esteem rather than the reverse. Since self-esteem rises with both age and education, we give the mean index not only for the four sex-marital-status groups, but also for the same four groups within sixteen age-education categories in Table 12.7.

Table 12.6

HUSBAND'S AND WIFE'S ATTITUDES AND THEIR AGREEMENT
(HUSBANDS IN 1975, WIVES IN 1976)

Attitude Response	Husband	Wife	Both	Both if Uncorrelated	Rank Correlation
Usually Felt Pretty Sure Life Would Work Out+	71.5	62.8	49.1	44.9	.18
Plans Ahead‡	49.2	37.9	22.7	18.6	.17
Usually Get to Carry Out Things the Way Expected⁘	64.8	54.6	40.1	35.4	.22
Nearly Always Finish Things§	81.1	70.7	59.2	57.3	.10

+The question was: Have you usually felt pretty sure your life would work out the way you want it to, or have there been more times when you haven't been very sure about it?

‡The question was: Are you the kind of person who plans his life ahead all the time, or do you live more from day to day?

⁘The question was: When you make plans ahead, do you usually get to carry out things the way you expected, or do things usually come up to make you change your plans?

§The question was: Would you say you nearly always finish things once you start them, or do you sometimes have to give up before they are finished?

NOTE: All questions left open-ended and coded on a five-point Likert scale. Most respondents accepted one phrase or the other without qualification.

Includes the 3,472 cases in which there was a stable couple both years and a wife's interview the second year, 1976

MTR #1191

Table 12.7

"SELF-ESTEEM" BY AGE, EDUCATION, SEX, AND MARITAL STATUS
(SUM OF FOUR QUESTIONS SCALED 1-5)

	Married		Not Married	
College Graduates	Men	Women*	Men	Women
Under 30	13.2	12.3	11.6	12.9
30-39	13.3	12.3	11.8	11.0
50-64	13.5	12.4	10.8	11.0
65 or older	13.8	11.1	14.3	12.1
Some Education beyond High School				
Under 30	11.5	10.3	9.9	8.9
30-49	12.0	10.8	11.1	10.3
50-64	12.1	10.9	10.9	8.9
65 or older	13.0	11.5	11.5	10.5
High School Graduates				
Under 30	10.1	9.4	8.9	7.8
30-49	11.2	10.4	11.1	7.8
50-64	12.1	10.5	6.2	9.2
65 or older	11.0	11.4	10.3	10.2
Less than 12 Years of School				
Under 30	8.5	7.0	6.9	5.7
30-49	10.3	8.3	5.7	6.1
50-64	10.4	8.5	9.5	7.6
65 or older	10.4	9.9	9.6	8.2
All	11.4	10.1	9.8	8.7
Standard Deviation	4.2	4.3	4.7	4.6
Number of Cases	3470	3472	637	1618

(20 - sum of scores) = ego-strength
self-esteem

*In 1976, others in 1975

MTR #1191

A consistent pattern holds for men to express considerably more self-esteem than women—married people more than single ones. In a few cases unmarried women expressed higher self-esteem than unmarried men in the same age-education group, particularly the young college graduates and the mature (aged 50 to 64) high school graduates. While age and education affect these self-ratings, there is not enough difference between men and women in the age and education distribution to distort the overall averages much. Unmarried women tend to be older and/or better educated than unmarried men, and the unweighted difference in their index differs for that reason, being 0.7 instead of the 1.1 in the weighted averages of the table (9.8-8.7).

It is clear from the powerful effects of age and education that failure to take them into account in studying self-esteem as a correlate of factors other than sex and marital status would lead to substantial spurious correlations. It is easy to understand why education is positively associated with self-esteem, but not so clear why it should rise with age. There has been much speculation and theorizing about the negative impact of retirement with its loss of a productive activity and drop in income, as to whether it left people with a sense of loss and dissatisfaction. If any such change in self-esteem does occur among each generation of individuals as they retire, it is being swamped by a large, intergenerational difference between a generally less complaining older generation and more critical succeeding ones.

Summary

Questions about time and money costs of housework and child care were divided between husbands and wives in the ninth wave of interviews, allowing a fuller analysis and probably better data. The time burden on working mothers is evident. Previous findings of the heavy reliance on informal, often unpaid methods of child care are reconfirmed, as is the very low frequency of missed wage work because of breakdowns in child care.

Wives' reports on their husbands' attitudes provide a picture of general agreement with the facts and with the wives' expectations. Husbands reported somewhat more attachment to work and somewhat fewer restrictions on work hours or location, but otherwise reports on commitment to work, job security, and restrictions on work hours or location were quite similar, and all followed similar age patterns.

Younger husbands were much more likely than their wives to feel that their job was likely to lead to a better job, and older husbands were more likely than their wives to report that their jobs required extensive experience on the job. We have already seen in earlier chapters of this volume that such differences in job quality account for substantial fractions of the sex differences in earnings.

Wives' reports on their own earnings, education, and experience correlate well with husbands' reports on the same items, particularly education, but the wives' reports are probably better. At least earnings are better explained on the basis of education and experience, using the wives' reports on all three.

Finally, husbands expressed more confidence in themselves than did wives, and there was very little correlation between paired spouses' responses to the same questions (asked a year apart).

References

Hill, Russell, and Stafford, Frank. "Time Inputs to Children." In Five Thousand American Families—Patterns of Economic Progress, Volume 11. Edited by James N. Morgan. Ann Arbor: Institute for Social Research, 1974.

Chapter 13

TRENDS IN DRIVING AND COMMUTING

James N. Morgan

Introduction

An important cost of earning a living is commuting to work. And an increasingly important part of that cost of commuting, for those who drive, is gasoline. Time costs of commuting in 1974 were reported in Volume V of Five Thousand American Families, "Appendix A" (1977) and gasoline costs in Volume IV (1976).

In the ninth wave of interviews, in 1976, we asked husbands and wives separately about their commuting in hopes of providing improved and updated estimates. These are combined here with an estimate of the higher gasoline prices to reestimate the burden of gasoline costs, as well as trends in mode, miles, and cost.

Working unmarried heads, husbands, and wives were asked how they got to work and how many miles it was, one way. On the basis of their weeks of work and whether they worked full or part-time, we estimated the number of trips and hence the annual miles driven to work and back. Unmarried heads and husbands were also asked how many miles the family drove in all its cars in 1976, an estimate which includes commuting to work. Where husband and wife drove to work together, we took the longer of the two trips to represent mileage driven, assuming the spouse was dropped off on the way. When anyone reported belonging to a car pool we took half the mileage, assuming that our respondent drove half the time.

Analysis

Trends in Mode of Commuting

There have been only small changes, if any, in the last few years in how people get to work. A barely visible increase in reported use of public transportation reached a peak in 1973, while reported use of car pools peaked in 1974, but rose again insignificantly between 1975 and 1976 (Table 13.1).[1] All the reports on mode in Table 13.1 are from

[1]It was not until the 1969 interview that we asked about mode, 1970 when we first mentioned and coded car pooling, 1975 when we first asked about wives' mode (including driving with husband), and 1976 when we first mentioned the possibility of husband driving with spouse. Hence, some trends require interpretation. In fact, the discrepancy

Table 13.1

TRAVEL MODE USED BY HEADS OF HOUSEHOLDS TO GET TO WORK
(As a Percentage of Commuting Heads)

	1970-1972 Average	1973	1974	1975	1976
Public Transportation	6.8	7.8	7.2	6.8	6.3
Car Pool	4.4	5.1	9.1	7.9	8.4
Drives Alone or with Members of Family Unit	80.0	80.4	77.1	77.9	78.3
Walk, Other	8.8	6.7	6.6	7.4	7.0
Total Who Travel to Work	100.0	100.0	100.0	100.0	100.0

Table 13.2

TRAVEL MODE USED BY WIVES TO GET TO WORK
AS REPORTED BY HUSBANDS IN 1975 AND WIVES IN 1976
(As A Percentage of Commuting Wives)

	Spring 1975	Spring 1976
Pulic Transportation	6.7	7.3
Car Pool	7.3	8.6
Drives	68.1	64.0
Rides with Husband	10.2	12.7
Walk, Other	7.7	7.4
Total Who Travel to Work	100.0	100.0

MTR #6070

unmarried heads or husbands about their own commuting. How wives get to work is given in Table 13.2 as reported in early 1975 by their husbands, and in early 1976 by the wives themselves. There is evidence that in 1975 the husbands underreported driving to work with their wives, so at least some of the apparent trend toward riding with husband is a methodological artifact.[2] We hope to correct this in 1978 by changing the question. (In 1977 commuting questions were not asked.)

What we have overall, then, is a persistent predominance by nearly eight in ten workers of commuting by private car. An eighth of those share with a spouse. As for the rest, about 8 percent belong to car pools outside the family, and the remainder are divided evenly between public transportation and walking or "other" (bicycle, work at home).

Total Miles of Commuting and Driving

Table 13.3 shows no important change in total commuting miles. There was perhaps a slight decline in the lowest three income deciles and some increase in the middle (fifth and sixth) deciles. The lowest income deciles of course contain many who do not commute at all because they are not working. On the other hand, there was apparently a small (6 percent) increase in total miles reported driven, spread throughout the income range. Table 13.4 shows annual car mileages for all families, and separately for car owners, since ownership varies with income level.

Commuting Mode and Commuting Miles by Income (Decile) Level

Any assessment of the distributional impact of policies affecting public transportation, costs of driving to work, or incentives to car-pooling, requires knowing the number in each income decile who would be affected. Table 13.5 shows that while all modes are used more frequently at upper income levels—because more people at those levels are working and commuting—the importance of the car rises dramatically with income.

But it is not just the mode but the mileage in that mode that is crucial. Table 13.6 summarizes the car mileage and commuting mileage by income decile, giving the commuting mileages separately for car and public transportation. For estimating the overall impact on each income level of changing costs of gas or of public transportation, the average mileage is used including zeroes for those who do not work or do not use that

---

mentioned in Chapter 12 between husbands' and wives' reports on driving with spouse would indicate that some husbands were saying they drove alone when they were actually driving with their wives.

[2]See Chapter 12 for comparisons of husbands' reports of their commuting mode with their wives' reports how they got to work. If one drove with spouse the other should also, but some husbands apparently reported driving to work without adding that they took their wives along.

Table 13.3

MEAN ANNUAL COMMUTING MILES OF FAMILY
IN 1974 AND 1975 BY INCOME DECILE
(All Families)

Family Income Decile	Cases, Unweighted N+		Mean Commuting Miles of Household‡	
	1974	1975	1974	1975
Lowest	738	733	376	333
Second	726	698	723	600
Third	661	703	1,761	1,618
Fourth	631	680	2,272	2,274
Fifth	604	555	2,563	2,888
Sixth	564	549	3,782	4,064
Seventh	521	495	4,591	4,288
Eighth	465	465	5,317	5,220
Ninth	428	419	6,042	6,036
Highest	387	379	5,566	5,547
Overall	5,725	5,670	3,300	3,274

+Excluding cases where commuting miles were not given, but including zeroes.

‡Where spouses drive together, only the longer trip of the two is counted. When either spouse pools with someone else, the mileage is cut in half--assuming respondent drives half the time.

MTR #6071, 1189

Table 13.4

MEAN TOTAL MILES DRIVEN IN 1974 AND 1975 BY INCOME DECILE

Family Income Decile, 1974	Upper Decile Limit		All Families				Car Owners			
			Unweighted N		Mean Annual Miles Driven		Unweighted N		Mean Annual Miles Driven	
	1974	1975	1974	1975	1974	1975	1974	1975	1974	1975
Lowest	$ 3,346	$ 3,499	703	720	2,850	3.734	211	220	7,236	8,432
Second	5,474	5,604	693	685	5,236	5,856	348	342	8,549	9,937
Third	7,253	7,682	618	682	8,310	9,615	418	451	11,065	12,404
Fourth	9,210	10,019	601	662	10,767	11,471	470	520	12,389	13,349
Fifth	11,500	12,199	575	563	12,600	12,881	483	495	13,953	13,983
Sixth	13,830	14,729	546	543	15,213	16,601	495	560	15,893	17,247
Seventh	16,496	17,663	505	503	16,911	16,424	467	466	17,355	17,156
Eighth	19,950	21,366	446	462	17,802	19,497	419	439	18,515	20,322
Ninth	25,985	27,314	412	427	20,514	21,360	407	417	20,691	21,633
Highest			374	392	24,549	25,567	369	386	24,821	25,847
OVERALL			5,473	5,639	13,547	14,374	4,087	4,236	16,077	17,029

Note: 252 Cases in 1974 and 223 cases in 1975 were not included because response to total miles question was NA or don't know.

MTR #6071, 1189

Table 13.5

PROPORTIONS OF HUSBANDS (OR SINGLE HEADS) AND OF WIVES WHO COMMUTED TO WORK BY VARIOUS MODES
(As Percentage of All Families)

	Husbands or Single Heads			Wives		
Family Money Income Decile	Public Transportation	Drives Alone	Car Pool or with Wife	Public Transportation	Drives Alone	Car Pool or with Husband
Lowest	2	11	3	0	1	0
Second	5	18	7	0	3	1
Third	5	37	5	0	6	3
Fourth	5	47	6	1	10	3
Fifth	3	54	6	1	15	6
Sixth	3	58	9	3	21	6
Seventh	4	61	8	4	22	7
Eighth	4	70	11	3	31	11
Ninth	5	71	9	4	40	7
Highest	6	73	6	2	38	7
All Income Deciles	4	50	7	2	19	5

MTR #1189

Table 13.6

CAR MILES AND COMMUTING MILES IN 1975, BY FAMILY MONEY/INCOME DECILES

	Total Miles Driven		(3) Commuting Miles (All Modes)	(4)	(5)	(6) Car Commuting	(7)	(8)	(9) Public Transportation	(10)	(11)
Family Money Income Deciles	All	Car Owning Families	Husband or Single Head	Wife	Both	Husband or Single Head+	Wife+	Both	Husband or Single Head ‡	Wife‡	Both
Lowest	3,734	8,432	405	23	420	2,472	1,363	333	1,504	542	31
Second	5,856	9,937	696	59	750	2,231	1,190	600	2,266	624	111
Third	9,615	12,404	1,702	169	1,867	3,499	1,822	1,619	3,235	3,430	166
Fourth	11,471	13,349	2,306	384	2,650	3,756	2,474	2,274	3,756	2,298	205
Fifth	12,881	13,983	2,694	579	3,208	4.009	2,656	2,888	5,190	2,196	186
Sixth	16,601	17,247	3,599	794	4,300	5,035	2,661	4,064	3,391	2,454	162
Seventh	16,424	17,156	3,926	847	4,673	5,234	2,542	4,288	5,101	3,017	226
Eighth	19,497	20,322	4,235	1,539	5,609	4,941	3,515	5,220	5,212	4,334	250
Ninth	21,360	21,653	5,201	1,761	6,701	5,860	3,289	6,036	10,134	6,235	703
Highest	25,568	25,847	5,001	1,505	6,380	5,456	2,978	5,547	10,132	6,604	766
	14,374	17,029	2,976	762	3,652	4,701	2,895	3,274	5,410	4,245	238
Number of Cases ⁑	5,639	4,236	5,743	5,789	5,676	3,083	1,263	5,676	327	129	5,862

+For car commuters only (49.8 percent of the husbands and 23.20 percent of the wives commuted by car).

‡For public transportation users only (3.86 percent of the husbands and 1.64 percent of the wives used public transportation).

⁑Numbers vary because of exclusion of those who did not give mileage and for husband-wife comparisons when they used the same mode because of inclusion only of those using that mode.

MTR #1189

mode. For comparing wives with husbands and single male or female heads, however, the mileage used is the average for those who actually commuted to work. Hence, columns 6 and 7 can be compared, but not added, and so can columns 9 and 10. Columns 3, 4, and 5 on total commuting miles and columns 8 and 11 on car and public transportation miles, are averages for everyone, except those who did not estimate their mileage. With respect to these columns, family mileage is also less than that of husband and wife combined because some of them drive together, and we tabulate vehicle miles.

It is clear that mileages increase with income, both because more people are commuting, and because those who do commute are going farther. The very high averages for a few upper income people using public transportation represent, of course, a very small fraction of the population.

The Burden of Rising Gasoline Prices

A balanced view of the effect of high and rising gasoline prices requires looking both at the average impact by income levels, and at the distribution within income groups. The average impact can be low in an income group because most people in that group do not drive, but some of those who do may drive a lot. At the lowest income deciles many do not work or do not have a car. But some low income commuters drive long distances, and many of them report no available public transportation. By the same token, however, the smaller the group who combine low income with a heavy burden of commuting miles, the easier it would be to provide some relief for them from the burden of rising gasoline prices or taxes.

Our estimates of gasoline costs for 1974 were based on assumptions of an average 55¢ per gallon for gasoline and an average of 13 miles per gallon or 4.2¢ per mile for gasoline. For 1975 we assume 5¢ per mile, based on 65¢ per gallon and the same 13 miles per gallon, or some combination of slight mileage improvement with a slightly larger price increase. The increase in the fraction of the total car stock reflecting subcompact cars with appreciably better mileage was small, and was partly replacing not the pollution-controlled gas guzzlers, but the more efficient pre-1971 models. The resulting estimates of gasoline costs for all driving as a fraction of family income are given in Table 13.7 for each income decile.

Even averaging over all families, there is a somewhat greater burden of gasoline costs at lower income levels. If we classify people not by income decile, but by income/needs deciles, the regressivity is greater, the percentage of income allocated to gasoline expenditures ranges from 7.6 percent for the lowest income/needs decile to 3.25 for the highest decile.

Table 13.7

MEAN GASOLINE EXPENDITURES BY TOTAL FAMILY MONEY INCOME, 1974 AND 1975
(All Families)

Family Money Income Decile	Cases, Unweighted N		Average Fuel Cost as a Percentage of Family Income	
	1974	1975	1974	1975
Lowest	696	720	4.4	6.5
Second	693	685	4.9	6.1
Third	618	682	5.5	7.2
Fourth	601	662	5.5	6.5
Fifth	575	563	5.2	5.8
Sixth	546	543	5.1	6.2
Seventh	505	503	4.7	5.1
Eighth	446	462	4.2	5.1
Ninth	412	427	3.9	4.5
Highest	374	392	3.0	3.5
	5,466	5,639	4.6	5.6

NOTE: 252 cases in 1974 and 223 cases in 1975 were not included because response to total miles question was NA or Don't Know. Seven cases were not included in 1974 because family money income was one dollar or less. In 1975 incomes of less than $100 were increased to $100. Percentages above 50 percent were truncated to 50 percent in both years.

The above figures assume 13 miles per gallon and gas price at 55 cents per gallon in 1974 and 65 cents per gallon in 1975, which means 4.2 cents per mile in 1974 and 5 cents per mile in 1975. Industry sources suggest that the increase was considerably less than the 10 cents we have used, so the year-to-year changes should be considered as a way of showing relative increases in different income groups, not absolute increments.

These are average ratios, not ratios of averages.

MTR #6071

Overall, the estimated fraction of income spent on gasoline rises from 4.6 percent to 5.6 percent, a 22 percent increase between 1974 and 1975. The relative increase in cost appears to be largest in the lowest income deciles. How we look at the burden, and its change, depends on the assumptions we make about the discretionary nature of the expenditure.

The vast bulk of driving is not commuting as Figure 13.1 shows, and it is tempting to assume that noncommuting driving is more discretionary. In the lowest income groups a smaller than average fraction of driving is commuting, but as we have reported earlier, alternative modes of getting to work are less likely to be available to these people than to others. About all we can do here is report separately on total driving and commuting car miles. But for these two kinds of costs it is the distribution that matters—the proportions who are spending different fractions of their income on gasoline for commuting or for driving.

Tables 13.8 and 13.9 show the distributions of estimated gasoline costs as a percentage of income by income deciles. Table 13.8 pertains to all driving, and Table 13.9 pertains only to commuting. Tables 13.10 and 13.11 give the same figures for blacks only. As shown in Table 13.8, a sizable percentage of families in the lowest two deciles are spending more than a fifth of their income on gasoline, 11 percent in the lowest decile and 9 percent in the next decile. Most of this driving is not commuting, however, and a substantial fraction of it might be discretionary. In Table 13.9 we note that only 1 percent of the 10 percent in the lowest decile report spending more than 20 percent of their income on gasoline for commuting, and some of them are only temporarily in that low income position. The results are similar for blacks, with even less "burden" from commuting since fewer of the blacks drive to work.

A tax credit for the gasoline costs of driving to work that exceeded some fraction of earned income would clearly not require a very large "tax expenditure" (loss in tax revenue), but would eliminate the excess burden from a very small number of people while allowing higher gasoline prices to encourage conservation generally. If the credit were based on commuting mileage rather than expenditures, it would not discourage economizing (car pooling, economy cars) even by those eligible for the tax credit.

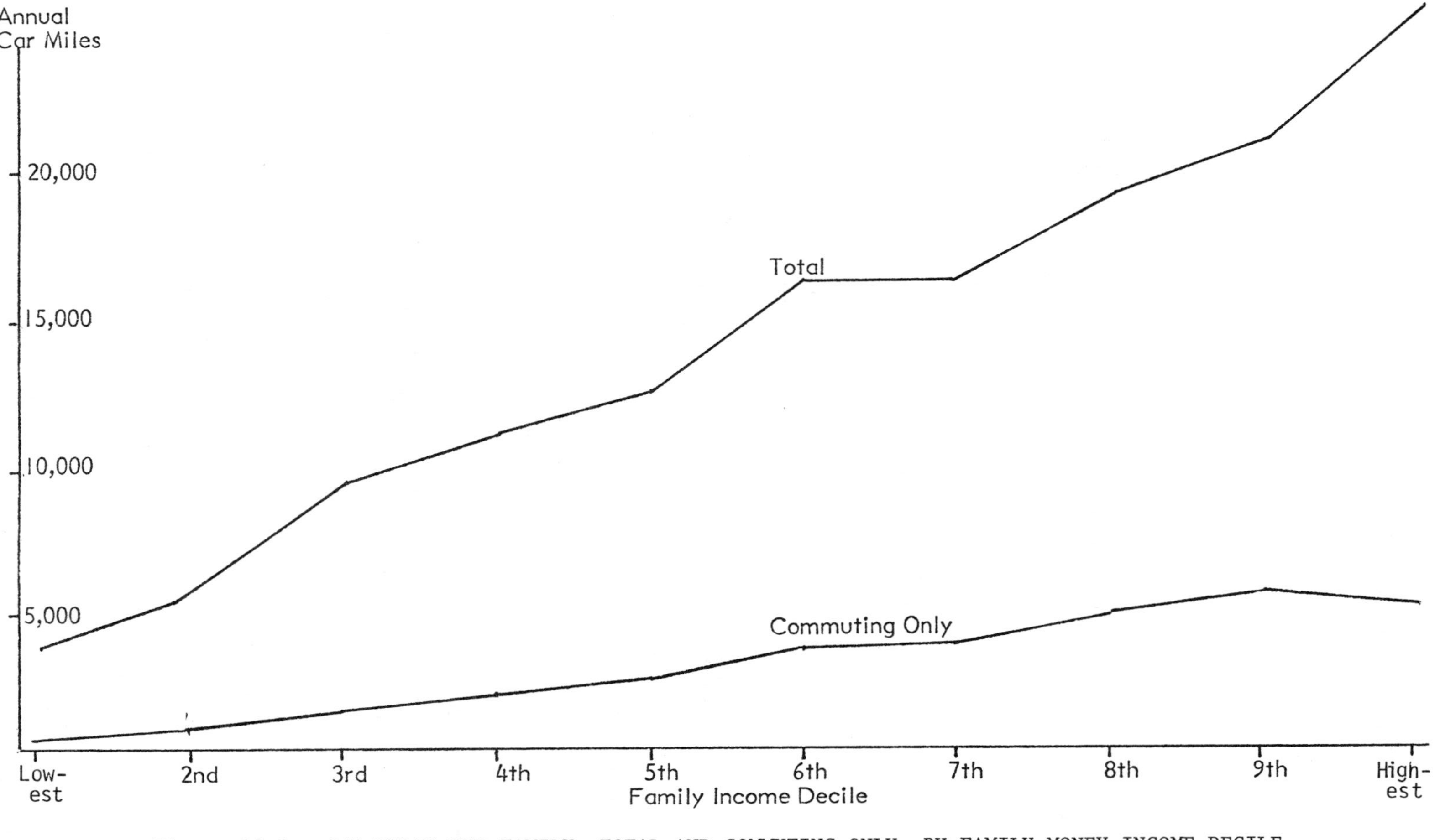

Figure 13.1. CAR MILES PER FAMILY, TOTAL AND COMMUTING ONLY, BY FAMILY MONEY INCOME DECILE

Table 13.8

GASOLINE COSTS FOR ALL DRIVING AS A PERCENTAGE OF INCOME
BY INCOME DECILE

Income Decile	Percentage of Income Spent for Gas							
	0	1-4	5-9	10-14	15-19	20 or More	Not Ascertained	Total
Lowest	55.9	12.3	7.3	6.2	3.0	11.1	4.1	99.9
Second	40.1	19.7	15.2	9.4	2.8	8.6	4.1	99.9
Third	20.9	27.1	23.4	10.2	5.9	7.0	5.6	100.1
Fourth	14.4	28.6	34.6	9.9	5.3	4.1	3.0	99.9
Fifth	7.8	39.1	37.6	9.8	2.4	0.7	2.7	100.1
Sixth	4.4	42.2	35.0	10.5	2.0	2.4	3.5	100.0
Seventh	4.5	53.5	29.5	8.2	2.0	0.3	2.0	100.0
Eighth	3.6	53.7	31.1	4.4	2.9	0.5	3.8	100.0
Ninth	1.3	61.5	29.6	5.1	0.5	0.5	1.6	100.1
Highest	0.9	80.9	14.0	3.0	0.6	0.0	0.7	100.1
All	15.4	41.9	25.7	7.7	2.7	3.5	3.1	100.0

NOTE: Assumes 13 miles per gallon and 65 cents per gallon.

MTR #1189

Table 13.9

GASOLINE COSTS FOR COMMUTING AS A PERCENTAGE OF INCOME
BY INCOME DECILE

Income Decile	Percentage of Income: 0	1-4	5-9	10-14	15-19	20 or More	Not Ascertained	Total
Lowest	85.9	9.3	1.3	0.9	0.3	1.0	1.4	100.1
Second	73.1	22.6	3.1	0.1	0.1	0.0	1.0	100.0
Third	53.9	36.0	6.0	1.3	0.4	0.1	2.4	100.1
Fourth	42.6	50.2	4.9	0.4	0.7	0.0	1.2	100.0
Fifth	33.7	59.0	2.7	0.6	0.3	0.0	3.7	100.0
Sixth	24.4	67.8	5.0	0.3	0.3	0.0	2.2	100.0
Seventh	23.7	68.3	4.2	0.2	0.3	0.0	3.2	99.9
Eighth	14.0	81.0	2.5	0.0	0.0	0.0	2.5	100.0
Ninth	12.4	82.3	2.0	0.1	0.0	0.0	3.1	99.9
Highest	13.7	82.0	0.6	0.0	0.0	0.0	3.7	100.0
All	37.7	55.9	3.2	0.4	0.2	0.1	2.4	99.9

NOTE: Assumes 13 miles per gallon and 65 cents per gallon.

MTR #1189

Table 13.10

GASOLINE COSTS FOR ALL BLACKS DRIVING AS A PERCENTAGE OF INCOME BY INCOME DECILES

Income Decile	Percentage of Income							
	0	1-4	5-9	10-14	15-19	20 or More	Not Ascertained	Total
Lowest	57	15	11	1	2	11	3	100
Second	38	23	14	12	2	6	5	100
Third	23	24	26	11	5	8	2	99
Fourth	13	29	33	9	4	6	6	100
Fifth	4	34	43	12	5	1	2	101
Sixth	5	32	46	13	2	2	0	100
Seventh	1	53	36	7	2	1	1	101
Eighth	1	49	36	4	3	2	5	100
Ninth	1	64	26	6	2	0	1	100
Highest	0	83	15	2	1	0	0	101
All	12	44	29	7	3	3	2	100

NOTE: Assumes 13 miles per gallon and 65 cents per gallon.

N = 1,352

MTR #1189

Table 13.11

GASOLINE COSTS FOR BLACKS COMMUTING AS A PERCENTAGE OF INCOME BY INCOME DECILES

Income Decile	Percentage of Income							
	0	1-4	5-9	10-14	15-19	20 or More	Not Ascertained	Total
Lowest	91	6	0	1	0	0	1	99
Second	70	24	5	0	0	0	1	100
Third	47	42	6	0	2	0	3	100
Fourth	40	52	7	0	2	0	0	101
Fifth	20	72	4	1	0	0	3	100
Sixth	22	73	3	1	0	0	0	99
Seventh	16	77	3	1	0	0	3	100
Eighth	11	86	1	0	0	0	2	100
Ninth	17	81	1	0	0	0	1	100
Highest	10	85	2	0	0	0	3	100
All	31	63	3	1	0	0	2	100

NOTE: Assumes 13 miles per gallon and 65 cents per gallon.

N = 1352

MTR #1189

Summary

Despite large changes in gasoline prices and attempts to develop public transportation and car pooling, the changes in how people get to work have been small and even appear temporary. One reason may be that commuting is only a fraction of most people's total driving, and that the gasoline cost for commuting is only rarely a substantial fraction of family income. If gasoline costs were salient, one would expect people to reduce their noncommuting driving first, and it is not apparent that they have done that. The average burden of gasoline costs on low income families is low partly because members of these families are less likely to be working, less likely to drive to work if they do work, and less likely to have a car. However, there are some low income families whose members drive long distances to work and for whom rising gasoline costs are a serious matter.

Chapter 14

TRENDS IN FOOD EXPENDITURES

James N. Morgan

Because estimates of family needs are based largely upon food needs and because the impact of rising food prices on families is of social and economic interest, the panel study included a limited set of questions about food expenditures at home and in restaurants. Since the sample was small and therefore provides an imprecise measure, it seemed appropriate to compare data from samples two-years-apart with the expectation that enough change would have occurred to be visible above the random noise. Here we compare 1976 food expenditure data with that of 1972 and 1974, reported by Greg Duncan in Five Thousand American Families, Vol. IV.

Although the survey questions asked about expenditure on food at the time of interview, we use the total income for the previous year in comparing expenditure with income. This produces some upward bias in the proportions of income spent on food if incomes and expenditures are continually rising. But we can compare such proportions in different years on the assumption that the trends are reasonably unbiased.

Figure 14.1 shows that the average ratio of food expenditure to income rose rapidly between 1972 and 1974, then subsided somewhat as incomes apparently rose faster than food prices. The same trend appears if we look separately at the top or at the bottom end of the income distribution.

It would be better to compare the ratio of food expenditures at the time of the 1975 interview with the income for 1975 as reported in 1976. However, the differences are small, as Table 14.1 shows. Overall, the percentage of income spent on food is exaggerated by less than 1 percentage point by not waiting a year for the ideal income report. The same pattern by income deciles appears. There are always some families who are temporarily in the lowest decile or who have recently dropped to that level whose food expenditures have not adjusted downward, and this lack of adjustment is slightly more apparent when current rather than last year's income is used.

Keeping in mind the small upward bias of the percentages, we can see from Table 14.2 that over the four years low income families persistently spent a higher

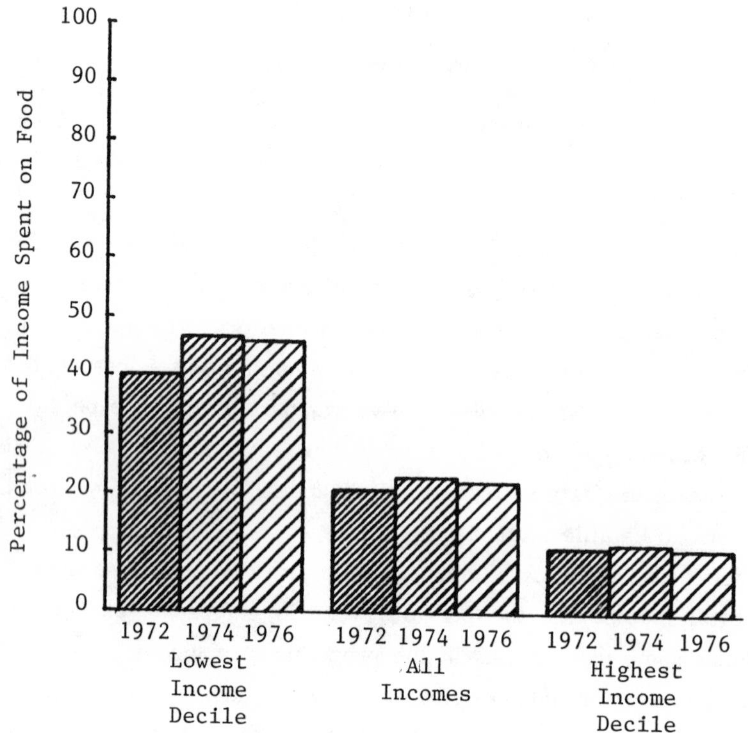

Figure 14.1. FOOD EXPENDITURES AS A FRACTION OF INCOME, BY INCOME GROUP

Table 14.1

FOOD EXPENDITURES AT TIME OF 1975 INTERVIEW
AS PERCENTAGE OF 1975 AND 1974 INCOMES

Income Decile of Year Used as Income base	Food Expenditure in 1975 as Percentage of 1975 Income	Food Expenditure in 1975 as Percentage of 1974 Income
Lowest	51.1	48.4
Second	30.6	32.8
Third	26.3	27.3
Fourth	22.4	23.2
Fifth	18.7	20.9
Sixth	17.0	18.1
Seventh	15.0	15.9
Eighth	13.9	14.6
Ninth	12.7	13.6
Highest	9.8	10.7
All	21.3	22.0

NOTE: Computed for families with same head from 1974 to 1976.

MTR #1195

Table 14.2

FOOD EXPENDITURE AS A PERCENTAGE OF INCOME BY INCOME DECILE FOR 1972, 1974, and 1976+

Income Decile	Home Food‡/Income			Total/Income∺			1972 Cigarette and Alcohol/Income
	1972	1974	1976	1972	1974	1976	
Lowest	36.0	42.7	45.1	40.1	46.6	45.8	6.2
Second	27.4	28.5	27.5	31.1	32.7	31.2	4.0
Third	22.4	24.0	24.7	25.1	28.0	28.2	3.3
Fourth	18.3	19.5	19.4	21.2	22.4	22.7	3.1
Fifth	16.7	18.1	16.5	19.1	20.8	19.5	2.7
Sixth	15.4	15.9	15.2	17.5	18.9	18.1	2.4
Seventh	13.6	15.0	13.4	15.8	17.6	16.2	2.1
Eighth	12.0	12.3	11.9	14.0	14.9	14.6	2.1
Ninth	11.2	12.0	11.1	13.1	14.3	13.4	1.4
Highest	8.9	9.4	8.3	10.8	11.4	10.6	1.2
Average	18.1	19.7	19.3	20.7	22.8	22.0	2.9

+See Table A7.1a for an explanation of reported income.

‡From the questions: "How much do you(FAMILY) spend on the food that you use at home in an average week?" "Do you have any food delivered to the door which isn't included in that?" For food stamp users, the cash paid for stamps is included in these expenditure figures but the bonus value of the stamps is not.

∺Including expenditures in restaurants from the question: "About how much do you (FAMILY) spend in an average week eating out, not counting meals at work or at school?"

MTR #7101

fraction of their income on food than upper income groups. Restaurant eating used to be considered a luxury, but it is clear from the table that it also accounts for a substantial fraction of total income at low-income levels.[1] Through 1972 we asked respondents to report their alcohol and tobacco expenditures separately from their food bills. Since we no longer remind them to separate these expenditures, it is possible that some people may now include these nonfood items in their grocery expenditure reports. Table 14.2 shows the fraction of income spent on alcohol and tobacco in 1972.

We can eliminate most of the problem of timing income and expenditures by looking at absolute food expenditures of families characterized by their decile position on the previous year's income.[2] Figures 14.2 and 14.3 show, respectively, the traditional income decile pattern and the pattern of expenditures according to income/needs, which is a better measure of ability to pay and hence of the burden of food costs. Since larger families within any income group are more likely to be in a lower income/needs decile and to spend more on food, the lines in Figure 14.3 are flatter, less income elastic, and imply that rising food prices are similar to a regressive tax.[3]

Restaurant expenditures are about as income elastic as home food expenditures, so the rapid rise in expenditures in the top deciles can be attributed fairly equally to both. The details are given in Appendix Tables A14.1a and A14.1b, while the actual incomes at the decile boundaries are shown in Table A14.1c.

The most substantial change between 1974 and 1976 was the increase in the proportion of families reporting some expenditures in restaurants (Table 14.3). This was accompanied by an increase in the reported amount spent. Had more people simply been reporting trivial amounts, the average expenditures would have dropped. The explosion of fast-food and other varied eating places, and the apparent high cost of grocery food may have contributed to this trend. Most of the increase occurred between 1974 and 1976, and the 1975 data indicate that there was somewhat more movement between 1974 and 1975 than from 1975 to 1976.

The increase was widespread, covering all levels of income/needs. Since there is an upper limit at 100 percent, neither the absolute nor relative increase is totally

[1]There is also a minor difference in procedure, the 1972 and 1974 data simply adding the average percentages of income spent at home and in restaurants to get a percent spent on all food, whereas in 1976 the third figure is an average of the ratios of total food expenditure to income. In the latter case the two components do not necessarily add to the average ratio of total expenditure to income.

[2]Some families will have moved into a different income decile, but their expenditures will not change the averages much, and the differences are largely offsetting.

[3]For previous analyses of the panel data on food expenditures, see Barlow (1974), Hymans and Shapiro (1974), and Benus, Kmenta and Shapiro (1976).

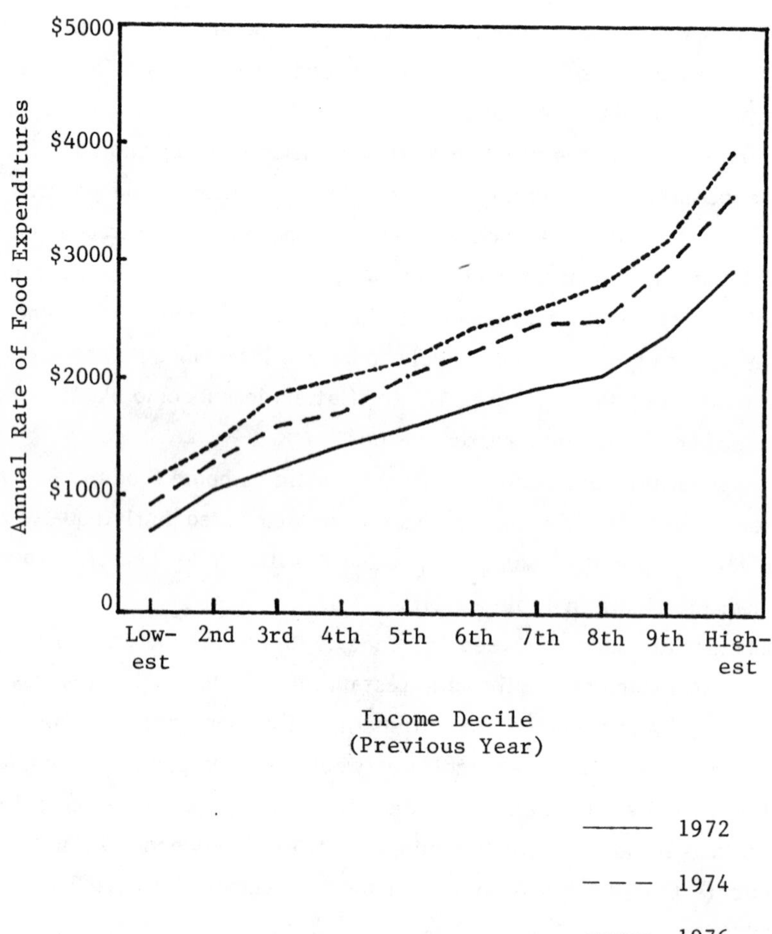

Figure 14.2. TOTAL (HOME AND RESTAURANT) FOOD EXPENDITURES BY INCOME DECILE, 1972, 1974, and 1976.

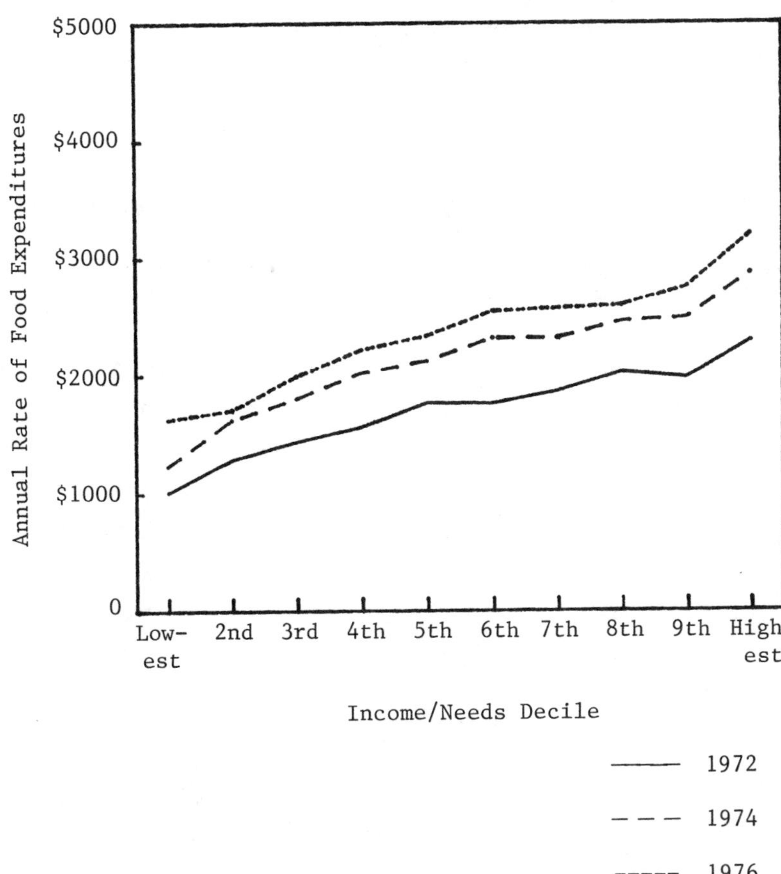

Figure 14.3. TOTAL (HOME AND RESTAURANT) FOOD EXPENDITURES BY DECILES OF INCOME/NEEDS

Table 14.3

RESTAURANT FOOD PURCHASE AND AMOUNT
BY INCOME/NEEDS FOR 1972, 1974, AND 1976

Income/Needs Decile	Percentage of Families Making Restaurant Expenditures in "Average" Week			Annual Dollar Restaurnat Expenditure for Families Eating Out		
	1972	1974	1976	1972	1974	1976
Lowest	30.3	32.5	48.6	198	338	359
Second	42.6	40.8	60.0	273	377	290
Third	53.3	56.1	72.2	245	308	311
Fourth	57.6	64.6	81.3	250	389	380
Fifth	67.1	63.2	85.0	289	392	385
Sixth	68.5	79.6	87.8	314	428	451
Seventh	79.6	83.2	88.7	362	450	453
Eighth	83.3	84.6	90.9	374	552	566
Ninth	86.1	87.8	94.6	417	542	638
Highest	89.9	88.7	96.1	619	777	884
Average	65.9	68.1	80.5	361	482	494

MTR #7101 and 1191, 1195

appropriate. Consequently, some analysts look at the proportion of restaurant users who formerly were not users. That proportion appears to be higher at the upper income levels. The relative increase in the proportion eating out is highest at the lowest income levels, however, and the absolute increase in the percentage is greatest at the middle income levels.

An economic interpretation would suggest that food prices were rising faster than the other costs of restaurants, giving restaurants a comparative advantage. A psychological interpretation might suggest that the larger relative price increases of food than of restaurant meals masked the fact that the absolute increase for the same food was higher in the restaurant. A marketing interpretation might suggest that the increasing variety of types of restaurants was opening up new markets by providing different mixes of food and service.

Summary

The patterns of food expenditures are reasonable, indicating that the data are usable for additional analysis. The trends indicate that no substantial adjustments or changes in household budgets are occurring, except for the increasing proportion who report <u>some</u> expenditures on restaurant meals.

References

Barlow, Robin. "The Incidence of Selected Taxes by Income Classes." In <u>Five Thousand American Families--Patterns of Economic Progress</u>, Volume II. Edited by James N. Morgan. Ann Arbor: Institute for Social Research, 1974.

Benus, Jacob; Kmenta, Jan; and Shapiro, Harold. "The Dynamics of Household Budget Allocation to Food Expenditures." In <u>Review of Economics and Statistics</u>, 58 (May 1976).

Hymans, Saul, and Shapiro, Harold. "The Allocation of Household Income to Food Consumption." In <u>Five Thousand American Families--Patterns of Economic Progress</u>, Volume II. Edited by James N. Morgan. Ann Arbor: Institute for Social Research, 1974.

Table A14.1a

MEAN ANNUAL FOOD EXPENDITURES BY
INCOME/NEEDS DECILE FOR 1972, 1974, and 1976+

Income/Needs Decile	Home Food‡					Restaurant Food‡‡					Total				
	Dollars Spent			Percentage Increase	Percentage Increase	Dollars Spent			Percentage Increase	Percentage Increase	Dollars Spent			Percentage Increase	Percentage Increase
	1972	1974	1976	1974/1972	1976/1972	1972	1974	1976	1974/1972	1976/1972	1972	1974	1976	1974/1972	1976/1972
Lowest	953	1,125	1,460	18	53	60	110	174	83	190	1,013	1,235	1,634	22	61
Second	1,172	1,472	1,538	27	31	117	153	174	31	49	1,289	1,626	1,712	26	33
Third	1,312	1,634	1,772	25	35	130	173	225	33	73	1,442	1,807	1,996	25	38
Fourth	1,418	1,773	1,910	25	35	144	251	309	74	115	1,562	2,024	2,220	30	42
Fifth	1,574	1,877	2,012	19	28	194	247	328	27	69	1,768	2,125	2,340	20	32
Sixth	1,549	1,977	2,150	28	39	215	341	396	59	84	1,764	2,318	2,546	31	44
Seventh	1,578	1,947	2,170	23	38	288	374	402	30	40	1,866	2,321	2,572	24	38
Eighth	1,714	1,994	2,080	16	21	314	467	515	49	64	2,028	2,461	2,595	21	28
Ninth	1,624	2,013	2,147	24	32	359	476	603	33	68	1,983	2,489	2,750	25	39
Highest	1,736	2,181	2,352	27	35	557	689	849	24	52	2,293	2,870	3,201	25	40
Average	1,463	1,800	1,959	23	34	238	328	398	38	67	1,701	2,128	2,357	25	39

+See Table A7.1a for an explanation of reported income and needs standard.

‡From the questions: "How much do you (FAMILY) spend on the food that you use at home in an average week?" "Do you have any food delivered to the door which isn't included in that?" For food stamp users, the cash paid for stamps is included in these expenditure figures but the bonus value of the stamps is not.

‡‡From the question: "About how much do you (FAMILY) spend in an average week eating out, not counting meals at work or at school?"

MTR #7101 and 1191

Table A14.1b

MEAN ANNUAL FOOD EXPENDITURES BY
INCOME DECILE FOR 1972, 1974, AND 1976+

Income Decile	Home Food‡					Restaurant Food‡‡					Total				
	Dollars Spent			Percentage Increase	Percentage Increase	Dollars Spent			Percentage Increase	Percentage Increase	Dollars Spent			Percentage Increase	Percentage Increase
	1972	1974	1976	1974/1972	1976/1972	1972	1974	1976	1974/1972	1976/1972	1972	1974	1976	1974/1972	1976/1972
Lowest	630	820	959	30	52	62	97	159	56	156	692	918	1,118	33	62
Second	921	1,118	1,251	21	36	121	163	182	35	50	1,042	1,281	1,433	23	38
Third	1,103	1,368	1,622	24	47	129	223	244	73	89	1,232	1,591	1,866	29	51
Fourth	1,230	1,491	1,718	21	40	195	220	293	13	50	1,425	1,711	2,011	20	41
Fifth	1,380	1,757	1,825	27	32	196	270	332	38	63	1,576	2,027	2,157	29	37
Sixth	1,548	1,873	2,044	21	32	217	361	391	65	80	1,765	2,235	2,435	27	38
Seventh	1,650	2,114	2,150	28	24	270	356	450	32	67	1,920	2,470	2,599	29	35
Eighth	1,747	2,065	2,293	18	31	292	437	520	50	78	2,038	2,502	2,813	23	38
Ninth	2,048	2,478	2,657	21	30	342	494	534	44	56	2,390	2,973	3,191	24	34
Highest	2,374	2,907	3,069	22	29	552	659	870	19	58	2,926	3,566	3,940	22	35
Average	1,463	1,800	1,959	23	34	238	328	398	38	67	1,701	2,128	2,357	25	39

+See Table A7.1a for an explanation of reported income.

‡From the questions: "How much do you (FAMILY) spend on the food that you use at home in an average week?" "Do you have any food delivered to the door which isn't included in that?" For food stamp users, the cash paid for stamps is included in these expenditure figures but the bonus value of the stamps is not.

‡‡From the question: "About how much do you (FAMILY) spend in an average week eating out, not counting meals at work or at school?"

MTR #7101 and 1191

Table A14.1c

UPPER LIMIT BOUNDARIES FOR INCOME AND INCOME/NEEDS DECILE FOR 1972, 1974, AND 1976 +

Decile	Income (Dollars)			Income/Needs Ratio‡		
	1972	1974	1976	1972	1974	1976
Lowest	2,600	3,047	3,499	1.00	1.18	1.40
Second	4,169	4,899	5,604	1.45	1.74	2.02
Third	5,769	6,554	7,682	1.91	2.29	2.68
Fourth	7,519	8,714	10,019	2.39	2.82	3.25
Fifth	9,133	10,867	12,199	2.83	3.37	3.88
Sixth	11,249	12,899	14,729	3.36	3.94	4.58
Seventh	13,275	15,365	17,663	3.99	4.63	5.39
Eighth	16,009	18,499	21,366	4.76	5.47	6.49
Ninth	20,799	23,519	27,314	6.10	7.03	8.23
Highest	--	--	--	--	--	--

+The 1976 report of income was for income received during the calendar year 1975.

‡The needs standard has been adjusted for inflation.

MTR #7101 and 1191

Chapter 15

SUMMARY OF OTHER RESEARCH

In this chapter we summarize some recent analyses of the Panel Study of Income Dynamics data being conducted here at The University of Michigan and elsewhere. A similar summary appeared in Volumes II, III, IV, and V, and here we attempt to bring up-to-date the list of research completed and in progress.

These analyses are in various stages of completion. Some have already been published in professional journals, some are currently at the "working paper" stage, and the remainder are just getting started.

The list of analyses is certainly not complete. The task of contacting everyone working with the Panel Study data is impossible, but our hope is that the following summaries will help to coordinate future research.

INDEX

Hanushek, Eric A. and Quigley, John M. Explicit Tests of the Human Capital Model and Intertemporal Adjustments of Relatives Wages.

Harrison, Bennett. How Americans Mix Work and Public Assistance: Implications for "Welfare Reform" Policy.

Hofferth, Sandra L. and Moore, Kristin. Work in Progress.

Johnson, Terry R. and Benus, Jacob M. An Econometric Analysis of Income Stability.

Levy, Frank; Vickery, Clair and Wiseman, Michael. The Income Dynamics of the Poor Project Report.

Lillard, Lee A. Estimation of Permanent and Transitory Response Functions in Panel Data: A Dynamic Labor Supply Model.

Lillard, Lee A. Dynamic Aspects of Earning Mobility.

Polachek, Solomon W. Occupational Segregation: Theory and Evidence.

Polachek, Solomon W. and Horvath, Francis W. A Life Cycle Approach to Migration: Analysis of the Perspicacious Peregrinator.

Theeuwes, Jules J. M. Family Labour Supply and Labour Force Participation Decisions.

Baker, Georgianne. Family Productivity: An Ecosystem Model.

SCHOOL EXPENDITURES AND THE ECONOMIC RETURNS TO SCHOOLING

John S. Akin, University of North Carolina
Irwin Garfinkel, University of Wisconsin
Published in The Journal of Human Resources, Vol. XII, No. 4 (Fall 1977).

The extent to which higher per pupil expenditures lead to any desirable outputs is an important policy question. We develop several alternative models which relate per pupil school expenditures to achievement orientation, verbal ability, years of schooling, and earnings. We use Panel Study data on males, age 30-55 in 1972, combined with state data on school expenditures from Biennial Surveys of Education and data on state income per capita from the Population Censuses. Our results indicate that the point estimate for the rate of return to increases in per pupil school expenditures is quite respectable for whites and very high for blacks irrespective of the model used. However, in one plausible model it is not possible to reject the hypothesis that the rate of return to whites is zero. In contrast, the results for blacks are not only consistently large, but also robust.

THE DETERMINANTS OF JOB SEARCH FOR EMPLOYED MALE WORKERS

Matthew Black, Mathematica Policy Research, Inc.

The labor market can be viewed as a sequence of events running from information acquisition, to mobility, to certain patterns of resource allocation. Within this context, adequate job information and mobile resources are crucial assumptions underlying the efficient operation of the labor market. This research attempts to place the dimension of mobility into sharper perspective by investigating the factors that prompt employed workers to engage in search activity. In particular, a model of search is developed and applied to a national sample of black and white male workers from the Michigan Panel Study of Family Income Dynamics. The empirical results are obtained from using a logistic model in which the dependent variable is the log-odds of the probability of undertaking search while employed at the time of the 1972 interview.

The empirical results offer strong corroboration of search theoretic models. In brief, whites react positively to relative wage opportunities, favorable market conditions, increased human capital stocks, remaining work years, and react negatively to search/relocation costs. Blacks react similarly to mobility costs and human capital, but appear to be insensitive to wage opportunities and search more when market conditions are threatening. Although both groups are sensitive to a large number of variables specified by search models, there also appears to be some important differences in the way the two racial groups interpret and respond to market wage and employment signals. The results are consistent with the notion that whites tend to view the labor market as a source of exploitable job opportunities while blacks, on the other hand, seem to be more concerned with job security and view the market as a threatening rather than benevolent force. The data, however, do not permit us to disentangle the factors underlying these differences (i.e., differences in (perceived) market risks associated with mobility versus personal variation in risk preferences).

SOCIAL SECURITY AND RETIREMENT DECISIONS

Michael J. Boskin, Stanford University and National Bureau of Economic Research
Published in Economic Inquiry, (January 1977).

Using data from the Panel Study of Income Dynamics, we follow a cohort of white married males through their sixties to estimate a model of retirement behavior. Using several definitions of retirement suggested in the literature, we find that the two key policy parameters of the social security system—the income guarantee and the implicit tax on earnings—exert an enormous influence on retirement decisions.

LABOR SUPPLY BEHAVIOR OF FEMALE HEADS OF HOUSEHOLDS

Andrew W. Braunstein, Rutgers University

This research examines the empirical labor supply behavior of female heads of households in the United States. Female-headed families are highly represented in the poverty population. Consequently, a careful study of the labor supply behavior of the group may provide useful information for policy makers charged with improving public programs directed at alleviating poverty.

The majority of existing studies treat labor supply behavior in a static framework. In addition, the implicit assumption is usually made that all individuals have freedom of choice in the hours of work decision.

In this research, labor supply behavior is formulated in a dynamic framework, under the contention that people look beyond current economic conditions in making their labor supply decisions. We separate our entire sample of female heads of households into two groups: those with freedom of choice in the hours worked decision, and those without that freedom.

The empirical analyses indicate little difference between the static and dynamic models in terms of key parameter estimates. However, parameter estimates for both the static and dynamic models vary greatly between the "free choice" and "choiceless" groups. Labor supply parameter estimates obtained for the "choiceless" group assume signs opposite from those expected on theoretical grounds, and they are very imprecise, as well. Since policy makers need reliable estimates of labor supply parameters, we have some evidence of the importance of insuring that those estimates are not contaminated by data on individuals who do not operate under the classical choice model.

ESTIMATING INDIVIDUAL MARGINAL VALUATIONS OF TRAVEL TIME SAVINGS

Jay Cherlow, State University of New York at Buffalo

The question of the proper valuation of marginal savings in travel time is more complex than it might appear. Several empirical studies, most of them based on observed modal choices, found similar mean values of 25 to 50 percent of the wage rate and this led some observers to conclude that such a value is the "true" value. However, theoretical analysis has shown that the marginal value of travel time savings need not be the same for all people, nor for the same person in all circumstances.

This study presents evidence derived from estimation of a multiple equation model of residential location choice which supports that viewpoint. The tremendous variation in the values for individual households suggests that previous studies which have reported only one value have been misleading. And since the use of a different sample resulted in estimated values quite different from those previously reported, this study should dramatize the danger of inferring values for use in one situation from those calculated in another. Additional studies of this type would be useful in order to isolate factors which account for variations in the value of travel time savings.

THE POVERTY LINE: ITS FUNCTIONS AND LIMITATIONS

Richard D. Coe, The University of Michigan
In Public Welfare 36 (Winter 1978), 32-36.

This article summarizes our findings on poverty and dependency in the short and long run.

MICROECONOMIC CONSEQUENCES OF CHILDBEARING IN THE UNITED STATES

James C. Cramer, University of California at Davis

This research examines the nature of the relationship between fertility and husband's income, and includes an exploratory look at husband-wife tradeoffs in employment and at the effect of fertility on family income. Couples who did and did not have a baby during 1970-73 are compared in terms of changes in employment and income in order to estimate the effects of fertility. Husbands who have a baby increase their employment by 11 percent, or 255 annual hours, relative to other husbands. They also increase their relative wage rates, so the average increase in husband's income associated with having a baby is $1267 (in 1969 dollars). Only a small part of this is due to changing jobs or to an increased rate of multiple job holding. Various factors associated with differential effects of fertility are examined, such as age, race, education, structural constraints, and wife's employment. Changes in husband's hours of employment have almost no association with changes in wife's employment. The net result of the opposing changes by spouses is an increase in family income associated with having a baby.

WIFE'S EMPLOYMENT AND PAID HELP

James C. Cramer, University of California at Davis

The relationship between wife's employment and paid help with housework and childcare was investigated as part of a project on fertility and female employment. The sample was restricted to wives under age 35 with at least one child under age 6. About half the sample were employed in 1971, but the nonemployed wives were nearly as likely to pay for help during 1971 (21 percent) as the employed wives (31 percent). The objective of the analysis was to estimate reciprocal causation models of employment and hiring help. Using data for 1969 and 1971 and controlling for such factors as wife's age, education, and number of children, both cross-lagged models and simultaneous-causation models indicate that wife's employment does not affect whether she hires help, but that hiring help does increase her employment. Analysis of the determinants of hired help yield results very similar to earlier reports on paid childcare among employed wives, so the extensions to paid housework and nonemployed wives seem credible as well as useful.

WORK IN PROGRESS

Walter Dolde, Carnegie-Mellon University

My research attempts to bifurcate the household section into wealth-constrained and liquidity-constrained groups. The latter should be much more sensitive to short-run macroeconomic phenomena, including stabilization policies. A life cycle model is posited and functional forms for year-to-year changes in housing, autos, and food expenditure are derived. The marginal rate of transformation between successive years is estimable. For the wealth-constrained it should approximate market interest rates. For the liquidity-constrained it is a shadow price which is much higher.

In addition to the expenditure data from the Panel Study, I use family size data, occupation, property income, and income data to construct life cycle profiles.

THE INTERRELATIONSHIP BETWEEN FERTILITY PATTERN AND TYPE OF OCCUPATION OF WORKING WIVES

Karen S. Edwards, Michigan State University, 1977

The strong inverse relationship between female employment and family size is often explained as alternate need gratification. The purpose of this study is to explore one aspect of this alternate need theory.

In reviewing the literature, a number of motivations for having children can be found. One of the major values reported by women is the opportunity to affiliate and nurture. This investigation was initiated to determine if specific occupations which vary in terms of their approximation of mothering roles, specifically nurturance and affiliation correlate differentially with fertility patterns of the employed wife.

It was hypothesized that women employed in "nurturant" occupations would demonstrate lower fertility and have fewer opportunities to nurture and affiliate at home as compared to other employed women of the same cohort group. Nurturant occupation was defined as employment in personal, health and educational service occupations. It was determined that these work activities are likely to be more rewarding in terms of opportunities to nurture and affiliate with others than employment in manufacturing, clerical or sales occupations. The relationships between fertility pattern and employment in these occupations was assessed using multiple linear regression analyses so that the effects of extraneous demographic variables could be controlled simultaneously.

A sample of stably married employed wives under the age of 53 was divided into three cohort age groups for separate analyses. These wives participated in the Panel Study from its inception through the wife's interview in the ninth year of data collection.

The results of this investigation indicates that employment in the "nurturant" occupations is not a significant variable in predicting fertility patterns. The hypothesized casual path from work gratifications to childbearing decisions was not supported. Opportunities to nurture and affiliate at home reflected in the number of children under 18 in the family unit was a significant variable in predicting employment in a nurturant occupation for the youngest cohort group, but the direction of the relationship was opposite to that expected by the proposed model.

EDUCATION, WAGE RATES, AND THE DIVISION OF LABOR BETWEEN HUSBAND AND WIFE

George Farkas, Yale University
In Journal of Marriage and the Family (August 1976).

Competing hypotheses relating the division of labor between husband and wife to their absolute level of education, their relative level of education, and their relative wage rates are identified, and are combined in a fully specified model. This model is estimated from panel data and it is found that neither the absolute educational level (subcultural) hypothesis nor the relative wage rate (economic) hypothesis can be rejected, although the strongest net effects are due to the presence of children. Implications for the further study of family behavior are drawn.

RISK AVERSION, RISK, AND THE DURATION OF UNEMPLOYMENT

Robert M. Feinberg, Pennsylvania State University
In Review of Economics and Statistics, Vol. LIX, No. 3 (August 1977).

This article presents estimates of a reduced-form equation derived from the job search theory and tests the following two hypotheses: (1) as the standard deviation of the distribution of potential wage offers increases, an individual's expected duration of unemployment will increase, ceteris paribus; (2) an individual who is more risk averse than another will have a shorter expected duration of unemployment, ceteris paribus.

The results presented here have demonstrated risk and attitudes toward risk to be determinants of an individual's duration of unemployment. Hypotheses (1) and (2), drawn from the job search theory but plausibly explained in alternative terms, have been generally confirmed by the data, especially the TOTAL samples. Further empirical work is needed to verify these results with other data samples.

RACIAL DIFFERENCES IN COMMUTING BEHAVIOR: NEW EVIDENCE FROM THE PANEL STUDY OF INCOME DYNAMICS

John L. Goodman, Jr., The Urban Institute
Mark Berkman, Harvard University
In Public Data Use, Vol. 5, No. 4 (July 1977).

Data from a national probability sample of metropolitan families reveal sharp racial differences in distance from home to work, commuting time, commuting speed, and mode of transportation. Black household heads are found to spend about 25 percent more time commuting per hour worked than do whites, even though blacks on average live slightly closer to their place of employment. The proportion of black workers using public transportation is three times the whites' proportion, and reliance on this slow mode of transportation accounts for about half of the difference between whites and blacks in commuting time and commuting speed. The paper mentions some housing market and labor market implications of the findings.

EXPLICIT TESTS OF THE HUMAN CAPITAL MODEL AND INTERTEMPORAL ADJUSTMENTS OF RELATIVES WAGES

Eric A. Hanushek and John M. Quigley, Yale University
A working paper (no. 767).

This paper extends the human capital model by considering the distinction between the actual labor market experience of workers and their potential experience gained simply by aging. This distinction permits the underlying parameters of the capital investment function and the rates of return to schooling and post-school investment to be estimated directly.

The existence of longitudinal data on individuals permits an investigation of the dynamics of temporal shifts in earnings curves for different classes of workers, at least in a crude manner. These longitudinal data also permit an independent, though somewhat exacting, test of the behavioral model using the same individuals as units of observation.

The estimates of the investment model appear quite consistent with the human capital formulation when estimated in level form. The implicit rates of return to post-school investment and the parameters of the underlying investment schedules seem plausible. "Growth adjusted" rates of return (those normalized for economic growth, price changes, and short run shifts in labor force demands) range between 3 and 9 percent. The investment profiles themselves (assumed to be linear) decline in a reasonable manner with a rate of decline that increases with level of schooling.

The intertemporal shifts in the earnings profiles are explained by GNP growth, price changes, and terms relating to specific race and schooling classes. Price changes are almost completely passed through to wage changes while the elasticity of the profiles with respect to GNP ranges is about .63. Over the period 1968 through 1974, the relative wages of blacks has risen while the relative wages of high school and college educated individuals has fallen. The decline has been more for high school than for college educated individuals.

Finally, there is some inconclusiveness in the explicit tests of the human capital investment model. This model should explain both the level and the growth of individual wages and earnings. However, when the model is estimated in its growth form, the plausibility of the human capital model is not supported. This may indicate a weakness of the data, but it may also indicate more serious conceptual problems.

HOW AMERICANS MIX WORK AND PUBLIC ASSISTANCE: IMPLICATIONS FOR "WELFARE REFORM" POLICY

Bennett Harrison, Massachusetts Institute of Technology

Theoretically, welfare can have a direct relationship to the labor market, an indirect relationship, or no relationship. There will be a direct relationship if people use work and welfare within the same time frame, either simultaneously or by moving back and forth between the two "states." Data from the PSID show that for periods of a year, the average incidence of mixing was only 5.3%. But the data for 1968-72 reveal a lot of "moving back and forth" from year to year, so much so that the cumulative probability of mixing was 16.3% for the sample as a whole (nearly four out of ten permanently poor households mixed work and welfare over the five-year period). Moreover, this 16.3% represents 92.0% of all "ever-welfare" households. Clearly the great majority of heads of "welfare households" had a job at some time or other. For welfare recipients, therefore, there is definitely a strong direct relationship to the labor market.

There will be an indirect relationship between work and welfare if, whether or not people actually work, labor market conditions significantly affect the extent of welfare utilization. Panel data show that this is indeed the case, even for the "pooled" sample of 2,688 observations, over 80% of which represent households in the upper two-thirds of the five-year (1968-72) U.S. distribution of family income. Local unemployment rates, the availability of high-wage jobs, and whether or not household heads were unionized were especially significant predictors of the absolute and relative utilization of welfare (industrial relations research suggests that unionized jobs tend to be higher paying and more stable than nonunion jobs. Therefore, workers in unionized jobs are less likely to need welfare, holding other things constant).

WORK IN PROGRESS
Kristin Moore and Sandra L. Hofferth, The Urban Institute

We are currently in the process of planning an analysis of the PSID to test hypotheses regarding the effects of adolescent childbearing on the lives of families and, especially, women. We are especially interested in explaining differentials in educational attainment, family size, labor force participation, and household income between early and late childbearers at different points in their lives. We expect to complete the analysis and have a final report by June 30, 1978.

AN ECONOMETRIC ANALYSIS OF INCOME INSTABILITY
Terry R. Johnson and Jacob M. Benus, Stanford Research Institute

This research develops an empirical measure of income uncertainty and examines the effects of future income uncertainty on consumption behavior. The empirical measure of income uncertainty developed in the paper is based on individuals' recent unexpected income fluctuations. It is assumed that an individual's earnings expectations are partly based on a human capital model of income determination. It is further assumed that individuals' expected earnings are also determined by unobservable personal characteristics such as ability and motivation.

The measure of income uncertainty is derived from an error components model of earnings. In such a model the random disturbance term is decomposed into two statistically independent parts: an individual specific effect which is invariant over time, and an effect that varies over both individuals and time. The individual specific effect captures income expectations associated with the unobservable characteristics. The remaining portion of the error term is used to form a measure of income uncertainty.

The empirical analysis is based on the Michigan Panel Study of Income Dynamics as well as the Seattle and Denver Income Maintenance Experiments. The results from both data sets suggest that future income uncertainty significantly reduces the demand for durable goods.

THE INCOME DYNAMICS OF THE POOR
PROJECT REPORT
Frank Levy, Clair Vickery, and Michael Wiseman, University of California, Berkeley

Each year a significant portion of the poverty population leaves poverty. In this paper, we define a sample of people who were poor in 1967. We then follow them over time to determine the extent to which poverty is a permanent phenomenon. The original sample represented 16.35 million people. We find this sample can be thought of as three separate groups. One is an underclass of 7.7 million people who were poor in 1967 and who remained poor through most of the next six years. The second group contained 4.1 million people who were poor in 1967 but who were out of poverty for five or six of the next six years. The third group contained about 4.4 million people who were poor half the time between 1967 and 1973.

We have found that the extensive writing on a "culture of poverty" is overdrawn in several respects. First, permanent poverty is a serious problem, but the permanent poor comprise only about one-half of the poverty population in any single year. Second, many of the poor—especially those in male-headed households—work significant numbers of hours, and their year-to-year changes in income are governed by the same kinds of permanent income models that govern income fluctuations in the rest of the society. The limited information available indicates that the children of poor households generally do not form poor households themselves.

ESTIMATION OF PERMANENT AND TRANSITORY RESPONSE FUNCTIONS IN PANEL DATA: A DYNAMIC LABOR SUPPLY MODEL
Lee A. Lillard, National Bureau of Economic Research, Inc., Stanford, California
Presented at the INSEE Conference on "Econometrics of Panel Data" in Paris, August 1977.

This paper emphasizes dynamic aspects of the labor supply decision, especially the distinction between responses of annual hours worked to long-run and to short-run changes in wage rates. The model assumes that log real average annual wage rates are predetermined by market conditions and include permanent individual wage differences, as well as a serially correlated transitory component of variation. Log annual hours of work are determined by a long-run labor supply response to the permanent wage and a short-run response to the transitory wage variation. Given the parameters of the dynamic model, one can easily analyze the role of wages, labor supply, and exogenous hours variation in the distribution of log real annual earnings over time. A major part of this paper is a description of the maximum likelihood estimation procedures.

In this paper, I present a method for estimating permanent and transitory response functions in panel data. The basic concept developed here is an analysis of the structural relationships among time varying economic variables, each of which have been decomposed into permanent and serially correlated transitory components. The permanent and transitory components can then be allowed to be related by different structural parameters. The more serial correlation in a transitory component, the more it will behave as a permanent one.

The method is applied empirically to estimate the parameters of a dynamic labor supply model. Wages are presumed to be predetermined from the viewpoint of each individual laborer. The wage rate (in logs) of any particular laborer at a particular point in time is composed of several components: a year effect representing year-to-year wage variation common to all individuals; an individual specific permanent (long run) wage level; and a serially correlated transitory (short run) deviation of that individual's wage rate from its permanent level. The individual permanent component is itself composed of the effect of measured and of unmeasured individual characteristics which affect wages. Annual hours of work is similarly composed of several components: a year effect representing year-to-year variation in hours common to all individuals; a labor supply response to permanent wage differences among persons; an individual residual or deviation from the aggregate long run labor supply function; an individual response to the personal transitory wage deviation from its permanent level; and a residual serially correlated transitory term representing involuntary transitory variation in hours (not on the aggregate transitory response function). All individuals are assumed to have the same transitory labor supply elasticity and the same degree of serial correlation in transitory variables.

The dynamic labor supply including errors of measurement can be straight-forwardly written as a LISREL model. Assuming normality for the relevant variables, maximum likelihood estimates of the parameters are obtained. Parameters are estimated for white males who are not disabled, retired or full time students during the panel period 1967-73. The model is estimated using annual hours of work and annual earnings in real 1970 dollars (equals hours plus wages in logs) since wages are not observed directly.

First the significance of measurement error is tested. It is quite significant for both hours and earnings. Measurement error accounts for 6.6 percent of observed variation in annual earnings and 17.4 percent of observed variation in annual hours of work. Controlling for measurement error in hours eliminates the usual negative bias in the labor supply elasticity widely cited in the literature when hours and earnings rather than hours and wages are observed. The permanent and transitory labor supply elasticities (response parameters) are found to be negative and not significantly different from each other (-.160 when constrained to be equal), while each is significantly different from zero. This equality result holds in various subgroups as well, e.g. schooling groups, experience groups and union status groups. The exception is husbands of wives who work all 7 years or who work some of the years. In the latter case the short run elasticity is more positive than the long run elasticity but remains negative. It appears that serial correlation in transitory wages is high enough (.823) to induce workers to behave as if they are permanent.

DYNAMIC ASPECTS OF EARNING MOBILITY

Lee A. Lillard, National Bureau of Economic Research
Robert J. Willis, National Bureau of Economic Research and Stanford University
NBER Working Paper, April 1977.

Uses seven year panel data from cross-section sample only (hence few blacks), 18-58 years old in 1967, not disabled, retired, or full-time student and with positive hours and earnings each year. Defines poverty as individual earnings less than half the CPS median for that year.

This paper proposes an econometric methodology to deal with life cycle earnings and mobility among discrete earnings classes. First, we use panel data on male log earnings to estimate an earnings function with permanent and serially correlated transitory components due to both measured and unmeasured variables. Assuming that the error components are normally distributed, we develop statements for the probability that an individual's earnings will fall into a particular but arbitrary time sequence of poverty states. Using these statements, we illustrate the implications of our earnings model for poverty dynamics and compare our approach to Markov chain models of income mobility.

In this paper, we present a methodology in which average life cycle earnings growth and the dynamics of the distribution of earnings—viewed either as a continuous distribution or in terms of mobility across a set of discrete earnings classes—can be analyzed within a common econometric framework using longitudinal data. The basic ingredient of our approach is an empirical (log) earnings function with an error structure that allows for permanent differences among individuals due to unmeasured variables and for first order serial correlation in the transitory components of a given individual's time-series of earnings. We call this error structure the "autocorrelated individual component model." Assuming normality of the permanent and transitory components, the intertemporal distribution of log earnings among individuals (holding measured variables constant) is multivariate normal with a correlation structure determined by the share of permanent variance in total variance and the degree of serial correlation. Earnings mobility is then analyzed by deriving the probability statements implied by the earnings function for arbitrary time sequences of earnings states (e.g. whether earnings are above or below an arbitrary poverty line) for a given individual (i.e. holding the permanent component constant) or for a group of individuals. The distribution of poverty probabilities across observationally identical individuals is also derived.

The methodology is illustrated using seven years of data on male earnings from the Michigan Income Dynamics Sample. The autocorrelated individual component model is estimated separately for blacks and whites, as well as for the total sample, using three successively more comprehensive sets of explanatory variables. The simplest model (no explanatory variables except time dummies) indicates that 73.1 percent of total variance in log earnings represents permanent earnings differences. Of the remaining 26.9 percent stochastic variation, 22.5 percentage points are due to purely stochastic variation, and 4.4 to serial correlation.

The variance components and serial correlation coefficients are of roughly similar magnitude for blacks and whites. The permanent component for blacks is about 44 percent larger than for whites, while their transitory component is about the same. Some caution concerning these and other racial comparisons is in order because of the relatively small number of blacks in our sample.

Explanatory variables in the more complex equations tend to leave the size of the permanent and transitory variance components unchanged but reduce the unmeasured permanent variance. For example, schooling, experience, and race explain 33 percent of observed annual earnings variation, but they explain 44 percent of the permanent earnings variation. Schooling, experience, race and the permanent component still explain 73 percent of total earnings variation. Within racial groups, schooling and experience alone explain 51 percent of the permanent component for blacks and 40 percent for whites.

We began this paper with several questions concerning the extent to which poverty is a permanent or transient status and, more broadly, the degree to which the distribution of earnings is characterized more by mobility or stratification. Since the analysis in this paper is confined to males who had earnings in a sequence of years, it cannot deal fully with such questions. A more complete analysis of poverty would consider family income, variations in family composition over time, unemployment and a variety of other issues. However, within their limitations, our model's implications for the mobility of blacks and whites into and out of poverty do suggest some tentative answers to these questions.

The poor are different from the non-poor. Those in poverty in a given year have permanently lower earnings than those not in poverty and are fifteen to twenty-five times as likely to be in poverty as much as six years later. Moreover, these differences are not solely the result of measured characteristics such as race, schooling and experience—these variables explain only about half of permanent earnings variation with the remainder due to unmeasured factors. Finally, although about 2.5 percent of whites and 9 percent of blacks are predicted to have earnings below the 1970 poverty line, the representative (i.e. median) person of either race had a negligible chance of falling into poverty in that year.

While the poor are different in the sense just described, it would be misleading to conclude that poverty is a permanent status. We find that of those individuals in poverty in a given year, about 55 percent of whites and 35 percent of blacks will be out of poverty in the following year. Another indication of mobility is that only 15 percent of whites and 35 percent of blacks who fall into poverty at some time during the three year period from

1967-70 are expected to be in poverty in all three years. It would also be misleading to conclude that our findings support the concept of a "culture of poverty" which is qualitatively distinct from the social and economic environment in which the majority of persons operate. Rather, our findings simply indicate that the majority of cross-section earnings variation is due to permanent rather than transitory factors. As a result, there is a considerable tendency for individuals to retain their position in the earnings distribution over time whether this position is in the lower, upper or middle portions of the distribution.

OCCUPATIONAL SEGREGATION: THEORY AND EVIDENCE

Solomon William Polachek, University of North Carolina, Chapel Hill
Presented at the Conference on Women in the Labor Market, Barnard College, Columbia University, New York (September 1977).

Currently human capital models are applied almost exclusively to explain earnings distribution. These models have been severely criticized because of their failure to explain existing occupational patterns. This paper introduces the concept of heterogeneous human capital so that optimal kinds as well as amounts of human capital can be determined. Inferences concerning occupational structure are obtained by assuming that each occupation requires different kinds of human capital.

The model is applied to analyze occupational segregation by sex. From Wave VI of the Income Dynamics Panel, it is found that if women were to have a full lifetime labor force attachment, then human capital considerations would dictate a 35 percent increase in the number of women professionals, a more than doubling of the number of women in managerial professions, and a diminution of the number of women in menial occupations in excess of 25 percent. These results for the first time indicate the potential strength of the human capital model in explaining occupational segregation by sex.

A LIFE CYCLE APPROACH TO MIGRATION: ANALYSIS OF THE PERSPICACIOUS PEREGRINATOR

Solomon W. Polachek and Francis W. Horvath, University of North Carolina, Chapel Hill
In Ronald Ehrenberg, Ed. Research in Labor Economics. JAI Press, 1977.

This paper creates a generalized theory of migration by embedding the mobility decision within a life cycle framework. In particular three aspects of migration, namely locational choice, periodicity of migration, and the impact of familial variables are considered.

Empirical implementation of the model is achieved by estimation using household data from the Income Dynamics panel. By utilizing a multi-equation specification, expected monetary gains are measured and explicitly used to account for household interstate migration. In addition, account is taken of the impact of past migration and household characteristics.

It is found that expected monetary gains affect migration decisions. A ten thousand dollar expected increase in the present value of husband's earnings increases the probability of interstate migration by six percent. Presumably because of intermittent labor force participation, expected increases in wife's wages are estimated to have a negligible effect. Further, past migration strongly influences current migration. Those that changed states within the last year have between a 10 and 20 percent greater probability of changing states again within the current year. Family characteristics are also important. Nearby relatives, children in school, wife's occupation, and education each influence mobility.

FAMILY LABOUR SUPPLY AND LABOUR FORCE PARTICIPATION DECISIONS

Jules J. M. Theeuwes, (Ph.D. Dissertation), University of British Columbia, 1975.

The main objective of this study has been the empirical estimation of family labour force participation decision functions. In this study I have used the binomial and multinomial logit model to estimate parameters affecting the probabilities of choosing a particular labour force participation alternative.

A theoretical contribution of this thesis to the econometric literature has been the development of a procedure which, in the context of the multinomial logit model, allows one to test whether decision taking is sequential or simultaneous.

In the empirical portion of this thesis I devoted considerable attention to the problem of predicting the potential wage rate for men and women who are not observed in the labour force. Although this wage variable is extremely important for theoretical reasons, problems involving actual estimation of a wage predictor, have been largely neglected in previous studies. The parameter estimates used in this study to approximate the unobserved wage rate were suspected of being biased (because of missing variables and structural difference problems). Whether the predictors have any desirable statistical properties (e.g., minimum mean squared error) is unknown and is an appropriate subject for further research. It is somewhat surprising that the use of predicted wage rates based on biased estimates yielded such significant results.

A substantial portion of the empirical research in this study has been the estimation and comparison of parameters of family labour force participation and labour supply decisions. I have attempted to discriminate statistically between the hypothesis that the parameters of supply and participation are either the same or different and found that the hypothesis of different parameters is more probable, a posteriori. In addition, the comparison of the parameters of family labour supply and labour force participation decisions has lead to interesting results, e.g., the substitution effect on both participation and supply behaviour of husband and wife. Another use of the estimated labour supply and labour force participation functions involved combining them to form unconditional labour supply functions. It was indicated that unconditional labour supply functions could be useful to evaluate the combined effect on supply and participation of a labour market policy.

FAMILY PRODUCTIVITY: AN ECOSYSTEM MODEL

Georgianne Baker, Arizona State University

Market work time, child care and housework time have been studied previously, but if they are substitutes for one another in families, a different approach is in order. This research proposes a family productivity variable: a measure of total productive time, combining market work time of all members, commuting time (part of market work time), child care and housework time. I use a subsample of 2,571 black and white families with both spouses present and between 18 and 63 years of age.

The analysis tests a family ecosystem model, where families adjust their outputs (productivity) when information about shifts in input resources and demands is acted upon. Inputs may be familial, environmental, or combine elements both internal and external to families.

Preliminary findings relevant to the family ecosystem output are the following: total family productivity averaged over 6,000 hours annually; market productivity was higher than home productivity; wives were more productive than their husbands. On the input side, the most important explanatory variables appear to be family life cycle (accounting for 26% to 39% of explained variance in productivity) or number of children in the family (accounting for 34% to 39% of explained variance). Income to needs ratio and spouses' occupation were important contributing predictors for market productivity or husband's productivity.

The study will continue to identify significant input variables and then consider issues of equity. The idea of individuals in families experiencing equity (or inequity) will be examined by looking at changes in relative contributions of spouses as inputs change. The idea of the family experiencing differential equity will be considered by comparing results for black and white families living in similar environments. Analysis will continue to be cross-sectional and then use time change measures. In so far as home productivity is affected by family system variations, substantial changes in non-market work hours can be projected over time.

Appendix A

RESPONSE RATES AND DATA QUALITY

For the last few years we have been able to report that we have found no adverse effects on the response rate or on data quality due to interviewing by telephone rather than in person and a small accompanying yearly increase in the number of interviews taken with someone other than the head of the family (usually a wife). The response rate remained constant and data quality, according to our measure of it, improved a little bit fom year to year.

Our 1976 findings were less straightforward. Although the number of telephone interviews increased slightly (Table A.2), so, to our surprise, did the number of interviews taken with the head of the family (Table A.3). This should have improved data quality, but it did not. More assignments than usual had to be made for missing information (Table A.4).

To confuse things still further, the response rate fell slightly (Table A.1). We think that this was due in part to the unfortunate wording of the government's informed consent statement which we are now required to send or read to all respondents.

However, probably all of these small aberrations should be blamed on a one year drop in efficiency brought on by overloading the interviewers with the 3,482 extra interviews with wives.

The 1977 response rate is back where it should be at 97 percent and there has been a small improvement in the accuracy of the data.

Table A.1

ANNUAL AND CUMULATIVE PANEL RESPONSE RATES[+]

Year	Percent: Annual	Percent: Cumulative
1968	76	76
1969	89	68
1970	97	66
1971	97	64
1972	97	62
1973	97	61
1974	97	59
1975	97	57
1976	96	55
1977	97	53

[+]The deceased, those too ill to be interviewed, and recombined families have not been removed from the base.

Table A.2

PROPORTION OF INTERVIEWS BY TELEPHONE

Year	Sample Size	Number of Telephone Interviews	Unweighted Percent of Sample
1968	4,802	--	--
1969	4,460	--	--
1970	4,655	67	1.4
1971	4,840	108	2.2
1972	5,060	134	2.6
1973	5,185	4,047	76.6
1974	5,517	4,554	82.5
1975	5,725	4,836	84.5
1976	5,862	5,360	91.4

Table A.3

PROPORTION OF FAMILY HEADS INTERVIEWED

Year	Total Sample	Proportion of Interviews by Head
1968	4,802	92.6
1969	4,460	93.1
1970	4,655	93.2
1971	4,840	93.3
1972	5,060	93.5
1973	5,285	91.1
1974	5,517	90.0
1975	5,725	88.3
1976	5,862	92.6

Table A.4+

TOTAL ACCURACY CODES ON HUSBAND AND WIFE INCOME VARIABLES

Year of Data	0	1	2	3	4 or More	Total
1968	94.0	2.5	2.6	0.2	0.8	100.0
1969	95.6	1.6	1.9	0.1	0.8	100.0
1970	96.9	1.3	1.3	0.1	0.5	100.0
1971	97.7	0.9	0.9	0.1	0.4	100.0
1972	97.8	0.8	1.1	0.0	0.3	100.0
1973	97.9	1.1	0.7	0.1	0.2	100.0
1974	98.2	0.9	0.7	0.0	0.2	100.0
1975	98.3	0.8	0.8	0.0	0.2	100.0
1976	97.0	1.2	1.6	0.1	0.2	100.0

+Table 4 is based on three variables:

Accuracy of Head's Labor Income
Accuracy of Wife's Labor Income
Accuracy of Asset Income of Head and Wife.

Accuracy here is determined by the number of assignments made by the editors in order to recreate data missing from an interview. The more assignments, the less reliable the data. The accuracy code values and their meanings are:

0. Adequate response: No assignments made.
1. Minor assignment: Response was inadequate, but estimates could be made within a probable error of under $300 or 10 percent of the assignment by using previous years' data or other data in the interview.
2. Major assignment: Response was inadequate and estimates had a probable error of at least $300 and at least 10 percent of the value of the assignment, using any information available in previous interviews or in the current one. Usually these values were assigned from an assignment table.

This table shows the sum of the accuracy codes for the three different income measures. The maximum number possible here would be six for married couples, four for single heads.

Appendix B

1976 QUESTIONNAIRES

Although the questionnaires, codes, and study procedures are described each year in a separate documentation volume, we reproduce the 1976 questionnaires in this appendix for readers without access to these volumes.

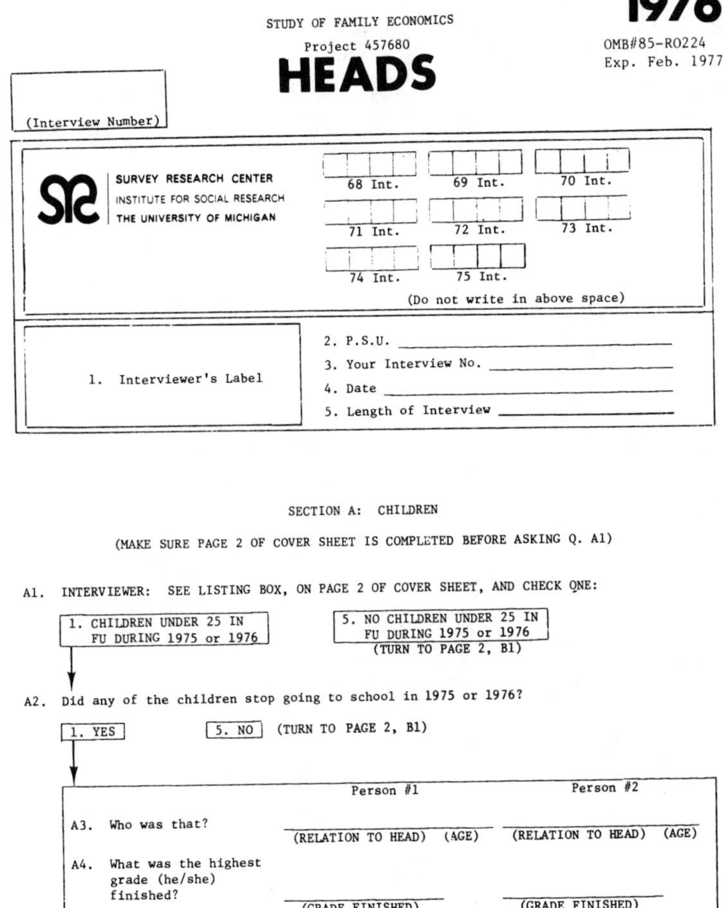

STUDY OF FAMILY ECONOMICS

Project 457680

HEADS

1976

OMB#85-R0224
Exp. Feb. 1977

(Interview Number)

SURVEY RESEARCH CENTER
INSTITUTE FOR SOCIAL RESEARCH
THE UNIVERSITY OF MICHIGAN

68 Int. 69 Int. 70 Int.
71 Int. 72 Int. 73 Int.
74 Int. 75 Int.

(Do not write in above space)

1. Interviewer's Label

2. P.S.U. ________

3. Your Interview No. ________

4. Date ________

5. Length of Interview ________

SECTION A: CHILDREN

(MAKE SURE PAGE 2 OF COVER SHEET IS COMPLETED BEFORE ASKING Q. A1)

A1. INTERVIEWER: SEE LISTING BOX, ON PAGE 2 OF COVER SHEET, AND CHECK ONE:

1. CHILDREN UNDER 25 IN FU DURING 1975 or 1976

5. NO CHILDREN UNDER 25 IN FU DURING 1975 or 1976 (TURN TO PAGE 2, B1)

A2. Did any of the children stop going to school in 1975 or 1976?

1. YES

5. NO (TURN TO PAGE 2, B1)

	Person #1	Person #2
A3. Who was that?	(RELATION TO HEAD) (AGE)	(RELATION TO HEAD) (AGE)
A4. What was the highest grade (he/she) finished?	(GRADE FINISHED)	(GRADE FINISHED)

SECTION B: TRANSPORTATION

(ASK EVERYONE)

B1. Is there public transportation within walking distance of (here) (your house)?

[1. YES] [5. NO] (GO TO B3)

B2. Is it good enough so that a person could use it to get to work?

____

____

B3. Do you or anyone else in the family here own a car or truck?

[1. YES] [5. NO] (TURN TO PAGE 3, C1)

B4. How many cars and trucks do you (and your family living here) own? ________

B5. During the last year how many miles did you and your family drive in (your car/all of your cars)?

____

____

(TURN TO PAGE 3, C1)

SECTION C: HOUSING

C1. How many rooms do you have for your family (not counting bathrooms)? ________

C2. Do you live in a one-family house, a two-family house, an apartment, or what?

[1. ONE-FAMILY] [2. TWO-FAMILY] [3. APARTMENT] OTHER ____________ (SPECIFY)

C3. Do you own the (home/apartment), pay rent, or what?

[1. OWNS OR IS BUYING] [5. PAYS RENT] (TURN TO PAGE 4, C12) [8. NEITHER OWNS NOR RENTS] (TURN TO PAGE 4, C15)

(IF OWNS OR IS BUYING)

C4. Could you tell me what the present value of your house (farm) is -- I mean about what would it bring if you sold it today?

$____________

C5. Do you have a mortgage on this property?

[YES] [NO] (GO TO C11)

		1st Mortgage	2nd Mortgage
C6.	About how much is the remaining principal on this mortgage?	\$________	\$________
(IF DON'T KNOW) C7.	How much are your monthly mortgage payments?	\$________	\$________
C8.	About how many more years will you have to pay on it?	________	________ (GO TO C10)

C9. Do you also have a 2nd mortgage?

[YES] → (RETURN TO C6) [NO] → (GO TO C10)

C10. Do your mortgage payments include property taxes

[1. YES] [5. NO]

C11. About how much are your yearly property taxes including city, county and school taxes?

$____________

(TURN TO PAGE 4, C17)

(IF PAYS RENT)

C12. About how much rent do you pay a month? $______

C13. Is heating included in your monthly rent?

1. YES | 5. NO

C14. Is this (house/apartment) rented furnished?

1. YES | 5. NO

(GO TO C17)

(IF NEITHER OWNS NOR RENTS)

C15. How is that? ______

C16. How much would it rent for if it were rented? $______ per ______ (MONTH, YEAR)

(GO TO C17)

(ASK EVERYONE)

C17. Have you (HEAD) moved since the spring of 1975?

1. YES | 5. NO (GO TO C20)

C18. What month was that? ______ (MOST RECENT MOVE)

C19. Why did you move? ______

C20. Do you think you might move in the next couple of years?

______ | 5. NO (TURN TO PAGE 5, D1)

(IF MIGHT MOVE OR WILL MOVE) → C21. Would you say you definitely will move, probably will move, or are you more uncertain?

1. DEFINITELY | 2. PROBABLY | 3. MORE UNCERTAIN

C22. Why might you move? ______

SECTION D: EMPLOYMENT

D1. We would like to know about what you do--are you (HEAD) working now, looking for work, retired, a student, a housewife, or what?

1. WORKING NOW → D2

2. ONLY TEMPORARILY LAID OFF → D2

3. LOOKING FOR WORK, UNEMPLOYED (TURN TO PAGE 13, E1)

4. RETIRED
5. PERMANENTLY DISABLED
6. HOUSEWIFE
7. STUDENT
8. OTHER ______ (SPECIFY)

(TURN TO PAGE 16, F1)

(GO TO D2 IF HAS JOB, OTHERWISE TURN TO PAGE 16, F1)

D2. What is your main occupation? (What sort of work do you do?)

______ OCC [|] IND [|]

(IF NOT CLEAR) → D3. Tell me a little more about what you do.

______

D4. What kind of business is that in? ______

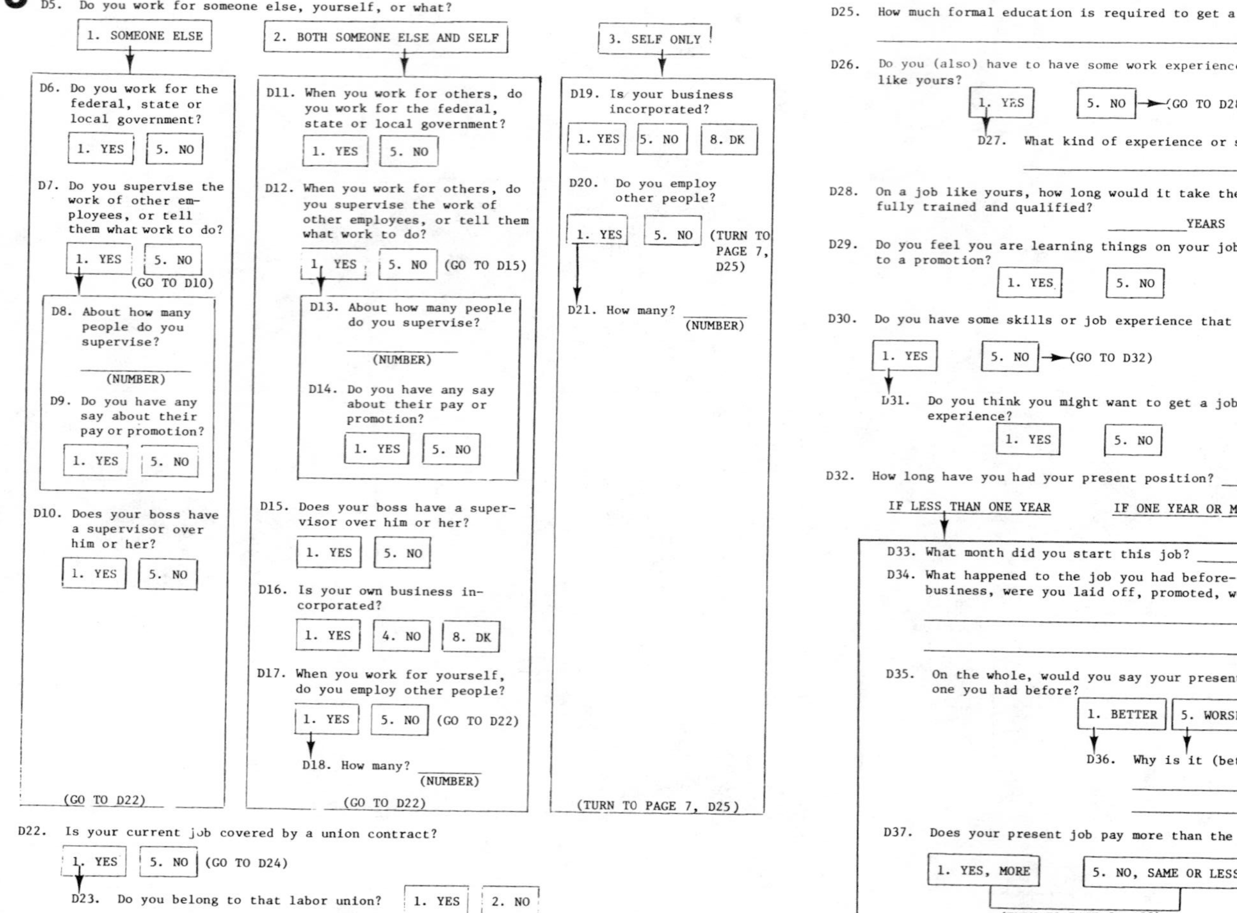

6

D5. Do you work for someone else, yourself, or what?

1. SOMEONE ELSE | 2. BOTH SOMEONE ELSE AND SELF | 3. SELF ONLY

[1. SOMEONE ELSE]

D6. Do you work for the federal, state or local government?

1. YES | 5. NO

D7. Do you supervise the work of other employees, or tell them what work to do?

1. YES | 5. NO (GO TO D10)

D8. About how many people do you supervise?

_______ (NUMBER)

D9. Do you have any say about their pay or promotion?

1. YES | 5. NO

D10. Does your boss have a supervisor over him or her?

1. YES | 5. NO

(GO TO D22)

[2. BOTH SOMEONE ELSE AND SELF]

D11. When you work for others, do you work for the federal, state or local government?

1. YES | 5. NO

D12. When you work for others, do you supervise the work of other employees, or tell them what work to do?

1. YES | 5. NO (GO TO D15)

D13. About how many people do you supervise?

_______ (NUMBER)

D14. Do you have any say about their pay or promotion?

1. YES | 5. NO

D15. Does your boss have a supervisor over him or her?

1. YES | 5. NO

D16. Is your own business incorporated?

1. YES | 4. NO | 8. DK

D17. When you work for yourself, do you employ other people?

1. YES | 5. NO (GO TO D22)

D18. How many? _______ (NUMBER)

(GO TO D22)

[3. SELF ONLY]

D19. Is your business incorporated?

1. YES | 5. NO | 8. DK

D20. Do you employ other people?

1. YES | 5. NO (TURN TO PAGE 7, D25)

D21. How many? _______ (NUMBER)

(TURN TO PAGE 7, D25)

D22. Is your current job covered by a union contract?

1. YES | 5. NO (GO TO D24)

D23. Do you belong to that labor union? 1. YES | 2. NO

D24. How long have you worked for your present employer? _______ (MONTHS) _______ (YEARS)

7

D25. How much formal education is required to get a job like yours?

____

D26. Do you (also) have to have some work experience or special training to get a job like yours?

1. YES | 5. NO → (GO TO D28)

D27. What kind of experience or special training is that?

____

D28. On a job like yours, how long would it take the average new person to become fully trained and qualified?

_______ YEARS OR _______ MONTHS

D29. Do you feel you are learning things on your job that could lead to a better job or to a promotion?

1. YES | 5. NO

D30. Do you have some skills or job experience that you cannot use on your present job?

1. YES | 5. NO → (GO TO D32)

D31. Do you think you might want to get a job some day which used that skill or experience?

1. YES | 5. NO

D32. How long have you had your present position? _______________

IF LESS THAN ONE YEAR | IF ONE YEAR OR MORE → (TURN TO PAGE 8, D38)

D33. What month did you start this job? _______________

D34. What happened to the job you had before--did the company go out of business, were you laid off, promoted, were you not working, or what?

____

_______________ 5. NO PREVIOUS JOB (TURN TO PAGE 8, D38)

D35. On the whole, would you say your present job is better or worse than the one you had before?

1. BETTER | 5. WORSE | 3. SAME → (GO TO D37)

D36. Why is it (better/worse)? _______________

____

____

D37. Does your present job pay more than the one you had before?

1. YES, MORE | 5. NO, SAME OR LESS

(TURN TO PAGE 8, D38)

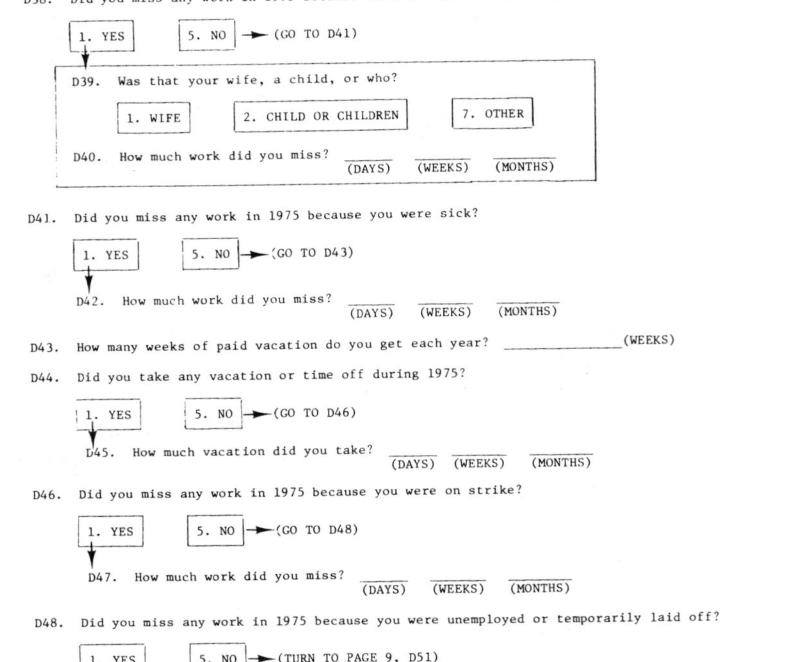

8

D38. Did you miss any work in 1975 because someone else in the family was sick?

[1. YES] [5. NO] → (GO TO D41)

D39. Was that your wife, a child, or who?

[1. WIFE] [2. CHILD OR CHILDREN] [7. OTHER]

D40. How much work did you miss? ______ (DAYS) ______ (WEEKS) ______ (MONTHS)

D41. Did you miss any work in 1975 because you were sick?

[1. YES] [5. NO] → (GO TO D43)

D42. How much work did you miss? ______ (DAYS) ______ (WEEKS) ______ (MONTHS)

D43. How many weeks of paid vacation do you get each year? ______________ (WEEKS)

D44. Did you take any vacation or time off during 1975?

[1. YES] [5. NO] → (GO TO D46)

D45. How much vacation did you take? ______ (DAYS) ______ (WEEKS) ______ (MONTHS)

D46. Did you miss any work in 1975 because you were on strike?

[1. YES] [5. NO] → (GO TO D48)

D47. How much work did you miss? ______ (DAYS) ______ (WEEKS) ______ (MONTHS)

D48. Did you miss any work in 1975 because you were unemployed or temporarily laid off?

[1. YES] [5. NO] → (TURN TO PAGE 9, D51)

D49. How much work did you miss? ______ (DAYS) ______ (WEEKS) ______ (MONTHS)

D50. Were those periods of unemployment or layoff all in one stretch, in two periods, or more than two?

[1. ALL IN ONE STRETCH] [3. TWO PERIODS] [5. MORE THAN TWO]

9

D51. Then, how many weeks did you actually work on your main job in 1975? ______ (WEEKS)

D52. And, on the average, how many hours a week did you work on your main job in 1975?

____

D53. Did you have any overtime which isn't included in that?

[1. YES] [5. NO] → (GO TO D55)

D54. How many hours did that overtime amount to in 1975? ______ (HOURS)

D55. Are you salaried, paid by the hour, or what?

[1. SALARIED]

D56. How much is your salary?

$__________ per __________

D57. If you were to work more hours than usual during some week, would you get paid for those extra hours of work?

[1. YES] [5. NO] (GO TO D63)

D58. About how much would you make per hour for that overtime?

$__________ (PER HOUR)

(GO TO D63)

[3. PAID BY HOUR]

D59. What is your hourly wage rate for your regular work time?

$__________ (PER HOUR)

D60. What is your hourly wage rate for overtime?

$__________ (PER HOUR)

(GO TO D63)

[7. OTHER]

D61. How is that?

____

____

____

____

D62. If you worked an extra hour, how much would you earn for that hour?

$__________

(GO TO D63)

D63. How many employee retirement or pension plans are you covered by, including Social Security?

[0. NONE] [1. ONE] [2. TWO] [3. THREE] [4. FOUR OR MORE] [8. DON'T KNOW]

10

D64. Did you have any extra jobs or other ways of making money in addition to your main job in 1975?

1. YES   5. NO → (GO TO D70)   OCC

D65. What did you do? ____________________

D66. Anything else? ____________________

D67. About how much did you make per hour at this? $__________(PER HOUR)

D68. And how many weeks did you work on your extra job(s) in 1975? ______ (WEEKS)

D69. On the average, how many hours a week did you work on your extra job(s)? ____________________(HOURS PER WEEK)

D70. Was there more work available (on your job/any of your jobs) so that you could have worked more if you had wanted to?

1. YES   5. NO OR DON'T KNOW

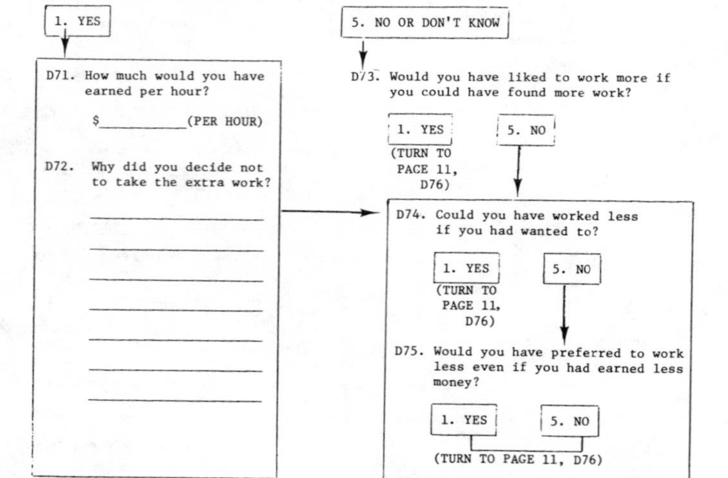

D71. How much would you have earned per hour?

$__________(PER HOUR)

D72. Why did you decide not to take the extra work?

D73. Would you have liked to work more if you could have found more work?

1. YES (TURN TO PACE 11, D76)   5. NO

D74. Could you have worked less if you had wanted to?

1. YES (TURN TO PAGE 11, D76)   5. NO

D75. Would you have preferred to work less even if you had earned less money?

1. YES   5. NO

(TURN TO PAGE 11, D76)

11

D76. About how much time does it take you to get to work each day, door to door?

__________(ONE WAY)   NONE → (GO TO D79)

D77. About how many miles is it to where you work? __________(ONE WAY)

D78. Do you use public transportation to get to work, have a car pool, drive by yourself, walk, drive with your wife, or what?

1. PUBLIC TRANSPORTATION   2. CAR POOL   3. DRIVE   4. WALK   5. DRIVE WITH WIFE   7. OTHER (SPECIFY) ______

D79. If you should lose your present job, what would you say were your chances for finding another job just as good as your present job in all respects? Would they be very good, good, not so good, or not good at all?

1. VERY GOOD   2. GOOD   4. NOT SO GOOD   5. NOT GOOD AT ALL

D80. Do you think you will keep on working for the next few years, or do you plan to quit?

1. KEEP ON WORKING (TURN TO PAGE 12, D84)   5. PLAN TO QUIT

D81. Why might you stop working?

D82. Would you then go back to work later?

1. YES   5. NO → (TURN TO PAGE 12, D84)

D83. When might you go back?

____

(TURN TO PAGE 12, D84)

D84. Are there better jobs you could get if you were willing to move and live somewhere else?

[1. YES] [5. NO] [8. DON'T KNOW]

D85. Are there better jobs around here that you might get if you were willing to go farther to work or work different hours?

[1. YES] [5. NO] [8. DON'T KNOW]

D86. Thinking back to when you started your present job, were there some limitations on where you could work or what hours you could work that were factors in taking this job?

[1. YES] [5. NO] → (GO TO D88)

↓ D87. What were these limitations? ____________________

____

____

D88. If you were to get enough money to live as comfortably as you would like for the rest of your life, would you continue to work?

[1. YES] [5. NO] [8. DON'T KNOW]

(TURN TO PAGE 19, G1)

E1. What kind of job are you looking for? ____________________

____

E2. What do you think your chances will be for getting a good job in that line of work--are they very good, good, not so good, or not good at all?

[1. VERY GOOD] [2. GOOD] [4. NOT SO GOOD] [5. NOT GOOD AT ALL]

E3. How much would you expect to earn? $__________ PER __________

E4. Will you have to get any training to qualify? ____________________

E5. Have you been doing anything in the last four weeks to find a job?

[1. YES] [5. NO] → GO TO E7

↓ E6. How many places have you been to in the last four weeks to find out about a job?

[0. NONE] [1. ONE] [2. TWO] [3. THREE] [4. FOUR] [5. FIVE OR MORE]

E7. Are there any limitations on where you could work or what hours you could work that would be factors in your taking a job?

[1. YES] [5. NO] → GO TO E9

↓ E8. What are these limitations? ____________________

____

E9. Are there jobs you could get if you were willing to move and live somewhere else?

[1. YES] [5. NO] [8. DON'T KNOW]

E10. How long have you been looking for work? ____________________

E11. Have you ever had a job?

[1. YES] [5. NO] → TURN TO PAGE 15, E34

↓

E12. What sort of work did you do on your last job? (What was your occupation?)

____________________ OCC [|] IND [|]

E13. What kind of business was that in?

____

E14. Did you supervise the work of other employees or tell them what to do?

[1. YES] [5. NO]

E15. What happened to that job--did the company go out of business, were you laid off or what? ____________________

14

E16. When did you last work? ______________________

[IF 1975 OR 1976] [IF BEFORE 1975] → (TURN TO PAGE 15, E34)

E17. Did you take any vacation or time off during 1975?

[1. YES] [5. NO] → (GO TO E19)

E18. How much vacation did you take? ______ (DAYS) ______ (WEEKS) ______ (MONTHS)

E19. Did you miss any work in 1975 because someone else in the family was sick?

[1. YES] [5. NO] → (GO TO E22)

E20. Was that person your wife, a child, or who?

[1. WIFE] [2. CHILD OR CHILDREN] [7. OTHER]

E21. How much work did you miss? ______ (DAYS) ______ (WEEKS) ______ (MONTHS)

E22. Did you miss any work in 1975 because you were sick?

[1. YES] [5. NO] → (GO TO E24)

E23. How much work did you miss? ______ (DAYS) ______ (WEEKS) ______ (MONTHS)

E24. Did you miss any work in 1975 because you were on strike?

[1. YES] [5. NO] → (GO TO E26)

E25. How much work did you miss? ______ (DAYS) ______ (WEEKS) ______ (MONTHS)

E26. Did you miss any work in 1975 because you were unemployed or temporarily laid off?

[1. YES] [5. NO] → (TURN TO PAGE 15, E29)

E27. How much work did you miss? ______ (DAYS) ______ (WEEKS) ______ (MONTHS)

E28. Were those weeks of unemployment all in one stretch, in two periods, or more than two?

[1. ALL IN ONE STRETCH] [3. TWO PERIODS] [5. MORE THAN TWO]

15

E29. Then, how many weeks did you actually work on your job in 1975?

______________ (WEEKS)

E30. And, on average, how many hours a week did you work when you worked?

______________ (HOURS PER WEEK)

E31. On your last job, how much time did it take you to get to work each day, door to door?

______________ (ONE WAY) [0. NONE] → (GO TO E34)

E32. About how many miles was it to where you worked? ______________ (ONE WAY)

E33. Did you use public transportation to get to work, have a car pool, drive by yourself, walk, drive with your wife, or what?

[1. PUBLIC TRANSPORTATION] [2. CAR POOL] [3. DRIVE] [4. WALK] [5. DRIVE WITH WIFE] [7. OTHER (SPECIFY) ______]

E34. If you were to get enough money to live as comfortably as you would like for the rest of your life, would you work?

[1. YES] [5. NO] [8. DON'T KNOW]

(TURN TO PAGE 19, G1)

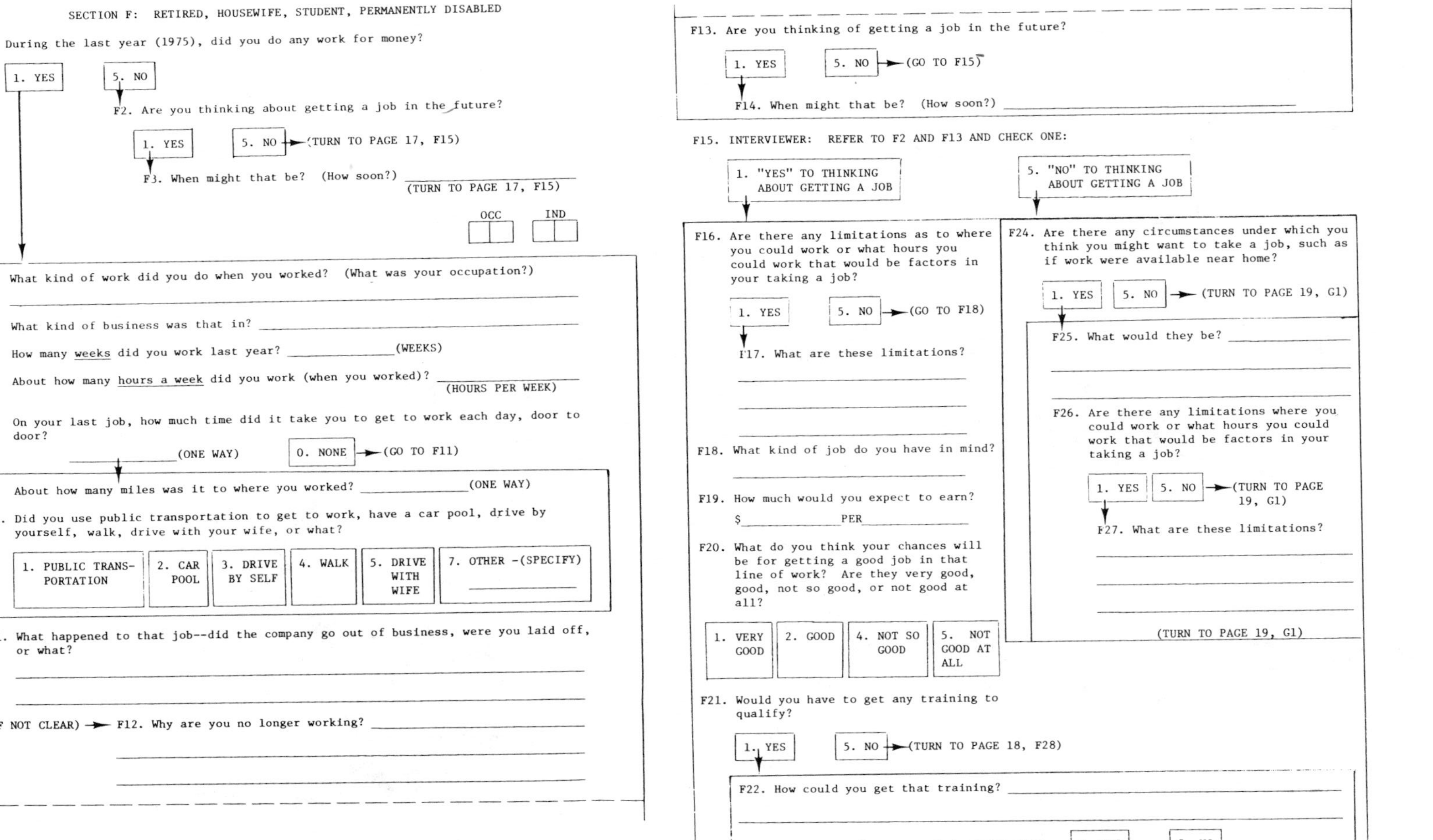

16

SECTION F: RETIRED, HOUSEWIFE, STUDENT, PERMANENTLY DISABLED

F1. During the last year (1975), did you do any work for money?

1. YES (GO TO F4) | 5. NO

F2. Are you thinking about getting a job in the future?

1. YES | 5. NO → (TURN TO PAGE 17, F15)

F3. When might that be? (How soon?) ________ (TURN TO PAGE 17, F15)

OCC ☐☐ IND ☐☐

F4. What kind of work did you do when you worked? (What was your occupation?)

F5. What kind of business was that in? ________

F6. How many <u>weeks</u> did you work last year? ________ (WEEKS)

F7. About how many <u>hours a week</u> did you work (when you worked)? ________ (HOURS PER WEEK)

F8. On your last job, how much time did it take you to get to work each day, door to door?

________ (ONE WAY) | 0. NONE → (GO TO F11)

F9. About how many miles was it to where you worked? ________ (ONE WAY)

F10. Did you use public transportation to get to work, have a car pool, drive by yourself, walk, drive with your wife, or what?

1. PUBLIC TRANS-PORTATION	2. CAR POOL	3. DRIVE BY SELF	4. WALK	5. DRIVE WITH WIFE	7. OTHER -(SPECIFY)

F11. What happened to that job--did the company go out of business, were you laid off, or what?

(IF NOT CLEAR) → F12. Why are you no longer working? ________

17

F13. Are you thinking of getting a job in the future?

1. YES | 5. NO → (GO TO F15)

F14. When might that be? (How soon?) ________

F15. INTERVIEWER: REFER TO F2 AND F13 AND CHECK ONE:

1. "YES" TO THINKING ABOUT GETTING A JOB (GO TO F16) | 5. "NO" TO THINKING ABOUT GETTING A JOB (GO TO F24)

F16. Are there any limitations as to where you could work or what hours you could work that would be factors in your taking a job?

1. YES | 5. NO → (GO TO F18)

F17. What are these limitations?

F18. What kind of job do you have in mind?

F19. How much would you expect to earn?

$________ PER ________

F20. What do you think your chances will be for getting a good job in that line of work? Are they very good, good, not so good, or not good at all?

1. VERY GOOD	2. GOOD	4. NOT SO GOOD	5. NOT GOOD AT ALL

F21. Would you have to get any training to qualify?

1. YES | 5. NO → (TURN TO PAGE 18, F28)

F22. How could you get that training? ________

F23. Are you getting any such training now? 1. YES | 5. NO

F24. Are there any circumstances under which you think you might want to take a job, such as if work were available near home?

1. YES | 5. NO → (TURN TO PAGE 19, G1)

F25. What would they be? ________

F26. Are there any limitations where you could work or what hours you could work that would be factors in your taking a job?

1. YES | 5. NO → (TURN TO PAGE 19, G1)

F27. What are these limitations?

(TURN TO PAGE 19, G1)

F28. Have you been doing anything in the last four weeks to find a job?

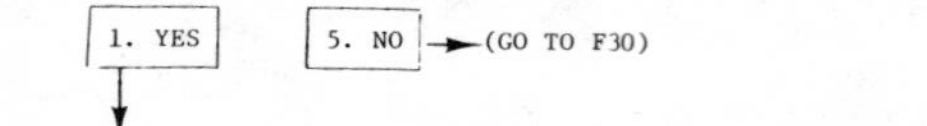

F29. How many places have you been to in the last four weeks to find out about a job?

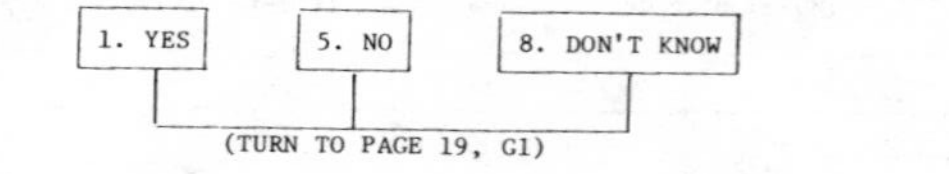

F30. Are there jobs you could get if you were willing to move and live somewhere else?

1. YES | 5. NO | 8. DON'T KNOW

(TURN TO PAGE 19, G1)

SECTION G: WIFE'S WORK, HOUSEWORK AND FOOD

(ASK EVERYONE)

G1. Are you married, single, widowed, divorced, or separated?

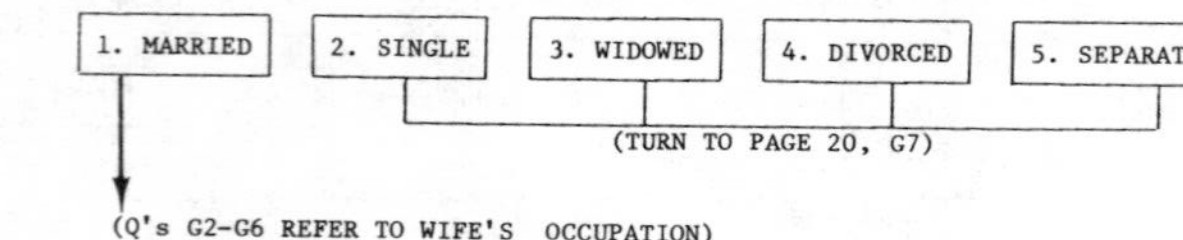

(Q's G2-G6 REFER TO WIFE'S OCCUPATION)

G2. Did your wife do any work for money in 1975?

1. YES | 5. NO → (TURN TO PAGE 20, G7)

OCC | IND

G3. What kind of work did she do? __________

G4. What kind of business is that in? __________

G5. About how many weeks did she work last year? __________

G6. And about how many hours a week did she work? __________

G7. About how much time do you (HEAD) spend on housework in an average week--I mean time spent cooking, cleaning, and doing other work around the house?

______________ HOURS PER WEEK

G8. INTERVIEWER: CHECK ONE

[FU INCLUDES PEOPLE OTHER THAN HEAD AND WIFE]

[0. ONLY HEAD OR HEAD AND WIFE IN FU] → (TURN TO PAGE 21, G13)

G9. Does anyone else here in the household (not including your wife) help with the housework?

[1. YES] [5. NO] → (TURN TO PAGE 21, G13)

	Person #1		Person #2		Person #3	
G10. Who is that?	(RELATION-SHIP TO HEAD)	(AGE)	(RELATION-SHIP TO HEAD)	(AGE)	(RELATION-SHIP TO HEAD)	(AGE)
G11. About how much time does (he/she) spend on housework in an average week?	______		______		______	

G12. Anyone else? [ ] YES → (ASK G10-11 ABOVF) [ ] NO → (TURN TO PAGE 21, G13)

G13. How much do you (FAMILY) spend on food that you use at home in an average week?

$______________(PER WEEK)

G14. Do you have any food delivered to the door which isn't included in that?

[YES] [NO] → GO TO G16

G15. How much do you spend on that food? $________ per________ (WEEK, MONTH)

G16. Did you or anyone else now living in your family receive or buy government food stamps last month?

[YES] [NO] → GO TO G21

G17. For how many members of your family were stamps issued? ________

G18. How much did you pay for the stamps? $________ per________ (WEEK, MONTH)

G19. How much food could you buy with the stamps? $________ per________ (WEEK, MONTH)

G20. You said you spend ______________ (MENTION AMOUNT IN G13) on food in the average week.

Did you include in that only the amount of money you actually spent or did you also include the extra value of the food you get with stamps?

[1. INCLUDES ONLY AMOUNT OF MONEY SPENT]

[5. ALSO INCLUDES EXTRA VALUE OF FOOD GOT WITH STAMPS (i.e., MONEY SPENT PLUS VALUE OF STAMPS)]

G21. Did you (FAMILY) use government food stamps (commodity stamps) in 1975?

[YES] [NO] → GO TO G26

G22. How much did you pay for the stamps in 1975? $________ per ________ (WEEK, MONTH)

G23. How much food could you buy with the stamps in 1975?

$________ per________ (WEEK, MONTH)

G24. Did you use food stamps regularly during all of 1975?

[YES] → GO TO G26 [NO]

G25. For how many months did you use food stamps in 1975?

________ MONTHS → (GO TO G26)

G26. About how much do you (FAMILY) spend eating out, not counting meals at work or at school?

$________ per ________ (WEEK, MONTH)

(ASK EVERYONE)

To get an accurate financial picture of people all over the country, we need to know the income of all the families that we interview.

H1. (INTERVIEWER: CHECK ONE)

1. FARMER, OR RANCHER | 5. NOT A FARMER OR RANCHER → (GO TO H5)

H2. What were your total receipts from farming in 1975, including soil bank payments and commodity credit loans? $________ A

H3. What were your total operating expenses, not counting living expenses? $________ B

H4. That left you a net income from farming of? A-B = $________ A-B

H5. Did you (R AND FAMILY) own a business at any time in 1975, or have a financial interest in any business enterprise?

1. YES | 5. NO → (GO TO H8)

H6. Is it a corporation or an unincorporated business, or do you have an interest in both kinds?

1. CORPORATION → (GO TO H8)
2. UNINCORPORATED
3. BOTH
8. DON'T KNOW

H7. How much was your (FAMILY'S) share of the total income from the business in 1975 -- that is, the amount you took out plus any profit left in?

$________

(ASK EVERYONE)

H8. How much did you (HEAD) receive from wages and salaries in 1975, that is, before anything was deducted for taxes or other things?

$________

H9. In addition to this, did you have any income from bonuses, overtime or commissions?

YES | NO → (GO TO H11)

H10. How much was that? $________

H11. Did you (HEAD) receive any other income in 1975 from:

(IF "YES" TO ANY ITEM, ASK "How much was it?" ENTER AMOUNT AT RIGHT)

(IF "NO" ENTER "0")

a) professional practice or trade?	$________	per ________
b) farming or market gardening, roomers or boarders?	$________	per ________
c) dividends, interest, rent, trust funds, or royalties?	$________	per ________
d) ADC, AFDC?	$________	per ________
e) other welfare?	$________	per ________
f) Social Security?	$________	per ________
g) other retirement pay, pensions, or annuities?	$________	per ________
h) unemployment, or workmen's compensation	$________	per ________
i) alimony? child support?	$________	per ________
j) help from relatives?	$________	per ________
k) the new Supplemental Security Income, the gold (tan, yellow) checks?	$________	per ________
m) anything else? ________ (SPECIFY)	$________	per ________

H12. Did anyone (else) not living here now help you (FAMILY) out financially -- I mean give you money, or help with your expenses during 1975?

YES | NO → (TURN TO PAGE 25, H14)

H13. How much did that amount to last year? $________

(DO NOT WRITE IN THIS SPACE)
HEAD TYPE INCOME:
L A T

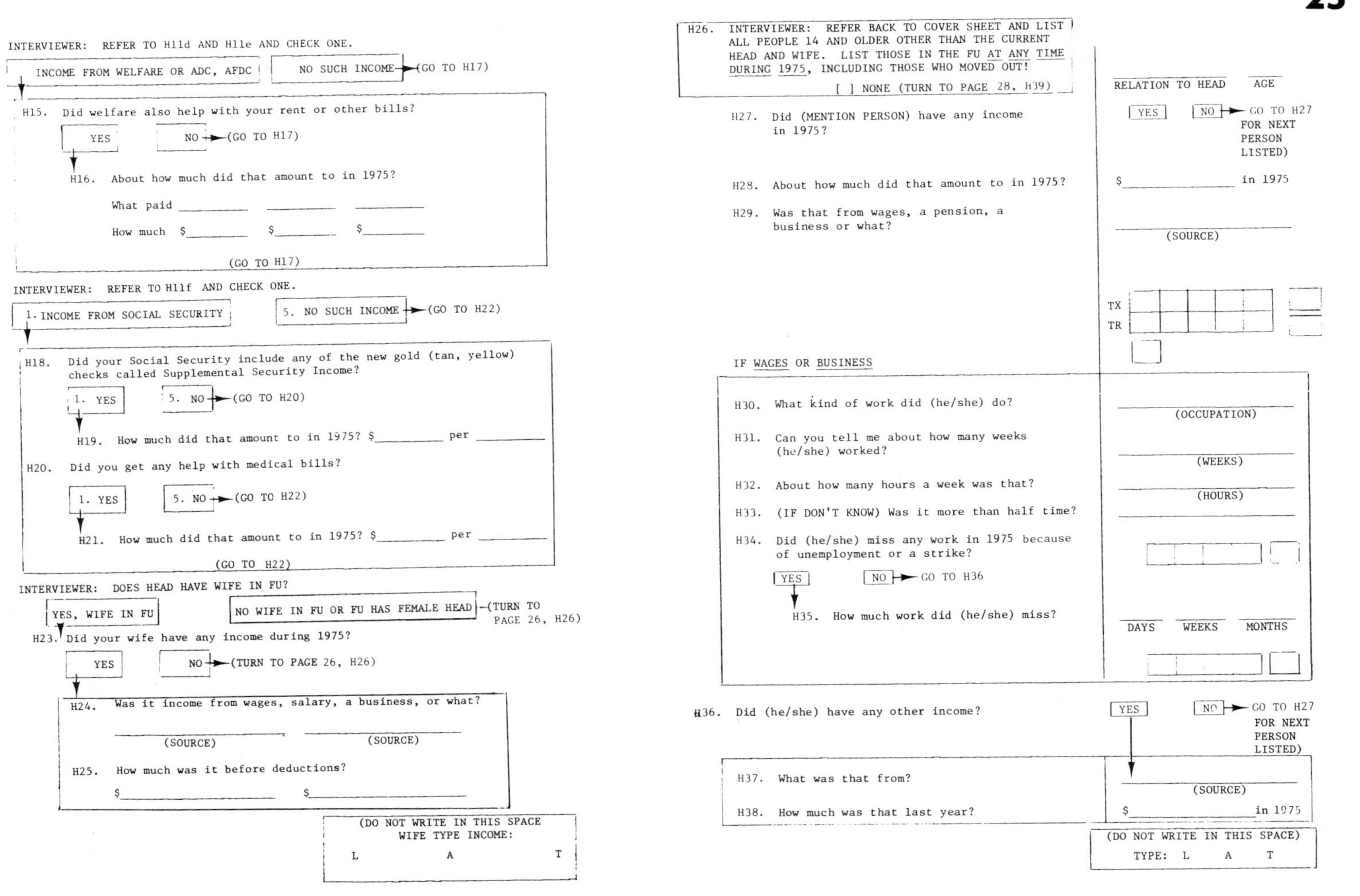

24

H14. INTERVIEWER: REFER TO H11d AND H11e AND CHECK ONE.

[INCOME FROM WELFARE OR ADC, AFDC] [NO SUCH INCOME] → (GO TO H17)

H15. Did welfare also help with your rent or other bills?

[YES] [NO] → (GO TO H17)

H16. About how much did that amount to in 1975?

What paid ________ ________ ________

How much $________ $________ $________

(GO TO H17)

H17. INTERVIEWER: REFER TO H11f AND CHECK ONE.

[1. INCOME FROM SOCIAL SECURITY] [5. NO SUCH INCOME] → (GO TO H22)

H18. Did your Social Security include any of the new gold (tan, yellow) checks called Supplemental Security Income?

[1. YES] [5. NO] → (GO TO H20)

H19. How much did that amount to in 1975? $________ per ________

H20. Did you get any help with medical bills?

[1. YES] [5. NO] → (GO TO H22)

H21. How much did that amount to in 1975? $________ per ________

(GO TO H22)

H22. INTERVIEWER: DOES HEAD HAVE WIFE IN FU?

[YES, WIFE IN FU] [NO WIFE IN FU OR FU HAS FEMALE HEAD] → (TURN TO PAGE 26, H26)

H23. Did your wife have any income during 1975?

[YES] [NO] → (TURN TO PAGE 26, H26)

H24. Was it income from wages, salary, a business, or what?

________ (SOURCE) ________ (SOURCE)

H25. How much was it before deductions?

$________ $________

(DO NOT WRITE IN THIS SPACE
WIFE TYPE INCOME:
L A T

25

H26. INTERVIEWER: REFER BACK TO COVER SHEET AND LIST ALL PEOPLE 14 AND OLDER OTHER THAN THE CURRENT HEAD AND WIFE. LIST THOSE IN THE FU AT ANY TIME DURING 1975, INCLUDING THOSE WHO MOVED OUT!

[ ] NONE (TURN TO PAGE 28, H39)

RELATION TO HEAD ________ AGE ________

H27. Did (MENTION PERSON) have any income in 1975?

[YES] [NO] → GO TO H27 FOR NEXT PERSON LISTED)

H28. About how much did that amount to in 1975? $________ in 1975

H29. Was that from wages, a pension, a business or what?

________ (SOURCE)

TX

TR

IF WAGES OR BUSINESS

H30. What kind of work did (he/she) do? ________ (OCCUPATION)

H31. Can you tell me about how many weeks (he/she) worked? ________ (WEEKS)

H32. About how many hours a week was that? ________ (HOURS)

H33. (IF DON'T KNOW) Was it more than half time? ________

H34. Did (he/she) miss any work in 1975 because of unemployment or a strike?

[YES] [NO] → GO TO H36

H35. How much work did (he/she) miss?

DAYS WEEKS MONTHS

H36. Did (he/she) have any other income?

[YES] [NO] → GO TO H27 FOR NEXT PERSON LISTED)

H37. What was that from? ________ (SOURCE)

H38. How much was that last year? $________ in 1975

(DO NOT WRITE IN THIS SPACE)
TYPE: L A T

RELATION TO HEAD AGE

[ ] YES [ ] NO → (GO TO H27 FOR NEXT PERSON LISTED)

$ ____ in 1975

(SOURCE)

TX

TR

(OCCUPATION)

(WEEKS)

(HOURS)

DAYS WEEKS MONTHS

[ ] YES [ ] NO → (GO TO H27 FOR NEXT PERSON LISTED)

(SOURCE)

$ ____ in 1975

RELATION TO HEAD AGE

[ ] YES [ ] NO → (GO TO H27 FOR NEXT PERSON LISTED)

$ ____ in 1975

(SOURCE)

TX

TR

(OCCUPATION)

(WEEKS)

(HOURS)

DAYS WEEKS MONTHS

[ ] YES [ ] NO → (GO TO H27 FOR NEXT PERSON LISTED)

(SOURCE)

$ ____ in 1975

RELATION TO HEAD AGE

[ ] YES [ ] NO → (GO TO H27 FOR NEXT PERSON LISTED)

$ ____ in 1975

(SOURCE)

TX

TR

(OCCUPATION)

(WEEKS)

(HOURS)

DAYS WEEKS MONTHS

[ ] YES [ ] NO → (GO TO H27 FOR NEXT PERSON LISTED)

(SOURCE)

$ ____ in 1975

(D O N O T W R I T E I N T H I S S P A C E)

TYPE: L A T | TYPE: L A T | TYPE: L A T

(T U R N T O P A G E 2 8, H 3 9)

(ASK EVERYONE)

H39. Did anyone else living here in 1975 have any income? (INCLUDING CHILDREN UNDER 14)

YES NO → (GO TO H41)

H40. Who was that?

RELATION TO HEAD AGE RELATION TO HEAD AGE RELATION TO HEAD AGE

(TURN BACK AND ASK H27-H38 FOR THESE ADDITIONAL MEMBERS)

H41. Did you get any other money in 1975 -- like a big settlement from an insurance company, or an inheritance?

1. YES 5. NO → (GO TO H43)

H42. How much did that amount to? $____ in 1975

H43. Do you help support anyone who doesn't live here with you?

1. YES 5. NO → (GO TO H48)

H44. How many? ____

H45. How much money did that amount to in the last year? $____ in 1975

H46. Were any of these people dependent on you for more than half of their total support?

1. YES 5. NO → (GO TO H48)

H47. How many? ____

H48. Do you belong to a labor union?

1. YES 5. NO

H49. Do you have any physical or nervous condition that limits the type of work or the amount of work you can do?

1. YES 5. NO → (GO TO H51)

H50. How much does it limit your work? ____

H51. Is there anyone (else) in this family who requires a lot of extra care because of (his/her) condition?

1. YES 5. NO → (TURN TO PAGE 29, J1)

H52. Who is that? ____ (RELATION TO HEAD) ____ (AGE)

SECTION J: WORK HISTORY

J1. How many years have you (HEAD) worked since you were 18?

_______ YEARS   [00. NONE] → (TURN TO PAGE 31, K1)

J2. How many of these years did you work full time for most of the year?

_______ (NUMBER OF YEARS)   [ALL] → (GO TO J4)

J3. During the years that you were not working full time, how much of the time did you work? _______

J4. Some people have stopped their regular work for a time for such things as military service, family responsibilities, or to go back to school. Have you ever stopped working for a year or more for any of these or other reasons and then gone back to work?

[1. YES]   [5. NO] → (TURN TO PAGE 31, K1)

J5. Was that only one period, or were there several periods of a year or more when you were not working?

[1. ONE PERIOD]   [2. SEVERAL PERIODS]

J6. When was the period you were not working? From when to when?

_______ (MONTH, YEAR) to _______ (MONTH, YEAR)

J7. What was the most recent period you were not working? From when to when?

_______ (MONTH, YEAR) to _______ (MONTH, YEAR)

[IF BEFORE 1955, TURN TO PAGE 31, K1]

J8. For what reasons did you stop working the last time? _______

J9. Did you get any training or skills during the time you were not working that you could use in a job?

[1. YES]   [5. NO]

J10. Why did you go back to work when you did? _______

J11. Did you go back to the same kind of work you had done before?

[1. YES]   [5. NO]

J12. Was it the same job?

[1. YES]   [5. NO]

J13. How did you find the job when you went back to work? Was it through a friend, an employment agency, a want ad, or what?

J14. How did you get the skills or qualifications for the job? Was it your regular education, previous work experience, some special training, or what?

J15. About how much did you earn when you went back to work?

$_______ per _______ (HOUR/WEEK/MONTH/YEAR)

J16. About how much would you have been earning at that time if you had been working all along?

$_______ per _______ (HOUR/WEEK/MONTH/YEAR)

J17. Why is that? _______

INTERVIEWER: REMEMBER TO FILL OUT "BY OBSERVATION" SECTION ON ALL INTERVIEWS

SECTION K: NEW HEAD

K1. INTERVIEWER: CHECK ONE

[1. FU HAS A NEW HEAD THIS YEAR] [5. THIS FU HAS THE SAME HEAD AS IN 1975] (TURN TO PAGE 34, L1)

K2. Now I have some questions about your family and past experiences. Where did your father and mother grow up? (FROM BIRTH TO 18 YEARS OF AGE)

ST, CO- FA [ ][ ][ ][ ][ ] Father: ______ (State if U.S., Country if foreign) ______ (COUNTY OR TOWN)

ST, CO- MO [ ][ ][ ][ ][ ] Mother: ______ (State if U.S., Country if foreign) ______ (COUNTY OR TOWN)

K3. What was your father's usual occupation when you were growing up? OCC [ ]

______

K4. Thinking of your (HEAD'S) first full time regular job, what did you do? OCC [ ]

______ [0. NEVER WORKED] (GO TO K6)

K5. Have you had a number of different kinds of jobs, or have you mostly worked in the same occupation you started in, or what?

______

K6. Do you (HEAD) have any children who don't live with you?

[ ] YES [ ] NO → (GO TO K9)

K7. How many? ______ (NUMBER)

1st [ ][ ]
2nd [ ][ ]
3rd [ ][ ]

K8. When were they born? ______ (YEAR BORN) ______ (YEAR BORN) ______ (YEAR BORN) # [ ][ ]

\# BY 25 [ ]

K9. Did you (HEAD) have any children who are not now living?

[ ] YES [ ] NO → (TURN TO PAGE 32, K11)

K10. When were they born? ______ (YEAR BORN) ______ (YEAR BORN) ______ (YEAR BORN)

K11. How many brothers and sisters did you (HEAD) have? ______ (SPECIFY NUMBER) [0. NONE] (GO TO K13)

K12. Were any of your brothers or sisters older than you?

[1. YES] [5. NO]

K13. Did you (HEAD) grow up on a farm, in a small town, in a large city, or what?

[1. FARM] [2. SMALL TOWN] [3. LARGE CITY] OTHER ______ (SPECIFY)

K14. In what state and county was that (EXAMPLE: ILLINOIS, COOK COUNTY)

ST, CO- H [ ][ ][ ][ ][ ] ______ (STATE) ______ (COUNTY)

(IF DON'T KNOW TO K14) → K15. What was the name of the nearest town? ______ (TOWN)

K16. What other states or countries have you lived in? (Including time spent abroad while in the armed forces.)

______

K17. Have you (HEAD) ever moved out of a community where you were living in order to take a job somewhere else?

[1. YES] → K19 [5. NO]

K18. Have you ever turned down a job because you did not want to move?

[1. YES] [5. NO]

K19. Were your parents poor when you were growing up, pretty well off, or what?

______

K20. How much education did your (HEAD'S) father have? ______

(IF LESS THAN 6 GRADES) → K21. Could he read and write? ______

K22. How much education did your (HEAD'S) mother have? ______

(IF LESS THAN 6 GRADES) → K23. Could she read and write? ______

K24. Are you (HEAD) a veteran?

[1. YES] [5. NO]

K25. How many grades of school did you (HEAD) finish?

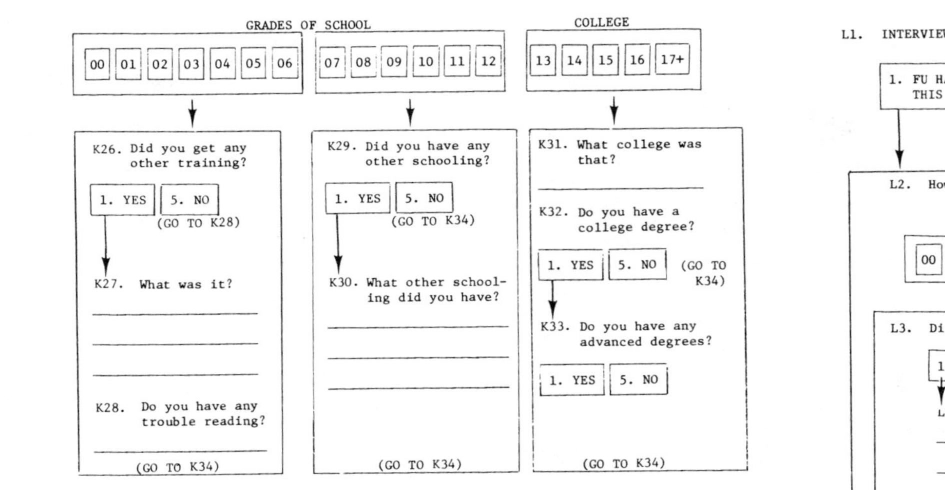

GRADES OF SCHOOL: 00 01 02 03 04 05 06 | 07 08 09 10 11 12

COLLEGE: 13 14 15 16 17+

K26. Did you get any other training?

1. YES → K27. What was it?
5. NO (GO TO K28)

K28. Do you have any trouble reading?

(GO TO K34)

K29. Did you have any other schooling?

1. YES → K30. What other schooling did you have?
5. NO (GO TO K34)

(GO TO K34)

K31. What college was that?

K32. Do you have a college degree?

1. YES → K33. Do you have any advanced degrees?
5. NO (GO TO K34)

1. YES 5. NO

(GO TO K34)

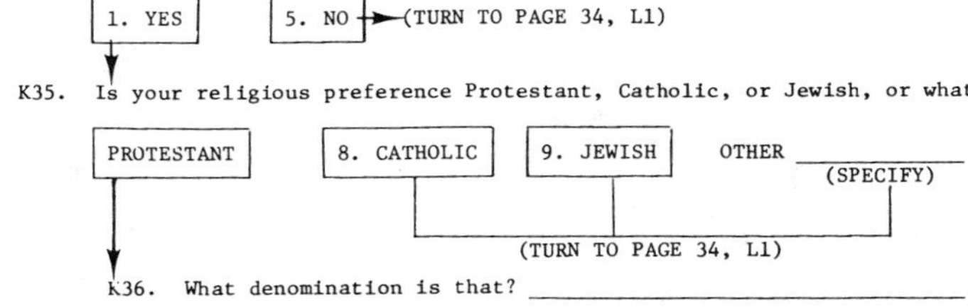

K34. May we record your religious preference?

1. YES
5. NO → (TURN TO PAGE 34, L1)

K35. Is your religious preference Protestant, Catholic, or Jewish, or what?

PROTESTANT → K36
8. CATHOLIC
9. JEWISH
OTHER ________ (SPECIFY)

(TURN TO PAGE 34, L1)

K36. What denomination is that? ____________________

SECTION L: NEW WIFE

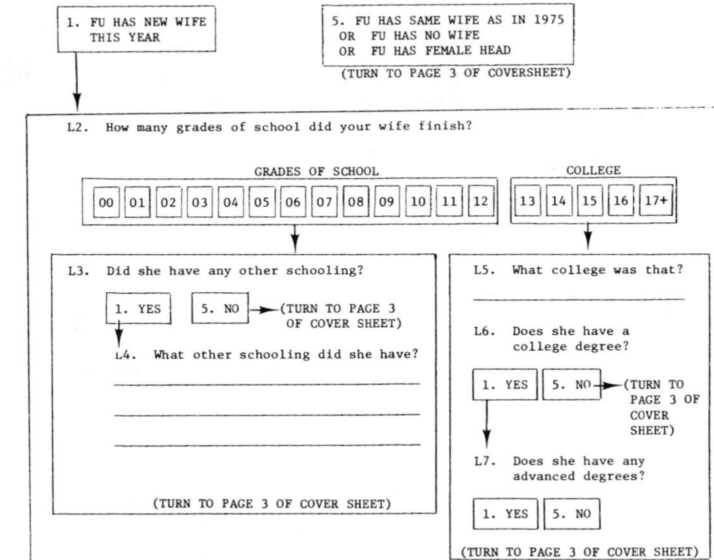

L1. INTERVIEWER: REFER TO COVER SHEET AND CHECK ONE:

1. FU HAS NEW WIFE THIS YEAR → L2

5. FU HAS SAME WIFE AS IN 1975 OR FU HAS NO WIFE OR FU HAS FEMALE HEAD (TURN TO PAGE 3 OF COVERSHEET)

L2. How many grades of school did your wife finish?

GRADES OF SCHOOL: 00 01 02 03 04 05 06 07 08 09 10 11 12

COLLEGE: 13 14 15 16 17+

L3. Did she have any other schooling?

1. YES → L4. What other schooling did she have?
5. NO → (TURN TO PAGE 3 OF COVER SHEET)

(TURN TO PAGE 3 OF COVER SHEET)

L5. What college was that?

L6. Does she have a college degree?

1. YES → L7
5. NO → (TURN TO PAGE 3 OF COVER SHEET)

L7. Does she have any advanced degrees?

1. YES 5. NO

(TURN TO PAGE 3 OF COVER SHEET)

SECTION M: BY OBSERVATION ONLY

M1. Who was respondent (relation to Head)? ______

M2. Number of calls ______

M3. Is this address inside of the city limits of a city of 50,000 or more? (INTERVIEWER: CONSULT ROAD MAP IF NECESSARY)

1. YES

M4. What city is that? ______

M5. How far is this DU from the center of that city?

1. LESS THAN 5 MILES
2. 5-14.9 MILES
3. 15-29.9 MILES
4. 30-49.9 MILES
5. 50 OR MORE MILES

5. NO

M6. What is the nearest city of 50,000 or more? ______

M7. How far is this DU from the center of that city?

1. LESS THAN 5 MILES
2. 5-14.9 MILES
3. 15-29.9 MILES
4. 30-49.9 MILES
5. 50 OR MORE MILES

M8. Is this address inside the city limits of a city of 5,000 or more?

1. YES 5. NO

WIVES

1976

OMB#85-R0224
Exp. Feb 1977

STUDY OF FAMILY ECONOMICS
Project 457680

(Interview Number)

SURVEY RESEARCH CENTER
INSTITUTE FOR SOCIAL RESEARCH
THE UNIVERSITY OF MICHIGAN

'68 Int. '69 Int. '70 Int.
'71 Int. '72 Int. '73 Int.
'74 Int. '75 Int.

(Do not write in above space)

1. Interviewer's Label

2. P.S.U. ______
3. Your Interview No. ______
4. Date ______
5. Length of Interview ______

SECTION A: BACKGROUND

A1. First I have some questions about your family and past experiences. Where did your father and mother grow up? (FROM BIRTH TO 18 YEARS OF AGE)

ST-FA

Father: ______
(State if U.S., Country if foreign)

ST-MO

Mother: ______
(State if U.S., Country if foreign)

A2. What was your father's usual occupation when you were growing up? OCC

______

A3. What was your mother's usual occupation when you were growing up? OCC

______

2

A4. How many brothers and sisters did you have? ______________ (SPECIFY NUMBER) [0. NONE] (GO TO A6)

A5. Were any of your brothers or sisters older than you?

[1. YES] [5. NO]

A6. Did you grow up on a farm, in a small town, in a large city, or what?

[1. FARM] [2. SMALL TOWN] [3. LARGE CITY] OTHER ______________ (SPECIFY)

A7. In what state and county was that? (EXAMPLE: ILLINOIS, COOK COUNTY)

ST, CO- H

______________ (STATE) ______________ (COUNTY)

(IF "DON'T KNOW" TO A7)→ A8. What was the name of the nearest town?

______________ (TOWN)

A9. How much education did your father have? ______________

(IF LESS THAN 6 GRADES)→ A10. Could he read and write? ______________

A11. How much education did your mother have? ______________

(IF LESS THAN 6 GRADES)→ A12. Could she read and write? ______________

3

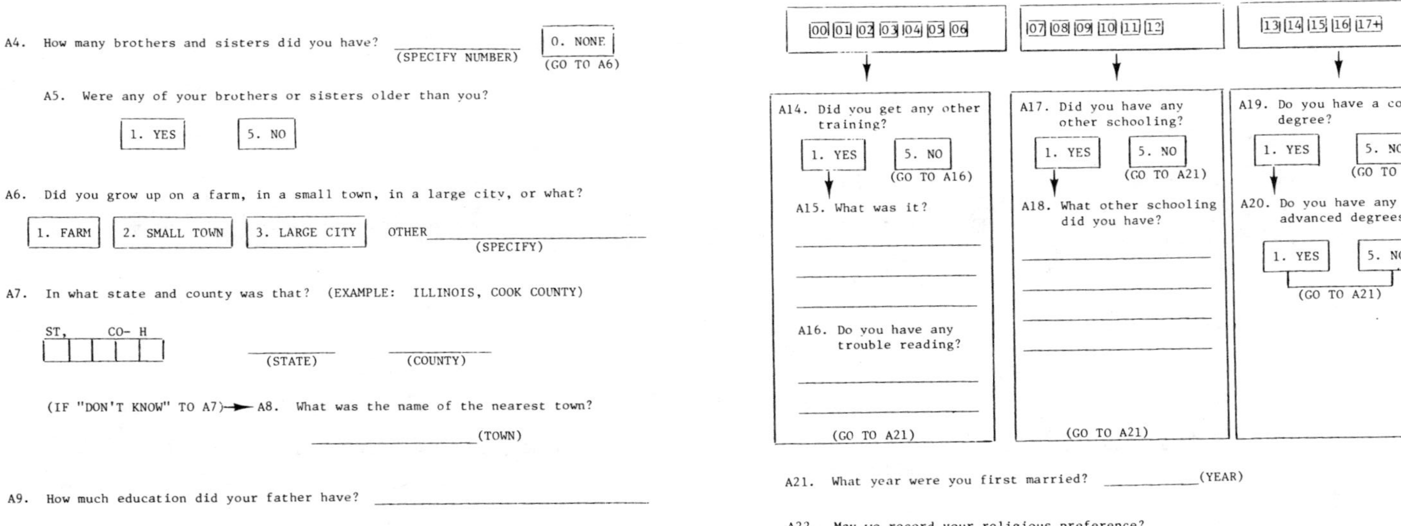

A13. How many grades of school did you finish?

[00] [01] [02] [03] [04] [05] [06] → A14. Did you get any other training? [1. YES] [5. NO] (GO TO A16)

A15. What was it? ______________

A16. Do you have any trouble reading? ______________

(GO TO A21)

[07] [08] [09] [10] [11] [12] → A17. Did you have any other schooling? [1. YES] [5. NO] (GO TO A21)

A18. What other schooling did you have? ______________

(GO TO A21)

[13] [14] [15] [16] [17+] → A19. Do you have a college degree? [1. YES] [5. NO] (GO TO A21)

A20. Do you have any advanced degrees? [1. YES] [5. NO] (GO TO A21)

A21. What year were you first married? ______________ (YEAR)

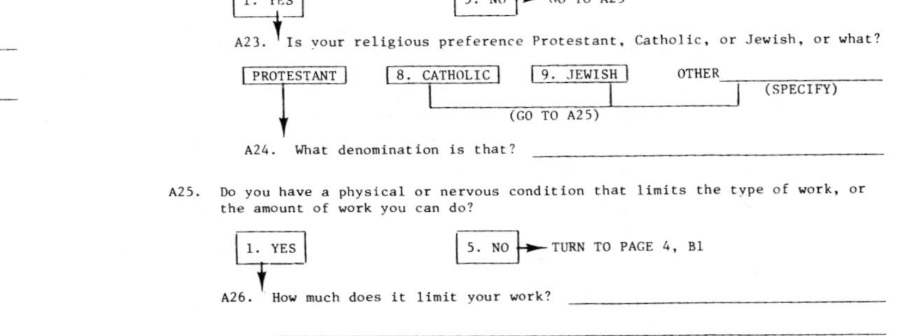

A22. May we record your religious preference?

[1. YES] [5. NO]→ GO TO A25

A23. Is your religious preference Protestant, Catholic, or Jewish, or what?

[PROTESTANT] [8. CATHOLIC] [9. JEWISH] OTHER ______________ (SPECIFY)

(GO TO A25)

A24. What denomination is that? ______________

A25. Do you have a physical or nervous condition that limits the type of work, or the amount of work you can do?

[1. YES] [5. NO]→ TURN TO PAGE 4, B1

A26. How much does it limit your work? ______________

SECTION B: HOUSEWORK

(ASK EVERYONE):

B1. About how much time do you spend on housework in an average week -- I mean time spent cooking, cleaning, and doing other work around the house?

_____________(HOURS PER WEEK)

B2. Do you pay for any help with the housework from someone outside your household?

[1. YES] [5. NO] → GO TO B4

B3. How much does this cost you per week? $__________(PER WEEK)

B4. Are there children under 12 living here with you, or were there in 1975?

[1. CHILD/CHILDREN UNDER 12 IN FAMILY NOW] [3. CHILD/CHILDREN UNDER 12 IN FAMILY IN 1975 BUT NOT NOW] [5. NO CHILDREN UNDER 12 IN FAMILY IN 1975/1976]

(TURN TO PAGE 7, C1)

B5. You said you spend ____________ (ANSWER TO B1) hours a week on housework. Are there times in addition to that when you are looking after the children or taking them places?

[1. YES] [5. NO] → GO TO B7

B6. About how many hours a week would that amount to on the average?

_______________(HOURS PER WEEK)

B7. Are there times when your husband looks after the children or takes them places?

[1. YES] [5. NO] → TURN TO PAGE 5, B9

B8. About how many hours a week would that amount to on the average?

_______________(HOURS PER WEEK)

(TURN TO PAGE 5, B9)

B9. Do you have a job now?

[1. YES] [5. NO] → TURN TO PAGE 6, B20

B10. How (are the children/is the child) taken care of while you work?

____

____

B11. (IF IN SCHOOL) - What about the time (he/she isn't)(they aren't) in school?

____

____

B12. How many hours per week are they taken care of? __________(HOURS PER WEEK)

B13. Do you pay for this with money, doing something in return, or what?

[1. MONEY] [3. BOTH MONEY AND DOING SOMETHING IN RETURN] [5. DOING SOMETHING IN RETURN] [7. OTHER (SPECIFY) ______________ (GO TO B18)]

B14. How much does that cost you per week?

$________ PER WEEK

(GO TO B18)

B15. How much does that cost you per week?

$_________PER WEEK

B16. How much time does that take per week?

________(HOURS PER WEEK)

(GO TO B18)

B17. How much time does that take per week?

__________HOURS PER WEEK

(GO TO B18)

B18. In the past year how many times did someone have to stay home from work to take care of the (children/child) because these arrangements broke down?

[1. FAIRLY OFTEN; 2 OR MORE TIMES PER MONTH] [2. ONCE A MONTH] [3. ONCE IN A WHILE; 3-11 TIMES PER YEAR] [4. RARELY; ONCE OR TWICE A YEAR] [5. NEVER] [9. DON'T KNOW]

(TURN TO PAGE 7, C1)

B19. Who was that? Was it you, your husband, or someone else?

____

(TURN TO PAGE 7, C1)

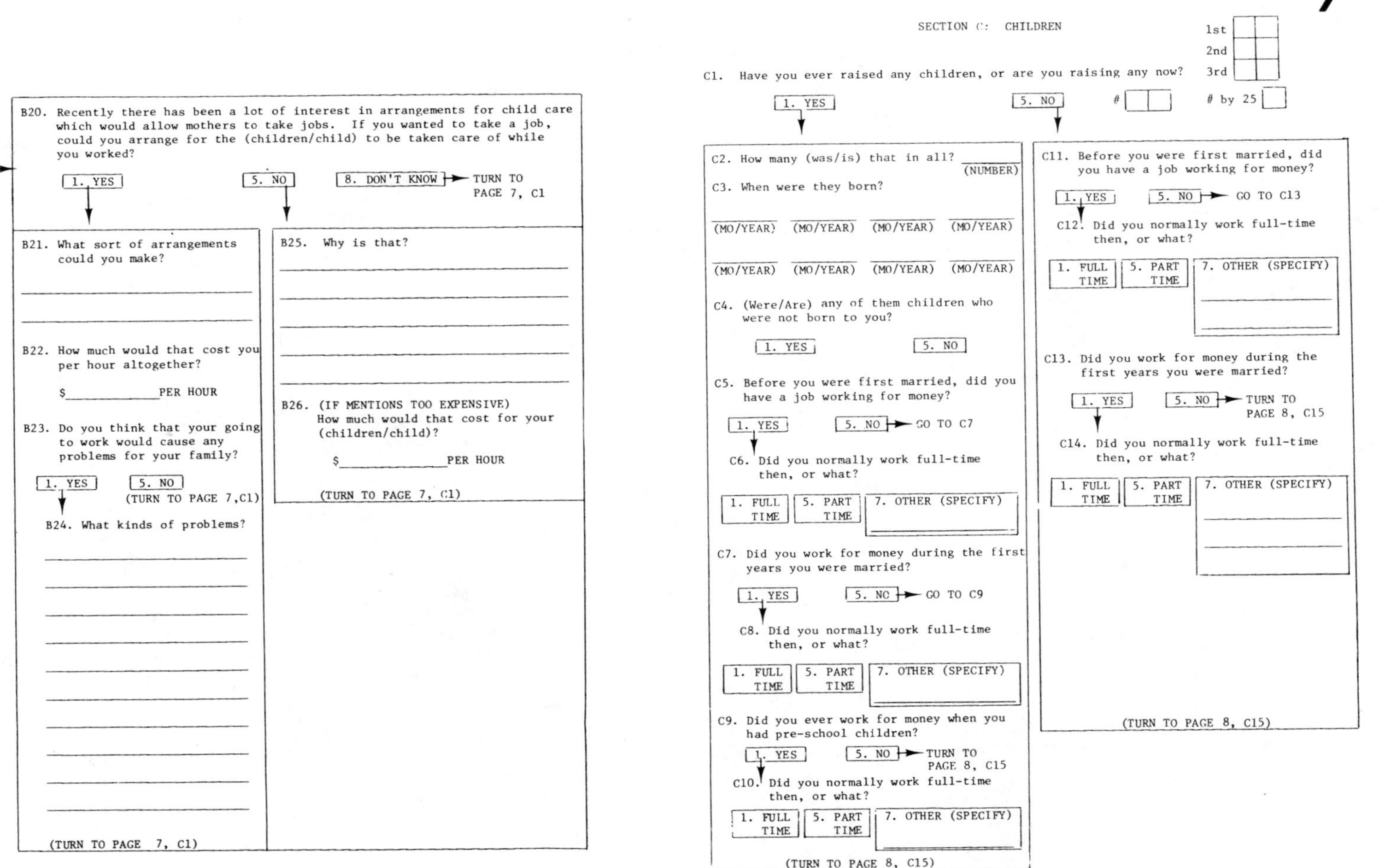

CHILDREN UNDER 12 IN FAMILY UNIT NOW AND WIFE IS NOT WORKING →

B20. Recently there has been a lot of interest in arrangements for child care which would allow mothers to take jobs. If you wanted to take a job, could you arrange for the (children/child) to be taken care of while you worked?

[1. YES] [5. NO] [8. DON'T KNOW] → TURN TO PAGE 7, C1

B21. What sort of arrangements could you make?

____

B22. How much would that cost you per hour altogether?

$________ PER HOUR

B23. Do you think that your going to work would cause any problems for your family?

[1. YES] [5. NO] (TURN TO PAGE 7,C1)

B24. What kinds of problems?

____

(TURN TO PAGE 7, C1)

B25. Why is that?

____

B26. (IF MENTIONS TOO EXPENSIVE) How much would that cost for your (children/child)?

$________ PER HOUR

(TURN TO PAGE 7, C1)

SECTION C: CHILDREN

1st [ ][ ]
2nd [ ][ ]
3rd [ ][ ]

C1. Have you ever raised any children, or are you raising any now?

[1. YES] [5. NO] # [ ][ ] # by 25 [ ]

C2. How many (was/is) that in all? ______ (NUMBER)

C3. When were they born?

(MO/YEAR) (MO/YEAR) (MO/YEAR) (MO/YEAR)

(MO/YEAR) (MO/YEAR) (MO/YEAR) (MO/YEAR)

C4. (Were/Are) any of them children who were not born to you?

[1. YES] [5. NO]

C5. Before you were first married, did you have a job working for money?

[1. YES] [5. NO] → GO TO C7

C6. Did you normally work full-time then, or what?

[1. FULL TIME] [5. PART TIME] [7. OTHER (SPECIFY) ______]

C7. Did you work for money during the first years you were married?

[1. YES] [5. NO] → GO TO C9

C8. Did you normally work full-time then, or what?

[1. FULL TIME] [5. PART TIME] [7. OTHER (SPECIFY) ______]

C9. Did you ever work for money when you had pre-school children?

[1. YES] [5. NO] → TURN TO PAGE 8, C15

C10. Did you normally work full-time then, or what?

[1. FULL TIME] [5. PART TIME] [7. OTHER (SPECIFY) ______]

(TURN TO PAGE 8, C15)

C11. Before you were first married, did you have a job working for money?

[1. YES] [5. NO] → GO TO C13

C12. Did you normally work full-time then, or what?

[1. FULL TIME] [5. PART TIME] [7. OTHER (SPECIFY) ______]

C13. Did you work for money during the first years you were married?

[1. YES] [5. NO] → TURN TO PAGE 8, C15

C14. Did you normally work full-time then, or what?

[1. FULL TIME] [5. PART TIME] [7. OTHER (SPECIFY) ______]

(TURN TO PAGE 8, C15)

C15. INTERVIEWER: CHECK ONE (REFER TO ITEM 1d, PAGE 2, OF BEIGE COVERSHEET
OR
ITEM 1b, PAGE 2, OF CORAL COVERSHEET)

1. WIFE IS UNDER 50 | 5. WIFE IS 50 OR OVER → TURN TO PAGE 9, C23

C16. Do you expect to have any (more) children?

1. YES | 5. NO | 8. DON'T KNOW (TURN TO PAGE 9, C21)

C17. How many children do you expect to have altogether?

C18. When do you think you will have your last child?

C19. Some women plan to look for a paid job as soon as all their children are in school; others try to keep a job with just maternity leaves; and still others have no plans for a paid job at all. How do you see your future job plans?

(TURN TO PAGE 9, C21)

C20. How sure are you that you will not have any (more) children)

(TURN TO PAGE 9, C21)

C21. How does your husband feel about having (more) children? Is he very much in favor of it, somewhat in favor of it, neither for nor against it, somewhat against it, or very much against it?

1. VERY MUCH IN FAVOR	2. SOME-WHAT IN FAVOR	3. NEITHER IN FAVOR NOR AGAINST	4. SOMEWHAT AGAINST	5. VERY MUCH AGAINST	8. DON'T KNOW

C22. How does your husband feel about (your working/the possibility of your working)? Is he very much in favor of it, somewhat in favor of it, neither in favor of nor against it, somewhat against it, or very much against it?

1. VERY MUCH IN FAVOR	2. SOME-WHAT IN FAVOR	3. NEITHER IN FAVOR NOR AGAINST	4. SOMEWHAT AGAINST	5. VERY MUCH AGAINST	8. DON'T KNOW

C23. INTERVIEWER CHECKPOINT:

1. CHILDREN UNDER 12 IN 1975 OR 1976 OR EXPECTS TO HAVE MORE CHILDREN

5. NO CHILDREN UNDER 12 IN 1975 OR 1976 AND DOES NOT EXPECT MORE CHILDREN (TURN TO PAGE 10, D1)

C24. About how much education do you think your children will have when they stop going to school?

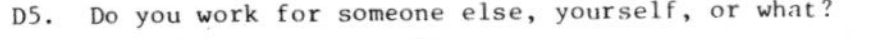

SECTION D: EMPLOYMENT

D1. We would like to know about what you do--are you (WIFE) working now, looking for work, retired, a full-time housewife, a student, or what?

- 1. WORKING NOW → D2
- 2. ONLY TEMPORARILY LAID OFF WORK → D2
- 3. LOOKING FOR WORK, UNEMPLOYED (TURN TO PAGE 18, E1)
- 4. RETIRED
- 5. PERMANENTLY DISABLED
- 6. FULL-TIME HOUSEWIFE
- 7. STUDENT

  (TURN TO PAGE 21, F1)
- 8. OTHER ________ (SPECIFY) (GO TO D2 IF HAS JOB, OTHERWISE TURN TO PAGE 21, F1)

D2. What is your main occupation? (What sort of work do you do?) ____________________ OCC [ ][ ] IND [ ][ ]

____

(IF NOT CLEAR) → D3. Tell me a little more about what you do.

____

____

D4. What kind of business is that in? ____________________

____

____

D5. Do you work for someone else, yourself, or what?

1. SOMEONE ELSE

D6. Do you work for the federal, state or local government?

1. YES 5. NO

D7. Do you supervise the work of other employees, or tell them what work to do?

1. YES → D8 5. NO (GO TO D10)

D8. About how many people do you supervise?

__________ (NUMBER)

D9. Do you have any say about their pay or promotion?

1. YES 5. NO

D10. Does your boss have a supervisor over him or her?

1. YES 5. NO

(GO TO D22)

2. BOTH SOMEONE ELSE AND SELF

D11. When you work for others, do you work for the federal, state or local government?

1. YES 5. NO

D12. When you work for others, do you supervise the work of other employees, or tell them what work to do?

1. YES → D13 5. NO (GO TO D15)

D13. About how many people do you supervise?

__________ (NUMBER)

D14. Do you have any say about their pay or promotion?

1. YES 5. NO

D15. Does your boss have a supervisor over him or her?

1. YES 5. NO

D16. Is your own business incorporated?

1. YES 5. NO 8. DK

D17. When you work for yourself, do you employ other people?

1. YES → D18 5. NO (GO TO D22)

D18. How many? ______ (NUMBER)

(GO TO D22)

3. SELF ONLY

D19. Is your business incorporated?

1. YES 5. NO 8. DK

D20. Do you employ other people?

1. YES → D21 5. NO (TURN TO PAGE 12, D25)

D21. How many?

_______ (NUMBER)

(TURN TO PAGE 12, D25)

D22. Is your current job covered by a union contract?

1. YES → D23 5. NO → GO TO D24

D23. Do you belong to that labor union? 1. YES 5. NO

D24. How long have you worked for your present employer? __________ (MONTHS) __________ (YEARS)

D25. How much formal education is required to get a job like yours?

____

D26. Do you (also) have to have some work experience or special training to get a job like yours?

[1. YES] [5. NO] → GO TO D28

D27. What kind of experience or special training is that?

____

____

D28. On a job like yours, how long would it take the average new person to become fully trained and qualified?

________ (YEARS) *OR* ________ (MONTHS)

D29. Do you feel you are learning things on your job that could lead to a better job or to a promotion?

[1. YES] [5. NO]

D30. Do you have some skills or job experience that you cannot use on your present job?

[1. YES] [5. NO] → GO TO D32

D31. Do you think you might want to get a job some day which used that skill or experience?

[1. YES] [5. NO]

D32. How long have you had your present position? ______________

(IF LESS THAN ONE YEAR) (IF ONE YEAR OR MORE, TURN TO PAGE 13, D38)

D33. What month did you start this job? ______________

D34. What happened to the job you had before--did the company go out of business, were you laid off, promoted, were you not working, or what?

______________________________ [5. NO PREVIOUS JOB] (TURN TO PAGE 13, D38)

____

____

D35. On the whole, would you say your present job is better or worse than the one you had before?

[1. BETTER] [5. WORSE] [3. SAME] → GO TO D37

D36. Why is it (better/worse)? ______________

____

D37. Does your present job pay more than the one you had before?

[1. YES, MORE] [5. NO, SAME OR LESS]

(TURN TO PAGE 13, D38)

D38. Did you miss any work in 1975 because someone else in the family was sick?

[1. YES] [5. NO] → GO TO D41

D39. Was that your husband, a child, or who?

[1. HUSBAND] [2. CHILD OR CHILDREN] [7. OTHER]

D40. How much work did you miss? ____ (DAYS) ____ (WEEKS) ____ (MONTHS)

D41. Did you miss any work in 1975 because you were sick?

[1. YES] [5. NO] → GO TO D43

D42. How much did you miss? ____ (DAYS) ____ (WEEKS) ____ (MONTHS)

D43. How many weeks of paid vacation do you get each year? ________ (WEEKS)

D44. Did you take any vacation or time off during 1975?

[1. YES] [5. NO] → GO TO D46

D45. How much vacation did you take? ____ (DAYS) ____ (WEEKS) ____ (MONTHS)

D46. Did you miss any work in 1975 because you were on strike?

[1. YES] [5. NO] → GO TO D48

D47. How much work did you miss? ____ (DAYS) ____ (WEEKS) ____ (MONTHS)

D48. Did you miss any work in 1975 because you were unemployed or temporarily laid off?

[1. YES] [5. NO] → TURN TO PAGE 14, D51

D49. How much work did you miss? ____ (DAYS) ____ (WEEKS) ____ (MONTHS)

D50. Were those periods of unemployment or layoff all in one stretch, in two periods, or more than two?

[1. ALL IN ONE STRETCH] [3. TWO PERIODS] [5. MORE THAN TWO]

14

D51. Then, how many weeks did you actually work on your main job in 1975? ______ (WEEKS)

D52. And, on the average, how many hours a week did you work on your main job in 1975?

______________ (HOURS PER WEEK)

D53. Did you have any overtime which is not included in that?

1. YES → D54. How many hours did that overtime amount to in 1975? ______ (HOURS)

5. NO → GO TO D55

D55. Are you salaried, paid by the hour, or what?

1. SALARIED

D56. How much is your salary?

$__________ per ________

D57. If you were to work more hours than usual during some week, would you get paid for those extra hours of work?

1. YES → D58. About how much would you make per hour for that overtime?

$__________ (PER HOUR)

5. NO → GO TO D63

(GO TO D63)

3. PAID BY HOUR

D59. What is your hourly wage rate for your regular work time?

$________ (PER HOUR)

D60. What is your hourly wage rate for overtime?

$________ (PER HOUR)

(GO TO D63)

7. OTHER

D61. How is that?

D62. If you worked an extra hour, about how much would you earn for that hour?

$__________

(GO TO D63)

D63. How many employee retirement or pension plans are you covered by, including Social Security?

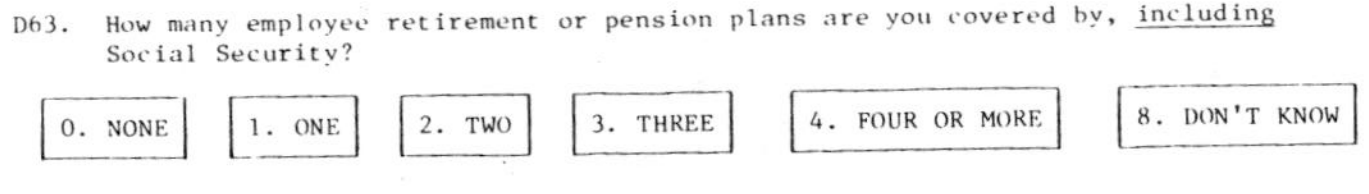

0. NONE | 1. ONE | 2. TWO | 3. THREE | 4. FOUR OR MORE | 8. DON'T KNOW

15

D64. Did you have any extra jobs or other ways of making money in addition to your main job in 1975?

1. YES

5. NO → GO TO D70

OCC

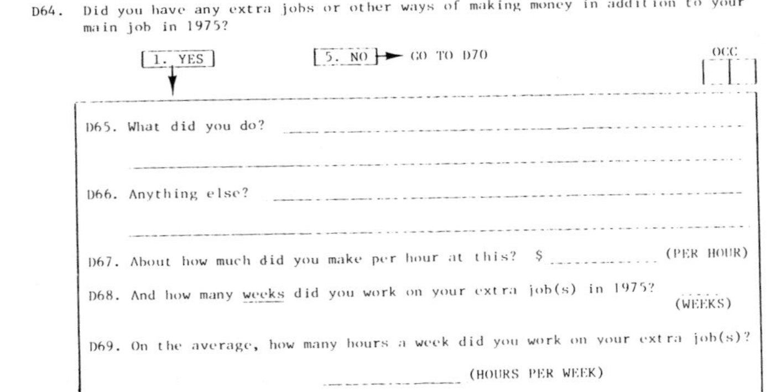

D65. What did you do? ______________________

D66. Anything else? ______________________

D67. About how much did you make per hour at this? $ ________ (PER HOUR)

D68. And how many weeks did you work on your extra job(s) in 1975? ____ (WEEKS)

D69. On the average, how many hours a week did you work on your extra job(s)?

__________ (HOURS PER WEEK)

D70. Was there more work available (on your job/on any of your jobs) so that you could have worked more if you had wanted to?

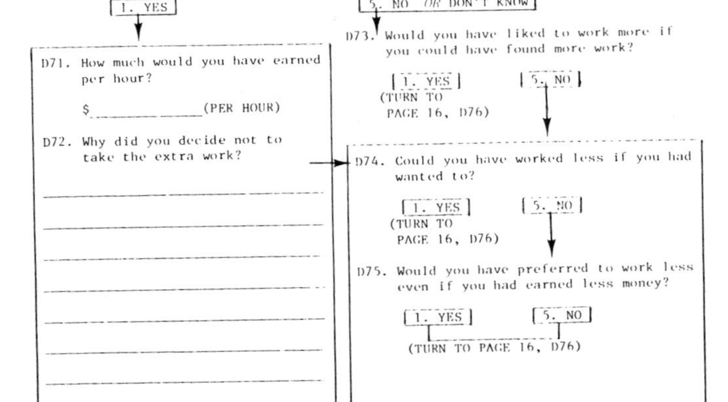

1. YES

D71. How much would you have earned per hour?

$__________ (PER HOUR)

D72. Why did you decide not to take the extra work?

5. NO *OR* DON'T KNOW

D73. Would you have liked to work more if you could have found more work?

1. YES (TURN TO PAGE 16, D76)

5. NO

D74. Could you have worked less if you had wanted to?

1. YES (TURN TO PAGE 16, D76)

5. NO

D75. Would you have preferred to work less even if you had earned less money?

1. YES | 5. NO

(TURN TO PAGE 16, D76)

D76. About how much time does it take you to get to work each day, door to door?

__________ (ONE WAY) [NONE] → GO TO D79

D77. About how many miles is it to where you work? __________ (ONE WAY)

D78. Do you use public transportation to get to work, have a car pool, drive by yourself, walk, ride with your husband, or what?

[1. PUBLIC TRANSPORTATION] [2. CAR POOL] [3. DRIVE] [4. WALK] [5. RIDE WITH HUSBAND] [7. OTHER (SPECIFY) __________]

D79. If you should lose your present job, what would you say were your chances for finding another job just as good as your present job in all respects? Would they be very good, good, not so good, or not good at all?

[1. VERY GOOD] [2. GOOD] [4. NOT SO GOOD] [5. NOT GOOD AT ALL]

D80. Do you think you will keep on working for the next few years, or do you plan to quit?

[1. KEEP ON WORKING] (TURN TO PAGE 17, D84)

[5. PLAN TO QUIT] ↓

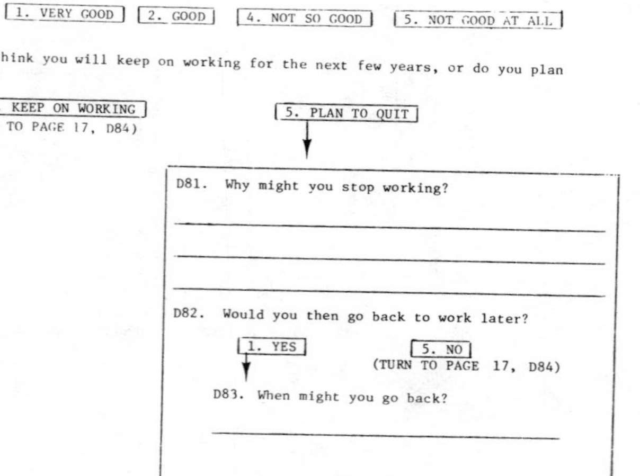

D81. Why might you stop working?

____

D82. Would you then go back to work later?

[1. YES] ↓ [5. NO] (TURN TO PAGE 17, D84)

D83. When might you go back?

____

(TURN TO PAGE 17, D84)

D84. Are there better jobs you could get if you were willing to move and live somewhere else?

[1. YES] [5. NO] [8. DON'T KNOW]

D85. Are there better jobs around here that you might get if you were willing to go farther to work or work different hours?

[1. YES] [5. NO] [8. DON'T KNOW]

D86. Thinking back to when you started your present job, were there some limitations on where you could work or what hours you could work that were factors in taking this job?

[1. YES] ↓ [5. NO] → GO TO D88

D87. What were these limitations? __________

D88. If you were to get enough money to live as comfortably as you would like for the rest of your life, would you continue to work?

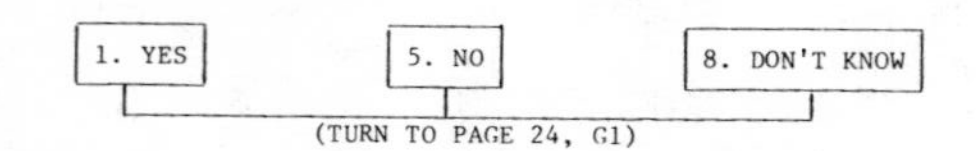

[1. YES] [5. NO] [8. DON'T KNOW]

(TURN TO PAGE 24, G1)

SECTION E: IF LOOKING FOR WORK, UNEMPLOYED IN D1

OCC [|]

E1. What kind of job are you looking for? ______________________

____

E2. What do you think your chances will be for getting a good job in that line of work -- are they very good, good, not so good, or not good at all?

[1. VERY GOOD] [2. GOOD] [4. NOT SO GOOD] [5. NOT GOOD AT ALL]

E3. How much would you expect to earn? $__________ PER__________

E4. Will you have to get any training to qualify? ______________________

E5. Do you belong to a labor union? [1. YES] [5. NO]

E6. Have you been doing anything in the last four weeks to find a job?

[1. YES] [5. NO] → GO TO E8

E7. How many places have you been to in the last four weeks to find out about a job?

[0. NONE] [1. ONE] [2. TWO] [3. THREE] [4. FOUR] [5. FIVE OR MORE]

E8. Are there any limitations on where you could work or what hours you could work that would be factors in your taking a job?

[1. YES] [5. NO] → GO TO E10

E9. What are these limitations? ______________________

____

E10. Are there jobs you could get if you were willing to move and live somewhere else?

[1. YES] [5. NO] [8. DON'T KNOW]

E11. How long have you been looking for work? ______________________

E12. Have you ever had a job? [1. YES] [5. NO] → TURN TO PAGE 20, E35

E13. What sort of work did you do on your last job? (What was your occupation?)

______________________ OCC [|] IND [|]

E14. What kind of business was that in?

____

E15. Did you supervise the work of other employees or tell them what to do?

[1. YES] [5. NO]

E16. What happened to that job--did the company go out of business, were you laid off, or what?

____

E17. When did you last work? ______________________

[IF 1975 OR 1976] [IF BEFORE 1975] → TURN TO PAGE 20, E35

E18. Did you take any vacation or time off during 1975?

[1. YES] [5. NO] → GO TO E20

E19. How much vacation did you take? ______ (DAYS) ______ (WEEKS) ______ (MONTHS)

E20. Did you miss any work in 1975 because someone else in the family was sick?

[1. YES] [5. NO] → GO TO E23

E21. Was that person your husband, a child, or who?

[1. HUSBAND] [2. CHILD OR CHILDREN] [7. OTHER]

E22. How much work did you miss? ______ (DAYS) ______ (WEEKS) ______ (MONTHS)

E23. Did you miss any work in 1975 because you were sick?

[1. YES] [5. NO] → GO TO E25

E24. How much work did you miss? ______ (DAYS) ______ (WEEKS) ______ (MONTHS)

E25. Did you miss any work in 1975 because you were on strike?

[1. YES] [5. NO] → TURN TO PAGE 20, E27

E26. How much work did you miss? ______ (DAYS) ______ (WEEKS) ______ (MONTHS)

E27. Did you miss any work in 1975 because you were unemployed or laid off?

[1. YES] ↓ [5. NO] → GO TO E30

E28. How much work did you miss? ______ (DAYS) ______ (WEEKS) ______ (MONTHS)

E29. Were those weeks of unemployment all in one stretch, in two periods, or more than two?

[1. ALL IN ONE STRETCH] [3. TWO PERIODS] [5. MORE THAN TWO]

E30. Then, how many weeks did you actually work on your job in 1975?

______ (WEEKS)

E31. And, on the average, how many hours a week did you work? ______ (HOURS PER WEEK)

E32. On your last job, how much time did it take you to get to work each day, door to door?

______ (ONE WAY) [0. NONE] → GO TO E35

E33. About how many miles was it to where you worked? ______ (ONE WAY)

E34. Did you use public transportation to get to work, have a car pool, drive by yourself, walk, ride with your husband, or what?

[1. PUBLIC TRANSPORTATION] [2. CAR POOL] [3. DRIVE] [4. WALK] [5. RIDE WITH HUSBAND] [7. OTHER - (SPECIFY) ______]

E35. If you were to get enough money to live as comfortably as you would like for the rest of your life, would you work?

[1. YES] [5. NO] [8. DON'T KNOW]

(TURN TO PAGE 24, G1)

SECTION F: RETIRED, HOUSEWIFE, STUDENT, PERMANENTLY DISABLED

F1. During the last year (1975), did you do any work for money?

[1. YES] → F4 [5. NO] ↓

F2. Are you thinking about getting a job in the future?

[1. YES] ↓ [5. NO] → TURN TO PAGE 22, F15

F3. When might that be? (How soon?) ______

(TURN TO PAGE 22, F15)

OCC [ ][ ] IND [ ][ ]

F4. What kind of work did you do when you worked? (What was your occupation?)

______

F5. What kind of business was that in? ______

F6. How many weeks did you work last year? ______ (WEEKS)

F7. About how many hours a week did you work (when you worked)? ______ (HOURS PER WEEK)

F8. On your last job, how much time did it take you to get to work each day, door to door? ______ (ONE WAY) [0. NONE] → GO TO F11

F9. About how many miles was it to where you worked? ______ (ONE WAY)

F10. Did you use public transportation to get to work, have a car pool, drive by yourself, walk, ride with your husband, or what?

[1. PUBLIC TRANSPORTATION] [2. CAR POOL] [3. DRIVE] [4. WALK] [5. RIDE WITH HUSBAND] [7. OTHER - (SPECIFY) ______]

F11. What happened to that job--did the company go out of business, were you laid off, or what?

______

______

(IF NOT CLEAR) → F12. Why are you no longer working? ______

______

______

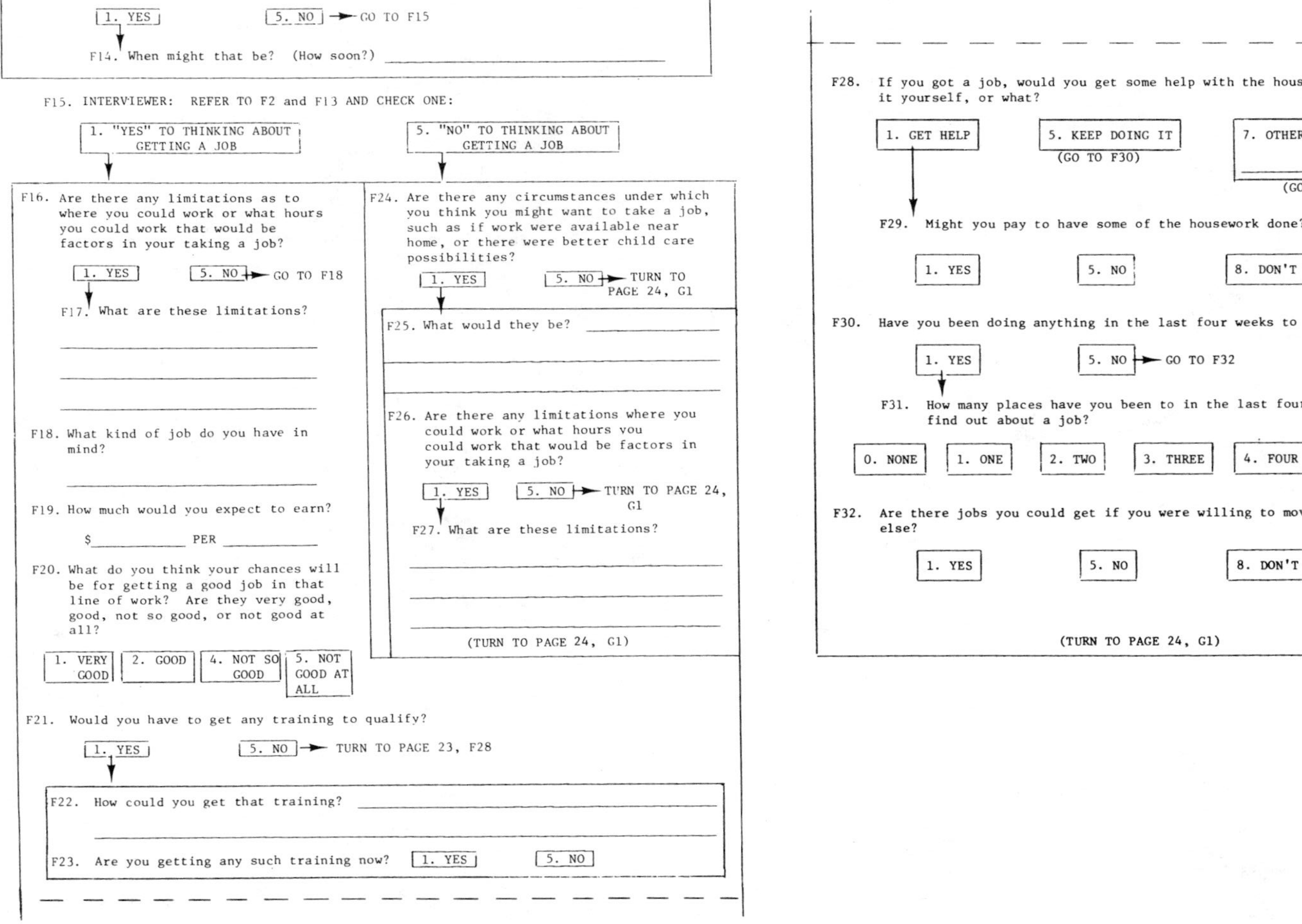

22

F13. Are you thinking of getting a job in the future?

[1. YES] [5. NO] → GO TO F15

F14. When might that be? (How soon?) ____________

F15. INTERVIEWER: REFER TO F2 and F13 AND CHECK ONE:

[1. "YES" TO THINKING ABOUT GETTING A JOB] [5. "NO" TO THINKING ABOUT GETTING A JOB]

F16. Are there any limitations as to where you could work or what hours you could work that would be factors in your taking a job?

[1. YES] [5. NO] → GO TO F18

F17. What are these limitations?

____

____

____

F18. What kind of job do you have in mind?

____

F19. How much would you expect to earn?

$________ PER ________

F20. What do you think your chances will be for getting a good job in that line of work? Are they very good, good, not so good, or not good at all?

[1. VERY GOOD] [2. GOOD] [4. NOT SO GOOD] [5. NOT GOOD AT ALL]

F24. Are there any circumstances under which you think you might want to take a job, such as if work were available near home, or there were better child care possibilities?

[1. YES] [5. NO] → TURN TO PAGE 24, G1

F25. What would they be? ____________

____

____

F26. Are there any limitations where you could work or what hours you could work that would be factors in your taking a job?

[1. YES] [5. NO] → TURN TO PAGE 24, G1

F27. What are these limitations?

____

____

____

(TURN TO PAGE 24, G1)

F21. Would you have to get any training to qualify?

[1. YES] [5. NO] → TURN TO PAGE 23, F28

F22. How could you get that training? ____________

____

F23. Are you getting any such training now? [1. YES] [5. NO]

23

F28. If you got a job, would you get some help with the housework, keep doing it yourself, or what?

[1. GET HELP] [5. KEEP DOING IT (GO TO F30)] [7. OTHER (SPECIFY) ________ (GO TO F30)]

F29. Might you pay to have some of the housework done?

[1. YES] [5. NO] [8. DON'T KNOW]

F30. Have you been doing anything in the last four weeks to find a job?

[1. YES] [5. NO] → GO TO F32

F31. How many places have you been to in the last four weeks to find out about a job?

[0. NONE] [1. ONE] [2. TWO] [3. THREE] [4. FOUR] [5. FIVE OR MORE]

F32. Are there jobs you could get if you were willing to move and live somewhere else?

[1. YES] [5. NO] [8. DON'T KNOW]

(TURN TO PAGE 24, G1)

SECTION G: WORK HISTORY

G1. How many years altogether have you worked for money since you were 18?

_____ (YEARS) 00. NONE → TURN TO PAGE 26, H1

G2. How many of these years did you work full time for most or all of the year?

_____ (YEARS) ALL → GO TO G4

G3. During the years that you were not working full time, how much of the time did you work?

_____

G4. Thinking of your first full time, regular job, what did you do?

_____ OCC

G5. Have you had a number of different kinds of jobs, or have you mostly worked in the same occupation you started in, or what?

_____

_____

G6. Some people have stopped their regular work for a time for such things as family responsibilities or to go back to school. Have you ever stopped working for a year or more for any of these or other reasons and then gone back to work?

1. YES 5. NO → TURN TO PAGE 26, H1

G7. Was that only one period, or were there several periods of a year or more when you were not working?

1. ONE PERIOD 3. SEVERAL PERIODS

G8. When was the period you were not working, from when to when?

_____ (MONTH, YEAR) to _____ (MONTH, YEAR)

G9. When was the most recent period that you were not working, from when to when?

_____ (MONTH, YEAR) to _____ (MONTH, YEAR)

IF BEFORE 1955, TURN TO PAGE 26, H1

G10. For what reasons did you stop working the last time? _____

_____

_____

G11. Did you get any training or skills during the time you were not working that you could use in a job?

1. YES 5. NO

G12. And, why did you go back to work when you did? _____

_____

_____

G13. Did you go back to the same kind of work you had done before?

1. YES 5. NO

G14. Was it the same job?

1. YES 5. NO

G15. How did you find the job when you went back to work? Was it through a friend, an employment agency, a want ad, or what?

_____

_____

G16. How did you get the skills or qualifications for the job? Was it your regular education, previous work experience, some special training, or what?

_____

_____

G17. About how much did you earn when you went back to work?

$_____ per _____ (HOUR/WEEK/MONTH/YEAR)

G18. About how much would you have been earning at that time if you had been working all along?

$_____ per _____ (HOUR/WEEK/MONTH/YEAR)

G19. Why is that? _____

_____

_____

_____

G20. Did you get more help with the housework and taking care of the children from your husband after you went back to work?

1. YES 5. NO

SECTION H: FEELINGS

INTERVIEWER: IF RESPONDENT SIMPLY REPEATS ONE OF THE ALTERNATIVES GIVEN IN A QUESTION, CIRCLE THAT WORD OR PHRASE.

Now I have some questions which ask you to describe yourself or your feelings about certain things. There are no right or wrong answers; we just want to know how you would describe yourself.

H1. Have you usually felt pretty sure your life would work out the way you want it to,

or have there been more times when you haven't been very sure about it?

____

H2. Are you the kind of person that plans her life ahead all the time,

or do you live more from day to day?

____

H3. When you make plans ahead, do you usually get to carry out things the way you expected,

or do things usually come up to make you change your plans?

____

H4. Would you say you nearly always finish things once you start them,

or do you sometimes have to give up before they are finished?

____

H5. Would you rather spend your money and enjoy life today,

or save more for the future?

____

H6. Do you think a lot about things that might happen in the future,

or do you usually just take things as they come?

____

(TURN TO PAGE 2 OF COVERSHEET)

SECTION J: BY OBSERVATION ONLY

J1. Who was respondent? (relation to Head) ______________________________

J2. Number of calls ______________________________

GLOSSARY

The following is a description of some of the technical terms used in this volume. For more details on the measures used in these analyses see the documentation series entitled A Panel Study of Income Dynamics: Volume I, Study Design, Procedures and Available Data, 1968-72; Volume II, Tape Codes and Indexes, 1968-72; 1973 Supplement (Wave VI); 1974 Supplement (Wave VII); 1975 Supplement (Wave VIII); and 1976 Supplement (Wave IX).

ACHIEVEMENT MOTIVATION - A personality measure from social psychology representing a propensity to derive satisfaction from overcoming obstacles by one's own efforts in situations where the outcome is ambiguous. It is believed to be developed by early independence training, to result in the taking of calculated but not extreme risks and in the raising of goals after success experiences. It was administered in the 1972 interview.

ASPIRATION-AMBITION - A seven-item index of attitudes and plans reflecting attempts to improve economic well-being; see Volume II of the documentation, p. 789. The items include the following:

Might move on purpose
Wanted more work, and/or worked more than 2500 hours last year
Might quit a job it if was not challenging
Prefers a job with chances for making more money to one more pleasant
Is dissatisfied with self
Spends time figuring out how to get more money
Plans to get a new job, knows what type of job and what it might pay
(Second and last items neutralized for those for whom they are inappropriate.)

ATTACHMENT TO LABOR FORCE - A set of measures indicating regularity of past, present and expected work, such as limits placed on job hours or location, absenteeism, plans to stop working.

BETA - A measure of the explanatory power of an independent variable when considered in a multivariate context.

BETA WEIGHTS - When the independent and dependent variables in the regression equation $Y = a + b_1X_1 + b_2X_2 + u$ are measured in their "natural" units (e.g., in dollars, years, hours) then the parameters b_1 and b_2 reflect the effect on Y of a one unit change in X_1 and X_2, respectively. If all variables are standardized so that each has a mean of zero and a standard deviation equal to one, then the equation becomes $Y = \beta_1 X_1 + \beta_2 X_2 + v$ and the β 's can be interpreted as the fraction of a standard deviation that Y changes as a result of a change of one standard deviation in the X's. The B's are regression coefficients (sometimes called "partial regression coefficients"), the β 's are beta weights or standardized regression coefficients. The unstandardized and standardized coefficients are related in the following way:

$$\beta_1 = \frac{b_1 \sigma_{x_1}}{\sigma_Y}$$

COGNITIVE ABILITY - See TEST SCORE

CONNECTEDNESS (to sources of information and help) - The following eight-item set of reported behaviors measuring the extent to which the respondent has friends or habits likely to keep him informed or provide help; see Volume II of the documentation, p. 793.

Attended PTA meeting within the year
Attends church once a month or more
Watches television more than one hour a day
Knows several neighbors by name (2 points if 6 or more)
Has relatives within walking distance
Goes to organizations once a month or more
Goes to a bar once a month or more
Belongs to a labor union and pays dues
(First item is neutralized for families without children).

COUNTY WAGE RATE for unskilled casual labor - An estimate of the wage rate for unskilled labor in the county where the respondent lives, secured by mail questionnaires sent each year to the state official in charge of unemployment compensation.

COUNTY UNEMPLOYMENT - An estimate of the unemployment rate in the county where the respondent lives, secured by mail questionnaires sent each year to the state official in charge of unemployment compensation.

CRAMER'S V - A measure of association between two nominal scale variables when they have no natural rank order. It is similar to the Chi-square measure except it is adjusted for the number of observations and is constrained to take on values between 0 and 1. The higher Cramer's V, the greater the association between the classifications.

DECILE - If all units are arranged in ascending order on some criterion such as income and each tenth marked off and identified, the ten groups formed are called deciles. The actual dividing points of incomes are given in Volumes II-VI of the documentation.

DEPRECIATION OF HUMAN CAPITAL - The process by which employee skills may become less valuable during periods of nonwork.

DESIGN EFFECT - The effect of departures from simple random sampling in probability samples, defined as the ratio of the actual sampling variance to the variance of a simple random sample of the same size.

ECONOMIES OF SCALE - As the size of a family increases, if the costs do not increase proportionately, then we say there are economies of scale in large families.

ECONOMIZING INDEX - An index of six reported behaviors taken to indicate parsimonious use of money; see Volume II of the documentation, p. 790.

Spent less than $150 a year on alcohol
Spent less than $150 a year on cigarettes
Received more than $100 worth of free help
Do not own late model car
Eat together most of the time
Spent less than $260 a year eating out
(The fourth item is neutralized for those not owning cars).

EFFICACY INDEX - An index composed of six self-evaluations which reflect a sense of personal effectiveness, and a propensity to expect one's plans to work out; see Volume II of the documentation, p. 787.

Is sure life will work out
Plans life ahead
Gets to carry out plans
Finishes things
Would rather save for the future
Thinks about things that might happen in future.

ELASTICITY - Refers to the response of the quantity of a good consumed to a change in price or in income. If the percentage change in the quantity of food consumed, for example, is greater than the percentage change in the price, then the demand for food is said to be price-elastic; if it is less than the percentage change in price, it is price-inelastic.

ETA^2 - A measure of the explanatory power of a set of subclass means based on a one-way analysis of variance. It is analogous to the R^2 from regression analysis and measures the fraction of variance on the dependent variable which is explained by a single categorical variable.

EXOGENOUS VARIABLE - Variables whose levels and changes are determined by forces independent of those being studied, as contrasted with endogenous variables which are dependent upon variables in the system.

EXPECTED VALUE - When a dependent variable is determined by a combination of systematic and random effects, the expected value is that part which can be predicted from the systematic relationship. In the case of regression, it is the value predicted by the regression equation.

F-TEST - A test of the significance of the proportion of the variance explained by a set of several predictors or several classifications of a single predictor; see STATISTICAL SIGNIFICANCE.

FAMILY - All persons living in a household who are related by blood, marriage, or adoption. In occasional cases an unrelated person has been included in the family unit if he or she shares expenses and is apparently a permanent member of the unit. The definition of family used in this study includes single person families. This contrasts with the Census Bureau convention of classifying single persons separately as "unrelated individuals."

FAMILY COMPOSITION CHANGE - Contains several dimensions, most of them related to the family's position in the standard life cycle: marriage, birth of first child, youngest child reaches age six and starts school, children leave home, one spouse dies. The sex and marital status of the head, the number of children, and age of the youngest are the main components.

FAMILY MONEY INCOME - Family income, unless otherwise designated, is the total regular money income of the whole family, including income from labor, capital, and transfers such as pensions, welfare, unemployment compensation, workmen's compensation, and alimony received by all members of the family. It does not include capital gains (realized or unrealized), irregular receipts from insurance settlements, or in-kind transfers such as food stamp bonus values.

FAMILY TAPE - A data file containing all the data on that family from all eight interviews. There is one record for each sample family. The final nine-year data tape includes only families interviewed in 1976 so that there are no partial records. Where there are several families derived from an original sample family, the early family information will appear on each of their records.

HEAD OF FAMILY - In nuclear families the husband is defined as the head. In families with a single adult, that adult, regardless of sex, is defined as the head. In ambiguous cases of more than one adult, the head is the major earner or the one who owns the home or pays the rent. Note that the head of the family may change due to marriage, divorce, or death. For splitoff families, the head is similarly defined.

HOUSEHOLD - Probability samples usually sample occupied dwellings, which may contain more than one household, which in turn may contain more than one family. However, the term household is often used loosely to mean family, since the number of individuals living with unrelated adults is very small. A family is a group of individuals related by blood, marriage, adoption.

HUMAN CAPITAL - The economically valued skills which result from the investment in one's self through education or other training.

IMPUTED RENT - A form of nonmoney income and consumption for home owners who can be thought of as in the business of renting a house to themselves. It is estimated by taking 6 percent of the owner's net equity in his house (house value minus remaining mortgage principal).

INCOME - Unless otherwise specified, this means total family money income including regular money transfers. (See FAMILY MONEY INCOME.) When a year is given, it is the year of the income, not the (later) year when the interview was taken.

INCOME/NEEDS RATIO - See NEEDS STANDARD

INDIVIDUAL TAPE - A data file with one record for each individual as of 1976, containing all the data for that individual over the whole period and all the data for the family that individual was in for each of the nine years. The tape contains some individuals who are not in the sample and are thus excluded from the analysis but who are necessary in order to derive family information for those in the sample. Individuals and families have separate weights; see WEIGHT and Volume I of the documentation.

INELASTIC - See ELASTICITY

INTELLIGENCE - See TEST SCORE

INTERRUPTION (OF WORK) - Any labor force withdrawal that is preceeded and followed by periods of market work.

LABOR FORCE WITHDRAWAL - Any period of non-work activity of a year or more after age 18 or school completion.

LEAST SQUARES ESTIMATION - That method of estimation which minimizes the squared deviations of the actual value from the predicted value of the dependent variable. Such estimators are sensitive to extreme cases and nonnormal distributions.

LINEAR REGRESSION - See REGRESSION

MOTIVATION - See ACHIEVEMENT MOTIVATION

MULTICOLLINEARITY - A problem arising in estimation if two or more predictors are highly intercorrelated. It thus becomes difficult to estimate the separate effects of these variables.

MULTIPLE REGRESSION - See REGRESSION

MONEY EARNINGS ACTS INDEX - An index of behavioral reports that the family is doing things to increase its money income including working long hours, getting to work on time, changing jobs, looking for a better job (see Volume II of the documentation, p. 794).

MTR - Tables and other computer output are indexed by a Machine Tabulation Request number for checking and filing purposes. The number appears at the bottom of some tables.

NEEDS STANDARD - An estimate of the annual income necessary for a family to meet basic needs. The standard is generated in the same way as the official federal poverty line; food needs are determined according to age and sex, as estimated and priced by the USDA (in Family Economics Review), and food costs are adjusted for economies of scale; this figure is then multiplied by a factor to allow for other needs also differentially greater for smaller families. The needs standard, based on the "low-cost" food plan is 1.25 times the official federal poverty standard, which is based on the "economy" food plan.

The absolute level is to some extent arbitrary and is not adjusted for inflation in later years, but the standard adjusts for differences in family size and structure so the status of families that differ in composition can be compared.

The needs standard is corrected for changes in family composition during the prior year, so that it is legitimate to compare it with the prior year's income. See Volume I of the documentation for further details.

NUMBER OF CASES - The actual number of families or individuals on which the estimate is based. The number does not reflect the proportion of the population represented by that group because of the differences in sampling and response rates. See WEIGHT.

NULL HYPOTHESIS - See STATISTICAL SIGNIFICANCE

ORDINARY LEAST SQUARES (OLS) - See REGRESSION

QUINTILE - If all cases are arranged in ascending order on some criterion such as income and each fifth is marked off and identified, these five groups are called quintiles.

PARTIAL CORRELATION COEFFICIENT (partial R^2) - The partial correlation coefficient (squared) is a measure of the marginal or added explanatory power of one predictive variable or set of variables, over and above all the other predictors. It can be thought of as the correlation of two sets of residuals, after removing the effects of all other predictors from both the dependent variable and the predictor in question. It is also the fraction of the remaining distance to perfect explanation (1.00) the multiple correlation (squared) is moved by the added predictor. It is the best measure of the "importance" of a predictor or group of predictors.

PERCENT OF POPULATION - The fraction of the weight-sum represented by a subgroup is an estimate of the percent of the population (of families or individuals) it represents. Aggregate estimates can be made by ratio-estimating procedures, i.e., multiplying the sample mean by the proportion of the population times an outside estimate of the aggregate number of families or individuals.

PLANNING INDEX- A subset of the efficacy index consisting of the following items:

Plans ahead
Prefers to save for future
Thinks about the future.

RATIO OF INVESTMENT - The proportion of ones earnings capacity which is spent on on-the-job training in a given time period.

REAL EARNING ACTS INDEX - A five-item index, with neutralization of the inapplicable items, reflecting ways of earning nonmoney income or investing in self; see Volume II of the documentation, pp. 789-90.

Saved more than $75 doing own additions or repairs
Saved more than $75 growing own food
Saved more than $75 repairing own car
Head was taking courses or lessons with economic potential
Head spent spare time productively.

R^2 - The fraction of variance in the dependent variable which is explained by the set of explanatory variables.

REGRESSION - A statistical technique which estimates the separate, independent effect of each of several predictors on a dependent variable. It minimizes the sum of the squared deviations from predicted values (see LEAST SQUARE ESTIMATION) and assumes that the dependent variable is a linear and additive function of the predictors and a random error term.

REGRESSION COEFFICIENT - The estimated effect of a predictor on the dependent variable obtained from a regression analysis. It shows the expected effect that a unit change in the predictor would have on the dependent variable if all other predictors were held constant.

RESERVATION WAGE - The minimum market wage which will entice a person to seek employment.

RISK AVOIDANCE INDEX - An index of six reported behaviors indicating the avoidance of undue risks; see Volume II of the documentation, p. 791.

Car (newest if several) in good condition
All cars are insured
Uses seat belts (2 points if all the time)
Has medical insurance or a way to get free care
Head smokes less than one pack of cigarettes a day
Have liquid savings (2 points if more than two months income in savings).

SIZE OF LARGEST CITY IN AREA - The primary sampling unit (PSU) is a county or (rarely) cluster of counties and the size of the largest city in that area is intended to reflect the number and variety of jobs, as well as differences in costs and standards of living. When the city is 50,000 or more, the area is a Census Standard Metropolitan Statistical Area.

SPLITOFF - A splitoff is someone who left a sample family and is living in a different household. Most splitoffs are children who left the parental home to set up their own households. When a couple is divorced, one of them is designated as the continuing family and the other is a splitoff.

STANDARD DEVIATION - A measure of the dispersion of a distribution of observations around their average (or predicted) value. If random effects are normally distributed, roughly two-thirds of the observations fall in a range of the mean plus or minus one standare deviation. It is equal to the square root of the variance and is denoted by the symbol σ. The standard deviations presented in the tables should be considered in the context of the design effect.

STATISTICAL SIGNIFICANCE - Traditional statistical inference tests the hypothesis that a finding (e.g., that some effect is greater than zero) is a chance result from the sample not existing in the population. If the probability is sufficiently small (e.g., less than 5 percent), this "null hypothesis" is rejected and it is believed that there is some effect which is "statistically significant."

In most initial searching of data for what matters, and in what form, the assumptions of statistical testing are violated because many alternative models are tried. In addition, there are problems of estimating sampling variance with complex samples.

TARGET POPULATION - Those families who were in the lowest 20 percent of the income/needs distirbution in any one of the five years, 1967-1971, or nine years, 1967-1975.

TEST SCORE - A 13-item sentence completion test developed as a culture-free, sex-free, and race-free measure of "intelligence." Of course, like all such measures, it may also test acquired skills or freedom from test anxiety. For further details, see Appendix F, Five Thousand American Families—Patterns of Economic Progress, Vol. I, p. 381-5.

TRAINING, FIRM-SPECIFIC - On-the-job training acquired with one's present employer that provides skills which are useful only for the present employer.

TRAINING-GENERAL - On-the-job training that provides skills which are useful to more than one employer.

TRUST IN OTHERS - An index composed of five self-evaluating items on trusting others, believing in the fairness of the system; see Volume II of the documentation, p. 788.

Does not get angry easily
It matters what others think
Trusts most other people
Believes the life of the average man is getting better
Believes there are not a lot of people who have good things they don't deserve.

T-TEST - Under certain assumptions, estimated regression coefficients have a frequency distribution known as the t-distribution. This fact can be used to form a test of significance for the coefficients, called the t-test. See also STATISTICAL SIGNIFICANCE.

WEIGHT - There are weights both for the file of individuals and families which make the weighted estimates representative of the national non-institutional population of the continental United States. They offset differences in sampling rates and response rates, and the extra probabilities of inclusion of those who married nonsample members. There will be more respondents in lower income and minority groups than the weighted proportions because of oversampling. The oversampling simply makes the estimates for those groups more reliable.

Weighted estimates essentially muptiply each case by a number representing the number of households it represents. Each digit of the weight represents 500 households.

WIFE - A legal wife; a female friend who has lived with a male head for a year or more.

YEAR - Interviewing was done in the spring of each year from 1968 through 1976, but the income questions refer to each previous year (1967-1975).